The NIV®

STANDARD LESSON COMMENTARY
1998 ~ 1999

International Sunday School Lessons

edited by

DOUGLAS REDFORD AND JONATHAN UNDERWOOD

published by
Standard Publishing
Eugene H. Wigginton, President
Mark A. Taylor, Publisher
Richard C. McKinley, Director of Curriculum Development
Carla Crane, Assistant Director of Curriculum Development
Jonathan Underwood, Senior Editor
Hela M. Campbell, Office Editor

Fifth Annual Volume

STANDARD PUBLISHING

Cincinnati, Ohio

FREE CD-ROM INCLUDED

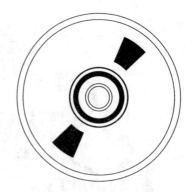

The electronic version of *The NIV® Standard Lesson Commentary* and the *QuickVerse® Library* STEP Book Reader are contained on the CD-ROM so you can:

- Instantly search the complete text of the Commentary for any word, phrase, or Bible reference. Search options include full-text, title-only, case-sensitive, and support of Boolean operators (AND, OR, NOT, etc.).
- Access related articles or information via hyperlinks within the text of each book. (Double-clicking on a highlighted word will access related articles.)
- Print lessons directly from the *QuickVerse® Library* or customize in any Windows® word processor

PLUS, you'll find additional reference titles locked on the CD. NOTE: These additional resources are made available for your convenience. Standard Publishing does not necessarily endorse the complete contents of any of them.

The electronic version of this book is fully compatible with the new Bible Software Industry standard for reference titles, STEP (Standard Template for Electronic Publishing).

System Requirements:
An IBM or compatible PC running Windows*, 6MB RAM, and 3MB hard drive space.
* Full compatibility requires Windows 95 or Windows NT 3.51 or later; partial compatibility achieved with Windows 3.1.

For technical support call Parsons Technology at (319) 395-7314.

© 1998
The STANDARD PUBLISHING Company
division of STANDEX INTERNATIONAL Corporation
8121 Hamilton Avenue, Cincinnati, Ohio 45231
Printed in U.S.A.

In This Volume

Special Features

Fall Quarter, 1998
Theme: *God Calls a People to Faithful Living*

Writers

Lesson Development ....*Orrin Root*	What Do You Think? ....*Kenton K. Smith*
Verbal Illustrations ....*Charles R. Boatman*	Reproducible Activities ....*Jonathan Underwood*
Discovery Learning ....*Richard A. Lint*	

Winter Quarter, 1998-99
Theme: *God Calls Anew in Jesus Christ*

Writers

Lesson Development .....*J. Michael Shannon (1-4),*	"Why Teach This Lesson?" ....*Richard W. Baynes*
Johnny Pressley (5-13)	Discovery Learning..............................*Alan Weber*
Verbal Illustrations ....*Gene Appel (1-4),*	What Do You Think? ....*David A. Baynes*
Robert C. Shannon (5-13)	Reproducible Activities................*Ronald G. Davis*

Spring Quarter, 1999
Theme: *That You Might Believe*

Writers

Lesson Development ....*Edwin V. Hayden (1-9),*	"Why Teach This Lesson?" ....*Richard W. Baynes*
Robert C. Shannon (10-13)	Discovery Learning ....*Howard Wakefield*
Verbal Illustrations ....*James G. VanBuren*	Reproducible Activities ....*Jonathan Underwood*
What Do You Think?...................*Kenton K. Smith*	

Summer Quarter, 1999
Theme: *Genesis: Beginnings*

Writers

Lesson Development ....*Larry Pechawer (1-4),*	Discovery Learning ....*Mark Plunkett (1-8),*
John W. Wade (5-13)	*Richard A. Lint (9-13)*
Verbal Illustrations ....*Richard W. Baynes*	Reproducible Activities..........*Mark Plunkett (1-8),*
What Do You Think? ....*David Morley*	*Jonathan Underwood (9-13)*

Index of Printed Texts, 1998-99

The printed texts for 1998-99 are arranged here in the order in which they appear in the Bible. Opposite each reference is the page number on which the lesson that treats the passage begins in this volume.

Introducing *The NIV®*
Standard Lesson Commentary

This is the fifth year teachers following the Uniform Lesson Plan have had available this popular commentary based on the *New International Version* of the Scriptures. Teachers familiar with *The NIV® Standard Lesson Commentary* will find in this volume all the features they have come to expect, plus a few new additions. A free CD-ROM was added last year and remains in this year's volume. New to this year's volume are some maps and chronological charts included with each quarter. By the end of the six-year series, you can compile quite a handy Bible atlas! Besides that, this year marks the first in a new Uniform Lesson "cycle," making 1998-99 a perfect time for new users to begin the series.

Whether you have used *The NIV® Standard Lesson Commentary* before or not, however, you will quickly find this volume a helpful companion in preparing your Sunday school lessons.

LESSON DEVELOPMENT

The first page of each lesson clearly identifies the title, Scripture, current unit, and lesson aims for the session. A thumb tab identifies the date the lesson will be taught so that it can be found quickly. The date is repeated on each page at the top outside corner.

The first item in the lesson development is a brief rationale for the lesson: **"Why Teach This Lesson?"** Tying the lesson theme to contemporary life, this section puts application at the forefront of your preparation. Then comes the lesson treatment itself, following a three-point structure: introduction, exposition, and conclusion. The **introduction** provides background and other useful information to set the stage, tie the current lessons with earlier ones, and generally give you a handle on the context for the current lesson.

Application from the start!

What follows is a **verse-by-verse Scripture exposition.** The text is printed in the *New International Version,* usually one verse at a time. Bold type sets the text off from commentary so you can read it easily, even if you just want to read through the passage without comment at first. The commentary is interspersed so you can relate the comments to the specific Scripture passage they illuminate.

Verse-by-verse exposition.

The **conclusion** leans heavily toward **application,** giving specific examples of how the principles of the lesson Scripture can be put to practice in real life.

Verbal illustrations, usually two to a lesson, help to illuminate the concepts of the lesson. These are found in the exposition section, providing yet another tool for you to illustrate the Scripture. These are set off in block quotes so they can be easily found or easily jumped over if you choose not to use them.

Verbal illustrations.

MARGINAL NOTES

Many of the most helpful features of this lesson commentary are found in the margins. Occasionally the text suggests some interesting point for discussion. These issues are raised under the heading of **"What Do You Think?"** The question is raised, sometimes from more than one perspective. The Scripture in the main section is relevant, and other Scriptures may also be suggested. No answers are given, however, because these are questions without pat answers. These will encourage your students to wrestle with the big issues without being trite.

Discussion starters.

"Visuals" are pictured in the margins, also. These are reproductions of the classroom visuals available from Standard Publishing each quarter to help your

Visual illustrations.

students visualize the points being made. Again, these appear in the margin alongside the Scripture or other part of the lesson where they are most appropriate.

Daily Bible readings.

Daily Bible readings, points to remember, and even prayer ideas are included in the margin near the end of each lesson.

DISCOVERY LEARNING

Student involvement!

For teachers who like to involve their students in the learning process, a page of **Discovery Learning** is included in each lesson. These alternate lesson plans are designed to get the students busy in Bible study and application to discover for themselves the timeless truths of the Scriptures. Each discovery learning plan includes an activity to begin the lesson, a Bible study activity, and an application activity.

Reproducible pages!

The last page of each lesson is a **reproducible page.** These, too, are designed to involve the students in discovery learning. Sometimes they are an integral part of the discovery learning plan. At other times, they provide optional activities that may be introduced at various points in the lesson. Marginal "Option" notes frequently call your attention to an activity on this page. Or you can start with the whole page and build your lesson plan around it, using the other resources in this book.

OPTIONS

Make it personal.

This is a lesson planner with lots of options! No matter what style you prefer—lecture, discussion, activities—you'll find resources to plan a great lesson. If you like variety, this will help you design an easy-to-teach lesson unique to your personality and that of your class. Or, if you like a ready-made plan you can teach with minimal preparation time, you'll find that, too. It's all here.

PLANNING SHEET

Map out your game plan.

Use the lesson planning sheet on page 10 to plan each of your lessons. The page is reproducible, so you can use it to fill in the blanks and plan out your complete lesson each week. List the options and features you have chosen for each lesson, and use it to guide you quickly and easily from one activity to the next.

EASY-TO-READ QUARTERLY FORMAT

NIV® BIBLE TEACHER

Some users of *The NIV® Standard Lesson Commentary* have wished for a quarterly format to use in teaching. Others have wished the type were a little larger and easier to read. Both those desires have been answered this year with the introduction of the *NIV® Bible Teacher,* available from your Christian bookstore or from Standard Publishing. It contains the same content as this volume but is published in four quarterly issues and in a larger typeface.

We Need Your Help

You can help us serve you better by completing this questionnaire. When you have done so, fold as indicated on the back. Glue or tape the ends together and mail the questionnaire to us. We will pay the postage. Thank you!

—The Editors

Teacher, please tell us a little about yourself:

In what age bracket are you?

- ❏ 20-30
- ❏ 41-50
- ❏ 61-70
- ❏ 31-40
- ❏ 51-60
- ❏ over 70

Check the highest level of formal education you have completed.

- ❏ 8th grade
- ❏ 12th grade
- ❏ college

(If college, how many years? _____)

How many years have you taught Sunday school? ___

Please tell us a little about your students:

Check the age range of your students. (Check all that apply.)

- ❏ 20-30
- ❏ 41-50
- ❏ 61-70
- ❏ 31-40
- ❏ 51-60
- ❏ over 70

Check the category that best describes the area from which your students come.

- ❏ city
- ❏ suburban
- ❏ rural
- ❏ small town

Check which best describes your class.

- ❏ men
- ❏ women
- ❏ both

Please tell us a little about your teaching:

What teaching method do you use most often?

- ❏ lecture
- ❏ discussion
- ❏ activities

Please list the versions of the Bible you prefer to use in your class.

First choice: _____

Second choice: _____

Third choice: _____

Please tell us what you think about *The NIV Standard Lesson Commentary*:

Do you think each lesson in the *Commentary* presents an important Bible truth?

- ❏ always
- ❏ usually
- ❏ sometimes
- ❏ seldom

Do you find the Lesson Aims helpful?

- ❏ always
- ❏ usually
- ❏ sometimes
- ❏ seldom

Do you find "Why Teach This Lesson?" to be useful?

- ❏ always
- ❏ usually
- ❏ sometimes
- ❏ seldom

Do you find the Lesson Introduction helpful?

- ❏ always
- ❏ usually
- ❏ sometimes
- ❏ seldom

Is the explanation of the Scripture adequate and appropriate for the age group you teach?

- ❏ always
- ❏ usually
- ❏ sometimes
- ❏ seldom

Do you find the Verbal Illustrations accompanying the explanation of the Scripture helpful?

- ❏ always
- ❏ usually
- ❏ sometimes
- ❏ seldom

Does the application presented in the lesson enable you to apply the Bible truths to your students' everyday lives?

- ❏ always
- ❏ usually
- ❏ sometimes
- ❏ seldom

Please give us your evaluation of the "Discovery Learning" section.

- ❏ very useful
- ❏ somewhat useful
- ❏ not useful

Please evaluate the "What Do You Think?" questions.

- ❏ very useful
- ❏ somewhat useful
- ❏ not useful

Do you use the *Adult Visuals*?

- ❏ always
- ❏ usually
- ❏ sometimes
- ❏ seldom

What teaching aids do you find most helpful?

- ❏ maps
- ❏ charts
- ❏ posters
- ❏ Bible art
- ❏ time lines
- ❏ filmstrips
- ❏ quizzes
- ❏ role-play scripts
- ❏ teaching games
- ❏ overhead transparencies
- ❏ other _____

Do you use the CD-ROM disk?

- ❏ always
- ❏ usually
- ❏ sometimes
- ❏ seldom

What additional features would you like to see on *The NIV Standard Lesson Commentary* CD-ROM?

Would you like to see *The NIV Standard Lesson Commentary* CD-ROM available separately from the book version?

Use the other side of this form to tell what features you like best about *The NIV Standard Lesson Commentary* and tell what features you would suggest to improve it.

BUSINESS REPLY MAIL
FIRST–CLASS MAIL   PERMIT NO. 760   CINCINNATI OH

POSTAGE WILL BE PAID BY ADDRESSEE

ADULT CURRICULUM DEPT.
STANDARD PUBLISHING
8121 HAMILTON AVE
CINCINNATI OH 45231-9943

FOLD HERE

Additional Comments:

PLEASE TAPE OR GLUE ENDS TOGETHER BEFORE MAILING.

Ready . . . AIM . . . Teach!

The Importance of "Lesson Aims" in Teaching

Do you ever wonder whether you are doing any good as the teacher of your class? Does it ever seem you are just passing time in class instead of accomplishing anything meaningful? If so, perhaps you need to take a second look at the "Lesson Aims" (also called "Learning Goals") included in each lesson.

Someone has said, "If you don't know where you are going, then any road will take you there." To know which is the right road, or the right way, one must know where it is he or she wants to be. The same is true in your teaching. Unless you have a clear idea of what you want to accomplish by the end of the class session—where you want your students to be, if you please—then there is no way to know just what you ought to spend your time doing in the class session.

What is your goal in teaching? Surely it is more than providing sixty minutes worth of diversion—you're not just "filling time." And you're not just trying to "cover" a particular portion of Scripture. No, you want more. You want your students to *know* something they may not have known before they came into your classroom. More than that, you want them to *understand* the truths and principles of Scripture that the lesson text presents. Finally, you want the students to *apply* to their lives those things they have come to know and understand.

That is the reason the editors of the *Standard Lesson Commentary* and *The NIV® Standard Lesson Commentary* have been spending so much time in formulating the lesson aims that appear in each lesson in the *Commentaries*. Usually there are three aims for a lesson. The first is a *content* aim. This aim addresses the issue of what facts the student should know as a result of having participated in the study of the assigned lesson text. Verbs like *recall*, *summarize*, and *tell* will frequently introduce such aims.

The second aim might be called a *concept* aim. This goal probes beneath the surface of the material to find the timeless principles underlying the facts reported in the Scripture text. This aim takes the learner beyond the knowledge of facts to understanding. This is a necessary link to bring the events of centuries gone by to relevance in our own day. Verbs like *relate*, *compare*, and *explain* will be more common in introducing these aims.

The third aim is what we might call a *conduct* aim. This is the goal that addresses the issue of application: how will the student's conduct change as a result of participating in this study? These aims may challenge the learner to *make a commitment* or to *suggest a specific action* that he or she can take in the coming week.

The concept aims are especially important in studying the historical narratives in Scripture. It is not enough to know the *facts* about the story of David's killing the giant Goliath. We must also understand the *principles* of faith and courage that moved David to action. Only then can we move on from the content aim—knowing the facts—to the conduct aim—applying this lesson to how we face the giants in our own lives. In some passages, especially in the epistles, the content may be more exposition than narration, more conceptual than historical. In these cases we may find that to know the content of the passage is to know the concept—so separate aims may not be needed. In these cases there may be only two aims instead of three.

No matter how many aims in a lesson, or whether you follow the ones here or develop your own, be sure to start your lesson preparation with a clear understanding of where you want to go. Only then will you be sure to get there!

WHERE ARE YOU GOING?

CONTENT AIM
  What does the text say?

CONCEPT AIM
  What does the text mean?

CONDUCT AIM
  What does the text demand of me?

Lesson Planning Page

List the aims here, either directly from the lesson or revised to suit your individual needs.

LESSON AIMS

Begin with an opening activity like the illustration from the beginning of the lesson, "Into the Lesson" from the Discovery Learning page, a discussion question, or some other appropriate opener.

GETTING STARTED

List in order the activities you will use. These include discussion questions, activities from the discovery learning page and the reproducible page—as well as key points from the commentary section.

LESSON DEVELOPMENT

I.

II.

III.

How will you bring the lesson to a climax, stressing the key point and desired action steps?

CONCLUSION & APPLICATION

Dismiss the class with an activity that reinforces the Bible lesson.

CLOSING ACTIVITY

Fall Quarter, 1998

God Calls a People to Faithful Living
(Old Testament Survey)

Special Features

Lessons

Unit 1. God Fashions a People

Unit 2. God's People Reject His Laws

Unit 3. God Works Through People

Unit 4. God Judges and Renews

About These Lessons

The lessons of the current quarter launch us on a new six-year study of the Bible. These lessons give an overview, or survey, of the Old Testament. It is hoped that this survey will help the student put into context the lessons learned from Old Testament Scriptures throughout the six-year period.

Sep 6

Sep 13

Sep 20

Sep 27

Oct 4

Oct 11

Oct 18

Oct 25

Nov 1

Nov 8

Nov 15

Nov 22

Nov 29

Here We Go Again

by Orrin Root

Six years ago, we began a cycle of lessons designed to lead us through the Bible in a span of six years. The cycle began with a survey of the Old Testament in thirteen lessons. That cycle was completed with the summer 1998 lessons, and now, with the fall 1998 quarter, we are ready to begin another six-year cycle. It should come as no surprise that we begin with a survey of the Old Testament in thirteen lessons.

This does not mean that we are repeating the lessons we used six years ago. When we plan to cover the Old Testament in thirteen lessons, obviously we have to leave some huge gaps between lessons. Six years ago we skipped the first eleven chapters of Genesis to begin with Abraham, the father of God's chosen people. This time we skip only two chapters at the beginning. We start with Genesis 3, which records the entrance of sin into the world.

After this first lesson from Genesis, we bypass the rest of the book and leap forward to consider the Hebrews' deliverance from slavery in Egypt. It looks as if

International Sunday School Lesson Cycle
September, 1998—August, 2004

YEAR	FALL QUARTER (Sept., Oct., Nov.)	WINTER QUARTER (Dec., Jan., Feb.)	SPRING QUARTER (Mar., Apr., May)	SUMMER QUARTER (June, July, Aug.)
1998-1999	God Calls a People to Faithful Living (Old Testament Survey)	God Calls Anew in Jesus Christ (New Testament Survey)	That You May Believe (John)	Genesis: Beginnings (Genesis)
1999-2000	From Slavery to Conquest (Exodus, Leviticus, Numbers, Deuteronomy, Joshua)	Emmanuel: God With Us (Matthew)	Helping a Church Confront Crisis (1 and 2 Corinthians)	New Life in Christ (Ephesians, Philippians, Colossians, Philemon)
2000-2001	The Emerging Nation (Judges, 1 and 2 Samuel, 1 Kings 1-11, 1 Chronicles, 2 Chronicles 1-9)	Good News of Jesus (Luke)	Continuing Jesus' Work (Acts)	Division and Decline (1 Kings 12-22, 2 Kings 1-17, 2 Chronicles 10-28, Isaiah 1-39, Amos, Hosea, Micah)
2001-2002	Jesus' Ministry (Parables, Miracles, Sermon on the Mount)	Light for All People (Isaiah 9:1-7; 11:1-9; 40-66; Ruth, Jonah, Nahum)	The Power of the Gospel (Romans, Galatians)	Worship and Wisdom for Living (Psalms, Proverbs)
2002-2003	Judgment and Exile (2 Kings 18-25, 2 Chronicles 29-36, Jeremiah, Lamentations, Ezekiel, Habakkuk, Zephaniah)	Portraits of Faith (Personalities in the New Testament)	Jesus: God's Power in Action (Mark)	God Restores a Remnant (Ezra, Nehemiah, Daniel, Joel, Obadiah, Haggai, Zechariah, Malachi)
2003-2004	Faith Faces the World (James, 1 and 2 Peter, 1, 2, 3 John, Jude)	A Child Is Given (Samuel, John the Baptist, Jesus) Lessons From Life (Esther, Job, Ecclesiastes, Song of Solomon)	Jesus Fulfills His Mission (Death, Burial, and Resurrection Texts) Living Expectantly (1, 2 Thessalonians, Revelation)	Hold Fast to the Faith (Hebrews) Guidelines for the Church's Ministry (1, 2 Timothy, Titus)

we are ignoring a lot of important material. But don't be alarmed. Next summer's studies will feature thirteen lessons drawn entirely from Genesis. (See the shaded portion of the cycle on the opposite page.) As we proceed through the thirteen lessons of this fall, we will find other large gaps in our study; but we can expect each gap to be partially filled through later studies.

Think of this fall's study as providing a framework that will aid us in putting future Old Testament studies in their proper context. (The time line found on page 16 will help you place the lessons in their proper historical context.) We need to be diligent in learning and remembering the framework. Then we will see how future lessons fit into the overall plan of the Old Testament. Notice how other lessons later in the cycle—often in the fall or summer quarters—continue our study of the Old Testament.

UNIT ONE: *GOD FASHIONS A PEOPLE*

SEPTEMBER

This unit of lessons reminds us of how God worked in a mighty way to establish a nation that would be his own special people—his own "treasured possession" (Exodus 19:5). **Lesson 1**, however ("God's Creation Marred by Sin"), focuses on the tragic entry of sin into the world through the disobedience of Adam and Eve in the Garden of Eden (Genesis 3). How grateful we should be that the second Adam, Jesus Christ, came to undo the work of the devil (1 Corinthians 15:45; Hebrews 2:14, 15)!

Lesson 2 ("God's People Delivered From Slavery") highlights God's deliverance of Israel, using Moses to lead them out of bitter bondage in Egypt. The events recorded in **Lesson 3** ("God's Expectations Made Plain") occurred forty years later. As the people of Israel stood on the verge of entering the promised land, Moses repeated the law that had been given nearly forty years earlier, not long after the Israelites had left Egypt (Deuteronomy 5:1-21). **Lesson 4** ("God's Actions Remembered") tells how God stopped the flow of the Jordan River while his people crossed on dry land to the other side. They erected two monuments in memory of this miracle (Joshua 4).

UNIT TWO: *GOD'S PEOPLE REJECT HIS LAWS*

OCTOBER

Lesson 5 ("Cycle of Sin and Judgment") calls attention to one of the most dismal periods of Israel's history—the period of the judges (about 1350-1050 B.C.). The Israelites became attracted to the gods of the people around them, whom they had failed to drive out of the land as God commanded. God's punishment (by means of oppression from pagan tribes) brought the nation back to obedience; but before long the people fell prey once again to idolatry. This happened many times in the span of about three centuries (Judges 2:11-23; 11:26). **Lesson 6** ("Demand for a King") notes how the people of Israel asked Samuel for a king. God granted this request, but he warned the people of what lay ahead for them (1 Samuel 8).

Our survey then moves past the reigns of Israel's first three kings (Saul, David, and Solomon) to the time when the kingdom was divided (931 B.C.). **Lesson 7** ("Jeroboam's Sin") tells how Jeroboam, the first king of the northern kingdom (Israel), set up two golden calves for the people in the north to worship. He also instituted other practices that were counter to what God had commanded.

UNIT THREE: *GOD WORKS THROUGH PEOPLE*

The lessons in the previous units show how God worked directly to deliver his people from bondage, to give them his laws, and to lead them into the land he had promised to give them. This next unit reminds us of the important truth that

God also works through people to accomplish his purposes. **Lesson 8** ("God Works Through Prophets") tells how Naaman, a leader of the Syrian army, came to Israel in search of healing from his leprosy. God healed him when he humbly followed the instructions of God's messenger Elisha (2 Kings 5:1-14).

NOVEMBER

Lesson 9 ("God Gives His Spokesman Courage") focuses on the ministry of the prophet Amos. God sent this shepherd/farmer to denounce the sins of the northern kingdom. The religious hierarchy, represented by Amaziah the priest, opposed the prophet; but God gave him courage to deliver his message of judgment on a sinful, complacent people (Amos 7).

Lesson 10 ("God Works Through Song Writers") is taken from Psalm 73. Asaph's song describes his own intense spiritual struggle and how he regained a proper perspective on his surroundings. Through this inspired songwriter, God works to help us through similar crises of faith.

UNIT FOUR: GOD JUDGES AND RENEWS

In 722 B.C., the northern kingdom of Israel was conquered by the Assyrians. Its people were scattered among various foreign countries (2 Kings 17:1-6). The southern kingdom of Judah exhibited far greater faithfulness toward God; and because of the godly leadership of King Hezekiah, God rescued Judah from the Assyrians (2 Kings 18:13–19:36). Eventually, however, evil kings guided the nation into wrongdoing. With the concluding unit of this quarter, we move forward to the time when the southern kingdom of Judah was under siege from the Babylonians. God's judgment was in the process of falling upon his stubborn, unrepentant people. **Lesson 11** ("False Hopes and Judgment") records the prophet Jeremiah's warnings to the nation. His words included a promise of God's judgment, "that will make the ears of everyone who hears of it tingle" (Jeremiah 19:3). But Jeremiah also extended God's gracious invitation to choose "the way of life" (Jeremiah 21:8).

Ezekiel, who was taken to Babylon in 597 B.C., served God as a prophet among the captives there. He gave the disheartened exiles God's promise that his people would be set free one day to return to their homeland (Ezekiel 37). This is the theme of **Lesson 12** ("Hope From God's Promise").

Lesson 13 ("Renewal and Worship") brings us to the year 445 B.C., when Nehemiah came to Jerusalem as governor of Judah. His first aim was to rebuild the city wall that had been destroyed more than a century earlier. The people worked enthusiastically, and the wall was completed in only fifty-two days (Nehemiah 6:15). Nehemiah, with the assistance of Ezra, then began to give attention to teaching the law of Moses to the people. By this time, the observance of the Feast of Tabernacles was at hand; and that festival was observed in the ancient way and with the joy that God intended for his people to experience (Nehemiah 8).

In approximately 430 B.C., the prophet Malachi wrote the final book of the Old Testament. It shows that the people of God were once again becoming negligent in their obedience, as their ancestors had done so many times before. This series of studies surveying the Old Testament demonstrates the need for a new covenant offering the forgiveness of sins and the power to conquer the power of sin in one's life. Such a covenant was foretold by the prophet Jeremiah (Jeremiah 31:31-34), and it was established by Jesus approximately four hundred years after the completion of the Old Testament Scriptures.

Today the church—those who have accepted God's gracious offer of forgiveness in Jesus—has much to learn from these studies surveying the Old Testament. We are now the people whom God calls to "faithful living." Are we living up to such a high and holy calling?

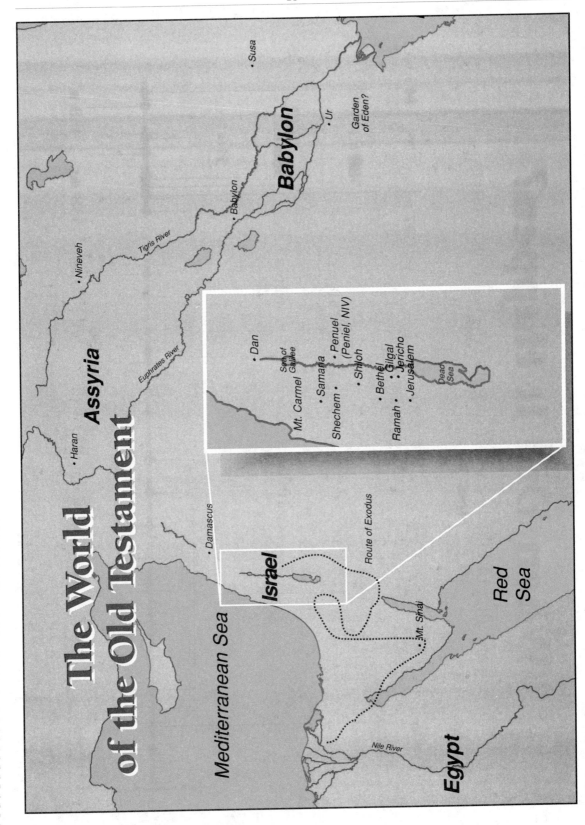

When Did It Happen?

(Time line of Old Testament events covered this quarter)

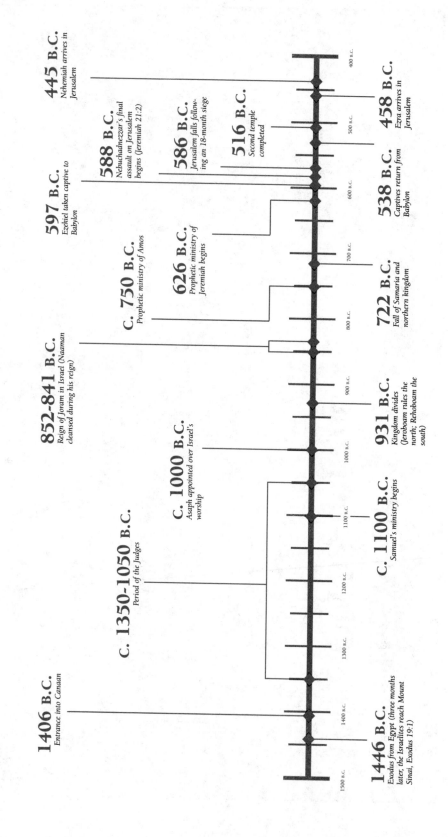

1406 B.C.
Entrance into Canaan

1446 B.C.
Exodus from Egypt (three months later, the Israelites reach Mount Sinai, Exodus 19:1)

c. 1350-1050 B.C.
Period of the Judges

c. 1100 B.C.
Samuel's ministry begins

c. 1000 B.C.
Asaph appointed over Israel's worship

931 B.C.
Kingdom divides (Jeroboam rules the north; Rehoboam the south)

852-841 B.C.
Reign of Joram in Israel (Naaman cleansed during his reign)

c. 750 B.C.
Prophetic ministry of Amos

722 B.C.
Fall of Samaria and northern kingdom

626 B.C.
Prophetic ministry of Jeremiah begins

597 B.C.
Ezekiel taken captive to Babylon

588 B.C.
Nebuchadnezzar's final assault on Jerusalem begins (Jeremiah 21:2)

586 B.C.
Jerusalem falls following an 18-month siege

538 B.C.
Captives return from Babylon

516 B.C.
Second temple completed

458 B.C.
Ezra arrives in Jerusalem

445 B.C.
Nehemiah arrives in Jerusalem

1500 B.C. 1400 B.C. 1300 B.C. 1200 B.C. 1100 B.C. 1000 B.C. 900 B.C. 800 B.C. 700 B.C. 600 B.C. 500 B.C. 400 B.C.

GOD'S CREATION MARRED BY SIN

WHY TEACH THIS LESSON?

"Nobody's perfect!" We say it so easily, and somehow that is supposed to lessen our guilt. We have become comfortable with sin. It is so common, it fails to disturb us as it should.

Perhaps a look at where sin began will help. Today's lesson will help your students see the tragic consequences of sin. Rather than get comfortable with sin, we need to feel the shame that was felt when sin was new. Use this lesson to help your students realize sin is still shameful!

INTRODUCTION

Steve was caught in the act. There were witnesses. His guilt could not be denied. At the advice of his attorney, he pleaded no contest. As a result, Steve was convicted of stealing a six-pack of beer.

When asked about the incident, Steve said that it was a joke—a part of the initiation into his college fraternity. But the storekeeper was not amused; the police were not amused; and the judge was not amused. Perhaps the older fraternity members were more guilty than Steve, but Steve was the one who had to spend time in jail instead of in class.

You can think of similar cases. Consider the boy who spends his after-school hours on the streets and gets involved with drugs. We can blame the pusher who entices him, the parents who abandon him to the streets, or the system that compels both parents to work in order to earn a living; but the boy is the one who suffers the addiction and has to endure detention in a juvenile facility.

A. AN ANCIENT RULE

The excuses may seem plausible, but they cannot overturn a fundamental principle: a person has to endure the consequences of what he does. This principle has been in operation for a long time, and it applies in matters much more serious than fraternity nonsense. Ultimately it is a matter of life and death. "The wages of sin is death," proclaimed Paul. But there was more to his message. Thanks to divine grace he could add, "The gift of God is eternal life in Christ Jesus our Lord" (Romans 6:23).

B. LESSON BACKGROUND

Today's lesson begins a survey of the Old Testament, entitled "God Calls a People to Faithful Living." Obviously, to conduct such a survey in only thirteen lessons is not an easy task. It requires being quite selective as to what Scriptures will be covered.

The book of Genesis itself is filled with several "high points." Within the space of just the first two chapters, the following events are described:

DEVOTIONAL READING
ROMANS 7:15-25a

LESSON SCRIPTURE
GENESIS 3

PRINTED TEXT
GENESIS 3:1-13

LESSON AIMS

After this lesson a student should be able to:

1. Describe the sin of Adam and Eve and its result.

2. Explain the nature and consequences of sin as they relate to God, man, and Satan.

3. Determine to obey God and resist Satan in one specific area of life.

KEY VERSE

Then the man and his wife ... hid from the LORD God among the trees of the garden.
—*Genesis 3:8*

LESSON 1 NOTES

WHAT DO YOU THINK?

Satan spoke through a snake in the garden. Today Satan spreads lies through a variety of impressive outlets: glossy magazines, books written in scholarly language, expertly crafted plays and films, and the like. Satan also uses glamorous people to propagate his false doctrines. Movie and television performers, professional athletes, successful businessmen, and smooth-talking politicians have all been recruited by the evil one to propagate moral and spiritual falsehoods. What are some ways we can resist such tactics?

The visual for lesson 1 is a map of the Old Testament world. You will find this map useful throughout the fall quarter.

God created the heaven and the earth.

God shaped the earth in wonderful ways, creating mountains and valleys, rivers, seas, and oceans, plains and rolling hills.

God made fish to swim in the sea, birds to fly in the air, and animals to walk on the ground.

God made man in his own image and gave him dominion over all the other creatures.

God appointed the man he created to be the caretaker of a lovely garden that provided food for both man and beast.

Realizing that it was not good for that man to be alone, God provided him with a wonderful "helper suitable for him" (Genesis 2:18)—a woman.

In the middle of this garden, God designated one tree from which the man and the woman were not permitted to eat. Disobedience to this command would bring death.

Within this year (during the summer quarter of 1999, to be exact) three entire months will be given to studies from Genesis. There we will be able to go into greater detail concerning some of the themes mentioned above and others that are found within this important book.

For now, however, we begin our Old Testament survey with one of the "low points" found in Genesis: "God's Creation Marred by Sin."

I. TEMPTATION (GENESIS 3:1-5)

Wise men of today look at the deteriorating slums of our great cities and say that poverty is the cause of crime; however, the first three chapters of Genesis are enough to tell us to look elsewhere for the cause. There was no poverty in Eden, yet that was where sin burst into bloom and brought forth its deadly fruit. Abundance is no shield against temptation.

A. THE TEMPTER (v. 1a)

1a. Now the serpent was more crafty than any of the wild animals the LORD God had made.

Crafty is a word that reminds us of human nature. Like each of us, it has both a good and a bad side. In a good sense, it means wise, sagacious, or perceptive. In a bad sense, it means cunning, sly, or tricky. Here it is used in its bad sense, as we see from the verses that follow. The *serpent* was the trickiest creature in Eden.

B. THE QUESTION (v. 1b)

1b. He said to the woman, "Did God really say, 'You must not eat from any tree in the garden'?"

The *woman* was Eve, wife of the first man, Adam (Genesis 3:20). The serpent approached her with a question, beginning with the phrase *Did God really say*. By expressing surprise that God would say, *You must not eat from any tree in the garden*, the serpent implied that he was unreasonable to say it. We might paraphrase the serpent's words as, "Is it possible that God said this? It sounds so silly."

Have you ever heard a snake talking? None of us has ever heard a snake use human language. While the Bible does not specifically say so, it is generally supposed that Satan took possession of this serpent and miraculously enabled it to speak the devil's own thoughts. Here, close to the beginning of the Bible, we see Satan in the guise of a serpent, and near the end of the Bible we see him described as "that ancient serpent" (Revelation 20:2). He is the same deceitful character throughout Scripture!

C. THE LAW (vv. 2, 3)

2, 3. The woman said to the serpent, "We may eat fruit from the trees in the garden, but God did say, 'You must not eat fruit from the tree that is in the middle of the garden, and you must not touch it, or you will die.'"

The woman was fully aware of the order given by God, recorded in Genesis 2:16, 17. *You must not touch it* is not included there, and so we are surprised to see Eve mention it here. Perhaps God had said more than is recorded in that verse, or perhaps the man and woman had made the addition in their own thinking. In any case, the woman fully understood that God wanted her and her husband to leave the *fruit from the tree . . . in the middle of the garden* alone.

D. THE LIE (vv. 4, 5)

4. "You will not surely die," the serpent said to the woman.

Now the *serpent* spoke more boldly. Flatly he accused God of lying. Why didn't the woman stop listening at that point? God's Word is true; he "does not lie" (Titus 1:2). Satan, on the other hand, "is a liar and the father of lies" (John 8:44). He seeks to contradict whatever God has said. But Eve kept on listening; and to this very day liars are denying the Word of God, and uncounted thousands of unwary people are listening to and liking what they have to say. All the attacks directed toward the Bible come down to the issue of truth: Can we trust what God has said? Is he telling the truth, or is he lying? Any amount of doubt that Satan can cast on this matter he will, just as he did with Eve.

5. "For God knows that when you eat of it your eyes will be opened, and you will be like God, knowing good and evil."

Having accused God of lying, the serpent proceeded to give the devil's twisted explanation of why God had lied. God wanted to keep something from his creatures, the devil claimed. The forbidden fruit would make Adam and Eve *like God*. God was afraid of competition, said the devil. God did not want the man and the woman to be all they could be. Today this argument is often stated as follows: "God doesn't want you to have any fun. His rules will only limit your freedom. Ignore them, and you'll really begin to live."

II. SIN (GENESIS 3:6)

With the benefit of hindsight, we easily see what the woman should have done. She should have said, "Get out of here! God said to leave this fruit alone, and that settles it!" But Eve kept on listening, kept on thinking, and allowed the devil's lie to guide her thoughts. Too many spend time thinking about the devil's offer when they should simply follow Jesus' example and say, "Get behind me, Satan!" (Matthew 16:23).

A. UNWARY THINKING (v. 6a)

6a. When the woman saw that the fruit of the tree was good for food and pleasing to the eye, and also desirable for gaining wisdom. . . .

The seed of doubt had been planted, and in Eve's mind it grew and blossomed. She kept looking at the forbidden *tree*, and what she saw seemed to confirm the devil's lie. She *saw that the fruit of the tree was good for food*. Obviously that fruit was edible, and in addition *it was pleasing to the eye*. How could it be bad when it looked so good? Besides all that, the fruit was *desirable for gaining wisdom*. That was evident in its name: "the tree of the knowledge of good and evil" (Genesis 2:17). Shouldn't one use every opportunity to learn more and to become wiser?

No doubt the fruit really was edible. No doubt it actually was pleasant to the eyes. No doubt it really is good to gain knowledge and wisdom. But God's Word

WHAT DO YOU THINK?

To contradict the clear teaching of the Word of God is to lie. Yet today we find no shortage of people ready and eager to contradict it. Shortsighted scholars claim to find inaccuracies within its pages. Entertainers mock its teachings. Many religious leaders substitute human philosophies for its eternal truths.

Under such circumstances, what should we believers do to defend the Bible? How important is it to be able to answer all the critics' charges? Why? What role does demonstrating the power of the gospel in our lives play in this defense?

OPTION

We do not know what kind of fruit was on the tree in the garden, but what kind of "fruit" tempts us? Use the reproducible page 24 to explore this issue.

WHAT DO YOU THINK?

What are some ways in which husbands and wives tempt one another to sin? What can husbands and wives do to be sure they are building each other up in the faith and not leading one another into sin?

is truth! If we do not keep that assurance firmly in mind, Satan is always ready to twist the truth to support his position, leading us to a false conclusion. Compare the qualities Eve found attractive in the tree with those that John says are part of "the world" that Christians are not to love: "the lust of the flesh, the lust of the eyes, and the pride of life" (1 John 2:16, *King James Version*).

B. UNWARY ACTION (v. 6b)
6b. She took some and ate it.

This seemed to be the only thing to do. If the fruit was pretty and tasty and promised good results, how could anyone refuse it?

There was another way, and that was to trust the Lord. He said to leave that fruit alone. He said it would do more harm than good. If we really put our trust in God and his Word, no lie is plausible enough, no argument is strong enough, and no facts are persuasive enough to make us disobey his plain command.

C. UNWARY SHARING (v. 6c)
6c. She also gave some to her husband, who was with her, and he ate it.

Was there any discussion between the two, any objection from Adam, or any persuasion by Eve? If there was, it is not recorded. The Scripture simply records the awful fact. Husband and wife now shared their guilt, just as they had been sharing their innocence.

How often have you compounded your sin by involving another unwary person in it with you?

EATING THE WRONG FOOD

During the Christmas shopping season in 1996, one of the most popular toys was a battery-powered Cabbage Patch Snack Time Kid doll. Unlike the ordinary Cabbage Patch doll that had been sold for years, this new version was able to "eat" a variety of fake food that came with it.

However, the Snack Time Kid turned out to have an appetite for food that it wasn't supposed to eat, sometimes with unfortunate results. After the gifts were unwrapped on Christmas morning, several children across America found that a stray lock of their hair "tasted" just as good to the Kid as the fake food it was supposed to "eat." One Kid even chewed the hair out of the scalp of a little girl, and because there was no "ON-OFF" switch, the doll had to be dismantled to free the child.

Our first parents, Adam and Eve, ate some food that brought even more disastrous results. Their simple act of taking a bite of the proverbial "apple" (although the specific fruit is not mentioned) had a calamitous effect on them and all who have followed them. With their sin came a dismantling of their paradise. Toil and suffering became a part of the human condition, not to mention the loss of intimate fellowship with God.

Human experience ever since that day so long ago confirms the truth that our Designer knew what he was doing when he warned Adam and Eve against eating the "forbidden fruit."

—C. R. B.

III. CONSEQUENCES (GENESIS 3:7-13)

A. SHAME (v. 7)
7. Then the eyes of both of them were opened, and they realized they were naked; so they sewed fig leaves together and made coverings for themselves.

Adam and Eve had been *naked* before, and in their innocence such a state had seemed normal and proper (Genesis 2:25). But now they were ashamed. Something was abnormal and improper about their nakedness, for sin had entered their lives.

B. FEAR (v. 8)

8. Then the man and his wife heard the sound of the LORD God as he was walking in the garden in the cool of the day, and they hid from the LORD God among the trees of the garden.

There are different kinds of fear. There is a wholesome and proper fear of God that is also referred to as reverence, awe, or submission. Unless this fear of God underlies our learning, our knowledge becomes flawed and twisted (Proverbs 1:7). Adam and Eve felt another kind of fear, a cringing fear that moved them first, to cover their nakedness (v. 7), and now, to hide from God. Think of the irony: the *garden*, which had been a place of fellowship with God, was now a place to hide from him. Such fear results from the guilt produced by sin.

C. EXPOSURE (vv. 9-11)

9. But the LORD God called to the man, "Where are you?"

The guilty *man* longed to be hidden. But God would not have it so. He was like the shepherd in search of his lost sheep (Luke 15:4). He asked the question *Where are you?* not for his sake (as though God did not know where Adam was), but to evoke Adam's confession.

10. He answered, "I heard you in the garden, and I was afraid because I was naked; so I hid."

No one can hide from God (Psalm 139:7-12). Adam quickly realized that, and told God where he was and why he had hidden himself. Some who are not so wise spend years trying to "hide" themselves in work or fun or riotous living, but God is not deceived. How much better it is to hear his voice and answer!

11. And he said, "Who told you that you were naked? Have you eaten from the tree that I commanded you not to eat from?"

Adam could not be hidden, and neither could his sin. God knows our sins as well. When will we stop our futile efforts to hide from him? When will we acknowledge our sin and seek his gracious forgiveness (1 John 1:9)?

D. EXCUSES (vv. 12, 13)

12. The man said, "The woman you put here with me—she gave me some fruit from the tree, and I ate it."

"It's not my fault." How often have you heard that excuse, or how often have you offered it yourself? Adam said, "It's Eve's fault. She gave me the fruit." Adam's excuse also included an element of blaming God as well, as he referred to *the woman you put here with me.* "You gave me that woman to be my helper. If you had given me one who was more obedient to you, I would have obeyed too. Don't you see it's not my fault?"

But the Word of God firmly rejects any and all excuses—whether Adam's, yours, or mine. You are responsible for your misdeeds; I am responsible for mine. "Each of us will give an account of himself to God" (Romans 14:12).

13. Then the LORD God said to the woman, "What is this you have done?" The woman said, "The serpent deceived me, and I ate."

Eve echoed her husband's excuse: "It's not my fault." "*The serpent deceived me.* It's his fault." She, like Adam, was trying to blame another party for what had happened. And like Adam's excuse, hers was to no avail.

Other consequences of this sinful act are described in the rest of the chapter. God's final word to Adam was a reminder of the sentence of death he now faced, just as God had said (v. 19). Satan's claim, "You will not surely die," was a lie.

Some critics of the Bible take delight in pointing out that Adam did not die at the time he ate the fruit, as God said he would (Genesis 2:17). In fact, he lived

WHAT DO YOU THINK?

People are still trying to hide themselves and their sins from God. Much of the busyness in which people are caught up today probably represents an unconscious effort to avoid thinking about God, sin, and eternity. People also hide in their pleasures. By keeping their minds occupied with food and drink, sex, recreation, and the like, they are able to keep God at a distance. Also, the epidemic abuse of drugs and alcohol is surely a means of hiding from God.

How can we convince people they cannot hide from God—and assure them that they do not need to?

WHAT DO YOU THINK?

Whom or what do people sometimes blame for their sins? Why do we do that? Why is it pointless to divert guilt from oneself to someone or something else? What benefits can come from owning up to our own sins? How?

PRAYER

How gracious you are, our Father and Creator! And how unworthy we are! With sorrow we confess that we too have disobeyed you. We beg you to forgive us through Jesus Christ our Lord, and we give ourselves to your service in grateful trust. Amen.

THOUGHT TO REMEMBER

Christ undid what Adam did.

DAILY BIBLE READINGS

Monday, Aug. 31—The Serpent As Tempter (Genesis 3:1-7)

Tuesday, Sept. 1—Disobedience Brings Fear (Genesis 3:8-13)

Wednesday, Sept. 2—Disobedience Has Consequences (Genesis 3:14-19)

Thursday, Sept. 3—Expulsion From the Garden (Genesis 3:20-24)

Friday, Sept. 4—Who Will Rescue Me? (Romans 7:15-25a)

Saturday, Sept. 5—No Condemnation (Romans 8:1-11)

Sunday, Sept. 6—Alive in Christ (1 Corinthians 15:12-22)

more than eight hundred years after his sin (Genesis 5:4, 5). So God was wrong, the critics say, or else the Bible does not truthfully report what he said. Bible students have pointed out at least three ways of reconciling these details:

1. In a spiritual sense, Adam did die when he ate from the forbidden tree. Spiritual death means alienation or separation from God. Such alienation is seen in Adam's attempt to hide from God among the trees (v. 8).

2. The Hebrew text in Genesis 2:17 literally says, "In the day you eat of it." The word *day* can designate a period of time, not necessarily a twenty-four hour period. For example, "Now is the day of salvation" (2 Corinthians 6:2). Paul wrote that centuries ago, and the day of salvation has not ended yet. Adam's sin ended his era of innocence and began his era of punishment; and within that era he died.

3. Literal, physical death is not instant. It is a long process, as we know when we see vitality dwindling in a man of eighty or ninety. Adam not only was sentenced to death at the moment he sinned; before the sun went down that very day, he actually began dying. From that time forward, the process of death went on unchecked until it was complete.

Perhaps all of these ingredients were involved in the sentence of death pronounced upon man. What is most important to acknowledge is that God kept his promise. Neither he nor his Word can be charged with error.

MAKING EXCUSES

The rookie pitcher's fast ball was *fast* and his curve had some "stuff" on it. Some observers thought he had a good career ahead of him. By August of his first year in the minor leagues, he was enjoying an 18-5 won-lost record. Then, diving after a ball in the outfield, he fell and cracked his shoulder. He would never pitch again.

The young pitcher could have made excuses for his bad luck and wandered off into some other career. Few people would have blamed him. But instead of making excuses, he focused on his other talents. By the time he set aside his spikes, bat, and glove for the last time, he had earned a record of 3,630 hits, 475 home runs, 1,949 runs scored, and 1,951 runs batted in. That player was Stan "the Man" Musial, one of the greatest baseball players of all time.

How we handle "bad luck" or foolish mistakes or terrible sins tells a lot about our character. Unfortunately, Adam and Eve did not fare well on this score. As soon as God approached them with the fact of their disobedience, they began to make excuses. We too sometimes find it easier to make excuses than to acknowledge responsibility for our failure, but God sees through our masks and calls our action *sin*. How much better it is to take responsibility for our actions, learn from our failures, and turn our lives in a new direction.

—C. R. B.

CONCLUSION

Adam sinned, and Adam died according to God's promise. So did Adam's children and grandchildren. So did our grandparents, and so shall you and I. "Sin entered the world through one man, and death through sin, and in this way death came to all men, because all sinned" (Romans 5:12). No one is exempt. From Adam to my ancestors and on to my grandchildren, the long funeral procession winds its way toward multiplied millions of tombs. Is there no escape?

Of course, there is a way of escape. "For God so loved the world that he gave his one and only Son, that whoever believes in him shall not perish but have eternal life" (John 3:16). Jesus said, "I am the resurrection and the life. He who believes in me will live, even though he dies; and whoever lives and believes in me will never die" (John 11:25, 26). What Adam did through his sin, Jesus undid by giving his life as a sinless sacrifice for us!

Discovery Learning

*This page contains an alternate lesson plan emphasizing learning activities. Classes
desiring such student involvement will find these suggestions helpful. The next page
is a reproducible activity page to further enhance discovery learning.*

LEARNING GOALS

After this lesson, each student will be able to:

1. Describe Adam and Eve's sin and its result.

2. Explain the nature and consequences of sin as they relate to God, man, and Satan.

3. Determine to obey God and resist Satan in one specific area of his or her life.

INTO THE LESSON

As you begin the lesson, write the word *freedom* on the chalkboard or a sheet of newsprint. Emphasize that God has given us the freedom to make choices. Ask the students to suggest some of the choices they made during the past week.

Most of the choices we make are routine and superficial. What will we wear? What will we have for breakfast? However, some choices are life-changing. Ask the students to suggest some of life's more important decisions. (Examples: what career to pursue, whom to marry, and how we will respond to Jesus' call to discipleship.)

Observe that, when temptation confronts us, we must choose to resist or to give in. In today's lesson, Adam and Eve chose to give in.

INTO THE WORD

Ask a volunteer to read Genesis 3:1-6. Class members should listen for factors that influenced Eve to choose to disobey God—like these:

1. *She entered into a dialogue with the tempter (vv. 1-3).* What should she have done?

2. *She allowed the tempter to plant a seed of doubt in her mind about the goodness of God (vv. 4, 5).* How should she have responded to the tempter's accusation that God was acting selfishly by forbidding access to the tree?

3. *She looked with lustful longing at something that was forbidden (v. 6).* How can we overcome the temptation to look with longing at something (or someone) God has forbidden?

4. *She involved someone else in her sin (v. 6).* What responsibility did Adam have to make a personal choice to resist temptation?

The sins of Adam and Eve resulted in some grave consequences. Direct your students to Genesis 3:7-13, asking them to identify the consequences of sin that appear in that passage.

First, Adam and Eve received firsthand experience of what sin is and how it feels to sin.

Second, they became aware of their nakedness (v. 7). In their pristine state, nakedness was no problem. Now that sin had corrupted their minds, it caused shame.

Third, sin broke their fellowship with God (v. 8). It made them afraid to face God.

Fourth, their sin put a strain on the relationship between Adam and Eve. When confronted by God over his sin, Adam put the blame on his wife (v. 12).

Divide the class into four groups to consider the consequences of sin spelled out in Genesis 3:14-19. Ask Group 1 to find aspects that relate to the serpent—Satan (vv. 14, 15); Group 2, aspects that relate to Eve (v. 16); Group 3, aspects that relate to Adam (vv. 17-19); Group 4, aspects that relate to the earth (vv. 17b, 18).

After five minutes, call for reports from the groups.

INTO LIFE

Begin the application part of the lesson by writing the word *responsibility* on the chalkboard or on a sheet of newsprint. The flip side of freedom is responsibility. We are free to make choices, but we must bear the responsibility for the choices we make.

Ask the students to list excuses people use to escape responsibility for bad choices. Here are some suggestions:

• "Everybody does it."

• "I had an unhappy childhood."

• "I was just doing what I was told."

• "If it feels good, why not do it?"

• "Life is too short to worry about what other people think."

Challenge your students to make wise choices—and then to take personal responsibility for the choices they make. If a bad choice resulted in a spiritual failure, they need to confess their sin and repent.

We all have areas where we are spiritually vulnerable—areas where Satan attacks repeatedly. Ask your students to think about the areas where they are most vulnerable. (Use the reproducible activity "It's So Tempting!" on the next page.) Ask, "What will you do during this coming week to obey God and resist Satan in the specific area of your life where you are most vulnerable?"

Challenge your students to make a commitment to stand firm and resist temptation. Close with a prayer of commitment.

It's So Tempting!

On each of the fruits on the tree below, write the name of something that tempts you today. For example, if you find it difficult to admit to a fault, you might write "Pride," or perhaps, "Telling the truth." Label as many as you can think of.

Look back at each temptation fruit that you listed. Is it connected to the lust of the flesh? If so, write a 1 next to it. Is it the lust of the eyes? Write 2. Is it the vain pride of life? Write 3.

Remember:

"You must not eat fruit from [this tree], or you will die."

GOD'S PEOPLE
DELIVERED FROM SLAVERY

LESSON 2

WHY TEACH THIS LESSON?

The deliverance of the nation of Israel from their bondage in Egypt is one of the most spectacular and memorable events in all of history. It was the basis for an annual celebration in Israel, and it typifies the deliverance from sin's bondage that God effected through Jesus.

It should also be the basis for reassurance and confidence for believers facing great trials today. Perhaps some of your class members are in distress. A married couple is questioning the validity of their vows. A parent is having trouble with a teenager. Another class member is under pressure at work to compromise his values. Some difficult decisions need to be made. The path ahead is not clear, and it looks frightening. Use this lesson to reassure them that the God who led Israel out of bondage will lead them, too.

INTRODUCTION

A. LEARNING FROM DISASTER

Last week we read how disaster came to Adam and Eve. They disobeyed God and lost their home in Eden. Later, their son Cain was born. We do not know if he was told about what had happened in Eden. If so, he did not learn from his parents' disaster. Cain murdered his brother, and in so doing brought a new disaster upon himself (Genesis 4:1-16).

Did Cain's children learn from his disaster? No, in fact it seems that each generation grew more wicked than the one before it. There were exceptions, of course. Enoch walked with God so well that God took him home, bypassing death (Genesis 5:21-24; Hebrews 11:5). For the most part, however, man's condition continued to deteriorate until "the Lord saw how great man's wickedness on the earth had become, and that every inclination of the thoughts of his heart was only evil all the time" (Genesis 6:5).

Such a state was intolerable. God destroyed most of mankind with a great flood, but saved one righteous family (Noah's) so that he could begin again (Genesis 6:9—8:22; 1 Peter 3:20).

B. A NEW BEGINNING

Did Noah's family all learn from the disastrous flood and walk faithfully with God? They did not. The new beginning proved to be merely the beginning of another slide toward increasing wickedness. The attempt to construct the tower of Babel, whose builders declared, "Let us . . . make a name for ourselves" (Genesis 11:4), gave evidence that man was still seeking to live in defiance of his Creator.

However, God did not destroy most of humanity again, as he had through the flood. Instead, he chose one man of faith to be the father of a nation that would

DEVOTIONAL READING
PSALM 105:37-45

LESSON SCRIPTURE
EXODUS 2:23-25; 5:1, 2; 11:1-8;
12:29-32; 15:1, 2, 19-21

PRINTED TEXT
EXODUS 2:23-25; 5:1, 2; 12:29-
32; 15:1, 2

LESSON AIMS

After this lesson a student should be able to:

1. Relate the details of Israel's exodus from Egypt.

2. Describe how God in his providence continues to grant victory and release to his people.

3. Pinpoint an area of life where he or she needs God's deliverance from the power of sin and death.

KEY VERSE

The Israelites groaned in their slavery and cried out, and their cry for help because of their slavery went up to God. God heard their groaning and he remembered his covenant with Abraham, with Isaac, and with Jacob.
—Exodus 2:23, 24

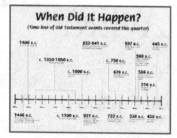

When Did It Happen?
(Time line of Old Testament events covered this quarter)

The visual for lesson 2 is a time line that you will find useful throughout the quarter. Locate the events of today's lesson on it.

WHAT DO YOU THINK?

The Hebrew people groaned under the weight of literal slavery. Jesus said, "Everyone who sins is a slave to sin" (John 8:34). It is obvious that many human beings today are slaves of sin. Some people are trapped in the tangled web of lying. Some people are snared in illicit sexual relationships. Some people are enslaved to alcohol or drugs.

What can we as individual Christians or as a church do to bring liberation to such people? Suggest specific ways of reaching these people with the gospel of Jesus Christ.

WHAT DO YOU THINK?

Of course, some people so enslaved seem not to realize they are in bondage. They do not groan; they celebrate. How can we take God's message of freedom to people who do not realize they are enslaved?

have God's special guidance and blessing—a nation designed to show the rest of the world how good and how profitable it is to obey God.

To begin this favored nation, God brought Abraham from Mesopotamia (Ur of the Chaldees) to the fruitful land east of the Mediterranean Sea. He promised that this land would belong to Abraham and his descendants (Genesis 13:14-17; 15:18-20; 17:8). They were required, however, to live in obedience to the Lord and his covenant (17:9).

C. LESSON BACKGROUND

After approximately two centuries in the land of promise, Abraham's descendants, seventy of them (Genesis 46:27), journeyed to Egypt to escape a great famine. These migrants were welcomed cordially and given a place in the most productive section of the land; for Abraham's great-grandson, Joseph, was a ruler in Egypt at this point and second in command only to the king. Within a few centuries, this family of seventy became a throng of, according to some estimates, two to three million.

The centuries following Joseph brought new leaders to the throne of Egypt and new policies for dealing with the increasing population of Hebrews. (It is possible that the various policies described in Exodus 1 reflect attempts by different Egyptian rulers to control the Hebrews.) The policies included: reducing the Hebrews to slavery and working them to death (v. 11), ordering each Hebrew baby boy to be killed upon delivery (vv. 15-19), and commanding that every Hebrew baby boy be thrown into the river (v. 22).

One boy escaped this last murderous edict and was brought up as a son of the king's daughter. However, at the age of forty he murdered an Egyptian and, to escape the wrath of the king, fled eastward across the desert to Midian (Exodus 2:11-15). There, while tending sheep, this man Moses was prepared by God to shepherd his people. In the meantime, the oppression of the Hebrews worsened.

I. THE BURDEN OF BONDAGE (EXODUS 2:23-25)

A. ISRAEL'S CRY HEARD (v. 23)

23. During that long period, the king of Egypt died. The Israelites groaned in their slavery and cried out, and their cry for help because of their slavery went up to God.

The *king of Egypt died,* but the new king brought no relief to the oppressed Israelites. Terribly overworked, and driven by the whips of brutal taskmasters, they *groaned in their slavery.* Apparently the practice of killing the baby boys had been discontinued. The Egyptians realized that the Hebrew males served a more useful purpose if allowed to grow and become numbered among the slaves.

At this point, the people's condition appeared hopeless. In their misery they *cried out* to the Lord. Both the verb *cried* and the noun *cry* in this verse suggest a loud cry, reflecting a desperate appeal for help from someone deeply troubled. Reading the record now, we see a bright glimmer of hope, for *their cry . . . went up to God.* However, they did not yet know that God had heard and was already planning an end to their misery.

B. GOD'S COVENANT REMEMBERED (v. 24)

24. God heard their groaning and he remembered his covenant with Abraham, with Isaac and with Jacob.

All told, the people of Israel had been enslaved more than four hundred years in Egypt (Genesis 15:13; Exodus 12:40). By now they must have been wondering if God knew or cared about their suffering. But he knew, and he cared deeply. He *heard their groaning:* he knew all about their distress. He *remembered his* covenant—the promise he had made to their ancestors. *Abraham* was the man whom God had called from Mesopotamia to begin a new nation. *Isaac* was Abraham's son; *Jacob* was Isaac's son. To each of these, God had given the promise that their descendants would live in the land of promise (Genesis 15:18-21; 26:1-3; 35:9-12).

The word *remembered* does not suggest God had forgotten his promise and only now remembered. He had been aware of his people's plight all along, and now the time for action had come. That God *remembered* his promise means that he would now take action according to that promise.

C. GOD'S LOVING CONCERN (v. 25)

25. *So God looked on the Israelites and was concerned about them.*

God not only heard the groaning of the Israelites; he also *looked* and saw all their suffering. For the phrase *was concerned about them*, the Hebrew text literally reads, "he knew." Thus by the use of two simple words ("looked" and "knew"), the stage is set for God's calling of Moses (Exodus 3, 4) to be the instrument through whom his people would be set free.

II. REQUEST REJECTED (EXODUS 5:1, 2)

For forty years Moses lived as a fugitive and a shepherd in Midian. Then God sent him back to Egypt to lead the Hebrew slaves to freedom (Exodus 3:9, 10).

A. MOSES' REQUEST (v. 1)

1. *Afterward Moses and Aaron went to Pharaoh and said, "This is what the LORD, the God of Israel, says: 'Let my people go, so that they may hold a festival to me in the desert.'"*

Aaron was Moses' older brother (Exodus 7:7). God had appointed him to help Moses in rescuing the enslaved children of Israel (Exodus 4:10-16). *Pharaoh* is another title for the king of Egypt (the two terms are used interchangeably in Exodus). This was most likely the successor of the pharaoh from whom Moses had fled forty years earlier (Exodus 2:11-15, 23).

The brothers first told the elders of the Israelites that God was about to set them free (Exodus 4:29-31), as Moses had been commanded (3:16, 17). *Afterward* they went to the king. Boldly they told him that God was saying, *Let my people go.* They did not yet tell him that the departure would be permanent; they asked only for permission to go into the *desert* for a religious holiday—*a festival* to the Lord. He later explained this as a "three-day journey into the desert" to hold a sacrifice to the Lord (v. 3). Apparently Moses was testing what Pharaoh's reaction to a very minor request would be.

B. PHARAOH'S DENIAL (v. 2)

2. *Pharaoh said, "Who is the LORD, that I should obey him and let Israel go? I do not know the LORD and I will not let Israel go."*

We wonder if the king was angry or only amused at this point. King though he was, it might be politically expedient for him to listen to Egyptian priests and defer in small ways to Egyptian gods. These Hebrews, however, were saying that the ruler of mighty Egypt was to take orders from the God of slaves. He must have found this ridiculous. His reply was unequivocal: he was not going to *let Israel go.*

CALL WAITING

The "call waiting" service offered by the telephone companies is either a blessing or a curse, depending on one's point of view. If the party we are talking to has "call

---

WHAT DO YOU THINK?

God was concerned about the sufferings of His people. How can we gain a stronger sense of God's concern for all who suffer today? How do John 3:16 and Mark 6:34 speak to this issue?

What about us? What are we doing specifically for the lost and others who suffer? How can we exhibit a greater compassion in this regard?

WHAT DO YOU THINK?

Pharaoh's stubborn resistance to the Lord is one of the striking details in the story of the ten plagues. People today can also be very stubborn. In spite of believers' appeals to trust in Christ and follow him, many unbelievers stubbornly cling to their own way of life. Even Christians can exhibit a Pharaoh-like stubbornness, such as when they resist God's call to sacrificial giving of their financial resources or God's challenge to undertake a position of spiritual leadership.

How can we soften our hearts and help others to soften their hearts to submit to the Lord—in all things?

How to Say It

Babel. BAY-bul.

Chaldees. Kal-DEEZ.

Enoch. EE-nock.

Mediterranean. MED-uh-tuh-RAY-nee-un.

Mesopotamia. MES-uh-puh-TAY-me-uh.

Midian. MID-ee-un.

Pharaoh. FAIR-o or FAY-roe.

What Do You Think?

Some Christians believe natural disasters in our own time are judgments on our culture even as the death of the firstborn in Egypt was a judgment on theirs. Of course, the disaster that rocked Egypt (death of the firstborn) was specifically prophesied for a specific purpose, so we should be cautious about drawing too close a parallel between it and disasters of our day. Still, natural disasters remind us that there is much that we cannot control. If our hope is anchored in this life only, we are at risk.

How can we use the fact of natural disasters to point people toward the Lord? What cautions do you think we should exercise in this?

waiting," it can seem like an impertinent imposition on our time: How could an unknown caller possibly be more important to the person we are conversing with than we are?

On the other hand, most of us have been on the phone at times when we wished we had an easy way to bring the call to a close. Now science has come to our aid! There is an inexpensive gadget that enables a person to duplicate the "call waiting" sound with the mere touch of a button. Appropriately enough, its trade name is "Gotta Go." When your patience with a long-winded caller or telemarketing agent wears thin, just push the button, click the phone off for a few seconds, and then tell your caller, "Sorry, but this is an important call; I've gotta go." However, like so many deceptive "solutions" to modern problems, this one works best if you can silence your conscience.

Pharaoh acted as if he had "call waiting" when Moses asked for permission for the Israelites to go into the wilderness to worship. He asked, "Who is the Lord? He's not important enough for me to talk to him." But Pharaoh eventually learned a lesson we all need to heed: it's very dangerous to "hang up" on God!

—C. R. B.

III. REQUEST GRANTED (EXODUS 12:29-32)

"Who is the Lord, that I should obey him and let Israel go?" Pharaoh asked. He received a clear and powerful answer to this question in the days that followed. The Lord is God! He controls things animate and inanimate, and uses them against people who defy him. The Egyptians saw this demonstrated mightily through the plagues that befell Egypt (Exodus 7:14—10:23). After the first nine, despite the devastation that Egypt had experienced, Pharaoh remained defiant. He told Moses, "Get out of my sight! Make sure you do not appear before me again! The day you see my face you will die" (Exodus 10:28). Thus the power of God was poised for the tenth and most fearsome plague.

A. Disaster (vv. 29, 30)

29. At midnight the Lord struck down all the firstborn in Egypt, from the firstborn of Pharaoh, who sat on the throne, to the firstborn of the prisoner, who was in the dungeon, and the firstborn of all the livestock as well.

What a *midnight* that was! *The firstborn of Pharaoh* was dead, and in every home *in Egypt* a similar disaster took place. Only Hebrew homes were spared. And in the stalls and pastures throughout Egypt, *the firstborn of all the livestock* were dead *as well*.

30. Pharaoh and all his officials and all the Egyptians got up during the night, and there was loud wailing in Egypt, for there was not a house without someone dead.

Apparently the dead did not die quietly in their sleep. Whole families were awakened during the midnight tragedy. *Pharaoh* in his royal palace was stricken with grief, and *all his officials* with him. Beyond the palace walls, *all the Egyptians* were grief-stricken as well. *There was loud wailing in Egypt*: cries of anguish rose from every home. Only in Hebrew houses was there no such mourning.

B. Permission (vv. 31, 32)

31, 32. During the night Pharaoh summoned Moses and Aaron and said, "Up! Leave my people, you and the Israelites! Go, worship the Lord as you have requested. Take your flocks and herds, as you have said, and go. And also bless me."

By this time, the king's haughty defiance had been replaced by humble deference. Filled with grief and terror, he could not wait for daylight. While it was still *night*, he sent messengers to bring *Moses and Aaron*. Hastily he granted all they had asked, urgently telling them to *leave* his country. Pharaoh was a beaten and broken man; his surrender was complete. The God of the Hebrews had carried out a tenfold curse, and had driven him to his knees. In his humiliation, Pharaoh begged Moses for a parting blessing instead of another curse: *And also bless me.*

When the people of Israel received word of their release from slavery, they were ready! They had not gone to bed that night. They had packed their goods. They had earlier celebrated their first Passover (Exodus 12:1-28), for death had passed over them and fallen on the Egyptians.

A GREAT PRICE

In 1967 a violinist at the University of California-Los Angeles (UCLA) borrowed a school violin for an off-campus practice session. After practice, the musician put the violin and its case on the roof of his car and drove off without thinking. That was the last he saw of the violin, which had been crafted in 1732 by the famed Antonio Stradivari.

In 1995, UCLA recovered this $800,000 violin, but not before a lawsuit and a payment of $11,500 to a descendant of the woman who found the instrument alongside a freeway on-ramp. Not knowing the violin's rightful owner, the woman's family had "held it captive" for twenty-eight years. The university concluded that $11,500 was a small price for the redemption of its prized violin.

The people of Israel had been "lost" for over four hundred years before God redeemed them from their captivity to the Egyptians. But when the time came for redemption, it was the Egyptians who paid a great price. During one terrible night, the firstborn in all the land—from Pharaoh's household to the firstborn cattle in the stable—had to give their lives as the price of Israel's freedom.

Whenever valuable property changes hands, whether it is human slaves or a precious musical instrument, there is a cost involved. As Christians, we may be thankful that when our freedom from sin was purchased, God himself is the one who paid the price, giving his only Son.

—C. R. B.

IV. PRAISE THE LORD! (EXODUS 15:1, 2)

Most know what happened after the Israelites left Egypt. Pharaoh had second thoughts about his decision to free the Hebrews. How could he have allowed such an enormous work force to escape? So Pharaoh summoned his army to seize Moses and Aaron, and to bring the runaway slaves back to their toil.

As the Egyptian troops approached the Hebrews' camp, Pharaoh concluded that the Hebrews were "hemmed in" against the Red Sea (Exodus 14:3), trapped in a virtual "no man's land." Then Pharaoh received another extraordinary answer to his earlier query, "Who is the Lord?" The Lord was the one who could push back the sea, leaving a wide stretch of dry land across it, with water standing like a wall on either side. Between those walls the fleeing Hebrews walked—millions of them, with their backpacks, loaded wagons, and animals. Pharaoh's troops hurried after them, but the walls of water collapsed, drowning the entire army.

Now the triumph over Pharaoh and his army was complete. The people of God were safely beyond the waters, and Pharaoh no longer possessed an army to go after them. It was time to celebrate!

A. THE LORD'S TRIUMPH (v. 1a)

1a. Then Moses and the Israelites sang this song to the LORD: "I will sing to the LORD, for he is highly exalted.

WHAT DO YOU THINK?

The Israelites sang a hymn to glorify God for the victory he gave. We, too, sing hymns, but if our hymns merely fill in time in our services, or if we sing mainly because it is a part of our worship that makes us feel good, then we have missed the point. Every hymn we sing should address God with praise or tell of his greatness to others. If they make us feel good, that is a by-product. They first and foremost give glory to God.

Think of a few of your favorite hymns. Why do you like them—because they glorify God or because you like the rhythm or the melody? How can we cultivate a preference for music that glorifies God over music that entertains?

PRAYER

We trust you, Father. Yours is the wisdom and yours is the power. Thank you for delivering us from the horrible slavery of sin through the gospel of our Lord Jesus. Help us to live daily by your power, so that sin will not have dominion over us. Use us to guide others to the freedom that we have found. In Jesus' name. Amen.

THOUGHT TO REMEMBER

Freedom from the bondage of sin is the greatest freedom of all.

DAILY BIBLE READINGS

Monday, Sept. 7—*Israelites Enslaved (Exodus 2:11-25)*

Tuesday, Sept. 8—*Moses Called (Exodus 3:1-12)*

Wednesday, Sept. 9—*"I AM WHO I AM" (Exodus 3:13-22)*

Thursday, Sept. 10—*Pharaoh Resists God (Exodus 4:27—5:9)*

Friday, Sept. 11—*God Repeats the Promise (Exodus 6:1-9)*

Saturday, Sept. 12—*Free at Last! (Exodus 14:19-25)*

Sunday, Sept. 13—*God Remembered the Holy Promise (Psalm 105:23-26)*

Moses took no credit for the Hebrews' deliverance. The triumph belonged *to the Lord,* and all his people knew it. The Lord had disciplined Egypt by means of the ten plagues, forcing Pharaoh to release the slaves; and when Pharaoh had changed his mind and attempted to reverse his decision, the Lord had won a final victory.

B. EGYPT'S DEFEAT (v. 1b)

1b. The horse and its rider he has hurled into the sea.

The Egyptian army had looked invincible with its thundering chariots and well-trained cavalry. The people of Israel had cried out in terror at the sight of them (Exodus 14:10). But with a single stroke, the Lord had ended their threat.

C. HELP FOR GOD'S PEOPLE (v. 2a)

2a. The LORD is my strength and my song; he has become my salvation.

Earlier on that very day, the Hebrews had felt themselves without *strength,* ready to go back to their life of slavery in Egypt (Exodus 14:11, 12). But they were never without strength when the Lord was with them. His strength was their strength, and before it Egypt was as feeble as the Hebrews felt before Egypt. The Lord was also their *salvation,* their deliverance, their preservation, their safety. For these reasons, he was their *song*—their hymn of praise and thanksgiving. Note the use of the personal pronoun *my;* these were meant to be words of praise for each Israelite to offer.

D. GRATEFUL PROMISE (v. 2b)

2b. He is my God, and I will praise him, my father's God, and I will exalt him.

This was now Israel's "pledge of allegiance." The Lord, Jehovah, *is my God*—the one I will worship, the one on whom I can depend, the one I will obey.

These grateful Hebrews were not lifting their *praise* to an unknown God. The Lord had been their God all their lives, even when they had been living in the misery of slavery. He had been the God of their fathers through the centuries since Abraham. We today who have faith in him and his Son are children of Abraham as well (Romans 4:23, 24; Galatians 3:29). The same Lord who made a way through the sea has opened ways for us through many difficulties, and will open more.

I will exalt him. Glory, honor, and highest praise to the Lord! This was the song of Moses and the grateful Hebrews. Is it not the song of every grateful Christian today?

CONCLUSION

The slavery in which Egypt held Israel for so many long years was cruel and oppressive. However, it is only one illustration of the slavery in which Satan has held mankind ever since the entrance of sin into the world. (See last week's lesson from Genesis 3.) In today's world, examples of such bondage are abundant. The sad irony is that so many believe that they are on the road to freedom. They, like Eve, have been duped by the father of lies (John 8:44).

This slavery has only one solution. It is found in the One who declared, "If the Son sets you free, you will be free indeed" (John 8:36). Hebrews 2:14, 15 tells us that Jesus came "so that by his death he might destroy him who holds the power of death—that is, the devil—and free those who all their lives were held in slavery by their fear of death."

Thank God that through Jesus, the chains of mankind's worst bondage can be broken.

Discovery Learning

This page contains an alternate lesson plan emphasizing learning activities. Classes desiring such student involvement will find these suggestions helpful. The next page is a reproducible activity page to further enhance discovery learning.

LEARNING GOALS

As a result of this lesson, each student in your class should be able to:

1. Relate the details of Israel's exodus from Egypt.

2. Describe how God in his providence continues to grant victory and release to his people.

3. Pinpoint an area of life where he or she needs God's deliverance from the power of sin and death.

INTO THE LESSON

Briefly summarize the historical background to build a bridge between last week's lesson and this lesson. (See sections B and C on pages 25 and 26.) Explain why the Hebrews were in Egypt and why they were slaves.

Introduce the lesson by asking your students if they have ever felt powerless. At one time or another we all feel as if we are being victimized by "the system" or an unfair law or a tyrannical boss or someone else. Ask your students to share some of their experiences with powerlessness. How did their powerlessness cause them to feel? How did they deal with their powerlessness?

The Hebrew slaves in Egypt knew all about powerlessness. They were oppressed and depressed, and no one came to deliver them. In today's lesson we look at what God did to get his people out of their predicament.

INTO THE WORD

God knows our situation. That comes through strongly in today's lesson. To demonstrate that, ask your students to look for the action verbs in Exodus 2:24 and 25, and then to explain how each action verb shows not only God's knowledge of our situation but also his concern.

1. God "heard" (v. 24). God hears everything that is said. But here the implication is that he heard with compassion, as a father listens to his children.

2. God "remembered" (v. 24). He remembered the covenant he had made with Abraham and his descendants. While the people had forgotten (violated) the covenant, God honored it.

3. God "looked" (v. 25). God's look implies action. When God looks, things happen.

4. God "was concerned" (v. 25). God was concerned about his people. He was moved to action by their plight.

Write the word *providence* on the chalkboard (or use the reproducible page that follows for a similar learning activity). Ask a volunteer to define or describe providence. (*Providence is God's provision for his people through miraculous or natural means, often unnoticed until later, when one can look back and see that God was at work through one's circumstances.*) Ask, "How can God's providence be seen in the situation of the Israelites in bondage in Egypt?" Draw special attention to Exodus 5:1, 2 and 12:29-32 of today's text. List the class's ideas on the chalkboard. Here are some suggestions:

1. By God's providence Moses was adopted by Pharaoh's daughter and reared with both the best Hebrew instruction and the best Egypt had to offer.

2. Moses spent forty years in the desert being prepared by God to lead his people.

3. Pharaoh's resistance (Exodus 5:1, 2) provided an opportunity for God to demonstrate his power over the Egyptian gods.

4. In the tenth plague (Exodus 12:29-32) Pharaoh was humbled before God, and the Israelites were delivered with Pharaoh's blessing.

5. When Pharaoh sent his army after the Israelites, God's providence delivered his people through the Red Sea, and the Egyptians were drowned.

When you have a good list of ideas, ask, "How does God in his providence continue to grant victory and release to his people?" Discuss how you and your students have seen God's providence at work.

INTO LIFE

It is proper to celebrate spiritual victories. Moses and the Israelites celebrated their victory over the Egyptians by singing a song of praise to God.

Read Exodus 15:1, 2. Then provide hymnals and ask the students to look for hymns that offer praise and thanksgiving to God. Compile a list of these hymns on the chalkboard. Your class might want to sing or recite in unison one of the hymns of praise.

God can deliver your students from the forces and the powers of evil just as surely as he delivered the ancient Hebrews. Hand out index cards, and ask each student to write down a specific area of life in which he or she needs God's deliverance. Then close with prayer, asking God to give your students the strength to trust him to provide the deliverance they need.

Looking for Providence

Providence is God's provision for his people through miraculous or natural means, often unnoticed until later, when one can look back and see that God was at work through one's circumstances. For example, we can see God's providence at work when Moses was adopted by Pharaoh's daughter, thus preserving alive the one whom God would use to deliver the Israelites. What are some other ways God's providence can be seen in the situation of the Israelites in bondage in Egypt? (Pay special attention to Exodus 5:1, 2 and 12:29-32.) Cite these on the chart below.

EVENT	REFERENCE	EVIDENCE OF GOD'S PROVIDENCE
Moses adopted by Pharaoh's daughter.	Exodus 2:1-10	Moses' life was spared and he was able to receive the best education Egypt had to offer, as well as spiritual training by his own mother—his Hebrew "nurse" (vv. 8, 9).

How have you seen God's providence at work in your own life?

Write a brief prayer of thanks and praise for God's providence.

GOD'S EXPECTATIONS MADE PLAIN

WHY TEACH THIS LESSON?

"Everyone talks about the weather, but nobody does anything about it!" That old line still makes us chuckle, and perhaps reminds us that we're not as powerful as we sometimes pretend. Lately the Ten Commandments have people talking, more about where they can or cannot be posted than anything else, but still they are being discussed. Perhaps we could say, "Everyone is talking about the Ten Commandments, but nobody is doing anything about them."

The Ten Commandments need to be more than a plaque on the wall or the topic of discussion in a politically charged debate. Use this lesson to help your students appreciate the purpose and goal of the Ten Commandments, and to put them into practice in their own lives.

INTRODUCTION

A. A GREAT ADVANTAGE

The people of Israel had been slaves in Egypt for generations. They had no experience with government, and no understanding of how to form a nation. Then suddenly they were free. Their bondage was behind them, but so were their homes and their means of making a living. Imagine how hard it would be to mold some two to three million people into a nation.

But the people of Israel had one great advantage: They were *God's* people. He was in charge. He showed them which way to travel; he fed them with manna; he brought water from the rock to quench their thirst. Most significant of all, he gave them laws to govern their emerging nation. Was ever another infant nation so well cared for? If Israel's obedience had been as reliable as the Lord's provisions, the results would have been remarkable.

B. LESSON BACKGROUND

By crossing the Red Sea, the people of Israel escaped from Egypt and entered the wilderness of the Sinai Peninsula. After two months of travel, they camped in a broad plain beside towering Mount Sinai. There they stayed for nearly a year, receiving God's laws from Moses and building the tabernacle as God had planned and instructed. God's laws covered many important areas of life, but the core of these laws was the Ten Commandments, which were written on two tablets of stone with "the finger of God" (Exodus 31:18).

In the second year of their journey, the people came to the border of the land God had promised them for their permanent home. There the people's faith fell prey to fear. Frightened by the big men and the fortified cities within Canaan, they refused to enter the promised land.

Because of their faithless spirit, the Israelites were sentenced to live in the desert for thirty-eight more years. The total number of years of wandering (forty)

DEVOTIONAL READING
ISAIAH 49:1-6
LESSON SCRIPTURE
DEUTERONOMY 5:1-21
PRINTED TEXT
DEUTERONOMY 5:6-21

LESSON AIMS

After this lesson, a student should be able to:

1. Recite the Ten Commandments.

2. Explain the relevance of these commandments today.

3. Suggest a means by which obedience to one specific commandment can be improved in one's personal life or in his or her community.

OPTION

Begin by seeing how many of the Ten Commandments your students can list. Use the reproducible activity on page 40.

KEY VERSE

I am the LORD your God, who brought you out of Egypt, out of the land of slavery. You shall have no other gods before me.
—Deuteronomy 5:6, 7

LESSON 3 NOTES

The visual for lesson 3 beautifully illustrates today's Key Verse (King James Version). Display it as you begin to discuss verses 5 and 6.

WHAT DO YOU THINK?

People may not bow before them in classic "pagan worship," but homes, automobiles, recreational vehicles, and similar possessions certainly appear to be idols to many people today. Others claim to worship God, but their concept of God has no basis in the truth revealed in Scripture. They have fashioned their own god as surely as did those who cast golden idols.

How can we help such "idolaters" see their need to worship the Lord God and him only? What can we do to guard ourselves from becoming idolaters?

was based on one year for each day of the forty-day mission to explore the land of Canaan (Numbers 14:34). Those adults who had balked at the border of Canaan died during those years of wandering, to be replaced by a new generation.

In the fortieth year of their wandering, the Israelites approached once more the border of the promised land. There Moses reviewed events from the past forty years. In it he repeated the Ten Commandments that had been given thirty-eight years earlier. Those Ten Commandments are the focus of our study today.

I. THE LORD AND YOU (DEUTERONOMY 5:6-11)

A. THE LIBERATOR (v. 6)

6. "I am the LORD your God, who brought you out of Egypt, out of the land of slavery.

Before revealing the contents of his law, God revealed himself and reminded the Israelites who he was. He was *the Lord your God.* Here *the Lord* represents the Hebrew name that has come into our language as "Jehovah" or "Yahweh." That name describes the I AM (Exodus 3:14): he is the only God who really exists. Next, God reminded the people that he had freed them from *the land of slavery.* That reminder served two purposes.

First, the people were reminded of God's power. Their release from *Egypt* had been accomplished by a series of mighty miracles: the ten plagues on Egypt and the marvelous opening of the Red Sea. The God who was powerful enough to bring his people out of Egypt would be powerful enough to bring them into the land of promise. They need not be afraid, as their fathers had been years before.

Second, the people were reminded of God's goodness to them. He had liberated them from generations of cruel slavery. Simple gratitude should move them to receive God's law and obey it gladly, and to move boldly into the promised land in spite of the dangers.

B. THE ONE AND ONLY (vv. 7-10)

7. "You shall have no other gods before me.

To many of us, this command against the worship of other gods may seem irrelevant, since there may be no pagan shrines or temples where we live. However, let us never forget our Master's warning: "You cannot serve both God and money" (Matthew 6:24). Paul adds that greed is idolatry (Colossians 3:5). Not all the world's idols are ugly carved statues made of gold, silver, or bronze. We are to "flee from idolatry" in any form (1 Corinthians 10:14).

8. "You shall not make for yourself an idol in the form of anything in heaven above or on the earth beneath or in the waters below.

This verse is not meant to forbid any artistic painting or sculpture. According to the book of Exodus, God ordered his people to make representations of various items as furnishings for the tabernacle: cherubim (25:18), almond flowers with their buds and blossoms (25:33), and pomegranates and bells (28:33, 34). On one occasion he even commanded Moses to fashion a snake (Numbers 21:8). To be understood, this verse must be read with the following one.

9. You shall not bow down to them or worship them; for I, the LORD your God, am a jealous God, punishing the children for the sin of the fathers to the third and fourth generation of those who hate me,

Now we see what verse 8 is saying: We must not make graven images and *bow down to them or worship them.* God is not *jealous* just because a sculptor prepares a beautiful statue; he is jealous when someone worships such a statue. Consider again the snake that Moses was commanded to construct. When it was used for God's stated purpose, it was a blessing; but in later years, when people began to worship it, it became an abomination and had to be destroyed (2 Kings 18:4).

God's jealousy is not an evil thing, as human jealousy usually is. He does not demand all our worship just for his own gratification; he demands it because it is bad for us to worship anyone or anything else. It is *sin*, and it will bring bad results to our *children* and grandchildren as well as to us.

While children do not share the guilt of their fathers unless they also do wrong, they may share some of the results of his wrongdoing. For example, a man engages in illicit behavior and contracts AIDS. He transmits it to his wife, and she passes it on to the unborn children in her womb. Or a man worships money and resorts to fraud for the sake of gain. He is caught, and then forced to pay a heavy fine in order to reimburse those he has defrauded. His children are reduced to poverty along with him. In addition, they are likely to lose the trust and respect of neighbors because of their father's wrongdoing.

10. But showing love to a thousand generations of those who love me and keep my commandments.

Here is the brighter side of the picture. When a man gives the Lord all his worship, all his allegiance, and all his obedience, the Lord blesses not only that man, but also his children and grandchildren who follow his example. Is there any doubt which way is the one to choose?

C. THE REVEREND (v. 11)

11. "You shall not misuse the name of the LORD your God, for the LORD will not hold anyone guiltless who misuses his name.

"Holy and awesome is his name" (Psalm 111:9). God's name is to be held in reverence, as God himself is. *Misuse* represents a Hebrew phrase that has varied meanings and can apply to much more than just swearing. This commandment is violated when God's name is used for any evil purpose; it is violated when his name is used lightly, frivolously, and with no meaning or purpose at all; it is violated when one swears falsely by God; it is violated when one swears profanely by God; and it is violated when one uses God's name as a mere expression of surprise, alarm, or indignation. "I don't mean anything by it," a man says to excuse such frivolous use of God's name. But this is part of what it means to *misuse* God's name. The name of the Lord should never be spoken or written without reverence.

II. THE SABBATH AND YOU (DEUTERONOMY 5:12-15)

A. A HOLY DAY (v. 12)

12. "Observe the Sabbath day by keeping it holy, as the LORD your God has commanded you.

The seventh day was to be made *holy*, or set apart from the others, and to be dedicated to rest from labor, as we see in the following verse. God had prepared the people for this commandment when he began providing manna for them (Exodus 16:22-30).

B. WORK AND REST (vv. 13, 14)

13. Six days you shall labor and do all your work,

As a rule, a man ought to *work* and earn his living. This is not only permitted, but commanded (1 Thessalonians 4:11, 12; 2 Thessalonians 3:10-12). But he ought to work no more than *six* days a week.

14. But the seventh day is a Sabbath to the LORD your God. On it you shall not do any work, neither you, nor your son or daughter, nor your manservant or maidservant, nor your ox, your donkey or any of your animals, nor the alien within your gates, so that your manservant and maidservant may rest, as you do.

WHAT DO YOU THINK?

What are some ways in which people misuse the name of God and the name of Jesus Christ?

One writer mentions a friend who bought a used car because "the Lord led" him to that specific car. But the car turned out to be a lemon! The writer questioned whether the Lord had really led his friend to make the purchase and wondered whether we take God's name in vain when we carelessly claim God's leading for our own decisions. What do you think?

WHAT DO YOU THINK?

The command to refrain from work on the Sabbath is not given to Christians in the New Testament. Some Christians, however, believe Sunday should be observed as a "Christian Sabbath." What do you think? How should Christians apply the fourth Commandment?

Ordinary daily *work* was to stop on the *Sabbath*. All the people were to rest: children as well as parents, slaves as well as masters, foreigners as well as Israelites. Even the domestic *animals* were to have a day of rest.

C. MEMORIAL OF DELIVERANCE (v. 15)

15. Remember that you were slaves in Egypt and that the LORD your God brought you out of there with a mighty hand and an outstretched arm. Therefore the LORD your God has commanded you to observe the Sabbath day.

According to Exodus 20:11, the *Sabbath* law was based on God's rest after creation, but in our text another thought is added. Verse 14 ends with the command that a Hebrew must give his slave a day of rest; verse 15 adds a reminder that the Hebrew himself had been a slave *in Egypt* until God had manifested his *mighty* power to set him free. The *Sabbath day* was to be a weekly reminder of God's rescue of the Hebrews and of his special covenant with them.

IT'S ABOUT TIME!

For some people in the United States, time stood still for a few minutes on November 18, 1883. For other people that day, time jumped forward. It all depended on which of the country's fifty-six time zones one lived in.

In earlier times, the shadow on a local sundial had been sufficiently accurate for most communities. As the modern era dawned, life became more complicated and timekeeping became more sophisticated: clocks were set according to a telegraph signal from an observatory that performed star sightings on clear nights.

The increasing popularity of travel by railroad is what precipitated the change to four "standard" time zones on that Sunday in 1883. Without a time standard, no one knew when a train was "on time."

God established the Sabbath as a standard by which Israel could measure the use of time. It was a holy day, set aside for the regular worship of God. It was a day of rest dedicated to remembering that God had delivered them from bondage—especially significant for a nation of freed slaves who had never known a "day off."

The New Testament does not include commandments regarding a "Sabbath" day, but it does indicate the significance of the first day of the week for Christians (Acts 20:7; 1 Corinthians 16:2). We do well to make this day a day in which we rest from our labors and remember the one who delivered us from our bondage to sin.
—C. R. B.

III. OTHER PEOPLE AND YOU (DEUTERONOMY 5:16-21)

The first four of the Ten Commandments deal with the duties of God's people toward him: worship him, not anyone or anything else; revere his name; observe his Sabbath. The other six commandments deal with one's duties toward others.

A. HONOR TO PARENTS (v. 16)

16. "Honor your father and your mother, as the LORD your God has commanded you, so that you may live long and that it may go well with you in the land the LORD your God is giving you.

This is named first among one's duties to others, perhaps because its results are so widespread and so far-reaching. God calls parents to teach his law to their children (Deuteronomy 6:6, 7), and children to honor their parents as well as God by learning and obeying that teaching. When these commandments are obeyed, generation after generation does right. The result is healthful, helpful, and peaceful living. Such living generally results in longer life, for obedient children do not destroy their lives by participating in self-destructive acts such as taking drugs, drinking alcohol, or provoking fights.

B. NO MURDER (v. 17)

17. *"You shall not murder.*

This commandment was not meant to forbid capital punishment. We know this because God's law commanded such punishment for a variety of acts: murder, striking or cursing a parent, kidnapping (Exodus 21:12-17); adultery, fornication, or rape (Deuteronomy 22:22-25); cursing God (Leviticus 24:15, 16); breaking the Sabbath (Exodus 31:14); witchcraft (Exodus 22:18); and idolatry (Exodus 22:20). Neither was the commandment meant to prohibit killing during a just and honorable war. God sent his people into the promised land with orders to "destroy . . . totally" the evil people living there (Deuteronomy 7:1, 2). But God's law forbade the willful taking of another human life.

C. NO ADULTERY (v. 18)

18. *"You shall not commit adultery.*

Promiscuous sex was popular among ancient pagans, as it is among unbelievers today. But God's law permitted sexual relations only between a man and a woman married to each other. As already noted, not only was *adultery* forbidden, but also rape and sexual immorality of any kind (Deuteronomy 22:22-25).

D. NO STEALING (v. 19)

19. *"You shall not steal.*

The right to ownership of private property is crucial for the security and stability of any society. Stealing is wrong, whether done by force, by stealth, or by deceit.

E. NO FALSE TESTIMONY (v. 20)

20. *"You shall not give false testimony against your neighbor.*

The term *false testimony* suggests perjury in a court of law. Such "false reports" were forbidden (Exodus 23:1). When applied to our conduct toward a *neighbor*, this commandment prohibits any attempt to twist the truth in our speech, whether by lying or gossip.

F. NO COVETING (v. 21)

21. *"You shall not covet your neighbor's wife. You shall not set your desire on your neighbor's house or land, his manservant or maidservant, his ox or donkey, or anything that belongs to your neighbor."*

Desire and *covet* may be regarded as synonyms. It is not wrong to want a wife or a house or a field; but it is wrong for anyone to have an envious wish for *anything that belongs to your neighbor*. Such envious wishing makes one unhappy, and may turn him into a thief.

All these commandments concerning relations with others are summed up in Leviticus 19:18: "Love your neighbor as yourself." If I really do that, I will not feel bad because my neighbor has a better house than I have. I will rejoice in his blessing as much as I would if the house were mine.

CONCERNED FOR OTHERS

Malden Mills is one of the last large textile mills remaining in New England. It is the largest employer in the village of Methuen, Massachusetts. But one night just before Christmas of 1995, the mill burned to the ground. Immediately fourteen hundred people were out of a job. They expected the fire to close the mill forever.

But the citizens of Methuen were not counting on the moral character of Aaron Feuerstein, the seventy-year-old owner of the mill. The morning after the fire, he said, "With God's help, we will overcome what has happened." Then he gave

WHAT DO YOU THINK?

It is interesting to note that obeying the command to refrain from coveting helps one in obeying some of the commands that precede it. The command to refrain from coveting someone else's wife could make the prohibition against adultery unnecessary. The command to refrain from coveting someone else's property could make the prohibition against stealing unnecessary. We may also wonder how often the dishonoring of parents, murder, and the bearing of false witness are the fruit of a heart set on covetousness.

At the same time, the advertising industry seems bent on getting us to covet! How can we guard against this dangerous and deadly sin? What safeguards can you suggest?

WHAT DO YOU THINK?

Some observers have pointed out that many people treat the Ten Commandments as though they were the "ten suggestions." Christians often claim they want to uphold the standard that God has set down in his Word. But what message is sent when Christian divorce rates approach the secular, or when a believer takes advantage of an opportunity for financial gain that he has not honestly earned?

To what degree is the church to blame for treating the Commandments as suggestions? What can we do to correct that?

THOUGHT TO REMEMBER

God's commandments are designed to add to, not take away, our enjoyment of life.

PRAYER

How gracious you are, our Father! How grateful we are for your forgiveness! Continue to bless us, we pray, and grant us wisdom, strength, and courage to do your will day by day. In Jesus' name. Amen.

every worker a paycheck and a $275 Christmas bonus. Two days later, Feuerstein announced that everyone would be paid for at least thirty days, and promised that the mill would be back in operation within ninety days. He later extended the pay for another thirty days. The mill was rebuilt on the promised schedule, and the grateful town now views this man as a hero.

The latter part of the Ten Commandments may be summarized as a demand that we be concerned for the welfare of others rather than our own desires. There are few better modern examples of this principle than Aaron Feuerstein. At a time in his life when he could have "picked up his marbles and gone home" (with few people blaming him for doing so), he demonstrated a godly concern for others that is worthy of emulation.

—C. R. B.

CONCLUSION

A. THE NATION GOD MADE

The nation God made possessed several advantages over others. First, its leader was faultless, all-wise, and all-powerful. He was the Lord, Jehovah, maker of Heaven and earth, the one and only God. Second, this faultless God let his people know exactly what he expected of them. The laws he gave were as faultless as himself. We have just surveyed the Ten Commandments. God also revealed additional laws to his people to govern the details of their daily living. These were exactly the laws needed in the nation God established. They stood for centuries, needing no additions or amendments.

The success of this nation depended not only on the excellence of the leader and his laws, but also on the response of the people. The faultless laws would not accomplish their purpose unless they were obeyed.

B. MAN-MADE NATIONS

No other nation can claim what ancient Israel could—that it is a nation God made. All other nations, both past and present, are man-made nations. This is not to belittle the influence of God in their making—at least some of them. Many Americans see God's hand at work in the founding of their nation. The collapse of the Soviet Union and the emergence of free nations that resulted may well be another example of God's providence. But God did not provide these nations with their constitutions or any of their laws. Congresses and parliaments meet almost continuously to make new laws and revise old ones.

Still, the success of any nation depends on its people more than on its leaders and its laws. Why haven't laws put a stop to murder? Because people are killers. Why does stealing continue in spite of laws? Because sneak thieves pilfer in darkness, armed robbers operate in daylight, and officials high in industry and government embezzle millions of dollars. Why does the tragic toll of death on the highways continue? Because people ignore the laws made for their safety.

The need is not for new laws as much as for new hearts. Any nation can rise to heights unexpected and marvelous if its people will go beyond the Ten Commandments and keep the commandments directed at the heart: "Love the Lord your God with all your heart and with all your soul and with all your strength" (Deuteronomy 6:5); and "Love your neighbor as yourself" (Leviticus 19:18).

The faultless covenant God made at Sinai included those commandments. However, that covenant was inadequate because people did not keep the commandments. So God offered a New Covenant whose crowning feature is forgiveness of sins (Jeremiah 31:31-34). Jesus Christ is the mediator of that better covenant (Hebrews 8:6). The hope of the world lies in turning to him and in leading others to open their hearts to his rule.

Discovery Learning

This page contains an alternate lesson plan emphasizing learning activities. Classes desiring such student involvement will find these suggestions helpful. The next page is a reproducible activity page to further enhance discovery learning.

LEARNING GOALS

As a result of this lesson, each of your students should be able to:

1. Recite the Ten Commandments.

2. Explain the relevance of these Commandments today.

3. Suggest a means by which obedience to one specific Commandment can be improved in his or her personal life or in the community.

INTO THE LESSON

Make several large "road signs" (speed limit, stop, etc.) and post them around the room. Begin the lesson by asking the students to imagine that there are no traffic laws: no speed limits, no stop signs, no yield signs, no one-way signs, no do-not-enter signs. Each person is free to drive in any way he or she desires. What would it be like to drive in such a "lawless" environment?

Ask, "What does this tell us about human nature? What does it tell us about the need for laws and the enforcement of those laws? What kind of society would we have if there were no laws?"

In today's lesson we look at the laws God gave his people after they were released from slavery and able to establish their own nation. Through these laws God told the people what he required of them and established a system of national order.

INTO THE WORD

The Ten Commandments are familiar to us all, but can any of your students recite the Commandments in order? Distribute copies of the reproducible page that follows and see how many can list all ten. Or have the Commandments listed on the chalkboard or on a large poster, and have the class read through the list in unison. Then cover all or part of one of them and have the class read through the list again—including the one that is covered. Keep covering more of the list and reading through the list together until the class can recite the entire list without seeing any of the words.

God's ten laws fall naturally into two categories: laws that govern our relationship with God, and laws that govern our relationships with other people. Divide the class into two groups. Group 1 will examine Deuteronomy 5:6-11 to see what the first four Commandments tell us about our relationship with God. Group 2 will examine Deuteronomy 5:12-21 to see what Commandments 5-10 tell us about our relationships with others.

Give Group 1 some magazines and ask them to create a montage of pictures, logos, and other symbols of items that can become "gods" to people today. The purpose here is to emphasize that whatever comes between us and God is an idolatrous item of worship.

Give Group 2 some newspapers and ask them to cut out several headlines. Then ask them to note which Commandment(s) was/were likely broken to result in each action that made the news. (If newspapers are not readily available, group members can write some typical headlines for this exercise.) The idea here is to see how disregard for God's law contributes to today's social ills.

After a few minutes have each group report. As Group 1 concludes its report, note that the collage deals with the first two Commandments, but there are two more that concern our relationship with God. Discuss the third and fourth Commandments with the class, using the "What Do You Think?" questions on page 35.

As Group 2 concludes its report, note that the tenth Commandment sums up many of the others. Use the "What Do You Think?" question on page 37 to discuss this issue.

INTO LIFE

Ask, "How important are these commands for us today? Why?" Your students' first reaction will be to affirm that the Ten Commandments are very important. Challenge them on this. Note that even very few Christians keep the fourth Commandment. Even if they do no work on Sunday, the Commandment says "the sabbath," which means "seventh," or Saturday. If we don't have to keep Saturday holy, why do we have to observe the other nine Commandments? This should lead to a probing of the principles behind each command. Observing the Lord's Day (Sunday) keeps the spirit of the fourth Commandment, just as watching our tempers is important to keeping the spirit of the sixth (Matthew 5:21, 22).

Remind your students that God has told us what he requires. Our task is to translate those requirements into standards for everyday living. In closing, tell your students to select one of the Ten Commandments that they have not been following as carefully as they should. Challenge them to make a conscious effort to improve its observance during the coming week.

The Ten Commandments

There is a lot of talk about the Ten Commandments, even in the news. Remember the Alabama judge who refused to remove the plaque of the Ten Commandments from his courtroom wall? For all our talk, however, do we really know them? How many of the Ten Commandments can you write without looking them up? Can you get them in the right order? Give it a try. Then read Deuteronomy 5:6-21 and see how well you did.

The first four Commandments concern our relationship with God. Write them here:

I.

II.

III.

IV.

The last six Commandments concern our relationship with each other. Write them here:

V.

VI.

VII.

VIII.

IX.

X.

GOD'S ACTIONS REMEMBERED

LESSON 4

DEVOTIONAL READING
PSALM 78:1-8

LESSON SCRIPTURE
JOSHUA 3:7—4:24

PRINTED TEXT
JOSHUA 4:1-3, 8-11, 20-24

Sep
27

WHY TEACH THIS LESSON?

"I don't remember." It's a common plea, but it usually brings trouble. The student who is asked by her teacher to recite certain facts is embarrassed to have to say instead, "I don't remember." The young husband is in big trouble if the wife asks about an anniversary and he has to reply, "I forgot."

God has always known that we humans can have short memories. So he does not berate us and make us feel guilty. He gives instead some helpful reminders, and he encourages us to set up reminders of our own. As we'll see in today's lesson, he told the Israelites to set up memorials to recall their crossing of the Jordan. His Son gave the church the Lord's Supper and said, "Do this in remembrance of me."

These are special reminders, but they are not the only ones. Use this lesson to encourage your students to make their own reminders of the good things God is doing in their lives. It might be as simple as a note carried in a wallet or jotted in the margin of a Bible. It might be more ornate, like a lovely embroidered Bible verse framed and hung on the wall in the living room. Some time in the future, perhaps when they are feeling discouraged, they will be glad to have such reminders.

INTRODUCTION

A. MEMORIES

How we love our memories! When I moved to Cincinnati, I found in a little downtown park a statue of William Henry Harrison. He served as the ninth President of the United States, but the statue shows him as a soldier, sitting tall on his handsome horse. Harrison's tenure as President lasted only thirty-one days, so his battlefield heroics outshine his White House career.

At the other end of the park is a statue of James A. Garfield. He, too, was a notable soldier, but the statue represents him in civilian clothes; for he is better remembered as the twentieth President of the United States.

Perhaps your town has a relic, statue, or monument dedicated to the memory of some person or event. This week we focus attention on a pair of monuments erected more than three thousand years ago. They served to commemorate an event that will not be forgotten while the world stands.

B. LESSON BACKGROUND

Last week we saw the people of Israel encamped on the east bank of the Jordan River. At this point, they had conquered two nations there and taken possession of their lands (Numbers 21:21-35). There Moses recounted the laws that God had given the people to follow, including the Ten Commandments (Exodus 20:1-17; Deuteronomy 5:6-21).

LESSON AIMS

After this lesson students should be able to:

1. Tell how Israel crossed the Jordan River and why they set up memorial stones.

2. Recall at least one spiritual milestone in their lives or in the lives of their families and church.

3. Praise and thank God for what he has done, as represented in these milestones.

KEY VERSE

In the future when your descendants ask their fathers, "What do these stones mean?" tell them, "Israel crossed the Jordan on dry ground."

— Joshua 4:21, 22

Moses died soon after this (Deuteronomy 34:1-8). After a month of mourning for him, it was time for the people to cross the Jordan and continue their conquests on the west side of the river. Joshua had already been appointed as Moses' successor to provide leadership for the people (Numbers 27:15-23).

The Bible records how the Jordan was flooded at the time the people prepared to cross (Joshua 3:15; 4:18). However, when the priests who were carrying the ark of the covenant placed their feet in the river, the waters miraculously separated. The waters from the north "piled up in a heap" (3:16), leaving an area of dry ground over which the people could cross. Priests carrying the ark of the covenant stopped in the middle of the dry riverbed. The waters did not come near them, but remained motionless until all the Israelites had crossed to the other side (v. 17).

I. MEMORIAL STONES (JOSHUA 4:1-3)

Even after all the people had reached the west bank of the river, the priests who carried the ark of the covenant remained standing in the middle of the dry riverbed. Another important matter needed to be taken care of, and they could not move on until it was.

A. SIGNIFICANT COMMITTEE (vv. 1, 2)

1, 2. When the whole nation had finished crossing the Jordan, the LORD said to Joshua, "Choose twelve men from among the people, one from each tribe,

The business at hand involved *the whole nation*, so the committee included *twelve men—one* taken *from each tribe*.

B. SIGNIFICANT STONES (v. 3)

3. And tell them to take up twelve stones from the middle of the Jordan from right where the priests stood and to carry them over with you and put them down at the place where you stay tonight."

Like the men who carried them, the *stones* represented the twelve tribes of Israel. The monument formed from these stones would become a monument for the entire nation, commemorating the crossing of the river by all twelve tribes. Nothing is said about the size of the stones, but it seems reasonable to suppose that each man chose a stone as big as he could easily carry to the bank.

II. MONUMENT IN THE RIVER (JOSHUA 4:8-11)

Verses 4-7 record how Joshua explained the purpose of the stones to the men who would carry them. The stones constituted a memorial of the miraculous crossing of the Jordan. We omit this explanation at this point because it is repeated in the last part of our printed text.

A. MISSION ACCOMPLISHED (v. 8)

8. So the Israelites did as Joshua commanded them. They took twelve stones from the middle of the Jordan, according to the number of the tribes of the Israelites, as the LORD had told Joshua; and they carried them over with them to their camp, where they put them down.

The *twelve stones from the middle of the Jordan* were carried to the bank as Joshua ordered. This verse also emphasizes that the command Joshua gave was not his own, but one that *the Lord* had given him. Then it repeats the fact that the stones represented *the number of the tribes of the Israelites*. However, before we read more about the significance of those stones, we are told how twelve other stones were selected and used.

WHAT DO YOU THINK?

God called for the use of stones in building a memorial to the Jordan River crossing. Jesus instituted the Lord's Supper by employing bread and grape juice in a memorial meal. What do you think—is this a precedent for our worship, suggesting that things should always be kept simple and common? Why or why not? If so, how do we explain the extravagance of the ark of the covenant that the priests carried, which was overlaid with gold inside and out? Solomon's temple had gold and silver and bronze in abundance. How do you know when to be simple and when to be extravagant in your expressions of worship?

B. LASTING MONUMENT (v. 9)

9. Joshua set up the twelve stones that had been in the middle of the Jordan at the spot where the priests who carried the ark of the covenant had stood. And they are there to this day.

The *New International Version* understands this verse as a summation of what transpired according to the preceding verse. Most other versions, however, see this verse as describing a second memorial that Joshua erected *in the middle of the Jordan at the spot where the priests . . . stood.* The NIV suggests this as an alternate reading in a footnote. The verse would then read, "Joshua also set up twelve stones in the middle of the Jordan. . . ."

In spite of the rendering we have here in the NIV, the original text seems to give better support to the dual-monument understanding, and nothing about the practicality of the idea seriously challenges this understanding. Some students believe that a monument in the river would have been useless because it would have been hidden by the water or because they believe the flowing stream would have soon demolished the monument. However, the Jordan River flows quite slowly—one writer calls it "sluggish"—and would not quickly dislodge such a monument. Large, heavy stones could have been used in the riverbed, since they did not have to be carried far. Probably the place chosen was a ford, where the river was shallow and fairly calm except in time of flood. If so, then it is likely that the top of the monument could be seen above the water during the dry season. If any stones were displaced, then travelers could replace them as they went by. A monument in the middle of the river would have served as a useful visual aid when parents explained to their children the meaning of the monument on the bank.

(Succeeding comments on the lesson text will be made based on the interpretation that there were two memorials.)

DID IT HAPPEN OR NOT?

Admiral Richard E. Byrd was long thought to have been the first person to fly over the North Pole. However, just a few years ago Byrd's long-lost diary was found in some archives at Ohio State University's Byrd Polar Research Institute; and the diary indicates that he may never have reached his goal. Experts at the Institute have determined that Byrd's navigational notes testify that he turned back two hours and one hundred sixty-five miles short of his goal.

A similar fate has dampened the assertions of Robert E. Peary, who claimed to have reached the North Pole by dogsled in 1909. Peary's claim had been controversial for many years, and has also been set aside recently by experts in the field of navigation.

When we hear that "heroes" have been either mistaken or willfully deceitful about what they have accomplished, we are disappointed. We like to trust in the authenticity of great events as they have been reported to us.

Israel's crossing the Jordan River on dry land was a moment of great significance. It was important that future generations have no doubt about what had happened. The building of a monument at the place of the event so soon after it had occurred served as a testimony to what God had done. As Christians we also would do well to remind ourselves of the memorials that testify to God's great works on our behalf.

—C. R. B.

C. SIGNIFICANT SPOT (vv. 10, 11)

10. Now the priests who carried the ark remained standing in the middle of the Jordan until everything the LORD had commanded Joshua was done by the people, just as Moses had directed Joshua. The people hurried over.

The visual for lesson 4 reminds us of some of the memorable things God did for Israel. Discuss, "What memorable things has God done for you?"

HOW TO SAY IT

Babylon. BAB-uh-lun.
Canaan. KAY-nun.
Gilgal. GIL-gal.
Jericho. JAIR-ih-co.
Shiloh. SHY-lo.

WHAT DO YOU THINK?

The priests stood in the middle of the Jordan riverbed while the people crossed, the stones were gathered, and the monument was built. All this time the water must have been piling up higher and higher. What kind of test do you think that would have been on the priests' faith? (We *can only imagine how the priests must have felt, but if the piling waters were in view, there was potential for doubt. The location of the city of Adam, Joshua 3:16, is unknown, so we do not know whether the heap of waters was visible to the people.)*

What tests your faith today? How do you stand firm when your faith is tested?

The *ark* was supported on long poles that extended in front of the ark and behind it. The two or more priests who carried the ark probably kept these poles on their shoulders. They stood still in the middle of the riverbed until all the people reached the other side, until the twelve stones had been carried out of the riverbed, and until the second group of twelve stones had been formed into a monument near where they stood. As long as the ark remained in that spot, the riverbed was dry.

The ark of the covenant was the visible symbol of God's presence and power. Its position at that spot in midstream indicated the power of God holding back the flow of the waters and piling them into a mountain upstream. The monument placed in that specific location would serve as a lasting memorial of such a wonderful event.

11. And as soon as all of them had crossed, the ark of the LORD and the priests came to the other side while the people watched.

When everyone was safe on the west bank of the river and the two memorials had been completed, *the priests* left their post in the middle of the river and carried *the ark* to the bank where *the people* were standing.

III. MONUMENT ON THE BANK (JOSHUA 4:20-24)

When the priests had carried the ark to the other side of the Jordan, the river returned to flood stage where it had been previously (vv. 15-18). The people then made camp at a place called Gilgal, which was beyond the reach of the flooded river. It was also situated near the east side of Jericho (v. 19), to which Joshua had already sent spies in preparation for the conquest of the city.

A. THE MONUMENT (v. 20)

20. And Joshua set up at Gilgal the twelve stones they had taken out of the Jordan.

The twelve stones were not squarely hewn blocks such as we might use for a monument. They were stones *taken out of the Jordan*—water-worn and probably not uniform in shape or size. *Joshua set* them *up* in a conspicuous pile. The text indicates nothing special about the design of the monument; it probably appeared to be nothing more than a loose pile of stones. But it was meant to serve a high and holy purpose. Passersby would notice the heap of stones and wonder how it came to be there. God intended for them to be told, as the following verses show.

WHAT DO YOU THINK?

God made special mention of using the memorial to the Jordan River crossing as a teaching tool. What are some common elements or symbols in our worship that may evoke questions from children or visitors and may yield a valuable teaching opportunity? How can we be sure more of us are ready to teach such lessons when questions are asked?

B. THE MEANING (vv. 21-23)

21. He said to the Israelites, "In the future when your descendants ask their fathers, 'What do these stones mean?'

The people of Israel were to gather three times a year for the feasts of Passover, Pentecost, and Tabernacles (Leviticus 23). Travelers coming to Shiloh (Joshua 18:1), and later Jerusalem, from east of the Jordan would likely ford the river at the place where the Israelites had crossed. Even if it were somewhat out of their way, they might deliberately choose to cross near the monument in order to see it. *Descendants* of the present generation would see the odd pile of stones and *ask* about it. That would give *fathers* a wonderful opportunity to tell how the power and goodness of God had been displayed at that very place.

22. "Tell them, 'Israel crossed the Jordan on dry ground.'

Travelers going to the Feast of Tabernacles in the autumn would probably find the river low enough to cross. Small children could be carried across, while adults probably would be wet to the knees or the waist. Children would be surprised to hear that anyone ever *crossed the Jordan on dry ground*. If the people were going to the Feast of Passover in the spring, the water would be higher and the children's amazement would be greater. "How did they do that?" they would ask.

23. For the LORD your God dried up the Jordan before you until you had crossed over. The LORD your God did to the Jordan just what he had done to the Red Sea when he dried it up before us until we had crossed over.

Through generations to come, the same explanation would be passed on from parents to children. If this trip took place in the autumn, children might see the pile of rocks in the river as they were crossing. Parents could then begin their teaching in midstream, promising to show the children the other monument on the bank.

This story of God's power and goodness would open the door for parents to tell of another miracle—the crossing of the *Red Sea* years earlier. Children would learn not only of wondrous events in the distant past, but also of God's continuing care for them as they walked over the ancient trail and crossed the same river that their ancestors had crossed.

LOOKING BACKWARD

Marathon running has become a very popular sport, with many large cities holding their own annual events. One of the strangest entries among the 22,000 who ran the 1987 New York City Marathon was Yves Pol. He ran the entire 26.2 miles backward!

The thirty-four-year-old Pol had two friends who ran alongside to warn him of any obstacles along the way. In spite of their help, he fell several times. Nevertheless, he finished in four hours and forty minutes, two and one-half hours behind the winner, but ahead of about half of his competitors.

Joshua's memorial of stones from the Jordan River was set up to cause Israel to look backward. He told the Israelites that in times to come, they should tell their children the meaning of those stones. In this way, the nation was never to forget what God had done for them. By looking backward into the past, they would maintain a proper appreciation of their present circumstances and could gain a perspective with which to face the future courageously. Unfortunately in the years to come, Israel would often forget to look back and, as a result, the people would lose their spiritual bearings.

Facing forward as we run the race of life is better than facing backward, but an occasional backward glance will help us to remember how God has upheld us in the past.   —C. R. B.

C. THE MESSAGE (v. 24)

24. He did this so that all the peoples of the earth might know that the hand of the LORD is powerful and so that you might always fear the LORD your God."

The miraculous stopping of the Jordan had a number of purposes. Obviously it was intended to get the people of Israel to the other side of the river. Another purpose is stated in the last part of this verse: *that you might always fear the Lord your God.* There were hard battles to be fought on the west side of the river. The people would have to face the fierce people and fortified cities that had frightened Israel some forty years earlier (Numbers 13:25—14:4). The present generation of Israel needed this assurance of God's power, an assurance that would make them *fear* him—that is, regard the Lord with such reverence and awe that they would be more afraid to disobey him than to go into battle against intimidating peoples and strong city walls.

An additional purpose reached beyond Israel. This miracle was performed *so that all the peoples of the earth might know that the hand of the Lord is powerful.* First

WHAT DO YOU THINK?

Apparently the memorial on the bank at Gilgal and the memorial in the river have both perished. What relevance do you see in this passage, then, since we cannot point to the stones and tell the story?

DAILY BIBLE READINGS

Monday, Sept. 21—Hear the Words of the Lord (Joshua 3:7-13)

Tuesday, Sept. 22—A Memorial Forever (Joshua 3:14—4:9)

Wednesday, Sept. 23—The Lord Exalted Joshua (Joshua 4:10-24)

Thursday, Sept. 24—The Conquest of Jericho Begins (Joshua 6:1-7)

Friday, Sept. 25—The Walls Came Tumbling Down (Joshua 6:12-25)

Saturday, Sept. 26—God's Covenant Transgressed (Joshua 7:1-9)

Sunday, Sept. 27—That the Next Generation May Know (Psalm 78:1-8)

THOUGHT TO REMEMBER

God is with us when we are with him.

WHAT DO YOU THINK?

The lesson writer points out how we tend to take many of God's blessings for granted, because they come to us continually. How can we overcome this tendency?

PRAYER

Thank you, Father, for the countless blessings that have made our lives happy, and thank you for the trials and disappointments that have made our spirits strong. Open our eyes to see the opportunities that lie ahead—opportunities for new conquests and new triumphs in your work. May we accept your leading and profit by both our triumphs and our troubles. Amen.

of all, some of the residents of Jericho likely witnessed the crossing, and would realize that the Israelites were equipped with something much greater than any human power. That news would spread quickly to other cities in Canaan. As it was, the people of Jericho were already frightened because they knew how Israel had crossed the Red Sea forty years earlier and conquered territories east of the Jordan (Joshua 2:8-11). Now they would recognize that the power that had opened the sea was still with Israel, and they would face these invaders with terror instead of confidence.

In addition, the people of that area were not isolated. Traders from distant places were constantly passing through. Soon the news of the stopped river and the mountain of water would be told in places as far away as Egypt and Babylon. More than three thousand years later, you and I are reading again this record, and we too are reminded that the hand of the Lord is mighty.

CONCLUSION

The people of Israel experienced many disappointments during their journey from Egypt to Canaan. Expecting an uneventful trip to a land flowing with milk and honey, they found themselves sentenced to forty years of hard living in the desert. More than once they thought of giving up their dream and going back to slavery in Egypt (Exodus 14:10-12; 16:1-3; 17:3; Numbers 14:1-4).

There were, however, an abundance of blessings along the way as well. There was manna every morning, and in times of need God provided an abundance of water. God gave the people victory over hostile desert tribes and other enemies east of the Jordan. He provided a dry path over which to cross the Jordan. He guided the people to a convincing triumph over Jericho. Then why did anyone ever think of going back to Egypt?

First, blessings that come continually are apt to be undervalued. The manna was there every day. Picking it up was part of the daily routine week after week and year after year. Soon people forgot that it was a special gift from God. Gathering it every morning, they may have come to think that they were earning their daily bread. When they forgot that God was with them continually and was the source of their blessings, they were ready to be discouraged by any disappointment or setback.

Second, even the greatest of our blessings tend to grow dim in our memories and lose their power to move us. That is the reason God desired that memorials be built to commemorate the crossing of the Jordan. That is the reason Jesus ordained the Lord's Supper—to remind us that he died so that we might live. "Do this in remembrance of me," he said (1 Corinthians 11:24). We need to count our blessings, both the tremendous and the tiny, and live to bless the Lord who blesses us.

We would do well to follow the example of Joshua and the Israelites. They set up two memorials in recognition of how God's mighty hand had worked on their behalf in the crossing of the Jordan River. These were to serve as valuable visual aids reminding the Israelites of God's goodness. Then they served as teaching tools by which parents could teach their children, and their children could teach *their* children, so that succeeding generations would also know the awesome power and love of God.

What about us? Do we receive God's blessings in a passive way, taking them for granted? Or do we take the time to establish our own "stones," in order to keep us mindful of God's faithfulness? If you have not done so, why not start assembling some "stones" of your own today—for yourself, your family, and your church? Such memorials will keep your faith focused on the "Rock of Ages"!

Discovery Learning

This page contains an alternate lesson plan emphasizing learning activities. Classes desiring such student involvement will find these suggestions helpful. The next page is a reproducible activity page to further enhance discovery learning.

LEARNING GOALS

After this lesson, your students should be able to:

1. Tell how Israel crossed the Jordan River and why they set up memorial stones.

2. Recall spiritual milestones in their lives or in the lives of their families and church.

3. Praise and thank God for what he has done, as represented in those milestones.

INTO THE LESSON

Before class, write these two open-ended sentences on the chalkboard or on a large poster: (If your class uses the student book, *NIV® Bible Student*, refer the students to page 19.)

The most significant experience of my life was when. . . .
To help me remember that experience, I. . . .

As the students arrive, direct them to the statements and tell them to think about how they would complete each statement. Then introduce the lesson by asking for personal responses. Encourage your students to talk about their significant experiences and what they do to remind themselves of good times.

We all use memorial devices to help us remember significant events and experiences: a first date, baby's first steps, a spiritual victory, a first car or house, a great battle. Mementos and memorials remind us of what happened and help us feel the way we felt in those times.

In today's lesson we learn about the value of spiritual memorials.

INTO THE WORD

Lay the historical groundwork for this lesson by telling the story of the miraculous crossing of the Jordan River (see the Lesson Background, pages 41 and 42). You may want to ask a student to do this for you.

An alternative method of presenting the story of the Jordan crossing is to divide the class into three-person groups and have the students pretend they are reporters covering the event for a newspaper. Give each group a different assignment, based on Joshua 3, for stories and sidebars related to the event. After about ten minutes, call for reports from each group.

Memorial stones play a significant role in this lesson. Ask the students to talk about some of the memorials and monuments they have seen. You can start the ball rolling by telling about a monument you have seen.

Tell your students to read Joshua 4:1-3, 8, 20-24, and then ask these questions:

• Why did the Hebrews set up memorial stones at the place where they crossed the Jordan? (To remind themselves of what God had done and to spark questions from those who did not know what had happened.)

• Who were to be told the story of what God had done for his people at the Jordan? (Future generations of Hebrews [vv. 22, 23] and anyone else who might ask [v. 24].)

Read Joshua 4:9-11, and ask these questions:

• What did Joshua do—perhaps while the twelve men were gathering the stones for the monument at Gilgal? (He set up another monument of twelve stones in the riverbed.)

• Why do you think he did this? (Marking the precise spot in the river where the priests stood would be a dramatic symbol and would serve as evidence that the event really did happen.)

• What might be the effect on future generations to see the pile of stones rising out of the water in the middle of the Jordan? (Their faith would be strengthened and God would be praised when they saw the clear evidence to support the story of God's stopping the Jordan.)

INTO LIFE

We do not need to see the same miraculous signs to believe in the God who has done these mighty deeds. We don't need for God to dry up a river or part a sea. We believe they happened just as we believe God raised Jesus from the dead. Discuss some of the reasons we can have faith even if we have not seen these events with our own eyes. (See John 20:24-31.)

Providentially, however, God does work even in our own lives in wonderful and faith-building ways. Hand out index cards, and tell each student to think of a time when God has done something wonderful or providential in his or her life. Then say, "Write a word or phrase on your card that reminds you of what God has done for you in the past. Then write 'Thank you, God,' on your card."

Next, give each person in the class a small stone. Tell your students to take these stones home and put them—together with the index cards—in a place where they will be seen every day to serve as reminders of what God has done in their lives.

The Story of the Stones

Read Joshua 4:1-3, 8, 20-24, and then answer the following questions:

1. Why did the Hebrews set up memorial stones at the place where they crossed the Jordan?

2. Who were to be told the story of what God had done for his people at the Jordan?

Read Joshua 4:9-11, and answer these questions:

1. What did Joshua do—perhaps while the twelve men were gathering the stones for the monument at Gilgal?

2. Why do you think he did this?

3. What might be the effect on future generations to see the pile of stones rising out of the water in the middle of the Jordan?

A Stone of My Own

Each day in your personal or family devotions this week, think of one specific way God has blessed you. Add a stone to a personal memorial to represent this blessing. If you do this in family devotions, give each person in the family a stone and ask each one to think of a blessing and to use this stone as a reminder of that. The second day repeat the procedure, asking each one to put the second stone with the first. Add a stone each day until each person has a pile of seven stones at the end of the week. (You may want to glue the stones together, especially if anyone wants to keep the memorial for any length of time.) Write the significance of each stone in your own memorial below:

1.

2.

3.

4.

5.

6.

7.

God Calls a People to Faithful Living

Unit 2. God's People Reject His Laws
(Lessons 5-7)

CYCLE OF SIN AND JUDGMENT

LESSON 5

WHY TEACH THIS LESSON?

A contemporary Christian song describes a situation in which a friend has fallen prey to an old temptation. The narrator thinks of giving up on her friend but recalls the love of God, that "He will never give up on you." Another singer cries out, "What's going on inside me? I despise my own behavior!" Both of these songs remind us that we often know better than we do. Again and again, it seems, we make the same mistakes we've made before.

If that scenario sounds familiar, then today's lesson offers both hope and a warning. As a nation, Israel repeatedly fell into sin and idolatry. The "cycle," as our title has called it, was more a spiral, with destruction of the nation looming ahead. That's the warning—continuing in this cycle may have dire consequences. The word of hope is that God was always there to restore Israel when repentance was renewed. He is still there for you and your struggling students as well!

INTRODUCTION

When World War I was heating up in Europe, Grandma observed that wars always brought lower moral standards and wild, reckless living. She had seen it during the Civil War, and now she could see it again. A prominent couple in our town was getting a divorce. The crime rate was increasing. Grandma thought a lady's bathing costume was indecent because the skirt barely covered the knee, and the calf of the leg was clad only in a stocking. Gloomily Grandma predicted a time when one marriage in ten would end in divorce, when we would not dare to leave home without locking the door, and when women would swim without stockings.

Sadly, Grandma's "prophecies" have come true—and to a degree that even she would not have dreamed possible.

A. THIS WORSENING WORLD

Becoming worse is not a phenomenon confined only to the twentieth century. The Bible tells how a spotless world became so corrupt that God destroyed it and started again with Noah and his family. Again, idolatry and sin became rampant; then God called Abraham to start a new nation that would be blessed by having his laws to know and obey. In spite of having such knowledge and in spite of having numerous opportunities to see God's mighty power at work, this nation repeatedly forsook the Lord and fell prey to idolatry and to all the vices that normally accompany idol worship.

B. LESSON BACKGROUND

When the Jordan River stopped to let the people of Israel cross, and when the walls of Jericho fell flat, God's people saw ample evidence of his power and had ample reason to trust and obey him. Similar evidence continued to mount as the

DEVOTIONAL READING
PSALM 78:17-32
LESSON SCRIPTURE
JUDGES 2
PRINTED TEXT
JUDGES 2:11-20a

Oct
4

LESSON AIMS

After this lesson, a student should be able to:

1. Describe Israel's repeated cycle in the time of the judges: peace and prosperity; growing disobedience to God; punishment; repentance; and the return of peace and prosperity.

2. Give examples of how a similar cycle has plagued the life of an individual, a family, or a nation.

3. Commit themselves, as followers of Jesus, to breaking this cycle in their lives or to helping another in doing so.

KEY VERSE

The LORD raised up judges, who saved them out of the hands of these raiders. Yet they would not listen to their judges.
—Judges 2:16, 17

Today's visual is a chart of the judges of Israel. Point out the periods of oppression that preceded the call of several of the judges and the periods of rest that followed.

WHAT DO YOU THINK?

The influence of the pagan peoples around them was one factor in the Israelites' tendency to forsake God. The Israelites had ceased to engage in actual warfare against their pagan neighbors. But they needed to recognize that there was still a spiritual war going on—a war for their minds and hearts.

We Christians must keep in mind that we are also at war (Ephesians 6:10-18). How can we combat the influence of ungodly neighbors and acquaintances? Suggest some "battle plans" for the following arenas:

Our schools

The offices of elected and appointed government officials

The media—television, movies, books and magazines, and the like.

people proceeded to take the promised land. On the positive side, God gave victory after victory to his people, even causing the sun to stand still on one occasion so they could successfully complete a battle (Joshua 10:12-14). On the negative side, a single act of disobedience resulted in an embarrassing defeat. Only when the sin was discovered and punished did God's blessing return (Joshua 7, 8).

In approximately seven years, God's people conquered as much land as they needed. They divided it among their tribes and settled down to peaceful living, though minor hostilities continued (Judges 1). Joshua and other godly leaders were a powerful influence for righteousness as long as they lived (Joshua 24:1-31; Judges 2:7). But in time that generation passed away, and there arose a generation that did not remember how greatly the Lord had helped his people (Judges 2:10).

How could this have happened? How could the knowledge of the Lord have disappeared so quickly from the people's thinking? God had told the people to teach his words diligently to their children (Deuteronomy 6:6, 7). Obviously this had not taken place; and because it had not, within one generation the law of God had faded from the people's memory. Any nation that fails to remember its history and respect its heritage is traveling a perilous path.

I. ISRAEL'S WORSENING CONDITION (JUDGES 2:11-13)

A. EVIL (v. 11)

11. Then the Israelites did evil in the eyes of the LORD and served the Baals.

Baal is a Hebrew word meaning "master" or "lord." The word Baals describes the various representations of the god Baal; for each town could have a Baal of its own, probably represented by a crude image in a shrine of some sort. His followers attempted to win his favor by offering sacrifices to him. While different towns may have held different myths about their Baals, it was generally believed that the god Baal controlled the fertility of people, animals, and crops. As a result, Baal worshipers often engaged in "religious" prostitution in order to induce Baal to grant fertility to themselves or their farms.

Of course, the Baals had no Ten Commandments by which their followers should live. They did not teach people to be unselfish, helpful, kind, or forgiving. People who served the Baals naturally did evil more and more as they became more oblivious to the Lord and his ways. Such is the consequence of making God in man's image.

B. INGRATITUDE (v. 12)

12. They forsook the LORD, the God of their fathers, who had brought them out of Egypt. They followed and worshiped various gods of the peoples around them. They provoked the LORD to anger.

Judges 1 tells how, in many cases, certain tribes of Israel failed to destroy the Canaanite inhabitants of the territories that had been allotted to them under Joshua. (God had clearly told them to do this, as Deuteronomy 7:1-5 states.) In the course of time, Israelites of the generations following Joshua's became acquainted with some of the pagans living near them. Perhaps those pagans did not seem to be as terrible as they were reported to be. After all, they were farmers and shepherds just like the Israelites. Wouldn't it be better for all concerned to try to work together?

The problem was that the Israelites began to turn from the true God to the various gods of the peoples around them. As noted earlier, these gods had no moral standards. As the worship of them increased among the Israelites, so did all kinds of wrongdoing, and so did the *anger* of the Lord. He had warned the people of this very danger (Deuteronomy 7:4, 5). Now his words were proving true.

C. WORSHIP OF OTHER GODS (v. 13)

13. . . . because they forsook him and served Baal and the Ashtoreths.

The *Ashtoreths* included imaginary goddesses that were associated with the various Baals (usually as their lovers). By serving such gods, the Israelites were violating the first Commandment: "You shall have no other gods before me" (Exodus 20:3). They needed a drastic "wake-up call."

II. PUNISHMENT (JUDGES 2:14, 15)

A. DEFEAT (v. 14)

14. In his anger against Israel the LORD handed them over to raiders who plundered them. He sold them to their enemies all around, whom they were no longer able to resist.

God's wake-up call came in the form of *raiders*, who originated from the pagan peoples nearby. They came to steal cattle, sheep, or grain as soon as it was threshed—and did not hesitate to kill anyone who was in their way.

In Joshua's time the army of Israel, with the help of God, had swept across the land, capturing cities and villages as it did so. But now the people of Israel had no such army. The men of the various tribes had settled in their towns and villages. They were not organized, trained, or equipped to resist these bands of raiders. Most significant, God no longer helped them; and for that reason, *they were no longer able to resist* their oppressors. That God *sold them* does not mean that God received any payment from the pagans; it means that he handed the Israelites over to *their enemies* as if they had been bought.

B. FAIR WARNING (v. 15)

15. Whenever Israel went out to fight, the hand of the LORD was against them to defeat them, just as he had sworn to them. They were in great distress.

The *hand of the Lord* signifies God's power at work. We saw in last week's lesson how that power had allowed the Israelites to cross the Jordan River (Joshua 4:23, 24). Now it *was against them to defeat them.* The bands of raiders were the weapon in God's hand to punish his people. Such punishment was designed to prevent a far greater tragedy—the people's continued descent into paganism and wickedness.

The Israelites could not claim that the punishment came without warning. Plainly and in clearest detail the Lord had promised this very punishment (and others) if the people disobeyed him (Deuteronomy 28:15-68; especially v. 25). That promise was as certain as the promise of blessing for obedience (Deuteronomy 28:1-14). This was no slap on the wrist; the people *were in great distress.*

A PARADISE THAT WASN'T

In 1905, the Colorado River overflowed its banks and broke through irrigation heads near the California-Mexico border. The floodwaters poured into the Salton Basin, a saline depression some thirty miles northeast of San Diego, California. The water created what is now called the Salton Sea, a huge lake more than two hundred feet below sea level. The lake has no outlet, but evaporation has reduced its size by about a third from its original surface area. Runoff into the lake has stabilized it at its current size, and the water is now more salty than that of the ocean.

About forty years ago, developers decided to turn the Salton Sea into a paradise of resorts, yacht clubs, golf courses, and seaside residential communities. However,

HOW TO SAY IT

Ashtoreths. ASH-toe-reths.
Baal. BAY-ul.
Caleb. KAY-leb.
Canaanite. KAY-nuh-nite.
Jericho. JAIR-ih-co.
Midianites. MID-ee-uh-nites.

WHAT DO YOU THINK?

The tremendous influence of the judges suggests that leadership among God's people is an awesome responsibility. What safeguards can leaders take to be sure they are leading the way God would want them to lead and are not leading God's people astray? What does this text suggest about the responsibility of Christians to submit to the leadership of godly leaders?

their plans have been stymied by some unanticipated problems. Because the water that now flows into the Salton Sea contains the runoff from agricultural irrigation and from untreated sewage and refuse from the large city of Mexicali, Mexico, the Salton Sea is not only getting more salty; it is also becoming increasingly polluted. The result is that the developers' dreams of a desert paradise have not come true. Their punishment for not doing sufficient research into their project was the loss of several million dollars' investment.

The Israelites thought they had moved to a paradise when they reached the promised land. It was a land that flowed "with milk and honey" (Numbers 13:27). But the Israelites thought they could live in that land without regard to the laws of the God who gave it to them. In that, they were terribly mistaken. For their disobedience to his commands, God allowed their enemies to overpower them.

Whatever "paradise" we seek to build on earth, this principle remains true: No place can be a paradise if we ignore or violate the laws of our Creator.　　—C. R. B.

III. RESCUE AND RENEWED EVIL (JUDGES 2:16, 17)

God's punishment accomplished its intended purpose: the distressed Israelites realized that they had turned away from God. In their misery they turned back to him and begged him for help. As we progress through the book of Judges, we see this same plea to the Lord recorded again and again (Judges 3:9, 15; 4:3; 6:6; 10:10, 15). The Lord's wondrous patience is seen in his response to these cries, for each time he provided the deliverance for which his people prayed.

A. DELIVERANCE FROM ENEMIES (v. 16)

16. Then the LORD raised up judges, who saved them out of the hands of these raiders.

How did God rescue his people from oppression when they turned to him with cries for help? He provided *judges*. A judge was a leader—one from among the people—who rallied them to take a brave stand against the enemies who were plundering them. Since the judge represented God's presence with the people, their resistance was successful; and their oppression ended. This happened again and again over approximately three hundred years (Judges 11:26).

The judges differed widely in their abilities and their actions. Deborah is described as someone who actually "judged" cases that were brought before her (Judges 4:5). Gideon is noted for his military leadership rather than for settling disputes. Samson was a one-man army. God used him to wreak havoc among the Philistines, but we are not given any detailed information about his teaching or judging.

B. DEPARTURE FROM GOD (v. 17)

17. Yet they would not listen to their judges but prostituted themselves to other gods and worshiped them. Unlike their fathers, they quickly turned from the way in which their fathers had walked, the way of obedience to the LORD's commands.

When an enemy had been defeated and robbery and oppression were ended, the judge who had led the people to victory would urge them to keep living in obedience to God so that peace and prosperity would continue. But the people *would not listen*. All too soon they lapsed again into idolatry and sin. As an unfaithful wife turns away from a good husband to seek pleasure with other men, unfaithful Israel turned away from the true God and *prostituted themselves to the gods* of the pagans. In so doing, they violated their covenant as God's people just as an unfaithful spouse violates the sacred covenant of marriage. *Their fathers* (including Joshua and Caleb) had gone in the way of righteousness—*the way of obedience to the Lord's commands*. In contrast, *they quickly turned from the way*.

DEFRAUDING GOD

Weddings are usually a time of hope and joy, with family and friends gathered to share with the happy couple as they start a new life together. However, a bizarre twist was given to the concept of marriage in Florida just a couple of years ago. The bride was hospitalized and lying in a deep coma, just hours from death. Before she died, her boyfriend forged a marriage license, and "married" her with the help of an unscrupulous notary public. Using the credit cards belonging to his dead "wife," the man then spent $20,000 fraudulently before he was arrested for the crime.

The Bible speaks in many places of the relationship of God and Israel as a marriage. But Israel seemed more like the faithless and fraudulent groom in the incident we have just related than a loving mate whose joy is found in being faithful. Israel's lack of faith and gratitude for her deliverance from slavery showed itself in her slide toward idolatry after God brought her safely to the promised land.

It is easy enough for us to look back at the Israelites and condemn their idolatry. We must not forget, however, that the church is the "bride of Christ." Dare we examine our lives to see if we have defrauded our Lord, who died for us so that we might be delivered from slavery to sin?   —C. R. B.

IV. REPEATED CYCLE (JUDGES 2:18-20a)

What is told briefly in verses 16 and 17 is now repeated in more detail. It is something that happened repeatedly in the approximately three centuries that we call the time of the judges.

A. GOD'S COMPASSION (v. 18)

18. Whenever the LORD raised up a judge for them, he was with the judge and saved them out of the hands of their enemies as long as the judge lived; for the LORD had compassion on them as they groaned under those who oppressed and afflicted them.

Whenever the Lord provided a leader for the Israelites, their *enemies were defeated*. The result was that the land had "peace" (Judges 3:11; 3:30; 5:31) until the people strayed from God once again. According to this verse, the slide into idolatry and sin was not as swift as we might think from verse 17. The Lord *was with the judge . . . as long as the judge lived*. The influence of the judge kept the people obedient. Sometimes the "peace" he provided lasted for forty years (Judges 3:11; 5:31; 8:28). In one case it lasted for eighty years (Judges 3:30).

B. GROWING DISOBEDIENCE (v. 19)

19. But when the judge died, the people returned to ways even more corrupt than those of their fathers, following other gods and serving and worshiping them. They refused to give up their evil practices and stubborn ways.

Peace, prosperity, and happiness might last forty years or eighty; however, *when the judge died* and when his influence no longer was present in the land, gradually *the people* began again to join in pagan worship. They began again to lie, cheat, steal, and kill. Stubbornly they continued in such *evil practices* until God withdrew his protection and allowed an enemy to conquer them.

C. GOD'S ANGER (v. 20a)

20a. Therefore the LORD was very angry with Israel.

It was not just the greed of the raiding bands that brought them into the land to devastate Israel; it was that *the Lord was very angry with Israel*. "The

---

WHAT DO YOU THINK?

The judges' influence lasted only as long as they lived. How can modern Christian leaders extend their influence beyond their lifetimes?

WHAT DO YOU THINK?

The responsibility for proper behavior fell not to the judge, according to today's lesson, but to the people. It was they who refused to learn or "to give up their evil practices and stubborn ways." What lessons do we need to learn from this text? What do you need to do to break out of, or to stay out of, a cycle of sin and judgment?

Lord is compassionate and gracious, slow to anger, abounding in love" (Psalm 103:8). But it would not be compassionate or merciful for him to let people go on forever destroying themselves. When the sin of Israel became intolerable, God's anger was hot, swift, and terrible. The kindest thing he could do for his people was to plunge them into terrible suffering, for in their suffering they realized what they were doing and stopped it. In suffering they turned to God and begged for help; and when they did so, his help was as swift and powerful as his anger. What then became of those innumerable desert dwellers who invaded and terrorized Israel? "All the Midianites ran, crying out as they fled" (Judges 7:21). The Lord's power was more than adequate when his people were ready to trust and obey him.

CONCLUSION

A. Slow Learners

In previous lessons we have seen that certain people were slow in learning to obey God. Let's suppose they were in "obedience school" and give them grades.

Lesson 1. Adam and Eve may have learned to obey, but their descendants became so disobedient that God drowned most of them. Give those people an F.

Lesson 2. The plagues taught Pharaoh to obey God; but then he had to have another lesson, and it cost him his army. Give Pharaoh an F.

Lesson 3. The people of Israel were privileged to receive the Ten Commandments from God, but they started breaking them before they saw them carved in stone. Give them an F for that session.

Lesson 4. Give an A to Joshua and his comrades. They led an obedient nation as long as they lived. But when they died, the people quickly forgot the Lord and all he had done.

How would you grade your church in its obedience to God? How would you grade yourself? Is your grade better or worse than it would have been a year ago?

B. Quick Forgetters

In this lesson we have seen that God used oppression by foreign powers to teach Israel to obey him. Once they learned in only seven years (Judges 6:1). Another time it took them forty years (Judges 13:1). Yet regardless of the time, their "learning" was short-lived. In one instance it was eighty years before they had to have another lesson (Judges 3:30). More often it was only forty years (Judges 3:11; 5:31; 8:28).

Today some of us who are older may think that people do not obey God as well as we did when we were young. What do you think? Are we going to need a lesson as severe as the kind that Israel received in the days of the judges?

C. Enrolling Learners

How can we bring more people to church and Sunday school so they will learn to obey God better? Give each of these plans a grade to indicate how effective you think it would be in your particular situation.

1. Advertise by newspaper, radio, or TV.
2. Have a revival meeting.
3. Have some sermons on obeying God.
4. Mail written invitations.
5. Invite people by telephone.
6. Send callers in person to invite people.
7. Plan a "Friend Day," and encourage each member to bring a neighbor.
8. Have a special class to teach Christians how to win others to Christ.

Discovery Learning

This page contains an alternate lesson plan emphasizing learning activities. Classes desiring such student involvement will find these suggestions helpful. The next page is a reproducible activity page to further enhance discovery learning.

LEARNING GOALS

As a result of this lesson, your students should be able to:

1. Describe Israel's repeated cycle in the time of the judges: peace and prosperity; growing disobedience to God; punishment; repentance; and the return of peace and prosperity.

2. Give examples of how a similar cycle has plagued the life of an individual, a family, or a nation.

3. Commit themselves, as followers of Jesus, to breaking this cycle in their lives or to helping another do so.

INTO THE LESSON

Begin the lesson by presenting the students with this challenge:

If you were devising the ideal strategy for being a victorious Christian in a basically non-Christian society and culture, which of the following elements would you include in your strategy?

• **Avoid** everyone who is hostile to the Christian faith.

• **Destroy** everyone who is hostile to the Christian faith.

• **Have only limited contact with** those who are hostile to the Christian faith.

• **Embrace with open arms** those who are hostile to the Christian faith for the purpose of winning them to Christ.

Encourage your students to explain their reasons for choosing the responses they choose.

When the Hebrews occupied the land of Canaan, God told them to exterminate all the Canaanites. But they failed to do that. In today's lesson we see what happened as a result of their being exposed to idolatrous religions and pagan practices.

INTO THE WORD

Fill in the historical bridge between last week's lesson and this lesson. (Use information from the Lesson Background on pages 49 and 50.) The time of the judges was one of the darkest periods in Israel's history. It was characterized by a repeating cycle of peace and prosperity; growing disobedience to God; punishment; repentance; deliverance and the return of peace and prosperity.

Distribute the reproducible activity "Round and Round We Go!" (page 56). Then divide the class into four groups to explore the text and describe each step in the cycle. Ask each group to read the printed text, Judges 2:11-20a, and then focus on a particular portion of the text to identify and describe one part of the cycle. Group 1 should focus on verses 11-13, 17, 19 (disobedience); group 2: verses 14, 15a, 20a (punishment); group 3: verses 15b, 18b (repentance); group 4: verses 16, 18a (deliverance and return to peace).

Allow ten minutes for study in the groups; then write "Peace and Prosperity" on the chalkboard. Draw a "cycle" like the one below, but without the labels. Have each group supply the proper labels as it gives its report.

INTO LIFE

God always expects his people to exert a positive influence on the people they live with and around. Unfortunately, after the death of Joshua the Hebrews forgot God and began to worship and serve the false gods of the Canaanites. Ask:

• Why did this happen?

• Why is it that a righteous person seems more likely to be influenced to go astray by a wicked environment than a sinful person is to be influenced to give up his sins and reform his life by a godly environment?

Ask your class members to suggest some of the dangers and hazards of living in a society that is basically non-Christian and hostile to Christ and the gospel. Discuss, "How can we safeguard ourselves from the influence of evil around us and strengthen our witness to the culture to lead people to Christ?"

In closing, emphasize that God is still in the business of delivering those who are bound by the consequences of their own self-destructive behaviors. Ask each adult to think about this question: "What do you want deliverance from today?" Offer a closing prayer, asking God to deliver your students from the things that bind them today.

Round and Round We Go!

Judges 2:11-20a illustrates a cycle that Israel repeatedly followed throughout the period of the judges. Read the text and label each part of the cycle below with a word that describes what happened in each segment.

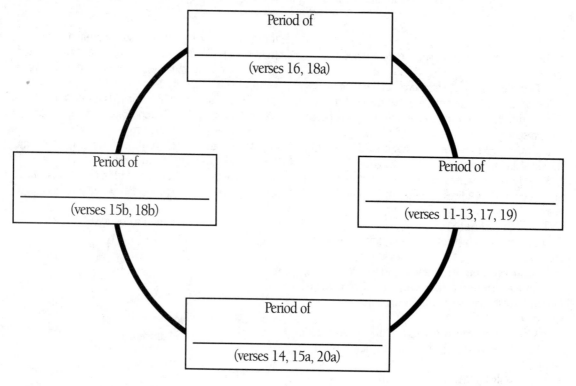

Period of
_____
(verses 16, 18a)

Period of
_____
(verses 15b, 18b)

Period of
_____
(verses 11-13, 17, 19)

Period of
_____
(verses 14, 15a, 20a)

Let Me Off, Please

We, too, can get caught up in a cycle of repeated sin. What can you do to break the cycle and follow the Lord more closely? List below some indicators that should warn you that you are taking sin too lightly and may be beginning to repeat the cycle of sin. Then list some positive action you can take to bring you back to the Lord's side.

DANGER SIGNS

CORRECTIVE MEASURES

DEMAND FOR A KING

LESSON 6

WHY TEACH THIS LESSON?

As Christians, "our citizenship is in heaven" (Philippians 3:20), but of course we are citizens of an earthly nation as well. As earthly citizens we have an obligation to be involved in the public square to try to effect positive change where we can. But with what tools will we work?

We may make a difference in public policy by the way we vote, by participating in demonstrations, or even by running for office and trying to make changes from within the system. But the opposing side is also voting and demonstrating and running for office. This is the secular arena, where our opponents are quite skilled.

So we pray and we share our faith. The opposing side has no arsenal against such things, so some believers believe we should wage our campaign exclusively in this spiritual arena. Other devout believers, however, feel that we cannot ignore the secular arena because the other side is so active there. Still, whatever we gain in the secular realm can be wiped away in the next elections.

Israel had some real needs, but her leaders looked for a secular solution—a king such as all the other nations had—to solve them. They should have looked to God. Let this lesson remind your students that every problem our society faces—abortion or racism or immorality or whatever—cannot be solved by a secular solution. We need God as our King!

INTRODUCTION

"I guess I'll hold my nose, vote for Smith, and hope he doesn't make too many mistakes." Thus a businessman regretfully announced his decision as an election drew near. The thought of voting for Candidate Smith was as repulsive to him as a foul odor; but the thought of voting for Smith's opponent was even worse. So he decided to do his civic duty and ended up voting for a candidate with whom he was not really satisfied.

Have you ever chosen between two candidates when you would have liked to vote against both of them? Or perhaps you chose one of two courses of action when you were against both of them. We usually refer to this as "choosing the lesser of two evils." Such dilemmas are not uncommon. They start early, like when Mom asks, "Do you want spinach or brussels sprouts?" Sometimes they take on moral value, as when we have to choose between keeping something in confidence and telling the secret to help a friend.

A. GOD'S DILEMMA

Even the Lord sometimes chooses the lesser of two evils. For example, he hates divorce (Malachi 2:16). Yet, when he gave laws to his people, he allowed for divorce in certain instances (Deuteronomy 24:1). Why? Because the alternative would have been worse. If a cruel, abusive man hated his wife and could not legally divorce her, he might treat her horribly. So, "because your hearts were hard," as Jesus put it (Matthew 19:8), divorce was allowed. This week's lesson tells of another time when God permitted something of which he did not approve.

DEVOTIONAL READING
PSALM 24:7-10

LESSON SCRIPTURE
1 SAMUEL 7:15—8:22

PRINTED TEXT
1 SAMUEL 7:15—8:9, 19-22

LESSON AIMS

After this lesson students should be able to:

1. Give the details of how Israel asked for and was given its first king.

2. Give examples of occasions when individuals have chosen a secular solution to a spiritual problem.

3. Suggest steps students can take to effect a spiritual solution to a current problem.

Oct
11

KEY VERSE

The LORD answered, "Listen to them and give them a king."
—1 Samuel 8:22

LESSON 6 NOTES

HOW TO SAY IT

Abijah. Uh-BYE-juh.
Beersheba. Beer-SHE-buh.
Gilgal. GIL-gal.
Levites. LEE-vites.
Levitical. Leh-VIT-ih-kul.
Mizpah. MIZ-pah.
Philistines. Fuh-LISS-teens or
    FILL-us-teens.
Ramah. RAY-muh.

WHAT DO YOU THINK?

Samuel's practice of traveling in a circuit made him more accessible to the people. How important do you think it is for a leader to be accessible? Why? Do you think a leader can be too accessible? Why or why not?

(Consider Matthew 20:25-28 and Exodus 18:13-23 in your discussion.)

B. LESSON BACKGROUND

Samuel was the last of the many judges who led Israel during the few troubled centuries after Joshua died and before there was a king. Samuel grew up in the tabernacle "before the Lord" (1 Samuel 1:22) and was reared by Eli, a priest who also judged Israel. Samuel was still rather young when the people of Israel realized that God had chosen him as a prophet (1 Samuel 3:19-21).

After Eli died, the Philistines harassed Israel for twenty years (1 Samuel 7:2). Then Samuel challenged the people to put away their false gods and rededicate themselves to serve the Lord alone (vv. 3, 4). Later, while Samuel was leading a time of confession and fasting, the Philistines prepared to attack Israel. The Lord came to his people's aid through a thunderstorm, and the Philistines were routed (vv. 5-14). They were kept under control "throughout Samuel's lifetime" (v. 13).

The first portion of our printed text summarizes Samuel's ministry in Israel.

I. A CHANGE REQUESTED (1 SAMUEL 7:15–8:5)

A. CIRCUIT JUDGE (vv. 15-17)

15. Samuel continued as judge over Israel all the days of his life.

The people of Israel gave their complete support to Samuel as their leader. Three reasons for this are easily seen.

1. Because Samuel's words had proved to be true, the people understood that he was a prophet of God (1 Samuel 3:19, 20).

2. Samuel had led the Israelites to a decisive victory over the oppressive Philistines (1 Samuel 7:3-11). The people accepted him as their leader as naturally as the United States accepted Washington's leadership after the American Revolution and Eisenhower's after World War II.

3. Experience showed that Samuel's judgments were just and right, and that he was a man of integrity. (See their later assessment of his character in 1 Samuel 12:4.)

16. From year to year he went on a circuit from Bethel to Gilgal to Mizpah, judging Israel in all those places.

Samuel "held court" in the three towns of *Bethel, Gilgal,* and *Mizpah.* These towns were fairly close to each other, and all were located in the territory of the tribe of Benjamin. Judges and preachers followed the same "circuit" strategy on the American frontier, where the population was sparse and travel was not easy.

It is probable that Samuel was not the only person who functioned in this capacity, especially since the territory that he covered was rather limited. Perhaps some of the cases that arose were handled by Levites in the various Levitical cities (Numbers 35:1-8). In addition, Samuel apparently organized a group of prophets (1 Samuel 10:5-10; 19:20), and they may have assisted him.

17. But he always went back to Ramah, where his home was, and there he also judged Israel. And he built an altar there to the LORD.

After holding court in the three places named in the preceding verse, Samuel would go back home to *Ramah.* That had been his parents' home (1 Samuel 1:19). Likely Samuel had inherited their property, or part of it. He *judged,* or held court, at Ramah also, thus making four stops in his circuit. He also *built an altar* in Ramah on which to offer sacrifices to *the Lord.*

B. DISAPPOINTING SONS (vv. 1-3)

1. When Samuel grew old, he appointed his sons as judges for Israel.

Perhaps Samuel's already heavy caseload was growing heavier, while he himself was losing energy as he *grew old.* It seemed reasonable to get some help, which Samuel found by appointing *his sons as judges.*

2. The name of his firstborn was Joel and the name of his second was Abijah, and they served at Beersheba.

Samuel's circuit was in central Israel. *Beersheba*, on the other hand, was approximately fifty miles away to the south. It was much more convenient for people in that part of the country to have a court closer to where they lived.

3. But his sons did not walk in his ways. They turned aside after dishonest gain and accepted bribes and perverted justice.

Samuel had managed the nation admirably, but he had not done so well with his *sons*. They had become selfish and greedy for *dishonest gain*. They did not care for law or *justice*; they saw their judgeship only as an opportunity to enrich themselves. They *accepted bribes*, selling each decision they made to the highest bidder.

C. CALL FOR A KING (vv. 4, 5)

4. So all the elders of Israel gathered together and came to Samuel at Ramah.

The corruption of Joel and Abijah was too evident to be hidden. News of it spread all over the country. *Elders* in the towns of Israel had supported Samuel and his exemplary leadership; but now they were alarmed, as they should have been, at the prospect of his sons' being in leadership roles.

5. They said to him, "You are old, and your sons do not walk in your ways; now appoint a king to lead us, such as all the other nations have."

Samuel had been known as a just judge for a long time, but he had been known even longer as a prophet of God (1 Samuel 3:20). With the help of the Lord, perhaps he would provide Israel with a *king* who would be as capable a leader as Samuel himself. With such a man in charge, peace and prosperity would continue. Besides, *all the other nations* around Israel had kings, and they seemed to be getting along quite well. If Israel was given a king who was better than any other, would it not become a nation more prosperous and respected than any other?

BEING LIKE EVERYONE ELSE

Sometimes it's good to be like everyone else—speaking the same language, for instance. Numerous regional dialects have added color to American speech, but they can also make it difficult for people from different regions to communicate.

Boontling is one such regional dialect. It developed in Boonville, a once remote village in northern California. Boontling has some two thousand words and phrases that differ from standard English. Several local men who were called to enlist in the army during World War I had to learn standard English before they could serve. However, cars, telephones, and television have erased Boonville's cultural distance from the "outside" world. Today, only a few old-timers speak Boontling. As one "boonter" said, "We've all piked for dusties now; our harpin' days are gone." ("We've all died off now; our speaking days are gone.")

Israel's problem was not that they wanted to communicate with their neighbors; they wished to be governed like them. They refused to hear from God that having a king as their neighbors did would lead to the same moral and spiritual problems their neighbors had. Wanting to be like the world is *still* a problem for the people of God, isn't it? —C. R. B.

II. A CHANGE CONSIDERED (1 SAMUEL 8:6-9)

Samuel had some thinking to do. Probably the request for a king was a surprise to him. He knew he had been judging justly, and he knew his judgment was acceptable to most of the people. Perhaps he did not realize how bad his sons were. So he was surprised when so many leaders came to him asking for a change.

WHAT DO YOU THINK?

Israel wanted to "be like all the nations." A similar desire to be like others creates problems for Christians. We may want to be like others in terms of money and possessions. The quest for material wealth can tempt us to employ ungodly methods to obtain it. The erosion of moral standards is, at heart, an attempt to be like others. When enough people view a behavior as acceptable, many others go along because they don't want to be "different."

How can we, as Christians, resist the temptation to compromise principles to be like others? How can we encourage others, especially young people, to take a stand?

A. SAMUEL'S FIRST REACTION (v. 6)

6. But when they said, "Give us a king to lead us," this displeased Samuel; so he prayed to the LORD.

The elders' request *displeased Samuel*. Probably he took the request personally. He felt that he was being rejected. (See verse 7.) After all Samuel had done for Israel, it seemed to him most ungrateful for the people to disregard the plan for leadership that he had proposed. (Perhaps, deep down, he was also displeased with himself and with his failure to do a better job with his sons.)

Additionally, Samuel knew enough about national affairs to know that a king would not solve Israel's problem. Having a king would be no better than having a judge, unless the king was a better man.

Despite the hurt he felt, Samuel reacted to the request in the right way. Instead of criticizing or denouncing the elders' appeal, he *prayed to the Lord*. Samuel preferred to give the elders no answer until he could give them God's answer.

B. GOD'S PERSPECTIVE (vv. 7-9)

7. And the LORD told him: "Listen to all that the people are saying to you; it is not you they have rejected, but they have rejected me as their king.

Now we see the real problem with the elders' request: It was a rejection of God and his rule over Israel. The problem was not so much the request—God had provided in the law for a time when *the people* would desire a king (Deuteronomy 17:14-20)—as the reason for the request. God had called Israel to be his own "treasured possession" (Exodus 19:5), distinct from all other nations. Now the elders were abandoning that call and asking to be like "all the other nations." They had forgotten that God was their real King.

Some students feel that, since God had made provision for a king in the law, then he must have expected Israel to have a king at some time. Some believe that God intended for David to be the first king of Israel, and that this request represented a case of the people running ahead of God and his timing.

8. As they have done from the day I brought them up out of Egypt until this day, forsaking me and serving other gods, so they are doing to you.

The people had been rejecting God ever since leaving *Egypt*—not all the time, but again and again. This was evident in our lesson last week.

9. Now listen to them; but warn them solemnly and let them know what the king who will reign over them will do."

Both in verse 7 and here in verse 9, we see that God told Samuel to *listen* to the elders and do as they asked. Why? As your own child grew toward manhood, didn't you sometimes decide that it was best to let him go his own mistaken way and learn from his error? So God let the people have their way, and later generations learned the disadvantages of having another *king* besides the Lord.

If you have ever decided to let your child go his own mistaken way, perhaps you also explained why you thought that way was mistaken. Likewise the Lord told Samuel to *warn* the people *solemnly* that having a king was not best for them, and to explain why. This protest is recorded in verses 10-18. A king, said Samuel, would become an expensive item for God's people to maintain. In time the people would cry to the Lord because of oppression by their king, just as they had cried because of oppression by enemies; but this time the Lord would not be as quick to respond.

III. A CHANGE ALLOWED (1 SAMUEL 8:19-22)

No doubt the elders had discussed their concerns at length before they approached Samuel. They thought the solution they proposed was the best

WHAT DO YOU THINK?

It is interesting to note how Samuel more than once responded to the elders' demands by praying to God, and how we sometimes wish that God would speak to us as he did to Samuel, making his answer clear! How can we understand God's answer to our prayers? How can we be sure we are acting according to his answer and not just as we think he should answer?

The visual for lesson 6 illustrates the prophet Samuel's warning the people of the consequences of having a king (1 Samuel 8:11-18).

possible one. Perhaps they felt so sure that they hardly heard Samuel's warning about what a king would cost the nation. At least we know they were not convinced by it. They repeated their request more emphatically, this time with additional support from the people.

A. REPEATED REQUEST (vv. 19, 20)

19. But the people refused to listen to Samuel. "No!" they said. "We want a king over us.

Usually these elders had gratefully accepted Samuel's leadership, but this time they resisted. Again they stated their desire, this time as a demand more than a request: *We want a king over us.*

20. Then we will be like all the other nations, with a king to lead us and to go out before us and fight our battles."

The elders repeated their wish to *be like all the other nations*. But Israel had been set apart to be different from all the nations, to be the one nation in all the world that was governed by God's law, and to be a living demonstration that the way of obedience to God is the best way there is. To be like all the nations would be to forsake the very purpose for which the nation of Israel had been created.

Another reason for the elders' request was that our *king* may *lead us*. They wanted the king to be responsible for enforcing the law and administering justice. We wonder if the elders hoped that a king would relieve them of their own leadership responsibilities. Obviously he would not. Even if Israel had a king, each of the elders would still be responsible for obeying the law and guiding the younger generation to obey it.

Finally, the elders desired that the king *go out before us and fight our battles*. They wanted the king to be responsible for Israel's national defense. But had they forgotten that there was a better protection already available—the protection of the Lord God Almighty? He would keep them safe if they would obey his law. He had proved that again and again. Was the desire for a king an attempt by the people to bypass their responsibility to obey God? If so, they were badly mistaken. No king (no matter how capable he might be) could take the responsibility of obedience from God's people.

SPIRITUAL MIDDLE AGE

People who have just entered the decade of their forties like to comfort themselves (and annoy younger people) with the boast that "life begins at forty." However, they often fail to complete the sentence: "Life begins (to become more troublesome) at forty." Forgetfulness, aches and pains where there used to be none, concerns for aged parents (not to mention "grown-up" but not yet mature children), wrinkles, thinning hair, and expanding waistlines all seem to be part of life that "begins at forty."

Now to the aid of such individuals comes a "middle-aged baby book" to help middle-agers remember all those bits of information that no longer come readily to mind: birth dates, anniversaries, waist size (as if they wanted to think about that!), Social Security number, E-mail address, and other facts and figures.

Israel seems to have been suffering from that middle-age scourge of forgetfulness. Things the people should have remembered seem to have been beyond their ability to recall when they most needed to do so. Among those items were God's dealings with Israel. He had been their king and provider from the time of Moses through the many years since he had brought them to the promised land. They forgot what God had done; they followed other gods; now they wanted another king.

Let us pray that we might be less forgetful of God's goodness than Israel was!

—C. R. B.

WHAT DO YOU THINK?

Apparently, the Israelite elders did not want to think through the consequences of asking for a king, so God told Samuel to show them what a king would do and how he would treat them. What are some present-day examples of human beings' acting without pondering the consequences of their actions? What harm has come to the church because of such short-sighted thinking? How can we develop an objective view of the future to consider potential results of our actions—both positive and negative?

DAILY BIBLE READINGS

Monday, Oct. 5—Hannah Prays for a Male Child (1 Samuel 1:3-11)

Tuesday, Oct. 6—Hannah Does As She Promised (1 Samuel 1:21-28)

Wednesday, Oct. 7—"Speak, for Your Servant Is Listening" (1 Samuel 3:1-10)

Thursday, Oct. 8—Samuel Administers Justice (1 Samuel 7:15—8:9)

Friday, Oct. 9—Samuel Listens to the People and God (1 Samuel 8:10-22)

Saturday, Oct. 10—Pray for All in Authority (1 Timothy 2:1-7)

Sunday, Oct. 11—Saul Recognized As King (1 Samuel 11:5-15)

PRAYER

What a wealth of opportunities you have placed before us, our Father! There are so many things that need to be done! Open our eyes to see them, we pray, and strengthen our will to do them. In Jesus' name. Amen.

B. DIVINE PERMISSION (vv. 21, 22)

21. When Samuel heard all that the people said, he repeated it before the LORD.

When the discussion was over, Samuel again went to *the Lord* in prayer. The decision in this matter would affect the nation for centuries to come. Samuel wanted it to be the Lord's decision, not his.

22. The LORD answered, "Listen to them and give them a king." Then Samuel said to the men of Israel, "Everyone go back to his town."

Again the Lord told Samuel to let the people have their own way, make their own mistake, and thus learn their own lesson. Samuel then told the assembled elders to go home and wait for God to make known his choice of a man to be king. Chapters 9 and 10 tell how this was done, resulting in the selection of Saul as Israel's first king.

CONCLUSION

Why didn't the elders of Israel come to Samuel and say, "Let us share the responsibility"? They could have said, "With your help we can do the judging in our towns. Our fellow citizens know us and respect us. We're not inspired prophets, but we can study the law together and know how to apply it. We can appeal to you for help when we have difficult problems."

Why didn't the elders say something like that? You know the answer. Seldom does anyone ask for added responsibility unless a salary goes with it. The elders wanted a king, not themselves, to be responsible for the national behavior and the national welfare.

A. WHO WANTS RESPONSIBILITY?

The United States elected a President in 1996. Shortly before the election, there was a so-called debate between the two leading candidates. Ordinary citizens were allowed to question the candidates.

The questions were not surprising. A schoolteacher asked a candidate if he would provide more funds for public education. A working mother inquired what help would be available for day care for her children. An owner of a small business wanted to know how a candidate would encourage small businesses. A naval man asked if there would be more pay for people in the armed services. No one asked what a President would expect of ordinary citizens or what a citizen could contribute to the general welfare. The universal question seemed to be, "What's in it for me?"

In essence, this was the primary concern of Samuel's two sons, who had become selfish and dishonest judges. It was also the issue being raised by the elders of Israel when they requested a king of Samuel. The king was to fight their battles, although God had been doing so all along! God, however, required obedience to his law. Perhaps with a king would come less responsibility on their part. This is often the thinking of those who seek to address spiritual problems by non-spiritual means.

The question, "What's in it for me?" may not necessarily be associated with greed or corruption. "We have left everything to follow you! What then will there be for us?" Simon Peter once asked of Jesus, and Jesus answered plainly. If we sacrifice much in serving him, even in this world we will get far more than we give; and in the world to come, we will have eternal life (Matthew 19:27-29). But God's people must also ask, "What can I give?" "How can I contribute?" "Where can I help?"

Look around your church. What needs to be done? What can *you* be responsible for doing?

WHAT DO YOU THINK?

The lesson writer suggests that some people never seem to get past the question, "What's in it for me?" How does the preoccupation with this question harm the church? How can we help people to think first of what's good for the Lord's kingdom instead of what's good for themselves?

THOUGHT TO REMEMBER

Meet your responsibilities. Don't try to pass them off to someone else.

Discovery Learning

This page contains an alternate lesson plan emphasizing learning activities. Classes desiring such student involvement will find these suggestions helpful. The next page is a reproducible activity page to further enhance discovery learning.

LEARNING GOALS

After this lesson, your students should be able to:

1. Give the details of how the Israelites asked for and were given their first king.

2. Give examples of occasions when individuals have chosen a secular solution to a spiritual problem.

3. Suggest steps they can take to effect a spiritual solution to a current problem.

INTO THE LESSON

Ask your students to imagine what would happen if they suddenly were transported to a land where everyone wore white. No colors, no creativity, no originality. Only white. Ask, "How long do you think it would take before you stopped wearing colorful clothes and began wearing only white?"

"Everybody does it. Why can't we be like everyone else?" How often have the parents in your class heard that refrain from their teenagers! Actually, we all want to fit in—parents and teens alike. Even those in our society who adopt bizarre and outlandish styles are trying to please others who dress and act the same way.

In today's lesson we hear the lament, "We want to be like everyone else."

INTO THE WORD

Samuel bridged the period of the judges and the prophetic age. He was the last judge and the first prophet.

For all his good qualities, Samuel shows that even a wise and godly leader does not always leave a great legacy.

Read 1 Samuel 7:15-17. Ask, "What good qualities do we see here in Samuel's life?" (He was faithful: he judged "all the days of his life"; he was accessible: traveling in a circuit; he was spiritual: he "built an altar . . . to the Lord.")

Now read 1 Samuel 8:1-9, 19-22. Observe that there was a real problem in Israel, and the elders were attempting to solve it with their proposal to Samuel. Divide the class into three groups to work on the following assignments. (Distributing copies of the reproducible page that follows may help you with this exercise.)

1. The problem. What was the problem the people identified? How serious a problem was it? (Samuel was old, so his influence would soon be gone, but his sons were corrupt; they would not lead as faithfully as Samuel had [v. 5].)

2. A secular solution. Israel's problem was spiritual, but the people chose a secular solution. What was it? Why was that attractive to them? (To have a king. This would make them more like other nations [v. 5] and give them a special leader to lead them into battle [v. 20].)

3. A spiritual solution. What spiritual solutions might they have come up with to solve their problem? What would you have suggested if you had been one of the Israelites? (They could have asked Samuel to appoint godly men to serve with him as judges and learn to serve in the same faithful way he had. They could have demanded that Samuel's sons be held accountable for their actions and either reform or give up their positions. Your students will have many good ideas.)

Observe that Samuel at first refused but later gave in. In between, he prayed. Discuss the importance of prayer when making a significant decision. (Use the "What Do You Think?" question on page 60 if you haven't already.)

Note also that God gave in to the people's request even though it was not in their best interest. Discuss why he would do that. Does God sometimes let us have our own way even though he knows it is not best for us? Can you think of some examples of this? (See "God's Dilemma" on page 57.)

INTO LIFE

Israel's desire to conform and be like everyone else led them to accept a secular solution to their problem (a change in government) rather than a spiritual solution (a change of heart).

Ask, "What are some spiritual problems facing our church and/or community today?" Make a list on the chalkboard as your students suggest items. These may include pornography, abortion, declining academic standards, crime, loss of faith in absolute truth, divorce, and others.

Ask the class to choose three or four of the problems and then assign a task force to consider each one. Each task force will answer two questions regarding the problem: (1) What are some secular solutions that have been implemented to deal with this problem? (2) What would be a spiritual solution to the problem, and how could we implement this solution?

Give the groups ten minutes to work; then ask for reports. Choose one of the spiritual solutions and take it on as a class project. Pray about it in your closing prayer.

Problems and Solutions

Read 1 Samuel 8:1-9, 19-22. There was a real problem in Israel, and the elders were attempting to solve it with their proposal to Samuel. What was the problem the people identified? How serious a problem was it? What solution did the people propose? Why was this secular solution attractive to the people? What better solution—a spiritual solution—might they have come up with? What would *you* have suggested if you had been one of the Israelites? Use the upper part of the chart below to record your answers.

THE PROBLEM	A SECULAR SOLUTION	A SPIRITUAL SOLUTION

In the lower part of the chart write one or two spiritual problems facing your church and/or community today. What are some secular solutions that have been implemented to deal with this problem? What spiritual solution to the problem can you suggest?

Make It Personal

What is the biggest problem facing you today—particularly, the one that could have the greatest impact on your relationship with the Lord?

What are you doing to address the problem?

Is this a spiritual solution or a secular one? What makes you think so?

What can you do differently to address this problem in a spiritual, Christ-honoring way?

JEROBOAM'S SIN

WHY TEACH THIS LESSON?

The boss decided the office needed an upgrade. Computers were the answer. The company had to have computers, but they were not in the budget. However, since the company did a lot of printing, it had a good bit of printing equipment, as well as a full-time printer. So the boss decided the company could buy its printing, liquidate the equipment, and lay off the printer—thus freeing capital with which to buy the computer equipment. He told the board of directors that buying outside printing would be less expensive than doing their own, so they approved the boss's plan. Any first-year accounting student with the numbers in front of him could have seen it was more expensive to buy printing, but that didn't matter. The boss wanted computers!

Jeroboam wanted a new kingdom. To get it, he had to replace the religion of the old kingdom with one of his own making. He told the people it was just as good. Anyone who knew God's law should have known better, but the people wanted a new kingdom, too. They approved the new king's plan.

Use this lesson to challenge your students to watch out for religious counterfeits. When someone says this new doctrine is "just as good," look in the Book!

INTRODUCTION

"Like father, like son." So says an oft-quoted proverb; however, there are many cases where it has been proved inaccurate. Last week we saw Israel's era of the judges end with the admirable work of Samuel, who was a prophet of God as well as a judge of Israel. In his old age he shared the work of judging with his sons, who, unlike their father, were greedy and corrupt. Unhappy at the prospect of having the people governed by such men, the elders of Israel asked Samuel to provide a king to rule the nation. The Lord told Samuel to grant this request, and Israel became a monarchy. Three kings ruled in succession before the time when the events recorded in this week's lesson occurred.

A. SAUL

The first king of Israel was Saul. He began his reign with an impressive victory over Israel's enemies; but later he became arrogant, foolishly going his own way instead of obeying the Lord. Eventually Saul's disobedience resulted in God's rejection of him and the choice of "a man after [God's] own heart" (1 Samuel 13:14). The record of Saul's reign is found in 1 Samuel 9–31.

B. DAVID

After Saul's death, David became king—first of his own tribe of Judah and then of all Israel. He built the nation of Israel into a great empire, subduing the surrounding pagan peoples. His later years were marred by his own scandalous conduct, and by two rebellions led by two of his sons. Still, David preserved a strong and stable empire, and turned it over to his son Solomon. Events of David's reign are found in 2 Samuel 5:1—1 Kings 2:12.

DEVOTIONAL READING
PSALM 48 9-14

LESSON SCRIPTURE
1 KINGS 12

PRINTED TEXT
1 KINGS 12:20, 25-33

LESSON AIMS

After this lesson students should be able to:

1. Describe the counterfeit religion Jeroboam established to consolidate his kingdom.

2. Contrast the counterfeit religion of Jeroboam with the true religion God had ordained.

3. Identify some counterfeit religious ideas that challenge the "faith . . . once delivered," and suggest ways to keep one's religion free of counterfeits.

Oct
18

KEY VERSE

After seeking advice, the king made two golden calves. He said to the people, "It is too much for you to go up to Jerusalem. Here are your gods, O Israel, who brought you up out of Egypt."
—1 Kings 5:28

You may find it helpful to display again the visual for lesson 1 and use it to locate some of the places mentioned in today's lesson.

WHAT DO YOU THINK?

Rehoboam failed to address the grievances of the people. As a result, the nation was split and most of it formed a new nation, one that turned quickly to idolatry. Similarly, churches are split when certain members feel their needs or wishes are not being addressed. Is it ever right to split or leave a church? Why or why not?

Consider the following Scriptures in your discussion: 1 Corinthians 1–4; Titus 3:10, 11; Hebrews 13:17.

C. SOLOMON

Gifted with special wisdom from the Lord, Solomon brought his country to the peak of its power and glory. The ancient empires of Egypt and Mesopotamia were both in periods of decline at that time, allowing Israel to reign supreme as the greatest empire of all. Yet with all his wisdom, Solomon ruined the latter part of his reign with foolish choices. He married several pagan wives and allowed them to desecrate Jerusalem with their pagan gods. Through excessive taxation and forced labor, he burdened his own people so heavily that they were on the verge of rebellion when his kingship ended. The record of Solomon's reign is found in 1 Kings 2:13—11:43.

D. LESSON BACKGROUND

While Saul, David, and Solomon all showed arrogance and folly in the latter part of their reigns, Solomon's son Rehoboam *began* his reign with a very foolish decision. When the people gathered to crown him king, they asked him to reduce the heavy burdens that Solomon had placed on them. Recklessly the young king vowed to increase their burdens instead. The greater part of the nation rebelled at this news. Judah, Rehoboam's own tribe, remained loyal to him, and the small tribe of Benjamin joined it; however, the northern tribes vowed to serve Rehoboam no more. They formed an independent nation and designated Jeroboam as their king.

Jeroboam had been an able administrator under Solomon; but when the king learned of a promise made by Ahijah the prophet to Jeroboam that he would one day become king of Israel, Solomon tried to kill him. Jeroboam then fled to Egypt (1 Kings 11:28, 37-40). Now he came back to govern the rebel nation in the north (thus fulfilling the prophet's words). That nation kept the name of Israel, while the portion loyal to Rehoboam was called Judah (1 Kings 12:1-24).

I. NEW NATION (1 KINGS 12:20, 25)

A. COMPLETING THE DIVISION (v. 20)

20. When all the Israelites heard that Jeroboam had returned, they sent and called him to the assembly and made him king over all Israel. Only the tribe of Judah remained loyal to the house of David.

Here *all Israel* refers to the people of the rebellious tribes. They were to be called Israel from that time forth. Many people of the northern kingdom knew Jeroboam, for he had served quite capably among them (1 Kings 11:28). He was also among the leaders who took their request to Rehoboam and heard his refusal to address their concerns (1 Kings 12:12, 13). Apparently the rebels trusted Jeroboam and were unanimous in choosing him to be their king.

The house of David describes the royal family. Rehoboam was its member on the throne, though no longer recognized by the northern tribes. At this point *only the tribe of Judah* was *loyal* to Rehoboam; but when he prepared to go to war to force the rebellious tribes to remain in his kingdom, the tribe of Benjamin joined Judah instead of siding with the rebels (v. 21).

B. CONSTRUCTING NEW CITIES (v. 25)

25. Then Jeroboam fortified Shechem in the hill country of Ephraim and lived there. From there he went out and built up Peniel.

Shechem, located in the *hill country* belonging to the tribe of *Ephraim*, had a long history before this. It had been particularly significant in the time of Joshua as a place where Israel gathered to renew its commitment to God (Joshua 24:1, 25). Jeroboam *fortified* it, making it a stronger, better defended city. Perhaps he also built a royal palace, for he *lived there*, making Shechem both his residence and his capital city for a time. Likewise Jeroboam *built up Peniel*, a city located east of the Jordan River. From there his troops could control the main route of travel and trade on that side of the river.

II. NEW PLACES FOR WORSHIP (1 KINGS 12:26-29)

According to the law of Moses, the men of Israel were required to assemble three times each year for the religious festivals of Passover, Pentecost, and Tabernacles (Exodus 23:14-17; Leviticus 23). Though given before Israel reached the promised land, these requirements looked forward to a special central place of worship in that land (Deuteronomy 12:5-7). For years that place had been the magnificent temple that Solomon had built in Jerusalem; but Jeroboam realized that continuing that practice constituted a threat to his newly gained power.

A. JEROBOAM'S DILEMMA (vv. 26, 27)

26. Jeroboam thought to himself, "The kingdom will now likely revert to the house of David.

Despite his efforts to establish his authority and fortify his defenses, Jeroboam was still unsure of how firmly he was in control. He began to think of a very unpleasant scenario. The people in the north might *revert* to Jerusalem to be ruled by Rehoboam, the king who belonged *to the house of David*. David was still recognized as a great national hero—the builder of Israel's empire. The people had rebelled without hesitation against his grandson when he had refused to lighten their financial burdens. Would they go back just as quickly if Rehoboam agreed to do what they asked? If they did, Jeroboam would likely have to flee again—assuming he could get away before being arrested and executed for treason.

27. "If these people go up to offer sacrifices at the temple of the LORD in Jerusalem, they will again give their allegiance to their lord, Rehoboam king of Judah. They will kill me and return to King Rehoboam."

Jeroboam knew that he needed the religious as well as the political support of the people if he were to reign successfully as their king. If they continued to view *Jerusalem* and Solomon's *temple* as their place of worship, Jeroboam's control in the north could be severely damaged. The three annual festivals in Jerusalem drew thousands of people, and included glorious ceremonies of worship in the stately temple. They were also festive occasions with joyful feasting, family reunions, and meetings of old friends. Would attending these gatherings cause them to regret their decision to sever ties with the house of David?

Jeroboam thought so, especially if Rehoboam reversed his earlier statement and promised lower taxes and less forced labor. Zealous men of Israel might then *kill* Jeroboam and *return to King Rehoboam*—back to the fold of David their hero. Jeroboam made plans to prevent this from happening.

B. JEROBOAM'S SOLUTION (vv. 28, 29)

28. After seeking advice, the king made two golden calves. He said to the people, "It is too much for you to go up to Jerusalem. Here are your gods, O Israel, who brought you up out of Egypt."

After seeking advice, Jeroboam devised a plan to keep the people of the north from going to Jerusalem. He *made two golden calves*. He then told the people, *It is too much for you to go up to Jerusalem*. They had asked for lighter burdens (v. 4); now Jeroboam was offering to remove the burden of a long trip to Jerusalem three times a year. That trip was *too much*; they could worship just as well much closer to home.

HOW TO SAY IT

Ahijah. Uh-HIGH-juh.
Elohim (Hebrew). El-oh-HEEM.
Ephraim. EE-fray-im.
Jeroboam. Jair-uh-BOE-um.
Levites. LEE-vites.
Mesopotamia. MES-uh-puh-TAY-me-uh.
Peniel. Pih-NYE-el.
Rehoboam. Ree-huh-BOE-um.
Shechem. SHECK-em or SHEEK-em.

WHAT DO YOU THINK?

Jeroboam instituted the new religious practices in his kingdom out of an effort at self-preservation. What are some evil practices that continue in our society because of the practitioners' concern for self-preservation? What special efforts might be needed to combat practices driven by such a self-preservation instinct?

Jeroboam's new religion consisted of a dangerous blend of truth and falsehood. He linked his religion with the act that led to Israel's establishment as a nation: their deliverance from slavery in *Egypt*. However, he credited this deliverance to the *gods* that were represented by the golden calves. Many Bible students note that pagan peoples often represented their gods as standing on the backs of bulls or calves. Apparently Jeroboam did not attempt to portray a deity; he simply erected the calves with no gods on their backs. The word rendered *gods* in this verse is the Hebrew *Elohim*, which is normally translated as *God*. In such instances, whatever verb, adjective, or pronoun is used with *Elohim* is, appropriately, singular. Here, however, the verb *brought . . . up* is plural. Jeroboam was not thinking of the one God. His act was a blatant violation of both the first and the second Commandments. It also opened the door for the entry of idolatry into the northern kingdom. As verse 30 notes, "This thing became a sin."

29. One he set up in Bethel, and the other in Dan.

Bethel was located at the southern end of Jeroboam's kingdom, just ten miles north of Jerusalem; *Dan* was situated at the northern end, north of the Sea of Galilee. A family could travel to the place that was more convenient.

EXOTIC RELIGIONS

"Exotic Plants, Animals Imperil U.S. Ecosystem" read the newspaper headline. The article beneath it described a number of "exotic" invaders: non-native (foreign) species that threaten the well-being of native species. Among those mentioned were the South Pacific brown tree snake (up to eight feet long) that is entering Hawaiian homes through the plumbing, the kudzu vine that is choking southern waterways, and the zebra mussel that is clogging parts of the Great Lakes and the Saint Lawrence Seaway. These are but a few of the forty-five hundred species of exotic plants and animals that have taken up residence in places where they often have no natural enemies.

Jeroboam should have known that there is no room in the human heart for two gods if one of them is the God of the Bible. Nevertheless, he attempted to import other "exotic" gods into Israel's worship. The result of this was disastrous for God's people; for in time, their idolatry destroyed them.

Each of us needs to ask himself, "Have *I* placed any other gods before my Father in Heaven?"

—C. R. B.

III. NEW SINS (1 KINGS 12:30-33)

Jeroboam tried to pretend that he was continuing the proper worship of Yahweh. In fact, he instituted a new system of worship. Verses 30-33 point out the system's features that were established by the king, not by the Lord.

A. IDOLS (v. 30)

30. And this thing became a sin; the people went even as far as Dan to worship the one there.

This thing (Jeroboam's counterfeit religion) *became a sin*. It explicitly violated the second Commandment: "You shall not make for yourself an idol . . . you shall not bow down to them or worship them" (Exodus 20:4, 5). Jeroboam's actions came to receive their own stigma in the biblical record, as both kings and the people of Israel in general were said to continue in "the sins of Jeroboam" (1 Kings 14:16; 15:30; 16:31; 2 Kings 3:3; 10:29, 31; 13:6; 14:24; 17:22). Because of these sins, God determined to destroy the house of Jeroboam "from the face of the earth" (1 Kings 13:34).

That *the people went even as far as Dan to worship* the golden calf placed there does not mean that the people worshiped only at Dan and not at Bethel; for the

WHAT DO YOU THINK?

Sometimes professing Christians will reject certain truths taught in the Bible. "My God is a loving God," they may say. "He could never send anyone to an eternal Hell." How would you answer, based on today's lesson text?

following verses repeatedly mention worship at Bethel. Perhaps we should understand the statement to indicate the zeal with which the people accepted the new religion. Observe the irony: it was "too much" for the people to go to Jerusalem, yet they were willing to journey to distant Dan in the north to participate in the sinful practices encouraged by Jeroboam.

B. PLACES AND PRIESTS (v. 31)

31. Jeroboam built shrines on high places and appointed priests from all sorts of people, even though they were not Levites.

The Hebrew text literally reads, "Jeroboam made a house of high places." Perhaps Jeroboam made a house, or a temple of some sort, for each of his golden calves. Such an act represented yet another attempt by Jeroboam to lure people in the northern kingdom from worship in the Jerusalem temple by providing a convenient substitute.

The phrase may also mean that Jeroboam built shrines on other high places, perhaps in addition to the main shrines at Bethel and Dan. This may indicate that he attempted to use already-existing shrines as places to worship the gods represented by the golden calves. That such additional sites existed throughout the northern kingdom is clear from 1 Kings 13:32, 33. Bethel, however, remained the most prominent place of worship, and the one at which the king himself made offerings (1 Kings 13:1).

As another ingredient of his counterfeit religion, Jeroboam appointed priests from all sorts of people, even though they were not Levites. First Kings 13:33 elaborates on this: "Anyone who wanted to become a priest he consecrated for the high places." The Lord had appointed Aaron and his descendants to be priests, and they were members of the tribe of Levi (Hebrews 7:5). Now, however, Jeroboam chose priests from other tribes. Second Chronicles 11:13, 14 tells us that legitimate priests and Levites from "all their districts throughout Israel" came to Judah, for Jeroboam did not allow them to carry out their appointed tasks. Perhaps he did this because the priests and Levites in his kingdom refused to take part in his idolatry, but this is not stated in the Bible.

C. FESTIVAL (v. 32)

32. He instituted a festival on the fifteenth day of the eighth month, like the festival held in Judah, and offered sacrifices on the altar. This he did in Bethel, sacrificing to the calves he had made. And at Bethel he also installed priests at the high places he had made.

In Judah the Feast of Tabernacles began on the fifteenth day of the seventh month (Leviticus 23:33-36). In yet another effort to lure people away from the worship in Jerusalem, Jeroboam instituted a similar feast in his domain and set its observance a month later than the Feast of Tabernacles. It has been noted that the change to the eighth month made this feast more convenient for farmers in the northern kingdom, where the harvest was approximately one month later than in Judah. He also offered sacrifices on the altar, perhaps similar to those prescribed for the Feast of Tabernacles (Numbers 29:12-39). Likely the priests' duties in Bethel resembled those of the priests in Jerusalem.

Thus Bethel housed a center of worship similar to the one in Jerusalem. No doubt it was smaller and less ornate than the one that Solomon had taken seven years to build in Jerusalem (1 Kings 6:37, 38), but it had all the proper religious ingredients, including priests, an altar, and sacrifices. The differences, however, were critical. The temple was not in the place God had chosen. The feast was not in the month God had appointed. The priests did not belong to the priestly tribe.

PRAYER

King of kings and Lord of lords! Rule in our hearts; rule in our minds; rule in our lives. Help us to pattern our will after your will, our thoughts after your thoughts, our acts after your desires. May we move closer to one another; but above all, may we stay close to you. Amen.

THOUGHT TO REMEMBER

Learn to want what God wants. Never settle for an inferior substitute.

The sacrifices were offered *to the calves* Jeroboam *had made.* The entire system was counterfeit!

D. CEREMONIES (v. 33)

33. *On the fifteenth day of the eighth month, a month of his own choosing, he offered sacrifices on the altar he had built at Bethel. So he instituted the festival for the Israelites and went up to the altar to make offerings.*

Here the counterfeit ceremonies are summarized. Sacrifices were offered and a *festival* was established in imitation of the ceremonies at Jerusalem. Yet none of it was commanded by the Lord; it was all of Jeroboam's *own choosing.* It was instituted by his own mouth, not by the mouth of the Lord. Thus it was doomed to fail.

CONCLUSION

A. A NATION DIVIDED

Among the nations of the world, Solomon's Israel was mightiest and most glorious. It is tragic that Israel became divided, and that it lost its power and glory, finally being dominated by other nations whose god was not Yahweh. Yet we must remember that the division of the nation was from the Lord (1 Kings 12:24).

Why did the Lord end the glory of his people? Because they no longer were behaving as his people should. Wise old Solomon had acted foolishly. He overburdened his people in order to enhance the glory of his kingdom (1 Kings 12:4). Worse than that, he married pagan wives and brought their idolatry to Jerusalem with them (1 Kings 11:1-13). The nation was no longer blessed, for Yahweh no longer was its one and only God.

Solomon's son Rehoboam might have been able to prevent the division of the nation, had he listened to the right counsel. But Rehoboam ignored the advice of the older and wiser men, who counseled him to "be a servant" by lessening the burden on the people (1 Kings 12:7). Instead, he followed the suggestion of those who were younger, and who wanted Rehoboam to establish himself as an aggressive, no-nonsense ruler. The result was full-scale revolt, and the division of God's people.

B. A NATION DECEIVED

Observe closely the subtle process by which Jeroboam drew the northern kingdom away from the true worship ordained by God in the law of Moses. He established a feast "like the festival held in Judah" (1 Kings 12:32), only his fell on the fifteenth day of the eighth month rather than the fifteenth day of the seventh month, as the law directed. Jeroboam ordained priests, but they were not taken from the tribe designated by God to be the source of priests. He encouraged worship, but it was the worship of false gods, in violation of the first and second Commandments. And all of this was done, claimed Jeroboam, to keep the people from having to go all the way to Jerusalem to worship.

Jeroboam's "conveniences" are a classic example of counterfeit religion at work. Most of us associate the term "counterfeit" with money. A counterfeit bill resembles the genuine brand so closely that it is usually hard for anyone except an expert to recognize the difference. The expert's job is to become so familiar with the genuine item that he can spot the counterfeit item with little trouble.

The application of this to God's people today should be clear. We need to become so familiar with God's Word that we cannot be led astray by "experts" or "scholars" who think they can improve on it.

WHAT DO YOU THINK?

The text tells us that Jeroboam set up a feast at a time of his own choosing." How does this human tendency to devise religious doctrines and practices of our own choosing affect the church today?

WHAT DO YOU THINK?

The lesson writer points out that it is a "subtle process" by which people are drawn away from the true worship ordained by God to a counterfeit. How can we tell whether a change is simply meeting the needs of contemporary people or is a compromise that may be the first step toward apostasy?

Discovery Learning

This page contains an alternate lesson plan emphasizing learning activities. Classes desiring such student involvement will find these suggestions helpful. The next page is a reproducible activity page to further enhance discovery learning.

LEARNING GOALS

Following this lesson, your students should be able to:

1. Describe the counterfeit religion Jeroboam established to consolidate his kingdom.

2. Contrast the counterfeit religion of Jeroboam with the true religion God had ordained.

3. Identify some counterfeit religious ideas that challenge the "faith . . . once delivered," and suggest ways to keep one's religion free of counterfeits.

INTO THE LESSON

The history of the church is filled with stories of people who have used religion to further their own political or financial ends. Ask your students to suggest some recent examples of false leaders in the church who have misled their people for personal profit.

The self-centered misdeeds of some former high-profile televangelists may still be fresh in your students' minds. Another example is Jim Jones, who in the name of religion led nearly a thousand people in an act of ritual suicide. A more recent example of a misleading leader is David Koresh, whose egocentric theology turned *Waco* into a word that inspires horror and grief.

Jeroboam was a leader in the tragic tradition of Jim Jones and David Koresh. He corrupted and perverted religion for his own selfish purposes. In today's lesson we will see what he did and why he did it.

INTO THE WORD

Fill in the events that happened in Israel's history since last week's lesson. (Refer to the Introduction and Lesson Background on pages 65 and 66.) The crisis that divided the kingdom is described in 1 Kings 12:1-17. Tell your students to read that passage and then discuss, "What role did Solomon's policies and practices play in the breakup of the united kingdom? What role did Rehoboam play in the breakup? What role did Jeroboam play?"

Distribute copies of the map on the next page. Ask the students to locate the northern kingdom of Israel, and then ask them to find Judah, the southern kingdom. Then have your students find the following towns on the map and describe why each is significant to this lesson:

- Shechem (v. 25).
- Peniel (v. 25).
- Jerusalem (v. 28).
- Bethel (v. 29).
- Dan (v. 29).

Lead your students in contrasting Jeroboam's counterfeit religion with the true religion that God had ordained and established. Write the following headings on the chalkboard: "Israel's True Religion" and "Jeroboam's Counterfeit Religion." (A similar activity appears in the student book, *NIV® Bible Student*.) Under the true religion heading write the following items:

1. The place of sacrifice was to be the temple at Jerusalem.

2. Priests were to come from the tribe of Levi only.

3. Images of God and idols were forbidden.

4. Three national feasts, or festivals, were to be observed at specified times each year: Passover, Pentecost, and Tabernacles.

5. Sacrifices were to be made to God alone.

6. Special incense was to be burnt to represent prayers offered to God.

Then ask the students to look for contrasting counterfeit elements in today's Bible passage (1 Kings 12:20, 25-33). Students may work individually or in groups. The following verses should reveal the necessary information to complete the chart: 1. v. 29; 2. v. 31; 3. v. 28; 4. v. 32; 5. v. 32; 6. v. 33.

INTO LIFE

Like the united kingdom, churches have been divided and congregations have been split apart when counterfeit ideas have been introduced to replace the genuine. Sometimes these are presented to make worship more "convenient." At other times they are introduced by leaders eager to make a name (and a profit) for themselves.

Ask your students to name some counterfeit religious ideas or practices. Make a list on the chalkboard as these are mentioned. Let the class brainstorm for a while, naming as many ideas as they can in a short period of time. Then review the list. Are any of these counterfeits being practiced in your church? If so, what can be done about it?

In closing, issue a call to integrity and genuineness. Challenge each student to do something specific during the coming week that would tend to focus attention on the true gospel in your church.

Two Nations

Use the map below to identify the Northern Kingdom of Israel and the Southern Kingdom of Judah. Locate the cities of Shechem (v. 25), Peniel (v. 25), Jerusalem (v. 28), Bethel (v. 29), and Dan (v. 29).

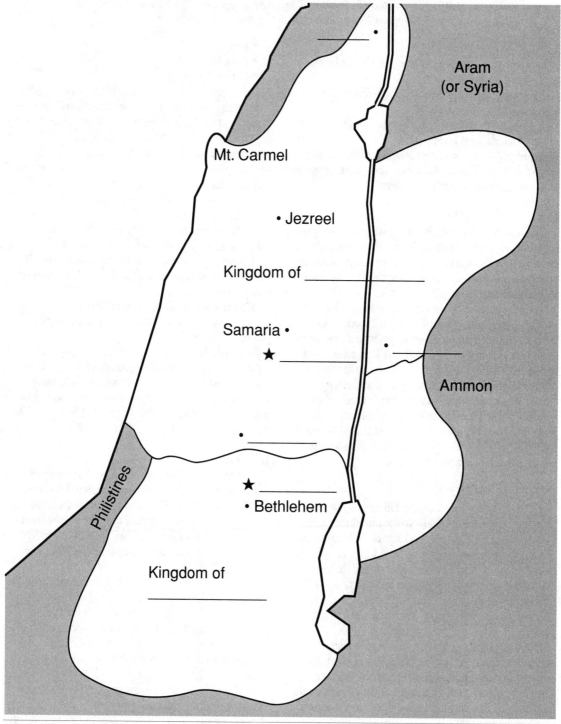

Unit 3. God Works Through People
(Lessons 8-10)

GOD WORKS
THROUGH PROPHETS

LESSON 8

WHY TEACH THIS LESSON?

"If it sounds too good to be true, it's probably false." Probably we've all heard that truism expressed so often that we really don't think we need another lesson on watching out for con men. Still, con men thrive, so the message must not be as well known as it seems.

This is not, however, another warning about things too good to be true. In fact, it's just the opposite. There is one grand truth that sounds incredible, completely illogical, and yet it is true. It is that sinners can be saved by the grace of God—not by works; in fact, to attempt to find salvation by works short circuits grace and salvation.

Perhaps Naaman, the subject of our lesson today, had heard that adage about things sounding too good to be true. At first he rejected the prophet's simple command to wash in the Jordan; it sounded too easy, too good to be true. But when he put his faith in God's word, he found healing.

The parallels between the events in this lesson and baptism are too obvious to need mention. More than that, however, this lesson will remind all your students that God's Word is true, even when it sounds unbelievable. When they put their faith in God and what he has said, they will be blessed beyond description.

INTRODUCTION

A. DIVIDED ISRAEL

The nation of Israel was divided after King Solomon's death, as we saw in last week's lesson. In the northern kingdom, known as Israel, King Jeroboam promptly instituted new religious practices that were continued by later kings. The Bible calls them "the sins of Jeroboam" (2 Kings 10:29). The presence of evil in the north sunk to new depths when King Ahab married a pagan princess (Jezebel), who seemed determined to make Baal worship the state religion of Israel (1 Kings 16:29-33).

B. PRESERVING THE TRUTH

In the troubled century following the division of the nation, God kept his truth alive and well in Israel by means of his prophets. Chief of these were Elijah and Elisha. In various places they gathered groups of faithful men, whom they trained to assist them in their prophetic tasks. The Bible calls them "the company of the prophets" (2 Kings 2:3, 5, 15). We have no idea how many of them there were; but when wicked Queen Jezebel set out to destroy the prophets, a hundred of them were saved by one man alone (1 Kings 18:13). The masses of people hesitated between allegiance to Yahweh and Baal (1 Kings 18:21); however, Elijah's heroic action on Mount Carmel brought them to declare their loyalty to Yahweh alone (vv. 20-40). When Elijah complained to God that he alone

DEVOTIONAL READING
2 SAMUEL 12:1-15
LESSON SCRIPTURE
2 KINGS 5:1-19
PRINTED TEXT
2 KINGS 5:1-14

LESSON AIMS

After this lesson students should be able to:

1. Retell the story of Naaman's healing.

2. Explain why Naaman found it difficult to obey God's prophet and what was the result when he did.

Oct
25

3. List some situations in which people find it difficult to obey God today, and suggest some ways to encourage them to do so.

KEY VERSE

"Have the man come to me and he will know that there is a prophet in Israel."
— 2 Kings 5:8b

LESSON 8 NOTES

HOW TO SAY IT

Abana. AB-uh-nuh.
Ahab. AY-hab.
Aram. AIR-um.
Aramean. Air-um-EE-un.
Assyria. Uh-SEAR-ee-uh.
Baal. BAY-ul.
Damascus. Duh-MASS-kus.
Elijah. Ee-LYE-juh.
Elisha. Ee-LYE-shuh.
Jehoram. Jeh-HO-ram.
Jehoshaphat. Jeh-HOSH-uh-fat.
Jeroboam. Jair-uh-BOE-um.
Jezebel. JEZ-uh-bel.
Joram. JO-ram.
Moab. MO-ab.
Naaman. NAY-uh-mun.
Omri. AHM-rye.
Pharpar. FAR-par.
Samaria. Suh-MEH-ri-uh.
Shechem. SHECK-em or
   SHEEK-em.
Syria. SEAR-ee-uh.

was faithful, the Lord replied that there were seven thousand others who had not fallen prey to idolatry (1 Kings 19:13-18).

C. LESSON BACKGROUND

During the troubled century following the division of Israel, there was intermittent war between Israel and Aram (also known as Syria)—the country to the north and east of the territory of Galilee. The Bible records a series of skirmishes that occurred during the reign of Ahab (1 Kings 20; 22:1-40). This tension provided the background for an incident that involved both these countries in a most unusual set of circumstances.

I. A SLAVE'S SUGGESTION (2 KINGS 5:1-3)

Our lesson story begins, not in Israel, but in Aram, the enemy country. However, a girl from Israel was living there.

A. A HAPLESS HERO (v. 1)

1. Now Naaman was commander of the army of the king of Aram. He was a great man in the sight of his master and highly regarded, because through him the LORD had given victory to Aram. He was a valiant soldier, but he had leprosy.

Naaman is introduced to us as *commander of the army of the king of Aram.* The king considered Naaman as *a great man . . . and highly regarded,* because he was a proven champion in battle. He had delivered Aram from a particular danger: perhaps an attack by Israel, or perhaps an attack by Assyria, which was gaining in strength as the ninth century B. C. progressed. The writer of this history knew that the *victory* was really the Lord's; Naaman was only his tool. Nevertheless, the writer notes that the commander was truly *a valiant soldier*—a genuine hero to his countrymen.

There was, however, a tragic side to Naaman's otherwise exemplary record: *he had leprosy.* Apparently people with leprosy were not isolated in Aram as they were in Israel (Leviticus 13:45, 46). It seems that Naaman was still able to command the Aramean army.

B. A CAPTIVE SLAVE (v. 2)

2. Now bands from Aram had gone out and had taken captive a young girl from Israel, and she served Naaman's wife.

As part of the ongoing warfare between *Aram* and *Israel,* raiding *bands* sometimes invaded Israel to steal what they could: stores of grain, sheep and cattle, and, in some cases, human captives to be used as slaves. Among the captives was a girl who was now a servant of *Naaman's wife.* We can only guess how *young* she was, but apparently she was old enough to help with some of the details of running a household.

C. A WORD OF HOPE (v. 3)

3. She said to her mistress, "If only my master would see the prophet who is in Samaria! He would cure him of his leprosy."

From this verse we can tell that the girl was old enough to realize that Naaman had an incurable disease and to be concerned about his health. Before leaving Israel, she had been old enough to know that marvelous miracles were done through Elisha, *the prophet who is in Samaria.* At this point, she had been in Aram long enough to become attached to her captors and to be concerned about their well-being. It appears that she had been kindly treated, for she spoke freely, and apparently was sincere in her desire to see Naaman healed of *his leprosy.* Knowing

WHAT DO YOU THINK?

The servant girl who waited on Naaman's wife could easily have been bitter about her captivity. In such a case she might have delighted to see her captor suffer. Instead, she seems to have been compassionate toward her enemy. How can we develop such a kindly spirit toward those who do us harm?

the Arameans were enemies of her native country, she probably assumed that there was no way Naaman could ever *see the prophet*, but she wished he could.

We noted in last week's lesson that Jeroboam established Shechem as the capital of the northern kingdom (1 Kings 12:25). One of the later kings of the north, Omri, established Samaria as the capital (1 Kings 16:24). This is the city where Elisha was residing.

PRISONERS OF WAR

War brings tragedies of many kinds, including some that affect innocent civilians. Early in World War II, Americans feared a Japanese invasion of the West Coast, so the United States military gathered 110,000 residents with Japanese ancestry into internment camps surrounded by barbed wire and guard towers. This was done in spite of the fact that more than two-thirds of these prisoners were loyal American citizens. After the war these internees were able to return to freedom, but four years of their lives had been lost, and many of them had lost all of their property. Amazingly, and to their credit, the vast majority of them returned to freedom with little hostility toward the United States.

The girl who served Naaman's wife was also a prisoner of war. We would understand completely if she had rejoiced in her master's poor health. Instead, she told Naaman's wife how he could be healed. As Jesus would say centuries later, doing good to those who do evil to us identifies us as children of the heavenly Father (Matthew 5:44, 45).   —C. R. B.

II. A KING'S PLEA (2 KINGS 5:4-7)

A. A WORD TO THE KING (v. 4)

4. Naaman went to his master and told him what the girl from Israel had said.

After the *girl* spoke to her mistress, no doubt she promptly told her husband about it. The Hebrew servant's suggestion was taken seriously. Perhaps we should not be surprised at this, for there was no other hope for Naaman. He would die unless a miracle occurred.

B. A QUICK RESPONSE (v. 5a)

5a. "By all means, go," the king of Aram replied. "I will send a letter to the king of Israel."

Enthusiastically *the king of Aram* told his general to go to Israel. Furthermore, the king volunteered to write *a letter to the king of Israel.* Apparently diplomatic channels were open between the two nations, in spite of the on-and-off war between them. Most likely this king of Israel was Joram (2 Kings 3:1), a son of Ahab. He must be distinguished from King Jehoram, who ruled Judah at the same time (2 Kings 8:16, 25, 29).

C. FROM KING TO KING (vv. 5b-7)

5b. So Naaman left, taking with him ten talents of silver, six thousand shekels of gold and ten sets of clothing.

The general expected to pay handsomely for his healing. Footnotes in the *New International Version* estimate that he took about 750 pounds of *silver* and 150 pounds of *gold*. Using those figures and the current prices of gold and silver, we can estimate that Naaman carried nearly a million dollars. Fine *clothing* also was highly valued in those days, and *ten* good suits would last the prophet a long time.

BUYING GOD'S FAVOR

In the spring of 1996 a new series of $100 bills went into circulation throughout the United States. The redesigned currency is supposed to be more difficult to counterfeit. It features a larger picture of Ben Franklin and other harder-to-duplicate features.

However, just one week after the bill went into circulation came the first known attempt to pass a fake copy of the new bill. The counterfeiter was a West Virginia teenager with a computer and laser printer. The bills weren't very good counterfeits, but that didn't stop the boy's uncle from trying to buy lunch with one of them at the local McDonald's! The boy was not arrested, because he apparently did not plan to circulate the bills (he even printed his own picture on some of them in place of Franklin's). His uncle, however, *was* arrested.

When Naaman went to Israel to seek a cure for his leprosy, he thought he could buy good health—a priceless commodity in anyone's estimation. Unlike the uncle in West Virginia, Naaman offered something of real worth. Gold, silver, and fine garments were the tokens with which he tried to buy the favor of God's prophet.

However, Naaman learned a lesson that is timeless: God's favor cannot be purchased. His grace is offered to those who have humble and contrite hearts and are willing to do what he says. This principle still holds true: we must come to God on his terms, not ours.

—C. R. B.

6. The letter that he took to the king of Israel read: "With this letter I am sending my servant Naaman to you so that you may cure him of his leprosy."

The Hebrew maiden had not claimed that the *king of Israel* could heal *leprosy*; she had said that the prophet could (v. 3). However, she had also said that the prophet was in Samaria; and Samaria was the capital city where the king of Israel lived. Apparently the king of Aram reasoned that King Joram would know it if a prophet in his city could heal leprosy.

7. As soon as the king of Israel read the letter, he tore his robes and said, "Am I God? Can I kill and bring back to life? Why does this fellow send someone to me to be cured of his leprosy? See how he is trying to pick a quarrel with me!"

Tearing one's own clothing was a way of expressing shock, dismay, or grief. *The king of Israel* felt all of these. An enemy king was demanding that he do something he could not possibly do. Then, because he could not fulfill those demands, Joram thought, the enemy king would respond by sending troops to punish him. This outlandish demand was simply a way of picking a fight; and Joram wanted no fight with the Arameans.

It should be noted that Joram's father (Ahab) had been defeated and killed when he had fought to recover some territory that Aram had taken from Israel (1 Kings 22:29-37). Now it seemed to Joram that Aram was looking for an excuse to start the war again, with the intention of seizing more of Israel's territory.

III. A PROPHET'S SOLUTION (2 KINGS 5:8-14)

Verse 7 probably records what Joram said to his advisers, while Naaman remained in a separate room and did not hear it. Perhaps Naaman was kept waiting for some time while the king and his counselors discussed how they could answer him. Meanwhile, word of the impossible demand leaked out, along with word of the king's fear. Swiftly the news spread throughout the city. There must have been a feeling of alarm everywhere, for no one wanted to resume the war with Aram. But Elisha was not alarmed. He knew that he could address Joram's concerns and grant the king of Aram's request.

A. THE PROPHET'S INVITATION (v. 8)

8. When Elisha the man of God heard that the king of Israel had torn his robes, he sent him this message: "Why have you torn your robes? Have the man come to me and he will know that there is a prophet in Israel."

WHAT DO YOU THINK?

How ironic that Naaman and the king of Aram seemed to have more faith in the God of Israel than Israel's own king! Why is it that we who know so well the Lord's mercies can sometimes forget them or fail to rely on his power? How can we maintain the childlike faith of the Israelite maid who initiated Naaman's journey of faith?

Why have you torn your robes? This was equivalent to asking, "What are you worried about?" All Joram had to do was to send his visitor to Elisha's house. There the visitor would learn that *there is a prophet in Israel.* Joram himself knew how Elisha had helped him during a battle with Moab (2 Kings 3:4-27), and was probably aware of several of Elisha's miracles (2 Kings 4). No doubt it was with great relief that the king sent Naaman to see the prophet.

B. THE PROPHET'S PROMISE (vv. 9, 10)
9. So Naaman went with his horses and chariots and stopped at the door of Elisha's house.

Can you imagine this demonstration of pomp and pride? Naaman's *chariots* were likely the finest in all Aram, except for the king's. He must have been accompanied by a formidable array of cavalry to protect the gold and silver that he carried. The entire entourage gathered at Elisha's door. The stage was set for a dramatic miracle. The general and his men were waiting with expectation.
10. Elisha sent a messenger to say to him, "Go, wash yourself seven times in the Jordan, and your flesh will be restored and you will be cleansed."

What a letdown! There was no dramatic miracle, no eloquent gesture, no loud cry to the Almighty, no striking ceremony whatsoever. The prophet himself did not even come out. He simply sent an unnamed *messenger* to tell his distinguished visitor to *go* and *wash* himself *seven times* in the *Jordan*, a little more than twenty miles away.

C. THE HERO'S FURY (vv. 11, 12)
11. But Naaman went away angry and said, "I thought that he would surely come out to me and stand and call on the name of the LORD his God, wave his hand over the spot and cure me of my leprosy.

Naaman went away angry. He had expected an impressive ceremony that would enhance his honor before his men and produce instant healing. His pride was deeply hurt.
12. Are not Abana and Pharpar, the rivers of Damascus, better than any of the waters of Israel? Couldn't I wash in them and be cleansed?" So he turned and went off in a rage.

Aram had *rivers* too—*better than any of the waters of Israel.* If bathing in a river would heal leprosy, what was the matter with those rivers? *In a rage* the general wheeled his chariot about and started back to *Damascus,* so angry that he scarcely remembered Elisha's promise, "You will be cleansed" (v. 10). In his anger, disappointment, and wounded pride, Naaman was returning home without the one thing he had come all those weary miles to get.

D. THE SERVANTS' SUGGESTION (v. 13)
13. Naaman's servants went to him and said, "My father, if the prophet had told you to do some great thing, would you not have done it? How much more, then, when he tells you, 'Wash and be cleansed'!"

For how many miles did Naaman and his men race down the road before his rage began to cool? We do not know. Perhaps, as reason began to return, he became ashamed of his childish tantrum. At some point, Naaman's *servants* ventured to approach him: *My father*—the term was respectful, but it also spoke of closeness and affection. *If the prophet had told you to do some great thing, would you not have done it?* Then why balk at a trivial request such as a sevenfold bath in the Jordan River? To Naaman's credit, he was able to recognize the common sense in his servants' advice; and he turned his chariot toward the Jordan.

He shall know that there is a prophet in Israel.

The visual for lesson 8 shows Naaman coming up from the water the seventh time, clean and whole. The caption reminds us of the prophet's promise in verse 8.

WHAT DO YOU THINK?
Naaman's pride got in the way of his accepting the prophet's solution. What are some ways pride hinders people from making the decision to accept Jesus Christ as Savior? How can we help them overcome this barrier?

THOUGHT TO REMEMBER
God's kingdom is forever, and so are you!

WHAT DO YOU THINK?

Naaman was healed only when he followed the Lord's instructions to the letter. Yet today many people seem to be looking for spiritual shortcuts rather than explicitly obeying God's instructions regarding salvation, holiness, worship, service, or any number of issues. What is the danger of such a practice? How can we emphasize the importance of strict obedience without becoming legalistic or minimizing the role of God's grace?

WHAT DO YOU THINK?

"God does not show favoritism but accepts men from every nation who fear him and do what is right" (Acts 10:34, 35). Naaman was from Aram, a political enemy of Israel. Still, God healed him. What does this suggest to you about the mission of the church and God's interest in people outside our own geographical or political borders? What programs does this suggest that we as a church ought to initiate or give renewed support to?

PRAYER

How wonderful are your works, our Father and our King! Thank you for the prophets, through whom we know about the marvels you have done and the marvels you will do. By your grace may we be good citizens of your kingdom, now and forever. In Jesus' name. Amen.

E. OBEDIENCE AND HEALING (v. 14)

14. So he went down and dipped himself in the Jordan seven times, as the man of God had told him, and his flesh was restored and became clean like that of a young boy.

Naaman's chariot stopped at the edge of the Jordan. The general waded into the "waters of Israel" that he had despised not long before (v. 12). He had been told to wash (v. 10), but apparently he did not take that to mean a thorough scrubbing. The record says that he *dipped himself* according to his instructions. Was he cleansed a little with each dipping so that after seven times he was clean, or did he come up diseased as ever for six times and then clean after the seventh? We are not told. All we know is that, after the seventh time, true to the prophet's word, *his flesh was restored and became clean like that of a young boy.*

We can be sure that a feeling of joy accompanied Naaman and his troops all the way back to Damascus. There they shared their joy with the king who had sent them on their journey. And surely joy filled the heart of one little Hebrew maiden.

CONCLUSION

What was the prophet thinking? Aram was the enemy. Aram had stolen some of Israel's territory, and had killed King Joram's father when he tried to reclaim it. Aram was a constant threat to Israel, and Naaman was the general of Aram's army. Wouldn't it be better to let him die from his illness than to show him the way back to health?

A. A GOOD ENEMY

Naaman commanded the army of Aram, Israel's enemy; but we see several indications that he was a man of fine character. In his military duties he appears to have been recognized as a genuine hero. In his home, he seems to have been so kind to a slave girl that she was genuinely concerned about his welfare. When disappointment and wounded pride caused him to reject Elisha's advice initially, he was willing to listen to the wise counsel of his servants and accept what Elisha said. After Naaman was healed, he went back to the prophet with deep gratitude, an offer of payment, and an earnest vow to worship Yahweh (2 Kings 5:15-19).

We know that no one on earth really deserves God's mercy, but this man, numbered among Israel's enemies, seems to have been more worthy than many men of Israel. Would he also be more worthy than some in the church today?

B. THE TEMPORARY AND THE PERMANENT

The nations of the world are temporary. God will pull down all of them. Only one kingdom will last forever. Hear Daniel the prophet: "In the time of those kings, the God of heaven will set up a kingdom that will never be destroyed, nor will it be left to another people. It will crush all those kingdoms and bring them to an end, but it will itself endure forever" (Daniel 2:44). To the apostle John, God gave this vision of the consummation of Daniel's prophecy: "The kingdom of the world has become the kingdom of our Lord and of his Christ, and he will reign for ever and ever" (Revelation 11:15). The greatest nation on earth will be pulled down, and so will the tiniest nation; but the kingdom of God and Christ will stand forever.

Should not every citizen of Christ's kingdom give attention to the King's commands? Should not his desires become ours? He said, "Go into all the world and preach the good news to all creation" (Mark 16:15). Should not every citizen of the world make haste to find his way into the kingdom of God? This is something permanent!

Discovery Learning

This page contains an alternate lesson plan emphasizing learning activities. Classes desiring such student involvement will find these suggestions helpful. The next page is a reproducible activity page to further enhance discovery learning.

LEARNING GOALS

Following this lesson your students should be able to:

1. Retell the story of Naaman's healing.

2. Explain why Naaman found it difficult to obey God's prophet and what was the result when he did.

3. List some situations in which people find it difficult to obey God today, and suggest some ways to encourage them to do so.

INTO THE LESSON

Write the following scrambled sentence on the chalkboard or on a sheet of newsprint:

know will there in that prophet is Israel he a

Have the students work in pairs or small groups to decipher the message. Award a token prize to the group who first comes up with, "He will know that there is a prophet in Israel."

Then ask your students, "What is a prophet?" Many will probably say a prophet predicts the future, but that was a minor role of the biblical prophet. Predicting the future served to validate the prophet's message. His first task was to speak for God to his generation.

Ask, "What, then, would be the value of knowing 'that there is a prophet in Israel'?" (Knowing there is a prophet presupposes there is a God for whom the prophet speaks.) In today's lesson we see one example of how God used the prophet Elisha to demonstrate his power.

INTO THE WORD

Make copies of the reproducible activity, "Order, Please," on the page that follows. Have the students work in small groups to arrange the statements in chronological order after you have a volunteer read the printed text, 2 Kings 5:1-14. (The statements are printed here in order for your convenience.)

1. Naaman becomes a leper.

2. A servant girl mentions there is a prophet in Samaria who can heal Naaman.

3. The king of Aram sends Naaman to the king of Israel to have him cured of leprosy.

4. The king of Israel thinks the Aramean king is trying to pick a fight with him, and he tears his clothing in grief.

5. Elisha sends a message to the king of Israel to have Naaman come to him, and "he will know that there is a prophet in Israel."

6. Through a servant Elisha orders Naaman to wash seven times in the Jordan River.

7. Naaman is angered, and he refuses to comply with the prophet's order.

8. Naaman goes to the Jordan and dips himself seven times.

9. Naaman is cured of leprosy.

Give the groups a few minutes to work; then ask someone which statement comes first. Work through the list so everyone has the correct order. Make comments as needed so everyone understands the significance of the events. For example, you'll want to point out Naaman's pride in initially refusing the prophet's order.

INTO LIFE

Naaman found it difficult to obey God because of pride. Probably all of your students have wrestled with that same problem. Ask, "What other factors sometimes make it difficult for us to obey God?" As the class suggests ideas, discuss how one might overcome the problem. Here are some possibilities to help you get started if the class is slow to respond:

Ignorance. Sometimes we just don't know what God has commanded. How can we help people know God's will so they can obey it?

Laziness. Sometimes God's commands require diligence and effort. Not everyone has the discipline to give that. How can we help people to develop self-discipline?

Lust. Any evil desire can be called lust, not just wrong sexual desires. Face it, sin can be fun, and many in our culture live to have fun. How can we help people see that there are some things—many things—more important than having fun?

Science. The prophet's command seemed contrary to natural law and did not make sense to Naaman, so he rejected it. But God doesn't always explain himself; he just asks for obedience. How can we learn to accept God's will even when it "doesn't make sense" to us?

For some people, salvation by grace doesn't make sense—they want to try to earn it. Close with a discussion of the importance of accepting God's grace by faith, including the importance of repentance and baptism. Design the discussion to help the students witness to others or to make their own confession of faith if they have not done so.

Order, Please

Read 2 Kings 5:1-14. Then close your Bible and arrange the following items in chronological order. To do this, write a 1 in the blank preceding the event that occurred first, 2 before the second, and so on. After you have completed the exercise, open your Bible and check your results for accuracy.

_____ The king of Aram sends Naaman to the king of Israel to have him cured of leprosy.

_____ Through a servant Elisha orders Naaman to wash seven times in the Jordan River.

_____ Naaman is cured of leprosy.

_____ A servant girl mentions there is a prophet in Samaria who can heal Naaman.

_____ Naaman becomes a leper.

_____ Elisha sends a message to the king of Israel to have Naaman come to him, and "he will know that there is a prophet in Israel."

_____ The king of Israel thinks the Aramean king is trying to pick a fight with him, and he tears his clothing in grief.

_____ Naaman is angered, and he refuses to comply with the prophet's order.

_____ Naaman goes to the Jordan and dips himself seven times.

Pride and Other Problems

Naaman found it difficult to obey God because of pride. What other factors sometimes make it difficult for us to obey God? List some on the chart below, cite an example of each one, and suggest how one might overcome the problem.

PROBLEM	EXAMPLE	SOLUTION

GOD GIVES HIS SPOKESMAN COURAGE

LESSON 9

WHY TEACH THIS LESSON?

"It's not my job."

"I could never lead someone to Christ. I don't know enough myself!"

"I did it last month. Let someone else take a turn."

With these and many other excuses we often excuse ourselves from participating in a ministry that needs attention in the church. If these sound familiar to your students, then they need to pay particular attention to today's lesson. Amos said he "was neither a prophet nor a prophet's son, but . . . a shepherd, and [a tender] of sycamore-fig trees." But then the Lord called him to prophesy to Israel. It was not his job, but the Lord had called. What else could he do but obey?

Perhaps the Lord does not call in as clear a voice as he called Amos, but he is calling each of us to ministry. This lesson will challenge your students to answer that call, even when it may lead them into a ministry where they never imagined they might serve.

INTRODUCTION

The north side of Hickory Hill was not for sledding. Everyone knew that. It looked good from the top, but the lower part of the slope was steeper; and it ended with a vertical drop of six feet into Stony Creek. The south side was not so steep, but it was safer.

Four boys brought their sleds to the hilltop after school. To their disappointment, the south slope was not in good condition for sledding. The sunshine had melted most of the snow, and what was left was too soft to bear a sled.

"Let's go that way," Bert challenged, pointing to the north. There was a short argument; but it ended when Bert sneered, "You're all chicken," and flung himself and his sled on the north slope.

"Who's chicken?" yelled Chuck, following only six feet behind. The other two launched themselves side by side, their elbows almost touching. It was wonderful, like riding on the wind!

Then they came to the steeper slope of the lower hill. Bert thrust his foot into the snow to stop his sled. Chuck crashed into him, followed by two more sleds and boys. The tangled mass plunged over the steep bank and broke through thin ice into freezing water.

A. ISRAEL'S SLIPPERY SLOPE

The history of the northern kingdom of Israel resembled the plunge of those boys into the icy water. Unable to resist the slippery slope of idolatrous pleasure, the nation plunged to disaster. King Ahab (encouraged by his wife Jezebel) led the nation on to the "steeper slope" by promoting the worship of Baal (1 Kings 16:29-33).

DEVOTIONAL READING
ACTS 4:13-22
LESSON SCRIPTURE
AMOS 6, 7
PRINTED TEXT
AMOS 6:1; 7:7-15

LESSON AIMS

After this lesson students should be able to:

1. Describe the call and courageous ministry of Amos.

2. Suggest some reasons a man like Amos was called instead of a "professional" prophet.

3. List some situations in which a "nonprofessional" minister might serve the Lord more fruitfully than a "professional."

Nov
1

KEY VERSE

Amos answered Amaziah, "I was neither a prophet nor a prophet's son, but I was a shepherd, and I also took care of sycamore-fig trees. But the Lord took me from tending the flock and said to me, 'Go, prophesy to my people Israel.'"

—Amos 7:14-15

For several years after Ahab's death, wicked Jezebel continued to promote the worship of Baal. God then commanded the prophet Elisha to anoint Jehu as king. Jehu was commissioned to destroy the house of Ahab (2 Kings 10:11). He proceeded to demonstrate his zeal for Yahweh by rounding up and killing the worshipers of Baal. The Lord then promised that four generations of Jehu's family would rule in Israel (v. 30).

Despite his zeal for the Lord's cause, Jehu did not put a stop to "the sins of Jeroboam"—the worship of the golden calves at Dan and Bethel (2 Kings 10:29). Other sins continued along with this idolatry, to the point that God used Aram (Syria) as his instrument to punish Israel (vv. 32, 33). However, the Lord was not yet ready to let Israel be destroyed (2 Kings 13:22, 23).

B. One More Chance

Nearly a century and a half after Jeroboam led Israel into idolatry through his counterfeit religious practices, another Jeroboam (generally referred to as Jeroboam II) came to the throne of Israel. He belonged to the fourth generation of Jehu's family. Like the kings before him, he continued in the sins of the first Jeroboam. Nevertheless, the Lord gave him victory over Aram, and he regained much of the territory that had been taken earlier from the north (2 Kings 14:23-27). Apparently the Lord was giving his people one more opportunity to respond to his goodness with faithful obedience. To reinforce his appeal, he sent the prophet Amos to denounce the sins of Israel and call for an end to them.

C. Lesson Background

Amos describes himself as one who was responsible for "tending the flock" at the time God called him to be a prophet (Amos 7:15). Amos 7:14 indicates that he also "took care of sycamore-fig trees." Clearly Amos was an ordinary man called to an extraordinary task!

Amos's home was in Tekoa (Amos 1:1), a town in the southern kingdom of Judah, about twelve miles south of Jerusalem. However, God sent him to minister in the northern kingdom of Israel. Amos spoke at Bethel (Amos 7:13), one of the sites where Jeroboam had set up one of his golden calves (1 Kings 12:28, 29).

As he began his message to Israel, Amos mentioned the pagan nations nearby. He named each one, spoke of its multiple transgressions, and foretold disaster to it (Amos 1:3—2:3). No doubt the people of Israel applauded all of that. He even pointed out the sins of Judah to the south (2:4, 5), which must have made the northerners feel rather smug.

But then Amos turned his attention to Israel (which probably brought the applause abruptly to an end!). He spoke openly of Israel's sins and its coming punishment: "'Therefore I will send you into exile beyond Damascus,' says the Lord" (Amos 5:27). Chapter 6 of Amos continues the prophet's denunciation of both Judah and Israel's sinfulness and complacency.

I. DISCOMFORT FOR THE COMFORTABLE (AMOS 6:1)

A. Woe to Judah (v. 1a)

1a. Woe to you who are complacent in Zion.

The word *woe* in the Old Testament often represents an expression of grief. The Hebrew word is pronounced with a wailing sound, similar to the cry of one who is grieving. Here it expresses the sorrows that would come to sinners who had closed their ears to the Lord's appeal through his prophets. Amos's words were directed to those who were *complacent*—unconcerned about their own sins or those of their countrymen. Complacent now, they would soon moan in grief.

What Do You Think?

Amos attempted to awaken his hearers from their ease and complacency. How important is it for someone to do that today? Why? Who should take on the job? How?

Originally *Zion* designated one of the hills on which Jerusalem stood. David captured this stronghold from the Jebusites (2 Samuel 5:6-9). Eventually the name Zion came to designate the entire city of Jerusalem (2 Kings 19:21; Psalm 48:2; Isaiah 1:8), as it does here.

B. WOE TO ISRAEL (v. 1b)

1b. And to you who feel secure on Mount Samaria.

Mount Samaria was a hill, some three hundred feet high, on which the city of Samaria was built. Samaria was the capital of the northern kingdom. Its elevation made it easy to defend against attack, and for that reason its leaders felt secure from any outside threat. Like those in Jerusalem, they were apathetic about the sins of their people, and oblivious to the punishment that loomed before them.

C. WOE TO THE LEADERS (v. 1c)

1c. You notable men of the foremost nation,
to whom the people of Israel come!

The first part of this appears to be directed specifically at the leaders of the nation. Thus the initial "woe" of this verse was targeted toward the leaders—both religious and political—*to whom the people of Israel* came for guidance and direction. These men should have been encouraging the nation to know and obey God's law, but they were leading the people away from it. For that reason, "woe" was coming both to the leaders and to the nation that they led. Chapter 6 goes on to describe the luxurious living of these self-satisfied men (vv. 3-6), and the disaster that was coming to them and to their cities (vv. 7, 8). Because they were first in rank and responsibility, they would be the first to be taken captive (v. 7).

II. THE PLUMB LINE (AMOS 7:7-9)

Chapter 7 begins with two visions describing the possible punishments that awaited sinful Israel. In the first vision, locusts "stripped the land clean" (v. 2). In the second, a great fire dried up the ocean and destroyed part of the land. In each case, Amos pleaded with the Lord not to punish Israel in such a brutal manner. The Lord relented and withdrew the threat. Then came a vision of a plumb line.

A. ISRAEL TESTED (vv. 7, 8)

7. This is what he showed me: The Lord was standing by a wall that had been built true to plumb, with a plumb line in his hand.

A *plumb line* is a string with a weight on the end, so it will hang straight down. Bricklayers use such a line to be sure that the wall they are building is perfectly vertical. In this vision, the Lord stood ready to test a wall that was already built.
8. And the LORD asked me, "What do you see, Amos?"

"A plumb line," I replied.

Then the Lord said, "Look, I am setting a plumb line among my people Israel; I will spare them no longer.

The wall to be tested was Israel. God's *plumb line* would show whether it was spiritually "straight" or not. If it was not, God would no longer *spare* the nation.

B. ISRAEL CONDEMNED (v. 9)

9. "The high places of Isaac will be destroyed
and the sanctuaries of Israel will be ruined;
with my sword I will rise against the house of Jeroboam."

Isaac was the father of Jacob; Jacob was given the new name of Israel; and *Israel* became the name of the nation descended from Jacob. In this poetic verse, both *Isaac* and *Israel* refer to the northern kingdom known as Israel. Tested by God's plumb line, that nation was not upright. A wall leaning to one side is likely to fall, and Israel's fall was drawing near.

High places and *sanctuaries* are places of worship. Israel's places of worship included Bethel and Dan (where Jeroboam's golden calves were) and other idolatrous sites as well. All those places of false worship were going to be *ruined*. They were out of line with God's law; they could not be permitted to stand.

The Lord had promised that Jehu's family would rule Israel for four generations (2 Kings 10:30). Jeroboam II was the fourth generation of that family. The Lord had blessed him and the nation with victory in battle and with prosperity (2 Kings 14:23-29), but they had not responded with obedience (v. 24). Now the rule of Jehu's family would end—and it would end violently. With the *sword* the Lord would *rise*, not against Jeroboam himself, but *against the house of Jeroboam*.

Second Kings records how this prophecy was fulfilled. Jeroboam's death ended the presence of stable government in the northern kingdom. Over the next thirty years there were six kings in the north, all of them evil in the Lord's sight. Four of them were killed by assassins who then seized the throne. The last four had to pay tribute to Assyria. The last one refused tribute and was taken captive. Samaria was then captured by the Assyrians, the people of Israel were deported to foreign lands, and the nation of Israel was no more. (The record of the reigns of these last six kings is found in 2 Kings 15:8-31; 17:1-6.)

III. THE PRIEST'S COMPLAINT (AMOS 7:10-13)

Having concluded our brief look at events after the time of Amos, we now go back to the time when Amos was preaching at Bethel. As might be expected, there was quite a protest when he denounced the sins of Israel and predicted its severe punishment.

A. AMAZIAH'S PROTEST (vv. 10, 11)

10. *Then Amaziah the priest of Bethel sent a message to Jeroboam king of Israel: "Amos is raising a conspiracy against you in the very heart of Israel. The land cannot bear all his words.*

This *Amaziah* was a *priest* who likely led in the worship of the golden calf at *Bethel*. Naturally he was not pleased to have a prophet from Judah proclaiming the destruction of the sanctuary in Israel and the demise of the king who had given Amaziah his job. Amaziah's first reaction was to complain to *Jeroboam king of Israel*. He claimed that Amos was spearheading a conspiracy against the king. Such preaching could not be tolerated.

11. *"For this is what Amos is saying:*
   "'Jeroboam will die by the sword,
   and Israel will surely go into exile,
   away from their native land.'"

It was true that Amos had predicted captivity for Israel (5:27; 6:7), but he had not said, *Jeroboam will die by the sword*. He had predicted violence only against Jeroboam's "house," or family (7:9). Probably Amaziah thought a bit of exaggeration would be more likely to stir the king to action, so he reported that the prophet had predicted a violent death for the king himself. How could any king let a preacher go on predicting his death?

B. AMAZIAH'S THREAT (vv. 12, 13)

12. *Then Amaziah said to Amos, "Get out, you seer! Go back to the land of Judah. Earn your bread there and do your prophesying there.*

WHAT DO YOU THINK?

Amaziah twisted Amos's words; he did not give a true report about Amos to the king. How should we respond when we or our church is misrepresented in the media or some other public forum?

(Consider Ephesians 4:15; 1 Peter 2:12; 3:16 in your discussion.)

If King Jeroboam issued any reply, it is not recorded. Perhaps he was wise enough to know that Amos was not a violent revolutionary. Perhaps he did send men to investigate Amaziah's claim. Perhaps Amaziah proceeded with his next threat without waiting for an answer. This was to advise Amos to *go back to the land of Judah*, from which he had come.

The term *seer*, while generally used respectfully of a prophet (1 Samuel 9:11; 2 Samuel 24:11), was used with contempt by Amaziah as he told Amos to *get out* of Israel. Perhaps he was alluding to the various visions that Amos claimed to "see." *Earn your bread there* suggested that he might be able to earn a living by preaching against Israel in Judah; but he could never expect people of Israel to pay him for denouncing their conduct and predicting their doom.

13. *"Don't prophesy anymore at Bethel, because this is the king's sanctuary and the temple of the kingdom."*

Here Amaziah's words took on the nature of a threat. The *temple* at *Bethel* was *the king's sanctuary*. Originally King Jeroboam I had it built; he put the calf there to be worshiped; he told the people to worship there; and he even burned incense on the altar (1 Kings 13:1). Who did this so-called prophet think he was—denouncing such a sacred place?

IGNORING BAD NEWS

Most of us prefer not to hear bad news. In fact, we practice hard at ignoring it. For example, scientists have been issuing warnings for years that the Pacific Northwest is ripe for an earthquake of epic proportions. About eleven hundred years ago, an area near Seattle rose twenty-three feet as a result of such a quake. In addition, there is evidence that Mount Rainier, just sixty miles from Seattle, could explode and send massive mud flows into the city. There is also the possibility of a *tsunami* (soo-*nah*-me)—a tidal wave—inundating Puget Sound as a result of an earthquake or volcanic explosion.

Traditionally—and very much in keeping with human nature—Washingtonians have given little heed to warnings of such disasters. They are no different from people elsewhere. Californians have long denied the possibility of being personally harmed by their frequent earthquakes. Midwesterners tend to "stay put," in spite of killer tornadoes, life-threatening blizzards, and devastating floods year after year.

So it is not surprising that the reaction of Israel to the divine judgment predicted by Amos was in words to this effect: "Go somewhere else with your prophecies of doom. If you can't say anything to make us feel good about ourselves, get lost!" The world still takes this approach to God's warnings about moral failure. Strange, isn't it? We haven't learned very much in the last 2,700 years!   —C. R. B.

IV. THE PROPHET'S ANSWER (AMOS 7:14, 15)

The priest of Bethel was a "professional." He was appointed by the king; he took his orders from the king; he was handsomely paid out of the offerings of worshipers. He could not understand a man like Amos, who was not concerned about his salary, the king's order, or his own safety. So Amos proceeded to explain how he had been called by Israel's real King.

A. NOT A PROFESSIONAL (v. 14)

14. *Amos answered Amaziah, "I was neither a prophet nor a prophet's son, but I was a shepherd, and I also took care of sycamore-fig trees.*

Before God called him, Amos was no *prophet*. Neither was he *a prophet's son*. This latter term may mean a "student" rather than a literal son. In Elisha's time there were groups of such students in several locations (2 Kings 2:3, 5, 7). Apparently such a group was like a boarding school. Sons of the prophets lived

WHAT DO YOU THINK?

Amaziah told Amos that he should go to his own land of Judah to do his prophesying. Today the pluralistic world seems to be telling the church to keep its preaching to itself—"Don't force your views on me." How should we respond to that?

(Consider Acts 4:20; 2 Corinthians 5:11, 20 in your discussion.)

The visual for today's lesson, showing Christians from many backgrounds teaching God's Word, challenges students to a ministry like Amos's.

What Do You Think?

Throughout history God has called people like Amos, out of common backgrounds, to be proclaimers of his truth. What is he calling you to do? How do you know? What will you do about it?

Thought to Remember

Do all that you do to the glory of God.

What Do You Think?

How can we objectively determine what our true capabilities are, and not what we wish they were? If you had a friend who was attempting to serve the Lord in a ministry for which he was not capable, would you tell him so? If so, how? If not, why not?

Prayer

Our Father, we are thrilled and thankful because you have supplied us and our brothers and sisters with numerous abilities and opportunities. By your grace may we find the places of service for which you have designed us, and may each one fill his place as you would have it filled. Amen.

together (2 Kings 6:1-7) and ate their meals together (2 Kings 4:38-44). Amos was not such a student. He was not trained to be a prophet; he did not choose to be a prophet; and he was certainly not one of the "professionals" who always gave the king the answer he wanted to hear (1 Kings 22:13). His life's work had been entirely different; he had been *a shepherd,* and he *also took care of sycamore-fig trees.*

B. Appointed by the Lord (v. 15)

15. "But the Lord took me from tending the flock and said to me, 'Go, prophesy to my people Israel.'"

This was how the shepherd/fig gatherer became a prophet. He had received his orders directly from *the Lord* himself. This was why he was unconcerned about his pay or his safety, or about offending the king. He was obeying the King of kings, and trusting him for whatever help or protection he needed.

CONCLUSION

There were numerous "sons of the prophets," whom God could have called to carry out his task; but he bypassed all of them and sent a shepherd to give his warning in Bethel, site of the king's idolatrous temple. There were hundreds of shepherds in Israel, yet the Lord sent one from Judah to travel northward and confront his people with their sins.

God knows the hearts of his people, and he knows their abilities as well. But God's call is not so obvious to us as it was to Amos, and it often seems that inspiration must be replaced by diligent study. How can a farmer know if he ought to be a preacher, and how can a preacher know if he ought to be a farmer?

"There's a place for every worker in the vineyard of the Lord." So begins an old song, but it ends with this plea: "Help me, Lord, from this time onward, find and occupy my place." Without such an unmistakable call as Amos received, how can I be sure what God wants me to do? Some simple questions may help.

1. What can I do? This is not as easy a question as it seems. Some of us have inflated opinions of our abilities. We handicap ourselves by being conceited and arrogant. Some of us are too modest. We handicap ourselves by underestimating our abilities. Paul advises each one of us not to think of himself more highly than he ought to think. On the other hand, one should not think of himself *less* highly than he ought to think. Each one needs to see himself clearly and objectively: he needs to think "with sober judgment, in accordance with the measure of faith God has given" (Romans 12:3).

2. What do I like to do? A happy worker is a better worker. I am not likely to be a great success in any work I dislike. On the other hand, work may be both pleasant and profitable to me, and still be unworthy of my time and effort. So, "What do I like?" is not the only question I must consider.

3. How can I best help other people? Most honest workers are helpful: the doctor, the lawyer, the farmer, the mail carrier, the grocery seller, and many others.

4. How can I best glorify God? Some glorify God by preaching the gospel. Others glorify him with honest and capable management in both the secular workplace and the church. Paul wrote, "Whatever you do, do it all for the glory of God" (1 Corinthians 10:31). Jesus said, "Let your light shine before men, that they may see your good deeds and praise your Father in heaven" (Matthew 5:16).

Discovery Learning

This page contains an alternate lesson plan emphasizing learning activities. Classes desiring such student involvement will find these suggestions helpful. The next page is a reproducible activity page to further enhance discovery learning.

LEARNING GOALS

After this lesson your students will be able to:

1. Describe the call and courageous ministry of Amos.

2. Suggest some reasons why Amos was called instead of a "professional" prophet.

3. List some situations in which a "nonprofessional" minister might serve the Lord more fruitfully than a "professional."

INTO THE LESSON

Before class, write COURAGE on the chalkboard or a sheet of newsprint. Then introduce the lesson by asking, "What was the most courageous thing you ever did?"

From this discussion develop a list of some of the things that require courage. Likely most items on your list will involve courage in the face of physical danger. Encourage the students to think also about issues of moral courage—like the determination to do what is right but unpopular or to speak the truth when no one wants to hear the truth.

In today's lesson we look at a man who had the courage to speak the truth even though that truth was unpopular. His courage came, not from an inner reservoir of human strength or will power, but from God.

INTO THE WORD

Direct your students to Amos 7:7-15 and ask them to look for evidences of who Amos was and what he did for a living.

- Amos was not a professional prophet. In other words, he was what many people today call "a layman" or a "volunteer" (v. 14).
- Amos was a "shepherd" (v. 14). He was called as he was "tending the flock" (v. 15).
- Amos was a tender of fruit (v. 14), which may mean either that he owned the fruit orchard or tended it for another.

Observe that Amos was a resident of Tekoa in the southern kingdom, but he went to Bethel to deliver his prophetic message. (Show Tekoa and Bethel on a map.) Ask the students what they know of Bethel. Some should remember that Jeroboam put one of his idols there (lesson 7).

The preaching of Amos at Bethel inspired anger on the part of Israel's religious establishment (vv. 12, 13). Ask the students how they would feel if a member of a church in a neighboring county came to your church to criticize and condemn the way your students are living.

Ask the students to suggest reasons Amos needed courage to perform his role. (This could be done in small groups or by the class as a whole.) Some ideas include the following:

- Amos was an "outsider." He left his own home in Tekoa of Judah to prophesy against Israel at Bethel.
- Amos declared an unpopular truth in the face of powerful opposition (v. 10).
- Amos was not a professional prophet (v. 14). Some might question his authority for his ministry.

Call attention to Amos's use of the image of a plumb line (vv. 1-8). Bring a plumb line to class to show those who may not be familiar with this device.

Ask, "What is the purpose of a plumb line?" (To show if a wall is "true"—is being built straight without leaning.) "What if the wall is not 'plumb'?" (It will be in danger of falling; the builder will tear it down to build a straight one.)

Then discuss: "What function might a plumb line serve in evaluating our spiritual lives?"

OPTION

Use the reproducible page that follows to explore and apply the plumb line metaphor.

INTO LIFE

Since Amos was a layman instead of a professional prophet, your students can identify with him and his mission. Ask your students to think about some situations in which a volunteer might be more effective than a professional minister:

- Being an influence for Christ on the job.
- Being a witness in the neighborhood.
- Being salt and light for friends and family.

As "nonprofessionals," your students have a unique opportunity to be witnesses for Christ on the job, in the community, and in the home. In closing, challenge each student to complete this open-ended sentence:

"During the coming week, I will have the courage to be a witness for Christ to. . . ."

Close with a prayer of commitment, asking God to help your students to be bold and courageous witnesses during the coming week.

God's Plumb Line

Read Amos 7:7-9 and answer the following questions.

What was God measuring with his plumb line?

What were the results of his measurements?

What would happen as a result of these measurements?

Now consider your own church and worship practices. If God brought his plumb line to church this morning, what features do you think he would find to be out of plumb?

What would you suggest to bring these features back to plumb?

What about your own life—not just when you are involved in worship or other church activities—but your daily routine. If the Lord dropped in on you at work or at home and had his plumb line with him, what features do you think he would find to be out of plumb?

The Lord said, "Look, I am setting a plumb line among my people Israel; I will spare them no longer."

What do you need to do this week to bring these things back in line with God's will?

GOD WORKS THROUGH SONG WRITERS

LESSON 10

WHY TEACH THIS LESSON?

Some people have a hard time with Scripture passages about the jealousy of God. "How can God, who is perfect, be jealous?" they wonder. Apparently, human jealousy is so common and so selfish that it's hard to imagine a different sort, a holy jealousy, that is compatible with the holy nature of God.

Indeed, human jealousy is all too common. Which of us has not been guilty of it from time to time, even if it is not a continual habit? Surely your students also fight the temptation to be jealous from time to time. Thus, they will appreciate this lesson. Asaph, the song writer, is candid about his own jealousy, so we can certainly identify with him. He also gives us some helpful insights on how to stop being jealous. More than identify with him, we can emulate him!

INTRODUCTION

"I was so tired of being poor!" That was Bob's excuse. He and Betty had agreed that she should leave her job to become a housewife and mother, but getting along on one salary was harder than they had expected. It was doubly galling because Jerry, Bob's college chum, was making money "hand over fist." His salary was no more than Bob's, but he seemed to have a golden touch with investments.

One day Jerry volunteered to let Bob in on a "sweet deal." It would make forty percent in a year, Jerry said, but he needed a few thousand dollars more to swing it. So Bob borrowed the money, using the equity in his home as security. He gave the money to Jerry, signed the papers Jerry put before him, and waited for his investment to turn a profit.

Unfortunately, the "sweet deal" turned out to be illegal. Because Bob's signature was on the papers, Bob is spending a year in prison. Betty is a single parent, and poorer than ever.

A. ASAPH'S STRUGGLE

Asaph could have sympathized with Bob. He felt frustrated because of his own meager circumstances when compared with those who were making money "hand over fist." Furthermore, those making the money were clearly people of ungodly character. Asaph was on the verge of a spiritual tragedy (rather than a financial one), but by the grace of God he found an answer. He wrote a song about his experience, and from that song we take today's text.

Asaph's song is one of a hundred and fifty collected over the centuries of Old Testament history into the book we call the book of Psalms. One of them is called "A prayer of Moses the man of God" (Psalm 90), so it would have been written approximately four hundred years before the time of Asaph. Others, such as Psalm 85, seem to have been written after Israel was released from captivity in Babylon, close to five hundred years after Asaph.

DEVOTIONAL READING
PSALM 27

LESSON SCRIPTURE
PSALM 73

PRINTED TEXT
PSALM 73:1-3, 12, 13, 16-18, 21-26

LESSON AIMS
After this lesson students should be able to:

1. Explain Asaph's envy and how he overcame it.

2. List several reasons believers sometimes envy unbelievers.

3. Suggest some ways Christians can encourage one another to keep an eternal, unenvious perspective.

Nov
8

KEY VERSE
As for me, it is good to be near God. I have made the Sovereign LORD my refuge; I will tell of all your deeds. —Psalm 73:28

B. LESSON BACKGROUND

Thus far in our survey of the Old Testament, we have had nine lessons in chronological order, though sometimes with wide gaps of time between lessons.

1. Adam and Eve bring sin into the world.
2. God's people escape from Egypt.
3. God's people receive his law.
4. God's people enter the promised land.
5. God's people are helped by judges.
6. Israel becomes a monarchy.
7. Israel is divided into two countries.
8. An Aramean general is healed in Israel.
9. Amos the prophet boldly confronts Israel with its sins.

Today's lesson does not follow Lesson 9 in chronological order. We go back to the time between when the events in Lessons 6 and 7 took place. David was king of Israel. Asaph was the chief of his musicians, whose duty was to help with the worship of the Lord in Jerusalem (1 Chronicles 16:4, 5; 2 Chronicles 5:12). Asaph is credited with writing twelve psalms (50, 73-83), although some of these reflect the time when Jerusalem was destroyed (74, 79, 83). These may have been composed by a member of "the descendants of Asaph," who comprised a group of singers during the period after the exile (Nehemiah 7:44).

I. A SHAKEN FAITH (PSALM 73:1-3, 12, 13)

Psalm 73 is a very personal psalm. Asaph writes from his own experience: his feelings and thoughts, his errors in judgment, and the firm conclusion that he eventually reached. His song is designed to help us reach the same firm conclusion when confronted with a similar spiritual crisis.

A. BASIC BELIEF (v. 1)

1. Surely God is good to Israel,
   to those who are pure in heart.

Asaph begins with a statement of faith. The rest of this song tells how he wavered in his belief, yet received an assurance that renewed his trust in God. At this point, however, the first line states his conviction that *God is good* to his people.

The second part of this verse repeats the first part, but with some modification. God is good *to those who are pure in heart*. This principle holds true for both Israel and the church: one will meet God's wrath instead of his goodness if one's heart is contaminated by evil motives, selfish desires, and malicious thoughts.

B. NEAR DISASTER (vv. 2, 3)

2. But as for me, my feet had almost slipped;
   I had nearly lost my foothold.

In some of the earlier lessons in this series, we noted the slippery slope by which the people of Israel sank to the depths of idolatry and sin. Asaph himself had been on a similar slope, on the verge of losing his spiritual *foothold*.

3. For I envied the arrogant
   when I saw the prosperity of the wicked.

Asaph is reflecting on a time when he *envied the arrogant*. At the time when he was struggling with his faith, the arrogant did not seem so foolish. Their lifestyle appeared quite desirable, for it was a lifestyle of *prosperity*. *Wicked* people were getting rich, and Asaph was jealous. One who feels such jealousy is tempted to link wealth with wickedness, and to join in wickedness for the sake of getting rich. Verses 4-11 elaborate on the pride, prosperity, and corruption of foolish,

WHAT DO YOU THINK?

"Surely God is good to Israel," Asaph said, and Christians also like to give God credit for the good things in their lives. However, the wicked are also "blessed" at times, but they do not give God credit. How would you answer a skeptic who said his—and your—blessings have nothing to do with God but are a result of hard work and personal effort?

WHAT DO YOU THINK?

Asaph was troubled by the economic prosperity the wicked in his day were enjoying. We also might envy the wicked for the same reason. How can we keep from envying such people?

wicked people who were doing remarkably well financially while appearing to thumb their noses at God.

ENVY

"I'm just a valet, but I play God for a second and take charge of their cars," was the smug claim of a valet parking attendant at a Los Angeles restaurant. He then explained how he treats people who do not meet his standards. Local celebrities who have expensive cars and are good tippers will be called by name. Their cars will be parked near the entrance to the restaurant. At the very least, if their cars are parked farther away, they will be given preferential treatment over "lesser" people.

But too bad for you if you own an older or inexpensive car. And if the valet remembers you as a poor tipper, you may wait "forever" for him to bring your car to you. And then he just may leave a big, smudgy handprint on your window as he slams your door shut on you.

This may not be a problem to those of us who live in the suburbs or small towns, but in big cities where parking is at a premium, parking valets may well seem like gods. Then we may *really* be tempted to envy people who are more "blessed" with fame and wealth and convenience than we. However, while we are envying them, we should not forget how they obtained their wealth or status. We must remember that there are greater blessings than a fancy car, a convenient parking place, or any of a myriad of other things that our culture tempts us to view as "essentials." —C. R. B.

C. SUMMARY (vv. 12, 13)

12. This is what the wicked are like—
always carefree, they increase in wealth.

Here Asaph describes what all of us have observed: *wicked* people—people who care nothing about what God says or thinks—*increase in wealth.*

13. Surely in vain have I kept my heart pure;
in vain have I washed my hands in innocence.

While the wicked were getting rich, Asaph was trying diligently to keep his *heart pure* and his *hands* clean: he was thinking right and doing right. But what did he get for his efforts? Nothing but trouble and pain: "All day long I have been plagued; I have been punished every morning" (v. 14). All his righteous living was *in vain*—useless and unprofitable. It wasn't fair!

II. A SURE FAITH (PSALM 73:16-18, 21, 22)

The wealthy wicked were not thinking straight. They believed that evil was good for them because it paid off financially. In his envy, Asaph had begun to entertain this same twisted outlook. His thinking needed to be straightened out!

A. PLACE OF STRAIGHT THINKING (vv. 16, 17)

16. When I tried to understand all this,
it was oppressive to me.

The wicked seemed to be blessed in spite of their wickedness; Asaph and other honest men were struggling in spite of their righteousness. The more Asaph thought about this injustice and *tried to understand* it, the more he felt oppressed, burdened, weighed down, and pained by what he saw.

17. . . . till I entered the sanctuary of God;
then I understood their final destiny.

A *sanctuary* is a holy place—a place set apart, or dedicated, to some sacred use or purpose. Before Solomon built the magnificent temple in Jerusalem, two humbler places might have been called *the sanctuary of God*. One was the ancient tabernacle at Gibeon (1 Chronicles 21:29); the other was the tent in Jerusalem

HOW TO SAY IT
  Asaph. AY-saff.
  Gibeon. GIB-ee-un

WHAT DO YOU THINK?

The psalmist was almost to the point of giving up. He felt it had been "in vain" that he had "kept [his] heart pure." Suppose a friend said, "I'm dropping out of church. It's just no use. I can't live the Christian life, and it hasn't done me any good to try. I still have a huge credit card bill, I can't afford the mortgage, and my husband's job just got cut out with downsizing."

How would you answer her?

WHAT DO YOU THINK?

Asaph gained victory over his temptation to envy the wicked when he "entered the sanctuary of God." True worship should help us to focus on God instead of

ourselves or others. This will help to realign our thinking. The writer of Hebrews tells us we need to be looking to Jesus (Hebrews 12:2). True worship helps us do that.

What features of our worship service help us to deal with envy and other temptations? What would you suggest that we add to provide more help in this area?

WHAT DO YOU THINK?

Asaph came to his senses when he looked beyond the immediate situation and saw the results of the wicked's behavior. There is nothing to envy in that! We, too, need to look more to the goal of our faith, to the eternal, and not get stuck in the temporal. Paul said whatever troubles we endure in this life "are not worth comparing with the glory" we will receive (Romans 8:18). What can the believer do to keep the eternal more in focus than the temporal, to remember the eternal glory we will one day share even when temporal wealth seems hard to come by?

where David had placed the ark of the covenant (1 Chronicles 16:1). Asaph was chief of the musicians who served "before the ark . . . regularly" (1 Chronicles 16:37). There he probably heard the teaching of the law, with its clear promise of blessing for obedience and cursing for disobedience (Deuteronomy 28). In the light of God's Word it was evident that any advantage gained by the wicked was only temporary. Asaph confessed, *then I understood their final destiny*.

B. PERSPECTIVE OF STRAIGHT THINKING (vv. 18, 21, 22)

18. Surely you place them on slippery ground;
    you cast them down to ruin.

Asaph himself had been close to *slippery ground*—close to the point at which men coast swiftly to *ruin*. He now realizes that the wealthy wicked whom he had envied were already there. Their final destiny would not change unless they changed their perspective as Asaph was now doing.

21, 22. When my heart was grieved
    and my spirit embittered,
I was senseless and ignorant;
    I was a brute beast before you.

Asaph realized that the time he had spent grieving what he did not have and feeling bitter toward those who had more was time wasted. It was not reasonable for him to envy those who were coming to ruin. The Hebrew word for *senseless* here describes the irrational behavior of a beast. This is consistent with the phrase *a brute beast* in the latter part of the verse. The term *ignorant* literally says, "I did not know." Asaph's envy of the wicked had arisen from ignorance and lack of clear thinking.

III. SECURITY WITH GOD (PSALM 73:23-26)

We can have the same assurance as Asaph that our senseless blunders need not condemn us forever. God is merciful and gracious. He would rather forgive than destroy. He is willing to be with us if we are willing to be with him. But he will not be with us in the pursuit of any selfish, greedy, or wicked way. Only by choosing to walk in godly ways can we be assured of his company.

A. COMPANIONSHIP (v. 23)

23. Yet I am always with you;
    you hold me by my right hand.

Yet, said Asaph—even though I was "senseless and ignorant" (v. 22)—*I am always with you*. God's care for me is not one degree less than what it was before I embarked on my path of erroneous thinking. The second part of the verse adds another precious thought. Though I have learned to think straight, it is not by my wisdom that I am able to escape the destruction facing the wicked. Though I am willing to exert all my strength to stay close to God, it is not by my strength alone that I am able to prevail: *you hold me by my right hand*.

B. GUIDANCE AND GLORY (v. 24)

24. You guide me with your counsel,
    and afterward you will take me into glory.

The privilege of being with God includes the privilege of being guided by him: by his *counsel*, which includes the wisdom of his Word. That leading is available to all of us if we make the effort both to know and to do what his Word teaches. *And afterward*, when I have followed God's leading faithfully, God *will take me into glory*. Even in this world there is a glory that comes to one who walks with

God over many years; but for the faithful follower of the Lord, there is more to come *afterward*. If this truth encouraged Asaph, how much more should it encourage us who live in the light of the empty tomb of Jesus?

C. THE ONE AND ONLY (v. 25)

25. Whom have I in heaven but you?
  And earth has nothing I desire besides you.

Heaven may have its angels—ten thousand times ten thousand, and more; but God is all I need. On *earth* I have family and friends and teachers and companions whose company I treasure; but all of them fade in comparison with God, whom I love with all my heart and with all my soul and with all my strength (Deuteronomy 6:5). I'll walk with him whether anyone else does or not.

D. SOURCE OF STRENGTH (v. 26)

26. My flesh and my heart may fail,
  but God is the strength of my heart
  and my portion forever.

My muscles, my mind, my motives, and my will are not enough to keep me walking faithfully with God in his way. My power fails, but his *strength* prevails. If my will is in accord with his will, and my mind agrees with his mind, and my motives are his motives, and my strength works with his strength, then with Asaph I can say, *God is . . . my portion forever.*

"AMAZING GRACE"

"Amazing Grace," by the eighteenth-century Englishman John Newton, perhaps more than any other Christian hymn has found a place even in the world of secular music. There is an amazing story behind this well-loved song.

During that tragic period of history when African warriors sold their captives to Western profiteers, many people with Christian backgrounds rationalized their participation in this "business." Newton was one such man. Though he had grown up in a Christian home, the young Newton left his faith behind when he went to sea.

He became captain of a slave ship and for years plied his gruesome trade, apparently without any influence from the faith he had once known. But the power of the gospel eventually overcame Newton, and he saw his trafficking in slaves for the awful sin that it was. Although he had amassed an ill-gained wealth that many would envy, through his conversion he came to realize that the grace of God and the gift of Heaven constituted a treasure worth far more:

  The Lord has promised good to me,
    His word my hope secures;
  He will my shield and portion be
    As long as life endures.

Newton's words echo those of Psalm 73:25, 26: "Earth has nothing I desire besides you. . . . God is the strength of my heart and my portion forever." —C. R. B.

CONCLUSION

Asaph was an extremely blessed man. As chief musician he was often in the Lord's sanctuary. He became acquainted with God's law; he led the sacred songs that praised it and reinforced its teaching.

As Christians, we are far more blessed than Asaph. Not only do we learn of the law and the Psalms in the sanctuary; we have them in our homes for daily study. We also have the books of the prophets who wrote after Asaph's time. Better still, we have the teaching of Christ and his apostles in the New Testament to add clarity and reinforcement to the lessons Asaph learned.

WHAT DO YOU THINK?

Asaph finally came to realize that, if he had God, he had enough (verse 25). Asaph's prayer is beneficial in causing us to take a fresh look at our priorities. We should be able to make that prayer our own. If not, then we are guilty of a form of idolatry, putting things or other persons ahead of God in our affections.

How can we help one another come to, and live with, the realization that a relationship with God through Jesus Christ is worth more than anything this world and its wealth have to offer?

It is good for me to draw near to God: I have put my trust in the Lord God.
Psalm 73:28

The visual for lesson 10 illustrates today's Key Verse, which provides a good point on which to close today's lesson.

PRAYER

Almighty and everlasting Father, how richly you have blessed us with your counsel! The call of riches is loud, and the call of pleasure is insistent; but above them all your Word calls us day by day to the road that leads us afterward to glory. May your power keep us on that road, we pray, and may your grace forgive us when we foolishly turn aside. Amen.

THOUGHT TO REMEMBER

Learn to view every circumstance from God's perspective.

DAILY BIBLE READINGS

Monday, Nov. 2—My Feet Had Almost Slipped (Psalm 73: 1-14)

Tuesday, Nov. 3—I Entered the Sanctuary of God (Psalm 73: 15-20)

Wednesday, Nov. 4—I Was Senseless and Ignorant (Psalm 73:21-28)

Thursday, Nov. 5— Reassurance Is Found in Worship (Psalm 27:1-14)

Friday, Nov. 6—The Fate of the Wicked (Psalm 37:1-13)

Saturday, Nov. 7—Integrity Is Affirmed (Psalm 26:1-12)

Sunday, Nov. 8—The Lord Is Our Protector (Psalm 121:1-8)

A. WATCH YOUR WANTING

"You shall not covet . . . anything that belongs to your neighbor" (Exodus 20:17). So said the law. Asaph violated that law when he envied the rich, even though they were wicked. Then in the sanctuary, he was reminded that he was envying people who were doomed to destruction. That was absurd.

It would be doubly absurd for us to fall into Asaph's error, especially when we have what Asaph never did—the teachings of Jesus and his apostles. Jesus said, "Watch out! Be on your guard against all kinds of greed; a man's life does not consist in the abundance of his possessions" (Luke 12:15). Paul wrote, "People who want to get rich fall into temptation and a trap and into many foolish and harmful desires that plunge men into ruin and destruction" (1 Timothy 6:9). We need to learn not to "hope in wealth, which is so uncertain, but to put [our] hope in God, who richly provides us with everything for our enjoyment" (v. 17).

What do you want most: to be rich, or to be with the Lord?

B. AFTERWARD

I know that my Redeemer liveth,
And on the earth again shall stand.

This joyous, triumphant hymn of Christian assurance is based on a similar statement of faith by Job (Job 19:25-27, *King James Version*). Asaph may have been acquainted with the book of Job. As a musician, he probably knew the song of David that joyfully ends, "I will dwell in the house of the Lord forever" (Psalm 23:6). From such sources, as well as from the direct inspiration of the Holy Spirit, Asaph seems to have expected not only God's guidance as long as he lived on earth, but also a glory that he would attain "afterward." Confidently he sang to the Lord, "You guide me with your counsel, and afterward you will take me into glory."

The New Testament casts a flood of light on what earlier saints could view only dimly. It tells us, "Christ Jesus . . . has destroyed death and has brought life and immortality to light through the gospel" (2 Timothy 1:10). "The gift of God is eternal life in Christ Jesus our Lord" (Romans 6:23).

Is that fair? It is much better than fair. It is *grace*. The gift of eternal life is available because God loved the world (John 3:16). Even when we were sinners he loved us—loved us so dearly that he gave his Son to die for us (Romans 5:8).

Yet even this matchless love is not irresistible. We can choose. We can accept the gift of eternal life, or we can receive the death that we have earned. Grievous sinners shall not inherit the kingdom of God (1 Corinthians 6:9, 10), but neither shall nice people who do not believe the good news of God's love (Mark 16:15, 16). Even church members who prefer to live like sinners can expect "judgment and . . . raging fire" (Hebrews 10:26, 27).

Asaph nearly slipped, lured by the prospect of riches; and today we see many attracted by that same temptation. Others are seduced by pleasures incompatible with godliness. Then there are multitudes who just do not care. Sin has no overpowering attraction for them, but they make no effort to live for God. They are just coasting—but they are coasting downhill.

Asaph found straight thinking in the sanctuary. Here is a good example for all who are running away from God, or being lured away, or just drifting away. Go to church, and take Christian teaching to heart. Have a little sanctuary at home, where the family searches the Scriptures together. Let your thinking be shaped by God's Word, and let your living follow your thinking. Then God will guide you by his counsel, and afterward receive you into glory.

Discovery Learning

This page contains an alternate lesson plan emphasizing learning activities. Classes desiring such student involvement will find these suggestions helpful. The next page is a reproducible activity page to further enhance discovery learning.

LEARNING GOALS

After this lesson, your students will be able to:

1. Explain Asaph's envy and how he overcame it.

2. List several reasons why believers sometimes envy unbelievers.

3. Suggest some ways Christians can encourage one another to keep an eternal, unenvious perspective.

INTO THE LESSON

Begin by asking your students to name their favorite Psalms. Several will likely say Psalm 23. Others may say Psalm 1. Ask if some would like to quote their favorite Psalms.

Psalms is a book of poetry. The writers—including David and Asaph—expressed their deepest feelings and thoughts in the poems that make up the book of Psalms. Point out that many of the hymns and gospel songs we sing as a part of worship are Psalms set to music.

INTO THE WORD

Psalm 73 begins by stating a basic belief that Asaph had arrived at as the result of a significant crisis in his life (v. 1). The rest of the psalm shows how he arrived at this basic belief.

Begin this part of the lesson by writing GOD IS GOOD on the chalkboard. Then ask students to answer the question, "How has God been good to you in the past week?"

Asaph began to describe the crisis in his life in verse 2. Suggest that most of the significant insights in our lives develop out of crises. Maybe some of your students can tell about a time when a crisis gave them a new spiritual insight or a clearer view of God and his goodness.

Get at the heart of the lesson by writing the following open-ended sentence on newsprint (or by referring the students to page 46 in the quarterly *NIV® Bible Student* book) and asking the students to suggest completions:

> *"When I see a wicked person who is successful and prosperous, I feel . . ."*

Urge students to be honest, and to express how they really feel. Their responses probably will fall into two categories:

• "It isn't fair!" This questions the goodness and fairness of God. But did God ever promise that life would be fair?

• "If the wicked prosper, what's the use of trying to be righteous and trying to do the right thing?" (see v. 13). This questions the value of right living—as if success and prosperity in this life were the only reasons for right living.

Does anyone feel sorry for them? The apparent prosperity of the wicked is often what keeps such people from seeing their need for a Savior. We should pity them rather than envy them.

Asaph was not thinking clearly. He was looking at life from the wrong perspective. Direct your students to Psalm 73:16-18. What did Asaph say he did to correct his faulty perspective? (He went to the sanctuary, probably the tent where the ark of God was kept. For us, this could mean a place of worship or any place where we can talk with God and meditate on his will.)

Asaph felt he had a legitimate gripe, and he took his complaint to God. Ask:

• What do you do when you feel God is being unfair?

• How do you express your complaints to God?

• How does God respond to your complaints?

INTO LIFE

Since we are human, and are surrounded by wicked people who prosper and good people who flounder, we are susceptible to the faulty thinking that afflicted Asaph. However, we have some advantages that the psalmist did not have. Ask your students to suggest what some of these advantages are. For example:

1. We have the completed Scriptures, which show the ultimate end of both the wicked and the righteous.

2. We have Jesus, who loved us and died for us.

3. We have the indwelling of the Holy Spirit.

4. We have two thousand years of Christian tradition.

5. We have the support and encouragement of fellow Christians, many of whom have already struggled with this issue.

Tell your students we need to make two responses to today's lesson: we need to remind each other of our blessings in Christ so we will not envy those who have earthly riches only, and we need to feel compassion for wicked and prosperous sinners. Distribute copies of the next page and allow a little time for the students to complete them. Challenge the students to do one thing during the coming week to encourage a fellow believer or reach out to a successful sinner. Close with prayer.

"If I Were Rich . . ."

Since we are human, and are surrounded by wicked people who prosper and good people who flounder, we are susceptible to the faulty thinking that afflicted Asaph. Read the following list and note which of the statements expresses a thought you have had at some time during your Christian experience.

____ 1. Bob makes so much more money than I do, and with half the education! I wonder what he's up to.

____ 2. I don't understand it. I've been faithful to the Lord for years, and it still seems like we just live hand-to-mouth. When are we going to have a little security?

____ 3. I could have a new car, too, if I didn't tithe!

____ 4. When I gave the contractor the check for the deductible, he said, "Keep it"; he would just bill the insurance company for $250 more than he charged so they would pay the whole thing. I told him no, but I wonder if I should have. I guess I'm just too honest!

____ 5. Hey, check out this book! It tells all the accounting tricks to hide income from our investments so we don't have to pay as much in taxes. It says these are the same tricks all the rich and famous use—that's why they're so wealthy and we're not!

"Earth Has Nothing I Desire Besides You"

Today's lesson suggests two types of responses to such statements as those listed above. First, we need to encourage each other and remind each other of our blessings in Christ. Then we will not envy those who have earthly riches only. Second, we need to feel compassion for wicked and prosperous sinners. Suggest a response to each of the statements above that would fall into one of these two categories. A suggested response is given for the first one to get you started.

1. Bob does seem to be quite successful, but I wonder whether he and Susan know the Lord. Let's invite them over for dinner and see if we can't find an opportunity to share our faith with them.

2.

3.

4.

5.

Think of someone you know who is financially successful but not a believer, or one who is a believer but struggling financially. What can you do this week to encourage this person?

FALSE HOPES AND JUDGMENT

LESSON 11

WHY TEACH THIS LESSON?

In forty days it will be Christmas. No doubt the Christmas decorations are already going up, and perhaps "Santa Claus" has even made an early appearance here or there. Christian parents are divided about what to tell the kids about Santa Claus. Some feel it's harmless fun to tell the legends of the old man who rides in a magic sleigh delivering toys to good little girls and boys on Christmas Eve. Others feel strongly that Santa Claus has no place in the Christian celebration of Christmas, and that telling children any story that is not true is wrong.

Whatever we do about Santa, surely we will also teach our children from infancy the true meaning of Christmas. Pity the child, though, who grows up in a home where Christ is not known, where Santa Claus offers his or her only hope for Christmas. Imagine the poor child, hoping Santa will even the score by bringing him as nice a present as the rich kid next door gets. Imagine the child of divorced parents who wants nothing from Santa except to get her parents back together. These are false hopes, doomed to disappointment.

Adults can have false hopes, too. They are not likely based on Santa Claus, but they are based on wrong perceptions of God, or on unreliable people, or merely on wishful thinking. Use this lesson to challenge your students to be sure their hope is the "living hope" the Bible tells us we can have in Christ Jesus. With anything less, we might as well believe in Santa Claus!

INTRODUCTION

More than a hundred years ago, according to an oft-repeated story, a missionary doctor took a microscope to his outpost in central Africa. He wanted to examine the water supply of a tribe that was plagued by sickness and early death.

As the doctor expected, he found the water contaminated with deadly bacteria. In that isolated place he could think of but one remedy. The natives would have to learn to boil their drinking water. To begin a campaign of education, the doctor asked the head chief to come and look through the microscope.

The chief was horrified when he saw the fearsome creatures wriggling in the water, but he had a ready solution. He picked up a heavy stone and smashed the microscope.

A. SMASHING MICROSCOPES AND DESTROYING VIRUSES

Two weeks ago we read how Amos exposed the deadly virus of idol worship in Bethel. Instead of working to destroy the virus, Amaziah, the priest of Bethel, tried to persuade Amos to take his message of doom back to Judah (Amos 7:7-13).

Last week we turned back to a time approximately two centuries before Amos. Asaph was infected with the viruses of greed and envy. When he "entered the sanctuary of God" (Psalm 73:17), he saw those deadly monsters exposed by the

DEVOTIONAL READING
JOSHUA 24:14-28

LESSON SCRIPTURE
JEREMIAH 19; 21:1-10

PRINTED TEXT
JEREMIAH 19:1-4, 10, 11; 21:1, 2, 8-10

LESSON AIMS

After this lesson students should be able to:

1. Summarize the warnings Jeremiah gave to Jerusalem in today's text.

2. List some of the false hopes that cause people to ignore God's warnings today.

3. Give thanks to God for Jesus, who gives us living hope in place of judgment.

Nov 15

KEY VERSE

This is what the LORD says: See, I am setting before you the way of life and the way of death.
—Jeremiah 21:8

HOW TO SAY IT

Ahaz. AY-haz.
Amaziah. Am-uh-ZYE-uh.
Ammonites. AM-uh-nites.
Asaph. AY-saff.
Assyria. Uh-SEAR-ee-uh.
Assyrians. Uh-SEAR-ee-unz.
Babylon. BAB-uh-lun.
Babylonians. Bab-uh-LOW-
nee-unz.
Gehenna. Geh-HEN-uh.
Hinnom. HIN-um.
Jehoiachin. Jeh-HOY-uh-kin.
Jehoiakim. Jeh-HOY-uh-kim.
Jeremiah. Jair-uh-MY-uh.
Josiah. Jo-SYE-uh.
Maaseiah. May-uh-SEE-yuh.
Manasseh. Muh-NASS-uh.
Malkijah. Mal-KYE-juh.
Molech. MO-lek.
Nebuchadnezzar. NEB-uh-kad-
NEZZ-er.
Pashhur. PASH-er.
Topheth. TOE-feth.
Zedekiah. Zed-uh-KYE-uh.
Zephaniah. Zef-uh-NYE-uh.

On the visual for lesson 13 (on the left side) is a map you may find useful for this lesson.

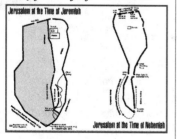

microscope of God's truth. Instead of smashing the microscope, he destroyed the viruses and gained renewed confidence in the Lord's promises.

This week we move forward to a time more than a century after Amos. Jeremiah was now exposing the viruses of idolatry and sin in Judah, as Amos had done in Israel. Instead of taking action against the viruses, people of Judah wanted to take action against Jeremiah (Jeremiah 26:8-11). But Jeremiah remained undaunted; he continued to expose the sins that were destroying Judah. Though the people did not silence him, neither did they heed him. In time, the nation fell to Babylon.

An epidemic is never stopped by smashing a microscope, and a nation is never preserved by ignoring the truth.

B. LESSON BACKGROUND

The book of Jeremiah is a collection of the messages that Jeremiah delivered during the approximately forty years of his ministry. In addition, the book includes important historical material. Many of Jeremiah's prophecies are not dated, including the one with which today's printed text begins. (The second portion, from chapter 21, names Zedekiah as king, so we are able to establish the time of that writing with more precision. Zedekiah was Judah's last king, so the events of chapter 21 come near the end of the nation, not long before the Babylonian captivity began.) Some students believe that the first section belongs to the time when King Josiah was leading Judah in obedience to God's law (2 Chronicles 34:29-33). Others link it to the time of Jehoiakim's reign, when Judah's subjection to Babylon had begun (see Daniel 1:1, 2). Jeremiah 19:3-5 seems to describe a time when the kings of Judah needed to be warned about their evil actions. Jehoiakim certainly merited such a warning (2 Kings 23:36, 37).

I. WARNING (JEREMIAH 19:1-4, 10, 11)

A. THE AUDIENCE (v. 1)

1. This is what the LORD says: "Go and buy a clay jar from a potter. Take along some of the elders of the people and of the priests.

This is what the Lord says. This lets us know that our text begins with instructions given by the Lord to Jeremiah. The *clay jar from a potter* was to serve as a visual aid for Jeremiah's message, much as another clay pot did earlier (18:1-10).

Jeremiah was told to gather an audience consisting of Judah's most respected leaders—*the elders of the people and of the priests.* Perhaps these men would be more apt to listen to what the prophet had to say.

B. THE PLACE (v. 2)

2. And go out to the Valley of Ben Hinnom, near the entrance of the Potsherd Gate. There proclaim the words I tell you.

The Valley of Ben Hinnom is sometimes called the valley of Hinnom (Joshua 15:8; 18:16; Nehemiah 11:30). It lay outside the south wall of Jerusalem. This is where the "city dump" was located. The Hebrew term for "valley of Hinnom" became, in Greek, "Gehenna," which is the New Testament word translated "Hell."

The Potsherd Gate was a gate leading to the dump. It could easily get such a name because the ground around it would be littered with fragments of broken clay pots discarded there.

C. THE MESSAGE (v. 3)

3. And say, 'Hear the word of the LORD, O kings of Judah and people of Jerusalem. This is what the LORD Almighty, the God of Israel, says: Listen! I am going to

bring a disaster on this place that will make the ears of everyone who hears of it tingle.

The phrase *kings of Judah* probably refers to the entire royal family. Only one of them was actually king, but the Lord wanted all of them (including those who would one day be king) to know about the message. Jeremiah's words applied to the powerful and mighty as well as to the common *people of Jerusalem*.

I am going to bring a disaster on this place. This was the heart of Jeremiah's message. So disastrous would Judah's punishment be that anyone hearing about it would find his *ears* tingling with the shock of the news. Similar language is found in 1 Samuel 3:11 and 2 Kings 21:12.

D. THE REASON (v. 4)

4. For they have forsaken me and made this a place of foreign gods; they have burned sacrifices in it to gods that neither they nor their fathers nor the kings of Judah ever knew, and they have filled this place with the blood of the innocent.

They have forsaken me summarizes the basic sin committed by the people of Judah. We should recall God's words concerning Israel when the elders requested that Samuel give them a king: "They have rejected me" (1 Samuel 8:7). This is what Jeremiah's countrymen had done. The rest of this verse lists some of the evils that had accompanied forsaking God.

First, the people had *made this a place of foreign gods.* Jerusalem was the place God had chosen, in order to put his name there (1 Kings 11:36). In a special sense, it was the city of God. But the people of Jerusalem had made the city a stranger to him. He did not want his name associated with such a sinful place.

Second, they had *burned sacrifices in it to* other *gods.* When Solomon dedicated the temple, he offered an abundance of sacrifices to the true God—the God of Israel (1 Kings 8:63). Now the temple was being used in the worship of false gods—gods unknown to the people, *their fathers*, and their *kings*.

Third, they had *filled this place with the blood of the innocent.* Taking *this place* to mean the Valley of Hinnom, some students think this refers to the burning of innocent children in sacrifice to Molech, the bloodthirsty god of the Ammonites. This sometimes took place in the Valley of Hinnom (Jeremiah 32:35). Among those who participated in this were King Ahaz and King Manasseh (2 Kings 16:2, 3; 21:1, 6).

However, in the verse before us it seems better to take *this place* to mean Jerusalem, where the acts by which innocent blood was shed were many. King Manasseh is said to have "shed so much innocent blood that he filled Jerusalem from end to end" (2 Kings 21:16).

Verses 5-9 continue the description of the sins of Jerusalem and the punishment that was imminent.

TAKING RISKS

So you think you're safe in your own home? Think again! While at home, during a typical year:

• 1 of every 400 Americans will be injured in bed by the headboard falling on them or the bed frame collapsing.

• 1 in 13 of us will suffer an injury requiring medical attention.

• 1 in 350,000 of us will be electrocuted.

Things get worse, or at least more tragic, when we step outside our front door:

• 1 in 40,000 of us will die as pedestrians in urban traffic accidents.

• 1 in 11,000 of us will die *inside* an automobile—about the same as the number of civil service or government workers who die in job-related accidents!

WHAT DO YOU THINK?

Jeremiah stood in a public place and declared "the word of the Lord" to the people of Judah. Once in a while you will still see a preacher standing in a public square preaching to the people who pass by. Most people do just that: they pass by without listening. How can we deliver "the word of the Lord" to our own generation, to the people of our community?

DAILY BIBLE READINGS

Monday, Nov. 9—I Went Down to the Potter's House (Jeremiah 18:1-11)

Tuesday, Nov. 10—I Will Bring Disaster on This Place (Jeremiah 19:1-9)

Wednesday, Nov. 11—I Will Smash This Nation and This City (Jeremiah 19:10-15)

Thursday, Nov. 12—Jeremiah Is Placed in the Stocks (Jeremiah 20:1-6)

Friday, Nov. 13—Jeremiah's Complaint (Jeremiah 20:7-18)

Saturday, Nov. 14—I Myself Will Fight Against You (Jeremiah 21:1-10)

Sunday, Nov. 15—They Have Forsaken the Covenant of the Lord God (Jeremiah 22:1-9)

The visual for lesson 11 illustrates Jeremiah's dramatic demonstration of the destruction coming on Jerusalem.

WHAT DO YOU THINK?

Jeremiah used the shattering of a clay jar as a means of symbolizing Jerusalem's approaching destruction. What are some symbols that could be used to visualize the corruption in our society and the dangers to which we have exposed ourselves?

These dangers and a multitude of others are discussed in *The Book of Risks* (1994), written by a University of Hawaii professor named Larry Laudan. Read it only if you're feeling especially brave! It is apparent that many risks must be accepted as the natural consequences of living in our complex, modern society.

But some risks we don't have to take: the punishment of ancient Judah reminds us that godlessness will bring certain retribution from the Lord. God's judgment came on those people because of their wicked behavior. If we are wise, we will learn from them and take the necessary steps to avoid such risks.   —C. R. B.

E. THE ILLUSTRATION (vv. 10, 11)

10, 11. "Then break the jar while those who go with you are watching, and say to them, 'This is what the LORD Almighty says: I will smash this nation and this city just as this potter's jar is smashed and cannot be repaired. They will bury the dead in Topheth until there is no more room.'"

As the climax to his brief message, Jeremiah was to *break the jar*, probably by hurling it to the ground so that it would shatter into pieces and be lost among the other fragments of pottery that lay near the Potsherd Gate. The jar would be beyond repair—a fitting description of how Jerusalem and its people would be crushed because of their disobedience.

Topheth was a place in the Valley of Hinnom where children were burned in sacrifice, most likely to the false god Molech (Jeremiah 7:31). It was to become the burial place of those sinners who would die during the siege and destruction of Jerusalem, and it would be filled to overflowing with their corpses.

GETTING OUR ATTENTION

"His employee's driving his car. So how come he's not worried?" The "he" in this case is a relaxed and smiling executive pictured in a magazine advertisement for a product called *DriveRight*. This "responsible driving monitor" is a computerized device that allows the boss to set the limits of speed and acceleration he will allow while employees drive his car.

When an employee/driver exceeds those limits, an alarm sounds a warning, indicating to the employee that the boss will have a record of the infraction. The boss will know how many times the limits have been violated as well as whether the errant employee has tried to tamper with the device. Presumably, the employee would receive appropriate discipline for violating the boss's driving standards.

Jeremiah's act of breaking the potter's vessel was God's way of getting Judah's attention and letting the people know that he was aware that they had violated his standards. God knew their long history of disregard for his will, both as individuals and as a nation.

Of course, God also knows when *our* behavior violates his standards. Jeremiah's words and actions are a warning to us as well: God is still serious about sin and its consequences.   —C. R. B.

II. ANOTHER WARNING (JEREMIAH 21:1, 2, 8-10)

For the next part of our printed text, we leap forward in time, perhaps about fifteen years. During these years, some important changes in Judah took place.

First, King Jehoiakim stopped paying tribute to Babylon. The consequences of such an act were predictable: Nebuchadnezzar returned to Judah with his army. During this time, Jehoiakim died and was replaced on the throne by Jehoiachin. After a reign of only three months, Jehoiachin surrendered to Nebuchadnezzar. He was taken to Babylon, along with the leading men of his government and the craftsmen and smiths (who were capable of making weapons). In all, ten

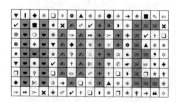

Solution to puzzle on p. 104
♥=h; ✍=o; ✈=p; ✉=e.

thousand captives were transported to Babylon. Zedekiah was left to be king in Jerusalem and to pay tribute to Babylon. The record of these events is found in 2 Kings 24.

Second, after ruling approximately eight years, Zedekiah stopped paying tribute. Nebuchadnezzar's troops returned and laid siege to Jerusalem for approximately a year and a half (2 Kings 25:1-3). With food supplies running dangerously low and despair running high, King Zedekiah sent a question to Jeremiah, with which the next part of our printed text begins.

A. THE KING'S QUESTION (vv. 1, 2)

1. The word came to Jeremiah from the LORD when King Zedekiah sent to him Pashhur son of Malkijah and the priest Zephaniah son of Maaseiah. They said:

Before relating *the word that came to Jeremiah from the Lord*, we are given the explanation of what called for it. Jerusalem was surrounded by overwhelming numbers of Babylonian troops, and *King Zedekiah* sent two of his advisers to the prophet Jeremiah with the question that follows.

2. "Inquire now of the LORD for us because Nebuchadnezzar king of Babylon is attacking us. Perhaps the LORD will perform wonders for us as in times past so that he will withdraw from us."

King Zedekiah understood that Jeremiah was a prophet *of the Lord*, so he asked Jeremiah to take his question to the Lord for an answer. Throughout Israel's history, the Lord had done many *wonders* on behalf of his people. At this point, Zedekiah may have been thinking especially of the Assyrian invasion a little more than a century earlier. The Assyrians had brought a massive army to capture Jerusalem, but the Lord had inflicted huge losses on them (2 Kings 19:35, 36). Would the Lord now perform yet another miracle and do away with the Babylonians? This was likely what the king wanted to know.

In verses 3-7 Zedekiah's question was answered in the plainest of terms. This time the Lord was going to fight against Jerusalem and Judah. He would not rescue them; he would turn them over to the Babylonians. The next verses of our printed text record the Lord's counsel to the people under siege in Jerusalem.

B. THE LORD'S ADVICE (vv. 8, 9)

8. "Furthermore, tell the people, 'This is what the LORD says: See, I am setting before you the way of life and the way of death.

Verses 3-7 were addressed to King Zedekiah (v. 3), but now we read a message to *the people*—those who were under siege in Jerusalem. The Lord was giving them a choice between *the way of life and the way of death*, much as Moses did centuries earlier (Deuteronomy 30:15).

9. "'Whoever stays in this city will die by the sword, famine or plague. But whoever goes out and surrenders to the Babylonians who are besieging you will live; he will escape with his life.

Jerusalem was going to be captured. That was certain (v. 10). Perhaps, however, this message was given soon after the Babylonian army arrived. The siege was going to last more than a year. The way of death (v. 8) was to stay in the doomed city. The food supply would be exhausted, and many people would die *by the famine*. In addition there would be a *plague*, an epidemic of disease. That would bring death to many. And when at last the invaders would breach the walls and force their way into the starving city, *by the sword* they would slaughter without mercy all who would seem inclined to resist them.

There was, however, another possibility: the people did not have to stay in the city and die there. The way of life (v. 8) was to go out and surrender *to the*

WHAT DO YOU THINK?

The common reaction to Jeremiah's message was to ignore it or to belittle it. Now Zedekiah wants Jeremiah to make inquiry of the Lord for him! Had the king noticed over time that Jeremiah's prophecies were unfailingly accurate—was he, even if reluctantly, coming to faith? Or was he simply hoping to get Jeremiah to say what he wanted to hear? Why do you think he called for Jeremiah? Why do you suppose he would be willing to believe Jeremiah now when he had not before? What lessons do you see in this event for us today?

WHAT DO YOU THINK?

In Jeremiah's time Judah was taking comfort in God's past acts of deliverance. He had rescued them before; surely he would rescue them again. Many people today trust in technology and education to solve the ills of society. Many have abandoned the God of the Bible. They have the false hope that God—if there is a God, they can never be quite sure—will surely save them if they are relatively good people. Their hope is vain.

How can we help people exchange the false hopes they cling to for hope in Jesus Christ?

WHAT DO YOU THINK?

Through Jeremiah the Lord told the people, "I am setting before you the way of life and the way of death." What significance, if any, do you see in this statement? How might it apply to our time and place?

Babylonians. One who chose to surrender would be taken to Babylon as a captive, but he would not die of starvation or be killed by the sword. He would be a part of the prey taken by the enemy, but he would *escape with his life*. The enemy might seize his goods and possessions as part of the spoils, but he himself would be kept alive.

As one might expect, such a message was not well received by the people of Jerusalem. Most of them considered Jeremiah's message "unpatriotic" and branded him a traitor (Jeremiah 26:8-11). He became the target of bitter opposition (37:11-15; 38:1-6). In the end, however, his message proved true, as God's words always do.

C. EXPLANATION (v. 10)

10. "'I have determined to do this city harm and not good, declares the LORD. It will be given into the hands of the king of Babylon, and he will destroy it with fire.'"

No longer was there any hope for Jerusalem, for the Lord himself had *determined to do this city harm*. The time of reckoning had come. *The king of Babylon* was going to conquer the city and *destroy it with fire*. The King of Heaven and earth had decreed it. If Zedekiah was hoping for a more positive word from God's prophet, he was sadly disappointed.

CONCLUSION

As we look back over the ten previous lessons and think of the long stretches of history between the lessons, two wonders stand out. They are God's patience and God's punishment.

A. GOD'S PATIENCE

God called the nation of Israel to keep his law and enjoy his blessing. He led that nation out of bondage in Egypt, but it was so rebellious that he thought of destroying it even before it reached the promised land (Exodus 32:9, 10). Yet his patience waited, and waited, and waited. We have seen in today's lesson how Judah finally reached a point when God's judgment could not be withheld. This was approximately eight hundred years after the deliverance of the people from Egypt.

Centuries later, God sent his Son to establish a new covenant with peoples throughout the world. Jesus laid the foundation for an eternal kingdom. Then he went back to Heaven, promising to come again. Even before that century was done, however, scoffers began to doubt his promise. Peter explained that Jesus is waiting patiently because God is "not wanting anyone to perish, but everyone to come to repentance" (2 Peter 3:9). Now nineteen centuries have passed, and he is still waiting—waiting for people to repent and be saved. What wonderful patience!

PRAYER

Merciful Father, we are saddened by the doom that befell Jerusalem, and saddened yet more by the thought of everlasting fire. Give us courage, we pray, and keep us faithful until we stand in your presence. Amen.

B. GOD'S PUNISHMENT

God's punishment has always been as certain as his patience. He waited eight hundred years for his chosen people to become what he desired them to be; but then he sent the Babylonians to destroy his temple and carry thousands into captivity in a distant land.

Today we live under the New Covenant established by Jesus. Sometimes we hear people say, "God is love. God is merciful and gracious. He would never condemn anyone to Hell." But Jesus said that one day he will say, "Depart from me, you who are cursed, into the eternal fire prepared for the devil and his angels" (Matthew 25:41). Whom will you believe?

THOUGHT TO REMEMBER

"I take no pleasure in the death of anyone, declares the Sovereign Lord. Repent and live!" (Ezekiel 18:32).

Discovery Learning

This page contains an alternate lesson plan emphasizing learning activities. Classes desiring such student involvement will find these suggestions helpful. The next page is a reproducible activity page to further enhance discovery learning.

LEARNING GOALS

Following this lesson your students should be able to:

1. Summarize the warnings Jeremiah gave to Jerusalem in today's text.

2. List some of the false hopes that cause people to ignore God's warnings today.

3. Give thanks to God for Jesus, who gives us living hope in place of judgment.

INTO THE LESSON

Introduce the idea of false hopes and ignored warnings by posing the following situations and asking your students to suggest some false hopes that would cause people to persist in harmful and self-destructive behaviors in each situation:

• A doctor warns a smoker that his cigarettes are killing him, but he doesn't want to give up smoking. *(False hope: "Other smokers may get cancer, but not me.")*

• A neighbor with whom you have been sharing the gospel refuses to respond to its message, saying "I'm just as good as So-and-so [a member of your church]. If he's going to Heaven, then I am, too." *(False hope: "I can get to Heaven on the basis of my good works and without Jesus Christ.")*

The people of Judah greeted Jeremiah's prophecies of divine judgment with the false hope that God would never destroy his own special people. In today's lesson we'll look at Jeremiah's prophetic messages and see how they apply to the false hopes held by people today.

INTO THE WORD

Provide some background information on the prophet Jeremiah. Using Jeremiah 1:1-3, do a brief lecture on who Jeremiah was and when he prophesied. Use a chronological chart (like the visual for lesson 2) to help you show when Jeremiah was prophesying and who the contemporary kings were. Note Jeremiah 1:13-19 and summarize his message and the general response God told Jeremiah to expect. Use Jeremiah 18:18 to illustrate how people responded to Jeremiah's message.

Now divide your class into groups to take a closer look at Jeremiah's message. Assign each group to find answers to one of the study questions below by studying Jeremiah 19:1-11; 21:1-10. (A similar activity appears on page 52 of the student quarterly, *NIV® Bible Student.*)

1. To whom was Jeremiah's message addressed? (See 19:1, 3, 11.)

2. What was the content of Jeremiah's message? (See 19:3, 6-9, 11.)

3. What precipitated Jeremiah's message? What had the people done to call forth the message? (See 19:4, 5.)

Point out verses 1, 2 of Jeremiah 21. Ask, "What false hope is implied in the king's question?" (That God would deliver his people and not allow the Babylonians to take Jerusalem.) Ask whether anyone knows why the king would believe such a thing. (Refer the class to 2 Kings 19:14-19, 35-37 for the answer.)

The people of Judah believed that God would not send judgment on his own special people and his own special city. Ask your students to suggest some false hopes that cause people to ignore God's warnings today. For example:

• "God loves us too much to punish us."

• "Those stories about God's judgment in the Old Testament are myths. God doesn't work that way."

• "Other people are a lot worse than we are."

In contrast to attractive and appealing false hopes, God offers true and genuine hope through Jesus Christ.

INTO LIFE

True and living hope—the hope that comes from God—is what makes life worth living. Hope in place of judgment is something to be thankful for. Ask a volunteer to read 1 Peter 1:3-5. (Or distribute the reproducible activity "Where Is Our Hope?" from the next page.) Note that our hope, individually and personally, is in Jesus Christ. While the people of Judah hoped in their nation as God's chosen possession, we who are in Christ have a personal hope in him.

In closing, hand each student a copy of the reproducible activity "Lord, We Thank You" from the next page and challenge each one to list on it five hopeful things that he or she would like to thank God for. Of course, we all can thank God for Jesus Christ. What else can they list?

When your students have compiled their lists, urge them to take the lists home and display them in a prominent place—perhaps fastened to the refrigerator with magnets. Every day they need to be reminded that God wants to give them hope rather than judgment. But if they reject the message of hope, judgment is sure.

Where Is Our Hope?

Something is missing from the following verse. To determine what it is, color the boxes on the grid below that contain symbols that match the symbols in the coded verse. Then replace the symbols with the appropriate letters and rewrite the verse.

"✈rais⊠ b⊠ t⊠ t♥⊠ G⊿d and Fat♥⊠r ⊿f ⊿ur L⊿rd J⊠sus C♥rist! In ♥is gr⊠at m⊠rcy ♥⊠ ♥as giv⊠n us n⊠w birt♥ int⊿ a living ♥⊿✈⊠ t♥r⊿ ug♥ t♥⊠ r⊠surr⊠cti⊿n ⊿f J⊠sus C♥rist fr⊿m t♥⊠ d⊠ad" (1 Peter 1:3).

Rewrite the verse below:

Lord, We Thank You

We all can thank God for Jesus Christ. Without Jesus, none of us would have any hope. List another five hopeful things that you would like to thank God for. Keep this list and post it where you will see it each morning. Start each day thanking God for the hope we have in Christ and for these items as well.

1.

2.

3.

4.

5.

HOPE FROM GOD'S PROMISE

WHY TEACH THIS LESSON?

The family had gathered around the bed of their loved one. He was dying, but they could not accept or admit that fact. They had pleaded with doctors and nurses to "do something," but there was nothing that could be done. They sat by the bed and wept. All hope was gone.

Elsewhere another family had gathered around the bed of a loved one. She, too, was dying, and they all knew it. They prayed and sang some hymns, and they spoke lovingly into her ear, not even knowing whether she could hear them. They told her they loved her and they were going to miss her, but they knew it was time for her to go home—and they were happy for her!

What made the difference for the second family is hope—the subject of our lesson today. All of your students have faced or will face the loss of loved ones. Use this lesson to equip them with "living hope" to handle those situations.

INTRODUCTION

Mourning was great in the village, for a popular citizen was dead. Throughout his days of illness, hope had gleamed brightly; but now hope was gone as well. Day after day the bereaved home was thronged with friends bringing comfort, but the shadow of grief remained.

Several days after the funeral, the family's best friend came to town and was led to the tomb. For a few moments, he stood weeping as others had. Then suddenly, in an authoritative voice, he called, "Lazarus, come out!"

Come out? Lazarus was not only dead; he was also so tightly bound in his grave clothes that he could not move even if he were alive. But that command could not be ignored. Lazarus did indeed "come out." Willing hands quickly loosened the grave clothes, and grief was dethroned by gladness.

Thus was demonstrated the truth so often illustrated in Scripture and in our own experience: "With God all things are possible" (Matthew 19:26).

A. DEATH OF HOPE

Centuries earlier there was great mourning in another location—the colony of Hebrew captives in the land of Babylon. Perhaps, in the early stages of captivity, the people of Judah still clung to some hope of liberation. But in 586 B.C. most of the people of Judah were dragged into captivity as well. Jerusalem and the temple were destroyed. Hope appeared dead, for there no longer was a home to which to return. The captives could only sit in Babylon and weep (Psalm 137:1-6).

B. LESSON BACKGROUND

We need to remember that the Hebrews' captivity in Babylon came in three phases.

DEVOTIONAL READING
REVELATION 21:1-7
LESSON SCRIPTURE
EZEKIEL 37
PRINTED TEXT
EZEKIEL 37:1-11a, 25-27

LESSON AIMS

After this lesson students should be able to:

1. Retell the story of the dry bones.

2. Compare the condition of the Jewish exiles with that of the church today.

3. Suggest a way to apply one of God's promises of hope to the church.

Nov
22

KEY VERSE

My dwelling place will be with them; I will be their God, and they will be my people.
—Ezekiel 37:27

LESSON 12 NOTES

HOW TO SAY IT

Abednego. Uh-BED-nee-go.
Ezekiel. Ee-ZEEK-yul or
   Ee-ZEEK-ee-ul.
Jehoiachin. Jeh-HOY-uh-kin.
Meshach. ME-shack.
Nebuchadnezzar. NEB-uh-kad-
   NEZZ-er.
ruah (Hebrew). RUE-ah.
Shadrach. SHAD-rack.
Zedekiah. Zed-uh-KYE-uh.

DAILY BIBLE READINGS

Monday, Nov. 16—The
Spirit Came Into Me (Ezekiel
3:22-27)

Tuesday, Nov. 17—The
Spirit Lifted Me Up (Ezekiel 8:1-
13)

Wednesday, Nov. 18—Can
These Bones Live? (Ezekiel 37:1-
14)

Thursday, Nov. 19—I Will
Make Them One Nation (Ezekiel
37:15-23)

Friday, Nov. 20—My
Servant David Shall Be Their
King (Ezekiel 37:24-28)

Saturday, Nov. 21—In
Visions of God (Ezekiel 40:1-4)

Sunday, Nov. 22—The Glory
of the Lord Filled the Temple
(Ezekiel 43:1-9)

Phase 1. When Babylonian troops first came to Judah in 605 B.C., they took only a few captives. Among them were Daniel and his three famous friends—Shadrach, Meshach, and Abednego (Daniel 1:1-7). Judah continued its national life as before, but had to pay tribute to Babylon.

Phase 2. After some years, Judah rashly rebelled against Babylon and refused to pay tribute. In 597 B.C., King Nebuchadnezzar and the army of Babylon returned. This time they took ten thousand captives, including the statesmen and politicians, the military leaders, and the craftsmen and smiths who made spears and swords. (It seemed unlikely that there would be another rebellion without either leaders or weapons.) The king of Babylon also took away the king of Judah (Jehoiachin), but he left another man of the royal family (Zedekiah) to rule the nation and to pay the tribute (2 Kings 24:1-17).

Phase 3. For approximately eight years King Zedekiah obediently paid the tribute, but in the ninth year he too rebelled. Again the Babylonians returned, and in 586 B.C. they destroyed Jerusalem. They took most of the survivors to Babylon, leaving only a few of the poor people to cultivate the land (2 Kings 25:8-12).

The prophet Ezekiel served as God's spokesman among the captives. He had gone to Babylon with the ten thousand who were taken during the second phase of the captivity, when King Jehoiachin was taken (Ezekiel 1:1-3). While others had hoped for an early release, Ezekiel foretold the end of Jerusalem. But now that Jerusalem had been destroyed and the nation was in the throes of utter despair, Ezekiel became the voice of hope to God's people.

Visions were a prominent part of the ministry of Ezekiel. Each is introduced by the phrase, "the hand of the Lord was upon me." These visions occur in four sections of the book. A vision of the glory of God begins the book (1:1—3:15), detailing Ezekiel's call to prophesy. Next is a vision of the abominations that were taking place in the temple (chapters 8-11). Perhaps the most famous vision is the one that is recorded in today's printed text from Ezekiel 37. The book closes with a detailed vision of a future temple (chapters 40-48).

I. PROPHECY OF LIFE (EZEKIEL 37:1-6)

A. PLACE OF DEATH (vv. 1, 2)

1. The hand of the LORD was upon me, and he brought me out by the Spirit of the LORD and set me in the middle of a valley; it was full of bones.

To be directed *by the Spirit of the Lord* is to be in a condition to receive his revelation, whether it is given in words, in a vision, or through tangible objects and visible events. *The hand of the Lord* represents his power in action. Ezekiel did not walk out to the valley; as he saw this happening, the Lord carried him there and put him down *in the middle of a valley,* which *was full of bones.*

2. He led me back and forth among them, and I saw a great many bones on the floor of the valley, bones that were very dry.

Having placed Ezekiel on the ground, the Lord *led* him to walk *back and forth among the bones* for a good look at them. Two facts were apparent: there were *a great many* of them, and they *were very dry.* Verse 9 describes them as "slain." It was as if there had been a terrible battle in the valley, killing countless thousands of men and leaving their bodies unburied. Wild animals and vultures had torn away the clothing and stripped the flesh from the bones. Perhaps the bones had lain in the valley for many years, dried and bleached by the wind and the sun.

B. QUESTION OF LIFE (v. 3)

3. He asked me, "Son of man, can these bones live?"
   I said, "O Sovereign LORD, you alone know."

You or I might have answered, "Certainly not! These bones have been dead for years. There's no possibility of life in them." But this *son of man* was a prophet. He knew that all things are possible with God. Wisely he waited for the Lord to reveal what the dried bones could do.

C. COMMAND TO PROPHESY (vv. 4-6)

4. Then he said to me, "Prophesy to these bones and say to them, 'Dry bones, hear the word of the LORD!

Prophesy to *dry bones*, long dead? Talking to them seemed like a waste of breath. But *the word of the Lord* is not like yours or mine. His power "gives life to the dead and calls things that are not as though they were" (Romans 4:17).

5. "'This is what the Sovereign LORD says to these bones: I will make breath enter you, and you will come to life.

It still sounded impossible, didn't it? Those bones had no lungs. How could *breath* get into them? The next verse mentions some details that needed to be addressed first before this could happen.

6. "'I will attach tendons to you and make flesh come upon you and cover you with skin; I will put breath in you, and you will come to life. Then you will know that I am the LORD.'"

Tendons tie bones together at the joints. *Flesh* here includes organs such as the stomach, liver, and lungs, along with blood vessels, nerves, glands, and whatever else goes into forming a human body. God's plan was to add completed bodies to the bones and then endow the bodies with life. They would become living human beings with minds, and they would know that the one who put them together was *the Lord*—the only one who can do something this magnificent.

II. LIFE AS PROPHESIED (EZEKIEL 37:7-10)

A. FROM BONES TO BODIES (vv. 7, 8)

7. So I prophesied as I was commanded. And as I was prophesying, there was a noise, a rattling sound, and the bones came together, bone to bone.

Promptly, as Ezekiel *prophesied* to the lifeless *bones*, they began to obey. Ezekiel heard *a noise*. Was this noise the same as the *rattling sound* mentioned next? Our translation would make it seem so. It does seem probable that two dry bones coming together would produce a click, and that multiplied thousands of clicks would produce a rattling sound. However, the Hebrew word rendered "noise" can also mean a "sound" or a "voice," while that translated "rattling sound" often describes an earthquake. Some students believe there was an initial sound, perhaps the call of God or of an angel, and then an earthquake, which brought the bones together. In any case, it was the power of God that brought the separated bones together. Miraculously they were joined *bone to bone*, each becoming attached to the very one it needed to join in order to form a complete skeleton.

8. I looked, and tendons and flesh appeared on them and skin covered them, but there was no breath in them.

Before his very eyes, Ezekiel saw the bones disappear from sight, encased in muscles, tendons, ligaments, and all the other components of human bodies. When the bodies were complete, *skin covered them, but there was no breath in them*. These people remained dead—dead as the dry bones had been.

B. FROM DEAD TO LIVING (vv. 9, 10)

9. Then he said to me, "Prophesy to the breath; prophesy, son of man, and say to it, 'This is what the Sovereign LORD says: Come from the four winds, O breath, and breathe into these slain, that they may live.'"

WHAT DO YOU THINK?

"Hear the word of the Lord." Ezekiel's vision illustrates the power of the Word of God. Of course, we will not appreciate the power of God's Word unless we expose ourselves to that power. Merely listening to a weekly sermon and/or Bible lesson will not provide adequate exposure. What can we do to develop a deeper appreciation for this power? What church programs might help believers develop such an appreciation? What can individual Christians do on their own?

(Consider 1 Thessalonians 2:13 and Hebrews 4:12 in your discussion.)

WHAT DO YOU THINK?

Ezekiel's vision, with the bones coming together, taking on flesh, and becoming whole bodies was quite impressive. But still, Ezekiel says, "there was no breath in them." Sometimes we can look good on the outside, but there is no breath or spirit in us, no enthusiasm for the Lord or his work. How can we be spiritually energized to do the Lord's work? What can we do to help energize others, especially young people?

WHAT DO YOU THINK?

When the bones became bodies and came to life as "a vast army," God said, "These bones are the whole house of Israel." The hopeless condition of the exiles was thus declared to be temporary—the nation would be brought to life again. And it would be the "whole nation"— not the fragmented Israel and Judah that had been since the death of Solomon. This should have brought great joy and hope to the exiles. What promises of the Bible bring you the greatest hope? Why?

Of course, some may have received the message with skepticism, as many receive the Word of God today. Others may have placed undue emphasis on the fact that the bones became an "army" and looked for a military solution to their predicament. What can we do to answer the questions of skeptics today, or to prevent misinterpretation of biblical promises?

This verse presents a problem to translators because the Hebrew word *ruah* can mean either *wind, breath,* or *spirit.* Regardless of the specific word used, the meaning of God's command is quite clear. There were so many thousands of *these slain* that an abundance of air was needed to fill their lungs and start them breathing. Therefore the Lord summoned the wind, or breath (or possibly God's Spirit as a source of life) to *come from the four winds* (that is, from every direction). It will bring air into every lung, and with that breath God will provide life.

10. So I prophesied as he commanded me, and breath entered them; they came to life and stood up on their feet—a vast army.

The *breath,* or wind, obeyed God's command as promptly as the bones had done. Pressing in from every direction, it filled the lungs of the dead; and suddenly the dead became alive. *They . . . stood up on their feet.* No estimate of their number is given, but they formed *a vast army.*

"THINGS GO BETTER WITH COKE"

There was a time when the only remedies for colds or the flu were foul-tasting patent medicines. It's no wonder that there has long been a market for sweeter remedies to help us endure life's common ailments.

Coca-Cola was introduced in 1886 as one such medical advance. It was first sold as a "brain and nerve tonic" that would cure "all nervous afflictions—Sick Headache, Neuralgia, Hysteria, Melancholy, Etc."

Today the secret formula no longer includes cocaine. Still, the stimulating effect of the caffeine in Coke and other cola drinks causes many people to feel much better after drinking one, especially if they are accustomed to drinking several a day. So it does seem to many people that "things go better with Coke."

The house of Israel had more than a mere moral headache. The nation was dead, and Ezekiel's vision of dried bones scattered across a valley was an accurate depiction of its moral condition. But God offered hope to his people if they would take the remedy he offered. It was a remedy far better than Coke: the word of the Lord would bring life to a people whose spirits were dead. It did then; it does now!

—C. R. B.

III. MEANING OF THE VISION (EZEKIEL 37:11a, 25-27)

A. LIFE FOR DEAD ISRAEL (v. 11a)

11a. Then he said to me: "Son of man, these bones are the whole house of Israel."

This metaphor is explained clearly in the rest of verses 11b–15, which are omitted from the printed text. With Ezekiel in Babylon were other captives from Judah. They were living and breathing, but they thought that their nation, *the whole house of Israel,* was dead—dead as those bones long bleached in the sun. Through Ezekiel, God assured them that the nation would be revived as the bones had been. Furthermore, the nation would be restored to its own land.

The promise was made to *the whole house of Israel,* both the northern kingdom (Israel) and the southern kingdom (Judah). More than three centuries before the Babylonian captivity, the nation had divided. Two centuries later, the northern kingdom had been crushed, and its people had been scattered among foreign lands. Now the people of the south were living in exile. But restoration would be experienced by the entire nation. This is clearly promised and illustrated in some of the verses omitted from our printed text (vv. 15-24).

B. A HOME FOR THE EXILES (v. 25)

25. "They will live in the land I gave to my servant Jacob, the land where your fathers lived. They and their children and their children's children will live there forever, and David my servant will be their prince forever.

See Psalm 137:1-6 for a powerful expression of the anguish of the captives in Babylon. Precious to those captives was the promise that they would live again in their own *land*, and that *their children* would *live there forever*. We must remember, of course, that the promised land was never promised unconditionally. The people of Israel could live there if they were obedient to God. If they were disobedient, they would be "uprooted from the land" (Deuteronomy 28:63, 64). Just as God promised, the people were "uprooted" and taken to Babylon for a time. Now they were to live in the land again, ruled by *David my servant*.

David himself had died long before the time we are studying, of course; but God had promised that members of his family would rule forever (2 Samuel 7:16). Thus the fulfillment of such promises as described here must be linked with the work of Jesus Christ. Jesus, the true son of David, has provided a way for us to enter the true promised land of Heaven (Hebrews 9:24). Even Old Testament saints knew that this was the land where they desired to live (Hebrews 11:13-16). Forever Jesus stands at the head of the church—of Christians who by faith are children of Abraham (Galatians 3:7) and constitute the Israel of God (Galatians 6:16) under the New Covenant. Other blessings of the kind only Jesus can provide are described in the remaining verses of our printed text.

Today's visual reminds us of the promise in verse 27. Discuss how this finds fulfillment in the church and in eternity. (See Revelation 21:3.)

C. AN EVERLASTING COVENANT (vv. 26, 27)

26. *"I will make a covenant of peace with them; it will be an everlasting covenant. I will establish them and increase their numbers, and I will put my sanctuary among them forever.*

The *covenant of peace* is the new covenant foretold in Jeremiah 31:31-34. Its crowning feature is this: "I will forgive their wickedness and will remember their sins no more" (v. 34). Today God's *sanctuary*, or holy place, is not a massive building of stone; he lives in each devoted Christian (1 Corinthians 6:19), and together these sanctuaries are built together into "a holy temple in the Lord" (Ephesians 2:21). This holy temple is "built on the foundation of the apostles and prophets, with Christ Jesus himself as the chief cornerstone" (v. 20). This is the church that Jesus is building, "and the gates of Hades will not overcome it" (Matthew 16:18). On such a foundation God places his people, and he has promised to *increase their numbers* as they "go into all the world and preach the good news to all creation" (Mark 16:15). This covenant is truly *everlasting*: it will never need to be replaced or amended.

27. *"My dwelling place will be with them; I will be their God, and they will be my people.*

The phrase *dwelling place* translates the same Hebrew word used to describe the tabernacle, which signified God's presence with his people prior to the building of the temple. The Lord is not content to be just an occasional visitor; through the presence of the Holy Spirit, he abides with us. He is our *God*: our Creator, our Ruler, and our Provider. We are his *people*: his creation, his obedient subjects, and the beneficiaries of his provisions.

RESTORED RELATIONSHIPS

Interesting things happen in carpools—so interesting that several governmental agencies in southern California sponsored a contest to discover the most memorable carpool experience.

Kimberly Arguelles won the contest. Her mother and stepfather died in an auto accident in Mexico in 1974. For a while Arguelles and her sister lived with their

WHAT DO YOU THINK?

God promised Israel and Judah several things in Ezekiel 37: reconciliation (vv. 11, 12), unity (v. 19), peace (v. 26), an everlasting covenant (v. 26), and his presence (v. 27). How can you apply each of these promises of hope to the church today?

(You might want to consider the following Scriptures in your discussion: Ephesians 2:4, 5 [reconciliation]; Ephesians 4:4-6 [unity]; Philippians 4:6, 7 [peace]; Hebrews 8:6-13 [new covenant]; and Matthew 28:20; Hebrews 13:5 [his presence].)

PRAYER

In a world of turmoil, Father, we are grateful for your promises and the hope they bring. By your grace and by your power, may each one of us be faithful even to the point of death, and at last be crowned with life eternal. Amen.

WHAT DO YOU THINK?

Some days our hope seems strong and bright, and on other days it seems to grow dim. What causes our hope to dim? How can we be faithful to God even when hope seems dim?

THOUGHT TO REMEMBER

"May the God of hope fill you with all joy and peace as you trust in him, so that you may overflow with hope by the power of the Holy Spirit" (Romans 15:13).

father in southern California; but as she reached her teen years, Arguelles became rebellious and was sent to live in Mexico with her grandmother. She refused to respond to her sister's attempts to communicate with her, and they lost track of each other.

In 1987, Arguelles returned to California to work. Her car broke down, so she joined a carpool. By the second day of ride-sharing, she discovered that a strangely familiar woman in her carpool was her long-lost sister! In mature adulthood, both women were able to put the past behind them and rejoice in the restoration of their relationship.

Ezekiel foretold the day when Israel's immature rebellion against God would be past. They would have learned an important lesson through their exile in a strange land. Their relationship with God would be restored through a growing spiritual maturity.

The good news of the gospel is that God specializes in restoring our relationship with him. Through Jesus, "the old has gone, the new has come" (2 Corinthians 5:17).

—C. R. B.

CONCLUSION

This lesson is well titled, "Hope From God's Promise." After the tragic events of 586 B.C., Israel was no more, or so its captive people thought as they wept by the streams of Babylon. They had no hope. Then came God's promise: Israel would live again. Hope was reborn in people who believed the Lord and his Word.

Throughout our survey of the Old Testament this quarter, mankind has failed repeatedly. With God, however, there is always reason to hope. There was always reason for Israel and Judah to hope, and there is always reason for God's people (the church) today to hope.

When we look at the impact of the church today, are we optimistic or pessimistic? Nearly two thousand years have passed since the church began, yet it still often seems weak, timid, and unsure of itself.

Is there hope for the church? Many believe that we are in a "post-Christian" age. The church and its message are no longer believed or considered relevant. Critics claim that the church has failed miserably in its task and deserves to be replaced by something more productive.

Jesus, the Head of the church, acknowledged that his church would not be perfect. He warned his disciples of false prophets, which "come to you in sheep's clothing, but inwardly they are ferocious wolves" (Matthew 7:15). Later, Paul told the Ephesian elders, "Even from your own number men will arise and distort the truth in order to draw away disciples after them" (Acts 20:30). Even in the days when the church was only a few years old, Paul knew that there would be threats against which the believers, and especially their leaders, would need to stand guard. Yet he also wrote a letter to this same church, confidently declaring that the church is the body of Christ, "the fullness of him who fills everything in every way" (Ephesians 1:23), and that the church is meant to be something "radiant" (5:27).

How can the church restore its "radiance"? Does it seem to be in a condition similar to that of the dry bones? Then let us heed the Word of God and obey the Head of the church. To a lukewarm church, Jesus said, "Here I am! I stand at the door and knock. If anyone hears my voice and opens the door, I will come in and eat with him, and he with me" (Revelation 3:20).

In a world where many voices clamor for the church's attention, only one voice matters. We must listen to Jesus. The Head of the church is the hope of the church.

Discovery Learning

This page contains an alternate lesson plan emphasizing learning activities. Classes desiring such student involvement will find these suggestions helpful. The next page is a reproducible activity page to further enhance discovery learning.

LEARNING GOALS

As a result of this lesson, your students should be able to:

1. Retell the story of the dry bones.

2. Compare the condition of the Jewish exiles with that of the church today.

3. Suggest a way to apply one of God's promises of hope to the church.

INTO THE LESSON

Begin by showing students a bone or a picture of a bone. (It would be even better if you could get your hands on a skeleton—even a small novelty or toy skeleton.) Ask, "What hope does a bone (or skeleton) have? What possibilities and potentials does a bone (or skeleton) have?"

Obviously, the answer to both questions is "None." However, as we will see in today's lesson, with God in the picture things are not always as they appear.

In today's lesson God took the prophet Ezekiel to a valley littered with the bones of warriors who had been killed in battle. God was using sun-bleached bones to illustrate that divine power can transform even a hopeless and desperate situation. There did not appear to be much hope for Judah and Israel in Ezekiel's day, but with God in the picture, things are not always as they appear.

This lesson is about finding hope in a seemingly hopeless situation. It is about seeing possibilities and potentials where none is apparent.

INTO THE WORD

This lesson is based on a dramatic vision seen by the prophet Ezekiel. Ask a volunteer to read Ezekiel 37:1-11a aloud for the class. Pass out index cards and ask students to list the steps it took to transform a valley of old bones into a great army. (The old spiritual "Dry Bones" is based on Ezekiel's vision. If you can find a tape of the spiritual, play it while the students complete their cards.)

• First, the bones needed to be joined with other bones to form skeletons. See verse 7.

• Then they needed connecting tissue (tendons) and vital organs and muscle (flesh). See verse 8a.

• They needed to be covered with skin. See verse 8b.

• More than anything else, they needed the breath of life. See verses 9, 10.

Divide the class into three-person groups and tell the students to study Ezekiel 37:11, 12, 25-27. Pose the following questions:

• Why were the bones in Ezekiel's vision a good representation of Judah and Israel? (vv. 11, 12).

• What did God promise Judah and Israel in verses 25-27?

• In what ways could God's promise of hope in verses 25-27 be applied to today's church?

INTO LIFE

Observe that there is not much of a difference between lifeless cadavers and professing Christians who do not demonstrate the fruit of the Spirit. Distribute copies of the reproducible activity on the next page and give the students time to complete the exercise in small groups or individually. Then discuss their results.

As you discuss this issue, note that the "dead" church in Sardis in Revelation 3:1-6 was urged to "wake up [and] strengthen what remains and is about to die." If our church seems dead and dry in any way, we need to offer the famous prayer, "Revive thy church, beginning with me."

Very often, those who complain about their church's being dead have unrealistic expectations of the church. They may confuse spiritual with spirited; they may be looking more for entertainment than for edification. Before we complain about our church, we need to make sure it is not we ourselves who need to draw nearer to God, repenting of arrogance and pride and giving him first place. Then, while we are praying for our own reviving, we can offer similar prayers for our minister, elders, teachers, and other members. If there is a problem with the church, nothing will help more than prayer and setting a good example of faithfulness and zeal.

Some of your students may especially need God's life-giving touch because of a situation in their lives. Maybe a loved one is ill. Financial problems may seem overwhelming. One may be bearing a load of emotional pain. Another's marriage may be falling apart. This lesson affirms that God's life-giving power is sufficient for even the most desperate and seemingly hopeless situation.

Close with a prayer that today will be a new beginning for your students—a transformation from despair to hope.

Dry Bones

The dry bones in Ezekiel's vision were an apt illustration of the plight of the exiles in Babylon. Perhaps they also illustrate some modern situations. Label each of the bones below with an identification of a person, church, or other entity that is suffering from spiritual "dryness." A couple have been labeled for you to get you started. How many more can you suggest?

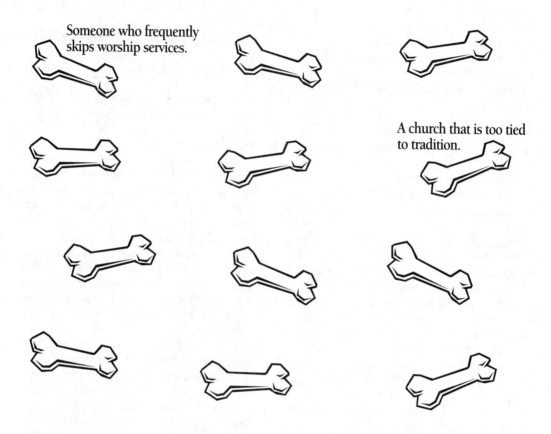

Someone who frequently skips worship services.

A church that is too tied to tradition.

Choose one of the personal situations from the bones above and suggest a way the person in question could find new spiritual life.

Choose one of the church situations from the bones above and suggest a way the church in question could find new spiritual life.

How about you? Are you feeling a little dry? What can you do to find new spiritual life?

RENEWAL AND WORSHIP

LESSON 13

WHY TEACH THIS LESSON?

The speaker was talking about worship. "True worship," he said, "should bring us into contact with the presence of God. Everyone present should have an awareness that God is there, too." Sleepy heads nodded. Yes, of course they should. There was no disagreement among the listeners, who had skipped their mid-morning break to attend devotions.

Then the speaker shocked his audience. "And that didn't happen at your church last Sunday!"

I found his remark rather brash. "How does he know? He wasn't at my church last Sunday. You just can't make a blanket statement like that," I thought.

Then he continued. "I know it didn't happen at your church last Sunday because you left!"

Well, he had me. I could not argue. If I had truly felt myself in the very presence of God Almighty, wild horses could not have dragged me away! Either the definition of worship was faulty, or my practice of it was. And if my worship practice was wrong, what else was not quite right in my life?

Use this lesson to challenge your students. If they want a renewed vitality in their spiritual lives, perhaps the way they approach worship is the place to start.

INTRODUCTION

A. THIS BACKSLIDING WORLD

Edmund Burke wrote, "All that is necessary for the triumph of evil is that good men do nothing." How often that truth has been demonstrated in times ancient and modern!

In Israel there were times of exemplary goodness. A dynamic judge, prophet, or king would lead the nation in obedience to God's law, and peace and prosperity would result. But when that leader died and his influence was no longer present, the people would quickly drift back into selfishness and sin.

Because of its wrongdoing, the nation of Israel was split into two smaller countries. Because of its wrongdoing, the northern kingdom was captured by Assyria and its people were scattered abroad. Because of its wrongdoing, the southern kingdom was taken in captivity to Babylon. Still, God did not abandon his people, but gave them another opportunity to resettle in the promised land. Liberation came about fifty years after Jerusalem was destroyed, and seventy years after the first captives were taken to Babylon.

B. RETURN FROM CAPTIVITY

In last week's lesson we noted that Israel's captivity in Babylon occurred in three phases. Now we note three phases in the return from captivity.

In 538 B.C., approximately fifty thousand of the captives traveled to Jerusalem. Enthusiastically they began to rebuild the temple. However, after laying the foundation, opposition to their project arose from some of the residents of the area. After nearly sixteen years of inactivity, two prophets, Haggai and Zechariah,

DEVOTIONAL READING
GALATIANS 3:23-29
LESSON SCRIPTURE
NEHEMIAH 8, 9
PRINTED TEXT
NEHEMIAH 8:13—9:3

LESSON AIMS

As a result of this lesson, your students should be able to:

1. Describe the observances renewed by the former exiles in today's text.

2. Tell why the observances were significant to their identity as God's people.

3. Commit to worshiping in such a way that his or her observances become times of genuine renewal and identification with God's people.

KEY VERSE

You alone are the LORD. You made the heavens, even the highest heavens, and all their starry host, the earth and all that is on it, the seas and all that is in them. You give life to everything, and the multitudes of heaven worship you.   —Nehemiah 9:6

Nov
29

HOW TO SAY IT

Assyria. Uh-SEAR-ee-uh.
Babylon. BAB-uh-lun.
Elijah. Ee-LYE-juh.
Elul. EE-lull or Eh-LOOL.
Ephraim. EE-fray-im.
Haggai. HAG-a-eye or HAG-eye.
Jeremiah. Jair-uh-MY-uh.
Levites. LEE-vites.
Nebuchadnezzar. NEB-uh-kad-
   NEZZ-er.
Nehemiah. Nee-huh-MY-uh.
Zechariah. Zek-uh-RYE-uh.

WHAT DO YOU THINK?

Our text describes the coming together of family leaders and religious leaders among the former exiles "to give attention to the words of the Law." How can we better equip family heads and church leaders to understand and practice the teachings of the Scriptures?

stirred the people to move forward with the project. The temple was completed in 516 B.C. amidst great celebration (Ezra 1-6).

In 458 B.C., Ezra led another group back from Babylon. He was a priest and a scholar, eager to teach God's Word. To his distress, he found that some of the people had intermarried freely with the pagan peoples of the land. Immediately he undertook to restore the purity of the nation (Ezra 7–10).

In 445 B.C., Nehemiah arrived with another group of Jews from Babylon, and with authority from the Persian king to rebuild the walls of Jerusalem. Vigorously he rallied the people to work, and the walls were finished in only fifty-two days (Nehemiah 1–6).

C. LESSON BACKGROUND

The intensive work on the walls was completed on the twenty-fifth day of Elul, which was the sixth month (Nehemiah 6:15). The people were then quickly organized for purposes of worship and security (Nehemiah 7:1-3). By the first day of the seventh month, they were prepared for a period of intensive Bible teaching. Ezra and his assistants taught them for half a day (Nehemiah 8:1-8), following a plan that is worthy of imitation by any Bible teacher: "They read from the Book of the Law of God, making it clear and giving the meaning so that the people could understand what was being read" (v. 8). The people grieved because they realized that they had not been obeying that law. However, Ezra and Nehemiah told them to rejoice instead, because they now understood the law and could obey it (vv. 9-12).

I. LEARNING FROM THE LAW (NEHEMIAH 8:13-15)

Now that the people had renewed their acquaintance with the law and their allegiance to it, the next step was to lead them in actual and active obedience to it.

A. SEARCHING THE SCRIPTURES (v. 13)

13. On the second day of the month, the heads of all the families, along with the priests and the Levites, gathered around Ezra the scribe to give attention to the words of the Law.

As noted in the Lesson Background, the first day of the seventh month was a day of reading from the law and rejoicing (v. 2). *On the second day*, a smaller group of leaders gathered for another session with *Ezra the scribe*. The word *scribe* literally means "writer," but the professional writers who copied the Scriptures by hand naturally became well versed in what they copied. Thus the term *scribe* became a name for a scholar and teacher like Ezra.

The leaders who met with Ezra included *the heads of all the families*, *the priests* (the primary leaders of worship), and *the Levites* (assistants to the priests). Their purpose was *to give attention to the words of the Law*.

B. FORGOTTEN CUSTOM (vv. 14, 15)

14. They found written in the Law, which the LORD had commanded through Moses, that the Israelites were to live in booths during the feast of the seventh month.

The feast of the seventh month is also called the Feast of Tabernacles. It should be noted that this word for *tabernacles* is not related to the word that describes God's dwelling place when the people were living in tents in the desert (Exodus 40:34-38). Instead, it describes the *booths*, or shelters, that the people were commanded to make from branches of trees; for this reason, this feast was also designated as the Feast of Booths. The feast lasted seven days, and on the day following it a special gathering of the Israelites was to take place (Leviticus 23:33-36). The people lived in booths in memory of the time when they had lived in booths or tents before they reached the promised land (Leviticus 23:39-43).

15. And that they should proclaim this word and spread it throughout their towns and in Jerusalem: "Go out into the hill country and bring back branches from olive and wild olive trees, and from myrtles, palms and shade trees, to make booths"—as it is written.

So that no one would forget, this feast and others were to be proclaimed publicly *throughout their towns* (Leviticus 23:4). Usually the announcement would have to be made well in advance, of course, so that people would have time to travel to *Jerusalem*. In this case, however, the people were already assembled for the reading of the law (vv. 2, 3), so it was easy to let them know about the feast.

It seems that *branches* might be gathered from any kind of trees that were thick with foliage, in order to provide sufficient shade in the booth. The *trees* named are likely the kinds that grew in abundance near Jerusalem. The feast was nicely timed before the end of the dry season, so that rain would not be a problem.

LOST TREASURES

We usually think of pawnshops as "other-side-of-the-tracks" establishments where hapless "down-and-outers" trade items of meager value for a bit of needed cash. Worse yet, pawnshops sometimes provide a venue where thieves can get money for stolen goods, with no questions asked.

But in Beverly Hills, California—home of some of the world's most famous "*up-and-outers*"—a "Jewelry and Loan" shop trades in more precious commodities. One young woman, seeking to finance a trip to Europe, recently pawned a 1920 Cartier twenty-eight carat diamond necklace and a matching Burmese sapphire bracelet for a total of $45,000. The dealer said that they were heirlooms of the family of the woman's husband: "It's old money. Sometimes young people don't care for this stuff. It's a shame, really." A shame, indeed!

Israel was in much the same situation regarding the law of God. Not appreciating what the law had symbolized in the history of God's family, several generations had allowed the words of the law to become forgotten. They were more concerned with the pleasures of the present than with the treasures of the past.

But in Nehemiah's time, a new generation of leaders arose who acknowledged the value of their heritage. When the book of the law was read, they realized the significance of the Feast of Tabernacles and began again to observe it. A lost family treasure was redeemed.   —C. R. B.

II. OBEYING THE LAW (NEHEMIAH 8:16-18)

It was on the second day of the seventh month that the leaders became aware of the law regarding the Feast of Tabernacles (v. 13). The feast was to begin on the fifteenth day of the same month (Leviticus 23:34). There was still plenty of time to prepare for it.

A. BUILDING BOOTHS (v. 16)

16. So the people went out and brought back branches and built themselves booths on their own roofs, in their courtyards, in the courts of the house of God and in the square by the Water Gate and the one by the Gate of Ephraim.

Probably every available open space in the city was used in constructing the *booths*. The flat *roofs* of houses could support *booths*. A big house might be built around a small courtyard or patio where a booth could be built. The large *courts of the house of God* (the temple) had room for many small booths.

WHAT DO YOU THINK?

The exiles had not been observing the Feast of Tabernacles— at least, not as they should have. When God's Word exposed their neglect, they set about to make things right. Do you think people today are as quick to make right a deficiency they find when they compare their lives to the Word? Why or why not? How can such a readiness be cultivated in people's lives?

SOLUTION TO PUZZLE ON P. 120

ACROSS:
1. assembly
4. quarter
7. regulation
8. wickedness
10. celebrated
12. house
14. booths
15. palm
17. Water
19. Ephraim
20. Joshua

DOWN:
2. shade
3. sackcloth
5. myrtle
6. foreigners
8. worshiping
9. second
10. courtyards
11. dust
13. olive
16. Ezra
18. sins

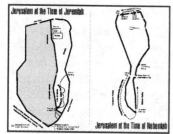

The visual for lesson 13 shows Jerusalem before and after the exile. Use the map on the right to locate places named in today's lesson.

WHAT DO YOU THINK?

The Feast of Tabernacles was an occasion on which the Jews remembered the difficult times of living in tents in the wilderness. What kind of past events or difficulties do you think Christians should commemorate? Why? How should we do it?

The Feast of Tabernacles recalled, not just the difficulty of the exodus, but that God was leading. How can believers celebrate the fact that God is leading today?

Inside each gate was a wide space, or *square*, where hundreds of men could be assembled to resist any invader who threatened to break down the gate and enter the city. These open spaces soon were green with booths.

This verse mentions two specific gates: *the Water Gate*, located on the east side of Jerusalem, and *the Gate of Ephraim*, which was the main gate on the north side of the city.

B. LIVING IN BOOTHS (v. 17)

17. The whole company that had returned from exile built booths and lived in them. From the days of Joshua son of Nun until that day, the Israelites had not celebrated it like this. And their joy was very great.

The Feast of Tabernacles had been observed on different occasions since *the days of Joshua son of Nun*. It was celebrated following the dedication of Solomon's temple (2 Chronicles 7:8-10) and the return of the captives from Babylon (Ezra 3:4). However, not since Joshua's time had the feast been celebrated with such joy. To the usual gladness of the feast was added the joy that resulted from keeping God's law more faithfully than it had been kept for some time.

RENEWING A GREAT TRADITION

Can you remember the days of steam locomotives? There was something awesome about the sound of one huffing and puffing up a mountain pass, and something strikingly beautiful in the billowing clouds of smoke and steam rising into a clear blue winter's sky as a locomotive and its train streaked across a snow-covered plain.

Things are more efficient today. Gone are the gritty particles of coal ash that settled on fresh-washed clothes hung out to dry. In their place is the vaporous exhaust of the diesel-electric locomotive. A mechanical roar and electric hum has replaced the powerful puffing of steam that symbolized the industrial age.

Because diesels are cheaper, cleaner, and easier to maintain, they began replacing steamers some fifty years ago. Steam locomotives are museum pieces now; but in order that their link to a romantic past may not be lost, many railroad museums around the country are training people to run the steamers and thus keep alive this legacy.

In the days of Nehemiah, the people of God had allowed a legacy to die. By failing to observe faithfully the Feast of Tabernacles, they had lost touch with the exodus—the event that gave them their national identity. As they renewed the great tradition of the feast, they were reminded that they had been wanderers until God gave them a home.

When properly observed, traditions remind us of who we have been and what we have become. We need to cherish our traditions—as individuals, families, and churches.

—C. R. B.

C. EARNEST BIBLE STUDY (v. 18)

18. Day after day, from the first day to the last, Ezra read from the Book of the Law of God. They celebrated the feast for seven days, and on the eighth day, in accordance with the regulation, there was an assembly.

Intensive Bible study was a daily part of the celebration, as *from the first day to the last, Ezra read from the Book of the Law of God.* Probably he or his assistants added explanation as it was needed, according to the pattern described earlier in verse 8. The congregation *celebrated the feast for seven days,* and then held *an assembly* on the following day, *in accordance with the regulation* prescribed in the law. See Numbers 29:12-39 for specific instructions about the sacrifices to be offered on each day of the feast.

III. HUMBLE WORSHIP (NEHEMIAH 9:1-3)

The feast covered the fifteenth through the twenty-first days of the seventh month; the solemn assembly that followed was on the twenty-second day. Apparently the people then had a day to prepare for worship of a different kind on the twenty-fourth day.

A. GRIEF FOR WRONGS (v. 1)

1. On the twenty-fourth day of the same month, the Israelites gathered together, fasting and wearing sackcloth and having dust on their heads.

Wise Solomon spoke of "a time to weep and a time to laugh" (Ecclesiastes 3:4). After listening to the law for half a day on the first day of the month, the people began to weep (Nehemiah 8:9). Probably they realized how far they had strayed from obeying the law. But now they knew what the law said. They could obey it instead of ignoring it. Their leaders encouraged them to rejoice (v. 10). Two weeks later the Feast of Tabernacles began. This was a joyous harvest festival that took place after the grapes and other fruits were gathered. It was also a time to rejoice because the people now had comfortable houses in which to dwell instead of the tents or booths where they had lived when they left Egypt (Leviticus 23:42, 43).

When the people met again *on the twenty-fourth day of the same month*, obviously they and their leaders had agreed that the time to weep had come. They *gathered together, fasting*. They wore uncomfortable clothing of rough *sackcloth*. They threw *dust on their heads*. These were traditional ways of expressing deep mourning (Job 2:12; Daniel 9:3).

B. SEPARATION AND CONFESSION (v. 2)

2. Those of Israelite descent had separated themselves from all foreigners. They stood in their places and confessed their sins and the wickedness of their fathers.

Earlier *those of Israelite descent had separated themselves from all foreigners* (people who were not Jews and did not worship the true God) under the influence of Ezra (Ezra 9, 10). If any unwise alliance with a pagan had been made since that time, it was now renounced.

Mingling with pagan foreigners had been a clear violation of the law (Deuteronomy 7:1-5). That specific prohibition was given because God knew that cordial associations with pagan peoples would turn his people away from him. The nation's experience over many centuries proved that this was true.

Humbly and sorrowfully the people of Israel *confessed their sins and the wickedness of their fathers*. These included their dangerous associations with pagans, but there must have been other sins as well. Recently these people had been listening to the reading of the law (Nehemiah 8:1-8, 18). That must have called their attention to various acts of dishonesty and unkindness among themselves.

C. READING AND WORSHIPING (v. 3)

3. They stood where they were and read from the Book of the Law of the LORD their God for a quarter of the day, and spent another quarter in confession and in worshiping the LORD their God.

They stood where they were. The standing posture is mentioned repeatedly in this section (vv. 2, 3, 4, 5). Apparently it was a sign of respect for God and his Word, and of their active participation in praise and confession. For *a quarter of the day*, or daytime (about three hours), they stood and *read from the Book of the Law of the Lord*. Probably Ezra and his assistants read aloud, while the people listened to the law and mourned their transgressions. Then they spent three more

WHAT DO YOU THINK?

We must keep ourselves separate from the pagans of our time, but we must also seek to influence them with the gospel. How can we accomplish these seemingly contradictory aims?

(Consider 2 Corinthians 6:14-17 in your discussion.)

WHAT DO YOU THINK?

The people of Israel engaged in a public confession of their sins. Should we encourage the public confession of sins? Why or why not? What difference would it make whether the sin being confessed were well known or relatively private, or whether the offender were a leader or not?

(See James 5:16.)

THOUGHT TO REMEMBER

True worship takes us from the world, in order that we may face the world on God's behalf.

hours in prayer, confessing their own wrongdoing and praising God's goodness. Most likely this meeting was held in the large outer court of the temple. In order to be seen and heard by the entire crowd, the worship leaders stood on the stairs leading up to an inner court (v. 4).

The rest of chapter 9 records some of the words of praise and confession. These words also review the national history of Israel. It is a lengthy record of God's power and goodness, and of Israel's ingratitude and sin. Chapter 10 then notes the people's fervent pledge "to follow the Law of God . . . and to obey carefully all the commands, regulations and decrees of the Lord our Lord" (v. 29).

CONCLUSION

A. GOD'S FAITHFUL PEOPLE

In every era God has had his faithful people—people who have done his will and enjoyed his favor. Noah was "a preacher of righteousness" (2 Peter 2:5) as he labored to build the ark, and he "found favor in the eyes of the Lord" (Genesis 6:8). Abraham heard the call of God and set out on a long journey, not knowing where he was going (Hebrews 11:8); and he brought blessing to all families of the earth (Genesis 12:1-3). Faithfully for over forty years Jeremiah gave God's word to an unbelieving people, and he lived to see God's word proved true. Mary said, "I am the Lord's servant. . . . May it be to me as you have said" (Luke 1:38); and she became the mother of God's Son and our Savior.

God's faithful people may feel lonely at times, for many unfaithful are choosing the wide road that leads to destruction (Matthew 7:13, 14). Elijah once thought that he was the only faithful one in Israel, but the Lord knew that there were seven thousand more (1 Kings 19:18).

Yes, God has his faithful people in the world today—people who not only do his will but also share his Word and help others do his will. In this world they may experience either prosperity or persecution, but in the world to come they will have joy forever.

B. GOD'S WORSHIPING PEOPLE

Today's lesson text provides some helpful insights on the subject of worship. Note the ingredients that made up the worship of those who gathered in Judah. There was Bible study: the leaders of the people assembled "to give attention to the words of the Law" (Nehemiah 8:13). This was followed by obedience; when the leaders found that the law required the people to live in booths during the feast of the seventh month, they encouraged the people to keep the law (vv. 14, 15). There was also "very great" joy once the people had followed the law's instructions (v. 17). Finally, there was an opportunity to confess sins and to demonstrate repentance through fasting, wearing sackcloth, and dealing decisively with sin (9:1, 2).

Let's take a close look at our worship today and raise some appropriate questions:

Is our time of worship characterized by a period of serious Bible study?

Do we challenge others to obey and apply the Scriptures?

Is there a spirit of gladness and joy as together we celebrate the Lord's goodness?

Is there a time for renewal through confession of sin?

We live in a day when worship is often designed to be convenient rather than convicting. The worship of those in Ezra and Nehemiah's day should challenge us who live under the New Covenant. Are we worshiping to please God or to please ourselves?

Discovery Learning

This page contains an alternate lesson plan emphasizing learning activities. Classes desiring such student involvement will find these suggestions helpful. The next page is a reproducible activity page to further enhance discovery learning.

LEARNING GOALS

As a result of this lesson, your students should be able to:

1. Describe the observances renewed by the former exiles in today's text.

2. Tell why the observances were significant to their identity as God's people.

3. Commit to worshiping in such a way that their observances become times of genuine renewal and identification with God's people.

INTO THE LESSON

If you have married couples in your class, ask, "How do you like to celebrate your wedding anniversary?" (If you have singles, ask how their parents or married friends celebrate.) Discuss why such a celebration is important. How does celebrating reinforce the commitment made in the past? What does a celebration say about the value of the relationship?

Then ask, "What events do we observe as a church, and why?" Your church may celebrate some of the traditional holidays like Mother's Day and Father's Day, Thanksgiving, Christmas, and others. You may also celebrate some days that are special to you as a congregation, like the anniversary of the church's founding or the dedication of its first building. At some point, someone is sure to mention the Lord's Supper. If no one does, you should mention it.

Observe that all of these remembrances are important to us as the people of God. They help to define who we are. The Jews had some special observances, too. But after seventy years in captivity in Babylon, many of these observances had been forgotten. Our lesson today shows how they renewed one of them.

INTO THE WORD

Use the information in the Lesson Background to set the stage for the events of today's lesson. If there are two creative men in the church (not members of your class so they can visit briefly and then exit), ask them to assume the roles of Ezra and Nehemiah and dress up in period costumes. (Bathrobes, with towels on their heads for turbans, would be okay.) They can present the background information to the class in first person.

If your class is large enough, divide it into groups of five to eight members each. Each group is to prepare a news story on the events of Nehemiah 8:13-18. The story, like one that might be broadcast on the evening news, should answer the famous questions "Who? What? When? Where? Why? and How?" Along with straight news ("just the facts"), the group could include a commentary feature, where one senior journalist explains the significance of the event. If the group members are creative, they could even choose some members to be residents of Jerusalem who are interviewed by news correspondents. Give them time to prepare the broadcast and, if there is enough time, an opportunity to perform it. (If there is not time for the performances in class, maybe the scripts could be used in an evening service or shared with a youth group.)

Then have a volunteer read Nehemiah 9:1-3. Ask the following questions:

1. The Feast of Tabernacles was concluded on the twenty-first day of the month and was followed on the twenty-second with a solemn assembly. What took place on the twenty-fourth day?

2. How did the Israelites demonstrate their sorrow?

3. Why did they separate themselves from foreigners?

4. What did they confess?

5. What role did the book of the law of the Lord play in their assembly?

INTO LIFE

Point out that as soon as the returned exiles learned from the Scriptures about the Feast of Tabernacles (or Booths), they put their new understanding of the Word of God into practice by doing what the Word said.

We have a great advantage over the former exiles. Where they were dependent on public readings to hear God's Word, we have copies available for our own reading. Discuss, "What added responsibility do you think we have over the former exiles because of our added opportunity to know God's Word?"

For the exiles, the Feast of Tabernacles became a great opportunity to incorporate a commemoration of their past into a meaningful worship experience. Discuss how we can incorporate the observances of special past events into a meaningful time of worship. Discuss ideas for special services as well as your weekly worship times. Then talk with the appropriate church leaders about implementing some of the better ideas.

Celebration Puzzle

There's no reason to be puzzled about the celebration of the Feast of Booths described in today's text. Read the following clues to solve the crossword puzzle below. Check Nehemiah 8:13–9:3 if you need help.

ACROSS

1. What was held on the eighth day, after seven days of feasting?
4. What part of the day was spent in reading the law?
7. The meeting that was held on the eighth day of the Feast of Booths was held "in accordance with the _____."
8. The people confessed the _____ of their fathers.
10. They _____ the feast for seven days.
12. Booths were put up in the courts of the _____ of God.
14. Israelites were to live in them during the feast of the seventh month.
15. Booths were made from the branches of this kind of tree.
17, 19. Two of the gates named where booths were made.
20. The Feast of Booths had not been celebrated like this since the days of what early leader?

DOWN

2. Booths were made from the branches of this kind of tree.
3. What were the people who gathered on the twenty-fourth day of the month wearing?
5. Booths were made from the branches of this kind of tree.
6. From whom had the Israelites separated themselves?
8. The people spent a quarter of the day in confession and in _____ the Lord.
9. The day of the seventh month that many gathered to give attention to the words of the Law.
10. The people built booths on their own roofs and in their _____.
11. What was on the heads of the people who gathered on the twenty-fourth day of the month?
13. Booths were made from the branches of this kind of tree.
16. The scribe.
18. The people confessed their _____.

Winter Quarter, 1998-99

God Calls Anew in Jesus Christ
(New Testament Survey)

Special Features

Lessons

About These Lessons

Having completed last quarter's survey of the Old Testament, we delve this quarter into an overview of the New. The good news is that God has called each of us into a reconciled relationship with him through the person of his Son Jesus. That truth comes through in each lesson of the quarter.

Dec 6

Dec 13

Dec 20

Dec 27

Jan 3

Jan 10

Jan 17

Jan 24

Jan 31

Feb 7

Feb 14

Feb 21

Feb 28

It Is Still Good News Today

by Johnny Pressley

"The beginning of the gospel about Jesus Christ, the Son of God" (Mark 1:1). So begins the New Testament writer Mark as he introduces his readers to his main subject, Jesus Christ, and to the biblical concept of a "gospel." Today we often refer to the "good news" of Jesus Christ.

The New Testament records for us the good news of Jesus—the story of his life on this earth, the lessons that he taught, and the spiritual legacy that he left behind for his followers. These three items—the life, teaching, and legacy of Jesus—are the essence of the New Testament message. They comprise the truths that we have grown up with in the church. One might wonder if there is anything more to be said on such familiar themes, and the answer is an unqualified *yes*. There is such a rich depth to the gospel story that we can always go back and find nuggets of truth that we had not noticed before.

The lessons for this upcoming quarter form a New Testament survey entitled, "God Calls Anew in Jesus Christ." It is hoped that the thirteen lessons will stimulate the minds of your students with new ideas to consider. Never forget, however, that there is also great value in looking afresh at truths we already know, not so much to learn new ideas as to enjoy the familiar company of old ones. Just as a wife never tires of hearing her husband say that he loves her, so also our souls are strengthened and renewed each time we hear again the Scripture passages we have grown to love. By them we continue to be challenged and encouraged. Our lessons may present an old familiar message, but it is still good news today.

THE LIFE OF JESUS

The first unit of lessons is entitled "The Good News of Jesus Christ." These four lessons will review some of the stories from the life of Jesus and show how they should impact our lives in a practical way.

Lesson 1, "The Son of God," will focus upon the divine nature of Jesus. This lesson reminds us that inside Jesus' human body was, as Paul says, "all the fullness of the Deity" (Colossians 2:9). The printed text combines the bold declarations of the opening verses of Hebrews with Peter's confession that Jesus is "the Christ, the Son of the living God" (Matthew 16:16).

Lesson 2, "The Gospel of Jesus Christ," will summarize some of the ingredients that make the church's message concerning Jesus so distinctive. Luke 1 represents the testimony of someone who did not see Jesus for himself, but who thoroughly researched the evidence and stated with confidence that the gospel story of Jesus is true. The opening verses of 1 Corinthians 15 give a succinct summary of the key elements in the story of Jesus—his death, burial, and resurrection. The first four verses of 1 John present John's eyewitness testimony to the story of Jesus, with John affirming that he actually saw, heard, and touched Jesus.

Lesson 3, "The Birth of Jesus," will focus on one of the most cherished biblical stories at the height of the Christmas season. The Luke 2 account will once again stir the heart with the familiar images of the "little town of Bethlehem," a baby in a manger, and angels announcing their "good news" to shepherds.

Lesson 4, "The Promise of Power," will touch upon the climax of Jesus' ministry on this earth as he prepared to ascend into Heaven. The lesson text from Luke 24 tells of a postresurrection appearance by Jesus that was typical of all the others recorded in the Gospels. Those who saw Jesus alive doubted at first, but were led to believe by the convincing evidence at hand—a nail-pierced body that they could see and touch. Jesus then commissioned his disciples to be his witnesses to others, who would then follow their lead in taking the gospel to all nations. As Luke 24 affirms, the evangelistic success of the apostles as well as the church ultimately derives from the powerful ministry of the Holy Spirit in the lives of Jesus' followers.

THE TEACHING OF JESUS

The second unit of lessons is entitled "Good News for Daily Living." These four lessons will focus upon the teaching ministry of Jesus in the Gospels. Each lesson will develop a different theme that often recurred throughout Jesus' ministry, showing once again the practical implications of his words for our lives today.

Lesson 5, "Love One Another," will use texts from three different Gospels to illustrate a key theme of Jesus' teaching ministry—that his disciples must learn to exhibit toward each other the same kind of self-sacrificing love that brought him to earth to die for their sakes. As the final text from John 13 will note, this kind of brotherly love is to be the distinguishing mark of those who have become followers of Christ.

JANUARY

Lesson 6, "Follow Kingdom Priorities," will use Luke 12:13-21 to challenge our natural attraction to money and possessions. The parable of the rich fool illustrates how easy it is to be blinded by prosperity and to forget our first duty to God and to others. The lesson's intent will not be to paint material blessings as wrong, but to remind us of the priorities by which we are to handle that which God gives us to enjoy.

Lesson 7, "Reverse the World's Standard," will use two stories from Matthew's Gospel that highlight the immature thinking of the apostles in their early years—when they argued among themselves about who should be "the greatest." This lesson will emphasize the humble servant-leader style required for ministry in the Lord's church.

Lesson 8, "Forgive One Another," will use Matthew 18 to teach a lesson on the grace and forgiveness that we have received from God and are expected to show to others. Jesus' parable of the servant who was forgiven but failed to show forgiveness to another will challenge us to "do unto others" as God has so graciously done to us.

THE LEGACY OF JESUS

The third unit of lessons is entitled, "Good News for Changing Times." These five lessons are taken from the book of Acts, the New Testament epistles, and Revelation. They are intended to represent how the early Christians sought to apply in their own culture and context the ideas that they learned from Jesus. It is hoped that their efforts will illustrate for us today how to apply the unchanging message of the gospel in a world that never ceases to change.

Lesson 9, "Knowing No Boundaries," will focus on an incident from Paul's missionary journeys that seems as fresh and relevant today as it was when it first happened. Acts 17 records the spread of the gospel into new territories, crossing previously untouched cultural and religious boundaries. As the world we know continues to "shrink" and as we encounter firsthand more of the peoples and cultures surrounding us, we will appreciate the lesson we can learn from Paul's first "cross-cultural" experience on Mars' Hill.

Lesson 10, "Obeying Civic Authorities," will touch on issues of continuing interest to modern Christians. In democratic countries Christians can be intimately

FEBRUARY

involved in the workings of government, with the right to vote and speak out on issues and even to seek political office—something impossible for most believers of the biblical era. Of course, the greater our privileges, the greater our responsibilities. As Christians we have the greatest burden of all citizens: a command from God to give obedience and respect to all authorities, acknowledging their legitimacy from God. Romans 13 gives guidelines for our duty to government, even when we do not like the policies of that government.

Lesson 11, "Building a Caring Community," will focus on the observance of the Lord's Supper, using Paul's teaching in 1 Corinthians 11. Starting with the primary purpose of this ceremony as a "remembrance" of Christ's death, we will look at another dimension of the Lord's Supper that is often missed—its message of unity among fellow believers who have also accepted the death of Christ for their salvation. The improper conduct of the church at Corinth teaches us not to partake "in an unworthy manner," thereby bringing God's judgment upon us.

Lesson 12, "Reconciling the World to God," will pick up on one of the grandest themes in Scripture—the meaning of Christ's death at Calvary. From 2 Corinthians 5 we will view the cross as a work of "reconciliation," in which Christ restored a peace and a friendship between man and God that was disrupted because of our sin. And as Paul emphasizes, the blessing of Calvary also comes with a duty—to speak as ambassadors of Christ and let others know that they too can be reconciled to God.

Lesson 13, "Living in Hope," is an appropriate way to end this New Testament survey. The lesson will focus on the promise that Jesus will one day return to gather the saints and take them home to Heaven forever. Titus 2 reminds us of the content of our hope, Hebrews 12 assures us of the security of our hope, while Revelation 1 reveals a heavenly vision of our hope. This will be a lesson of both celebration and challenge, encouraging us to live out the hope of which we speak and sing.

The "good news" of Jesus Christ, demonstrated by his life on earth, proclaimed through his teachings, and living on in his spiritual legacy to the church, is indeed still good news today. Let us faithfully carry out our mission as Christ's ambassadors, declaring to a lost world, "Be reconciled to God!"

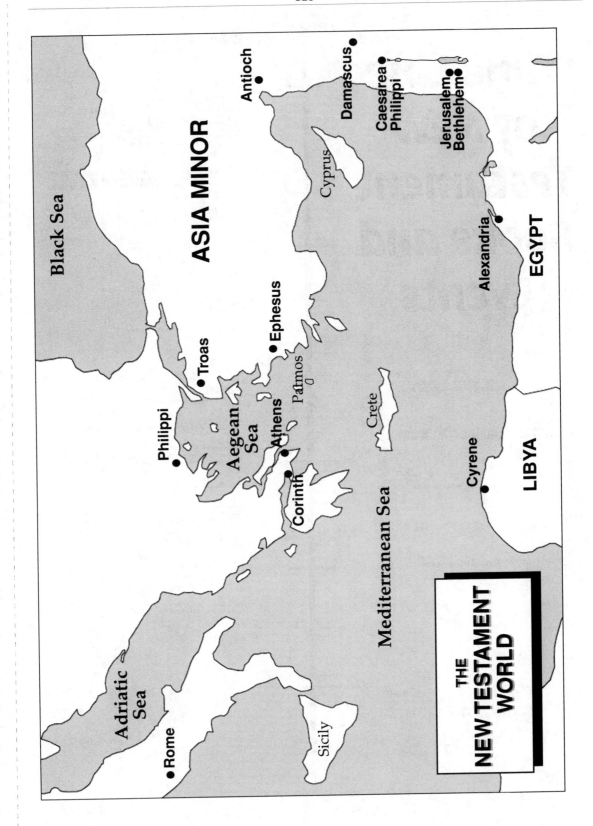

THE NEW TESTAMENT WORLD

Time Line of New Testament Books and Events

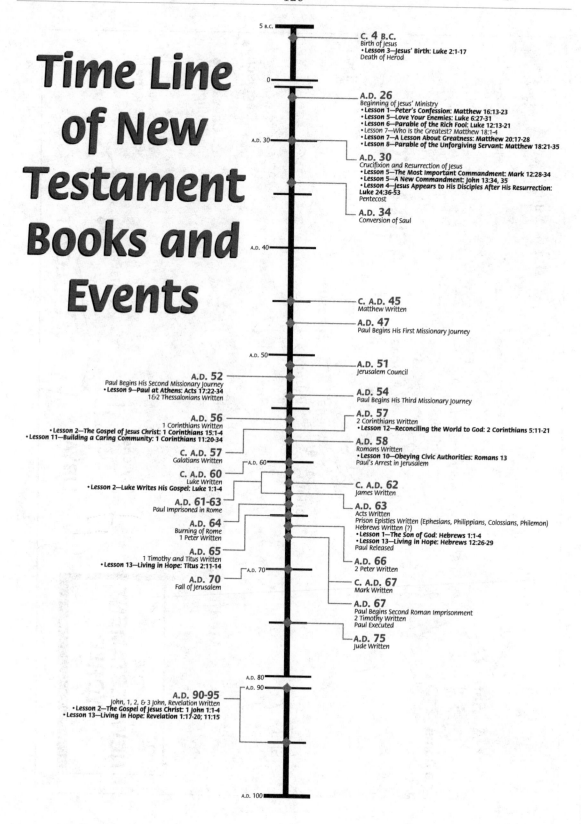

5 B.C.

C. 4 B.C.
Birth of Jesus
• Lesson 3—Jesus' Birth: Luke 2:1-17
Death of Herod

0

A.D. 26
Beginning of Jesus' Ministry
• Lesson 1—Peter's Confession: Matthew 16:13-23
• Lesson 5—Love Your Enemies: Luke 6:27-31
• Lesson 6—Parable of the Rich Fool: Luke 12:13-21
• Lesson 7—Who Is the Greatest? Matthew 18:1-4
• Lesson 7—A Lesson About Greatness: Matthew 20:17-28
• Lesson 8—Parable of the Unforgiving Servant: Matthew 18:21-35

A.D. 30

A.D. 30
Crucifixion and Resurrection of Jesus
• Lesson 5—The Most Important Commandment: Mark 12:28-34
• Lesson 5—A New Commandment: John 13:34, 35
• Lesson 4—Jesus Appears to His Disciples After His Resurrection: Luke 24:36-53
Pentecost

A.D. 34
Conversion of Saul

A.D. 40

C. A.D. 45
Matthew Written

A.D. 47
Paul Begins His First Missionary Journey

A.D. 50

A.D. 51
Jerusalem Council

A.D. 52
Paul Begins His Second Missionary Journey
• Lesson 9—Paul at Athens: Acts 17:22-34
1&2 Thessalonians Written

A.D. 54
Paul Begins His Third Missionary Journey

A.D. 56
1 Corinthians Written
• Lesson 2—The Gospel of Jesus Christ: 1 Corinthians 15:1-4
• Lesson 11—Building a Caring Community: 1 Corinthians 11:20-34

A.D. 57
2 Corinthians Written
• Lesson 12—Reconciling the World to God: 2 Corinthians 5:11-21

C. A.D. 57
Galatians Written

A.D. 58
Romans Written
• Lesson 10—Obeying Civic Authorities: Romans 13
Paul's Arrest in Jerusalem

C. A.D. 60
Luke Written
• Lesson 2—Luke Writes His Gospel: Luke 1:1-4

C. A.D. 62
James Written

A.D. 61-63
Paul Imprisoned in Rome

A.D. 63
Acts Written
Prison Epistles Written (Ephesians, Philippians, Colossians, Philemon)
Hebrews Written (?)
• Lesson 1—The Son of God: Hebrews 1:1-4
• Lesson 13—Living in Hope: Hebrews 12:26-29
Paul Released

A.D. 64
Burning of Rome
1 Peter Written

A.D. 65
1 Timothy and Titus Written
• Lesson 13—Living in Hope: Titus 2:11-14

A.D. 66
2 Peter Written

A.D. 70
Fall of Jerusalem

C. A.D. 67
Mark Written

A.D. 67
Paul Begins Second Roman Imprisonment
2 Timothy Written
Paul Executed

A.D. 75
Jude Written

A.D. 80

A.D. 90

A.D. 90-95
John, 1, 2, & 3 John, Revelation Written
• Lesson 2—The Gospel of Jesus Christ: 1 John 1:1-4
• Lesson 13—Living in Hope: Revelation 1:17-20; 11:15

A.D. 100

God Calls Anew in Jesus Christ

Unit 1. The Good News of Jesus Christ
(Lessons 1-4)

THE SON OF GOD

WHY TEACH THIS LESSON?

The "golden text" of the Bible (John 3:16) is closely followed by this promise of Jesus that also serves as a warning: "Whoever believes in him is not condemned, but whoever does not believe stands condemned already because he has not believed in the name of God's one and only Son" (John 3:18). Verse 36 of the same chapter reiterates: "Whoever believes in the Son has eternal life, but whoever rejects the Son will not see life, for God's wrath remains on him." John expresses the same thought again in his first letter: "He who has the Son has life; he who does not have the Son of God does not have life" (1 John 5:12).

Is there any more important reason for teaching Bible lessons than generating saving faith among your students? It is a life-and-death matter of their spiritual destiny!

INTRODUCTION

A. CHRISTIANITY IS JESUS

Consistently in surveys that address religious matters, more than ninety percent of the people in America report believing in God. Not nearly that many believe in Jesus. It is not enough to admire Jesus or proclaim him to be a great teacher or prophet. What makes Christianity distinctive is its belief that Jesus is divine, and that he is uniquely the Son of God. Some people may describe themselves as Christians who do not hold these beliefs. They would not, however, meet the biblical criteria. Christianity is founded upon Jesus—not just his teachings, but also his person and work.

Today's lesson is the first in a survey of the New Testament, and also the first in a unit on Jesus. Its contents go right to the heart of the matter: Who is Jesus? Matters of eternal significance will be determined by our answer.

B. LESSON BACKGROUND

Our discussion today is based on two very different biblical texts. The first is a selection from the opening verses of the book of Hebrews. The most difficult question surrounding this book is its authorship. Unlike other epistles or letters in the Bible, this one does not bear the author's name. This is appropriate, since the author wanted to lift up Christ. Some believe Paul to be the author. Others have speculated that the writer may have been John the apostle, Apollos the great preacher, Barnabas, Priscilla and Aquila, or a number of others. After all the speculation, we must conclude that we do not know with certainty who wrote the book. We do know that it appears to have been written to Jewish believers who were considering abandoning their Christian faith to return to Judaism. The author proclaims the superiority of Jesus and of the Christian faith.

The second part of the printed text comes from the Gospel of Matthew. It highlights a pivotal discussion between Jesus and his disciples, focusing particularly on Peter.

DEVOTIONAL READING:
ISAIAH 11:1-10

LESSON SCRIPTURE:
HEBREWS 1:1-4; MATTHEW 16:13-26

PRINTED TEXT:
HEBREWS 1:1-4; MATTHEW 16:13-23

LESSON AIMS

After this lesson, a student should be able to:

1. Describe the unique character of Jesus, the Son of God, as illustrated in today's text.

2. Explain why Jesus must be accepted as "Son of God" or not at all.

3. Make a confession of faith in Jesus, the Son of God, and determine to share that confession with someone this week.

KEY VERSE

Simon Peter answered, "You are the Christ, the Son of the living God." —Matthew 16:16

The visual for lesson 1 will be useful throughout the quarter. It will help you place the events studied and the biblical texts in chronological order.

WHAT DO YOU THINK?

What does it mean to be created in God's image? What separates us from the other living creatures God made? Think in terms of our abilities to reason, create, and communicate ideas; the choices we make and how we make them; how we love and express love; and most important, the kind of relationship we can have with God.

As the "exact representation" of God, Jesus does not merely share some features in common with God, as we do; he is God. In what ways are we limited where Jesus is unlimited (even if God's image in us were not distorted by sin)?

I. CHRIST'S SUPREMACY DESCRIBED (HEBREWS 1:1-4)

A. THE WORD OF GOD TO MAN (vv. 1, 2)

1. In the past God spoke to our forefathers through the prophets at many times and in various ways.

The author of Hebrews begins his treatise with a tribute to the majesty of Jesus. He recalls that *God* has always had a desire to communicate with his creation. He has, in fact, spoken *in the past . . . at many times and in various ways,* and he has done so *through the prophets.* These were inspired verbal messages. However, these men did not communicate all that God desired mankind to know. The author of Hebrews was eager to call attention to a message from God that was far superior—one to which many of the prophets pointed in their preaching (1 Peter 1:10).

2. But in these last days he has spoken to us by his Son, whom he appointed heir of all things, and through whom he made the universe.

Jesus has come *in these last days* as a unique messenger of God. He is not just another prophet; as God's *Son,* he embodies God's Word. The beginning of John's Gospel notes how the Word, which was "with God in the beginning" (John 1:2), "became flesh and made his dwelling among us" (v. 14).

The reference to Jesus' arrival in the *last days* should be interpreted in light of how the New Testament uses this phrase. It does not refer to the end of time, but rather to the final stage of God's redemptive plan. The Old Testament era is considered the former days, or "the past" (Hebrews 1:1). The New Testament era, beginning with Jesus' first coming and concluding with his return, is viewed as the *last days* (see also Acts 2:16, 17; 1 Peter 1:19, 20; 1 John 2:18).

In addition, Jesus is *heir of all things.* This is another way of describing the sonship of Jesus. He is God's Son in a special sense—one not achievable by any human being. As the second person of the Godhead, he was also a participant in the creation of the world (John 1:3). According to the author of Hebrews, Jesus was the one *through whom* God *made the universe* and all that is part of it, both seen and unseen.

B. THE IMAGE OF GOD TO MAN (v. 3)

3. The Son is the radiance of God's glory and the exact representation of his being, sustaining all things by his powerful word. After he had provided purification for sins, he sat down at the right hand of the Majesty in heaven.

The author continues to wax eloquent in his lofty tribute to Jesus. He describes Jesus as *the radiance of God's glory* (John 1:14). He is also *the exact representation of his being.* The Greek word translated "exact representation" is a term that applied to an impression made by a seal or stamp, which left behind an image of itself. It was the kind of stamp used by a government official or person of wealth to seal a document, to signify its authenticity as legally representing the person who sent it. In other words, Jesus bears the stamp of the heavenly Father's image, and has revealed to us the Father's nature and character (John 14:9).

Jesus is also *sustaining all things by his powerful word.* He keeps the world from falling apart; "in him all things hold together," says Colossians 1:17.

The final half of this verse calls our attention to the cross, where Jesus *provided purification for sins.* When he finished his redemptive work, he *sat down at the right hand of the Majesty in heaven.* This signifies that his work is completed, and contrasts his accomplishment with that of the Old Testament priest, who "day after day . . . stands and performs his religious duties; again and again he offers the same sacrifices, which can never take away sins" (Hebrews 10:11).

C. THE SALVATION OF GOD FOR MAN (v. 4)

4. So he became as much superior to the angels as the name he has inherited is superior to theirs.

In today's world, many have become fascinated by *angels*. We now have movies, television programs, books, and even a magazine devoted solely to angels. Certainly the angels who appear in the Scriptures are magnificent creatures, inspiring awe and wonder. But they are not worthy of worship. Only Jesus is worthy of worship because he is *much superior to the angels*. He has a greater inheritance and a greater *name*. An angel is simply a messenger. The ministry of angels is significant, but their splendor pales in comparison to Jesus as God's Son. The writer elaborates on this point in the remainder of Hebrews 1.

THE FLOODLIGHTS SHINE ON JESUS

We've all seen buildings that are surrounded by floodlights and beautifully illuminated at night. Sometimes you can see them for miles. The owner of such a building may have spent thousands of dollars on the floodlights, yet seldom does anyone say, "Wow! Look at those floodlights! Aren't those the most impressive floodlights you've ever seen?" Instead, people say, "Wow! Look at that building! Isn't it magnificent?" When the lights are installed correctly, they draw attention to the building, not to themselves.

God's angels do not call attention to themselves. They simply point to Jesus. Don't give your worship and allegiance to the angels, but to the One on whom the angels shine their "floodlights." Only Jesus can give you truth, meaning, hope, and salvation. —G. A.

II. CHRIST'S SUPREMACY DECLARED (MATTHEW 16:13-23)

As we continue our study of Jesus as God's Son, we move not only from one book to another, but from one kind of literature to another. We move from Hebrews, an epistle or letter, and go to an eyewitness account of the life of Christ—the Gospel according to Matthew. Our text from Matthew focuses on a critical teaching encounter between Jesus and his disciples.

A. A PROBING QUESTION (vv. 13-15)

13. When Jesus came to the region of Caesarea Philippi, he asked his disciples, "Who do people say the Son of Man is?"

It is significant that this encounter took place after heightened tensions had developed between Jesus and the Pharisees and after a series of miracles (Matthew 14:13—16:12). The time had come for Jesus to probe *his disciples* concerning how they interpreted these events.

The incident recorded here took place in the *region of Caesarea Philippi*. This city was built by Herod Philip, a son of Herod the Great who is called "tetrarch of Iturea and Traconitis" (Luke 3:1). Although Herod the Great had arranged to divide his kingdom among his sons upon his death, all the Herods ruled at the pleasure of Caesar (Tiberias), the Roman emperor. Herod Philip wanted to curry favor with Caesar, so he called this city Caesarea. His own name was attached to the city to distinguish it from the other Caesarea, which was located near the Mediterranean Sea.

Jesus asked his disciples, "*Who do people say the Son of Man is?*" The term *Son of Man* was used at times as a title for the Messiah in the Old Testament. The term can also be used simply to mean "I." Jesus is asking, "Who do people say I am?"

14. They replied, "Some say John the Baptist; others say Elijah; and still others, Jeremiah or one of the prophets."

WHAT DO YOU THINK?

Angels are "ministering spirits sent to serve those who will inherit salvation" (Hebrews 1:14). Think of the Bible accounts of angels appearing to people (like Joseph, Mary, the shepherds). What were they doing? What more did Jesus accomplish than conveying a message? How is what Jesus did superior to what angels could do? How is his identity superior to that of angels?

VISUALS FOR THESE LESSONS

The Adult Visuals *packet* contains classroom-size visuals designed for use with the lessons in the Winter Quarter. The packet is available from your supplier. Order No. 292.

The disciples offered several answers to Jesus' question. *Some* believed Jesus to be *John the Baptist* returning from the dead. The record of John's Gospel is clear that John the Baptist was not the Messiah (John 1:8, 19-27; 3:28).

The disciples also reported that some said that Jesus was *Elijah.* Elijah was a popular prophetic figure. The prophet Malachi (Malachi 3:1; 4:5, 6) declared that Elijah would be God's messenger, preceding the coming of the Messiah. Jesus explained that this prophecy was fulfilled in John the Baptist (Matthew 11:10-14). According to the words of the angel Gabriel, John came "in the spirit and power of Elijah" (Luke 1:17).

Still others claimed that Jesus was *Jeremiah.* Jeremiah was another great prophet who was revered because of his courage and his passion for God's truth. Jesus, however, was not any of these. He was no mere man or prophet.

15. "But what about you?" he asked. "Who do you say I am?"

Now Jesus made the question much more personal, directing it to the disciples and asking, *"Who do you say I am?"* This was a question they had to face, along with everyone who has ever heard of Jesus. It is one thing to report what others say; it is quite another to declare what you believe.

B. AN INSPIRED ANSWER (vv. 16, 17)

16. Simon Peter answered, "You are the Christ, the Son of the living God."

True to his personality, *Simon Peter* was the first to speak. In most cases, he said (or did) the wrong thing, but here he was right on target. He *answered* that Jesus is the *Christ.* The word *Christ* is a title. It is the Greek equivalent to the Hebrew word *Messiah.* It means "anointed one." Peter went on to say that Jesus is the *Son of the living God.* This went beyond a declaration of messiahship, for Peter could have had in mind a human Messiah. Peter was declaring his conviction that Jesus was no mere mortal. He was God in the flesh.

17. Jesus replied, "Blessed are you, Simon son of Jonah, for this was not revealed to you by man, but by my Father in heaven.

Jesus responded to Peter's answer by calling him *blessed.* This is the same word as that used in the Beatitudes, and it is not easy to translate into English. Some have suggested that "happy" or "joyful" are good translations.

Why was Peter *blessed*? The confession he made was not one whose source was mere human reasoning. It was a confession that required spiritual sensitivity and discernment. Peter was responding to a truth *revealed* by God through Jesus' words and works.

C. AN ENCOURAGING PROMISE (vv. 18-20)

18. "And I tell you that you are Peter, and on this rock I will build my church, and the gates of Hades will not overcome it.

The interpretation of this verse has been subject to much discussion. In responding to Peter's confession, Jesus declared, *On this rock I will build my church.* Was he talking about Peter? Or was he talking about the confession itself and the truth it contains? The latter seems to be the most appropriate answer. Would Jesus build his church on a human foundation? That is doubtful. On one level this might make sense, since the Bible teaches that the church was built on the foundation of the apostles and prophets (Ephesians 2:20). But can one man be the rock? Only one person deserves that designation: Jesus himself.

Part of what makes this verse problematic is that Peter's name means "rock." However, when Jesus said, "On this rock I will build my church," He was using a Greek word (*petra*) that was slightly different from the Greek form of Peter's name (*petros*). The difference may be expressed as follows: "You, Peter, are just a

WHAT DO YOU THINK?

What practical difference does it make whether Jesus was just one more great religious teacher or the Son of God?

Jesus was a great moral teacher. But part of his teaching was about himself—he claimed to be the Son of God. What advantages are there to being the Son of God over just being a great teacher?

WHAT DO YOU THINK?

Jesus anticipates the church storming the gates of Hell. Where do you see your church waging the battle against the forces of evil and death? What evidence can you cite that the church is prevailing?

What form of evangelistic outreach have you and your church been trying? Are you demonstrating God's love by meeting needs in your community?

small pebble; but on this bedrock [the truth of who I am] I will build my church." Jesus was using a play on words that was most appropriate in the language of the New Testament.

Furthermore, Jesus promised that *the gates of Hades will not overcome* the church. This word is a general term for the abode of the dead, both good and bad. Other times it describes death or the powers of death. The latter is most likely its meaning here. Notice also that the church is pictured as on the march—not in a defensive mode. Jesus' description is not one of the church behind its gates, withstanding the assault of the powers of death. He describes the church pounding on the gates of death and prevailing over them. Jesus' church is a victorious church.

19. "I will give you the keys of the kingdom of heaven; whatever you bind on earth will be bound in heaven, and whatever you loose on earth will be loosed in heaven."

This verse is part of Jesus' great promise, but it also is a bit problematic. Peter was told that he would be given *the keys of the kingdom of heaven*. Keys are used in opening doors, allowing people to enter buildings or rooms. This is why Peter is often the main character and doorkeeper in many folk tales about people entering the gates of Heaven. Peter used the keys given to him not to make up his own rules of admission, but to outline God's terms of admission into the Christian life on the day of Pentecost (Acts 2:38).

Jesus appears to say that any judgment Peter makes *on earth* will be acknowledged as binding in *heaven*. This phrase "binding and loosing" does speak of a special authority, but it is an authority to declare judgment, not to determine it. A better translation of Jesus' words (and one followed in the *New American Standard Bible*) might be, "Whatever you shall bind on earth shall have been bound in heaven, and whatever you shall loose on earth shall have been loosed in heaven."

20. Then he warned his disciples not to tell anyone that he was the Christ.

Jesus then gave *his disciples* what must have seemed a strange command. They were not to tell anyone that he was *the Christ*. Why not? Jesus will set his own time for the cross. He will lay his life down; it will not be taken from him (John 10:18). Jesus did not want to arouse the crowds at this point, or give the authorities reason to question his ministry. This command was given for a specific occasion and a specific need. Today we are no longer under any obligation to keep the truth about Jesus quiet. Rather, we are obligated to share it wherever we go.

SEARCH AND RESCUE

Who can forget the heart-wrenching images in the aftermath of the bombing of the federal building in Oklahoma City in 1995? The scenes of grieving family members, dead children, and horrific destruction linger in our minds.

Among the scenes that few of us will ever forget are those involving the incredible rescue operations conducted by emergency personnel. For many days they kept reentering the fragile, collapsing structure at the risk of their own lives. Weren't they afraid it might collapse on them? Of course. Weren't they afraid there might be additional explosives that could yet be detonated? Of course. But the larger fear that they had for the ones still trapped overcame their fears for themselves.

It is true that Jesus did not want his disciples to tell anyone that he was the Christ, according to today's text (Matthew 16:20). However, his command to us is to be his witnesses "to the ends of the earth" (Acts 1:8).

We may have many fears about sharing our faith with our friends, family, and co-workers. Perhaps we're afraid that someone will be more intelligent than we are.

HOW TO SAY IT

Apollos. Uh-PAHL-us.
Aquila. ACK-will-uh.
Caesarea Philippi. Sess-uh-REE-uh Fuh-LIP-pie or FILL-uh-pie.
Elijah. Ee-LYE-juh.
Gabriel. GAY-bree-ul.
Iturea. It-you-REE-uh.
Jeremiah. Jair-uh-MY-uh.
Malachi. MAL-uh-kye.
petra (Greek). PEH-trah.
petros (Greek). PEH-tross.
Priscilla. Prih-SILL-uh.
Sanhedrin. San-HEED-run or SAN-huh-drin.
Tiberias. Tie-BEER-ee-us.
Traconitis. Trak-o-NYE-tus.

DAILY BIBLE READINGS

Monday, Nov. 30—She Will Name Him Immanuel (Isaiah 7:10-17)

Tuesday, Dec. 1—A Child Has Been Born to Us (Isaiah 9:1-7)

Wednesday, Dec. 2—A Vision of Peace (Isaiah 11:1-10)

Thursday, Dec. 3—He Was Wounded for Our Transgressions (Isaiah 53:1-12)

Friday, Dec. 4—Arise, Shine, for Your Light Has Come (Isaiah 60:1-7)

Saturday, Dec. 5—God Has Spoken by His Son (Hebrews 1:1-4)

Sunday, Dec. 6—You Are the Christ! (Matthew 16:13-26)

PRAYER

Above all else, dear God, I want to know your Son. In him I see you. In him I understand your grace. In him I discover your love. Thank you for putting a face on yourself by sending us Jesus. Thank you for his sacrifice and suffering for us. We worship and serve a suffering Savior. In the name of him who bears the scars. Amen.

WHAT DO YOU THINK?

Jesus told Peter that rejecting the way of suffering was thinking like men and not like God. Can you give any examples of believers today thinking like the world and not like God?

We also know of believers who deny themselves in order to be more obedient to the will of God. They restrict their material wants in order to contribute to the church outreach project, or sacrifice a vacation in order to serve short-term with a foreign mission or work in Vacation Bible School. What are some other examples? What impact do you think such service has on the people who notice it?

THOUGHT TO REMEMBER

Words cannot express or the mind fathom the majesty of Jesus.

Maybe we'll lose the respect of others. Maybe we've fumbled some attempts in the past.

What can keep us motivated to share with others in the face of these fears? A greater fear—the fear that if we don't keep sharing, others will spend eternity without Jesus Christ and thus without hope.

Christmas is just around the corner. Let's share the good news of this season with someone who needs Jesus.   —G. A.

D. A SOLEMN WARNING (vv. 21-23)

21. From that time on Jesus began to explain to his disciples that he must go to Jerusalem and suffer many things at the hands of the elders, chief priests and teachers of the law, and that he must be killed and on the third day be raised to life.

Jesus followed up on this "mountaintop experience" with a disturbing announcement: the Messiah must die. Jesus knew the when, where, and how of his death. He even told the *disciples* of his resurrection—a promise that (as shown by their reaction now as well as their behavior just after his death) they appeared to ignore.

Jesus also told who would instigate his suffering. The *elders* was a general designation of the Jewish leaders. The *chief priests* were those in charge of the temple and its procedures. *Teachers of the* Jewish *law,* or lawyers (Luke 11:45, 46, 52) were respected authorities. These three groups made up the Jewish ruling council called the Sanhedrin.

22. Peter took him aside and began to rebuke him. "Never, Lord!" he said. "This shall never happen to you!"

Peter, who had just spoken in such exemplary fashion, now returned to his characteristic rashness. He told Jesus that the scenario he had just described must not *happen.* His words constituted a *rebuke*—a strange way to talk to a person that he had just affirmed to be Christ and Lord.

23. Jesus turned and said to Peter, "Get behind me, Satan! You are a stumbling block to me; you do not have in mind the things of God, but the things of men."

In contrast to Jesus' earlier compliment of Peter's faith, we now see a bluntness in Jesus' response to Peter's folly. Jesus said, *Get behind me, Satan.* Earlier Jesus called attention to the meaning of Peter's name ("rock"). Now Peter has become a *stumbling* stone.

What did Jesus' addressing Peter as *Satan* mean? The word *Satan* means "adversary." When it is used as a proper name, it signifies the ultimate adversary—the devil himself. Here, by calling Peter *Satan,* Jesus may have been saying that Peter was speaking and acting as an adversary of God's plan and purpose. Any attempt to stop Jesus from facing the cross was an attempt to oppose the will of God.

CONCLUSION

Napoleon was reported to have said that he knew men, and that Jesus was no mere man. As we study the text from Hebrews and the Good Confession of Peter, we see that the Bible does not give us the option of believing that Jesus is a mere man. Jesus is Lord, Christ, and so much more. He is beyond description. It is interesting that most world religions try to find some way to fit Jesus into their scheme, for such is the force of his powerful influence. Frequently, however, the emphasis that these religions place on Jesus is far less than what the Scripture says he must receive.

We must accept Jesus on his terms, not ours. We need to find a place for Jesus as he is, and he is no mere man.

Discovery Learning

This page contains an alternate lesson plan emphasizing learning activities. Classes desiring such student involvement will find these suggestions helpful. The next page is a reproducible activity page to further enhance discovery learning.

LEARNING GOALS

After this lesson the student will be able to:

1. Describe the unique character of Jesus, the Son of God, as illustrated in today's text.

2. Explain why Jesus must be accepted as "Son of God" or not at all.

3. Make a confession of faith in Jesus, the Son of God, and determine to share that confession with someone this week.

INTO THE LESSON

Write the heading *"Bible Names and Descriptions of Jesus"* on a large poster or on the chalkboard. (Waxed butcher paper also works well.) Select a student to act as "scribe" to write the responses students give. Ideas for names and descriptions include Immanuel, Almighty God, the way, the truth, and the life, the bread of life, etc.

At the end of this exercise, add the name Son of God to the list (or circle it if it is already there). Tell the class that today we will explore more descriptions with special attention given to the name Son of God.

INTO THE WORD

Explain that this quarter's study is a survey of the New Testament. The first four lessons highlight the basic gospel story, including Jesus' birth, life, death, and resurrection. Today, we see a wonderful snapshot of his character.

Ask the students to read Hebrews 1:1-4 and Matthew 16:13-23 and to list every name or description of Jesus they can find. This task may be accomplished in small groups, in pairs, or as a whole class. List the answers on another poster. Note: This exercise is included in the student book. Answers should include *his [God's] Son, heir of all things, he made the universe, the radiance of God's glory, the exact representation of his being, sustaining all things, provided purification for our sins, sits at the right hand of the Majesty, superior to the angels, has a superior name, Son of Man, Christ, Son of the living God,* and *Lord.*

Ask the class to explain the significance of each name or description. Refer to Scripture or the lesson commentary as needed. Then discuss the following questions.

1. Why did some think Jesus was John the Baptist, Elijah, Jeremiah, or one of the prophets? (See Matthew 14:1, 2; Malachi 4:5, 6; John 3:2.)

2. Of all the descriptions of Jesus given in our text, why is Peter's response "the Son of the living God" so special?

What is the great significance of Jesus as God's Son? (As Son of God, he is divine—equal with God. His word is greater than that of the prophets; see Hebrews 1:1, 2.)

3. Within 500 years of Jesus' ascension, distorted views of Jesus began to arise. Some denied that Jesus was God, saying that Jesus was only a man. Others denied that Jesus was human and insisted that Jesus, being God, couldn't really have suffered and died. What ramifications do these views have for the Christian faith? (If Jesus were a mere man, he would have been sinful as we are. He could not atone for sin unless he were sinless; see 2 Corinthians 5:21. If he were God and not man, he also could not atone for sin; see Hebrews 4:15.)

4. The Arians believed there was a "level of being" between humans and God. They saw Jesus as inferior to the Father, though superior to human beings. Why is this view of Jesus inadequate? (Review the commentary notes on Hebrews 1:2, 3; Matthew 16:16.)

5. Our lesson commentator says that in Peter's confession, he was saying that Jesus is no mere mortal. He is God in the flesh. Why would this become the premise upon which Jesus would build his church? (Jesus is fully God, having existed eternally and having the power and nature of God. He was also fully human, experiencing all human emotions and temptations. In order for him to complete God's plan of salvation, he had to be both God and man.)

Ask a volunteer to read John 8:39-59. Ask, "Why were the Jews going to stone Jesus?" (They accused him of blasphemy because he claimed to be equal with God. It is on that basis that we must accept Jesus—or else we must reject him as a liar!)

INTO LIFE

Give each student a sheet of paper or a 3x5 card with the following question written on it: "Suppose you were asked by a non-Christian friend, 'Who is Jesus?' In light of today's study, what would you say? List five to ten key views you now hold about Jesus that would be important for your friend to know." Ask class members to work on this project in pairs. After the project, allow a few students to share their answers with the whole class.

Challenge each class member to identify a friend with whom he or she will try to create an opportunity to share these convictions about Jesus.

Ask the pairs that worked together to share these names and pray for each other's commitment.

God's Redemptive Scheme:
"Easy as 1 . . . 2 . . . 3!"

Look at verses 1-3 of Hebrews 1. Can you summarize God's redemptive scheme with three basic truths taken from those verses respectively?

1. God _____.

_____.

2. God _____.

_____.

3. The Son _____.

_____.

Who Is the Son?

Jesus' question of Matthew 16:13 is still *the* relevant question, a question each person *must* answer. Often the question is answered wrongly. But the two texts of today's study give correct answers. Make the two lists suggested here.

WRONG ANSWERS	RIGHT ANSWERS

THE GOSPEL OF JESUS CHRIST

LESSON 2

WHY TEACH THIS LESSON?

"And that's the gospel truth!" people sometimes glibly declare as they defend their own credibility. The origin of that saying can be traced to the early believers who announced the Good News with full confidence in its veracity. Until recent years, most people accepted the reliability of the gospel records without question.

Today, perhaps more than in previous eras, the "death, burial and resurrection" of Jesus needs to be validated. A strong defense of the gospel as history, not myth or legend, should be made by those who believe it to be "the power of God for salvation." Seekers after truth need to be persuaded by the Christian evidences that the biographical accounts of Jesus' life and ministry are absolutely true, inspired by God. That is the purpose of this lesson.

INTRODUCTION

A. PASSING THE FAITH ALONG

Have you ever watched a relay race? The most important part of the race is the passing of the baton. No matter how speedy the team members, a fumbled baton is almost certain to cost them the race. For this reason, relay teams spend hours practicing the passing of the baton.

Most of us have something we wish to pass on to our children. Perhaps it is property, money, or family heirlooms. However, the most important item to pass on is our faith. We owe much to the writers of the New Testament. They and their colleagues have given us a clear picture of Jesus. We can decide whether or not to believe them, but we cannot say that we don't know what they believed. Even those who do not believe must come to the conclusion that these men believed in Jesus with all their hearts. They knew Jesus, they were certain of who he is, and they wanted others to know of their certainty. The job now belongs to us. We have to make sure that the message is passed on to the next generation. Let's not drop the baton!

Last week's lesson dealt with the identity of Jesus as God's Son. This week we look at the substance of the apostolic preaching about Jesus. We will seek to learn what the early preachers told their audiences about Jesus. What was the message that "caused trouble all over the world" (Acts 17:6)?

B. LESSON BACKGROUND

The New Testament writers were insistent on establishing the truth of their message. They wanted people to know that Jesus was real, not a creation of their imaginations. They wanted to confirm that people saw, heard, and touched him. Today's lesson looks at three texts from three different writers, who each in his own way sought to provide evidence of the reality of Jesus. The first witness is Luke. Known as "our dear friend Luke, the doctor" (Colossians 4:14), Luke may

DEVOTIONAL READING:
COLOSSIANS 1:15-20

LESSON SCRIPTURE:
LUKE 1:1-4; 1 CORINTHIANS 15:1-4; 1 JOHN 1:1-4

PRINTED TEXT:
LUKE 1:1-4; 1 CORINTHIANS 15:1-4; 1 JOHN 1:1-4

LESSON AIMS

After this lesson a student should be able to:

1. Summarize the testimony of Luke, Paul, and John regarding the gospel.

2. Tell why the historical foundation of the gospel makes it worthy of our acceptance and belief.

3. Give thanks to God for the firm foundation of our faith.

KEY VERSE

We proclaim to you what we have seen and heard, so that you also may have fellowship with us. And our fellowship is with the Father and with his Son, Jesus Christ. —1 John 1:3

have been a convert of the apostle Paul. In Philemon 24, he is listed among Paul's "fellow workers." Luke is also the author of the book of Acts.

The second witness is the apostle Paul himself. Paul had been reared outside of Palestine but was well acquainted with the Jewish faith and traditions. He was educated by the great rabbi Gamaliel (Acts 22:3), and was also a Pharisee (Philippians 3:5). Paul was not one of the original twelve apostles. In fact, he was at first violently hostile to the Christian cause (Acts 26:9-11). But Jesus called him to become an apostle to the Gentile (non-Jewish) world (Acts 26:12-18). Paul was eminently qualified for this task because he was well educated, knew the Scriptures well, and had lived in the Gentile world. He wrote more of the New Testament than any other writer.

Our third witness is the apostle John, known as the beloved apostle. He was one of the first of Jesus' disciples along with his brother, James, and his fishing partners, Peter and Andrew. John was part of Jesus' "inner circle"; he, along with Peter and James, witnessed certain events that the other disciples did not (Luke 8:51; 9:28; Mark 14:33). He stood with Jesus' mother at the cross as Jesus was dying (John 19:25-27). It appears that he was the last of the apostles to die, yet we shall see that his writing reveals a knowledge of Jesus that had deepened, not diminished, over the years.

I. LUKE'S TESTIMONY (LUKE 1:1-4)

Luke's testimony is contained in the prologue to his Gospel, in which he sought to establish for the record the historical accuracy of his account.

A. RECEIVED FROM EYEWITNESSES (vv. 1, 2)

1. Many have undertaken to draw up an account of the things that have been fulfilled among us.

While we generally think of four Gospels, Luke writes that *many* in his day had *undertaken to draw up an account of the things that have been fulfilled among us.* Just what records did he have in mind? There is no way of knowing. Was he referring to the Gospels we have in our Bibles? They may be included, but Luke surely was also including some accounts that were not inspired and have not been passed down to us. The implication here is that not all the many accounts were trustworthy, so Luke took in hand to provide an orderly account so that Theophilus and others could "know the certainty" (v. 4) of the facts of the gospel.

Each of the four Gospels had a particular theme and point of view. Each writer organized his material to make a specific point. While much of the information in Luke can be found in Matthew and Mark, Luke had certain themes he wanted to explore and a particular method that he wanted to employ. The inspiration of Scripture still allows the individual writer the use of his own personality and writing style. Notice that in Luke's case (see verse 2), the Holy Spirit inspired him to talk to eyewitnesses. The doctrine of inspiration does not require that every word of Scripture be supplied by God directly. Inspiration is the process by which God guarded the words that were written, whether they came by revelation from God, from the author's memory or research, or from another source. Together, revelation and inspiration have produced for us a Bible that is reliable and trustworthy, completely inerrant in the original manuscripts.

2. Just as they were handed down to us by those who from the first were eyewitnesses and servants of the word.

Who were the *eyewitnesses* to whom Luke refers? Surely the apostles must be included among them. In Acts 6 the apostles delegated the care of the needy widows to seven men of sterling character so that they could devote themselves

WHAT DO YOU THINK?

Luke notes that there were many accounts of Jesus' life. Four inspired ones are included in the New Testament. How does the presence of more than one Gospel encourage your faith? What is gained by having more than one account of any event, that we would not have with just one account? Would we have more or less reason to believe? Would we have a greater or lesser perspective of what happened? Why?

to prayer and to the "ministry of the word" (Acts 6:4). They were, then, *servants of the word.* No doubt there were other eyewitnesses as well. Luke could easily have spoken to Mary, the mother of Jesus, and others of the women who supported Jesus' ministry (Luke 8:2, 3). He could have talked to Jesus' brothers.

Those who view the stories of Jesus as legends or myths have to reckon with the brief period of time between when the events took place and when the written works began to appear. There were people alive who could verify the truthfulness of the accounts. Matthew, Mark, and Luke were written approximately thirty years after Jesus' death. It takes much longer than thirty years to create a legend.

WHERE ARE THE CRITICS?

Imagine that you picked up the newspaper tomorrow and saw a headline that read, "Preacher Raises Dead Elephant Back to Life." Wouldn't you be a bit skeptical? Wouldn't you have doubts?

Well, then, imagine as you continued reading that you discovered that the person making the incredible claims was your preacher, and that this miracle was allegedly done in your home church at a time when you know you were present. Wouldn't you let the newspaper and everyone else know, "Hey, I was there! My preacher didn't raise a dead elephant back to life!" And if your preacher started appearing on talk shows and news programs, and people seemed to be buying his story, wouldn't you raise some strong objections? Of course you would!

An important part of the credibility of the life, miracles, and resurrection of Jesus is the absence of the critics. Eyewitnesses wrote down their records of Jesus' life, and these have been preserved for us in the Bible. These records circulated soon enough after the events themselves that others could have stepped forward and challenged these claims if they were not true. The silence of the critics testifies loudly to the accuracy of the eyewitnesses' reports. —G. A.

B. AN ORDERLY ACCOUNT (vv. 3, 4)

3. *Therefore, since I myself have carefully investigated everything from the beginning, it seemed good also to me to write an orderly account for you, most excellent Theophilus.*

Luke claims that he had *carefully investigated everything from the beginning.* He gathered information by talking to the apostles and other witnesses concerning the events of Christ's birth, life, death, and resurrection. Luke was also determined to write *an orderly account.* We do not know if this means chronological order or thematic order. Slight differences in the arrangement of events in the Gospels make chronology difficult to determine with much precision. Luke's Gospel seems to be mostly chronological, with a few exceptions.

Luke was writing to a man named *Theophilus.* Who was he? The name *Theophilus* means "friend of God" or "lover of God." Many Bible students believe that this was a name for all friends and lovers of God wherever they may be. If these students are right, then *Theophilus* simply represents all Christians. Others suggest that Theophilus was an otherwise unknown Christian who was the recipient of Luke's account of Jesus' life as well as his account of the early church found in Acts. There is even a suggestion that Theophilus may have been a Roman official connected with Paul's trial in Rome. Those who hold this position believe that Theophilus was involved in Paul's defense in court, and needed an orderly account of the life of Jesus in order to learn more about the Christian message.

Luke uses the title *most excellent* in referring to Theophilus. Such a title would normally be used for an official (see Acts 23:26), or some other person of great prominence. Perhaps Theophilus was a benefactor who supported Luke in the production of his writings.

WHAT DO YOU THINK?

We now know of several apocryphal gospels—spurious accounts of Jesus' life that contain obvious errors and exaggerations. What reasons can we give for trusting that the New Testament accounts of Jesus are believable? Look at who the Gospel writers were, what their relationship to Jesus was, and what they themselves stated they were trying to do. What criticisms of their accounts might have been made by unbelievers? What would they have said in their defense against such critics?

HOW TO SAY IT

Corinth. KOR-inth.
Corinthians. Kor-IN-thee-unz.
Damascus. Duh-MASS-kus.
Gamaliel. Guh-MAY-lee-ul.
Gnosticism. NAHSS-tih-sizz-um.
Gnostics. NAHSS-tiks.
Pharisee. FAIR-ih-see.
Theophilus. Thee-AHF-ih-luss.

4. So that you may know the certainty of the things you have been taught.

Here it appears that Theophilus knew something of Jesus but needed to be assured of the *things* about which he had been *taught*. Perhaps he was a believer who needed an accurate standard by which to measure all that he was hearing about Jesus. In the biblical records, we too have an accurate standard by which to measure the teachings of those who claim to be spiritual guides.

II. PAUL'S TESTIMONY (1 CORINTHIANS 15:1-4)

Paul's testimony is found toward the end of his first letter to the church at Corinth. It is part of his teaching concerning the basic facts of the gospel, of which some Corinthians seemed unsure. This troubled church needed advice in many areas, but they needed special help with their doctrine.

A. THE POWER OF THE GOSPEL (vv. 1, 2)

1. Now, brothers, I want to remind you of the gospel I preached to you, which you received and on which you have taken your stand.

Paul reminds the Corinthians of *the gospel* he had *preached* to them. The word gospel means "good news" and is related to the Greek word from which our English word "evangelism" comes. Paul says that this is a gospel that had been *received*. In other words, the Corinthians had responded to the message about Jesus. It was also a gospel in which they could *stand*. It was something in which they had placed their total confidence. It was not a new message to the Corinthians, but they needed to be reminded of what it had accomplished in their lives.

2. By this gospel you are saved, if you hold firmly to the word I preached to you. Otherwise, you have believed in vain.

Here Paul describes the gospel as that which *saved* the Corinthians. However, their responsibilities were not completed; they were to *hold firmly* to what Paul had *preached*, or else they will have *believed in vain*. Such warnings to saved people are found in other portions of the New Testament (Colossians 1:21-23; Hebrews 6:4-6; 2 Peter 1:10; 3:17).

B. THE PERSON OF THE GOSPEL (vv. 3, 4)

3. For what I received I passed on to you as of first importance: that Christ died for our sins according to the Scriptures.

Not only had the Corinthians received the gospel (v. 1); Paul himself had *received* it. Paul was not one of Jesus' original twelve apostles. He was, however, qualified to be an apostle, since he had seen the resurrected Lord when Jesus appeared to him on the road to Damascus (Acts 9:1-9). Paul writes of receiving the gospel message "by revelation from Jesus Christ" (Galatians 1:12).

What is the substance of this gospel? First, it centers on the death of Jesus Christ on the cross. Paul says that this death happened *according to the Scriptures*. For Paul *the Scriptures* meant the Old Testament, particularly those portions that predicted the death of Jesus. No doubt he had in mind passages such as Isaiah 53 that foretold the suffering that Jesus experienced.

This death had a specific purpose: *Christ died for our sins*. The word translated *sins* pictures an archer missing the mark. Whether sins of omission or commission, all sins involve missing God's mark. Jesus, the perfect Lamb of God who never missed that mark, died in the place of all persons, who without exception have missed it (Romans 3:23). The cross thus allows God to be both loving (by saving lost mankind) and just (by punishing sin) at the same time.

4. That he was buried, that he was raised on the third day according to the Scriptures.

WHAT DO YOU THINK?

Luke spoke of "eyewitnesses" and "servants of the word" who delivered the news of Jesus to others. Paul also speaks of preaching the gospel that he received. Delivery of the gospel seems as important as receiving it! How did you first receive the news of Jesus? Why did you believe it to be accurate? What are you doing to deliver it faithfully to others?

The Bible is now widely available. Even so, many people rely only upon what they hear about the Bible, or upon what they are taught. What does this mean for the church in terms of its teachers? its missionaries?

Paul also stresses that Jesus *was buried*. Why would he bother with this detail? Perhaps Paul was countering arguments we sometimes hear today—that Jesus was not really dead, that perhaps he merely "swooned" on the cross. Of course, if there had never been an actual death and burial, then the resurrection loses its significance. This is the next important fact of the gospel: Jesus *was raised*.

This resurrection, notes Paul, was also accomplished *according to the Scriptures*. What Old Testament Scriptures speak of a resurrection? General references to this can be found in Job 19:25, 26; Psalm 16:10; and Isaiah 53:10, 11. As for being raised *on the third day*, Paul may have been thinking of the words of Hosea 6:2 or of Jonah 1:17. In subsequent verses (5-8), Paul lists six specific appearances of the risen Christ. Adding this information to the Gospels, we have a total of at least eleven separate appearances. That is far too many for the resurrection to be dismissed as the product of mere rumor, wishful thinking, or mass hallucination.

ONLY JESUS CAN RESCUE

If you were in a boat out on the open sea and fell overboard, but didn't know how to swim, what would you want your friends in the boat to do? Certainly their encouragement to "hang in there" and "stay above the water" would be welcome. They could even model for you how to swim or how to tread water. They could tell you stories about how they fell overboard one time and survived. But sooner or later, wouldn't you hope that they would throw you a life preserver? At some point you would have to be rescued, because your situation is a matter of life and death.

In 1 Corinthians 15:1-4, Paul tells us that the substance of the gospel message is the death, burial, and resurrection of Jesus Christ. Yet many times in our witnessing it seems as if this message is noticeably absent. We may talk about the exciting church we're a part of and all that is happening there. We may talk about how Jesus' wisdom for living has helped us find meaning and significance as a single person, or in our marriage, or in our family. We may talk about how the power of Jesus Christ has helped us overcome addictive behaviors, or a sinful past, or a painful season of grief. And there's a time to talk about all of that.

But unless there is a time where we get down to basics and talk about the cross and the empty tomb, we are not sharing the true gospel. Sooner or later we've got to throw people a life preserver—because all that can save a person from drowning for eternity is the death, burial, and resurrection of Jesus Christ!   —G. A.

III. JOHN'S TESTIMONY (1 JOHN 1:1-4)

John's testimony concerning Jesus is taken from the first four verses of his first epistle. Although the name of the author does not appear in the letter, there are sufficient similarities in language and style between this letter and the Gospel of John to indicate that the apostle John was the writer.

A. I HAVE SEEN HIM (v. 1)

1. *That which was from the beginning, which we have heard, which we have seen with our eyes, which we have looked at and our hands have touched—this we proclaim concerning the Word of life.*

The opening of John's first letter is reminiscent of the opening of his Gospel. His Gospel begins with, "In the beginning was the Word," and his epistle commences with, *That which was from the beginning*. In both cases John is stressing the eternal nature of the Son of God. His Gospel also stresses that "the Word became flesh and made his dwelling among us" (John 1:14). Here in this letter he describes Jesus as that *which we have heard, which we have seen with our eyes, which we have looked at and our hands have touched*.

DAILY BIBLE READINGS

Monday, Dec. 7—An Orderly Account (Luke 1:1-4)

Tuesday, Dec. 8—The Good News Paul Proclaimed (1 Corinthians 15:1-4)

Wednesday, Dec. 9—That Which We Have Seen and Heard (1 John 1:1-4)

Thursday, Dec. 10—Those Who Do God's Will (1 John 2:15-29)

Friday, Dec. 11—We Are Children of God (1 John 3:1-10)

Saturday, Dec. 12—We Should Love One Another (1 John 3:11-24)

Sunday, Dec. 13—God Is Love (1 John 4:13-21)

PRAYER

Dear Father, help me not only to pass the faith along to the next generation, but to appreciate the great heritage that my spiritual ancestors have passed down to me. Although I have not seen Jesus with physical eyes, I have seen him with the eyes of faith. May I never lose the vision. In Jesus' name. Amen.

WHAT DO YOU THINK?

How does it add confidence to your faith to know that John and the other apostles were such close companions of Jesus? How does it help you to know that almost every one of the apostles went to a martyr's death defending the truth of those claims?

One may ask, "What is the difference between saying *we have seen with our eyes* and *we have looked at*?" The second phrase is more intense. A casual glance may account for the report, "We have seen," but a steady gaze is suggested by, "We have looked at." It may carry the connotation of looking intently or looking with understanding.

John wants his readers to know assuredly that Jesus was no legend or myth. Just as Jesus is called "the Word" in John's Gospel, here John calls him *the Word of life*. John's emphasis on seeing, looking at, and touching Jesus may have been an attempt to counter an early form of false doctrine that came to be called Gnosticism. The Gnostics held many odd beliefs that challenged certain essentials of the Christian faith. Among their views was the idea that all flesh is absolutely evil, and that Jesus, if holy, could not have appeared in human flesh. John denies such teaching and reminds his readers that Jesus had a real body. He was not a phantom.

B. I HAVE SHARED HIM (v. 2)

2. *The life appeared; we have seen it and testify to it, and we proclaim to you the eternal life, which was with the Father and has appeared to us.*

Here Jesus is called *the life*. This is partly because of his resurrection, but also because he is the source of life. This life was *with the Father*, but has now been given to human beings. It is *eternal life*, inseparably connected to Jesus himself. Just as Jesus is the Word made flesh, he is eternal life made flesh.

C. I HAVE FELLOWSHIP WITH HIM AND YOU (vv. 3, 4)

3. *We proclaim to you what we have seen and heard, so that you also may have fellowship with us. And our fellowship is with the Father and with his Son, Jesus Christ.*

The partnership, or *fellowship*, that we experience with other Christians is a result of the testimony concerning Jesus being passed from believer to believer. We who are alive today have not *seen and heard* Jesus as John did. We accept the testimony of eyewitnesses such as he, and this brings us into fellowship with the *Father*, the *Son*, and all others who have fellowship with them.

4. *We write this to make our joy complete.*

John could never experience true and complete *joy* unless others shared in the knowledge he had of Christ. Those who know Jesus and have accepted his offer of salvation can always experience a joyous fellowship with each other (even when they are meeting for the first time!).

CONCLUSION

Some people try to place Jesus in the same category with legends such as King Arthur and Robin Hood. Luke, Paul, and John will not let us do that. It takes hundreds of years to build a legend. All of the New Testament was written within the lifetime of those who had knowledge of the events recorded therein. Many could have stepped forward to counter any false information. Had there been any "cleverly invented stories" (2 Peter 1:16) within the early church's preaching, they would have been exposed, given the hostility of so many to the church's message.

Clearly something dramatic and wonderful happened to the disciples. We may choose not to believe what Luke, Paul, and John have written, but no one should do so unless and until he has examined the testimony of men such as these. Jesus is a person rooted in history. Few if any modern scholars, no matter how skeptical, doubt that Jesus of Nazareth existed. They may argue over how much they trust the biblical account of his life, or whether he was who he claimed to be. But there is no way to escape him. Jesus has changed history. He has changed countless lives. He is "the real thing."

Discovery Learning

This page contains an alternate lesson plan emphasizing learning activities. Classes desiring such student involvement will find these suggestions helpful. The next page is a reproducible activity page to further enhance discovery learning.

LEARNING GOALS

After this lesson each student will be able to:

1. Summarize the testimony of Luke, Paul, and John regarding the gospel.

2. Tell why the historical foundation of the gospel makes it worthy of our acceptance and belief.

3. Give thanks to God for the firm foundation of our faith.

INTO THE LESSON

Ask the class to suppose you had a book in which the author claimed to have seen a working time machine. "Time travel is no longer science fiction," the author claims. "It is here!" Ask, "What would it take for you to believe the story?" Different kinds of evidence probably will be demanded, but the basic source will be testimony from witnesses. Who else has seen it? What tests have been run to verify the performance of the machine? What credentials do the people testing it have that we can believe them?

People want the same thing when it comes to believing in Jesus. Who saw him and can verify his existence? Who witnessed his actions, and what credentials do the witnesses have that we should believe them?

The Bible offers many witnesses to Jesus. Our lesson today will consider the testimony of three of them. One was an eyewitness and very close associate of Jesus. One was an unbeliever who became convinced when Jesus made a dramatic appearance to him. And one was a careful historian who spoke with eyewitnesses and carefully researched the matter. (See if the class can identify the three witnesses from those descriptions before they know the texts for today's lesson.)

INTO THE WORD

Choose three good readers to read aloud today's Scripture texts: Luke 1:1-4; 1 Corinthians 15:1-4; 1 John 1:1-4. Then provide the students with the following list of statements. Ask the class to read each statement and to match it with the witness (Luke, Paul, or John) who might likely have made the statement. (Answers are provided here for your convenience.) Have the students work on the activity individually or in small groups; then go over the list together. Use information from the commentary to explain or reinforce important points raised.

1. Many people have written about the life of our Lord, but some of those accounts are not accurate and may cause confusion. I wrote to establish a certain record, one that people could count on. (Luke)

2. We know what we're talking about. We saw Jesus; we heard him; we touched him. You can believe our testimony about him. (John)

3. I wasn't there with Jesus, but I talked to a lot of people who were. (Luke)

4. My preaching is just what the Lord told me and what the Scriptures affirm was to happen: Jesus died, was buried, and rose again. (Paul)

5. Jesus was no mere man. He existed from the beginning. He was with the Father before, and then was made known to us in human form. (John)

6. The good news about Jesus has saving power when it is received and believed. (Paul)

7. I have a very clear understanding of the details of Jesus' life, so I have written an orderly account of it. (Luke)

8. I have not written a "Gospel," but I preach the gospel all over the world—just as I preached it to you in Corinth. (Paul)

9. Won't it be grand when our fellowship with one another and our fellowship with the Father and with Jesus are made perfect in Heaven? That is eternal life! (John)

INTO LIFE

Remind the class that Luke tells us of many other testimonies and writers not included in the Scriptures. Many of these were not inspired, but were the natural expressions of believers wanting to share with others what they had come to believe.

That process continues to this day. Songwriters in particular write their testimonies, and we can enjoy them and use them to express something of our own faith. Ask the students to name some of their favorite songs about Jesus. (Sing a few of these hymns and choruses if you have time.)

One hymn that summarizes much of what we have been discussing is "How Firm a Foundation," by Norman J. Clayton. This hymn celebrates the certainty we can have for our faith because of the testimony of the Bible. Close the class period with prayers of thanks for the Scriptures and with a singing of this hymn.

Gospel = ?

The word *gospel* means "good news" and is related to the Greek word from which the English word *evangelism* derives. In the following word table, select a word from each column and see how many thoughts or "definitions" of *gospel* you can find.

G	O	S	P	E	L
GENEROSITY	OF	SALVATION	PASSION	EFFECT	LAW
GIFT	OBEDIENCE	SATISFY	PATIENCE	ENABLE	LEARNER
GLAD	OFFERS	SAVE	PEACE	ENCOURAGE	LIBERTY
GLORIFY	ONLY	SEEK	PENITENCE	END	LIFE
GOD	OMNIPOTENCE	SIN	PEOPLE	ESTABLISH	LIGHT
GOD'S	OPEN	SONG	PLEAD	ETERNAL	LIMITLESS
GOOD	OPTION	SPIRIT	PLEASE	EVANGELIZE	LISTEN
GRACE	OVERWHELM	STILL	PRAISE	EVERYONE	LOVE

Feel free to change word endings as you work. Write one of your "best" efforts here:

_____

(Sample: "Grace overwhelms sin; please evangelize learners!")

Credible Witnesses

Luke, Paul, and John—in today's text selections—stand as credible witnesses to the gospel story. Draw lines across from each witness to the truths each emphasizes.

LUKE—

PAUL—

JOHN—

- ○ saw with his own eyes
- ○ got eyewitness accounts
- ○ "received" revelation
- ○ carefully investigated
- ○ wanted believers to be certain
- ○ preached what he wrote
- ○ equates gospel with life
- ○ equates gospel with salvation

THE BIRTH OF JESUS

LESSON 3

DEVOTIONAL READING:
ISAIAH 9:2-7
LESSON SCRIPTURE:
LUKE 2:1-20
PRINTED TEXT:
LUKE 2:1-17

Dec
20

WHY TEACH THIS LESSON?

Why, indeed! These texts get far more than average attention in church settings. Is it necessary to rehearse these well-known facts annually? Yes, for two reasons.

Every Christmas season finds more people attuned to the message of the Gospel than at other times. The general knowledge that Christmas began as a recognition of Christ's birth still opens doors that we must walk through!

Second, this time of year also provides so many rivals that we need to remind people of the truth. Christmas cards and TV specials offer many humanistic explanations of the "true meaning of Christmas"—family, love, peace, giving, and a host of other good and noble concepts. These fall short, however, of the gospel story of a "Savior" who is "Christ the Lord." That is why you will teach this lesson!

INTRODUCTION

A. HERE WE ARE AGAIN

Did you hear about the man who took his preacher to task for preaching on the same subjects over and over again? He said, "All you ever talk about are the birth of Jesus and the resurrection of Jesus." The man quickly turned red when his wife said, "That's because the only times you come are on Christmas and Easter!"

Why do we need to talk about Jesus' birth again? It is probably the most familiar part of the Bible. We revisit it year after year at Christmastime. Nevertheless, there are many traditions that have grown up around Christmas that are not really biblical. The story seems so familiar, but occasionally we discover that we do not really know it as well as we thought. It is important to remind ourselves of the significance of Jesus' birth and its implications for today's confused world.

In an unassuming way, Luke tells us how God came down, not only in human form, but as a baby. Have we become so used to hearing this truth that it has lost some of its wonder? It is good for us to step back at this time of the year and take a fresh look at the Christmas story. Think of what it means: God on earth. God in Bethlehem. God in a manger. God on a cross. These are some of the mysteries of what we call the incarnation.

Besides being appropriate for this Sunday before Christmas, today's lesson is a fitting follow-up on last week's lesson, which stressed the trustworthiness of the New Testament record concerning Jesus. Today we return to that specific time and place in history when God entered our world in the person of Jesus.

B. LESSON BACKGROUND

Virtually all we know about Jesus' birth comes from Matthew and Luke. Mark begins with a brief description of John the Baptist's ministry and jumps immediately to Jesus' baptism. John begins by considering Jesus' preexistence. It is Matthew and Luke who lead us to Bethlehem. Matthew gives us the story of the angelic appearances to Joseph, the visit of the wise men, and the journey of Mary, Joseph, and Jesus to Egypt. Luke records the birth of John the Baptist, the announcement to Mary by the angel Gabriel that she would become the mother of God's Son, and the account of the birth itself in Bethlehem.

LESSON AIMS

After this lesson students should be able to:

1. Retell the familiar story of Jesus' birth, as recorded in Luke.

2. Explain the significance of the details reported by Luke.

3. Commit themselves to telling others the good news of the Savior—as the shepherds did.

KEY VERSE

Today in the town of David a Savior has been born to you; he is Christ the Lord.   —Luke 2:11

The visual for lesson 3 illustrates the angel's message that a Savior has been born. His light is not just for the little town of Bethlehem, but for the whole world.

WHAT DO YOU THINK?

In Caesar's decree we see a human explanation for why Jesus was born in Bethlehem. Of course, we know God's providence was at work to arrange for his prophecies to be fulfilled. We can see that both explanations are accurate, depending on your point of view. One is just more limited than the other; the second takes the larger view, the bigger picture. How can you convince the skeptic that this larger view is true?

Do you think knowing this bigger picture is a result of faith—or the source of it?

How should we view the interaction of the human and the divine in the events of life?

Luke's is the only account that includes the visit of the shepherds near Bethlehem. One of the unique characteristics of Luke's Gospel is his interest in common people and those whom society regarded as outcasts. Only Luke mentions the parable of the good Samaritan (10:25-37), the parable of the prodigal son (15:11-32), the story of the rich man and Lazarus the beggar (16:19-31), the cleansing of the ten lepers (17:11-19), and Jesus' meeting with the despised tax collector Zacchaeus (19:1-10). Shepherds were looked upon with disdain by many, because they tended to be a rather crude group of men. In addition, their work with animals often left them ritually unclean.

Even though many details in the Christmas story are very familiar to us, let us see if we can recapture what it would be like to hear this story for the very first time. Let us never lose our sense of wonder and celebration at the "good news of great joy," that to us a Savior is born!

I. SETTING OF JESUS' BIRTH (LUKE 2:1-7)

A. THE RULERS (vv. 1, 2)

1. In those days Caesar Augustus issued a decree that a census should be taken of the entire Roman world.

As a careful historian, Luke fixes the birth of Jesus in a particular historical context. He places the event during the reign of *Caesar Augustus*, who was the first emperor of Rome. The word *Caesar* means "ruler" and became the title used by subsequent Roman rulers. The name *Augustus* means "exalted"; thus the first Roman emperor was designated "exalted ruler."

A *census . . . of the entire Roman world* was taken for taxation purposes. This world would have included any territories under Rome's control. Some skeptics have claimed that Luke is in error because such an empire-wide census is not recorded in Roman history. But this is not a valid reason to conclude that it never happened. Such a practice would have been consistent with Roman policy in occupied territory. In fact, there is a reference to another census, taken later than the one mentioned here, which Luke also notes in Acts 5:37.

Isn't it ironic that as renowned as Caesar Augustus was, and as important as he thought he was, he is probably most famous for what is said about him in connection with the birth of Jesus in a remote part of his empire? Truly, "God chose the weak things of the world to shame the strong" (1 Corinthians 1:27).

2. (This was the first census that took place while Quirinius was governor of Syria.)

Some say that Jesus could not possibly have been born *while Quirinius was governor of Syria*, for there are non-biblical records of his being governor later. However, there is evidence that suggests Quirinius held the office of governor for two terms, and the first coincides with the time of Jesus' birth. Luke's account was written within a generation of the event itself. Luke, who has already spoken of his concern for careful research (Luke 1:1-4), would not likely have included this detail if he did not have a sound basis for doing so. Justin Martyr in A.D. 140 claimed to have documentation to prove that Jesus was born under Quirinius.

B. THE COUPLE (vv. 3-5)

3, 4. And everyone went to his own town to register. So Joseph also went up from the town of Nazareth in Galilee to Judea, to Bethlehem the town of David, because he belonged to the house and line of David.

Joseph lived in a region called *Galilee*, a name that means "circle." The word describes a cluster of small towns that formed a rough circle near the Sea of Galilee. *Nazareth* was a small town in Galilee, covering probably no more than seven acres in Jesus' day.

From Nazareth, Joseph and Mary traveled approximately eighty miles to *Bethlehem*, a small town just five miles south of Jerusalem, to *register* for the census. Such a trip normally took about three days, perhaps longer for one in Mary's condition. The journey was necessary since Mary and Joseph were both descendants of David, and Bethlehem—being King David's hometown (1 Samuel 16:1, 13)—was considered *the town of David*. Perhaps this journey also served as a means of escaping the wagging tongues of those in Nazareth who may have had their own theories of the cause of Mary's pregnancy.

The name *Bethlehem* means "house of bread." It was a fitting birthplace for one destined to become the Bread of Life.

5. He went there to register with Mary, who was pledged to be married to him and was expecting a child.

Mary . . . was pledged to be married to Joseph. A pledge was considered much more binding than an engagement. If a pledged woman's husband died, she was considered a widow. The problem for Joseph, of course, was Mary's pregnancy during the period while she was pledged. If not for angelic intervention, he would have "divorced her quietly" (Matthew 1:19).

By this time Mary was *expecting a child*. Just how far along she was at the time of the journey to Bethlehem is uncertain. The biblical text simply describes her as pregnant, with nothing to suggest how many months remained until the time of birth. The context implies that the time was fairly close.

C. THE TIME (vv. 6, 7)

6. While they were there, the time came for the baby to be born.

While in Bethlehem, Mary gave birth. This is what had been prophesied about the birth of the Messiah (Micah 5:2). "The time had fully come" (Galatians 4:4).

7. And she gave birth to her firstborn, a son. She wrapped him in cloths and placed him in a manger, because there was no room for them in the inn.

When Jesus was born, he was *wrapped in cloths*. This was the usual procedure with newborns. These bands of cloths were tightly wrapped to provide the infant with warmth, protect his extremities, and provide a sense of security. Thus Jesus was treated like any other infant in his day. Unlike any other newborn, he was *placed . . . in a manger*, which describes a feeding place for the animals. We usually assume that this feeding place was in a stable. Quite possibly it was in a cave.

Mary and Joseph found themselves in such lowly surroundings because *there was no room for them in the inn*. Sometimes the innkeeper is treated in Christmas pageants as cruel and heartless. Luke says nothing of any innkeeper, although most likely there was one. Perhaps he should be commended for finding a quiet, out of the way place where Mary could give birth. Ancient inns were often crowded, noisy places that could be dangerous as well. This may have been especially true on this occasion, given the circumstances that had forced many to make the journey to Bethlehem in compliance with the emperor's decree.

Jesus is referred to as Mary's *firstborn*. This implies that Mary had other children after Jesus. In fact, the Gospels do tell us that Jesus had brothers and sisters (Matthew 13:55, 56; Mark 6:3).

GOD AS A MAN

Radio commentator Paul Harvey says that the story he is asked to repeat most often is about a farmer, his wife, and their young daughter. The mother and little girl attended church, but the father did not. He said he refused to believe in God because it just wasn't reasonable to him that God would come down from Heaven and become a man.

HOW TO SAY IT

Caesar Augustus. SEE-zer Aw-GUS-tus.
Quirinius. Kwih-RIN-ee-us.
Gabriel. GAY-bree-ul.
Immanuel. Ih-MAN-you-el.
Syria. SEAR-e-uh.
Zacchaeus. Zack-KEY-us.

WHAT DO YOU THINK?

Mary laid the infant Jesus in a manger. Apparently, Jesus was born in some kind of stable or corral close to animals. Why do you think God did not intervene to provide a "better" setting for the birth of the Savior? If it had been up to you, how would you have arranged the circumstances of his birth to achieve the greatest effect? In choosing the setting he did, what do you think God was trying to say about his Son?

On the Sunday night before Christmas, the farmer's wife and little girl asked him to attend the children's Christmas program at the church, but he declined. It was bitterly cold when they left, so the farmer sat by the fire in the living room and read the newspaper. Before long he started hearing little thuds on the big picture window—first one, then another, and then another. He went to the window and realized that some birds were trying to get in where it was warm.

So the farmer went out and opened the barn doors so that the birds could get out of the cold, but the birds ignored him. He did all he could to entice them and even drive them in, yet nothing worked. He asked himself, "How can I get those birds into the barn?" Then he thought, "You know, if I could just become a bird, I could lead them in." Just as that thought came to him, the church bells began ringing, and he realized what he had said. He fell to his knees in the barn and prayed, "Oh, dear God, I believe now, because I understand."

God became a little baby that night in Bethlehem so he could lead human beings like us into Heaven.

—G. A.

II. ANNOUNCEMENT OF JESUS' BIRTH (LUKE 2:8-17)

A. THE RECIPIENTS (v. 8)

8. And there were shepherds living out in the fields nearby, keeping watch over their flocks at night.

The story now moves to the *fields* near Bethlehem, where *shepherds* were *keeping watch over their flocks at night*. Some people believe that the birth of Jesus could not have happened anywhere near December 25 because that would be in the rainy season, and shepherds would not be out in the field that time of year. It is possible, however, that these sheep were being raised for use in the temple sacrifices in Jerusalem (since Bethlehem was not far from Jerusalem). In that case these shepherds may well have needed to be in the field throughout the year. Still, the critics may be right. We simply do not know what time of year Jesus was born. Let's just praise God that he was born—of that we can be certain!

It is fascinating to note that God chose to make the announcement of his Son's birth to humble people, not to the wealthy, the powerful, or the famous. Had we been in charge of planning this event, we might have arranged for the Messiah to be born into a king's family, a priest's family, or at least a family of significant wealth and influence. We might have sent angels to announce the birth in Herod's palace or the temple in Jerusalem.

God's ways, however, are not like man's ways (Isaiah 55:8). He had his own plan, and according to that plan it was necessary that Jesus be born to humble people and then announced to humble people. As noted earlier, shepherds were not high on the social ladder and were treated by most as outcasts. The announcement of the gospel came first to the down and out, rather than the high and mighty.

B. THE MESSENGERS (vv. 9-14)

9. An angel of the Lord appeared to them, and the glory of the Lord shone around them, and they were terrified.

The quiet night was dramatically interrupted by *an angel of the Lord*. Perhaps this was the same angel (Gabriel) who made other significant announcements relevant to the birth of Jesus (Luke 1:19, 26). The immediate response to such an angelic messenger was often fear (Mark 16:5, 6; Luke 1:11, 12; Acts 10:3, 4). The shepherds are described as being *terrified*. The Greek text literally says, "They feared a great fear."

10. But the angel said to them, "Do not be afraid. I bring you good news of great joy that will be for all the people.

WHAT DO YOU THINK?

Shepherds existed on one of the lower rungs of the social ladder. God chose to reveal what he was doing, not to the religious establishment, but to these shepherds. Who would be the modern-day equivalent of shepherds (in terms of social class) in your community? What efforts are you or your church making to reach them with the good news?

It makes sense that the angel's first words were *Do not be afraid*, thus responding to the shepherds' terror. The angel had *good news*, not bad, to convey. Furthermore, this good news is for *all the people*. This implies that Jesus will be a universal Savior, sent not for Jews alone, but for the whole world.

11. *"Today in the town of David a Savior has been born to you; he is Christ the Lord."*

Here is the essence of the good news: the world has a *Savior*, who is *Christ the Lord*. The word *Christ* means "Messiah" or "anointed one" and would have been understood by any Jew. The word *Lord* was a title with greater meaning to Gentiles, who would have had no concept of the Jewish Messiah. Once again, Bethlehem is called *the town of David*, because it was King David's hometown. Here in David's town the greatest Son of David *has been born*.

THE SIGNIFICANCE OF THE INSIGNIFICANT

In 1809 Napoleon was sweeping across Europe with blood, destruction, and French rule in his wake. Nothing else that year seemed as significant in the scope of world events as his exploits.

In that year of 1809 many babies were born, but who had time to notice when history was being made by Napoleon? However, during that year William Gladstone and Alfred Tennyson were born in England. Oliver Wendell Holmes and Edgar Allan Poe were born in Massachusetts. A young physician and his wife named their infant son Charles Robert Darwin. And in a Kentucky log cabin Abraham Lincoln was born.

Today only those who are true history buffs can name more than two or three of the battles of Napoleon. But these seemingly insignificant births that so few noticed had an impact that is still felt.

Twenty centuries ago the world was watching Rome in all of its splendor. The Roman Empire stretched from the Atlantic to the Euphrates, and from the Rhine to the Sahara. All eyes were on Caesar Augustus as he demanded a census in order to raise taxes. Who would have even noticed a young Jewish couple making their way to Bethlehem? But while Rome was making history, God was about to arrive. Most of the world would miss this birth of the King of kings.

Today, in the midst of all that we think is so important, let us not overlook the significance of this humble birth.
—G. A.

12. *"This will be a sign to you: You will find a baby wrapped in cloths and lying in a manger."*

The angel gave the shepherds a *sign*. The newborn is *wrapped in cloths and lying in a manger*. The cloths were not particularly unusual (this was the customary practice with infants), but being in a manger was quite out of the ordinary. Only one baby in Bethlehem would fit that description.

13. *Suddenly a great company of the heavenly host appeared with the angel, praising God and saying . . .*

The one *angel* was then joined by *a great company of the heavenly host*. We often think of them as singing their message, but the Bible simply reports that they said it. The angels were *praising God* for the wonderful news that they were privileged to tell the shepherds.

14. *"Glory to God in the highest, and on earth peace to men on whom his favor rests."*

The angels' message proclaimed *glory to God in the highest*, focusing on Heaven's response to God's wondrous gift. The phrase *on earth peace to men on whom his favor rests* seems different from the familiar "on earth peace, good will toward men" of the *King James Version*. Both translations emphasize the *peace* the Messiah has come to bring—a peace "not . . . as the world gives" (John 14:27).

Gracious God, clear away the clutter of this season and close our ears to the sound of the cash register, so that we may truly thank you for the gift of your Son. We thank you for the way in which you sent him. We thank you for those who were the first witnesses. Help us never to lose our sense of awe and wonder at what this season really means. We pray in the name of our Savior, Christ the Lord. Amen.

THOUGHT TO REMEMBER

Christ needs to be born twice. He was born in Bethlehem, and he wants to be born again in your heart.

DAILY BIBLE READINGS

Monday, Dec. 14—John the Baptist's Birth Foretold (Luke 1:5-17)

Tuesday, Dec. 15—Gabriel Visits Mary (Luke 1:26-38)

Wednesday, Dec. 16—"My Spirit Rejoices in God My Savior" (Luke 1:39-55)

Thursday Dec. 17—The Lord's Hand Was With Him (Luke 1:57-66)

Friday, Dec. 18—The Child Grew and Became Strong in Spirit (Luke 1:67-80)

Saturday, Dec. 19—Joseph Went From Nazareth to Bethlehem (Luke 2:1-7)

Sunday, Dec. 20—Good News of Great Joy (Luke 2:8-20)

C. THE RESPONSE (vv. 15-17)

15. When the angels had left them and gone into heaven, the shepherds said to one another, "Let's go to Bethlehem and see this thing that has happened, which the Lord has told us about."

Immediately the *shepherds* determined to travel *to Bethlehem* and investigate the sign given them. They showed admirable discernment in recognizing that what they had witnessed was not a dream or hallucination; it was something *the Lord* had *told* them.

16. So they hurried off and found Mary and Joseph, and the baby, who was lying in the manger.

The shepherds *hurried off,* signifying how important they thought the good news was. It did not take long for them to find *Mary and Joseph, and the baby.* Many of us procrastinate in telling others about Jesus (and we know far more about him than the shepherds did!). Such good news should set our feet running.

17. When they had seen him, they spread the word concerning what had been told them about this child.

These shepherds became evangelists and witnesses as they *spread the word concerning what had been told them about this child.* If it is true that these shepherds were responsible for keeping watch over the temple lambs, then there is truly something special about their being given the first opportunity to visit the Lamb of God who would one day take away the sins of the world.

CONCLUSION

A. I WONDER

Christmas has been so overtaken by the secular dimensions of the holiday that it is easy to lose the sense of wonder that should be associated with it. Even Christians can get caught up in the commercialism of the season, allowing spiritual priorities to take a back seat. Perhaps it would help if we could capture the spirit of the old Christmas carol that says,

> I wonder as I wander out under the sky,
> How Jesus, the Savior, did come for to die
> For poor, ornery people like you and like I—
> I wonder as I wander out under the sky.

We must never allow the Christmas story to be reduced to the level of a fairy tale. If we grasp its reality and its glory, as Luke wanted us to, then we cannot help but be caught up in the wonder of it all. Christmas is a wonderful time of the year, but the most wonderful part about it is what God was doing for us.

B. MOVING IN AT CHRISTMASTIME

On Christmas Eve in 1908, a young seminary student named Toyohiko (Toy-o-hee-ko) Kagawa (Kuh-gah-wuh) moved into the worst slums of Kobe (Ko-bee), Japan. He felt that he could never understand the people and minister to them unless he shared their lot. Soon he was taking in the poor and homeless. Eventually he had to acquire more houses in order to take care of the expanding needs of others. In time Kagawa became synonymous with Christian charity.

It is fitting that Kagawa moved in at Christmastime to minister to the needs of others, for it was at Christmas that God came down to the "slums" of earth to minister to our needs. Who, knowing the joys of Heaven, would voluntarily leave it to live on this planet? The answer is: Someone who loved us more than we can ever comprehend.

Discovery Learning

This page contains an alternate lesson plan emphasizing learning activities. Classes desiring such student involvement will find these suggestions helpful. The next page is a reproducible activity page to further enhance discovery learning.

LEARNING GOALS

After this lesson students should be able to:

1. Retell the familiar story of Jesus' birth, as recorded in Luke.

2. Explain the significance of the details reported by Luke.

3. Commit themselves to telling others the good news of the Savior—as the shepherds did.

INTO THE LESSON

As soon as students arrive, ask each one to complete a worksheet as described below (or refer the student to the appropriate page in the student book, *NIV Bible Student*). The worksheet should have these instructions at the top: "Read Matthew 1:18—2:23 and Luke 1:26-56; 2:1-20. Identify which author tells about the events and people listed below by initialing them as 'M' (Matthew) or 'L' (Luke). If the person or event is not mentioned in the Bible but there is a traditionally held belief about it, mark it 'T' (Tradition)."

Below the heading, list the following (without the answers that are in parentheses): Magi (M), Herod (M), Caesar Augustus (L), the innkeeper (T), Immanuel (M), Mary's donkey (T), the names of the Magi (T), the flight to Egypt (M), an angel appears to Joseph (M), Gabriel appears to Mary (L), cloths (L), the manger (L), the star over a stable (T), Mary's visit with Elizabeth (L), the announcement to the shepherds (L), the little drummer boy (T).

Give the students a few minutes to work; then review the lists for accuracy. Explain that the accounts in Matthew and Luke are the only records we have of Jesus' birth. We need to pay careful attention to what they say so that our celebration of the Lord's birth focuses on the spiritual significance first and foremost.

INTO THE WORD

Read the printed text, asking the students to listen for words or events they do not understand or would like clarified. An alternative to reading the text would be to have an "honored guest" read it by way of an audio or video recording. After the reading, invite the students to ask questions about this text.

Using the lesson commentary, provide clarification on some of the details of the text. The following should be discussed and/or explained:

a. The significance of Caesar Augustus's name.

b. The dating of Jesus' birth.

c. First-century marriage customs, especially how they were "pledged to be married" (v. 5).

d. The purpose of wrapping Jesus in cloths.

e. Why God chose to announce his Son's birth to humble shepherds rather than the rich or the power brokers.

f. The significance of the title "Christ."

INTO LIFE

Explain that the significance of the incarnation of Jesus is often lost in the celebration traditions of Christmas. Ask the class to call out all the Christmas celebration traditions and symbols they can recall (e.g., Christmas tree, fruitcake, gifts). Have a class member list these on a visual. Then review the list and ask the class to cite items on the list that are distinctly related to the incarnation.

Remind the class of the importance of remembering the reason for the celebration. In his book, *The Screwtape Letters*, C. S. Lewis's devil, Screwtape, wrote to his nephew: "I shudder to think what might happen if too many Christians should suddenly remember what Christmas is all about."

Ask the class members to take three or four minutes to write an answer to the question, "What would be the situation of our world if Jesus had not come? Why?" After the project has been completed, ask volunteers to share their thoughts with the entire class.

Next, issue this challenge: "Suppose you were asked to explain the significance of Christmas to a friend. What would you say to him or her?" Ask each student to share his or her thoughts with one other class member.

Remind the students that such an opportunity may present itself in the next few days before Christmas. However, in many situations, we need to create a window of opportunity to speak with a friend or family member about this important subject. Ask each class member to identify someone who needs to know the good news the shepherds heard. Then, ask for ideas on how to create a window of opportunity to share the significance of the incarnation with that person.

In closing, challenge your students to open that window and share the joy of Christ's coming with the persons they have identified.

Historical Marker

If there were a historical marker at the Bethlehem city limit, how might it read regarding the most important thing ever to have happened there? Write it as an objective state historian might.

Consider how it might be different if written by an excited Christian believer. Which one best represents the way you would want it to read? Why?

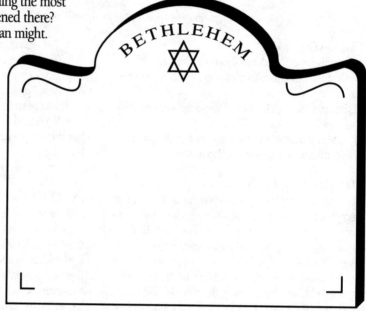

BETHLEHEM

Let All Men Know
the King of Kings . . .

A Royal Decree

Luke begins his recounting of Jesus' birth with a "historical marker," a decree of the leader of the Roman Empire. Jesus is "God's Decree." What is it that God is decreeing? Finish the Royal Decree to the left.

If an angel were reading it, how would it be articulated and emphasized? How would it be a different reading by an excited Christian believer? How would *you* read it?

THE PROMISE OF POWER

LESSON 4

WHY TEACH THIS LESSON?

Is your life soaring, or just boring? Charles Swindoll poses that question in his book, *Living Above the Level of Mediocrity*. It is a good question for end-of-the-year personal inventory.

Sadly enough, many Christians live a boring existence. They need to plug into the power of the living Christ—our resurrected Lord. And there is no wrong time to embrace the truths of today's lesson. Students can be spiritually empowered by consideration of these texts.

Jesus came to bring to us *abundant* life, "life to the full" (John 10:10). With his presence and power, all of his followers can soar on the winds of his Spirit.

INTRODUCTION

A. ANYONE HERE NEED POWER?

Jesus' resurrection had a lasting impact on the church and the world. The risen Christ turned his disciples from doubters to doers. He turned fearful men into forceful men. This he did by convincing them of his victory over death. They realized that if Jesus had power over death, then he had power over any circumstance they would face.

Many people today feel that they lead powerless lives. They are unable to meet the demands placed on them. To the disciples, taking the gospel to "all the world" (Mark 16:15) must have seemed impossible. (It seems overwhelming to us today.) Nevertheless, they undertook the task with great vigor and determination. They fearlessly proclaimed their faith in Jesus wherever they went. This they could not have done without the power that the resurrected Christ provided. Today, if we find ourselves continually overwhelmed by life's challenges, our primary problem may be a lack of power.

A preacher was traveling through Tennessee not long after the Tennessee Valley Authority started building the great hydroelectric dams. These dams produced huge amounts of electricity for the rural inhabitants of that state. As he traveled, the preacher noticed a small house that was located near a dam but was still using kerosene lamps. The residents were close to the power source, but they were not plugged into it. So it is with many who are near Jesus but are not plugged into his power. Jesus' resurrection provided power for the early church. He can provide power for today's church as well.

Last week's lesson considered the beginning of Jesus' earthly life. This week we look at the end of his earthly life and the effect of his resurrection on his disciples. Last week we focused on the baby in the manger, this week on the risen Lord.

B. LESSON BACKGROUND

Today's lesson examines one of the accounts of Jesus' appearances following his resurrection. Usually we consider this subject only at Easter, but it is beneficial to consider at any time the blessing of what it means to serve a living Savior. And it is appropriate, as we prepare to enter a new year, to remind ourselves that our Savior is the same "yesterday and today and forever" (Hebrews 13:8).

DEVOTIONAL READING:
JOHN 16:1-11
LESSON SCRIPTURE:
LUKE 24:13-53
PRINTED TEXT:
LUKE 24:36-53

Dec
27

LESSON AIMS

After this lesson each student should:

1. List the proofs Jesus provided for his resurrection when he appeared to the disciples.

2. Explain how those proofs answer those who doubt Jesus' resurrection.

3. Determine to fill each day with worship and joy in the power of the risen Christ.

KEY VERSE

I am going to send you what my Father has promised.
—Luke 24:49

All four Gospels (along with 1 Corinthians 15:5-8) tell about Jesus' postresurrection appearances. Whatever differences exist in the accounts are minor and do not pose any significant problems. In fact, newspaperman Louis Cassels once said that the small differences we encounter in the Gospels are the mark of a true testimony. If every account were exactly alike, one would suspect some measure of collusion. With careful study, all accounts of the resurrection can be harmonized.

What impact did Jesus' postresurrection appearances have on his disciples? This is the question we want to consider in today's lesson. What did Jesus accomplish through these appearances? And what does he want his disciples—both then and now—to do?

I. JESUS COMFORTS HIS FRIENDS (LUKE 24:36-43)

The disciples were in despair. They had lost a friend; but more than that, they had lost the leader on whom they had pinned all their hopes. They had come to believe that he was the Messiah—and now he was gone. It is not hard to imagine their sorrow.

Jesus' first order of business was to comfort his disheartened disciples. He may have appeared to them in the same room in which he shared the Last Supper with them. That supper spoke of Jesus' impending death. The meal soon to be shared will celebrate his life.

A. HE INVITES INVESTIGATION (vv. 36-40)

36. While they were still talking about this, Jesus himself stood among them and said to them, "Peace be with you."

This is the third appearance of the risen Christ recorded by Luke and apparently the same one mentioned by John in John 20:19-23. If so, we should note that John records that "the disciples were together, with the doors locked" (v. 19). Jesus was not restricted by locked doors, even though, as we shall see, he was not a spirit.

Luke does not tell of Jesus' appearance to Mary Magdalene (John 20:11-17) or to the other women (Matthew 28:8-10). The first appearance in Luke is to an otherwise unknown disciple named Cleopas and his companion on the way to Emmaus (Luke 24:13-32). Upon recognizing the Lord, the two returned to Jerusalem, where they learned that Jesus had also appeared to Simon Peter (Luke 24:33, 34). Luke is the only Gospel writer to mention the appearance to Peter, though Paul confirms it in 1 Corinthians 15:5.

At this point, story after story was beginning to confirm that Jesus had indeed risen from the dead. While Cleopas and his companion were talking, *Jesus himself stood among them.* His greeting was, *Peace be with you.* This was a common first-century greeting among the Jews. Variations of it are still used today.

37. They were startled and frightened, thinking they saw a ghost.

In spite of Jesus' greeting of peace, the disciples were *startled and frightened.* The word *frightened* in the Greek text comes from a word that is the source of our English word "phobia." The disciples thought that they had seen a *ghost.*

If this story were a fictitious account, it probably would not portray the disciples as still entertaining doubts about Jesus' resurrection. But the Bible is an honest book. It reveals these people as they really were. This should not *discourage* us; it should *encourage* us. These men, who became leaders of the New Testament church, were people just like us.

38. He said to them, "Why are you troubled, and why do doubts rise in your minds?

Jesus asked the disciples why they were *troubled.* He himself had predicted these events (Mark 8:31; 9:31; 10:34); thus they should not be so surprised that

WHAT DO YOU THINK?

By the time Jesus appeared to the disciples in today's text, he had already appeared to Mary Magdalene (John 20:11-17), the other women (Matthew 28:8-10), two on the road to Emmaus (Luke 24:13-33), and Simon Peter (Luke 24:33, 34). Why, then, do you suppose the disciples were so afraid and slow to believe when Jesus appeared to them?

Once your mind is made up, what kind of persuasion does it take to change it?

his words had been fulfilled. Furthermore, at this point they had ample evidence for the resurrection: the empty tomb; the testimonies of Mary Magdalene, the two on the road to Emmaus, and Peter; and Jesus' own presence with them now. *39. "Look at my hands and my feet. It is I myself! Touch me and see; a ghost does not have flesh and bones, as you see I have."*

Jesus then allowed the disciples to *touch* him. He wanted to assure them of the truth of his resurrection. They needed to know that he was, in fact, the same individual who had died on the cross. The crucified Savior was now the living Lord. That is the reason he still bore the scars of Calvary in his *hands* and *feet*. The disciples were not hallucinating. This was not a *ghost*; this was someone with *flesh and bones*. Later, Jesus invited doubting Thomas to touch him in order that he too could be assured that Jesus was alive (John 20:27).

Reading this passage, some have wondered about the resurrection body that is promised to Christians. Will our resurrection bodies still show scars and physical handicaps? It is important to distinguish between Jesus' experience and ours. Regarding the resurrection, Paul writes in 1 Corinthians 15:44, "It is sown a natural body, it is raised a spiritual body." Yet Jesus' resurrection body, as he took care to demonstrate, was not "spiritual." Jesus' resurrection was followed by numerous "flesh and blood" appearances meant to convince his disciples that he was alive. Such is not the case with our resurrection; for when Jesus comes, those believers who have died will be raised from the dead and will "meet the Lord in the air" (1 Thessalonians 4:17). We will then receive the kind of "spiritual body" that Jesus received following his ascension, in order to dwell with his Father where "flesh and blood" cannot be present (1 Corinthians 15:50).

40. When he had said this, he showed them his hands and feet.

Having offered the invitation to touch him, Jesus proceeded to show the disciples the wounds in his *hands and feet*. These were consistent with those received on the cross. Sometimes people who were crucified were simply tied to the cross, but we know that Jesus was nailed to his. Seeing the wounds settled any doubts that the disciples may have had concerning the individual standing before them. This was without question Jesus—the crucified One, now risen from the dead.

FROM SADNESS TO JOY

In December a few years ago, Frank and Bet Forest were getting ready for their daughter Page to come home from college. Page was a freshman and their only child. It seemed as though the college she attended in Oklahoma was a million miles from their California home. The thought of her being home for Christmas filled every moment with anticipation.

Frank and Bet headed for the airport and couldn't help but laugh at themselves when they realized they were a full hour early. About thirty minutes before Page's flight was due to arrive a voice announced, "Will persons waiting for flight number . . ." The rest of the announcement was a blur. Frank and Bet were escorted to another room where a representative of the airlines explained that there had been an accident. Page's flight had crashed on takeoff from Denver. All the passengers were believed to have been killed.

Frank and Bet made their way back home. Standing in their living room they hugged and cried, unsure what to do. A few minutes later the phone rang. The voice at the other end said, "This is Mrs. Hastings with the airline. Your daughter missed the plane. She's all right."

If you can imagine how those parents felt upon hearing such news, then you know something of how the disciples must have felt when Jesus came and stood among them and they realized, "He is alive!"   —G. A.

HOW TO SAY IT

Alexandria. Al-iks-AN-dree-uh.
Cleopas. KLEE-uh-pass.
Emmaus. Em-MAY-us.
Magdalene. MAG-duh-leen or
    Mag-duh-LEE-nee.
Ptolemy. TAHL-uh-me.
Zechariah. Zek-uh-RYE-uh.

The visual for lesson 4 illustrates Jesus' promise to send the Holy Spirit to empower the apostles (verse 49).

WHAT DO YOU THINK?

Luke says the disciples "still did not believe it because of joy and amazement" (v. 41). They found it hard to believe Jesus was alive because it was "too good to be true." Do you think some people today do not believe because the idea of eternal life and forgiveness of sins seems too good to be true? Why or why not? How can we help people believe that, in this case, something too good to be true really is true?

WHAT DO YOU THINK?

The text suggests that with a clearer understanding of the Scriptures (see vv. 44, 45), the disciples could have had a better understanding of what was happening. How? What errors could they have avoided?

Can the study of the Bible help us to interpret and understand historical events in our time? What about personal events in our lives? In what ways?

What are we doing to make sure that people in our church have a good understanding of the Scriptures so they can understand what God's plan is and work in harmony with it?

WHAT DO YOU THINK?

Jesus made clear that his suffering and death were part of God's plan. How does that help us understand suffering in our lives? Do you think suffering is part of God's plan and meant to serve a purpose?

How do you explain suffering when it seems to be senseless and without purpose? Do you try to

B. HE SHARES FELLOWSHIP (vv. 41-43)

41-43. And while they still did not believe it because of joy and amazement, he asked them, "Do you have anything here to eat?" They gave him a piece of broiled fish, and he took it and ate it in their presence.

Then Jesus said something that must have appeared just as curious as the invitation to touch him. He asked the disciples if they had *anything . . . to eat.* Certainly Jesus could have provided food miraculously, for himself and the disciples. No doubt this action served as yet another proof that he was the same person who had been crucified. A "spirit" would not be able to partake of such food.

II. JESUS CONFIRMS HIS RESURRECTION (LUKE 24:44-46)

Having provided a series of "many convincing proofs" (Acts 1:3) that he was the resurrected Jesus, Jesus now demonstrated the significance of the resurrection by pointing to the testimony of the Old Testament Scriptures.

A. HE OPENS THE SCRIPTURES (v. 44)

44. He said to them, "This is what I told you while I was still with you: Everything must be fulfilled that is written about me in the Law of Moses, the Prophets and the Psalms."

Jesus moved from the realm of personal experience to the Scriptural support for his resurrection. He spoke specifically of *the Law of Moses, the Prophets and the Psalms.* This was a characteristic way to summarize the entire Old Testament. The Jews in Jesus' day usually referred to the categories of the Law, the Prophets, and the Writings; but since the book of Psalms is the first book found in the Writings, it was sometimes used to designate this third category.

Jesus also reminded the disciples that he had spoken to them of these matters before. Now, with the evidence of the resurrection before them, they were capable of a greater understanding of God's master plan. That plan included events, foretold in the Scriptures, that *must be fulfilled.*

B. HE OPENS THEIR MINDS (vv. 45, 46)

45. Then he opened their minds so they could understand the Scriptures.

What does the phrase *then he opened their minds* mean? Most likely this refers to the understanding that came with Jesus' explanation of what the Old Testament Scriptures taught concerning him. It was the same method that he used with the men on the road to Emmaus, as he "explained to them what was said in all the Scriptures concerning himself" (Luke 24:27). Such understanding was also provided when Jesus taught his disciples "about the kingdom of God" during the forty days between his resurrection and ascension (Acts 1:3).

46. He told them, "This is what is written: The Christ will suffer and rise from the dead on the third day.

Again, Jesus emphasized that his death and resurrection were part of a plan. The Scriptures' message was clear: *the Christ will suffer.* A suffering Messiah had not been easy for the disciples to accept (Matthew 16:21, 22). This is why so many failed to recognize Jesus as the Messiah, and why many saw the cross as a "stumbling block" (1 Corinthians 1:23).

Jesus specifically mentioned the prophecies of the resurrection on *the third day.* This has troubled some students of the Bible, because they cannot account for three full days in the scriptural record. But in the normal speech of that time, a span of "three days" could cover any portion of any of those days. Jesus was crucified on Friday; therefore, he spent part of Friday, all of Saturday, and part of Sunday in the tomb. The expression would have made perfect sense to the disciples.

III. JESUS COMMISSIONS HIS DISCIPLES (LUKE 24:47-49)

Jesus' next concern was to prepare the disciples for the challenge of world evangelism. This must have seemed an impossible task to them, yet Jesus did not issue the command without also promising adequate help.

A. HE ISSUES A CHALLENGE (v. 47)

47. *"And repentance and forgiveness of sins will be preached in his name to all nations, beginning at Jerusalem.*

Here Jesus alludes to what will happen on the Day of Pentecost. In *Jerusalem,* Peter will preach a sermon emphasizing *repentance and forgiveness of sins* (Acts 2:38). Following the *beginning* of its proclamation on that day, the message was then to go out to *all nations.* We must not hear these words without considering their fulfillment in Acts 2 and without accepting the challenge in our day to take the gospel to *all nations.*

B. HE ISSUES A PROMISE (vv. 48, 49)

48, 49. *"You are witnesses of these things. I am going to send you what my Father has promised; but stay in the city until you have been clothed with power from on high."*

Jesus did not command these men to be his *witnesses* without supplying the necessary power for such a mission. This power *from on high* was the Holy Spirit (Acts 1:8). Sending the disciples out to win the world without the power of the Holy Spirit would have been like sending a child out in the wilderness to trap his own food with just a pocketknife. The equipment would not be appropriate for the task. Jesus promised that the disciples would be *clothed* with the Holy Spirit. He would surround and envelop them like a robe.

However, all of this would not take place immediately; the disciples were to *stay in the city* of Jerusalem. It almost seems as if Jesus is telling them, "Hurry up . . . but wait." Yet the waiting will be worthwhile, for the work Jesus has commissioned these men (and us) to do cannot be done without the aid and assistance that the Holy Spirit brings.

IV. JESUS COMPLETES HIS MISSION (LUKE 24:50-53)

Even though Jesus appeared to his followers several times, the appearances could not continue indefinitely. The promised Spirit could not come until Jesus went away (John 16:7). The stage was being set for Jesus' ascension.

A. HE ASCENDS INTO HEAVEN (vv. 50, 51)

50. *When he had led them out to the vicinity of Bethany, he lifted up his hands and blessed them.*

This event took place in *the vicinity of Bethany,* which was located on the south side of the Mount of Olives. Bethany was the home of Mary, Martha, and Lazarus (John 11:1). While Luke's account reads as though the ascension immediately followed the events described in verses 36-49, we know from the book of Acts that Jesus spent forty days instructing his disciples prior to his ascension (Acts 1:3). Since there were fifty days between Passover and Pentecost, this left ten days between Jesus' ascension and the Day of Pentecost.

Prior to his ascension, Jesus *lifted up his hands and blessed them.* The Greek word for *blessed* is a word that gives us the English word "eulogy." Literally it means "to speak well of." But when Jesus gave this blessing to his disciples, it meant much more than well-wishing. It carried the impact of his full authority as Lord and Christ.

fit it into God's plan and say there must be some purpose we don't know? Is suffering supposed to happen? Why or why not?

DAILY BIBLE READINGS

Monday, Dec. 21—Jesus Himself Came Near (Luke 24:13-27)

Tuesday, Dec. 22—Stay With Us, for It Is Nearly Evening (Luke 24:28-35)

Wednesday, Dec. 23—Peace Be With You (Luke 24:36-43)

Thursday, Dec. 24— Everything Must Be Fulfilled (Luke 24:44-53)

Friday, Dec. 25—I Will Not Leave You as Orphans (John 14:15-24)

Saturday, Dec. 26—The Holy Spirit Promised (John 14:25-31)

Sunday, Dec. 27—Your Grief Will Turn to Joy (John 16:12-28)

WHAT DO YOU THINK?

After Jesus ascended, the disciples "returned to Jerusalem with great joy." How can we cultivate that same kind of joy in the lives of believers today? What helps you personally to experience a sense of joy in the knowledge of Christ's resurrection and ascension? In what ways is the presence of the Holy Spirit in our lives better for us than Jesus' physical presence in the world?

51. While he was blessing them, he left them and was taken up into heaven.

Jesus then ascended *into heaven*. A fuller account of this is found in Acts 1:9-11. Jesus *left them*, "and a cloud hid him from their sight" (v. 9). Then "two men dressed in white" (apparently angels) reminded the disciples that "this same Jesus . . . will come back in the same way you have seen him go into heaven" (vv. 10, 11).

B. THE DISCIPLES OBEY (VV. 52, 53)

52, 53. Then they worshiped him and returned to Jerusalem with great joy. And they stayed continually at the temple, praising God.

The disciples obeyed Jesus immediately and *returned to Jerusalem*. Notice that the attitude of terror with which our text began (v. 37) has now been replaced with *great joy*.

It is interesting that Luke's Gospel ends in about the same place it begins. After his opening remarks (1:1-4), he takes his readers to the temple where Zechariah heard the news regarding the birth of his long-awaited son. Now, at the conclusion, the disciples of Jesus go to the temple to worship the Son of God.

Luke's account may seem to end somewhat abruptly, since it does not record the coming of the promised Holy Spirit. That is because Luke's Gospel is only part one of his writing. Luke will continue his account in part two: the book of Acts. This tells the story of how the disciples fulfilled what Jesus commanded them to do following his resurrection. The risen Christ provided them with the peace, the proof, and the power to take the gospel "to the ends of the earth" (Acts 1:8).

CONCLUSION

A. THE WRONG SIDE OF EASTER

James Stewart, the great Scottish preacher, once declared that this world is living on the wrong side of Easter. What did he mean by that? He meant that most people act as if Jesus had never risen from the grave. They are as solemn and discouraged as the disciples were before they saw the risen Lord. The sad fact is that many people live as if there were no resurrection. The mood of some churches would cause some to think that the Savior is not alive. Nothing has done the Christian cause a greater disservice than the grimness that sometimes accompanies Christian commitment. Who would want to be part of such an organization? The existence of the church is one proof of the resurrection. Let's resolve that our attitude as part of the church will be another.

When Julius Caesar came to Alexandria, Egypt, the residents showed him the coffin of Alexander the Great. They then asked him if he wanted to see the coffin of the Egyptian ruler Ptolemy. He replied, "I came to see a king, not a corpse." When we come to church, we come to see a King, not a corpse! We need less mourning and more celebration, less fear and more confidence, less apathy and more commitment.

PRAYER

Father, help us to recognize that, until we call on your power, we have not used all our power. Thank you for making us partners in your great enterprise of taking the gospel to the world. Like the disciples of old, may we accept your mission and depend on your power to accomplish it. Through the powerful name of Jesus, amen.

B. FEEL THE POWER

Some time ago, a television ad promoting professional football featured people talking about their passion for football. The ad concluded with a player looking into the camera and saying with great intensity, "I feel the power." When it comes to our Christian commitment, we should ask, "Do we feel the power?" Jesus calls and equips us to carry out the glorious task of fulfilling his Great Commission. How committed are we to doing this? Are we placing ourselves at his disposal to accomplish his mission?

Now that you have considered the challenge of this lesson, do you "feel the power"?

THOUGHT TO REMEMBER

"You will receive power" (Acts 1:8).

Discovery Learning

This page contains an alternate lesson plan emphasizing learning activities. Classes desiring such student involvement will find these suggestions helpful. The next page is a reproducible activity page to further enhance discovery learning.

LEARNING GOALS

After this lesson each student will be able to:

1. List some of the proofs Jesus provided for his resurrection when he appeared to the disciples.

2. Explain how those proofs answer those who doubt Jesus' resurrection.

3. Determine to fill each day with worship and joy in the power of the risen Christ.

INTO THE LESSON

Prepare and display a very large poster with the word "Power" printed at the top. If possible, also attach a picture (perhaps from a comic book cover) of a superhero. Ask the class members to recall the names of comic book, television, or mythological heroes who had super powers (e.g., Superman, the "bionic woman," or Hercules).

After listing some heroes, remind the class that these are fictional. But the supernatural resurrection of Jesus is historical fact. The resurrection also turned Jesus' disciples from fearful doubters into forceful doers. But they had to tap into the power of the Holy Spirit, whom he promised to send them.

Use the illustration of the TVA dams that is given on page 151. Point out that knowing *about* Jesus is not enough. We must be plugged into the power he has promised. This study will help us tap into that power.

INTO THE WORD

Briefly review the Lesson Background; then read today's printed text. Have the class form groups of four or five people each, and give each group one of the following tasks. (Print each assignment on an index card to be given to the appropriate group. You will also need to make available information from the commentary section of this lesson to give to groups 1 and 3.) Each group should select a spokesperson to report its work to the class. If you have a large class, more than one group can do the same assignment. Just allow each group to report and contrast their findings. Of course, if you choose not to use groups, these assignments may be used for discussion items for the entire class.

Group 1. Jesus Comforts His Disciples.

Read Luke 24:36-43. Tell how the disciples' fear and doubt can actually encourage us today. (They had to be convinced Jesus was alive, so we also can be convinced.)

Cite and comment on the evidences Jesus offered that he is alive. (Physical presence; they saw him; they heard him; he ate with them.)

Group 2. The Resurrection Is Part of God's Plan!

Read Luke 24:44-46. Use a concordance to find some Scriptures from the Law of Moses (Genesis— Deuteronomy), the Prophets (this includes the books we call "history"), and the Psalms that foretell Jesus' death and resurrection. Check Peter's sermon in Acts 2:22-36 for some ideas.

Group 3. Jesus Commissions His Disciples.

Read Luke 24:47-53. Describe Jesus' simple strategy for spreading the gospel. (See also Acts 1:8.) How was that task accomplished in the early church? How was God's promise to give "power from on high" accomplished? (See Acts 2:1-21.) How does that promise to the apostles help us today? (The Spirit inspired the Scripture, 2 Peter 1:21; the Spirit is still active, living in Christians, Acts 2:38; he equips us for spiritual ministry, 1 Corinthians 12:4; he intercedes for us, Romans 8:26, 27).

Allow each group to work for ten or twelve minutes. Then ask the spokesperson from each group to report the results of the group's work.

INTO LIFE

Tell the class that the record makes it apparent that the resurrection of Jesus transformed the lives of the disciples. Write the words "Living on the Wrong Side of Easter" on a visual, explaining that James Stewart, a great Scottish preacher, once declared that this world is living on "the wrong side of Easter." Ask them, "Why would he say that? What do you suppose he meant?" Use the lesson commentary (page 156) to guide the discussion.

Additional questions may include, "If people choose to live on the right side of Easter, how will that affect their worship?" "How does living on the right side of Easter affect one's lifestyle and witness?"

Distribute index cards (and pens, if needed). Ask each student to write, "I will live on the right side of Easter this week by . . ." Have each student complete the sentence with some way he or she will fill each day with worship and joy in the power of the risen Christ. If there is time, ask volunteers to share their responses. Close with prayer.

What Are You Wearing?

The question, "What to wear?" is a dominant one in most Western cultures. Taken ethically rather than stylistically, "What do most modern people *wear?*" On the following "paper dolls" write in what most "wear." (One sample is written in to get you started.)

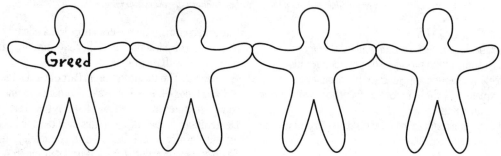

What Does the Christian Wear?

Jesus told his apostles they will be "clothed with power from on high." The only thing that distinguishes Christians from non-Christians is "what they wear." Check the following texts for the Christian's "wardrobe." Write the appropriate "attire" on the Christian figures given. Texts: Galatians 5:22, 23, Ephesians 6:13-17, 1 Peter 5:5, Revelation 3:4, 5. Feel free to add relevant "accessories."

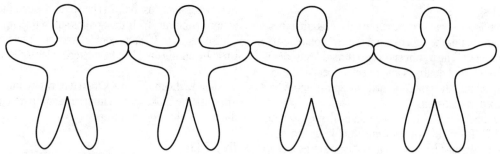

Friends Waver . . . Jesus Stabilizes

In today's text, Luke pictures a group of uncertain, anxious friends of Jesus who seem to be tottering at his death. But he also describes the loving, resurrected Lord. For each of the disciples' weaknesses, Jesus offers strength; for each doubt, Jesus offers proof. Fill in the following:

Wavering	STABILITY
The disciples are afraid	Jesus _____
The disciples "see a ghost"	Jesus _____
The disciples misunderstand messianic prophecy	Jesus _____
The disciples huddle in weakness	Jesus _____

LOVE ONE ANOTHER

LESSON 5

WHY TEACH THIS LESSON?

Isn't it Tina Turner who sings, "What's Love Got to Do With It?"? You may not be certain about the full import of that lyric, nor should it necessarily pique your interest. One thing is sure, she is not singing about Christian discipleship. Jesus repeatedly admonishes his followers to love God unreservedly, and to love each other unconditionally.

Love has *everything* to do with the Christian life. Unselfish, unashamed and unrestrained devotion is the essence of kingdom faithfulness and loyalty. Love, as Paul reminds us in 1 Corinthians 13, is the most excellent of all the spiritual gifts and disciplines. Without it, everything else we are and do is of little significance. This lesson will be a clear reminder of love's priority.

INTRODUCTION

A. YOU'RE GOING TO LOVE THIS

Perhaps there are no greater words that a person can hear than, "I love you." As children we felt a sense of security when parents and teachers expressed their love to us. In our courting days many of us freely spoke these words as our affection for another grew. Later as parents our hearts seemed to melt when we heard our own children say these magic words to us. Some of us are blessed with hearing them spoken by a grandchild or great-grandchild.

Unfortunately, our affinity toward love has also led to a certain amount of unclarity regarding the meaning of the word. We talk about how much we *love* a good pizza or an ice cream treat, how we *love* to play basketball or watch a baseball game, or how we would *love* to have someone come visit us sometime. We *love* sunny days and walking on the beach and would *love* to stay and talk some more if only we had the time. We introduce a program by telling our audience, "You're going to *love* this." Is it any wonder that we have trouble arriving at a clear, simple definition of the word *love*?

In several passages in the Gospels, Jesus teaches us the true meaning of love. He describes the nature of love and gives practical examples of how it should be expressed. And to motivate us toward this kind of love, he reminds us of how he himself demonstrates love to us. Anyone confused about the meaning of love would do well to learn from Jesus what love truly is and how it is expressed.

B. LESSON BACKGROUND

It was nothing new for the Jews of Jesus' day to hear one of their teachers talk about love. The Old Testament contains many verses that speak of God's love for us and our duty to love others (Leviticus 19:18, 34; Deuteronomy 6:5; 7:8, 9; Joshua 22:5; 1 Kings 10:9; Psalm 146:8). But first-century Judaism was also keenly interested in the concepts of wrath and vengeance. Throughout their history the Jews had suffered much at the hands of invading armies and oppressive overlords. In the first century they were chafing under the political restraints of Rome's domination of their country. Thus it is not surprising that Jews of that day often spoke of their feelings of anger toward their enemies. In addition, one of the frequent

DEVOTIONAL READING:
1 JOHN 4:7-12

LESSON SCRIPTURE:
MARK 12:28-34; LUKE 6:27-36;
JOHN 13:31-35

PRINTED TEXT:
MARK 12:28-34;
LUKE 6:27-31;
JOHN 13:34, 35

Jan 3

LESSON AIMS

After completing this lesson a student should be able to:

1. Describe love according to what Jesus taught in today's text.

2. Tell why loving God first and one's neighbor as himself is the essence of the law.

3. Look for a practical way to express love to God and for a neighbor.

KEY VERSE

By this all men will know that you are my disciples, if you love one another. —John 13:35

themes of the book of Psalms is the prayer that God would bring vengeance upon the enemies of his oppressed people (Psalms 6:10; 18:3, 40; 56:9; 66:3; 72:9; 132:18; 139:19-22). This mind-set was so pervasive that the work of the promised Messiah was typically viewed from this perspective. As John the Baptist's father, Zechariah, put it, the Messiah was to come that Israel might be given "salvation from our enemies and from the hand of all who hate us" (Luke 1:71).

It is against this background that Jesus' teaching on love stood out. He elevated love to the high status that God intended it to have from the beginning, even going so far as to maintain that God expects us to love our enemies rather than wish them harm. Jesus placed our God-given duty to love in settings that seemed awkward to his contemporaries (and probably seem that way for many of us today!). God's kind of love will test the boundaries we have erected in our thinking, and will challenge us to reach out much farther than we have imagined.

I. THE GREATEST COMMANDMENTS (MARK 12:28-34)
A. LOVING GOD (vv. 28-30)
28. One of the teachers of the law came and heard them debating. Noticing that Jesus had given them a good answer, he asked him, "Of all the commandments, which is the most important?"

The discussion found in Mark 12 occurred on Tuesday of Jesus' final week, just three days prior to his crucifixion. On this occasion Jesus sought to teach in the temple, but he was constantly interrupted by his enemies. The chief priests, teachers of the law, and elders (Mark 11:27), the Pharisees and Herodians (12:13), and the Sadducees (12:18), all took turns sending representatives to challenge Jesus with a supposedly difficult question. They hoped that Jesus would give a weak or offensive answer that would turn the crowds against him and give the religious leaders an occasion to arrest him. Each time, however, Jesus responded with an answer that challenged the hypocrisy of the religious leaders and left the crowd even more supportive of him.

The question in our text was put forward by *one of the teachers of the law*, a group of scholars who were experts in the intricacies of rabbinical law. Perhaps this man originally approached Jesus as part of those who came to trap him (Mark 11:27), yet there was something that set him apart from the others. Or perhaps he was passing by when *he heard them debating* and stopped to listen.

This scribe thought that Jesus had *given* his questioners *a good answer*. His motive was not the deep animosity felt by his colleagues. Instead, he possessed a sincere appreciation for Jesus' wisdom and a curiosity about his views on Jewish law.

29. "The most important one," answered Jesus, "is this: 'Hear, O Israel, the Lord our God, the Lord is one.

Both the scribe's question and Jesus' answer reflected a long-standing debate among Jewish scholars of that day over the question of which was *the most important* commandment. First-century Judaism had systematized the instructions written by Moses and created a list of approximately 613 commands, with 248 of them positive ("do this . . .") and 365 negative ("do not . . ."). According to the rabbinical literature now available to us, much fervor was applied to the debate over which of the 613 commands was to be given priority by a Jew.

For those scheming to undermine Jesus' ministry, this multiple choice question looked promising. No matter which command Jesus suggested as the *most important*, his enemies could argue for other possibilities, thereby suggesting that Jesus was not as wise as he claimed or even implying that he may not really care about the commandments he passed over in his answer. What they did not

WHAT DO YOU THINK?

Why was the scribe who questioned Jesus so interested in his answer? Did he seem more interested in academic knowledge or practical obedience? What is the difference? Knowledge is necessary before any obedience can take place, but how can you be filled with knowledge about a subject and fail to translate it into behavior? What should be the goal of knowledge we strive for in the church today, and how can we reach that goal?

count on was Jesus' proposing an answer that would make so much sense that it would be impossible to refute.

In his statement of the most important commandment, Jesus quoted Deuteronomy 6:4, 5. Jewish tradition referred to verse 4 as the *shema*, a Hebrew word that means "hear," because this is the first word in the Hebrew text of this passage (*Hear, O Israel . . .*). The *shema* was held in such high esteem that it was quoted as the invocation for every synagogue service (and is still used as such in Jewish services today).

The reason this passage was so highly valued by the Jews was that it succinctly expressed the monotheism (belief in one God) that formed the foundation of the Jewish faith. Though the tendency in ancient times was to worship many gods, Judaism held the distinctive view that there is only one God. The *shema* was treasured as a clear, concise summary of this view.

30. "'Love the Lord your God with all your heart and with all your soul and with all your mind and with all your strength.'

By quoting the verse that followed the *shema*, Jesus proposed that the *entire* passage be treated with great esteem, not just the first part. That is, one's priority should be not only to believe that there is just one God, but also to *love* that one God. The Scripture text that defined one's most important belief also supplied his most important command.

It is possible to take the different terms Jesus uses (*heart, soul, mind, strength*) and treat them as distinct aspects of man's nature, thereby drawing several implications about the way in which we are to love God. However, knowing the Jewish penchant for speaking in "parallelism" (that is, repeating an idea several times with phrases that are roughly synonymous), we cannot say for certain whether Jesus intended for us to make such fine distinctions. What we can reasonably conclude from Jesus' statement is that our love for God should spring from our entire being, impacting every aspect of life.

B. LOVING OTHERS (vv. 31-34)
31. "The second is this: 'Love your neighbor as yourself.' There is no commandment greater than these."

Jesus had not been asked to list the *second* greatest commandment, but he took this opportunity to teach a more complete view of our primary duty to God. This second quotation is taken from Leviticus 19:18. In first-century Jewish thought, this was recognized as a legitimate command; however, its full force was often blunted by attempts to limit the scope of the word *neighbor.* Recall one man's attempt to "justify himself" by asking Jesus, "Who is my neighbor?" (Luke 10:29).

There is no commandment greater than these. Loving God and loving our neighbor are God's highest expectations for mankind. Why should these two loves be so closely linked? Because the latter logically follows from the former. One who truly loves God cannot help but love those who carry within them the image of God.

32. "Well said, teacher," the man replied. "You are right in saying that God is one and there is no other but him.

This is not the kind of admission that we would expect from one working within the ranks of those attempting to discredit Jesus. But then, sometimes truth is so powerful that an honest man cannot deny it, no matter how much he may dislike the source of that truth.

33. "To love him with all your heart, with all your understanding and with all your strength, and to love your neighbor as yourself is more important than all burnt offerings and sacrifices."

WHAT DO YOU THINK?

What does wholehearted love for God look like in terms of everyday life?

Look at a monogamous marriage as an example. How can you tell the difference between wholehearted love in a marriage and loyalties that are divided? What kinds of alternatives can take the place of wholehearted loyalty to a marriage partner?

Are you committed to God wholeheartedly, or does the evidence point to divided loyalty? What do you need to do to improve on your commitment?

WHAT DO YOU THINK?

Why do the commands to love God and to love our neighbor stand above all the other commands of God? What are the differences between these two commands and the other Commandments?

Can love be commanded? What kind of love are we talking about? Where do feelings come in?

Use the visual for lesson 5 to illustrate the truth that love must be demonstrated with action. Only active love can declare our discipleship.

It is not uncommon for Christians to assume that Old Testament saints were saved by lawkeeping and sacrifices, whereas we under the New Covenant are saved by grace and faith. However, animal sacrifices could not atone for sin (Hebrews 10:1-4). Furthermore, all who were saved in the Old Testament age were saved by faith in God and his promises (as noted in Romans 4; Galatians 3:6-9; and Hebrews 11:13-16, 39, 40). Therefore it should not surprise us to discover that the prophets often stated the principle that the attitude of the heart is much more important to God than the sacrifices offered on an altar (see Hosea 6:6; Micah 6:8). The scribe's words were an insightful summary of the message of the Old Testament. It is no wonder that Jesus was pleased with his answer.

34. When Jesus saw that he had answered wisely, he said to him, "You are not far from the kingdom of God." And from then on no one dared ask him any more questions.

Here was a man who was not yet in full stride with God's messianic plan, but he was *not far* off. Perhaps he was like the religious leaders John mentions (12:42, 43), who believed in Jesus but would not admit it because "they loved praise from men more than praise from God." Or perhaps he was moving in the right direction but just had not come to faith yet. We do not know any more about him, but we can hope that he was one of those who later accepted Jesus as the promised Messiah, perhaps on the Day of Pentecost.

II. LOVE YOUR ENEMIES (LUKE 6:27-31)

A. HOW TO RESPOND TO THEM (vv. 27-30)

27, 28. "But I tell you who hear me: Love your enemies, do good to those who hate you, bless those who curse you, pray for those who mistreat you.

Earlier in his ministry, Jesus explained the true nature of love in his teaching. The "sermon" found in Luke 6, delivered by Jesus on a "level place" (Luke 6:17), may have been given on a different occasion from the famous Sermon on the Mount (Matthew 5–7), but the two texts are very similar in style and content. In both sermons, Jesus declared that the love God manifests and commands is unconditional, acting with kindness even to those who are anything but kind.

How is it possible to feel love toward those who would hurt us? The answer is that we have not been commanded to *feel* love, but to act in a loving manner. The love described by the Greek word *agape* involves a decision of the will, not a feeling of the heart. It is a decision to treat others in a kind and considerate way, regardless of how we actually *feel* about them.

29. "If someone strikes you on one cheek, turn to him the other also. If someone takes your cloak, do not stop him from taking your tunic.

Our natural tendency (and the accepted practice of modern society) is to say, "If you hit me, I will hit you back." But *agape* love says, "I will not stoop to your level; I will not hit back." *Agape* love chooses not to retaliate. Thus Jesus said that he could have called upon twelve legions of angels to destroy his enemies (Matthew 26:53); instead, he allowed them to arrest him and literally strike his cheek without reprisal (John 18:22). He felt free to challenge the actions of those who slapped him (v. 23), but he did not strike back at them.

30. "Give to everyone who asks you, and if anyone takes what belongs to you, do not demand it back.

Here is a legitimate question to consider: Does Jesus want us to be doormats for people to step on and trample? Do we always have to stand by and let others hurt us and take advantage of us? Not necessarily. For example, Paul was not opposed to Christians seeking restitution when they have been wronged; but if the manner in which we seek redress damages our public witness for Christ, then he

WHAT DO YOU THINK?

Does Jesus really expect us to love our enemies, or is this some kind of hyperbole? If he means it, how can we honestly do it? Do you need to have feelings of love for your enemy?

Suggest some practical ways of loving one's enemies in both passive ways (like refusing to retaliate) and active ways.

would rather that we choose to "be wronged" and "be cheated" for the sake of the gospel (1 Corinthians 6:1-7). Perhaps the key question is: "What is at stake if I exercise my rights?" In other words, will the cause of Christ suffer loss in order for me to gain, or will my loss serve to advance the cause of Christ?

Sometimes the most *agape* thing we can do is to let people know that we could seek retaliation for their unkindness, but for the sake of Christ we choose not to do so. Thus the position of strength is not found in beating your enemy, but in letting him know that today he is a beneficiary of your grace. By this reaction, a gospel seed can be planted within a sinful heart.

B. HOW TO TREAT OTHERS (v. 31)

31. "Do to others as you would have them do to you."

From childhood most of us have memorized some version of Jesus' Golden Rule: "Do unto others as you would have them do unto you." Something similar to this has been expressed by most ancient philosophers and religions. Perhaps that is because this principle is built within the nature of man by God. We do seem to have a natural instinct toward self-preservation, and we soon learn from experience that how we treat others has implications for how we will be treated in turn.

Our tendency is to oppose rules restricting what we can do, and we will do evil if we think we can get away with it. But given the possibility that someone might follow our evil lead and retaliate by doing evil to us, we recognize the value of restraint. Jesus' "do as you would have others do to you" rule makes sense, in many cases even to an unbeliever.

THE HAZARDS OF HATRED

It was a very old twelve-gauge shotgun, passed down through the family for three generations. Its owner wouldn't let anyone shoot the gun. "It kicks so bad," he said, "it can kill at both ends." No doubt that was not literally true of the old shotgun, but it is literally true of hatred. It wounds the hater as much as the one hated.

Some time ago, newspapers reported that a terrorist in the Middle East had blown himself up with the bomb he intended for others. If we allow ourselves to hate someone, we do him great harm; however, we do ourselves more harm. Harry Emerson Fosdick said, "Hating people is like burning down your house to get rid of a rat."

During the Civil War, Abraham Lincoln once referred publicly to the people of the Confederacy as erring human beings, not as foes to be exterminated. An older woman criticized him for speaking kindly of his enemies, when, according to her, he ought to be thinking of destroying them. "Why, Madam," said Lincoln, "do I not destroy my enemies when I make them my friends?"

The great American poet Edwin Markham stated it well in this little verse:

> He drew a circle that shut me out—
> Heretic, rebel, a thing to flout.
> But Love and I had the wit to win:
> We drew a circle that took him in.   —R. C. S.

III. LOVE YOUR FRIENDS (JOHN 13:34, 35)

A. JESUS' EXAMPLE (v. 34)

34. "A new command I give you: Love one another. As I have loved you, so you must love one another.

Agape love requires that we treat others with kindness and consideration. It does not allow us to act with rudeness or meanness or spite. In this passage, we also learn that *agape* demands even more than this: we must *love one another* the

---

HOW TO SAY IT

agape (Greek). *uh-GAH-pay.*
Confucius. Con-FEW-shiss.
Herodians. Heh-ROE-dee-unz.
*monotheism. mah-nuh-THEE-
    izz-um (th as in thin).*
Pharisees. FAIR-ih-sees.
Sadducees. SAD-you-sees.
shema (Hebrew). shih-MAH.
Zechariah. Zek-uh-RYE-uh.

DAILY BIBLE READINGS

Monday, Dec. 28—*Which Commandment Is the Most Important? (Mark 12:28-34)*

Tuesday, Dec. 29—*Love Your Enemies (Luke 6:27-36)*

Wednesday, Dec. 30—*Evidence of Discipleship (John 13:31-35)*

Thursday, Dec. 31—*Rooted and Established in Love (Ephesians 3:14-19)*

Friday, Jan. 1—*Love Fulfills the Law (Romans 13:1-10)*

Saturday, Jan. 2—*Love Builds Up (1 Corinthians 8:1-6)*

Sunday, Jan. 3—*God Abides in Those Who Love (1 John 4:7-12)*

What Do You Think?

Christians are to be known by their love for one another. Would you characterize your Christian family as being polite and "nice" to each other, or really loving each other? How are you showing love among your Christian friends? Can this love be seen and recognized by others? How could you do more?

Prayer

Heavenly Father, help us to love one another even as you and your Son have expressed your love toward us, through the bounty of your creation and the blessings of your redemption. In Jesus' name, amen.

Thought to Remember

Love should be the trademark of the Christian. Is your trademark easy to read?

way Jesus has *loved* us. That kind of love is a self-sacrificing love that ultimately led him to die on the cross for our sakes.

The occasion for Jesus' *new command* was the last supper in the upper room on the Thursday evening prior to his death. With Calvary just hours away, Jesus went on to explain what it means to love as he has loved us: "Greater love has no one than this, that he lay down his life for his friends" (John 15:13). More than a warm feeling, more than kindness and consideration, love is ultimately a willingness to help someone else, no matter what it may cost you to do so.

B. The Christian's Trademark (v. 35)

35. *"By this all men will know that you are my disciples, if you love one another."*

When a friend betrays your confidence or hurts your feelings, the test of Christian character will be whether you seek revenge or choose to overlook how he or she has wronged you. When a husband no longer has feelings of love toward his wife, the test of Christian character will be whether he abandons his wife or chooses to continue to treat her in an honorable way. When members of the church disagree with each other over a decision, the test of Christian character will be whether they alienate themselves from each other or choose to continue to regard one another as brothers and sisters in Christ. *Agape* love is the distinguishing mark of a heart that has truly been changed by the love of Christ.

The Iron, Silver, and Golden Rules

Even people who know very little about the Bible can quote the Golden Rule in some form: "Do unto others as you would have them do unto you." This rule stands in contrast to two other rules. One we may call the Iron Rule. It is stated as follows: "Whatever others do to you, do you also to them." This is the rule of retribution. Many live by this rule, but Jesus taught us that we should never try to get even.

The second rule we may call the Silver Rule. It is a great improvement over the Iron Rule; for it says, "What you do not want done to yourself, do not do to others." This was the rule of Confucius. It is a good rule, but it is entirely negative. It demands only that we refrain from doing wrong, but it requires nothing in terms of positive action.

The Golden Rule, however, stands far above both of these. It is positive. It requires far more of us than the Silver Rule, for it goes beyond not doing evil to doing good. It demands that we go beyond the minimum. We cannot say, "I am as good as my neighbors." We have to be better than they. We have to be like Christ!

—R. C. S.

CONCLUSION

Legal contracts can be long and tedious. Logical arguments in the realms of science and philosophy can become rather complex. Explanations and excuses for wrong behavior can meander aimlessly. Usually, when all is said and done, what we need is a succinct summary of the key issues at stake. As we sometimes say, "Here it is in a nutshell."

The Bible is filled with hundreds of commandments and guidelines, which could seem overwhelming. However, the key commandments can be put "in a nutshell." To love God and to love one's neighbor are the greatest and second greatest commandments. Echoing Jesus' teaching, the apostle Paul writes, "The commandments, 'Do not commit adultery,' 'Do not murder,' 'Do not steal,' 'Do not covet,' and whatever other commandment there may be, are summed up in this one rule: 'Love your neighbor as yourself'" (Romans 13:9).

The world needs to see our Christianity demonstrated, not by lengthy and detailed explanations of our beliefs, but, "in a nutshell," by our love.

Discovery Learning

This page contains an alternate lesson plan emphasizing learning activities. Classes desiring such student involvement will find these suggestions helpful. The next page is a reproducible activity page to further enhance discovery learning.

LEARNING GOALS

After this lesson, a student should be able to:

1. Describe love according to what Jesus taught in today's text.

2. Tell why loving God first and one's neighbor as himself is the essence of the law.

3. Look for a practical way to express love to God and for a neighbor.

INTO THE LESSON

Before the students arrive, arrange the chairs in circles or around tables, with four or five chairs per group. At each group supply a worksheet as described below. (Or refer the groups to the Discovery Learning page in the student book, *NIV Bible Student.*)

Write the heading "Confusing Definitions of Love" at the top of the worksheet. Then write the following instructions: "Define *love* as the word is used in each of the following expressions." Follow that with a list of expressions, including but not necessarily limited to these:

I love classical music. Puppy love. Forty serving love (a score in tennis). I love my country. We'd love to have you visit us. We love a sunny day. I love my husband. "Love your neighbor."

Allow six or eight minutes for the groups to discuss their definitions; then share answers quickly. Observe that our many uses and definitions of the word love have produced some confusion. When Jesus says, "Love God" or "Love your neighbor," what does he mean?

INTO THE WORD

Early in the week, ask a class member to read the lesson commentary notes on the *shema*. The class member should be ready to give a very brief report to the class on the history and significance of the *shema*. Call for the report just before Group 1 reveals the results of their discussion of question 2.

Keep the class in the groups formed earlier (at least three groups) and give each group one of the following assignments:

Group 1. Love Your Neighbor (Mark 12:28-34)

1. Do you think the scribe asked this question because of animosity he had learned from his colleagues, appreciation for Jesus' wisdom, or curiosity about Jesus' view on Jewish law. Why?

2. In citing the most important commandment, Jesus quoted Deuteronomy 6:4, 5. Why do you think Jesus connected the concept of the one God to the command to love God first and foremost? How is that relevant to us?

3. Jesus was asked to cite only one commandment, but he added a second commandment: "Love your neighbor." Why do you think he added this commandment to answer the scribe's question? Consider these options: It teaches a more holistic view of our primary duty to God; these two commands comprise a summation of all God's commands; if we love our neighbor, we are being like God, who loves all people.

Group 2. Love Your Enemies (Luke 6:27-31)

1. Which of the following best defines "love" as it is expressed toward our enemies? Why? (a) a feeling or emotion, (b) a decision of the will, (c) an idealistic but unattainable goal.

2. What is the primary benefit of loving our enemies? (a) peacemaking, (b) demonstrating how to be a doormat that people can walk on, (c) frustrating our enemies, (d) demonstrating Christ's love.

3. Who benefits most when we love our enemies—we, the enemies, or God? Why?

Group 3. Love Your Friends (John 13:34, 35)

1. Do you think the emphasis of Jesus' new commandment is on (a) our feelings, (b) our determination or will, or (c) our behavior?

2. What is distinctive about the love practiced by Christians? How does it tell people that we are Jesus' disciples, and not just "nice people"?

Allow fifteen minutes for discussion; then review the questions and expand the discussion to include the whole class. Use the lesson commentary to fill in the gaps and answer any questions.

INTO LIFE

Ask each student to write on an index card the words "I will better express my love for God by . . ." Allow thirty seconds for the students to write their answers; then ask one student to pray and ask God to bless this commitment. Do a similar exercise with the words "I will express love to a neighbor by . . ." and "I will express love to an 'enemy' by . . ." Close with a prayer of thanks for God's love and ask his help in expressing love.

Matthew, Luke, or John?

Which of the three Gospel writers includes each of the following principles of Christian living in today's texts? Write **M, L,** or **J** on the line to the right of each.

1. **Loving one another** includes enemies as well as friends. _____

2. **Loving one another** characterizes Christ's disciples. _____

3. **Loving one another** comes *second* in life's overall scheme. _____

4. **Loving one another** is simply imitating Christ. _____

5. **Loving one another** is more important than burnt offerings and sacrifices. _____

6. **Loving one another** involves a non-possessive attitude. _____

I, You, or They?

How does each of the people in the following incidents violate Christ's principles of loving one another?

Carl told the preacher, "I don't have the time to serve on the Benevolence Committee, but I'll donate $500 to their budget for the year. That's just as good, isn't it?"

Joe buys coffee for his whole office staff . . . only when Larry is out for the day. Larry is always trying to make him look bad.

Carlene regularly affirms that she believes in God and Christ. But when invited to a worship occasion or a Bible study, she refuses. She says, "I believe . . . but I don't have time or interest for such things."

FOLLOW KINGDOM PRIORITIES

WHY TEACH THIS LESSON?

Money management endows those who *have* it, but those who *lack* it are impoverished. It is a subject of popular interest, and thousands of entrepreneurs exploit the seemingly universal desire to possess its "secrets." All of us want to know how to have more money, to save more money, to pay less taxes on our money, and to invest more money more wisely.

Jesus said more about money and possessions than about many other topics. Yet most folk ignore his valuable advice. Today's text reviews one of Christ's "seminars on estate planning." Every student needs this information and inspiration. The Christian perspective on money management prioritizes "treasures in heaven" and idealizes being "rich toward God." That is a sensible approach for any generation.

INTRODUCTION

A. A FOOL AND HIS MONEY

Many of the fairy tales and fables that we learned as children cautioned us against those who would try to cheat us out of our money. Remember the story of "Jack and the Beanstalk"? Jack's mother called the young boy foolish because he let a crafty charlatan talk him into trading the family cow for a handful of beans. Fortunately for Jack, the beans turned out to be valuable after all. But then, fairy tales often have magical endings. In real life, a trade like that would not lead to a chest of gold, but to an overwhelming sense of how foolish we have been. The con man's credo is our word of warning: "A fool and his money are soon parted."

In Luke 12 Jesus tells a parable about a fool and his money. In this case, the story is not about a man who foolishly loses his money; it is about a man who saves his money in a foolish way. Neither problem is desirable, but the latter is more serious. The first scenario is often a matter of foolish judgment. However, the man in Jesus' story exhibited a foolishness that derives from an ungodly attitude, and ultimately will result in divine condemnation.

B. LESSON BACKGROUND

Luke 12 presents a collection of highlights from Jesus' teaching ministry. All of the incidents could have occurred on the same day, but it is likely that Luke is presenting a summary of the kinds of topics that Jesus often spoke about as he traveled from town to town. Jesus probably spoke these teachings in about the middle of his three-and-a-half-year ministry. During this period Jesus spent most of his time in the region of Galilee, where he was regularly confronted with crowds likely numbering in the thousands. Luke 12:1 describes the crowd gathered on this occasion as "many thousands."

Chapter 12 begins with Jesus rebuking the hypocrisy of the Pharisees. He then proceeded to challenge his hearers concerning their perspective on life. Jesus

DEVOTIONAL READING:
HABAKKUK 3:17-19
LESSON SCRIPTURE:
LUKE 12:13-34
PRINTED TEXT:
LUKE 12:13-21

Jan
10

LESSON AIMS

This lesson should encourage each student to:

1. Tell the setting for, and the significant details of, Jesus' parable of the rich fool.

2. Contrast the world's materialistic view of wealth with what it means to be "rich toward God."

3. Assess his or her own priorities and make a commitment to put God first, being content with the blessings he gives.

KEY VERSE

Watch out! Be on your guard against all kinds of greed; a man's life does not consist in the abundance of his possessions.
—Luke 12:15

taught that godly people should not worry about how they will protect and care for their lives because God is concerned about their welfare and is ready to come to their aid. What a disappointment it must have been for Jesus then to hear someone in the crowd petition him to help him get more money! Jesus used this opportunity to teach a lesson on true riches.

I. SEEK AFTER TRUE RICHES (LUKE 12:13-15)

A. AN INAPPROPRIATE REQUEST (vv. 13, 14)

13. Someone in the crowd said to him, "Teacher, tell my brother to divide the inheritance with me."

Here is a familiar sight for our day and time: family members squabbling over an *inheritance*. Many of us can tell "horror stories" about brothers and sisters fussing over the terms of a will, arguing for why they deserve to get certain items, and eyeing each other's "take" to see whether anyone is getting more than his or her share. How sad that at a time when family members need to pull together, they can be so easily pulled apart over material property.

The Mosaic law had given certain instructions regarding inheritance disputes, such as the provisions in Deuteronomy 21:15-17 for a fair distribution to a son whose mother had fallen into disfavor with his father. By the time of Jesus, rabbinical law had created an elaborate system of guidelines for the distribution of an estate among the heirs.

We are not given enough information in this verse to know why the man who spoke up felt that he was being cheated out of his portion of the family inheritance. Maybe he had a legitimate complaint, maybe not. Regardless, Jesus used the occasion to discuss the evils of covetousness and greed.

14. Jesus replied, "Man, who appointed me a judge or an arbiter between you?"

Why did Jesus refuse this man's request? Obviously not because he lacked a knowledge of Jewish law or the wisdom to make such a judgment. Most likely Jesus saw this as an unwelcome diversion from his divinely appointed ministry. It was not his mission to serve as a financial consultant or to resolve legal matters. Jesus' calling was to a work of much greater significance than redistributing money and property. His greatest desire was the redemption of the world from sin.

This is why Jesus put limits on the healing miracles he performed. He was pleased on many occasions to heal the sick in order to provide supernatural credentials for his claim to be the Messiah and the Son of God. In such cases his healings furthered his ministry. But when the crowds tried to dominate his time by demanding more healings, he had no qualms about slipping away from a town so that he could resume teaching somewhere else (Luke 4:42-44). Jesus understood that he had not been sent by the Father simply to be a doctor for physical ills. As important as such work is, it was not his primary calling. Jesus remained focused upon his divinely ordained purpose.

Could he not, however, make one exception here and help this man without upsetting his ministry? Jesus knew the Galilean multitude well. Once they got a taste for what he could do, they always wanted more. After he fed the five thousand, the crowd repaid his act of compassion by trying to block his departure and later demanded that he continue to provide them with bread (John 6:14-27). Jesus knew when it was best for the sake of his ministry to "just say no."

Would this man suffer an injustice because Jesus refused to assist him? No; there were sufficient legal venues for resolving inheritance issues. Perhaps he had been rejected already by the courts or he was attempting to circumvent the process by taking advantage of the authority the crowds ascribed to Jesus. Whatever the case, Jesus stated that this was not a matter appropriate for his attention.

WHAT DO YOU THINK?

Jesus refused to arbitrate a dispute over an inheritance. Our lesson writer says to do so "was not his mission," that his calling was "to a work of much greater significance." In what ways can we be tempted to stop short of Jesus' calling of bringing redemption and participate in lesser (though good) activities?

What is your congregation doing to encourage your young people to enter vocational Christian ministry?

WHAT DO YOU THINK?

Just as Jesus had a work of greater significance than arbitrating legal disputes, so the church has a greater work as well. However, Paul suggests the church is a better place to settle disputes within the body than the secular courts (1 Corinthians 6:1-8). If two church members asked the church to settle a financial dispute, under what circumstances would it be better to decide the dispute within the church, and when would it be better to keep it out of the church?

B. A WARNING AGAINST GREED (v. 15)

15. Then he said to them, "Watch out! Be on your guard against all kinds of greed; a man's life does not consist in the abundance of his possessions."

The tension that characterized this situation prompted Jesus to issue a warning against greed. The Greek word that is used here has an interesting etymology. The word literally means "to thirst for more." The imagery is that of a person who has finished a drink and yet still feels thirsty. Water is ideal for quenching thirst, but some beverages such as soft drinks can feel satisfying for the moment, only to leave you wanting a refill. Salty peanuts and potato chips have a similar effect on our hunger, drawing us back to them until we realize too late that we have eaten much more than we should have. A lust for material possessions can be just as strong or stronger.

Is it wrong, then, for us to desire our fair share from an inheritance, or to expect to be treated fairly in a business deal, or to ask for an honest wage for an honest day's work? Not necessarily. The problem Jesus is addressing is the matter of priorities. He is concerned about a heart that cares more about accumulating material wealth than about seeking after spiritual treasure. Isn't that what this man has done? When out of a crowd of thousands he had the privilege to speak to Jesus, he missed the opportunity to seek spiritual guidance and blessing. Instead, his thoughts were focused upon things that satisfy for a short while on this earth and then are no more. We can seek a good income on behalf of our families with a clear conscience as long as we do not allow such concerns to interfere with our devotion and service to God.

II. HAVE CONCERN FOR OTHERS (LUKE 12:16-19)

A. A TIME OF BLESSING (vv. 16, 17)

16. And he told them this parable: "The ground of a certain rich man produced a good crop.

This story is identified by Luke as a *parable*, which means that it is not a description of an actual event, but a realistic story of an experience that could happen often enough that Jesus' listeners could easily imagine it.

17. "He thought to himself, 'What shall I do? I have no place to store my crops.'

This rich farmer was enjoying a bumper crop. By God's providence he was being blessed with a higher return than he had anticipated. This raises the question: Was there anything wrong with this man's being rich? The Bible does not condemn the possession of riches. It is more concerned with our attitude toward material things, the means by which we attain them, and the way we use our abundance. Many godly men such as Abraham and Job possessed material wealth, and there is no indication in the Bible that this was unacceptable.

The classic statement that links money with evil actually says that it is "the *love of money*" that is "a root of all kinds of evil," not necessarily the possession of money (1 Timothy 6:10). As this lesson will demonstrate, there is nothing inherently wrong with enjoying the blessings God has given us, as long as we follow his rules and avoid the kind of foolish mistakes illustrated by the farmer in this parable.

B. RUINED BY SELFISHNESS (vv. 18, 19)

18. "Then he said, 'This is what I'll do. I will tear down my barns and build bigger ones, and there I will store all my grain and my goods.

What a problem to have! More income than you anticipated and no place to put it all! Some have wondered why this man would not simply build additional *barns* rather than *tear down* the old ones and put new ones in their place. It may be that he was acting out of pride and just wanted to trade in the old models for

WHAT DO YOU THINK?

Who do you think is more prone to give in to the temptation of covetousness, the rich or the poor? Why?

Do you consider yourself to be rich or poor? Compared to what?

Visual for lesson 6

This humorous poster will provide fuel for discussion as your class considers the plight of those who are not "rich toward God."

WHAT DO YOU THINK?

What good things might be true about someone with many possessions (he's a hard worker, etc.)?

What good things might be true about someone with few possessions (she's generous, etc.)?

Why are possessions a poor measure of a person's life or worth? What other measures may be more revealing?

the new ones he could now afford. But it is more likely that he was working with a limited amount of nonfarming land that would support a structure like a barn; thus, to have bigger barns he had to use the space occupied by the smaller barns. We can give him the benefit of the doubt on this issue, because his problem was not so much the new barns as the motive behind the new barns.

19. "'And I'll say to myself, "You have plenty of good things laid up for many years. Take life easy; eat, drink and be merry."'

Here is the slogan often associated with the pleasure-seeking, hedonistic mindset: *eat, drink and be merry.* Now, to be fair to this rich man, our text does not imply that he was seeking sensual pleasure or drunkenness. His sin was his self-centered attitude that gave no thought to how his blessings could be used to bless others.

Many a commentator has noted how this man's brief speech is overrun with first-person pronouns. "What shall *I* do? *I* have no place to store *my* crops . . . this is what *I'll* do. *I* will tear down *my* barns . . . there *I* will store all *my* grain and *my* goods . . . *I'll* say to *myself.* . . ." Why would this man need more storage? He was already a rich man. At no time did he consider that there might be a better way to use his surplus than to simply hoard it all for himself. It was not his enjoyment of wealth that was the problem; it was his failure to acknowledge God or to consider the needs of others.

Some wonder whether this parable implies that planning for retirement is inappropriate for a Christian. To some it appears that this man might not have been punished by God if he had continued working with his hands, rather than living off the wealth he had set aside for retirement. It has also been argued by some that laying aside money for retirement implies a lack of trust that God will provide for his people.

None of these arguments will stand up under careful scrutiny. Scripture never encourages us just to sit back and wait for God to do everything for us. Rather, it commends those who are industrious. "Go to the ant, you sluggard; consider its ways and be wise" (Proverbs 6:6). The "wife of noble character" who engages in a variety of projects to provide for her family "can laugh at the days to come" because of the preparations she has made (Proverbs 31:25). The Bible portrays Joseph in Egypt as a wise man because he heeded God's forewarnings regarding the future and filled the storehouses with grain to be reserved for the years of famine (Genesis 41:25-36).

Occasionally we Christians can come up with ideas that have the appearance of being very spiritual but in fact are lacking in good common sense. Jesus sometimes gives us a gentle rebuke regarding such matters. For example, after commending a shrewd manager for using his master's money in a way that profited himself, Jesus noted that "the people of this world are more shrewd in dealing with their own kind than are the people of the light" (Luke 16:8). In a different context, he stated a principle that contains some relevance to our question: "Be as shrewd as snakes and as innocent as doves" (Matthew 10:16). We want to be innocent of wrongdoing, but this does not mean that we have to be foolish. The person who makes no plans whatsoever for the future because he believes God will supply all he needs is likely to find himself coming up short.

USE YOUR HEAD

A minister once told of discussing with his leaders his need for life insurance. One of the men objected. He said that a minister should not worry about such things. He claimed that the minister's concern demonstrated a lack of faith. "Don't you believe that God will take care of you?" he asked. The minister wisely replied, "I believe God already took care of me when he put a head on my shoulders."

To use Jesus' words in Luke 12:15 as an excuse not to plan for the future is to misunderstand him completely. There is no sin in life insurance. There is no sin in saving. The problem with this rich farmer was that when he thought he was prepared for the future, he was thinking only of his short-term future. He completely ignored his long-term future.

While it is commendable to plan for our future on this earth, we ought to be all the more concerned that we prepare for our ultimate future in eternity. We are not fools when we look ahead. But we are certainly as foolish as the man in our lesson if we prepare only for the body and make no preparation for the soul.

Therefore, when you use your head to plan for your retirement, which you may live long enough to experience, also use your head to prepare for the one thing that we all will certainly experience: eternity.

—R. C. S.

III. BE THANKFUL TO GOD (LUKE 12:20, 21)

A. THE GIVER OF ALL WE HAVE (v. 20)

20. *"But God said to him, 'You fool! This very night your life will be demanded from you. Then who will get what you have prepared for yourself?'*

Preoccupied with himself, the rich farmer in this parable rejoiced in his blessings without any recognition of the source of those blessings. In his words there is no acknowledgment of the providence of God. There is no consideration for what God's will might be regarding his abundance. There is no mention of any word of thanks. Thus the God who is the giver of all the rich man's wealth reminded him of another great truth: God is the giver of his life as well. On the *very night* in which the farmer uttered his self-serving speech, God took away his *life* and canceled his dreams.

We have all heard the expression, "You can't take it with you." We know it is true that when we die we must leave behind all of our possessions. What an irony it would be should death come sooner than we anticipated, and many of the things we accumulated for our own pleasure are actually used by someone other than ourselves. This is the question that the rich farmer in our parable had not yet considered. If death unexpectedly interfered with his long-range plans, *then who will get what you have prepared for yourself?* David's words offer a similar perspective: "Man is a mere phantom as he goes to and fro: He bustles about, but only in vain; he heaps up wealth, not knowing who will get it" (Psalm 39:6).

B. WORTHY OF ALL OUR GRATITUDE (v. 21)

21. *"This is how it will be with anyone who stores up things for himself but is not rich toward God."*

Herein lies a summary of the sin of our rich farmer. He was so focused upon his own desires as he amassed *things for himself* that he gave no thought to how he might use his blessings to benefit others. God was nowhere to be found in his plans, because his self-centered attitude had blinded him to the need to be *rich toward God*.

Today's lesson is intended to prompt all of us to assess our attitude toward material things. This is an evaluation we need to do periodically, because we know that the love of money can be very seductive. But let us be careful not to draw erroneous conclusions from this parable. Scripture does not teach that it is wrong to have money and possessions, or to take pleasure in the good things we can attain through our labor. Life is to be enjoyed as long as we do so with a spirit of thankfulness, and act according to the moral guidelines of God's Word. "For everything God created is good, and nothing is to be rejected if it is received with thanksgiving, because it is consecrated by the word of God and prayer" (1 Timothy 4:4, 5).

WHAT DO YOU THINK?

Why was the rich farmer in the parable called a fool? What do you think he would have done differently if he had been wise? If you became suddenly rich, what would you do with the money? In what ways would you change how you live?

WHAT DO YOU THINK?

How does one become "rich toward God"? What are the benefits of this kind of wealth?

PRAYER

Our heavenly Father, who watches over our every moment and provides what your wisdom knows is best, help us to be faithful servants and wise stewards of all the blessings you have given to us. In Jesus' name, amen.

THOUGHT TO REMEMBER

"Seek first his kingdom and his righteousness, and all these things will be given to you as well" (Matthew 6:33).

DAILY BIBLE READINGS

Monday, Jan. 4—*Be on Guard Against All Kinds of Greed (Luke 12:13-21)*

Tuesday, Jan. 5—*Do Not Worry About Your Life (Luke 12:22-34)*

Wednesday, Jan. 6—*Greed Takes Away Life (Proverbs 1:8-19)*

Thursday, Jan. 7—*Money Alone Does Not Satisfy (Ecclesiastes 5:1-10)*

Friday, Jan. 8—*Amassing Wealth Unjustly Is Hazardous (Jeremiah 17:5-11)*

Saturday, Jan. 9—*Beware the Sin of Covetousness! (Micah 2:1-5)*

Sunday, Jan. 10—*Greed Is Self-Defeating (James 5:1-6)*

It is legitimate for Christians to seek to better themselves, advance in their jobs, and work for promotions. It is wrong to pursue such goals with a heart of covetousness. What is required is an attitude of *contentment*. Biblical contentment does not mean that we must stay as we are and must never seek advancement. It means that we will continue to be happy with how the Lord is blessing us, regardless of whether or not we advance any further. Contentment sees items that would be nice to possess, but acknowledges that we do not have to have them to be happy. "For we brought nothing into the world, and we can take nothing out. But if we have food and clothing, we will be content with that" (1 Timothy 6:7, 8).

Contentment never forgets the priority of spiritual riches over material possessions. When there is a conflict between the two, we know what has the greatest value for us in the long run. "Store up for yourselves treasures in heaven, where moth and rust do not destroy, and where thieves do not break in and steal" (Matthew 6:20).

HOW MUCH DID HE LEAVE?

Those of us who were fortunate enough to grow up in small towns had a great advantage. We had the chance to sit around the country store and listen to the conversations of people older and wiser. A lot of wisdom was exchanged on those worn benches outside the crossroads store. On one occasion the men in a certain town were discussing a recent death in the community. "How much did he leave?" asked one. Some speculated that the amount was quite large. Others thought it was modest. One old man hit the nail on the head. "How much did he leave? He left it all." And so will we.

You cannot cash a check or use your *Visa* card in the world to come. Job said it well: "Naked I came from my mother's womb, and naked I will depart" (Job 1:21). But while we must leave all our treasure behind and can take nothing with us, we can send it on ahead. Jesus spoke of storing up treasures in Heaven (Matthew 6:20). How do we do that? We do it by investing our treasure in people who are going to Heaven! Much of the money we make we lose. All of the money we have made and kept we will leave. The only money that we can really keep is the money we give away in God's service. Then we are being "rich toward God," as Jesus said.

It matters little the amount of your net worth here. It matters terribly, and it matters for all eternity, whether or not you are rich toward God.   —R. C. S.

CONCLUSION

The end of December has many traditions associated with it. It is a time to put away the Christmas decorations, close out the year's financial records, make New Year's resolutions—and open a pile of sweepstakes letters. Who has not dreamed at some time or another about what it would be like to win a sweepstakes or inherit a vast fortune? We imagine what we could do with all that money: the debts we would pay off, the luxuries we could buy, or the assistance we could give to our families. Some of us may even dream about how we could use some of that wealth for our favorite ministries and missions. We like to think that we would be wise stewards of our new-found riches if we ever received such a windfall.

Of course, we know better than to expect money to fall into our laps. Most of us will never have an income that provides great wealth (although we know that by the standards of many in the world, we in our society are in most ways "rich"). Even so, whatever amount of material blessings we are able to accumulate will come to us with a God-given responsibility: to cultivate a godly attitude that focuses on spiritual priorities, seeks opportunities to be generous with others, and always maintains a spirit of gratitude to God for his many blessings.

Discovery Learning

This page contains an alternate lesson plan emphasizing learning activities. Classes desiring such student involvement will find these suggestions helpful. The next page is a reproducible activity page to further enhance discovery learning.

LEARNING GOALS

Today's lesson should enable each student to:

1. Tell the setting for, and the significant details of, Jesus' parable of the rich fool.

2. Contrast the world's materialistic view of wealth with what it means to be "rich toward God."

3. Assess his or her own priorities and make a commitment to put God first, being content with the blessings he gives.

INTO THE LESSON

Before class begins, write on the chalkboard, "A fool and his money are . . ." Provide paper and pens or pencils and ask the students to complete the sentence in as many ways as they can. Give them about three minutes (or use the time while they are arriving and proceed when everyone is present), and then ask for volunteers to share their answers.

Option: Sometime before class take a survey of elementary children who may not be familiar with the popular expression about a fool and his money and ask them to complete the statement. Report on the results as you begin class.

Make the transition to Bible study by noting, "We're all familiar with the proverb, 'A fool and his money are soon parted.' But it's not always true. As our lesson today reveals, sometimes it is not reckless *spending* that makes one a fool; it may be reckless *hoarding*."

INTO THE WORD

Begin the Bible study by reading the printed text. Then ask, "What is the purpose of a will?" Use the lesson commentary notes on verses 13 and 14 to guide the discussion. Conclude by telling the class that there are two key thoughts in today's text that will guide the remainder of the study. They precede and conclude Jesus' parable. The first thought tells us what life is not: "a man's life does not consist in the abundance of his possessions" (v. 15). The concluding statement defines a fool and implies who is wise: "anyone who stores up things for himself but is not rich toward God."

1. Verse 15 tells us to beware of covetousness. What is the danger of covetousness?

2. What earned this man the title "fool"? Was he wrong in planning for early retirement? Why or why not?

3. Compare today's parable with the story of the rich young ruler in Luke 18:18-25. Do you think Jesus condemns riches? (Teacher: play devil's advocate on this one. The easy answer is, "No, Jesus doesn't condemn riches," but the temptations of the rich are great and Jesus' warnings about them can sound like a condemnation of wealth itself. Make sure the students are thinking through the warnings carefully and not just saying no because they hope to be rich someday!)

Point out to your students that the rich fool's error was not in acquiring wealth. He erred in giving the wealth a higher priority than God and by taking full credit for its acquisition. It is not a sin to acquire wealth. It is a sin to deem that wealth more important than God. The *love* of money is a root of evil (1 Timothy 6:10).

Ask your students to list aloud several earthly indicators of great wealth and success (fancy cars, summer homes, and the like). Next, ask your students to list items that make one rich toward God. Ask, "What is the difference between these two lists?" The major difference is the immortal maxim, "You can't take it with you."

Conclude this section by having verses 15 and 21 read aloud by two good readers. Observe that these verses summarize the key points of the Bible study.

INTO LIFE

Ask the class to suggest one-word descriptions of the life of this fool. Words such as *selfish* and *godless* should surface. Explain that these are qualities we do not want in our lives if we are to be rich toward God.

Ask a couple of volunteers to read Philippians 4:11-13, 19 and 1 Timothy 6:6-10. Ask the class to contrast the attitude Paul urges in these verses with the attitude of the farmer in Jesus' parable. What new insights do these verses give about the concept of being "rich toward God"?

Probably all of us would like to be "rich." Most of us, however, will not be—at least, not by the standards we usually employ to measure worldly wealth. But all of us can be rich toward God. Close with prayer, confessing that we all yield occasionally to the temptation of covetousness and asking that your students will find the joy that comes from generosity, contentment, and putting God first in their lives.

Financial Planning

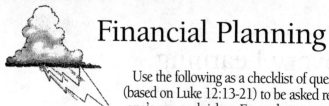

Use the following as a checklist of questions (based on Luke 12:13-21) to be asked regarding one's personal riches. For each one you answer "Yes," put a check (✔) in the space to the left.

____ (1) Did I get this money at someone else's loss? ____

____ (2) Did I "pester" God for this money? ____

____ (3) Does this money come of greed? ____

____ (4) Do I consider this money to make me what I am? ____

____ (5) Was my *first* thought upon receiving this prosperity how to make it even more? ____

____ (6) Do I think savings/investment *before* I think sharing? ____

____ (7) Am I content with what is sufficient for now . . . or do I have to consider years to come? ____

____ (8) Is my money for personal comfort and fun . . . first and foremost? ____

____ (9) Do I feel compelled to leave a major financial heritage behind when I die? ____

____ (10) Will this money allow me to bless Christ's kingdom? ____

Can you relate each question to a verse of today's text? For each, put a verse number to the right.

From the 1960's through the 1980's, a popular program to encourage growth in giving and other stewardship was called "Faith Promise." Consider a personal faith promise and complete the following statement.

Date _____

"As God blesses me financially in this new year, I will _____

_____

_____."

_____
Signed

REVERSE THE WORLD'S STANDARD

WHY TEACH THIS LESSON?

Is humility the forgotten virtue? Today's society seems to be so full of self that humble service and sacrificial submission are foreign concepts. Best-selling books, recordings, and movies expose the public's preoccupation with pride. Personal success and celebrity are the exclusive life-goals of millions. To be known, to be lauded, to be served—these are the rewards most sought after.

Even when Jesus lived on earth, position, power, and prestige were primary goals of the majority. Christ's teachings and example were revolutionary in this regard.

Human nature hasn't changed; selfishness remains the chief drive and motive of the carnal-minded. Affluence, leisure, and independence have fed some of our worst instincts. We need to hear and heed the Lord on this; we need to see and emulate his servanthood. This lesson is an opportunity to "stop, look, and listen."

INTRODUCTION

A. FEELING YOUNG AGAIN

Why is it that the older we get the more we appreciate the beauty of childhood? Judging by some of our popular expressions, you would think that we adults have a fascination with our long-lost childhood years. We speak of a grown man enjoying a hobby or a game with great enthusiasm as going through his "second childhood." When ridiculed for being an "overgrown kid" or "acting like a child," many of us are having so much fun that we consider the remark a compliment. It was an adult author who wrote the fantasy story of Peter Pan and the children living in a Never-Never Land, where one could always remain a child. We observe the innocence of a boy and a girl in love, and with longing desire we think, "Oh, to be young and in love again." And many of us have been heard to joke, "I would not mind being a child again as long as I could skip the teenage years." Childhood certainly looks inviting to those of us who can no longer experience it.

Perhaps this nostalgic feeling can help us appreciate those occasions when Jesus used children to illustrate the nature of the Christian life. Not only does the imagery of childhood easily draw our attention, but it also portrays important spiritual lessons that we all must heed.

B. LESSON BACKGROUND

Today's lesson places us in the period of the final six months of Jesus' ministry. During this time, Jesus began to speak more plainly to his disciples regarding the nature of his mission, telling them details about his imminent arrest, trial, and execution. He also gave increased attention to the more difficult themes of his message: the full commitment, hardship and sacrifice, and radical changes in thinking and acting that following him requires.

DEVOTIONAL READING:
GALATIANS 5:13-15
LESSON SCRIPTURE:
MATTHEW 18:1-4; 20:17-28
PRINTED TEXT:
MATTHEW 18:1-4; 20:17-28

Jan
17

LESSON AIMS

As a result of this lesson a student should:

1. Summarize what Jesus said about humility and greatness in today's Scripture texts.

2. Contrast the world's standards of greatness with Jesus' standards.

3. Identify someone who models Jesus' standard of greatness, and express his or her appreciation to that individual this week.

KEY VERSE

Whoever wants to become great among you must be your servant.   —Matthew 20:26

It was time for Jesus' followers to learn that being his disciple meant more than just enjoying companionship with Jesus. Discipleship still demands that we move away from the world's standard and become someone different, someone Christlike.

I. A HUMBLE SPIRIT (MATTHEW 18:1-4)

A. NOT SEEKING AFTER HONOR (v. 1)

1. At that time the disciples came to Jesus and asked, "Who is the greatest in the kingdom of heaven?"

The twelve *disciples* were men with great potential for service and leadership in Jesus' *kingdom*. Otherwise, Jesus would not have selected and trained them for such important work. Even so, during these early years of training for their future ministry, the disciples were often very immature and foolish. On more than one occasion, the Gospel writers record how they argued among themselves about what ranking each one of them deserved in the kingdom that Jesus was preparing to establish. This would not be something they would want to admit aloud to others, especially to Jesus. Matthew's account of this episode simply says that they put the question of *who is the greatest* to Jesus. The parallel account in Mark 9:33, 34 fills in what we might have guessed: the disciples refused to admit to Jesus that they "had argued about who was the greatest."

Such petty fussing must have been a great disappointment for Jesus. According to the two previous chapters of Matthew, he had begun to reveal to his disciples the dangers that awaited him in Jerusalem (Matthew 16:21; 17:22, 23). They should have been focusing more on his words and how they could encourage and support him. Instead, they were more concerned about how they might attain advancement and honor within the ranks of Jesus' followers.

B. BECOMING AS A CHILD (vv. 2-4)

2, 3. He called a little child and had him stand among them. And he said: "I tell you the truth, unless you change and become like little children, you will never enter the kingdom of heaven.

Jesus declared that his disciples must *become like little children* if they wished to *enter the kingdom of heaven*. There are so many good qualities that children possess that are worthy of our imitation: the simplicity of their lives and priorities, the way they can speak with frankness and unabashed truthfulness, and their unconditional trust in and dependence on those who watch over them. While all of these traits are exemplary, the next verse indicates the particular quality Jesus had in mind at this time.

4. Therefore, whoever humbles himself like this child is the greatest in the kingdom of heaven."

Humility was the virtue that the apostles needed to learn, especially on this occasion when they were arguing over who among them was the *greatest*. A *child* does not succumb to such foolishness. At that stage in life, he or she is filled with an unpretentious spirit that feels no need to have one's ego stroked. Competition may occur at this age over a desirable toy or a parent's affection, but there is little concern for building up one's own self-esteem while putting others in their place. The simple feeling of being loved and valued for being oneself is satisfaction enough.

All of this changes as we grow older and are told that we live in a "dog-eat-dog" world where in order to survive we must "look out for number one." We readily adapt to this new way of thinking, and childhood innocence is quickly lost. Jesus challenges us to reach back into our past and retrieve the humble

WHAT DO YOU THINK?

We don't like to admit it, but many of our disputes are, at heart, arguments about who is greatest. How does this old argument find expression in the church today?

How can we pursue the way of humility that Jesus modeled? Can you think of Scripture verses that point out the attitude we should have (e.g., Romans 12:10 and Philippians 2:3-5)?

WHAT DO YOU THINK?

Jesus said we need to "become like little children." But in Ephesians 4:14, Paul said we are to "no longer be infants." How would you respond if a friend said this was evidence of contradictions in the Bible? Read 1 Corinthians 14:20. How is a "childlike" attitude a good one, but a "childish" attitude a bad one?

spirit that we once exhibited as a child. To do so we must stop casting a competitive eye on those around us. When others do well and are honored and rewarded, we should wish them our best rather than envy their success. We should rejoice in the thought that we have family and friends, as well as a heavenly Father, who love us for who we are and not on the basis of how we measure up against others.

II. A DETERMINED WILL (MATTHEW 20:17-23)

A. JESUS' WARNING (vv. 17-19)

17. Now as Jesus was going up to Jerusalem, he took the twelve disciples aside and said to them . . .

Matthew 20 moves us a few months after the previous episode in chapter 18 to the final days of Jesus' ministry. Jesus is *going up to Jerusalem* for the Passover celebration that will also be the occasion for his arrest and crucifixion. He is apparently just days away from his journey to Jericho where he healed two blind men (Matthew 20:29-34), followed immediately by his triumphal entry into Jerusalem on a donkey (Matthew 21:1-11). Jesus *took the twelve disciples aside* so that he could tell them some information not intended for the general populace.

18. "We are going up to Jerusalem, and the Son of Man will be betrayed to the chief priests and the teachers of the law. They will condemn him to death.

This is the third recorded occasion in Matthew where Jesus gave his disciples a clear and specific description of the *death* that awaited him. Throughout most of Jesus' ministry, he had used symbolic language and parables to describe the nature of his ministry. Only during the final six months following Peter's famous confession near Caesarea Philippi did he begin to speak "plainly" regarding this matter (Mark 8:31, 32).

In his first prediction, Jesus declared that he would be killed in Jerusalem. He identified his assailants as the "elders, chief priests, and teachers of the law," also known as the Sanhedrin, the ruling body of the Jewish people. He also affirmed that he would be "raised to life" on the third day following his death (Matthew 16:21). The second prediction repeated much of this information, but added one detail: he would be *betrayed* by one of his companions into the hands of his enemies (Matthew 17:22, 23). This third prediction also included many of these same details.

19. ". . . and will turn him over to the Gentiles to be mocked and flogged and crucified. On the third day he will be raised to life!"

At this point, Jesus' third prediction of his death gave some new information to the disciples. While the Jewish leaders had already been designated as playing a significant part in his death, Jesus here indicated that they would *turn him over to the Gentiles* in order to accomplish the execution. This agrees with the political realities of that day. The Jews were under the rule of the Roman Empire and did not possess the authority to execute a criminal. If the Jews wanted to see a criminal executed, they would need to convince the Roman governor that a Roman capital law had been violated.

This third prediction also included the additional information that Jesus would be *mocked* and *flogged* prior to his death. And then, in perhaps the most amazing detail of all, Jesus specifically identified the means of his death: crucifixion. The disciples did not grasp any of this information at the time. They assumed that Jesus was still speaking in symbols; thus they were completely caught off guard, even as they watched the predicted events unfold one by one.

Consider how this episode demonstrates Jesus' strength of will. He did not walk into a trap unwittingly. He possessed a full knowledge of the horrible

The visual for lesson 7 reminds us of today's key verse, that whoever wants to be great must achieve that status through humble acts of loving service.

WHAT DO YOU THINK?

The lesson writer notes that it took great strength of character for Jesus, knowing what awaited him in Jerusalem, to go there. In what situations do Christians need similar strength? How is that strength made available to us?

HOW TO SAY IT

Caesarea Philippi. Sess-uh-REE-uh Fuh-LIP-pie or FILL-uh-pie.
Gethsemane. Geth-SEM-uh-nee.
Jericho. JAIR-ih-co.
Joses. JOE-sez.
Magdalene. MAG-duh-leen or Mag-duh-LEE-nee.
Patmos. PAT-mus.
Salome. Suh-LO-me.
Sanhedrin. San-HEED-run or SAN-huh-drin.
Zebedee. ZEB-uh-dee.

suffering that awaited him in Jerusalem. The average man would probably flee from such danger if given the opportunity, but not Jesus. He knew that mankind's eternal destiny depended upon him. He later shuddered in the Garden of Gethsemane as the decisive moment approached. But he did not depart from carrying out the will of his heavenly Father.

B. NOT SEEKING POSITIONS (VV. 20, 21)

20. Then the mother of Zebedee's sons came to Jesus with her sons and, kneeling down, asked a favor of him.

The woman in this story is called *the mother of Zebedee's sons,* who were James and John (Matthew 4:21; Mark 10:35). She is referred to one other time in the Gospels as one of three women who watched "from a distance" as Jesus died (Matthew 27:55, 56). It seems likely that she is the "Salome" mentioned in Mark's account of the women who witnessed the crucifixion (Mark 15:40). Both Gospels name "Mary Magdalene" and "Mary the mother of James the younger and of Joses," but where Matthew refers to "the mother of Zebedee's sons," Mark names "Salome." Even more intriguing is the possibility that in John's listing of the women at the cross, this woman could be the one described as the sister of Jesus' mother Mary (John 19:25). It is not certain that any of the lists includes everyone who was present, so we cannot be sure about this identification; but if it is correct, then James and John would have been Jesus' cousins.

21. "What is it you want?" he asked. She said, "Grant that one of these two sons of mine may sit at your right and the other at your left in your kingdom."

It should not surprise us to see a mother looking out for what she perceives to be the best interests of her children. We should understand, though, that she was not acting alone. According to Mark's account of this incident, James and John actually expressed this request (Mark 10:35-37). Most likely the mother put the initial request to Jesus, and then Jesus insisted that James and John speak up for themselves. Which one of the three first came up with the idea cannot be determined, but Jesus' response was specifically directed to the two disciples.

THE RIGHT-HAND MAN

Because the majority of people are right-handed, it has become proverbial to say that someone who is most important to your work or success is called your "right-hand man." The Bible even uses this figure of speech when it says that Jesus "sat down at the right hand" of God (Hebrews 1:3).

However, there are some books on the subject of gaining influence and power that suggest just the opposite. They claim that if you are present at a corporate board meeting, the most powerful place to sit is on the *left* of the chairman. (Of course, to those facing the chairman the one on *his left* is actually on *their right!*) But Jesus' disciples were not aware of all this. They regarded the person on the right as the most powerful and influential, and the one on the left as the second most powerful and influential.

If Jesus had granted the request of James and John, would that have brought the discussion to an end? Don't you suppose that the two of them would then have gotten into an argument over which one got to sit on the right side? Likely they would have. But Jesus refused to be drawn into such controversy over positions. Such debates are part of the devil's strategy. He used it with James and John, and he still uses it today: get people thinking about power and position. Then they will forget about the church's real task, and its progress will come to a screeching halt.

—R. C. S.

C. FOLLOWING JESUS' EXAMPLE (vv. 22, 23)

22. "You don't know what you are asking," Jesus said to them. "Can you drink the cup I am going to drink?" "We can," they answered.

Jesus' statement *you don't know what you are asking* was true in more ways than one. First, there was apparent in this request a misunderstanding of the nature of Jesus' kingdom. The disciples' thinking was being influenced by the traditional Jewish understanding of an earthly kingdom with thrones to sit on and armies to command. It was not until after Pentecost that these men finally grasped the idea of a spiritual kingdom that focuses on hearts committed to the lordship of Jesus.

James and John also had no idea of how much trouble they were asking for. They saw sitting next to Jesus as a position of honor. But they failed to take into account the opposition that Jesus had been facing throughout his ministry, and the suffering and death that he had recently predicted. To stand next to Jesus is to stand at the "ground zero" of hardship and persecution.

Jesus challenged James and John's request because he knew that their motive was self-serving. He wanted them to take a more realistic view of what it means to serve him and stand by his side. There is certainly a heavenly glory awaiting those who follow Jesus, but to follow him there we must first be willing to follow him in the path of suffering (Luke 24:25, 26).

23. Jesus said to them, "You will indeed drink from my cup, but to sit at my right or left is not for me to grant. These places belong to those for whom they have been prepared by my Father."

We are so accustomed to associating the word *cup* with the Lord's Supper that we could easily read the wrong idea into this passage. Jesus' *cup* was the suffering associated with Calvary, as he himself indicated when in the Garden of Gethsemane he prayed that this "cup" be taken away if possible (Matthew 26:39). His distress would not be that which courageous men are accustomed to handling, for he would experience an agony beyond our comprehension.

Certainly James and John did not realize all of this when they asked to be seated next to Jesus. They were rebuked for their selfish motives, and rightly so. But it is to their credit that Jesus also commended them. He knew that one day they would change their attitudes and become humble servants who would walk the path of suffering, not for their own glory, but for the praise and glory of their Master. Eventually James would be executed for his Christian faith (Acts 12:2), while John would be exiled to the island of Patmos (Revelation 1:9). They would ultimately be welcomed into glory, but only after they first learned humility.

III. A SERVANT'S HEART (MATTHEW 20:24-28)

A. NOT CONTROLLING OTHERS (vv. 24-27)

24. When the ten heard about this, they were indignant with the two brothers.

Were the other *ten* disciples *indignant* because the selfish request of James and John was unbecoming for a disciple of Jesus? More likely they were upset that the two brothers had presumed to place themselves above the rest. No doubt each of them had reasons why he himself should be seated at Jesus' side instead of one of the other disciples. Jesus' ensuing rebuke indicates that all of these men still had much to learn about the heart of a true disciple of Jesus.

25. Jesus called them together and said, "You know that the rulers of the Gentiles lord it over them, and their high officials exercise authority over them.

The power model of leadership used by authority figures in politics, military life, and business uses coercion, intimidation, and the threat of stiff penalties to achieve desired goals. Decisions are often unilateral, dictated from the top to

DAILY BIBLE READINGS

Monday, Jan. 11—A Child Among Them (Matthew 18:1-4)

Tuesday, Jan. 12—Not to Be Served, But to Serve (Matthew 20:17-28)

Wednesday, Jan. 13—I Have Set You an Example (John 13:1-15)

Thursday, Jan. 14—The Strong Ought to Help the Weak (Romans 15:1-6)

Friday, Jan. 15—I Am Unworthy (Genesis 32:3-12)

Saturday, Jan. 16—Humility Comes Before Honor (Proverbs 15:25-33)

Sunday, Jan. 17—Humble in Spirit (Isaiah 57:15-21)

WHAT DO YOU THINK?

Jesus' definition of greatness is very different from the world's. Do you think it is appealing to the world or repulsive? Why?

Do you know someone who has authority but does not deserve it? What is this person like? Do you know someone who deserves authority but does not have it? What qualities do you think of as "deserving" of authority? Do these match Jesus' idea of greatness? Why or why not?

those on the bottom. In such a system, a person learns to play by the rules and advance, or eventually be trampled on by everyone else.

26, 27. *"Not so with you. Instead, whoever wants to become great among you must be your servant, and whoever wants to be first must be your slave—*

In contrast, the *servant* model of leadership guides people along by persuasion, wisdom, and godly example. Decisions are made, not to advance the leader's own interests and wealth, but for the good of those he leads. This is noticeably different from the way the world operates. But if the world's standard had been acceptable to God, Jesus would not have shown us a better way.

THE GREATEST IN THE KINGDOM

A certain king was very successful and well known. He had defeated all his enemies, and his people lived in peace and prosperity. To honor the king, they held a great banquet. Many attended and paid tribute to the king with their gifts.

That night one of the king's trusted counselors awakened him, greatly worried. "I've just dreamed a terrible dream," he told the king. "I dreamed that the greatest man in the kingdom is going to die tonight." Immediately the king stationed guards at the door to his room, in the corridors, and at the door to the palace. He could not sleep. The next morning, however, he felt fine. He told the counselor, "You had me scared for no reason at all," and put him in chains.

Later that day, the king went on a tour of his capital city. All the people cheered him until he reached the poorest part of the city. Here the crowds were not cheering. They told the king, "It's not that we don't wish you well, but a man in our neighborhood died last night. You wouldn't have known him, but he was a slave in your palace. He didn't have much money, but if anyone was in need he managed to help. He had a hard life, but he was always cheerful and happy. He died last night."

The king stopped his tour. He released his counselor. He told his advisers, "I am going on a long journey. I may never come back. My son will rule in my stead." The king never returned. But some noticed a new slave in the palace, doing what the old slave had done. The man looked remarkably like the king.   —R. C. S.

B. IMITATING OUR LEADER (v. 28)

28. *"Just as the Son of Man did not come to be served, but to serve, and to give his life as a ransom for many."*

There is no question that as our Creator and Redeemer, Jesus has absolute authority over all. He has the right and power to demand anything he wishes, and to treat us any way he chooses. Yet the example that he set for us in the incarnation was that of a humble servant who was fully dedicated to doing the will of God, even to the point of suffering on a cross. This is still the standard for anyone who would be his disciple.

CONCLUSION

Many times I have spoken with students or friends who have quit their jobs before finding other employment. When I ask why they would quit before they had another job lined up, they say, "I just could not stand to work another day being treated like that!"

I may question the wisdom of my friends' timing, but I understand their frustration in working for an employer who uses his authority in a manner that breaks morale. The world's approach to authority may seem to get results; but it is demeaning to those on the bottom, and ultimately unfulfilling for those on the top.

The lesson for today challenges us to "reverse the world's standard." If we are going to "quit" anything, let us quit playing by the world's rules and follow the model of Jesus. Let us develop a servant's heart.

PRAYER

Our Father in Heaven, break down within us the remnants of worldly pride and selfishness, so that we may serve you and those around us in a humble manner, for your glory and honor. In the name of Jesus. Amen.

THOUGHT TO REMEMBER

"The Son of Man did not come to be served, but to serve, and to give his life as a ransom for many" (Matthew 20:28).

Discovery Learning

*This page contains an alternate lesson plan emphasizing learning activities. Classes
desiring such student involvement will find these suggestions helpful. The next page
is a reproducible activity page to further enhance discovery learning.*

LEARNING GOALS

As a result of this lesson, a student should:

1. Summarize what Jesus said about humility and greatness in today's Scripture texts.

2. Contrast the world's standards of greatness with Jesus' standards.

3. Identify someone who models Jesus' standard of greatness, and express his or her appreciation to that individual this week.

INTO THE LESSON

Before class, prepare enough slips of paper to tape one to the bottom of every chair in the classroom. On a third of the slips write, "I became a Christian through the influence of _____."

On the second third write, "_____ is someone who has helped me in my Christian walk."

On the remaining third write, "Someone who has given freely of himself or herself for the sake of the Lord is _____."

Ask each person to reach under his seat, remove the slip of paper he or she finds there, and write the name of an individual who fits the description on the slip of paper. Give the students about two minutes, and then instruct them to pair up with another person with the same assignment. Once each student has a partner, ask the group to spend five minutes telling each other why the individuals named fit the descriptions. Then ask volunteers to share their responses with the whole class.

Tell the class that the definition of greatness varies with different people's perspectives and goals. Some would name people of power. Some would name people of authority. But the people your class has named are better examples of what Jesus meant by "greatness." The beauty of his definition is that every person can become great in the grandest kingdom of all.

INTO THE WORD

Ask a volunteer to read Matthew 18:1-4; 20:17-28. (Or use a VCR to show a video dramatization of the text. Some very good ones are available.)

Use a flip chart or a couple of sheets of poster board to help the students follow the movement of the text and remember the principles gleaned in this study. Put this heading on the first page of the flip chart or poster board: "Lessons From Little Children About Greatness."

After reading or viewing Matthew 18:1-4, give a brief lecture about why Jesus would use children for illustrations. (The commentary section of this book will help you prepare the lecture.) Then ask and discuss the following questions:

1. Why do you suppose the disciples asked, "Who is the greatest in the kingdom of heaven?"

2. What did Jesus mean by, "Unless you change and become like little children, you will never enter the kingdom of heaven"?

3. What did Jesus teach us about humility in verse 4?

4. What are the specific lessons you learn about greatness and humility from this teaching? (Make a list of the students' answers on the flip chart or poster board.)

On the second page of the flip chart or poster board, print this heading: "Lessons From Grown-up Kids About Greatness." After reading or viewing Matthew 20:17-28, do a short lecture on the specific details Jesus was giving about his future in verses 17-19. Then, from verse 20, explain "Zebedee's sons." These "grown-up kids" presented another opportunity for Jesus to teach a lesson on greatness.

Ask these discussion questions:

1. Why would this mother ask such a bold favor of Jesus?

2. What was Jesus saying to James and John with his question about his "cup"? What was he implying about their future?

3. What was Jesus telling them—and what does he say to us—about greatness?

4. Contrast the model of the "rulers of the Gentiles" with Jesus' model of greatness in verses 25-27.

INTO LIFE

When a person strives for greatness in the world, he strives to better himself. Often he is oblivious to how his pursuit damages those around him. Jesus' model starts with helping others first. What personal greatness we achieve is awarded us by God, our Father.

In closing, ask each student to think of a person he considers great by Jesus' standard. Ask your students to think of a way to thank this person for services rendered. Often, this thanks can take the form of a letter, a prayer, a phone call, or even a service rendered in return. Close the class with prayer, and challenge the students to appreciate those who are great by Jesus' standard.

Good (Jewish) Mothers!

In both of today's texts, we have evidence of a loving—if perhaps "pushy"—mother. Examine each of these attributes and decide how today's texts represent each concept. At the end add one or two "Good Mother Sayings" of your own.

The good mother makes certain her child is in the right place at the right time.

The good mother wants the very best for her child.

The good mother speaks up on behalf of her child.

The good mother risks herself for the sake of her child.

The good mother encourages her child to speak up for herself or himself.

The good mother. . . .

The good mother. . . .

The Master Teacher

In every era, master teachers have used audiovisual aids to help learners understand and remember conceptual truth. The Master Teacher set a worthy example in the Matthew 18 text: He used "a little child" to represent the ideal kingdom person. Read each of the following Scriptures. Identify what the Master Teacher used to visualize his lesson; identify the truth he was teaching.

	ITEM	TRUTH
MATTHEW 22:17-21	_____	_____
MATTHEW 6:28-30	_____	_____
MATTHEW 26:26-28	_____	_____
JOHN 20:24-27	_____	_____
ACTS 2:1-4	_____	_____

The Hardest Lesson of All

Of all the hard lessons on greatness that Jesus teaches in today's texts, which would you call "the hardest lesson of all"?

FORGIVE ONE ANOTHER

LESSON 8

WHY TEACH THIS LESSON?

"Selective forgetters"—that's what we are! We easily forget names, dates, appointments, promises, shopping lists, sermons, and where we parked the car. But we rarely forget slights, slanders, insults, offenses, hassles, conflicts, and betrayals. Why is that? To make matters worse, the older we get, the more we seem to forget items in the first category, and the less likely we are, it seems, to forget wrongs like the ones in the second list. We might forget before suppertime what we ate for lunch, yet harbor a grudge over an incident that happened decades ago.

Some of the difference is linked to an unforgiving spirit. We don't forget what we won't forgive. We must be reminded of our need to be *forgiven,* and of our need to be *forgiving.*

This lesson is such a reminder.

INTRODUCTION

A. ANIMAL PSYCHOLOGY

Those who study animal behavior will tell us that animals have an instinct for "learning" from their experiences. If a dog is hit with a rolled-up newspaper each time he jumps up onto a sofa, he will soon be conditioned to stay off the sofa. A cat that is sprayed with water each time she scratches the side of a chair quickly learns to stay away from that chair. A mouse that bumps his nose a few times on a barrier placed in the middle of a maze will soon learn not to go down that portion of the maze.

Mankind approaches the experiences of life with certain God-given advantages over the animals. We have greater reasoning abilities, we can devise a plan in our minds and determine to see it through, and we can make freewill decisions. In short, we possess the image of God.

Why is it, then, that we are so often slower than the animal kingdom to learn from our mistakes? Too often we repeat the same errors that brought us trouble before, forgetting the lessons learned from previous experiences. As for positive reinforcement, we readily feel appreciation for those who show kindness to us; but then we fail to see the logical implication: people would appreciate us in like manner if we showed them the same kindness that we have received. Life's classroom has much to teach us, but we have to pay attention.

B. LESSON BACKGROUND

Poor Peter! In the Gospel accounts, he tries so hard to come up with clever things to say; but more often than not, his great ideas end up looking pretty lame. We read the incidents recorded in the Gospels and talk about Peter's penchant for "putting his foot in his mouth." In today's text he attempts to make a perceptive observation regarding forgiveness, and then finds himself on the receiving end of a short sermon.

But think how easy it would be for any of us to make the mistake Peter made. Jesus had just finished giving instructions regarding a brother who "sins against you," explaining how to discipline someone who refuses to deal responsibly with

DEVOTIONAL READING:

PSALM 103:6-14

LESSON SCRIPTURE:

MATTHEW 18:5-35

PRINTED TEXT:

MATTHEW 18:21-35

LESSON AIMS

Today's lesson should encourage each student to:

1. Tell how Jesus illustrated the limitless grace of God and the duty that believers have to imitate his grace.

2. Explain the relationship between receiving God's grace and showing grace to others.

3. Attempt this week to resolve a conflict in such a way as to demonstrate God's grace at work in his or her life.

Jan
24

KEY VERSE

If you forgive men when they sin against you, your heavenly Father will also forgive you. But if you do not forgive men their sins, your Father will not forgive your sins. —Matthew 6:14, 15

his sin when confronted with it (Matthew 18:15-20). It would be natural to assume that certain people may not deserve to be forgiven, especially if they keep repeating the same sin.

What Peter failed to consider in his thinking was that immediately before Jesus gave the "sinning brother" instructions, he had told the parable of the lost sheep (Matthew 18:12-14). Here Jesus painted a beautiful picture of the heart of God. As our Shepherd, he understands how easy it is for sheep to get lost; but because he values us so much, he does not abandon us to our folly. Instead, he does whatever he can to rescue even one sheep and restore it to the fold. True, there are appropriate times for tough measures when discipline should be applied, but even that should be done in harmony with a grace that desires an individual's restoration. Judgment should not begin until grace has had a hearing.

I. FORGIVE AS OFTEN AS ASKED (MATTHEW 18:21, 22)

A. A REASONABLE PLAN (v. 21)

21. Then Peter came to Jesus and asked, "Lord, how many times shall I forgive my brother when he sins against me? Up to seven times?"

There is nothing in this text to indicate how Peter arrived at the number *seven* as his limit. Some have theorized that there may have been a rabbinical tradition of requiring forgiveness up to three times. With this in mind, Peter is said to have generously doubled the minimum number and then added one more for good measure. Whatever the reason for Peter's choosing the number seven, it is clear that he desired to set some kind of limit on forgiveness.

Apparently Peter was thinking that a person does deserve a second chance, but only so many "second chances." A person who continues to do the same wrong over and over is evidently not very serious about quitting, and not very sincere when he says, "I'm sorry." To keep on forgiving such a person unconditionally might very well tempt a sinful heart to take advantage of one's goodness. Clearly stated ultimatums and limits could serve as a much-needed wake-up call. What Peter proposed was not unreasonable.

B. GRACE EXPLAINED (v. 22)

22. Jesus answered, "I tell you, not seven times, but seventy-seven times.

Jesus did not question Peter's logic, but he challenged him to consider a better plan: grace. The biblical idea of grace is to treat a sinner better than he deserves to be treated. It is the nature of grace to go beyond what is reasonable and fair to something that is admittedly undeserved. Grace does not ask us to do something that is less than fair; rather, it challenges us to be more than fair.

Grace is not an easy path to take. In fact, it requires a measure of spiritual maturity in order to maintain such a posture. After all, it is possible that a sinful heart may try to take advantage of your gracious disposition. And it is not easy to watch a person do wrong and yet go unpunished.

Perhaps grace would be an easier course of action if we also saw its positive aspects. A sinner who knows that we have forgiven him and will not pay him back could walk away feeling smug about his sin; however, being the beneficiary of grace has a way of stirring up a guilty conscience and melting a sinful heart (Romans 12:17-21). That is why it can be beneficial, when we forgive someone, to make it clear that we are doing so as a gracious choice, and not out of weakness or necessity. Forgiveness done well can be an opportunity for a persuasive gospel witness. As for someone's taking advantage of us, we can rest assured that God will one day "balance the scales" so that those who abuse us will pay, while we will be blessed with so much more than we ever lost.

WHAT DO YOU THINK?

Have you ever been offended by someone more powerful than you, and you could do nothing about it? Have you ever been offended and had the perfect opportunity to retaliate? What did you do? What is hard about forgiving in each case? How can we forgive "as a gracious choice, and not out of weakness or necessity"?

Who benefits most from forgiveness, the giver or the receiver? Why?

Let us not then read Jesus' number *seventy-seven times* as a replacement limit for Peter's suggestion. Jesus was making a play on words based on Peter's comment. He used a large number that does not lend itself to record keeping; for it is not his intent that we keep count of the wrongs we have forgiven, but that we forgive indefinitely.

LOSING COUNT

The man has collected clocks for years. He has hundreds of them—small clocks, large clocks, old clocks, new clocks. Every room of the house has at least a dozen or two. If someone asks, "How many clocks do you have?" his answer is: "I don't know. My grandchildren try to count them every time they come to visit. They get up to about eight hundred, and then they can't remember which ones they've counted and which ones they haven't. They lose count."

Isn't this what Jesus had in mind when he gave his reply to Peter's generous offer to forgive seven times? To try to keep track of seventy-seven wrongs becomes a tiring, frustrating exercise. One soon loses count of such record keeping, and realizes that it is not worth the effort. The *New English Bible* translates 1 Corinthians 13:5 as follows: "Love keeps no score of wrongs." Keeping score is exactly what we often do. And after our enemy has run up the score to a certain point, we decide that it is time for us to get even.

Sometimes people have missed the point of Jesus' words in the Sermon on the Mount: "If someone strikes you on the right cheek, turn to him the other also" (Matthew 5:39). They claim, "Jesus said to turn the other cheek, but he didn't say what to do after that!" But of course, Jesus *did* say what to do after that; he said it in today's lesson. Keeping score demands that we keep on remembering. Forgiving demands that we also try to forget. That may be the hardest part of forgiving, but it is also the most rewarding.

                         —R. C. S.

The visual for lesson 8 puts the words of the king of the parable (vv. 32, 33) in the mouth of Jesus. On the cross he forgave us so much—can't we forgive our brothers and sisters?

II. FORGIVE REGARDLESS OF THE COST (MATTHEW 18:23-27)

A. A STAGGERING DEBT (vv. 23-25)

23. *"Therefore, the kingdom of heaven is like a king who wanted to settle accounts with his servants.*

Parables are stories that are taken from real life and used to illustrate spiritual truths. The most frequently used imagery in Jesus' parables for representing the interaction of God and mankind is that of a king and his subjects.

The *servants* in this parable should not be thought of as slaves who worked for minimal compensation or nothing at all. It is more accurate to view them as managers who were commissioned by the king to invest his resources in projects that would bring a handsome return. For the king to *settle accounts* involved a summoning of each manager to the court to report on his investment of the king's money.

24. *"As he began the settlement, a man who owed him ten thousand talents was brought to him.*

There is no way to put an exact dollar figure on *ten thousand talents* and expect it to remain accurate in an age when monetary values change daily. But we can come up with a rough idea that will enable us to appreciate the message of Jesus' parable. A denarius in New Testament times was equal to one day's wages, that is, what a person would be paid for one day's work on a typical manual labor job. One talent was worth approximately six thousand denarii, or six thousand days of labor. Ten thousand talents would thus be the equivalent of the income from sixty million work days! Once such a sum of money was lost, it would be virtually impossible to repay the debt. The only viable option was to sentence the debtor to prison.

25. *"Since he was not able to pay, the master ordered that he and his wife and his children and all that he had be sold to repay the debt.*

Both Jewish and Roman law contained certain provisions for dealing with loan defaults and financial mismanagement. A debt repayment plan was a possibility if the size of the debt was manageable. When repayment was not feasible, a person had the option of recouping some of his losses through the sale of the debtor's property and family. While this seldom, if ever, covered the full debt, it at least provided the satisfaction of seeing the debtor receive a stiff punishment.

It may seem strange and cruel to us to include the *wife* and *children* in such a penalty. This reflects the view (common in ancient cultures) that the head of a household acted in behalf of the rest of the household; thus, when he was guilty, so were they to a certain extent.

B. GRACE BESTOWED (vv. 26, 27)

26. *"The servant fell on his knees before him. 'Be patient with me,' he begged, 'and I will pay back everything.'*

This debtor's plea was totally unrealistic. No matter how patient the king chose to be, the servant would never be able to *pay back everything.* The only hope that remained was that his king might bestow grace upon him.

27. *"The servant's master took pity on him, canceled the debt and let him go.*

The *master,* or king, is the hero of this parable. He is the model of grace in action. We have no way of knowing how much this loss affected him financially. No matter how you look at it, to lose the equivalent of millions of dollars had to hurt! To forgive a *debt* this size could happen only at a great cost to the king. Grace is not an easy course to follow.

Jesus would have us learn to forgive no matter what the cost. After all, is that not the way God has dealt with us? By his grace he has arranged a plan of redemption that allows us to be forgiven of our debt of sin, but only at the unthinkable cost of the life of his Son.

The king's action teaches us something else about grace: it cannot be demanded; it can only be requested. No one can require that you forgive them. No one who owes you a debt can obligate you to write off that debt. It is the nature of grace that it must be a gift freely given, or it is not really grace. The king in Jesus' parable was under no obligation to the debtor. He acted out of *pity,* not necessity.

III. FORGIVE AS YOU HAVE BEEN FORGIVEN (MATTHEW 18:28-35)

A. A LESSON FORGOTTEN (vv. 28-31)

28. *"But when that servant went out, he found one of his fellow servants who owed him a hundred denarii. He grabbed him and began to choke him. 'Pay back what you owe me!' he demanded.*

The amount *a hundred denarii* is the money an average worker would earn for one hundred days of manual labor. Sometimes a teacher today who wants to contrast the size of the two debts will liken the second debt to a few pennies or a few dollars. This actually damages the credibility of the story, for no court of law, Jewish or Greek, would imprison a man for such a small amount. However, one hundred denarii was an amount significant enough to call for legal action.

In modern terms, the difference in the two debts would be equivalent to the difference between owing a few thousand dollars and owing several million. The latter is beyond hope of repayment, while the former is manageable and could be resolved with a little patience. Our *servant,* however, was not in the mood for any patience or grace.

WHAT DO YOU THINK?

The master was moved by compassion to forgive his servant. How can we develop compassion as a motivation to be more forgiving?

Think about a time you were in debt to someone and it was forgiven, or you felt guilty about offending someone, and the person forgave you. How did you feel before? After? How did this change your outlook on this person?

WHAT DO YOU THINK?

The "unforgiving servant" had a legal obligation to repay his debt. He failed but was treated as if he had done right. Later he had a legal right to demand repayment of the debt owed to him. But when he did so, he was treated as an evildoer. Do you think some might find this irony to be unfair? Why or why not? How would you explain it to a friend who was struggling with the concept of God's justice?

29. "His fellow servant fell to his knees and begged him, 'Be patient with me, and I will pay you back.'

One would think that this plea would have had a familiar ring to our servant, since he himself had uttered these same words not long before. The old expression is so true: "How quickly we forget!"

30. "But he refused. Instead, he went off and had the man thrown into prison until he could pay the debt.

How could a person *pay* a *debt* while sitting in a *prison*? One way was through a system by which the prison farmed its inmates out as slave labor. A prisoner would then be credited with a small amount of money that could be applied directly to his debt. Obviously it would take a long time to pay off a debt in this manner, but it could be done after several years.

A faster way for a prisoner to repay a debt was to call upon his family and friends to rescue him from his dire circumstances and pay his debt for him. These people might act out of compassion, or they might simply desire to remove an embarrassment to the family. The person who forced a debtor into imprisonment would not care how he got his money, just as long as he got it.

31. "When the other servants saw what had happened, they were greatly distressed and went and told their master everything that had happened.

The *other servants* would be other men whom the king considered responsible enough to serve as managers of his large estate. As we might expect, men working the same job would naturally form a fraternal relationship, perhaps with some mutual assistance and even friendly competition for honors. And as this story indicates, over time they would develop a concern for the welfare of each other that would prompt them to stick up for one of their own who was not treated properly.

B. GRACE DENIED (vv. 32-35)

32, 33. "Then the master called the servant in. 'You wicked servant,' he said, 'I canceled all that debt of yours because you begged me to. Shouldn't you have had mercy on your fellow servant just as I had on you?'

The *master* did not argue on the basis of what the law demanded, because legally the *servant* was not required to cancel a *debt* (even though he had just had his own debt canceled). This was simply a matter of common courtesy, evident to the king, the fellow servants, and (Jesus apparently assumed) to his hearers as well. No law was required in this matter. It should be natural for a person who has received a grace in the "millions" to demonstrate a similar grace with a much lesser debt. Rightly so is this man called a *wicked servant*.

34. "In anger his master turned him over to the jailers to be tortured, until he should pay back all he owed.

The cancellation of the ten thousand-talent debt was rescinded and the wicked servant sent to prison. One might wonder how a debt earlier forgiven could legally be reinstated. Perhaps there was some stipulation in Roman law that allowed for putting conditions on a debt cancellation. Perhaps this was simply a matter of royal prerogative. In the case of God's forgiveness, however, we know how this works. The justification for sin that we enjoy now is always conditioned upon whether or not we continue to live by faith (Colossians 1:21-23; Revelation 2:10). Those of us who do not live by grace could one day lose the grace we now enjoy (Galatians 5:4).

To say that the wicked servant would suffer until he could *pay back all he owed* was not to imply that repayment was possible. This debt was too great to be repaid. Jesus was saying that this person would not be released from his torture as

---

HOW TO SAY IT

denarii. dih-NAIR-ee or dih-NAIR-eye.

denarius. dih-NAIR-ee-us.

DAILY BIBLE READINGS

Monday, Jan. 18—No Stumbling Blocks! (Matthew 18:6-14)

Tuesday, Jan. 19—Dealing With a Sinning Brother (Matthew 18:15-20)

Wednesday, Jan. 20—How Often Must I Forgive? (Matthew 18:21-35)

Thursday, Jan. 21—Restore Transgressors! (Galatians 6:1-5)

Friday, Jan. 22—"Be Kind . . . Compassionate . . . Forgiving" (Ephesians 4:25-32)

Saturday, Jan. 23—God Forgives; So Should We (Psalm 103:6-14)

Sunday, Jan. 24—I Will Remember Their Sins No More (Hebrews 10:11-25)

long as any debt remained—and we know that there will always be a debt remaining. This was actually a creative way of referring to an eternal suffering, thus providing a good analogy to Hell.

35. "This is how my heavenly Father will treat each of you unless you forgive your brother from your heart."

Forgiveness seems to work by a variation of the Golden Rule: "So in everything, do to others what you would have them do to you" (Matthew 7:12). It is appropriate to practice forgiveness, so that those you forgive will in turn be gracious with you when you do them wrong. But our greater concern is not the forgiveness of man, but the forgiveness of our *heavenly Father*. We "do to others" as we would have God do to us.

Jesus' warning is clear. We who refuse to *forgive* others jeopardize our status with God. To refuse to forgive after we have been forgiven of so much is a "slap in the face" of Almighty God. It suggests a lack of appreciation for what God has done, perhaps even an insincerity in our appeal for mercy. We dare not be cheap with a grace that cost God so much.

FREQUENT FORGIVER POINTS?

All the major airlines now offer their passengers "frequent flyer points." Sometimes one can also accumulate points by using a certain credit card or long distance service. If you accumulate enough points, you can get a free ticket to fly on the participating airline.

At first glance this concluding verse in today's printed text sounds like a plan for "frequent forgiver points." This is especially true if we combine it with the portion of the Lord's Prayer that says, "Forgive us our debts, as we also have forgiven our debtors" (Matthew 6:12). It sounds as if each time we forgive someone, we earn the forgiveness of one of our sins. (If that were true, we'd better hope that others do a lot of harm to us, so we can build up enough points to get forgiveness for all our sins!)

But Jesus was not talking about a one-for-one exchange. His meaning is this: when we are unforgiving, we build a shell around our hearts that even the grace of God cannot penetrate. If, having been forgiven by God, we do not forgive others, we show that we have not realized the magnitude of God's forgiveness of us. When we have done so, we will want to treat others as God has treated us.

This is not a merit system. We earn no merit badges. We accumulate no points. We do show what kind of persons we are and whether we understand what it means to be saved by grace.   —R. C. S.

CONCLUSION

Even those of us who do not play baseball know the expression, "three strikes—you're out." In baseball there are rules and boundaries. So also in life. We have deadlines for turning in school assignments and filing income taxes. We have limits on the number of trips we can make to the salad bar. We have honor codes at military academies that require immediate expulsion for violations. We learn to play by the rules or "we're out." This is the way most of life needs to be in order to work effectively. After all, how is the other team ever going to get a time at bat if there are no limits on strikes?

Not so with forgiveness. As Peter learned, there are no limits on how often we are to forgive others. We who have received an immeasurable amount of grace from God have a responsibility to be as gracious as we can with others. If we cannot forgive the lesser debts against us, why should we expect God to forgive our debt of sin? Three strikes . . . seven strikes . . . seventy-seven strikes . . . let us not think of limits, but rather let us think of, and rejoice in, God's abounding grace!

Discovery Learning

This page contains an alternate lesson plan emphasizing learning activities. Classes desiring such student involvement will find these suggestions helpful. The next page is a reproducible activity page to further enhance discovery learning.

LEARNING GOALS

Today's lesson should encourage each of your students to:

1. Tell how Jesus illustrated the limitless grace of God and the duty that believers have to imitate his grace.

2. Explain the relationship between receiving God's grace and showing grace to others.

3. Attempt this week to resolve a conflict in such a way as to demonstrate God's grace at work in his or her life.

INTO THE LESSON

Write the following open-ended sentences on poster board to display before students arrive.

"A time an acquaintance offered forgiveness that I did not deserve was . . ."

"One occasion I really struggled with forgiving someone was . . ."

"The biggest barrier to forgiving someone is . . ."

Prepare three cans or baskets, each labeled with one of the three open-ended sentences above. Ask each person to jot an answer on a piece of paper. Do not sign names. Ask the students to drop the papers into the appropriate can or basket. At random, draw three slips of paper from each can and read the answers.

Make the transition from this activity to Bible study by admitting to the class that forgiveness is not an easy thing to do. Forgiveness is unnatural. But Jesus forgave us, and he expects us to forgive each other. In today's lesson, Jesus illustrates the grace of God and the duty believers have to imitate his grace.

INTO THE WORD

Distribute handouts as described below (or refer the students to the proper page in *NIV Bible Student*). Have a transparency or poster prepared with the same information.

On the handout, write the following headings across the top: *Person, The Offender, The Debt,* and *Action.* Under *Person* write the following in a vertical column: Peter, King (first time), Servant, King (second time), and Heavenly Father.

Have a volunteer read Matthew 18:21-35 aloud. Then ask the students to work in groups of two or three to complete the handouts. Next to each "person" listed in column 1, the students should write who offended

the person ("offender"), how ("debt"), and what the person did about it ("action"). After the groups have completed their work, review the parable with the whole class by completing the chart on the overhead transparency or poster as volunteers give you information. As you complete the chart, comment on how the events of the parable illustrate God's forgiveness of our debts or sins. For example, the servant could not repay his debt, and we do not have any way to repay our debt for sin.

Ask the class, "Do you think Jesus' primary objective was to answer Peter's question about forgiving someone or to teach about God's grace? Why?" (Note: Jesus accomplished both objectives with this parable.)

Discuss the lesson writer's statement: "The biblical idea of grace is to treat a sinner better than he deserves to be treated." How does that define God's grace toward us?

Do a brief summary, stressing that the king is a model of grace in action (see the commentary on verses 27 and 35). Jesus wants us to learn to forgive, no matter what the cost.

INTO LIFE

These questions will help students apply the lesson to their personal lives:

a. Would there be forgiveness of the debt or forgiveness of our sins without asking for it or without repentance? Why or why not? (See the notes on verse 27.)

b. The definition, "Grace is to treat a sinner better than he deserves to be treated," can also be applied to our relationship with persons who have offended us. What are the positive aspects of this kind of behavior? What kind of impact could forgiveness have on the offender? (See the commentary on verse 22.)

c. Why is practicing forgiveness good for the one who forgives? List the answers to this question on a chalkboard or poster board.

To conclude the lesson, ask the class to recall persons they've forgiven or have not yet forgiven. Remind them forgiveness is not easy, but God expects it of us. Challenge them to resolve at least one conflict this week in such a way as to demonstrate God's grace.

Just before the closing prayer, ask someone to lead the class in singing the chorus, "Change My Heart, O God."

To Forgive or Not to Forgive:
That Is the Question

Jesus quickly and thoroughly disagreed with Peter's forgiveness quotient. And poor Peter thought he was being so agreeable! Today's lesson writer draws a number of conclusions about forgiveness. Do you Agree or Disagree with his statements? Circle your status for each.

A D 1. "We are often slower than the animal kingdom to learn from our mistakes."

A D 2. "Clearly stated ultimatums and limits could serve as a much-needed wake-up call."

A D 3. "Judgment should not begin until grace has had a hearing."

A D 4. "Forgiveness done well can be an opportunity for a persuasive gospel witness."

A D 5. "Jesus would have us learn to forgive *no matter what the cost*." (Italics added)

A D 6. "Grace cannot be demanded; it can only be requested."

A D 7. "It should be natural for a person who has received a grace in the 'millions' to demonstrate a similar grace with a much lesser debt."

A D 8. "Those of us who do not live by grace could one day lose the grace we now enjoy."

A D 9. "We who refuse to *forgive* others jeopardize our status with God."

A D 10. "We dare not be cheap with a grace that cost God so much."

Setting Limits on Grace

Peter's concept of setting limits on grace is totally rejected by Christ. Which of the following schemas represents your own attitude toward forgiveness: is it "boxed in," with limits? Or is it limitless?

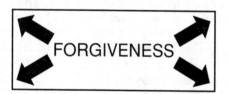

KNOWING NO BOUNDARIES

LESSON 9

WHY TEACH THIS LESSON?

Christians are surrounded by foreign cultures. We are a significant minority, if not a "silent majority." Our values, convictions, and codes of conduct distinguish us from most of our neighbors.

Our worldview, our sense of priorities, our personal agendas do not match. Though we speak the same language, our philosophies, our loyalties, and our perspectives are likely to differ from those of the general populace.

Are we prepared to share our faith with these "odd" folks? That's what cross-cultural evangelism means: personal witnessing to people who are different. People with different backgrounds, education, incomes, and ideas—they all need Jesus and the abundant life he came to bring.

The apostle Paul ventured far "out of his element" to preach in Athens. His example, documented in this lesson, can be instructive to us as we consider leaving our comfort zones to become "all things to all men so that by all possible means" we might win some (1 Corinthians 9:22).

INTRODUCTION

A. ONE LEG AT A TIME

It is our natural tendency to feel anxious and ill at ease when unfamiliar situations arise. For example, we are easily intimidated when we first encounter someone who is distinguished or famous because of personal achievements, power and prestige, or education and expertise. We wonder if we can handle our end of a conversation with such an individual without looking awkward and foolish.

Yet what a pleasant surprise to discover, after getting to know a person, that he or she is not that different from us. In fact, most people whom we hold in high esteem turn out to be ordinary people just like us. As the saying goes, "They put their pants on one leg at a time just as we do."

In Acts 17 the apostle Paul stepped out of his "comfort zone" as he moved from preaching the gospel to his Jewish brothers and sisters to discussing religion with "professional" Greek philosophers in Athens. Luke (the writer of Acts) does not record how Paul felt about this new experience; but if he was like most of us, he probably felt a certain amount of "fear and trembling." Yet Paul found the courage to stand before these highly intelligent scoffers and speak to them in a way that actually challenged their thinking.

How did he do it? We will note in today's study that Paul identified some ideas and concerns that he and the Athenians shared. Both believed that they were made by a divine Creator, that they had a religious duty to seek out this Creator, and that they needed to find a way to appease him for the wrong things they had done. Paul came to realize that these new people in this strange culture were not much different from himself. This sense of identity allowed him to break through the cultural and intellectual boundaries that tend to intimidate, in order that he might present to them the gospel that they needed to hear.

DEVOTIONAL READING:
PSALM 96
LESSON SCRIPTURE:
ACTS 17:16-34
PRINTED TEXT:
ACTS 17:22-34

LESSON AIMS

As a result of studying this lesson, a student should:

1. Summarize the content and the results of Paul's message before the Areopagus.

2. Compare the methods of Paul in trying to reach a Greek audience with current methods of reaching our secular culture.

3. Suggest one specific way the student can reach beyond his comfort zone to share the gospel with someone whose religious and cultural backgrounds are different from his own.

Jan
31

KEY VERSE

God . . . commands all people everywhere to repent. For he has set a day when he will judge the world with justice by the man he has appointed. He has given proof of this to all men by raising him from the dead.

—Acts 17:30, 31

LESSON 9 NOTES

B. LESSON BACKGROUND

As the story of Acts 17 unfolds, we find Paul in the early stage of his second and longest missionary trip. His ministry thus far had been primarily in Asia Minor (what we know today as Turkey). But evangelistic boundaries began to crumble in Acts 16:9, 10 when Paul received a heavenly vision challenging him to go to Macedonia (modern-day Greece). There was great significance in this move, because it represented the advancement of the gospel from beyond its Middle Eastern beginnings to a European culture. It marked Paul's entrance into the world of cross-cultural evangelism.

Once in Macedonia, Paul continued to use his proven evangelistic strategy of first seeking out the Jewish synagogue in a new town and using his own Jewish identity as a point of contact for preaching the gospel of Jesus Christ. When he finally arrived in Athens, Paul quickly made contact with the local synagogue (Acts 17:17). He also witnessed about Christ in the open marketplace, and it was here that he encountered the philosophers of Athens. Two different schools of Greek philosophy, the Epicureans and the Stoics, began to challenge Paul in open debate. They resisted his teaching, calling him a "babbler" who was "advocating foreign gods" and "bringing some strange ideas" (vv. 18-20). They brought him to a meeting of the Areopagus, where Athenians and foreigners gathered to debate the latest ideas.

A lesser man might have been frightened away by such a challenge, back to the familiar comfort of the Jewish synagogue. But Paul saw an opportunity to present the gospel here; for as skeptical as they were, the Greek philosophers were also very much intrigued by new ideas (v. 21). Paul accepted their invitation to speak in a more formal setting. He took the unchanging gospel and presented it in a way best suited to challenge the hearts and minds of a different kind of hearer, thereby showing us how the good news can penetrate the boundaries that often separate us from others.

I. OUR CREATOR GOD (ACTS 17:22-25)

A. EVIDENT TO ALL MEN (vv. 22, 23)

22. Paul then stood up in the meeting of the Areopagus and said: "Men of Athens! I see that in every way you are very religious.

The location for Paul's address was known as the *Areopagus*. This was an open-air court on an elevated plateau in the middle of Athens. It was the place where the Athenian Supreme Court deliberated, as well as one of several locations where public disputations were held. The term can refer either to the location where the group met or to the group itself.

Paul was able to *see* something about the religious character of the people of Athens by observing their public idols and temples. It has been estimated that first-century Athens may have had two to three thousand idols on display. This would have been overwhelming to a Christian who was a first-time visitor. Perhaps that was part of what Luke meant when he said that Paul was "greatly distressed" (Acts 17:16) at the sight of the idols.

Paul began his remarks by describing the *men of Athens* as *very religious*. Some wonder how Paul could have referred to idol worshipers in such a seemingly positive manner. He may have been using a mild compliment to "soften up" his audience, so that they might give him a fair hearing. Some have suggested that Paul intended to be ambiguous (the Greek word translated *religious* is rendered "superstitious" in the *King James Version*). Thus, by making the Athenians wonder whether they had just been complimented or criticized, he would have given them further reason to listen carefully to what else he had to say.

WHAT DO YOU THINK?

Athens in Paul's day was the crossroads of philosophical thought (see Acts 17:21). Planting a gospel seed in that soil was an important step. What forum in our community or nation might be comparable? How can we gain a hearing for the gospel in such an important field? How did Paul get invited to speak in the meeting of the Areopagus? What pattern does this suggest for us?

WHAT DO YOU THINK?

The Athenians were a "very religious" people. What issues must Christians address in sharing the gospel with "religious" people today? How do you stand up for the truth of the Bible without demeaning others or their beliefs? How did Paul handle it?

23. *"For as I walked around and looked carefully at your objects of worship, I even found an altar with this inscription:* TO AN UNKNOWN GOD. *Now what you worship as something unknown I am going to proclaim to you.*

We do not know the occasion for setting up an anonymous *altar,* but we can imagine how it was used thereafter. The city of Athens apparently intended to pay tribute to every religious personage that existed, without slighting even one. This would be a daunting challenge if one did not know for certain how many gods there are. An undesignated altar, however, could serve as a "miscellaneous" object of worship to cover any god that may have been inadvertently missed.

It is interesting that Paul could take something evil (a pagan altar) and turn it into an occasion for teaching the truth. Here is a principle worthy of note: to commend someone for a good thing he is doing does not necessarily imply that you approve of everything he does. Sometimes Christians will stubbornly refuse to acknowledge anything good in churches or religions different from their own for fear that it will appear that they have compromised their convictions. However, to recognize *both* strengths and weaknesses in another is not only the honest thing to do, but, as Paul demonstrates, it can also pave the way for further dialogue and teaching.

B. BIGGER THAN WE IMAGINE (vv. 24, 25)

24. *"The God who made the world and everything in it is the Lord of heaven and earth and does not live in temples built by hands.*

As Paul looked for some common ground with the Athenians from which he could present the gospel, he began with the most fundamental of beliefs: the existence of a divine Creator. As Paul explains in Romans 1, mankind has always sensed that someone wise and powerful must have put together all that we see (Romans 1:20). All of nature, from living beings to inanimate objects to the heavenly bodies, possesses an intricacy and beauty that testifies to an intelligent Designer. In theology we speak of this concept as "general revelation," that is, the testimony that creation gives on behalf of its Creator.

Nature does not reveal the name of our Creator, nor does it speak in great detail regarding his nature or his expectations. But the Athenians had demonstrated their acknowledgment of the existence of a Creator (though their method left much to be desired). Now Paul was testing them to see if there was a genuine desire to know more about this God who was yet unknown to them.

25. *"And he is not served by human hands, as if he needed anything, because he himself gives all men life and breath and everything else.*

The city of Athens contained several pagan temples. In fact, the Areopagus was located within sight of the most important worship center of that time—the Parthenon. This view provided Paul with the perfect occasion to present the idea that the Creator does not dwell "in temples built by hands" (v. 24), nor does he require the services or gifts of man in order to maintain his existence. Anyone capable of creating a universe is obviously too big to fit inside a building suited for man, and is far too powerful to require assistance from someone as small as man.

Such an argument as this would sound reasonable to the Greek philosophers whom Paul was addressing. In fact, by the first century many of the educated Greeks and Romans no longer believed the ancient pagan myths, though they retained a belief that there was some kind of divine Creator. Paul's description of the Creator was meant to appeal to the thinking of the "modern" philosopher of the first century.

HOW TO SAY IT

Aratus. AIR-uh-tus.
Areopagite. Air-ee-OP-uh-gite.
Areopagus. Air-ee-OP-uh-gus.
Athena. Uh-THEE-nuh (th as in thin).
Athenians. Uh-THIN-e-unz.
Athens. ATH-unz.
Cleanthes. Clee-AN-theez.
Corinth. KOR-inth.
Corinthians. KOR-in-thee-unz.
Damaris. DAM-uh-ris.
Dionysius. Die-oh-NISH-ih-us.
Epicureans. Ep-ih-CURE-ee-unz.
Epimenides. Ep-ih-MEN-ih-deez.
henotheism. HEH-nuh-thee-ih-zum (th as in thin).
Macedonia. Mass-uh-DOE-nee-uh.
Nebuchadnezzar. NEB-uh-kad-NEZZ-er
Parthenon. PAR-thuh-non.
Pericles. PAIR-ih-kleez.
Stoics. STOH-iks.
Zeus. Zoose.

The visual for lesson 9 is a dramatic reminder that the Lord Jesus will one day judge the whole world. Display it as you begin to discuss verse 31.

A TEMPLE BUILT BY HANDS

We do not know how many hands it took to build the magnificent temples in Athens to which Paul could easily point as he spoke before the Areopagus. We do know that it took fifteen years (from 447 to 432 B.C.) to build one of them: the Parthenon. This temple to Athena, the Greek goddess of wisdom, required countless quarrymen, haulers, carpenters, stonecutters, sculptors, goldsmiths, workers in ivory, and painters. On a frieze located between the temple's outside columns and its walls, workmen carved and painted 350 figures of men and women and 125 horses. Thousands of tons of marble were hauled from a quarry ten miles away. The cost was astronomical. A little over two years after it was built, Pericles, the ruler who inspired and commissioned it, died. Soon after that the worship of Athena died as well.

We marvel that so much effort went into building a temple for a god that never has existed. Our God is the living God, and as Paul told the Athenians, no temple "built by hands" is adequate to house him. How humbling the thought that the only temple where God longs to dwell is us (1 Corinthians 3:16; 6:19)!

—R. C. S.

II. OUR RELIGIOUS DUTY (ACTS 17:26-29)

A. TO SEEK AFTER GOD (vv. 26-28)

26. *"From one man he made every nation of men, that they should inhabit the whole earth; and he determined the times set for them and the exact places where they should live.*

Without mentioning the name of Adam, Paul declared that the human race originated from *one man.* Greek philosophy did not typically speak this way; and yet the philosophers could readily grant that humanity had to begin somewhere small, then grow to the size it had now become.

As for Paul's description of God's involvement in political affairs, the Old Testament declares that God's hand is "stretched out over all nations" (Isaiah 14:26). To King Nebuchadnezzar, Daniel declared, "He [God] changes times and seasons; he sets up kings and deposes them" (Daniel 2:21).

All of this is in keeping with Paul's statement to the Athenians that God determines how long he will allow each nation to stand, and how far each nation may advance in conquest. Exactly how he does all of this is not certain to us, because from our perspective the workings of God in the world are very discreet. Even so, we must pray about social and political issues, believing that God is actively involved in the affairs of mankind, though we may not always know how.

BLOOD TYPES

Most people have one of four blood types: A, B, AB, and O. Until quite recently you could not put type A blood into a type B person, or vice versa. Blood donors who were type O, however, could give blood to anyone.

Just recently, however, scientists have come up with a substance that can coat the molecules of blood so that one need not find a donor with the same type of blood that he has. Does this confirm Paul's statement that God has created the nations "from one man" (Acts 17:26)? Yes, it does, for the blood types do not divide along any racial or ethnic lines. The pigment of your skin has no bearing on the type of blood you have in your veins. The color of your hair or eyes has nothing to do with the type of blood you have. The land of your family's origin has no bearing on the type of blood you have.

Of course, Paul was not giving a lecture on biology or human anatomy. He was talking about the fact that we are all human and that we all have a common ancestry in our Creator. No race is superior to another, and no ethnic group is better

DAILY BIBLE READINGS

Monday, Jan. 25—"God . . . Commands All People Everywhere to Repent" (Acts 17:16-34)

Tuesday, Jan. 26—Cornelius Is Instructed by an Angel (Acts 10:1-8)

Wednesday, Jan. 27—Peter's Vision (Acts 10:9-16)

Thursday, Jan. 28—Peter Welcomes the People From Cornelius (Acts 10:17-23a)

Friday, Jan. 29—No One Is Impure or Unclean (Acts 10:23b-33)

Saturday, Jan. 30—God Shows No Partiality (Acts 10:34-48)

Sunday, Jan. 31—Salvation Is for Everyone (Romans 1:8-17)

than another. God does not honor such distinctions, and we should not take notice of them. We are all made in the image of God. Jesus died for all of us.

—R. C. S.

27. *"God did this so that men would seek him and perhaps reach out for him and
find him, though he is not far from each one of us.*

Once one realizes that a Creator exists, he should naturally desire to know
more about this Creator—who he is, what he is like, and how one can please
him. Paul expresses a similar idea in Romans 1 when he explains why God is
angry with pagans who have seen his general revelation, yet refuse to *seek* him.
"What may be known about God is plain to them, because God has made it
plain to them. For since the creation of the world God's invisible qualities . . .
have been clearly seen, being understood from what has been made. . . . For although they knew God, they neither glorified him as God nor gave thanks to
him" (Romans 1:19-21). This is religious duty in its most elementary form,
something with which Paul's philosophy-minded listeners could agree.

28. *"'For in him we live and move and have our being.' As some of your own poets
have said, 'We are his offspring.'*

Paul tells us something about his own education by citing two statements
from ancient Greek literature. These quotations were meant to highlight man's
special relationship to his Creator. *In him we live and move and have our being* was
apparently written by a poet from Crete named Epimenides, who lived around
600 B.C. *We are his* [God's] *offspring* was first recorded by the third-century B.C.
Greek philosopher Cleanthes in his "Hymn to Zeus," and then later repeated by
the poet Aratus (at around 270 B.C.) in a poem entitled, "Phenomena."

Why would Paul quote material from pagan sources? To do so would enhance
his credentials in the eyes of this critical and skeptical audience. By showing that
he was well versed in their literature, Paul would appear to them as a learned
man worthy of their time and attention. By giving the Greek poets credit for
knowing some truth about God, he would be more likely to be judged an honest
and fair-minded man by the Athenians. And, in fact, Cleanthes' "Hymn to Zeus"
is recognized as a pivotal work in influencing Greek thought toward an acceptance of monotheism—a belief in one god rather than in many.

Christians need to be acquainted with the literature, music, art, and other elements of their surrounding culture. Often we can use these to illustrate the futil-
ity of life without Christ and the need of the world for the abundant life that only
Jesus can give.

B. TO THINK OF HIM CORRECTLY (v. 29)

29. *"Therefore since we are God's offspring, we should not think that the divine
being is like gold or silver or stone—an image made by man's design and skill.*

Having established some intellectual rapport with his audience, Paul could
present a more direct criticism of their position. Bowing to an idol does not make
sense, and men as intelligent as these philosophers should have known better.

III. OUR FINAL JUDGMENT (ACTS 17:30-34)

A. ALL WILL BE JUDGED (vv. 30, 31)

30. *"In the past God overlooked such ignorance, but now he commands all people
everywhere to repent.*

Even when linked with good intentions, idolatry is always an offense against
God. All through the Old Testament age, God was gracious enough to restrain
his anger at such *ignorance* and not bring the fury of Hell upon the nations at

WHAT DO YOU THINK?

*Paul displayed both a thor-
ough understanding of Scripture
and a familiarity with the Greek
culture and literature of the day.
To what extent is that a precedent
for Christians today to follow?*

*Evangelical Christians, one
skeptic said a few years back, are
"ignorant" and "easily led." Can
you think of an occasion when
the skeptic appeared to be right?
How can Christians refute this
idea by argument, or prove it
wrong by their conduct?*

WHAT DO YOU THINK?

*Many of the Athenians prac-
ticed "henotheism": they worshiped one god but acknowledged
that there were other gods worshiped by others. What similarities do you find between Athens
and our culture?*

*How would you argue against
the idea that all belief systems
must be accepted as equally
valid—that "we all worship the
same God, just by different
names"?*

WHAT DO YOU THINK?

Paul did not spend a long time in Athens, perhaps because it was a relatively resistant field. His preaching met with greater results in Corinth and Ephesus, and there he spent much more time. What can we conclude? Should we spend the most time in fields that look the most promising? How should we evaluate church programs and evangelistic efforts—especially in resistant fields?

PRAYER

Father, grant us the courage to reach out beyond where we feel safe and secure, and to touch people we have never imagined touching before. In Jesus' name, amen.

THOUGHT TO REMEMBER

"Go into all the world and preach the good news to all creation" (Mark 16:15).

that time. But whereas he *overlooked* that disobedience, he will not do so forever. There will be a day of judgment in which those who have offended him will pay dearly, unless they *repent* of their sin.

31. "For he has set a day when he will judge the world with justice by the man he has appointed. He has given proof of this to all men by raising him from the dead."

The Athenian philosophers would readily grant that a Creator exists. They could concede the logic of Paul's description of man's religious duty to that Creator (though they might not have appreciated his criticism regarding idols). And if they were honest, they would have to admit that they had considered the possibility that one day they may have to give an account to this Creator regarding how they have treated him. Paul builds upon this natural instinct and declares with certainty: you will be condemned by the Creator whom you have offended, if you do not respond to his plan of salvation.

Some are troubled that the name of Jesus is not mentioned in this account. But this is obviously a summary of Paul's message. (We assume that he preached longer than the five minutes it takes to read these verses in Acts.) It may be that during the complete sermon, Paul mentioned Jesus several times. It was Paul's preaching of "Jesus and the resurrection" (v. 18) that led to his being invited to speak before the Areopagus. That Jesus' name is not mentioned in this brief summary should not concern us.

B. A MIXED RESPONSE (vv. 32-34)

32, 33. When they heard about the resurrection of the dead, some of them sneered, but others said, "We want to hear you again on this subject." At that, Paul left the Council.

For some of the philosophers, Paul lost his credibility as a logical thinker when he spoke of a *resurrection of the dead*. Others were interested in hearing Paul defend his case for the resurrection, but assumed they had plenty of time to debate this new issue later. What a tragedy to see people put off until it is more "convenient" a decision with eternal implications (Acts 24:25)! This should challenge us to make sure that we are ready today to face the One who will pass eternal judgment on us.

34. A few men became followers of Paul and believed. Among them was Dionysius, a member of the Areopagus, also a woman named Damaris, and a number of others.

We know nothing about *Dionysius, a member of the Areopagus,* or *Damaris,* except what is said in this passage. We would do well just to focus on what we are told: Dionysius, Damaris, and some unnamed friends gathered to hear a man present a new philosophy, but went home having received new life through Jesus Christ the Savior.

CONCLUSION

Your local theme park opens a new ride. For the first few weeks the line is two or more hours long, and yet the ride lasts no more than five minutes. As much fun as it may be, was it worth the trouble you went through to get on?

The cultural and intellectual boundaries confronting Paul at the Areopagus put his ministry skills to the test. The pressure would have been great; the results, somewhat disappointing. Was it worth the effort, Paul? Absolutely, he would say. A new mission field was breached, a nucleus of believers was formed, and the seed of truth was planted in a pagan land. From such a small beginning as this, great things can happen in God's kingdom. From such small steps as these, boundaries once thought impenetrable by the gospel are removed.

Discovery Learning

This page contains an alternate lesson plan emphasizing learning activities. Classes desiring such student involvement will find these suggestions helpful. The next page is a reproducible activity page to further enhance discovery learning.

LEARNING GOALS

As a result of studying this lesson, a student should be able to:

1. Summarize the content and the results of Paul's message before the Areopagus.

2. Compare the methods of Paul in trying to reach a Greek audience with current methods of reaching our secular culture.

3. Suggest one specific way to reach beyond his comfort zone to share the gospel with someone whose religious and cultural backgrounds are different from his own.

INTO THE LESSON

Before class begins, prepare letter-sized posters to be hung from the ceiling in various parts of the room. Print one of these religious or secular groups on the front and back of each poster: *Mormons, Jehovah's Witnesses, Muslims, Jews, New Agers, Humanists, Secular Scientists.* Feel free to add any other group to this list. As the students enter the classroom, ask them to select a sign that identifies a group with which they are at least somewhat familiar and stand under that sign. Make sure the class is evenly dispersed. If too many people choose a particular sign, ask a few students to join one of the other groups.

Ask the groups to sit together and give each group a poster board and this assignment: "Identify (1) some good practices or beliefs of people in this group and (2) some faults in their beliefs. Write your information in large print on the poster and select one person to report your information to the class."

After you have allowed each group to report its findings, remind the class how intimidating it is to share our faith with someone whose belief system is very different from our own. Yet the apostle Paul models a method of doing so. He identifies something good about the belief and uses this as a way to introduce the truth. Say, "Each of you knows something about one of the beliefs we have posted about the room. You have shared the good and the bad about them. How can we use this knowledge to introduce the Lord? Let's see how Paul did this."

INTO THE WORD

Use the information in the commentary section to develop a brief lecture on the background for this magnificent teaching event. Explain that this event is a practical model of cross-cultural teaching, one of the most intimidating challenges we may face as we try to share Christ.

Prepare a poster or transparency with the following information on it. (Do not include the material in italics.)

PAUL'S MODEL OF EVANGELISM
What did Paul observe in Athens? (vv. 16, 22, 23)
Idols and pagan altars.
How did he capture attention? (vv. 22, 28)
He dubbed the Athenians "very religious," referred to the altar to the unknown god, and cited Greek poets.

PAUL'S MESSAGE
• The common ground (vv. 24, 25)
The existence of a divine Creator. (Be sure to explain "general revelation" from the lesson commentary notes on vv. 24-27.)
• Who is God? (vv. 24-26, 29)
He is not an idol, and he is not dependent on man. He is the Creator.
• What has God done? (vv. 24-26)
He has given life and breath to all men. He has created the many nations and has determined their place and time in history.
• God's expectation (vv. 30, 31)
God expects all men to come to repentance.

THE MIXED RESPONSE (vv. 32-34)
Various Athenian responses included rejection, procrastination, and acceptance.

After reading the text, ask the class members to help you complete the outline. Use the information in italics to assist you.

Note that Paul's trip to Athens was not a comfortable experience. He was "put on the spot" by some of the greatest thinkers in Athens. Paul performed well, however. Rather than attack his audience's beliefs, he identified the strengths and weaknesses of the Athenian religion and used that as a springboard into a discussion of Christ.

INTO LIFE

Turn to the posters created in the lesson introduction and ask how we could use Paul's model to reach people in these groups. Ask each student to think of one person who falls into one of the categories posted. Encourage each one to implement Paul's model and introduce that person to the gospel.

Athenian Political Correctness

The Athenians of Paul's day were "enlightened," or so they thought. They made every effort to be "politically correct"! Examine the text to identify a verse or verses that might suggest the following "politically correct" views and behaviors.

_____ —did not want to offend anyone's religion

_____ —wanted everyone to have opportunity to present his or her views

_____ —affirmed there was a brotherhood of man and a fatherhood of God (gods!)

_____ —believed that all are the offspring of God (the gods!)

_____ —let logic and natural "science" determine what they would believe

Pauline Theological Correctness

Paul's "political correctness" was simple: he wanted to "become all things to all men so that by all possible means I might save some" (1 Corinthians 9:22). But to do that he would never compromise theological correctness. Examine the text to identify a verse or verses that affirm the following basic theological doctrines.

_____ —God is essentially unknown to many

_____ —God created the world and everything in it

_____ —the Creator is also Lord of Heaven and earth

_____ —God is not contained in a physical temple

_____ —God gives life to people

_____ —God controls nations and history

_____ —God wants people to find him

_____ —God expects people to repent of sin

_____ —God has appointed a man for judgment

_____ —that man lived, died, and has been resurrected

P.C. Meets T.C.

Every day in one's life "political correctness" meets "theological correctness." The Christian must be prepared for the conflict. What sort of problems arise when the two stand face to face? What is the best way to resolve the problem? How does Paul's example—by the Spirit—give help . . . and hope?

OBEYING CIVIC AUTHORITIES

LESSON 10

WHY TEACH THIS LESSON?

When Henry David Thoreau published his essay, "On the Duty of Civil Disobedience," in May of 1849, it was largely ignored. One hundred fifty years later it is regarded as a pinnacle work, having influenced the likes of Mahatma Gandhi in India and Dr. Martin Luther King, Jr., in the United States. If a law of government is "of such a nature that it requires injustice to another," Thoreau wrote, then it is the duty of the just to "break the law."

Many Christians endorse this concept of civil disobedience. Citing the example of Peter, who declared, "We must obey God rather than men!" (Acts 5:29), some Christians today approve of a wide variety of lawbreaking in the name of God. This lesson urges caution on this issue, even as it notes Peter's example. Paul makes it clear that civil disobedience is the exception for the Christian rather than the rule. Given the frustration many Christians feel about their government, this is a timely lesson.

INTRODUCTION

A. PATRIOTISM

Every country in the world has a flag, its own banner that identifies not just a political and geographical boundary, but a people. Bound together by history and tradition, and often by ethnic ties, this people takes its place among the many peoples of the world. When many of the flags of the world hang together, as they may during the Olympic Games or other international athletic competition, one can always pick out his own country's flag. Its unique colors or striping or emblem always stands out. We are proud of our flag because we are proud of our country.

We feel a similar pride—a surge of patriotism—each time we see a military parade, with soldiers decked out in their dress uniforms and marching proudly to a patriotic tune. When our national anthem begins to play, we are instantly on our feet, standing proudly, perhaps searching for that flag of which we are so proud. As the music comes to an end, a tear may trickle down our cheek. An impartial observer of all of this would conclude that we must possess a great respect for our country.

So why is it, then, that crime persists, with citizens hurting their fellow citizens? Is not every violation of the law an affront to the country in which we take such pride? Why do average citizens, including Christians, feel that there is no real harm in violating certain laws—like speed limits, for example? Since we Christians should strive to be genuine in all things, perhaps it is time that we brush up on the basics of citizenship.

B. LESSON BACKGROUND

Today's text is taken from an epistle written by the apostle Paul to a church living in the most important city of his day—the imperial city of Rome. Paul shared with so many others a fascination with Rome, expressing in this letter his long-standing desire to one day visit and minister in this city (Romans 1:10-13). His

DEVOTIONAL READING:
1 PETER 2:13-17
LESSON SCRIPTURE:
ROMANS 12:9—13:14
PRINTED TEXT:
ROMANS 13

LESSON AIMS

After today's lesson students should be able to:

1. Summarize Paul's teaching on good citizenship in Romans 13.

2. Explain why a Christian should show respect to civic authorities even when their views and actions are questionable.

3. Suggest at least one way to be a better Christian citizen, and begin to implement it in the coming week.

Feb
7

KEY VERSE

Everyone must submit himself to the governing authorities, for there is no authority except that which God has established. The authorities that exist have been established by God.

—Romans 13:1

HOW TO SAY IT

Belshazzar. Bel-SHAZZ-er.
Nebuchadnezzar. NEB-uh-kad-
NEZZ-er.

WHAT DO YOU THINK?

What is the result when citizens refuse to "submit . . . to the governing authorities"?

Think of an instance where Peter disobeyed civil authority (Acts 3). Still, he counsels Christians to "submit . . . to every authority instituted among men" (1 Peter 2:13). When is civil disobedience in order?

dream was fulfilled just a few years later (in a way he likely did not anticipate), when he was taken to Rome as a prisoner (Acts 28).

The epistle to the Romans does not reveal a specific occasion that prompted Paul to write. It does not indicate that there was any previous communication between Paul and the Romans. There do not seem to be any controversial issues that Paul has been called on to address. The letter reads more like a doctrinal treatise in which Paul uses twelve chapters to examine the grand theme of salvation by grace.

Chapter 13, from which our Scripture text comes, likewise does not indicate that it was occasioned by a previous question or problem. Perhaps Paul decided to develop the subject of a Christian view of government and citizenship, because he assumed that Christians living in the capital of the Roman Empire would have a great interest in this. Whatever their concerns with such matters may have been, we know that subsequent generations of Christians have struggled with the issue of what is the proper way to relate to a secular government, especially when that government is hostile to our religious convictions. What Paul tells the church at Rome has abiding relevance for church-state relationships in today's world as well.

I. OBEDIENT CITIZENS (ROMANS 13:1-7)

A. FOR GOD'S SAKE (vv. 1, 2)

1. Everyone must submit himself to the governing authorities, for there is no authority except that which God has established. The authorities that exist have been established by God.

The Christian's primary duty to civic laws and officials is to *submit himself,* or be obedient. This is a God-given responsibility of *everyone* without exception.

There is a problem, though. Could Paul really be saying that God is responsible for oppressive dictators and regimes that persecute the church? Perhaps he is best understood as saying that God has ordained the *principle* of civic government. The heart of man is so sinful that he will repeatedly take advantage of his neighbor if he thinks he can get away with it. That is why it is in the best interest of all of us to have some kind of civic *authority* over us, to keep us in check when we consider hurting each other. No one form of government has been established in God's Word as the ideal, but the legitimacy of governing authority has been *established by God.* Even a bad government is still God-ordained, because it is still better than the anarchy of no government at all.

None of this should be thought to imply that God condones the wrong actions of a government. The prophet Daniel, for instance, informed kings such as Nebuchadnezzar and Belshazzar that God would hold them responsible for the misuse of their God-given authority (Daniel 4:19-28; 5:18-23). Whether the individual is good or bad, we remain obligated to submit to legitimate authority, even if he is as bad as the infamous persecutor Nero—the ruler of the Roman Empire when Paul penned these words.

2. Consequently, he who rebels against the authority is rebelling against what God has instituted, and those who do so will bring judgment on themselves.

One who *rebels against* a civic *authority* participates in an implicit rebellion against the God who gives authorization to all rulers. It is quite likely that a person defying an earthly power would have no intent to oppose God. His complaint would be solely against the ruler he perceives as undeserving of his submission. Regardless of what we intend, however, we will be judged on the basis of what God perceives. Respect for authority, even bad authority, is necessary simply because it is what God expects of us.

B. FOR YOUR OWN SAKE (vv. 3, 4)

3. For rulers hold no terror for those who do right, but for those who do wrong. Do you want to be free from fear of the one in authority? Then do what is right and he will commend you.

Rulers hold no terror for those who do right. An honest citizen should not be afraid of government officials. After all, if their job is to punish lawbreakers, then we who are not lawbreakers have nothing to *fear* when we see them or when they drive through our neighborhood.

4. For he is God's servant to do you good. But if you do wrong, be afraid, for he does not bear the sword for nothing. He is God's servant, an agent of wrath to bring punishment on the wrongdoer.

It may seem surprising to see Paul refer to a government official as *God's servant.* Yet anyone in such a position is to be viewed in this manner because he is the human instrument whom God uses to effect justice on earth.

Paul notes that God uses an earthly ruler to be an agent of wrath to bring punishment on the wrongdoer. This phrase calls to mind Paul's earlier words in Romans 12:17-19, where he teaches that individuals are not permitted to repay anyone "evil for evil." Should you hurt me, I am not to strike you back, curse you back, or shoot you back. We as individuals have no authority, from the state or from God, to try to punish someone who has done us great harm. "'It is mine to avenge: I will repay,' says the Lord." We are to allow God to administer vengeance as he sees best.

However, God's plan is not always to wait until Judgment Day. Just six verses after Paul's declaration of God's vengeance (12:19), we are told that even on this earth he will punish some of the wrong done to us. His agent of justice is government. Criminal penalties by a human court are a God-appointed means for getting some relief from the injustices we suffer from criminal activity. Paul himself was not averse to using the legal system of his day to avoid being mistreated (Acts 16:35-39; 22:22-29).

One of the ongoing debates within society and the church is just how much vengeance is appropriate for a fallible, human government to take. Some are opposed to the use of deadly force in law enforcement, the execution of murderers, and even the support of one's country in warfare. Those who take such a position believe that only God has the right to take a human life—even that of a hardened criminal. This position has the appearance of taking the moral high ground, but it fails to take into account the clear teaching of Scripture about government's role as God's appointed avenger.

When God started creation all over again with Noah and his family, he not only authorized the practice of execution, but also the agent. "Whoever sheds the blood of man, by man shall his blood be shed; for in the image of God has God made man" (Genesis 9:6). The nation of Israel fought many wars under the authorization and guidance of divine revelation. Soldiers such as Cornelius were told how to receive remission of sins (Acts 10:43), but no soldier was told in Scripture to discontinue his military service. When Paul was on trial in a Roman court, he did not challenge the state's right to execute him if they found him guilty of a capital crime; he only insisted that he was not guilty (Acts 25:11).

Christians should support a government's pursuit of justice. Anyone who serves as an agent of government is doing something legitimate and honorable, according to biblical precedent. Of course, any Christian who does not feel comfortable using an instrument of deadly force should refrain for the sake of conscience. But he should not expect that everyone else must do as he does, for God has declared that human governments are to *bear the sword* as his servant.

WHAT DO YOU THINK?

If it is the duty of governments to be a terror to the evil, how is that best accomplished?

What happens if the people in a government, or the people of a country, cannot agree on what is good and what is evil? What if they cannot agree on who is responsible for evil actions?

WHAT DO YOU THINK?

How can government officials be "God's servants" even if they are not part of the church? Does this mean that church and state should not be "separated"? How can God work through government even if it is not obedient to him?

The state should enforce the right and oppose evil. Where do we get our ideas of what is right and what is wrong?

C. FOR CONSCIENCE' SAKE (vv. 5-7)

5. Therefore, it is necessary to submit to the authorities, not only because of possible punishment but also because of conscience.

Paul has made the theological case that it is our duty to *submit to the authorities* lest we show disrespect to God, who has ordained such authority. He has given the pragmatic reason that it is wise to obey our authorities so that we will not have to face their *punishment* for our disobedience. Now Paul points out the personal reason that we must obey lawful authority: *because of conscience.*

Whenever we violate or take lightly the rules of those who have authority over us, we know deep within ourselves that we are wrong. Do you want to have a good feeling about yourself? Then do what is right. Do it because God commands it, but also because deep within yourself, you know it is right.

6. This is also why you pay taxes, for the authorities are God's servants, who give their full time to governing.

If we are to be obedient to our governing *authorities,* we must do so even when they demand *taxes.* Few of us enjoy parting with our money, especially when we have reason to believe that it will not be used wisely. But we cannot justify resisting authority at any point, including the payment of taxes. Jesus himself spoke clearly to this issue when he said, "Give to Caesar what is Caesar's, and to God what is God's" (Matthew 22:21).

Though Christians have a duty to pay whatever taxes are demanded, we may find it necessary in some cases to challenge the amount of taxes required and the way our tax money is used. As noted earlier, it is helpful to consider the occasions in Paul's ministry when he protested questionable acts of the civic authorities. In a representative form of government, in which there are legitimate means for citizens to express their views, Christians should feel free to offer their perspective, though always through proper means and always in a Christlike spirit.

7. Give everyone what you owe him: If you owe taxes, pay taxes; if revenue, then revenue; if respect, then respect; if honor, then honor.

Here is a good summary of our responsibility toward our civic leaders. There is some repetition of concepts here for the sake of emphasis. For instance, *taxes* and *revenue* are essentially the same thing, as are *respect* and *honor.*

II. LOVING NEIGHBORS (ROMANS 13:8-10)

A. GIVING WHAT IS DUE (v. 8)

8. Let no debt remain outstanding, except the continuing debt to love one another, for he who loves his fellowman has fulfilled the law.

Some have understood the Bible to forbid Christians from either lending money with interest or borrowing money from others. It is true that the law of Moses did have regulations regarding interest, but with guidelines for fair dealings, not a total prohibition of interest on loans (Exodus 22:25; Deuteronomy 23:20). It is also true that Jesus taught that we should "lend . . . without expecting to get anything back" (Luke 6:35); however, the context was not business dealings, but confrontational situations where we are to love our "enemies" and show kindness to people who do not deserve kindness from us.

As for borrowing money, the New Testament does not prohibit this. Someone might argue, "But is that not what Paul is saying in this passage: *let no debt remain outstanding*"? In the context of this chapter, the *debt* Paul has in mind has to do with our civic duty—such matters as obedience, civic service, taxes, and respect. He has not mentioned financial issues. Still, it is good advice to try and stay as free from financial debt as possible—not because Paul commands it but because it is wise stewardship of the resources that God has given us.

WHAT DO YOU THINK?

What if we believe a public official has done things that make him or her unworthy of honor? How should we regard that official? What should be our conduct toward him, considering his official position?

What kind of witness are this driver's bumper stickers yielding now? The visual for lesson 10 draws a practical application to today's lesson title.

When it comes to giving the obedience and respect due to those who have authority over us, we should never come up lacking. To our neighbors we have a duty as well: to show them love and kindness each time we interact with them.

DEBTS AND DEBTORS

Debt is something we all understand. The national debt of the United States changes daily, but at the time of the writing of this illustration it was well over five *trillion* dollars! Often we hear news reporters talking about the credit card debt of consumers in this country. It, too, has reached astronomical proportions. Perhaps you are concerned about your personal debt. Without debt, however, there would be no banks; for banks cannot exist without borrowers.

What did Paul mean when he said, "Let no debt remain outstanding" (Romans 13:8)? Did he intend for the entire world of banking and finance to collapse? No—the meaning is that we should incur no debt that we cannot repay. In fact, we should repay every debt but one. That is a debt that can never be repaid: the debt to *love one another.*

It is interesting that the same Paul who said, "Let no debt remain outstanding" also said, "I am obligated" (Romans 1:14). Paul recognized a spiritual debt that can never be completely "paid in full." While as Christians we must be honest, must pay our bills, and must not take on debts we cannot repay, we will never be able to repay the debt of love. As Isaac Watts wrote in his great hymn, "At the Cross":

> But drops of grief can ne'er repay
> The debt of love I owe:
> Here, Lord, I give myself away,
> 'Tis all that I can do!
>
> —R. C. S.

B. NEVER DOING HARM (vv. 9, 10)

9, 10. The commandments, "Do not commit adultery," "Do not murder," "Do not steal," "Do not covet," and whatever other commandment there may be, are summed up in this one rule: "Love your neighbor as yourself." Love does no harm to its neighbor. Therefore love is the fulfillment of the law.

Here Paul lists four of the last five of the Ten Commandments (Exodus 20:13-17), treating them as *neighbor* commandments. Apparently he sees the first four commandments as focusing upon God, the fifth as honoring parents, and the remainder as dealing with how to treat our neighbors. Each one of the four prohibitions listed represents an action that is unkind and unloving, bestowing *harm* upon one's neighbor. Thus, Paul declares, all of the "neighbor commandments" of Scripture can be summed up in a simple rule: *Love your neighbor as yourself.*

III. GODLY SAINTS (ROMANS 13:11-14)

A. NOTHING TO HIDE (vv. 11-13)

11. And do this, understanding the present time. The hour has come for you to wake up from your slumber, because our salvation is nearer now than when we first believed.

It was Paul's concern that Christians begin acting like the Christ whose name they wear. Why such urgency? The answer: *Our salvation is nearer now than when we first believed.* Some see this as a reference to the second coming of Christ, and then wonder why Paul mistakenly assumed that it would occur soon ("the day is almost here," v. 12). It is good to remember that New Testament writers could speak of Christ's return as "soon," and yet understand this as being from God's perspective and not necessarily ours (as in 2 Peter 3:8, 9).

However, what Paul more likely had in mind was not the end of all time, but of our individual timetables. Each one of us has a limited amount of time to

DAILY BIBLE READINGS

Monday, Feb. 1—Hate What Is Evil; Cling to What Is Good (Romans 12:9-21)

Tuesday, Feb. 2—Be Subject to the Governing Authorities (Romans 13:1-7)

Wednesday, Feb. 3—Love Does No Wrong to Its Neighbor (Romans 13:8-14)

Thursday, Feb. 4—Walking Blamelessly (Psalm 15:1-5)

Friday, Feb. 5—Accept the Authority of Every Human Institution (1 Peter 2:11-17)

Saturday, Feb. 6—Everything We Need for Life and Godliness (2 Peter 1:2-11)

Sunday, Feb. 7—A Living Sacrifice (Romans 12:1-8)

PRAYER

Our Father in Heaven, the Ruler above all earthly authorities, help us to practice in our relationships and our daily contacts the kind of love and respect that we owe to each other, knowing that it will be a tribute to our love and respect for you. Amen.

THOUGHT TO REMEMBER

"Give everyone what you owe him: If you owe taxes, pay taxes; if revenue, then revenue; if respect, then respect; if honor, then honor" (Romans 13:7).

WHAT DO YOU THINK?

Paul writes, "Live by the Spirit and you will not gratify the desires of the sinful nature" (Galatians 5:16). He then lists the "fruit of the Spirit" and says, "Against such things there is no law" (v. 23).

Can you be reasonably certain of being in accordance with civil laws if you follow Paul's advice? Why or why not?

Can morality be legislated? Is being legally innocent the same as living morally? Why or why not?

"work out" our salvation (Philippians 2:12). Those who are not taking seriously their duty to pursue godly living had better *wake up* before their time runs out. *12, 13. The night is nearly over; the day is almost here. So let us put aside the deeds of darkness and put on the armor of light. Let us behave decently, as in the daytime, not in orgies and drunkenness, not in sexual immorality and debauchery, not in dissension and jealousy.*

The best way for a Christian to live in a secular world is to practice a godly lifestyle that can be displayed boldly for all to see. Christians are encouraged not to cultivate any of the *deeds of darkness,* such as sexual *orgies, drunkenness, sexual immorality, debauchery, dissension,* and *jealousy.* Instead, we must *put on the armor of light* and *behave decently,* being authentic in our conduct and unashamed of what others will see.

NIGHT CREATURES

Many of God's creatures are seen only at night: the bat, the possum, the raccoon, and the owl, to name a few. The psalmist recognized that night is the time that God has arranged for certain creatures to be active: "You bring darkness, it becomes night, and all the beasts of the forest prowl" (Psalm 104:20).

In the moral and spiritual realms, night is associated with evil. Deeds are done in darkness that would never be done by day. Many do not feel a need to lock their doors during the daytime, but almost everyone locks the doors at night. If you have ever been in a bar or a liquor lounge, you may have noticed that such places are always dark. Darkness is associated with the penalty for evil (2 Peter 2:17; Jude 6, 13).

Jesus, on the other hand, is always associated with light and with day (John 1:5; 3:19; Ephesians 5:13, 14). He is the Light of the world (John 8:12), and he calls his people to be lights in the world (Philippians 2:15). To be "light creatures" (not "night creatures") means that we do nothing of which we would be ashamed. Our lives are open books. We have nothing to keep in secret. In the words of an old gospel song, we are "stepping in the light."
—R. C. S.

B. LIVING FOR CHRIST (v. 14)

14. Rather, clothe yourselves with the Lord Jesus Christ, and do not think about how to gratify the desires of the sinful nature.

The secret to living a life others will respect is to live the way Jesus lived. It is true that his enemies nailed him to a cross. But the opposition was always against his messianic teaching, not his personal conduct. You cannot go wrong if you choose to ignore *how to gratify the desires of the sinful nature,* and instead *clothe yourselves with the Lord Jesus Christ* and follow his leading.

CONCLUSION

Have you ever been in the following situation: Your car breaks down while you are traveling out of town, and you feel helpless. Then comes a total stranger who offers to look under your hood, or change your flat tire, or take you to get some gas. When he has your car running again, there is a question that you naturally ask: "What do I owe you?"

This is the question that Paul wants us to ask of our government, our community, and our neighbors. Do we Christians have any special responsibilities as citizens and neighbors? The answer is a firm *yes.* We are to obey our civic authorities, regardless of whether or not we like them. We are to treat our neighbors with kindness, regardless of how they treat us. We are to live such decent lives in our communities that people will respect us, even if they do not care for our faith. We have a duty to be the best citizens and neighbors we can be, for that is what God has called us to be.

Discovery Learning

*This page contains an alternate lesson plan emphasizing learning activities. Classes
desiring such student involvement will find these suggestions helpful. The next page
is a reproducible activity page to further enhance discovery learning.*

LEARNING GOALS

After today's lesson, students will be able to:

1. Summarize Paul's teaching on good citizenship in Romans 13.

2. Explain why a Christian should show respect to civic authorities even when their views and actions are questionable.

3. Suggest at least one way to be a better Christian citizen, and begin to implement it in the coming week.

INTO THE LESSON

Before class begins, hang a long sheet of butcher paper (several large poster boards will also work) on the wall with these words printed at the top, "Patriotism means . . ." As students arrive, provide them with markers and ask each person to write an answer or draw a symbolic picture to express his or her definition of patriotism. Be sure you have enough space that three or four students may be writing at the same time. This activity is often called a "graffiti wall."

Begin the session with a review of the "graffiti wall." You may need to ask some students for clarification of their responses or pictures. Note the variety of understandings of and feelings about patriotism. Using the Introduction of the commentary section (page 199), briefly comment on the irony between our expressions of patriotism and our sometimes unpatriotic behavior.

Remind your students that it is easier to be patriotic when all is well. How would their view of patriotism change if they did not live in a free country? How would they respond to a government that persecuted Christians? Should we obey the laws of our land? If so, then why do so many Christians violate speed limits? Today's text drills right into the core of the Christian's relationship with the government. And, for some, its teachings may be uncomfortable.

INTO THE WORD

Using the lesson commentary, begin with a brief lecture on the background of today's text.

Prepare a handout with the following tasks and questions. Ask the class members, in groups of three, to answer the questions quickly and briefly. (Several groups may be given the same task.)

1. Write a paraphrase of verse 1, making its principles clear to contemporary Christians.

2. According to Paul, why should Christians be obedient to secular governments? (vv. 2-5)

3. Why are governing officials called "servants" in verses 4 and 6?

4. What is the meaning of Paul's statement that the ruler is "an agent of wrath to bring punishment on the wrongdoer"? (v. 4)

5. What are some practical applications of good citizenship that Paul cites in verses 7-14?

Allow ten minutes; then call for reports. Observe that this teaching raises some tough questions. Discuss the following issues:

1. Does verse 1 suggest God is responsible for oppressive regimes that assault human rights or even persecute the church? Explain. Can and will God use evil governments to accomplish his will? Why or why not?

2. Does verse 2 suggest that such efforts as the failed resistance at Tiananmen Square in China (1989) or the American Revolution were wrong? Can you cite biblical justification for rebellion against a corrupt government? To what extent, or in what cases, is "resistance" like protests, demonstrations, or blocking access to public buildings justified? (See also the question on page 200.)

3. Paul's concern in verses 11-13 is that Christians begin acting like Christ even though oppressed. What are some of the major behavioral concerns that Christians are facing in today's free world? What advice would you offer to parents about how to live as Christians in a free society? To teens?

These issues may require more study than you have time for. If some students have strong opinions but cannot support them biblically now, suggest they do some research during the week and come prepared to support them next week.

INTO LIFE

Remind the class that patriotism is more than a feeling of pride or allegiance. It involves understanding God's ordination of the concept of government and his expectations for living as good citizens. And it involves everyday practical behavioral issues—like obeying the speed limit. Ask the class to share other everyday practical applications to good citizenship. List these on a chalkboard. Conclude by asking students to identify and implement at least one principle of good citizenship they have discussed today.

Citizenship Grade

At one time in America's past, school children were given a "Citizenship" grade. They were evaluated for how well they conformed to the social needs and goals of the class and the school. Paul's writing to the Romans—of all the world's citizens!—on civic duty is not only interesting but even a bit startling. Fill out the following "Report Card" checklist based on Romans 13:1-14. Put an X on each line to show your own standing between "Good Citizenship" and "Needs Improvement."

	NI	GC
Submits to Proper Authority	_____
Believes Government is God-ordained	_____
Believes Government Officials are God's Servants	_____
Feels Guilty About Breaking Government Laws	_____
Pays Taxes Due	_____
Respects Government Officers	_____
Pays Personal Debts	_____
Loves Neighbors as Self	_____
Behaves Decently	_____

Overall Grade: A B C D F

Civics Questions

Any study in civics attempts to answer certain basic questions. What are your answers to the following core questions? How well do your answers align with those the Spirit reveals through Paul?

What are the essential purposes of government?

To the Christian, is there a moral base to legality?

What is the role of taxation in government?

How to such codifications as the Ten Commandments relate to contemporary government systems?

How does God relate to the ordination of government?

Which is the "best" form of government?

God Calls Anew in Jesus Christ

Unit 3. Good News for Changing Times

(Lessons 9-13)

BUILDING A CARING COMMUNITY

LESSON 11

WHY TEACH THIS LESSON?

We hear much rhetoric these days about "family values," and that is an important topic. Christians also should be concerned about "church-family values." Centuries ago, the apostle Paul addressed the same theme in his epistles, most particularly the letters written to Christians in Corinth. "First Church" at Corinth was a troubled congregation. Most of their problems were related to poor church-family values.

Today's text points up a basic essential for body life among disciples: sensitivity and thoughtfulness in worship and fellowship settings. The observance of the Lord's Supper especially should be characterized by discernment of Christ's body—his physical body that was broken at Calvary, and his spiritual body, the church, God's kingdom on earth.

Will the world "know we are Christians by our love"—our love for each other? Yes, if we take these Scriptures seriously.

INTRODUCTION

A. I COULDN'T CARE LESS

Many popular expressions go through a process of change, taking on a new form and yet retaining something of the old. Sometimes the new expressions make sense, sometimes they are absurd, but always they are interesting. Take, for instance, the old standard, "I couldn't care less." Its meaning is clear: "I have no interest in what you are saying or thinking; my interest level is at zero." The shorter version, "I could care less," is generally understood to mean the same thing; however, it actually says the opposite: "I *could* have less interest than I have." And if economy of words is desirable, there is always the succinct, "So?" No matter how a child says it, the message comes through loud and clear to the parent or teacher: here is an attitude that needs adjustment!

Christians must not be people who "couldn't care less." We should have a genuine interest in others that listens when they speak and gives their ideas a fair hearing—even when we disagree. We should hear their concerns and seek appropriate ways to respond. We are not permitted to "tune out" others because we do not care. We are called to be a community that cares.

B. LESSON BACKGROUND

The church at Corinth still has a reputation as a congregation with lots of problems. They had the unique "privilege" of receiving a letter from the apostle Paul in which every one of its sixteen chapters addressed something these people were doing wrong. Paul knew them well, having ministered with them for a year and a half (Acts 18:11) and having kept in touch with them by means of letters and through reports from others (1 Corinthians 1:11; 5:1; 7:1; 11:18).

DEVOTIONAL READING:

1 CORINTHIANS 12:14-27

LESSON SCRIPTURE:

1 CORINTHIANS 11:17-34

PRINTED TEXT:

1 CORINTHIANS 11:20-34

LESSON AIMS

As a result of this lesson students should:

1. Tell what Paul said about the meaning and purpose of the Lord's Supper, and how the Corinthians' behavior violated that.

2. Explain the relationship between the Lord's Supper and the spirit of community that should characterize a church.

3. Make a commitment to partake of the Lord's Supper in a manner worthy of Christ and the community of believers.

Feb 14

KEY VERSE

A man ought to examine himself before he eats of the bread and drinks of the cup. For anyone who eats and drinks without recognizing the body of the Lord eats and drinks judgment on himself.

—1 Corinthians 11:28, 29

Paul viewed the Corinthians' problems as very serious and potentially damaging to the stability of their fellowship and their relationship with God. Even so, he did not "write off" the Corinthians. He still considered them among "those sanctified in Christ Jesus" (1 Corinthians 1:2). As we read Paul's admonitions in chapter 11, let us humble our hearts and be prepared to change where change is needed.

I. WORSHIPING AS ONE (1 CORINTHIANS 11:20-22)

A. ACTING AS ONE BODY (vv. 20, 21)

20. When you come together, it is not the Lord's Supper you eat.

The church at Corinth regularly gathered *together* for corporate worship. According to 1 Corinthians 16:2, this took place on "the first day of every week," or, every Sunday (see also Acts 20:7).

Paul claimed that what the Corinthians were doing during their worship service was *not the Lord's Supper.* This is evidence that the Lord's Supper was a regular weekly feature in New Testament worship. Had eating the Lord's Supper not been expected when they would *come together,* the fact that they didn't would have warranted no comment from Paul. The obvious implication is that observing the Lord's Supper was expected each week when they came together—that they were, in fact, going through the motions of observing it with the bread and the juice—but they were doing it in such a way that their observance did not deserve to be called "the Lord's Supper."

21. For as you eat, each of you goes ahead without waiting for anybody else. One remains hungry, another gets drunk.

The church at Corinth apparently had a practice of eating the Lord's Supper in conjunction with a church fellowship meal. After all, it would be difficult to imagine why Paul would speak of some going *hungry* and some being *drunk* with just the small portions used during the Lord's Supper.

Probably the practice of having a larger meal with the Lord's Supper was followed to imitate the original institution of the ceremony by Jesus during his final Passover supper in the upper room. Churches who did this would either have the Lord's Supper at some point during their meal, or shortly thereafter. This is a practice that could be done today if a church so desired, because there is biblical precedent. However, there is no biblical evidence that *every* church in the apostolic age did this. Corinth is the only first-century church we know that observed the Lord's Supper in the context of a larger meal.

The error of the Corinthians is implied in verse 21 but more precisely stated in verse 18. The church was divided into groups or cliques that would not fellowship with each other. Thus, in the eating of church meals, believers would share their food only with their friends. As a result, some were overlooked, while others overindulged. The unity for which Jesus prayed (John 17:20, 21) and the love of one another that he taught (John 13:34) were apparently nonexistent at Corinth.

B. LOVING EACH OTHER (v. 22)

22. Don't you have homes to eat and drink in? Or do you despise the church of God and humiliate those who have nothing? What shall I say to you? Shall I praise you for this? Certainly not!

When Paul asked, *Don't you have homes to eat and drink in?* he was not condemning the practice of serving the Lord's Supper with a meal, but the uncaring manner in which the Corinthians ate their meal. He questioned whether the Corinthians intended to *despise the church of God* and *humiliate* each other. The attitude he was condemning was the very opposite of the love he would define in chapter 13. Love would not be so rude and inconsiderate, nor would it hurt and offend.

WHAT DO YOU THINK?

The Corinthians went through the form of observing the Lord's Supper, but they were not keeping its function intact. What were they doing? How can this same kind of problem occur in our worship today? How can we keep our worship from becoming empty and devoid of legitimate function?

How do you "participate" in worship and in Communion?

WHAT DO YOU THINK?

Some believers think that Paul's words ("Don't you have homes to eat and drink in?") condemn the practice of having fellowship meals in the church building. Do you agree or disagree? Why?

How were the practices of the Corinthians failing to show love for each other?

II. FOCUSING ON CHRIST (1 CORINTHIANS 11:23-26)

A. HIS BROKEN BODY (vv. 23, 24)

23. For I received from the Lord what I also passed on to you: The Lord Jesus, on the night he was betrayed, took bread, . . .

For I received from the Lord. Paul could not give firsthand testimony regarding the institution of the Lord's Supper, because he had not been one of the apostles present in the upper room. His information had been given to him by divine revelation, perhaps during the three-year period that he spent by himself in Arabia in preparation for his ministry (Galatians 1:15-18).

24. and when he had given thanks, he broke it and said, "This is my body, which is for you; do this in remembrance of me."

At some point during the Passover supper, Jesus paused and *broke* a piece of bread. We know it would have been bread made without yeast because it was required that there be no yeast anywhere in a Jewish house during the whole week leading up to the Passover celebration. Most churches today have chosen to use unleavened bread for the Lord's Supper, not only because that is what Jesus would have used, but because of the appropriateness of the symbolism. Since leaven is often used in Scripture to represent sin (Luke 12:1; 1 Corinthians 5:6-8), unleavened bread is a good reminder of what we want our lives to be in Christ.

The purpose for the broken piece of bread is that it serves as a *remembrance* of how Jesus' body was "broken" on the cross of Calvary. The bread itself is not the body of Christ, but it represents or symbolizes the body of Christ.

What brings Calvary to our minds during the Lord's Supper is not the bread itself, but the fact that we eat a *broken* piece of bread. That is the reason some churches prefer to serve a larger loaf for Communion. Each worshiper breaks off a piece of bread in order to participate personally in the symbolism. However, even the use of precut wafers can carry the symbolism when we remember that each little piece was "broken" from a larger portion.

B. HIS SHED BLOOD (v. 25)

25. In the same way, after supper he took the cup, saying, "This cup is the new covenant in my blood; do this, whenever you drink it, in remembrance of me."

During the institution of the Lord's Supper, the bread and the juice were not given to the disciples at the same time. The bread was broken during the meal, but the cup was presented *after supper.* The probable reason for this was that Jesus wanted to wait and use the "third cup" of the Jewish Passover meal for his Lord's Supper memorial. In a traditional Passover service, there were four occasions when the participants would drink a cup of the fruit of the vine. Each cup had a distinctive theme, often accompanied by prescribed words, songs, and prayers. The first two cups were taken prior to the main meal, and the latter two cups were taken after the meal. The third cup was called the Cup of Redemption, which celebrated the fact that God had redeemed Israel from bondage in Egypt and that he continues to redeem his people in times of distress. It is likely that this was the cup Jesus used for the Lord's Supper, giving it a new and richer meaning than before—a celebration of the ultimate redemption that God would give his people through the death of his Son on the cross.

The message of the cup is much the same as that of the bread. The broken body of Jesus produced blood—the blood that ushered in a *new covenant* (Hebrews 9:11-14), by which sins can be forgiven and forgotten (8:12). Just as many churches prefer to use unleavened bread for the observance of the Lord's Supper, they prefer unfermented grape juice.

WHAT DO YOU THINK?

How important, if at all, do you think it is that the church follow the precedent of using unleavened bread in the Lord's Supper? For the Passover meal, what was the unleavened bread supposed to symbolize (Deuteronomy 16:3)? In the New Testament, what did leavening often symbolize (1 Corinthians 5:7, 8)? Is either of these ideas relevant to the Lord's Supper? Why or why not?

HOW TO SAY IT

agape (Greek). uh-GAH-pay.
Arabia. Uh-RAY-bee-uh.
Corinth. KOR-inth.
Corinthians. Kor-IN-thee-unz.

THE CUP OF BLESSING

In his series of poems *Idylls of the King*, Alfred Lord Tennyson told a story that had in some form already circulated in England as one of the legends surrounding King Arthur. Sir Galahad saw a vision of the very cup that Jesus used when he instituted the Lord's Supper. It was called "the Holy Grail." He and the other knights embarked on a long and fruitless search to find this cup.

Suppose the cup had been found. Would Communion then mean more to us than it already does? Would that enhance our observance of the Lord's Supper? Not at all. However, we *do* have something from the upper room. We have the presence of Jesus himself. That is enough to make Communion holy, no matter the kind of cup we use. It is his presence and our reverence, humility, and prayerful attitude, that give meaning to the Supper. The kind of table on which the emblems rest, the kind of utensil from which they are poured or into which they are poured, the kind of building in which we meet—all of these are really unimportant. What is in our hearts is most important. And what happens in our lives as a result is essential.

Let the cup then stand for what it symbolizes: Jesus' sacrifice for us and our response of loving remembrance to him.

—R. C. S.

C. HIS REDEMPTIVE DEATH (v. 26)

26. For whenever you eat this bread and drink this cup, you proclaim the Lord's death until he comes.

The simple ceremony that Jesus instituted in the upper room was intended to be observed by his disciples *until he comes* to take us to our heavenly home. It is meant to insure that every Sunday when we gather for worship, we will give at least a few minutes to remembering Christ's death—the most important event in history, the key to our salvation, and the reason we are gathered as a church.

This fundamental meaning of the Lord's Supper has some practical implications for us. Our thoughts should not wander to other concerns; rather, we should make a serious effort to reflect upon Calvary and its significance for us. Likewise, those who present a "Communion meditation" should refrain from discussing other subjects or telling entertaining stories. They should seek to direct our thoughts where they belong for the next few moments—to the redemptive death of Jesus our Savior.

III. EXAMINING OUR HEARTS (1 CORINTHIANS 11:27-34)

A. TO REMOVE UNWORTHY MOTIVES (vv. 27-32)

27. Therefore, whoever eats the bread or drinks the cup of the Lord in an unworthy manner will be guilty of sinning against the body and blood of the Lord.

WHAT DO YOU THINK?

Who is permitted to participate in the Lord's Supper? Who is qualified to participate? Who is responsible to determine who may partake?

Paul raises an issue that has puzzled many readers and troubled the conscience of some as they have approached the Lord's Supper. What is an *unworthy manner* of partaking of the *bread* and the *cup*? The immediate context is focused upon one problem in particular. The church at Corinth was in a state of division, yet had the gall to take part in a ceremony that symbolizes the unity of the body of Christ!

While the primary focus of the Lord's Supper is upon Calvary, Paul also notes a secondary imagery in 1 Corinthians 10:17: "Because there is one loaf, we, who are many, are one body, for we all partake of the one loaf." My individual piece of bread was broken from a larger, single loaf, just as yours was. I may partake of the Lord's Supper in a quiet meditation of my own, but the small piece should remind me that I am a member of a larger fellowship. To participate in a sacred ceremony that symbolizes unity, while willfully being at odds with my Christian brother or sister, is an act of hypocrisy. Of course, the same can be said for meeting with the body at all while willfully at odds with a brother or sister.

Some people wonder if they should stay away from the Lord's Supper while they are wrestling with sinful issues in their lives, lest they be guilty of partaking *in an unworthy manner*. It was not Paul's intention here to keep people away from the Lord's Supper. Believers with a genuine concern for the sin in their lives benefit from being at the Lord's Supper and seeing afresh the sacrifice that will remove their sins entirely if they repent of them. The Lord's Supper does not push sinners away; it draws repentant sinners to it so that their thinking can be challenged and their lives renewed.

28. A man ought to examine himself before he eats of the bread and drinks of the cup.

Rather than abstinence, Paul urges examination. Every time we prepare to partake of the Lord's Supper, we should first *examine* ourselves and ask whether there is any fellow believer from whom we are estranged, or toward whom we have bitterness, or against whom we hold a grudge. If such is the case, we must immediately release that bitterness and repent of it. Some would even suggest that we should not partake until we have first made an effort at reconciliation, though their appeal to Matthew 5:23, 24 is not conclusive.

Paul's purpose was not to tell when we should and when we should not partake of the Lord's Supper. Instead, he was giving directives for a proper observance, in a right spirit and in full fellowship with the body. As long as we seek to partake in such a manner, we can have a clear conscience at the Lord's Supper.

SELF-EXAMINATION

With cancer so prevalent, health care professionals are urging both men and women to do careful self-examinations. They publish literature that tells you what signs to look for. News reports on television provide relevant information. They claim that many lives can be saved by careful self-examination.

The Lord's Supper is an occasion for spiritual self-examination. What danger signs should we look for? Pride is one. Selfishness is another, along with harboring a divisive spirit. So is self-indulgence, even in something otherwise good and proper. We need to detect these early warning signs before the cancer of sin destroys us.

Certainly no one can come to Communion, conduct a self-examination, and not find something. This does not mean that we should not partake. It does mean that we should recognize our weaknesses, repent of our sins, and resolve to do better and to be better. To diagnose our own condition is to go a long way toward curing that condition.

Often cancer in the human body can be cured. Always cancer of the soul can be cured if we follow the prescriptions of the Great Physician. To ignore what we discover in our self-examination would be more dangerous than to ignore the signs of malignancy in the human body. To recognize signs of spiritual sickness, confess them, repent of them, and find forgiveness for them can lead us to full recovery and renewed spiritual health.

—R. C. S.

29. For anyone who eats and drinks without recognizing the body of the Lord eats and drinks judgment on himself.

It is a sin to partake of the Lord's Supper when we are at odds with a Christian brother or sister. To do so will make us "guilty" (v. 27) before God and liable for divine *judgment*. This understanding helps us to grasp what Paul means when he speaks of partaking *without recognizing the body of the Lord*. The *body* refers to the church. To "recognize the Lord's body" means to envision the unity of all believers and to realize that our alienated brother or sister is still a partner with us in Christ's church. We are under obligation to do our part to reestablish unity where we have allowed it to lapse.

WHAT DO YOU THINK?

How should one properly prepare for the Lord's Supper?

How do you examine yourself, and for what? Do you recognize sin in your life? Have you confessed that with a repentant heart and asked the Lord's forgiveness?

Display the visual for lesson 11 as you discuss verse 29. Discuss the implications of "recognizing the body of the Lord" in a proper observance of the Lord's Supper.

PRAYER

Heavenly Father, help us to grow in our concern for each other so that we can truly be one body in Christ, in whose name we pray, amen.

THOUGHT TO REMEMBER

"Because there is one loaf, we, who are many, are one body, for we all partake of the one loaf" (1 Corinthians 10:17).

DAILY BIBLE READINGS

Monday, Feb. 8—More Harm Than Good (1 Corinthians 11:17-22)

Tuesday, Feb. 9—Do This in Remembrance of Me (1 Corinthians 11:23-26)

Wednesday, Feb. 10—Origin of the Passover (Exodus 12:1-13)

Thursday, Feb. 11—A Day of Remembrance (Exodus 12:14-28)

Friday, Feb. 12—The Passover for the Whole Congregation of Israel (Exodus 12:43-51)

Saturday, Feb. 13—Remember This Day (Exodus 13:1-16)

Sunday, Feb. 14—One Body, Many Members (1 Corinthians 12:14-27)

30. That is why many among you are weak and sick, and a number of you have fallen asleep.

Here Paul mentions additional consequences of disregarding the unity of the body of Christ. His reference to becoming *weak and sick* and to falling *asleep* could describe a weakening of our moral character. But it is also possible that Paul is referring to physical ailments that may be used in our lives as disciplinary measures to break down our complacency and lead to repentance. This would be consistent with verse 32, which refers to the Lord disciplining us. He wants to see us reform our sinful attitudes before it is too late and we receive the eternal condemnation that he has planned for the rest of the world.

31, 32. But if we judged ourselves, we would not come under judgment. When we are judged by the Lord, we are being disciplined so that we will not be condemned with the world.

How can we avoid being *judged* by God and receiving the accompanying penalties, spiritual and otherwise? We must judge *ourselves* (recall the exhortation to "examine" ourselves in v. 28) and then seek reconciliation where we find it is needed.

B. TO PRACTICE CONSIDERATION (vv. 33, 34)

33, 34. So then, my brothers, when you come together to eat, wait for each other. If anyone is hungry, he should eat at home, so that when you meet together it may not result in judgment.

And when I come I will give further directions.

From now on, when the Christians at Corinth *come together,* for a fellowship meal or any other purpose, they are advised to show consideration for *each other.* Anyone present at a fellowship meal who thinks he is too *hungry* to *wait* for others to arrive should have eaten something *at home.*

To build a strong church, the members must learn to exercise love and patience *for each other.* This was practical advice for a church whose thinking was not only foolish, but sinful. The Corinthians now knew what they had to do to address this particular problem; if other matters remained unresolved, Paul promised to *give further directions* when he returned to Corinth.

CONCLUSION

Have you ever had to discipline a dog for doing something wrong, such as jumping up on your furniture or chewing on your shoes? You know the routine. You hit him with a rolled-up newspaper and tell him "bad dog." The dog's typical response is to run away with his head down, his ears hanging low, and his tail tucked between his legs. It is a sight so pitiful that it can make you wonder if you did the right thing. But God designed a dog so that he rebounds quickly. As soon as you summon him back, he comes running with head up and tail wagging, eager for your affection. He acts as if you never touched him, yet in the future he will be more cautious around your furniture and your shoes. A lesson has been learned, and the friendship remains intact.

Paul's second epistle to the Corinthians indicates that the church at Corinth did make some changes after Paul's first hard-hitting letter. They felt the sting of his rebuke and humbly repented (2 Corinthians 7:8, 9). Of course, they could have responded with a bitterness that would have aggravated their problems within the church. However, they made the better choice; and Paul's second letter expressed the confidence he had in them (7:16).

Whenever we are challenged by our study of God's Word, may we have the strength to respond as well as the church at Corinth.

Discovery Learning

This page contains an alternate lesson plan emphasizing learning activities. Classes desiring such student involvement will find these suggestions helpful. The next page is a reproducible activity page to further enhance discovery learning.

LEARNING GOALS

After this lesson the student will be able to:

1. Tell what Paul said about the meaning and purpose of the Lord's Supper, and how the Corinthians' behavior violated that.

2. Explain the relationship between the Lord's Supper and the spirit of community that should characterize a church.

3. Make a commitment to partake of the Lord's Supper in a manner worthy of Christ and the community of believers.

INTO THE LESSON

Before the students arrive, write the words "A Very Special Communion Service" on the chalkboard or on a large poster at the front of the classroom. As the students arrive, ask them to be thinking of Communion services that particularly impressed them with the significance of the Lord's Supper. Perhaps it was a special service in your own church, or perhaps some of your students have participated in special observances while they were traveling.

When it is time to begin, ask for some volunteers to share their experiences. Write down some key features of these services on the chalkboard or poster.

Move into Bible study by explaining that there are many forms of sharing the Lord's Supper. Some of the differences are minor variations of procedure. Other differences, rooted in a theology of Communion, are more significant. Today's lesson will introduce us to a church that had drifted into a Lord's Supper tradition that was divisive to the local church and was offensive to the Lord. In it we will discover principles for our Communion observances.

INTO THE WORD

Form study groups of no more than five people in each group. Larger classes can have more than one group doing the same project. Give each group a written copy of one of the following tasks. Note: the tasks may also be used as discussion guides for the class as a whole.

Group 1. Read 1 Corinthians 11:18, 20, 21. Create a detailed verbal picture of how you visualize the Corinthian church sharing in the Lord's Supper. Detail all the problems and obstacles to a rich fellowship and experience in this church's Communion service.

Group 2. Read 1 Corinthians 11:24-26. Explain the rich symbolism in the Lord's Supper. Compare the biblical symbolism with the special features noted earlier (see "Into the Lesson").

Group 3. Read 1 Corinthians 11:27-34. Make a presentation on the significance of church fellowship in the Lord's Supper, and the idea of partaking "unworthily" or in an "unworthy manner."

Allow each group adequate time to discuss their tasks and formulate their presentations. After they have made their presentations, use the "bad dog" illustration on page 212 to demonstrate the changes in the Corinthian church before Paul sent his second and more accepting letter to them.

INTO LIFE

Ask each group to work together again to write a Communion meditation that reflects their research. If there is not enough time to write the meditation, ask them to simply make a few notes about what they would stress in their presentation.

Group 1. Please write a three- or four-minute Communion meditation that begins with, "What might Paul say if he were writing to our church about our Communion practices?"

Group 2. Please write a three- or four-minute Communion meditation that begins with, "The impact of Communion lies, partly, in the symbols of the bread and the cup. . . ."

Group 3. Please write a three- or four-minute Communion meditation that begins with, "The words 'unworthily' or 'in an unworthy manner' are words for every Christian to heed. . . ."

Ask a spokesman from each group to read the meditation that the group has prepared. You might also submit these meditations to your church newsletter to be adapted for a series of instructional articles celebrating the richness of the Lord's Supper.

Conclude the lesson by asking for testimonies from volunteers about what they learned that will impact how they celebrate the Lord's Supper. The closing prayer time can be done in the same small groups used earlier. Ask each person to make a silent or oral commitment to share in the Lord's Supper in a worthy manner that honors the Lord and brings credit to the fellowship of believers.

God's Caring Community: The Church

The church, God's caring community, has a variety of positive characteristics. Though the Corinthian church failed at some, Paul encouraged them to live in wholeness, oneness . . . community! How many positive characteristics can you find in the following word puzzle? Write them to the right, as you find them.

```
C  H  U  R  Y  C  G  E  M  E
C  L  E  H  T  N  C  C  E  M
A  O  H  C  I  U  H  A  M  I
R  V  M  R  N  R  U  E  O  T
E  E  A  M  U  E  M  P  R  L
C  H  D  P  U  R  I  T  Y  A
S  H  C  R  H  N  L  T  U  E
R  C  E  P  O  H  I  H  A  M
C  H  U  R  C  C  T  T  C  P
H  C  H  U  R  C  Y  H  Y  H
```

_____
_____
_____
_____
_____
_____
_____
_____
_____
_____

The Lord's Supper, Not

The Corinthian church was "celebrating" something the apostle Paul said was "not the Lord's Supper." It had become something divisive and chaotic. Characterize their attitudes and behaviors.

_____
_____
_____
_____

The Lord's Supper, Yes

The ideal church needs to make the Lord's Supper a truly unifying and worshipful experience. Characterize this ideal church in contrast to the Corinthian church.

_____
_____
_____
_____

(For example, the Corinthian church meal showed socioeconomic class differences—as in 1 Corinthians 11:22; the ideal church keeps the occasion simple and classless, as all are equal in Christ.)

RECONCILING THE WORLD TO GOD

LESSON 12

WHY TEACH THIS LESSON?

A church-growth pollster surveyed members of nearly 1,000 churches a few years ago, posing only one question: "Why does the church exist?" Most answers indicated that the church's purpose is to minister to members and their families. Only 11% responded, "The purpose of the church is to 'seek and save the lost.'"

Perhaps such attitudes have prompted many congregations in recent years to formulate a "mission statement" for their local body of believers. These statements clarify the purpose of the church, and express the vision of its leaders.

Christians need to know we are saved to serve. Those who have been reconciled to God are to become ministers of reconciliation, ambassadors of redemption. No lesson is needed more in this day of self-centered, maintenance-minded churches.

INTRODUCTION

A. IT'S FOR A WORTHY CAUSE

Do you remember the floods of 1997? Maybe you live in an area that was not affected, so for you the floods were nothing more than a story on the news several evenings. But for many people in the Ohio River Valley and the northern plains the spring floods were a life-changing experience. Some of the older residents in those areas could tell stories of earlier floods, but for most of them it was a "once in a lifetime" event. Property loss was high, and loss of life was tragic. However, what may be remembered longer than the devastation of the floods is the volunteer aid that responded to the need.

In both areas volunteer relief assistance arrived with great haste and abundance. Churches and civic groups collected donated supplies and shuttled them to the flood areas for distribution. Groups of people drove in from great distances to spend a few days cleaning and rebuilding. Sometimes the volunteers and supplies came in faster than organizers could manage them, prompting appeals to wait until a call was issued for more. Such a response is what happens time and time again when a heart-touching need is presented to the public. People will rally together for what they believe to be a worthy cause.

Paul devoted his adult life to the ministry of the Word. He preached the gospel all over the known world, establishing new churches and then nurturing them through visits and letters. But Paul knew that there was a limit to how much one man could do, so he recruited people he had converted to join him in ministry. He wrote in his epistles of the world's great need—of people alienated from God and from each other, in danger of being lost for eternity. He hoped that Christians would respond to a spiritual need as well as they do to a natural disaster. He believed that if followers of Jesus could get a vision of a lost and dying world, they would rally together for the worthiest of all causes.

DEVOTIONAL READING:
1 PETER 2:18-25

LESSON SCRIPTURE:
2 CORINTHIANS 5:11-21

PRINTED TEXT:
2 CORINTHIANS 5:11-21

LESSON AIMS

As a result of participating in this lesson, students should:

1. Explain what Paul said about the means and message of reconciliation with God.

2. Compare and contrast the way sinners are reconciled to God with other types or occasions of reconciliation.

3. Accept God's offer of reconciliation or plan to share his offer with someone else who needs to accept it.

KEY VERSE

God was reconciling the world to himself in Christ, not counting men's sins against them. And he has committed to us the message of reconciliation.
—2 Corinthians 5:19

Feb
21

B. LESSON BACKGROUND

As noted in last week's lesson, Paul's first epistle to the church at Corinth gave a stinging rebuke to the Corinthians for their many sinful attitudes and practices. While most of the Corinthians accepted Paul's rebuke and repented (2 Corinthians 7:8, 9), some of them apparently took offense at Paul's tone and words. Some were asking, in effect, "Who does Paul think he is, talking to us like that?" Considering how strongly Paul defends his apostleship in 2 Corinthians, some of the scoffers must have been challenging his credentials, perhaps noting that he was not one of the original twelve, or that he had once been a persecutor of the church. In some cases, Paul does go on the defensive in behalf of himself and his ministry. See, for example, 2 Corinthians 3:1, 2; 4:1, 2; 6:3; 7:2; 10:7—11:33; 12:17-19.

However, in chapter 5 (from which today's text is taken), Paul takes the offensive. He challenges friend and foe at Corinth to put aside their bruised feelings and petty fussing in order that they might concentrate upon the higher calling that God has put before all Christians. Paul challenges the Corinthians, not to fight him, but to join him as partners in the ministry of reconciliation.

I. A MISSION TO ACCOMPLISH (2 CORINTHIANS 5:11-15)

A. NOT FOR PERSONAL GAIN (vv. 11-13)

11. Since, then, we know what it is to fear the Lord, we try to persuade men. What we are is plain to God, and I hope it is also plain to your conscience.

In response to his critics at Corinth who challenged his authority and his motives, Paul begins this section of 2 Corinthians by explaining his devotion to preaching. He has taken on an evangelistic ministry of trying to *persuade men* to accept Christ. He does this, not for his own sake, but for the sake of those whom he persuades.

In the preceding verse, Paul has mentioned that all must "appear before the judgment seat of Christ." For those outside of Christ, that will be a time to view with *fear,* but for those in Christ it will be an occasion of joy. Paul did not want the judgment to be a fearful experience for anyone, so he worked to persuade everyone to come to Christ.

The charges being made against Paul were patently false. He had no ulterior motives or insatiable ego behind his ministry. Paul declared that his life and ministry were *plain* to both *God* and man. He was not operating under any "hidden agenda."

12. We are not trying to commend ourselves to you again, but are giving you an opportunity to take pride in us, so that you can answer those who take pride in what is seen rather than in what is in the heart.

We are not trying to commend ourselves to you again. Several times in 2 Corinthians, Paul provides details regarding his ministry, his background, and his apostolic authority. But Paul insisted that he was not providing any new information to the Corinthians; instead, he was simply reminding them of what they already knew. He hoped that his reminder would provide them with *an opportunity to take pride in us,* that is, it would encourage them to speak up for him when his critics became especially spiteful.

Paul's critics are described as those who *take pride in what is seen rather than in what is in the heart.* Apparently some of their criticism of Paul was grounded in certain external matters that they found objectionable. Perhaps there was something about Paul's appearance that they did not like. Some believe that Paul's "thorn in the flesh" (2 Corinthians 12:7-10) was a physical abnormality, though this is only speculation. Perhaps there was something about Paul's speaking style

HOW TO SAY IT

Corinth. KOR-inth.

Corinthians. Kor-IN-thee-unz.

reconciliation. rec-un-sill-e-AY-shun.

WHAT DO YOU THINK?

We are often cautioned about being too pushy in evangelism, about "cramming the gospel down people's throats." Yet Paul said, "We try to persuade men." What is the difference between persuasion and being too pushy? How can we follow Paul's example without becoming offensive?

Why are we to be "fishers of men," not "hunters of men"? What is the difference between fishing and hunting?

In regards to your own evangelistic efforts, are you too pushy or too timid?

that his critics found wanting, since he himself acknowledged that he did not speak with the "eloquence or superior wisdom" that some valued so highly (1 Corinthians 2:1-5).

Whatever their specific complaints may have been, Paul charged his critics with being superficial. The true measure of a person is not found in outward appearances, but in the character of the heart.

13. If we are out of our mind, it is for the sake of God; if we are in our right mind, it is for you.

Apparently Paul's mental stability was also being challenged. Paul's response was to turn the charge around and make it look ridiculous. Are we *out of our mind?* Then it would be because we are "crazy" about God. Of course, Paul was not admitting any incompetence; he was simply responding "tongue in cheek" to the critics' charge. The second part of the verse expresses what was closer to reality. Paul saw himself as someone of *right mind*, which was evident in the way he had devoted his life to serving God and others rather than himself.

B. COMPELLED BY LOVE (vv. 14, 15)

14. For Christ's love compels us, because we are convinced that one died for all, and therefore all died.

Paul develops a logical argument in this verse and the next. It actually begins with the premise *that one died for all*, a reference to Christ dying on the cross for all sinners. If this is true (and we know it is), then it implies that *all died.* How so? Paul is picturing Christ's death as a substitutionary atonement. We sinners had a penalty we owed to God because of our sin. Christ was willing to pay that penalty for us as our substitute. We would expect the penalty that he paid to be the same as the penalty we owed. Therefore, Paul is reasoning, if what Christ did for us was to die, then this reveals the condition that Christ came to remedy as our substitute: *all died.*

Why such clever reasoning here? Paul was simply explaining his motive for ministry. Since he along with everyone else was once "dead in sin" until Jesus paid his penalty for him, he felt a great burden in his heart to find some way to "repay" Jesus for loving him enough to do what he did at Calvary. As Paul says, *Christ's love compels us.*

15. And he died for all, that those who live should no longer live for themselves but for him who died for them and was raised again.

Now Paul completes his logical progression by arguing that every person for whom Christ died should feel in his heart the same constraint that Paul feels toward his preaching. All who have been saved by the death of Christ should feel compelled to serve with full devotion the One who saved them.

II. A MOTIVE TO INSPIRE (2 CORINTHIANS 5:16, 17)

A. NOT LIMITED BY WHAT WE SEE (v. 16)

16. So from now on we regard no one from a worldly point of view. Though we once regarded Christ in this way, we do so no longer.

Paul had come to realize that the *worldly point of view* was an inadequate standard by which to measure any individual. At one time he had *regarded Christ in this way.* But all of this had changed. Paul *no longer* judged people by the world's perspective; instead, he saw them the way God sees them. He learned to view every person the same way, as someone created in God's image with dignity and value. Christ considered that individual so valuable that he was willing to give up everything he had in Heaven in order to save him. Paul's thought was, "How can I do any less?"

B. SEEING WHAT WE CAN BECOME (v. 17)

17. Therefore, if anyone is in Christ, he is a new creation; the old has gone, the new has come!

Once we begin to see others from God's perspective, we will not only see their inherent dignity but also their potential *in Christ*. Those we can persuade to yield to Christ in faith will have their inner character completely reworked. When we who have been radically changed by Christ consider what a difference he could make with our family and friends, how could we not make every effort to persuade each of them to let Christ make him a *new creation* as well?

The Corinthians could easily have testified to the dramatic change that being *in Christ* could produce. Some of them had been sordid characters of the worst kind (1 Corinthians 6:9-11). But they had been "washed" in the blood of the Lamb, "sanctified," and "justified in the name of the Lord Jesus Christ and by the Spirit of our God" (v. 11). In other words, they were "in Christ."

NEW CREATURES

When the first Europeans came to Australia, they found many new creatures that they had never seen before. We can imagine their excitement when they first saw the kangaroo! Here also they found the emu, the kiwi, and the duck-billed platypus. It was a continent filled with new creatures.

Christians are new creatures never seen before the coming of Christ. And it is still true that when a sinner becomes a Christian, he becomes a new creature. His physical appearance may be the same, but if you watch his life, you will know that something has happened. He is not the person he used to be!

A minister was at a gas station when one of the newer members of his church walked in. The minister said to the man who owned the gas station, "Do you know Fred?"

The owner answered, "Yes, I know him."

Then the minister asked, "Do you know anything good about him?"

The owner replied, "I know that he made a great change in his life."

That man had become a new creature, and it was obvious to all who knew him! If you become a Christian and no one can tell the difference, you have to wonder whether anything really happened.

Of course, the gas station owner was not entirely correct. It was not the man himself who had made such a radical change in his life. Only the Lord can make new creatures. They come from his hand, not from our best efforts. What God did at creation he does again in conversion.

—R. C. S.

III. A MESSAGE TO PROCLAIM (2 CORINTHIANS 5:18-21)

A. NOTHING ELSE GOD CAN DO (vv. 18, 19)

18. All this is from God, who reconciled us to himself through Christ and gave us the ministry of reconciliation.

To understand the *ministry of reconciliation*, we must first understand the concept of *reconciliation*. The basic idea is to take two persons who are in disagreement and help them resolve their differences so that they can resume their normal relationship. For example, when management and labor are in a contract dispute, their normal working relationship is interrupted. When negotiations reach an impasse, a mediator is brought in to help them resolve their differences. The mediator's job is essentially to listen as each side states his case, determine where each has legitimate claims against the other, and then help the two sides work out a reasonable solution to which both can agree.

At Calvary Jesus Christ acted as the mediator between God and sinful man. We had no legitimate charge against a holy God, for he has never done us wrong.

WHAT DO YOU THINK?

It is hard for some people to recognize that sin has put them at enmity with God and in need of reconciliation. How can we expose their need and bring about reconciliation?

But because of our sin against God, he did have just cause for punishing us with death. The mediator's judgment against us would have been devastating, but he graciously offered to pay the penalty for us in order to bring a resolution to this dispute. This offer was above and beyond the duty of a mediator; but then, Christ is no ordinary mediator. So it is that all sinners who agree to these terms and allow Christ to pay their death penalty for them can be *reconciled* to God, restored to a peaceful relationship with the One our sins have alienated.

We who have been reconciled to God by Christ are not to rest comfortably in our new standing. We have been given *the ministry of reconciliation*. We have a duty to announce to others what they need to do if they want to be reconciled to God as we have been.

19. That God was reconciling the world to himself in Christ, not counting men's sins against them. And he has committed to us the message of reconciliation.

No one should ever imagine that God was a bystander at Calvary, observing what went on, then deciding how to respond. The cross was part of God's "set purpose and foreknowledge" (Acts 2:23). God was *reconciling the world to himself.* Reconciliation was neither our idea nor our doing; it was entirely of God.

Because of the work of Christ on behalf of his people, God is no longer *counting men's sins against them.* We need to understand that our biggest obstacle to a relationship with God is the guilt of our sin. The idea of being guilty means to deserve punishment because one has done wrong. Sin makes us guilty in the eyes of God and deserving of his punishment. (It should be noted that we do not always feel guilty, but we are in fact guilty just the same.) For those of us who through faith claim the death of Christ for our sins, God will not "count" the guilt of our sins; instead, he will mark our debt "paid."

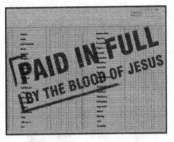

The visual for lesson 12 illustrates our need for Jesus to act in our behalf to pay the debt we could not pay.

SHUTTLE DIPLOMACY

It is only since the advent of the jet airplane that diplomats have been able to engage in what is called "shuttle diplomacy." Now it is quite common. Two nations are at odds. They're about to go to war—or may already be at war. A diplomat from a third nation undertakes to be the peacemaker. He flies back and forth between the warring countries. In some instances, he is able to bring the two nations to the peace table, where at least some dialogue can begin.

Our Lord Jesus did not need to engage in shuttle diplomacy to reconcile man and God. He came only once from Heaven to earth and accomplished that reconciliation—not by skillful negotiation, but by his sacrificial death. This is the amazing truth of the gospel.

Today we who have been reconciled to God serve as Christ's ambassadors, or "diplomats," in order to bring others into the same reconciliation. He did it with his death. We do it with our lives. We do it when we tell of his death and how it brings us from sin into salvation. All Christians have been called to the ministry of reconciliation.

—R. C. S.

B. AN OFFER TO ACCEPT (vv. 20, 21)

20. We are therefore Christ's ambassadors, as though God were making his appeal through us. We implore you on Christ's behalf: Be reconciled to God.

Here is one way to summarize our gospel message to the world: *be reconciled to God.* Paul's phrasing is intended to add one more thought to the picture of two disputing parties in mediation. After a mediator works out a plan for reconciliation, each party in negotiation must then decide whether or not to agree to the terms. Usually as one party agrees to the terms, he reaches his hand out across the table for a handshake that will "seal the deal." He has decided that he

WHAT DO YOU THINK?

How is our role as Christians in the world like that of an ambassador? Of what are we an ambassador? What is our job relative to the one who sent us?

What conclusions about our "government" can people draw based on your character and conduct?

PRAYER

Our Father in Heaven, we thank you for your mercy and grace, for loving us so much that you would give us the privilege of coming back home to you. Thank you, in Jesus' name. Amen.

THOUGHT TO REMEMBER

"We implore you on Christ's behalf: Be reconciled to God" (2 Corinthians 5:20b).

DAILY BIBLE READINGS

Monday, Feb. 15—*The Love of Christ Urges Us On (2 Corinthians 5:11-15)*

Tuesday, Feb. 16—*There Is a New Creation! (2 Corinthians 5:16-21)*

Wednesday, Feb. 17—*Justification and Life for All (Romans 5:18—6:4)*

Thursday, Feb. 18—*Alive to God in Christ Jesus (Romans 6:5-11)*

Friday, Feb. 19—*God's Gift Is Eternal Life (Romans 6:12-23)*

Saturday, Feb. 20—*Instructed by Law; Saved by Grace (Romans 7:1-13)*

Sunday, Feb. 21—*Thanks Be to God! (Romans 7:14-25a)*

is ready to be reconciled to his adversary. He now asks his adversary to do the same, to "be reconciled" to him.

In a spiritual sense, God stands even now with his hand reaching out across the table. He has agreed to the terms of Christ the mediator. He has accepted his substitutionary death at Calvary. He is ready to shake hands and "seal the deal." Through our preaching, he is pleading with sinful man: *be reconciled to God.* There is nothing more that God needs to do for our salvation. It now remains for each individual to decide whether or not to accept the terms of reconciliation.

This wonderful news will not be communicated unless those who have already been reconciled do so. Thus we Christians are Christ's *ambassadors* or royal representatives. We speak in his behalf a message he has given. We are not permitted to modify or compromise it, for it is not our message. We speak what Christ has told us to say. It is the same message that was once delivered to us: *be reconciled to God.*

21. God made him who had no sin to be sin for us, so that in him we might become the righteousness of God.

The pronouns of this verse should first be identified in order to grasp the meaning. The one *who had no sin* is Jesus Christ. His sinless character is clearly affirmed in Scripture (Hebrews 4:15; 7:26) and supported by the Gospel accounts of his life.

At Calvary Jesus was *made . . . to be sin for us.* This is another reference to the substitutionary atonement, by which Jesus assumed the guilt of our sins and paid their penalty. This should not be read so as to imply that Jesus actually became a real sinner. He took the place of sinners, and he was punished as a sinner should be punished; but he will always be the one who in reality *had no sin.*

And never forget the other side of the substitution. Christ took on the guilt of our sins so that *in him we might become the righteousness of God.* We could never pass the judgment bar of God on the basis of our own record of good deeds; for no matter how much good we could show, it would never be enough to make up for our sins against God. That is why God's grace allows us to assume Christ's perfect record even as he assumes our guilt. We stand before God fully reconciled to him, not on the basis of our good deeds, but because he allows us to wear the righteousness of Christ.

CONCLUSION

Have you ever noticed the advertisements for the Runaway Teen Hotline? It is a free service for youth who have run away from home, but now desire help in contacting their parents to find out if they can come back home. If you are a parent and have noticed the ads, you probably also have felt somewhat ill at ease. A runaway child is a parent's worst nightmare. Were it to happen to any of us, our days would be filled with anxiety, and our nights would give little relief. Each time the phone rang, we would pray to hear a familiar voice say the words, "I want to come home."

Jesus told a parable of a "prodigal son" who, after leaving his family and squandering his father's money, wondered whether he would be welcomed back home. He prepared a speech to win over his father. He was ready and willing to admit his mistakes and plead for a second chance. But what he found at home surprised him—a father running to him, having anxiously watched for his son's return. All along the father had been ready for a reconciliation. It was just a matter of waiting for the son to decide to come back home.

This is the gospel message that the world needs to hear. The Father loves us. He longs for us to stop running and come home.

Discovery Learning

This page contains an alternate lesson plan emphasizing learning activities. Classes desiring such student involvement will find these suggestions helpful. The next page is a reproducible activity page to further enhance discovery learning.

LEARNING GOALS

As a result of participating in this lesson, students should:

1. Explain what Paul said about the means and message of reconciliation with God.

2. Compare and contrast the way sinners are reconciled to God with other types or occasions of reconciliation.

3. Accept God's offer of reconciliation or plan to share his offer with someone else who needs to accept it.

INTO THE LESSON

Option 1. If your class sits around tables, have enough cutouts of butterflies on the tables for each student to have one. As students enter, ask them to decorate the butterflies with markers or crayons you provide. Explain that, because of the way a butterfly is transformed from a caterpillar, it has become a symbol of new life. Ask each student to print the words, "If anyone is in Christ, he is a new creation," on his or her butterfly. Point out that our new life in Christ becomes a reality when our relationship with God changes. The key word in today's study is "reconciliation."

Option 2. Begin by asking the following question: "Suppose you could be appointed an ambassador to any nation you chose. What nation would you choose and why?" Allow each student to share his or her answer with one other student. Then ask, "What would be your job? What does an ambassador do?" Discuss this briefly with the entire class.

Tell the class that our text calls us to be ambassadors. But we will have to read the text to discover our target group and discover our task.

INTO THE WORD

Prepare a handout with two columns. In column one print the text in four sections: 2 Corinthians 5:11-13; verses 14 and 15; verses 16 and 17; and verses 18-21. Place the heading "Personal Notes" over column 2.

Begin this section by distributing the handouts and giving a brief lecture on the background of the text. (See page 216.)

Ask a class member to read the first section, verses 11-13. Then ask the following discussion questions and encourage the students to make notes on their handouts during the discussion.

1. What is Paul's motive for ministry?

2. Why does Paul offer an opportunity for his readers to take pride in him?

3. Can you paraphrase verse 13 to clarify Paul's thoughts?

Ask another volunteer to read verses 14 and 15. Using the commentary, lecture on the logical progression in these verses. Emphasize the substitutionary atonement Christ offers for our sins. Also emphasize Paul's call to service in verse 15.

Ask a third volunteer to read verses 16 and 17; then ask why Paul would say, "We once regarded Christ from a worldly point of view." What was in Paul's background that would make him say this about himself? Also ask how a person becomes a "new creation" (v. 17).

Read verses 18-21. Make a few comments about the basic concept of reconciliation and the concept of a mediator (see pages 218, 219). Ask, "How does Jesus act as a mediator between God and man? How did he go beyond the duty of an ordinary mediator?"

Then reread the text, substituting the name of Jesus for the pronouns: "God made [Jesus] who had no sin to be sin for us so that in [Jesus] we might become the righteousness of God." Also read Isaiah's wonderful description of Christ's substitutionary atonement from Isaiah 53:4, 5.

Conclude this section by explaining the term "the righteousness of God" (page 220).

INTO LIFE

Summarize the text by explaining that there are two important messages in today's study. The first is to "be reconciled to God," to get our relationship with God resolved. God has done his part with Jesus' substitutionary sacrifice. He now waits for our response. (Invite class members who want to talk more about this to tell you. Meet with them after class to discuss this.)

The second message is a reminder that we are ambassadors of God. Ask class members to affirm their commitment to be ambassadors in closing prayer groups.

If you used the butterfly option in the lesson introduction, ask class members to post this on the bathroom mirror for one week as a joyful reminder of their new life.

Making Friends for God

One of the primary meanings for the word *reconcile* is "to make friendly again" or "to win over to a friendly attitude." The verb is appropriate for trying to get two warring nations to agree to peace, or for counseling a husband and wife who are on the verge of divorce. It is as appropriate for the one who encourages friendship in strangers as it is for the Christian who wants to fill a ministry of reconciliation between sinners and Christ. What is it that the conciliator does in each of the relationships mentioned above? Can you create an acrostic for the procedures? Use words, phrases, or complete thoughts for each letter.

R _____

E _____

C _____

O _____

N _____

C _____

I _____

L _____

E _____

Old Friend-isms!

Consider how these old adages about friendship are true in the ministry of reconciliation.

"Friends don't let friends drive drunk!"

"A friend in need is a friend indeed!"

"A mutual enemy is the strongest bond for friendship!"

"A friend loves at all times!"

"To have a friend one must be a friend"

"There are no breaks in a circle of friends!"

The God Friend

There is no typographical error in the heading atop this paragraph. God has demonstrated what friendship can and should be. In today's text from 2 Corinthians 5, can you find a verse or some verses that reveal how God's friendship works in each of the following ways?

____ He sees right through us, but loves us anyway.

____ He realizes we are more than height, weight, and appearance.

____ He would go so far as to die for us.

____ He knows we can become new and better.

____ He did not wait for us to become lovable.

____ He can overlook our flaws and weaknesses.

____ He trusts us to help him make other friends.

Unit 3. *Good News for Changing Times*
(Lessons 9-13)

LIVING IN HOPE

LESSON 13

WHY TEACH THIS LESSON?

As this century draws to a close, interest in "end-time" prophecy escalates. Many date-setters predict that, since history seems to neatly divide itself into 2000-year periods, the end of the 20th century A.D. marks the close of the Christian era.

The thrust of this lesson will not speculate as to dates and times when the Lord will return or when the world will end. The emphasis here is the Christian hope of a heavenly kingdom where peace will reign and praise will prevail forever. Christians who are blessed with prosperity and freedom need frequent reminders of our future hope of glory. Satisfaction and contentment here can obscure the matchless abundance of life eternal that is promised in eternity. Let these apocalyptic Scriptures rekindle your (and your students') anticipation of "the prize for which God has called [us] heavenward in Christ Jesus."

INTRODUCTION

A. PRACTICE WHAT YOU PREACH

Can you picture the irony of this scene? Inside a barber shop is a man getting a haircut. Leaning against the wall outside is the sign he has been carrying around on the street: "The world will end today." You have to wonder if the man is serious about what he is preaching.

This probably sounds like possible subject matter for a cartoon. Surely no one would actually do this—would he? How about the preacher who uses Scriptures and charts to predict an immediate date for Christ's return while at the same time putting away funds into a retirement plan for the future? (Some actually do!) What is lacking in both of these illustrations is consistency. The time-honored adage, "Practice what you preach," surely applies.

We need to ask ourselves how well we "practice what we preach" regarding the second coming. We say we believe that Christ will return one day to judge the world. Have we done everything we need to do to be ready to stand before the Judge? We say we want to live forever in the presence of God. But are we preparing now for that kind of existence by saying no to our sinful habits (since we cannot practice them there), by spending as much time as we can in personal devotion and corporate worship (since we will be worshiping continually there), and by actively participating in Christian service (since we will be serving our King forever)?

We need to do more than just talk and sing about the return of Christ. We need to live in a way that shows that we are serious about our hope for the future.

B. LESSON BACKGROUND

The Old Testament prophets spoke often of a coming Messiah who would bring salvation and judgment to the world. The common assumption by Jews in the time of Christ was that all of this would occur in one messianic appearance. But as the Gospels tell us, Jesus explained that he had come primarily "to seek

DEVOTIONAL READING:
1 PETER 1:3-9

LESSON SCRIPTURE:
TITUS 2:11-14; HEBREWS 12:18-29; REVELATION 1:14-20; 11:15-19

PRINTED TEXT:
TITUS 2:11-14; HEBREWS 12:26-29; REVELATION 1:17-20; 11:15

LESSON AIMS

As a result of today's lesson students should:

1. Summarize what today's texts tell us about the return of Jesus and how that gives us hope.

2. Compare the Christian's perspective on living in hope with the secular concept of living to "make a difference" in the present world.

3. Tell one activity or behavior each of them practices—or will begin to practice—because of the hope he or she has in Christ Jesus.

KEY VERSE

While we wait for the blessed hope—the glorious appearing of our great God and Savior, Jesus Christ.
—Titus 2:13

Feb
28

HOW TO SAY IT

Ephesus. EF-uh-sus.
Hades. HAY-deez.
Haggai. HAG-eye *or* HAG-a-eye.
Judaism. JOO-duh-izz-um *or*
    JOO-day-izz-um.
Messianic. Mess-e-AN-ick.
Patmos. PAT-muss.
Sinai. SYE-nye *or* SYE-nay-eye.

WHAT DO YOU THINK?

Does grace make the presence of sin unimportant in your life? What is grace supposed to accomplish with regard to our conduct?

How has receiving God's grace taught you to say no to ungodliness? With all the temptations around us, how can we stay motivated to live godly lives?

and to save what was lost" (Luke 19:10). Later, he would return to carry out judgment upon the lost as well as the saved (Matthew 25:31-33).

The New Testament epistles (such as Titus and Hebrews) provide the clearest picture of how the original messianic plan is to be understood. Their purpose is to instruct all Christians, who are already enjoying the blessings of Christ's first coming, how to prepare for the remaining messianic work of the second coming.

The book of Revelation is well known as a book of prophetic themes; however, its primary purpose should never be overlooked. Like the epistles, it encourages those who live between the first and second comings of Christ, not to set dates for his return but to set their lives in order.

I. PRACTICING A GODLY LIFESTYLE (TITUS 2:11-14)

The letter to Titus was written by the apostle Paul. Titus was a young preacher serving on the island of Crete (Titus 1:5). The epistle is filled with practical guidelines for life in the church, regarding both its organization (elders and their qualifications) and the proper conduct of individual members.

A. THE WAY GRACE DEMANDS (vv. 11, 12)

11. For the grace of God that brings salvation has appeared to all men.

Some of the grandest biblical themes regarding our *salvation* are summarized in this verse. Salvation derives from the work of *God,* not from our initiative. Salvation is made possible by the *grace* and mercy of God, not because we deserved it. Salvation is intended for *all* people and not just for a select few. Though freely given, this salvation includes certain responsibilities that cannot be ignored.

12. It teaches us to say "No" to ungodliness and worldly passions, and to live self-controlled, upright and godly lives in this present age.

The grace of God obligates us to live the kind of life described in this verse, not in order to earn our salvation, but because we are compelled to express our gratitude in this way. A heart truly changed by God's grace will reflect that change by rejecting the path of *ungodliness,* that is, saying *no* to any temptation to do something that violates God's standards.

Paul also warns against the influence of *worldly passions.* This calls to mind John's counsel not to "love the world . . . for everything in the world—the cravings of sinful man, the lust of his eyes and the boasting of what he has and does—comes not from the Father but from the world" (1 John 2:15, 16). Though we live *in this present age,* we are called to live differently.

This passage also lists three of the many virtues that should be developed in the life of a Christian. First, we should strive to be *self-controlled.* The basic idea of the Greek word is of someone who has so much discipline that he does not allow other people or things to push him around or to dictate his agenda. He makes decisions with a clear head and rational thinking, not because of emotions or coercion. The Greek word behind *upright* refers to being fair and above board in one's dealings. A *godly* person is someone who seeks to imitate the moral qualities of God emphasized in Scripture, such as holiness, love, mercy, patience, and faithfulness. These virtues and many others like them are the distinguishing marks of a person who has been changed by God's grace.

B. THE WAY GOD INTENDED (vv. 13, 14)

13. While we wait for the blessed hope—the glorious appearing of our great God and Savior, Jesus Christ, . . .

The second coming of Christ is our *blessed hope* in that it is the one event in the future toward which we have directed our lives. While the death and resurrection of Christ are the essence of our faith, the return of Christ is the essence of our hope.

The phrasing of this passage in the Greek text poses some difficulties for us in translation and interpretation. It is not typical to speak of God *appearing* when referring to the second coming, but the idea is not inappropriate. Most likely, Paul is referring to Jesus by a divine title, as *our great God and Savior.* This is consistent with Paul's teaching that in Christ "all the fullness of the Deity lives in bodily form" (Colossians 2:9; see also Romans 9:5; Philippians 2:6).

LIVING WITH HOPE

The Talmud is a commentary on the Old Testament Scriptures and is regarded highly by Jews. It teaches that the first question we will be asked at the judgment will be, "Did you live with hope?" However, the question about hope is properly a question for life now, not judgment in the future: "Are you living with hope now? What is the basis for your hope?"

In common usage, hope has come to mean a rather vague wish that we do not really expect to be fulfilled. But hope in the Bible is not vague, nor is it just wishful thinking. Biblical hope is something strong and resilient. It is "an anchor for the soul, firm and secure" (Hebrews 6:19). It is able to sustain us in any circumstance we face.

During the days of Communist rule, people in Romania used to greet one another by asking, "How are you today?" The typical answer was, "Better than tomorrow!" But Christians in that country sang and believed the words of the old hymn: "My hope is built on nothing less than Jesus' blood and righteousness." In a situation that seemed politically hopeless and economically hopeless, Christians found their hope in Jesus to be of supreme value.

Whatever our circumstances may be, we can rejoice that our lives are never hopeless. In Christ we have help for the present and hope for the future. —R. C. S.

The visual for lesson 13 is both a good illustration of our Golden Text (Titus 2:13) and a helpful reminder of the hope we have in Christ.

14. *Who gave himself for us to redeem us from all wickedness and to purify for himself a people that are his very own, eager to do what is good.*

Note how this passage affirms that God's purpose in saving us is not simply to get us out of trouble, but to change us into a new kind of people. We are expected to sever ties with *all* practices that entangle us in any form of *wickedness.* We are to be a pure people, cleansed from both the guilt and the moral contamination of sin. We are to join with others who have also been saved, thus forming *a people that are* [God's] *very own.* This means that we are his exclusive property, to be used in any way he chooses. We are to be *eager* in practicing good works that help others and glorify God.

II. SERVING A HEAVENLY KINGDOM (HEBREWS 12:26-29)

The book of Hebrews was written by an unknown yet inspired author to a community of Jewish Christians who were considering abandoning the Christian faith and returning to Judaism (Hebrews 10:35). Chapter 12 (vv. 18-22) likens Judaism to Mount Sinai, where Moses received the Ten Commandments and the law. The appearance of Sinai was terrifying, marked by fire, dark clouds and smoke, thunder and lightning, and an earthquake (Exodus 19:16-18). It is the nature of Judaism, the writer argues, that it instills within its adherents a sense of separation from God; because it reminds them of their sin and their guilt, yet offers no real solution (Hebrews 10:1-4).

The Christian faith, on the other hand, is like Mount Zion, the mountain upon which the city of Jerusalem was built. (Mount Zion is one of several biblical symbols for Heaven.) In contrast to Judaism, Christianity proclaims a sacrifice

WHAT DO YOU THINK?

Think of a Christian you know who might be regarded as a "religious fanatic." What aspects of his behavior might cause him to be labeled that way? What makes this person so eager for doing good? What can we learn from such a person?

Is the person labeled this way because he really takes his enthusiasm too far, or because society disapproves of him?

that will remove our guilt (Hebrews 10:11-14), thus opening the way for us to move one day to the "heavenly Jerusalem" (Hebrews 12:22).

A. NEVER TO BE DESTROYED (vv. 26, 27)

26. At that time his voice shook the earth, but now he has promised, "Once more I will shake not only the earth but also the heavens."

The writer observes that God's *voice shook the earth* when Moses received the law at Sinai. The next time God speaks such a powerful word will be at the end of time. His voice will then *shake* everything—the earth as well as the heavenly bodies. The writer refers to a portion of the Old Testament in this verse (Haggai 2:6) in order to strengthen his appeal to his readers, whose background, as we have noted, was in Judaism.

27. The words "once more" indicate the removing of what can be shaken—that is, created things—so that what cannot be shaken may remain.

When the ultimate shaking comes, all *created things,* that is, the material universe, will collapse. Everything we value from this life will exist no longer. All that will remain will be *what cannot be shaken.*

In contrast, spiritual realities cannot be touched by an earthquake. Our relationship with Christ, our brotherhood within the church, the fruit of our service—these and other blessings will continue after the end of time. They are secure on the heavenly Mount Zion.

B. OUR DUTY AS CITIZENS (vv. 28, 29)

28, 29. Therefore, since we are receiving a kingdom that cannot be shaken, let us be thankful, and so worship God acceptably with reverence and awe, for our "God is a consuming fire."

Once again we see a familiar theme. Reflecting on the heavenly life that we hope to inherit one day has implications for how we should live our lives now on this earth. The thought of *receiving a kingdom* in Heaven should move us to *be thankful.* We should want to *worship God* through giving ourselves as "living sacrifices" (Romans 12:1), because we appreciate how much he has done for us.

Note also how this passage brings in another motive for our godly lives and service: the reality of Hell. We should serve God *with reverence and awe,* not only because we appreciate his grace, but also because we do not want to face the *consuming fire* of his wrath.

III. TRUSTING AN ALMIGHTY SAVIOR (REVELATION 1:17-20; 11:15)

The apostle John wrote the book of Revelation while in exile on the island of Patmos (Revelation 1:9). It is usually dated at sometime near the end of the first century.

A. HIS POWER OVER DEATH (1:17, 18)

17. When I saw him, I fell at his feet as though dead. Then he placed his right hand on me and said: "Do not be afraid. I am the First and the Last.

While in a state of worship one Lord's day (1:10), John received a vision of Jesus. He saw the Lord adorned in glorious garments that were symbolic of his great power and authority (1:12-16). The sight was beautiful, yet terrifying at the same time. John *fell at his feet as though dead.*

Jesus tried to calm John's fears with a gentle touch and encouraging words. He called John's attention to his eternal nature, identifying himself as the *First and the Last* of everything, the One who has no beginning and no ending.

WHAT DO YOU THINK?

The writer of Hebrews contrasts the things that can be "shaken" with those that can't. Why do so many people trust in shaky things like material wealth or temporal power? How can we persuade them to put their faith in the eternal and almighty God? How might your own reputation as a Christian help to persuade such people?

18. *"I am the Living One; I was dead, and behold I am alive for ever and ever! And I hold the keys of death and Hades.*

John well knew that at one time Jesus was *dead*; he had been present at the crucifixion (John 19:26, where John is described as the disciple whom Jesus loved) and had seen him die. John knew where to go to find Jesus' tomb, so we assume he saw him buried as well (John 20:1-4). John was also one of the first witnesses to the resurrection of Jesus (John 20:5-8, 19). Now, as John's life and ministry were threatened by a hostile emperor, he received a vivid reminder that the One whose church the emperor sought to destroy was alive and well.

Jesus is described as having *the keys of death and Hades.* Hades refers to the place where people go when they die to await judgment. Jesus had been there for three days and had broken free, taking with him the keys that lock a person into death permanently. Such imagery implies not only that Jesus is the Conqueror of death, but that he has the power to release us from death's grip after we die. In other words, this vision dramatized the Christian's hope that one day Jesus will resurrect the saints to everlasting life so that they may live with him in Heaven.

THE KEEPER OF THE KEYS

A man once told how during his youth, his father was the janitor of the high school he attended. There were some disadvantages to that; for example, often the father had to stay and work after school. But there was one great advantage. If the boy and some of his friends wanted to get into the gym and play basketball on weekends, they could go right to the boy's father. Why? Because he had the keys! To have the keys is to have power. So we should be encouraged by today's lesson when we learn that Jesus has "the keys of death and Hades."

A Sunday school teacher who had never been to Bible college or seminary saw to the heart of this verse. He said, "So the Devil doesn't even have the keys to his own house." That's a very helpful insight. It reassures us that Christ always has more power than Satan. It tells us which side is going to win. It also reminds us that in Christ we become stronger than Satan. "The one who is in you is greater than the one who is in the world" (1 John 4:4).

We should be alert to the influences of Satan, but we should not be afraid of his power. He doesn't even have the keys to his own house!   —R. C. S.

B. HIS AUTHORITY OVER THE CHURCH (vv. 19, 20)

19. *"Write, therefore, what you have seen, what is now and what will take place later.*

John was not given this vision simply that he might watch and learn. He was explicitly commissioned to record it all (Revelation 1:11) and then send it to seven specific churches in Asia Minor (modern western Turkey). This is an area where, according to the early church fathers, John served (particularly in Ephesus) during the later years of his life.

John's writing was to consist of three parts (not of equal length). *What you have seen* referred to the vision he had just witnessed in chapter 1. *What is now* referred to the messages Jesus was about to give to the seven churches (chapters 2 and 3). *What will take place later* designated the visions John was yet to see—in other words, the remainder of the book (chapters 4–22).

20. *"The mystery of the seven stars that you saw in my right hand and of the seven golden lampstands is this: The seven stars are the angels of the seven churches, and the seven lampstands are the seven churches.*

Determining the meaning of the symbolism in the book of Revelation can be challenging. Perhaps the best place to find clues is the Old Testament, because

DAILY BIBLE READINGS

Monday, Feb. 22—The Blessed Hope (Titus 2:11-14)

Tuesday, Feb. 23—What Cannot Be Shaken Remains (Hebrews 12:18-29)

Wednesday, Feb. 24—Do Not Be Afraid (Revelation 1:12-20)

Thursday, Feb. 25—He Will Reign Forever and Ever (Revelation 11:15-19)

Friday, Feb. 26—A Living Hope (1 Peter 1:3-9)

Saturday, Feb. 27—The Hope to Which God Has Called Us (Ephesians 1:15-23)

Sunday, Feb. 28—A New Heaven and a New Earth (Revelation 21:1-8)

most of the figures in Revelation have clear parallels in the Old Testament prophets. We may not be certain regarding our conclusions, but a person who studies this background thoroughly can make some reasonable suggestions.

Of course, the best interpretations are those that are given to us by John himself. In the verse before us, he records Jesus' explanation of the meaning of two of the symbols in the vision he had seen. *The seven stars* were *the angels of the seven churches*, while *the seven lampstands* were *the seven churches* of Asia Minor.

Understanding the seven churches presents no difficulty for us, since we have already been given their names (v. 11). However, *the seven angels* still presents some confusion because we are not sure what kind of "angels" a church has. Some assume this refers to guardian angels, but why would Jesus send a letter to guardian angels? The Greek word used here literally means "messengers," which could designate either a heavenly messenger (an angel) or an earthly messenger (such as an elder or a preacher). Perhaps the seven messages were to be sent to the preacher of each congregation, who would then read the letter aloud.

Regardless of what the stars symbolize concerning the seven churches, the meaning of this stirring vision is clear. Jesus appears "among the lampstands" (1:13). Thus, he is present with his people—the churches. In dramatic form John's vision teaches what Matthew 28:20 declares: "Surely I am with you always, to the very end of the age."

C. HIS FINAL TRIUMPH (11:15)

15. The seventh angel sounded his trumpet, and there were loud voices in heaven, which said: "The kingdom of the world has become the kingdom of our Lord and of his Christ, and he will reign for ever and ever."

The book of Revelation is filled with action—seven seals being broken, seven trumpets being sounded, seven bowls of plagues being poured out, along with a host of other symbolic actions. We cannot always be certain about how to interpret what is happening, but usually we can see enough to learn a valuable lesson.

As a case in point, we may not understand as fully as we would like the meaning of the first six trumpets and all the disasters that are associated with them. However, when the *seventh angel* blows the last of the trumpets, we know without a doubt of the final triumph of Christ and his people.

Many will not read the words of the verse before us without thinking of the majestic "Hallelujah Chorus" that is part of Handel's *Messiah*. Let us endeavor to make certain that we are part of the heavenly kingdom of Christ, so that we can one day join the great voices of the "Hallelujah Chorus" in Heaven.

CONCLUSION

Most of us know what it is like to take a test in school. Often the teacher passes out the test questions face down, and then, when every student has a copy, she announces, "Begin!" The test may seem to go well for a while; however, there is usually a sense of panic whenever students realize that the allotted time is nearing an end. Eventually they are either relieved or terrified to hear the teacher say, "Time's up!"

The above scenario provides us with an appropriate way to look at the second coming of Christ. Your life and mine may be considered a kind of "test." We cannot know for certain when the day of "grading" (Judgment Day) will take place. We must live lives of consistent godliness each day, in anticipation of what one of our texts calls "the blessed hope." We need to be secure in our knowledge that whatever comes first (our death or Jesus' return), we belong to Jesus. For the Christian, "time's up" means that eternal life has just begun!

Discovery Learning

This page contains an alternate lesson plan emphasizing learning activities. Classes desiring such student involvement will find these suggestions helpful. The next page is a reproducible activity page to further enhance discovery learning.

LEARNING GOALS

As a result of today's lesson students should:

1. Summarize what today's texts tell us about the return of Jesus and how that gives us hope.

2. Compare the Christian's perspective on living in hope with the secular concept of living to "make a difference" in the present world.

3. Tell one activity or behavior each of them practices—or will begin to practice—because of the hope he or she has in Christ Jesus.

INTO THE LESSON

Divide the class into small groups of three to five persons and give each group one or two hymnbooks and a piece of poster board. Ask the groups to look for songs about Heaven (often found under "Eternal Destiny, Heaven, Everlasting Life" in the index). Ask them to list every word or phrase used by hymn writers to describe Heaven (e.g., pearly gates, mansions, glory, beyond the river, etc.). Hang their posters in front of the class when they are finished. You may highlight the variety of descriptive phrases. Allow volunteers to tell which descriptions particularly touch them and why.

Comment that many hymns, while describing the joy of Heaven, also remind us we have something to do while we are waiting for this fantastic place. A good example is "When We All Get to Heaven." List the words and phrases from this hymn that tell us how to live while here on earth.

Point out that the hymn writers simply reflect the writers of Scripture. The Scriptures remind us of our wonderful goal, yet they also remind us how to live while we are waiting.

INTO THE WORD

Place three poster boards with the following headings at the front of the class: "How to Live," "Our Hope," and "Characteristics of Our Almighty Savior."

Copy the printed text on handouts to give to each class member. Tell the class to listen when the text is read for what the Scriptures tell us about how to live (mark these on their handouts with an "L"), words that describe our hope (mark these "H"), and words that describe our Savior ("S").

Read Titus 2:11-14 and give the students time to mark their texts. Ask one student to write each word or phrase on the corresponding poster as class members recite them.

Use the commentary section to define or clarify the phrases "say 'No' to ungodliness," "worldly passions," "self-controlled," "upright," "godly," "blessed hope," "great God," "redeem," and "a people that are his very own." Emphasize that while the death and resurrection of Jesus are the essence of our faith, the return of Christ is the essence of our hope.

Read Hebrews 12:26-29, giving the students time to mark their texts and entering their answers on the posters. Use the commentary to explain the background to and significance of this text. Ask for definitions of "a kingdom that cannot be shaken" and "consuming fire" (see page 226).

Do the same exercise with Revelation 1:17-20 and 11:15. Ask why John would fall at the Lord's feet "as though dead." Comment on the significance of the word "living." Then ask the class to help you define "the keys of death and Hades" and the sevens (stars, candlesticks, churches, and angels). Conclude by emphasizing the transfer of power and the eternal reign of the Lord in 11:15.

INTO LIFE

Point to the three posters you have just completed. Tell the class that God wants us to enjoy the assurance that he will conquer death and has created an eternal kingdom for us. That assurance gives us a hope that should change our values, our lifestyles, and our commitments.

Write on the chalkboard "Living in Hope" and "Living to Make a Difference." Observe that there are many good non-Christian people who want to "make a difference" in this world. Ask the class to suggest differences in the Christian's perspective on "living in hope" and the secular view of "making a difference." Note their responses under the headings on the chalkboard. Then use the "Time's Up" illustration on page 228. This is an appropriate way to think about the second coming of Christ.

Give each class member a three-inch by five-inch card with these words printed on it: "Because I am Heaven bound, I will . . ." Ask each student to identify one activity or behavior pattern he or she needs to change or strengthen in order to bring glory to God. Close the class session by asking God to hear and bless each commitment.

God's Great *Grace* (Titus 2:11)

The Christian's hope is based in God's grace. By the Spirit, Titus reveals the marvelous grace of God. Complete each of the following from Titus 2:11-14.

1. The grace of God brings _____Salvation_____

2. The grace of God has appeared _____to all men_____

3. The grace of God teaches us to say _____No to ungodliness____

4. The grace of God teaches us to live ___self-controled, upright + godly lives.___

5. The grace of God makes us eager to _____do good_____

♩ing the ♩ongs of *Hope*

From what great hymn of hope does each of the following lines come? Read verse 13 of Titus 2, then sing (or hum!) each of the hymnwriters' words.

"His grace has planned it all/'Tis mine but to believe"

"And though this world with devils filled/Should threaten to undo us"

"When shall I reach that happy place/And be forever blessed?"

"I'm so glad I learned to trust thee/Precious Jesus, Savior, Friend"

"When all my labors and trials are o'er/And I am safe on that beautiful shore"

"Come we that love the Lord/And let our joys be known"

Grace and Hope's Outcome: *Praise!*

As the Hebrew writer reveals: "We are receiving a kingdom that cannot be shaken; let us be thankful, and so worship God acceptably with reverence and with awe!" (12:28, 29). Everyone who knows the grace and has the hope will—as John does in Revelation 1:17—fall at his feet in worship. Clip the following verse of praise based on the Revelation texts and carry it with you for an occasional "Burst of Praise!" this week.

> Praise the One who's First and Last,
> Alpha and Omega, Praise!
> Praise the One who died but liveth,
> Resurrected Lord of Days!
> Praise the King of Kingdom Endless,
> He who reigns forever, Praise!

Spring Quarter, 1999

That You May Believe
(Gospel of John)

Special Features

Lessons

Unit 1: Jesus' Coming Calls for Faith

Unit 2: Jesus Is Raised to Life

Unit 3: Jesus Declares God's Message

Unit 4: Jesus Prepares His Followers

About These Lessons

This quarter will be a faith builder. These thirteen lessons from the Gospel of John will remind your students of some of the reasons they put their faith in Jesus Christ and will equip them to share that faith with others.

Mar 7

Mar 14

Mar 21

Mar 28

Apr 4

Apr 11

Apr 18

Apr 25

May 2

May 9

May 16

May 23

May 30

The Business of Believing

by Edwin V. Hayden

I was filling out a position questionnaire from the political party that gets most of my support. The first part was easy: what did I believe about each of several issues being contested between "our" party and "theirs"? A penciled mark in the proper box would record my position on each point. On most questions, I knew my responses would please the pollsters.

Then the party's questions became more difficult. Would I support my opinions with a financial contribution at this or that level? Substantial sums were suggested to indicate a substantial degree of support. Then I was asked if I would campaign for the party in my neighborhood and represent it as a poll watcher in the forthcoming election. Now the issue had become not only what I believed, but how far I was willing to follow my belief. Later mailings would present the party's position in a way designed to strengthen my faith in its principles and increase my commitment to it.

A GOSPEL WITH A GOAL

In his Gospel, John deals in a better way with our faith in Jesus Christ as Lord. John doesn't begin by asking questions; he starts with a firm declaration of Jesus as the bodily revelation of God—"The Word became flesh and made his dwelling among us" (John 1:14). He then continues with a factual account to establish his claim. He doesn't make repeated demands on the reader for increasing commitment; he sets forth Jesus' own claims concerning who he is and what he demands of his followers. Innumerable blessings are promised for those who believe and irreparable loss for those who will not. In conclusion John makes plain his plan and purpose for writing. He has told what is most important about Jesus, "that you may believe that Jesus is the Christ, the Son of God, and that by believing you may have life in his name" (John 20:31).

Who is the *you* to whom John's Gospel is addressed? He doesn't say. The approach and appeal are so general that it might have been directed to "Dear Reader" or "To Whom It May Concern." Yet the contents are so personal that John might have called each reader by name. What, moreover, is meant by *believing*? Obviously the word includes all that was suggested by my political opinion poll, but much more. It involves life and living, for now and eternity. It invites the first-time reader to consider and acknowledge the truth of what John has written. It also challenges the lifelong follower of Jesus to a higher and deeper commitment.

FOUR DIMENSIONS OF FAITH

Scripture uses *belief*, or *faith*, in four distinct but related ways. In the phrase *the faith* it signifies that which is believed. For the Christian, that embraces the truth embodied in Jesus Christ and revealed through him and his chosen apostles. It is "the faith which was once for all entrusted to the saints" (Jude 3). That belief is to be kept, defended, and proclaimed, in full recognition that those committed to other beliefs (or faiths) will resist its claims and will need to see a consistent, patient demonstration of Christlike living before they are likely to believe in him.

Second, *believing* is an act of the will—a voluntary response to evidence. For the Christian, "faith comes from hearing the message, and the message is heard through the word of Christ" (Romans 10:17). John's Gospel sets forth God's

Word with the purpose of persuading its readers that Jesus is indeed God's Son and the promised Messiah (John 20:31).

Next, *faith* describes a trust and commitment that is built on one's conviction of what is truth. It causes one to think, feel, and act on the basis of his belief. So Jesus insisted that those who *believe* (trust) in God will not be unduly concerned about material security (Luke 12:28), frightened by troubling circumstances (Mark 4:40), or upset by the prospect of death (John 14:1).

A fourth aspect of *faith* is better known as faithfulness, a steadfastness in doing as belief directs. We sometimes call it "keeping the faith." Jesus once told some wavering followers that they did not believe, and John adds, "Jesus had known from the beginning which of them did not believe and who would betray him" (John 6:64). The Lord's grand assurance in Revelation 2:10 must not be neglected here: "Be faithful, even to the point of death, and I will give you the crown of life." We can be sure that he will be faithful to that promise!

Our lessons for the forthcoming quarter are designed to build a steadfast *faith* in Jesus Christ as Lord. They are arranged in four units according to four different emphases. The texts, taken from thirteen of John's twenty-one chapters, begin with the first chapter of John and proceed through its contents, though not always consecutively.

BELIEVE!

MARCH

Unit 1 ("Jesus' Coming Calls for Faith") occupies the four weeks in March. Texts are taken primarily from John 1, 3, and 4.

Lesson 1 ("The Word Became Flesh") ties John's introduction (John 1:1ff) with his statement of purpose (20:30, 31). His Gospel is designed to establish the fact that Jesus, the eternal Word made flesh, is God's Son and the Messiah.

Lesson 2 ("John the Baptist Testifies of Jesus") is taken from John 1:19-34. It presents the ministry and message of the man who came preaching and baptizing to prepare the way for Jesus.

Lesson 3 ("Nicodemus Visits Jesus"), from John 3:1-17, sets forth Jesus' demand for a new birth "of water and the Spirit." The lesson text includes the Golden Text of the Bible (John 3:16), with its grand announcement of salvation for believers in God's only begotten Son.

Lesson 4 ("A Woman Brings Her Village to Jesus") recounts Jesus' conversation with a woman of Samaria by Jacob's well (John 4). When he identified himself as the Messiah, the enthusiastic woman brought her neighbors to meet Jesus, and many came to believe in him.

BELIEVE WHAT?

APRIL

Unit 2 ("Jesus Is Raised to Life") provides lessons for the first two weeks in April (Resurrection Sunday and the week following). These lessons present the facts described in 1 Corinthians 15:1-4 as the essence of the gospel: the death, burial, and resurrection of Jesus.

Lesson 5 ("Jesus Is Crucified and Resurrected") is from John 19 and 20, including the touching account of Jesus' resurrection appearance to Mary Magdalene. Read the full account of Jesus' arrest, crucifixion, and resurrection in John 18–20.

Lesson 6 ("Jesus Appears to His Disciples"), from John 20:19-29, recounts two events a week apart from each other. Thomas, who was absent on the first occasion, was present to see the risen Christ on the second and to voice his faith. Jesus declared that those who believe in him without having seen him are "blessed."

THE BUSINESS OF BELIEVING

BELIEVE IN WHOM?

The theme of Unit 3 ("Jesus Declares God's Message") provides lessons for two weeks in April and one in May. It describes qualities and characteristics in Jesus that demand our faith in him as God's Son and our Lord.

Lesson 7 ("Jesus, the Bread of Life"), from John 6, depicts the feeding of more than five thousand persons with five small loaves and two fishes, and follows that with Jesus' presentation of himself as the Bread of life eternal for all mankind.

Lesson 8 ("Truth That Sets People Free") comes from John 8:12, 21-36. It highlights teaching that Jesus gave in the heat of controversy in Jerusalem during the Feast of Tabernacles. He is the Light of the world. He is God's eternal Son. His way is the way of truth. He is God's appointed means by which mankind can be freed from slavery to falsehood, sin, and death.

Lesson 9 ("Death That Gives Life"), from John 12, presents material from Jesus' last public teaching session. He was soon to die, but that was necessary in order to provide the life that he came to give to others. Tragically, many still refused to believe in Jesus, and some who believed were afraid to admit it.

BELIEVE AND DO

Unit 4 ("Jesus Prepares His Followers") will cover the last four weeks in May. All texts for this unit come from Jesus' final evening with his disciples before his betrayal and arrest. Jesus instructed them, and through them all believers, in the kind of life that is lived by faith in him.

Lesson 10 ("Jesus Teaches Servanthood") is taken from John 13:1-17. It tells of Jesus' object lesson on servanthood, when he washed his disciples' feet.

Lesson 11 ("Jesus, the True Vine"), from John 15:1-17, calls attention to another vivid object lesson. Just as the fruit-bearing branch of a grapevine cannot live and bear grapes unless it maintains a vital connection with the trunk, so spiritual life and usefulness are impossible without a constant, vital connection with Jesus. Love is cited as an example of Christian fruitfulness.

Lesson 12 ("The Spirit Empowers Loving Obedience") is based on texts from John 14 and 16. The Comforter, sent to be with the apostles after Jesus' departure, would remind them of all he had taught and would guide them in all truth. Such a promise assures us of the trustworthiness of the New Testament Scriptures.

Lesson 13 ("Jesus Prays for His Disciples"), from John 17, focuses on what has been called Jesus' high priestly prayer. First, he prayed to be glorified so that his Father would be glorified. Then he prayed for the apostles to be kept united in him, strong in faith, and untainted by the world. Finally, Jesus prayed for unity among future believers so that others would also believe.

Here, then, is a series of lessons in which we draw near to the center of the apostles' (and the Holy Spirit's) purpose in giving us the Bible; the center of Jesus' purpose in coming to earth; and the center of God's purpose for all creation! What we do with these lessons will make a difference, not only to those we teach, but to God himself! What an awesome thought!

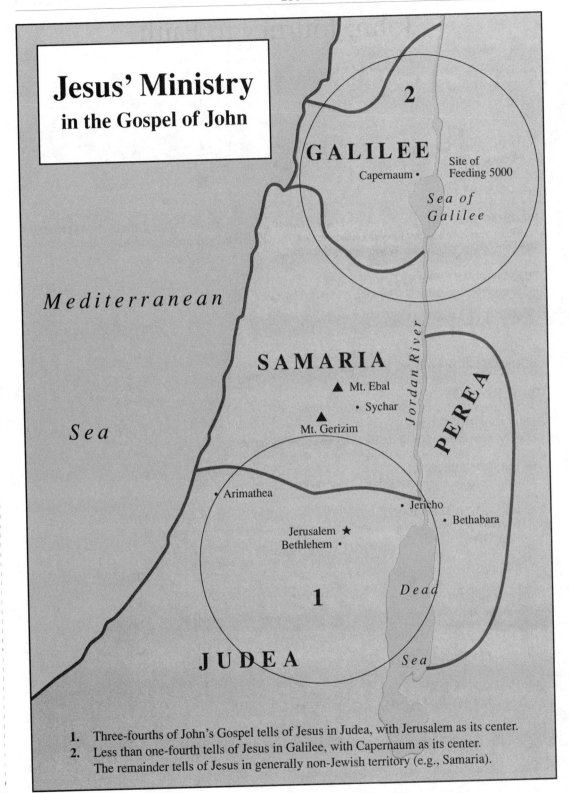

Jesus' Ministry
in the Gospel of John

GALILEE

Capernaum •

Site of
Feeding 5000

*Sea of
Galilee*

Mediterranean

SAMARIA

▲ Mt. Ebal

• Sychar

▲
Mt. Gerizim

Sea

Jordan River

PEREA

• Arimathea

• Jericho

• Bethabara

Jerusalem ★
Bethlehem •

Dead

1

JUDEA

Sea

1. Three-fourths of John's Gospel tells of Jesus in Judea, with Jerusalem as its center.
2. Less than one-fourth tells of Jesus in Galilee, with Capernaum as its center.
   The remainder tells of Jesus in generally non-Jewish territory (e.g., Samaria).

John: Journey to Faith

A FEW MONTHS	**PROLOGUE** The Word became flesh	*JOHN 1:1-18*	*LESSON 1*
	BAPTISM	*JOHN 1:29-34*	*LESSON 2*
	WATER TURNED TO WINE "He thus revealed his glory, and his disciples put their faith in him" (John 2:11).	*JOHN 2:1*	
ONE YEAR	**FIRST PASSOVER**	*JOHN 2:13*	
	NICODEMUS VISITS JESUS "We know you are a teacher who has come from God. For no one could perform the miraculous signs you are doing if God were not with him" (John 3:2).	*JOHN 3*	*LESSON 3*
	THE SAMARITAN WOMAN AT JACOB'S WELL "Many of the Samaritans from that town believed in him" (John 4:39).	*JOHN 4:1-42*	*LESSON 4*
ONE YEAR	**SECOND PASSOVER***	*JOHN 5:1*	
	HEALING AT THE POOL OF BETHESDA/CONTROVERSY WITH PHARISEES "If you believed Moses, you would believe me" (John 5:46).	*JOHN 5*	
ONE YEAR	**THIRD PASSOVER**	*JOHN 6:4*	
	FEEDING OF THE 5000/BREAD OF LIFE "We believe and know that you are the Holy One of God" (John 6:69).	*JOHN 6:5-71*	*LESSON 7*
	THE FEAST OF TABERNACLES "Even as he spoke, many put their faith in him" (John 8:30).	*JOHN 7, 8*	*LESSON 8*
	LAZARUS RAISED AT BETHANY "Many of the Jews who had come to visit Mary, and had seen what Jesus did, put their faith in him" (John 11:45).	*JOHN 11:1ff.*	
A FEW DAYS	**FOURTH PASSOVER**	*JOHN 12:1*	
	SON OF MAN TO BE LIFTED UP "Many even among the leaders believed in him. But because of the Pharisees they would not confess their faith . . ." (John 12:42).	*JOHN 12*	*LESSON 9*
	JESUS WASHES THE DISCIPLES' FEET	*JOHN 13*	*LESSON 10*
	FAREWELL DISCOURSES ". . . so that the world may believe that you have sent me" (John 17:21).	*JOHN 14–17*	*LESSONS 11-13*
	THE TRIALS AND CRUCIFIXION	*JOHN 18, 19*	*LESSON 5*
	THE RESURRECTION "Blessed are those who have not seen and yet have believed" (John 20:29).	*JOHN 20, 21*	*LESSON 6*

*John does not specifically mention this as a Passover, but most agree that the "feast" mentioned in John 5:1 was the Passover.

THE WORD BECAME FLESH

LESSON 1

WHY TEACH THIS LESSON?

Probably there is not a person in your class who does not believe Jesus is the Son of God or that he came to earth in a flesh-and-blood human body. So this lesson about the Word made flesh may seem like summer re-runs on TV—been there; done that!

If you allow that mind-set to settle in, you will have missed one of your greatest teaching moments of the year. This lesson is more than an affirmation of the fact of the incarnation. This is an opportunity for your students to commit themselves to the mission of the Incarnate Christ, who has returned to Heaven and left us to carry on the task at hand. For those who would rather see a sermon than hear one, your students can be, in a sense, "the word made flesh." You won't find anything that exciting on TV this summer!

INTRODUCTION

A. "SHOW ME"

A man in our town liked to tell why he was an atheist. He recalled walking one day through a wooded area when his mind turned to thoughts of God. "Is there really a God?" he wondered. He sat down on a convenient log to ponder the question and considered how he could settle the matter once and for all. He decided to ask God (if indeed there were a God) to show himself in some convincing demonstration, now!

Nothing happened. The man was left among the trees with no recognizable voice or vision. So he got up and went on, a confirmed atheist. God had failed to provide the proof the man ordered.

From earliest times men have wanted to see God or witness special proofs of his existence. The Pharisees pestered Jesus with demands for miraculous signs (Matthew 12:38, 39; 16:1-4). Near the close of his earthly ministry, even one of Jesus' own disciples pleaded, "Show us the Father" (John 14:8).

That, however, was exactly what Jesus had been doing throughout his earthly ministry. It may not have been the kind of revelation of God that people were looking for, but it was an infinitely better demonstration than they could have imagined. Today's lesson deals with this subject of how "the Word became flesh."

B. LESSON BACKGROUND

Today's printed text includes portions of both the introduction and the conclusion to the fourth Gospel. The writer does not identify himself by name. However, by comparing material in this Gospel with that in the other three, we conclude that the writer was the apostle John, son of the fisherman Zebedee (Matthew 4:21). This "disciple whom Jesus loved" (John 13:23; 19:26; 20:2; 21:7, 20), along with his brother James, were among the Lord's first disciples. It is generally assumed that John was directed to Jesus by John the Baptist, whom he and Andrew had followed earlier (John 1:35-40).

Jesus nicknamed James and John "sons of thunder" (*Boanerges*) from their highly temperamental personalities (Mark 3:17; 9:38-41; Luke 9:49-55). Even

DEVOTIONAL READING
1 JOHN 4:1-6

LESSON SCRIPTURE
JOHN 1:1-18; 20:30, 31

PRINTED TEXT
JOHN 1:1-18; 20:30, 31

LESSON AIMS

After this lesson a student should be able to:

1. State the identity and mission of Jesus as the incarnate Word.

2. Compare Jesus' mission with John's purpose for writing his Gospel.

3. Express a commitment to living in harmony with Jesus' identity and mission.

KEY VERSE

The Word became flesh and made his dwelling among us. We have seen his glory, the glory of the One and Only, who came from the Father, full of grace and truth.   —John 1:14

so, John was so completely transformed by his acquaintance with Jesus that he came to be known as the apostle of love—a theme that permeates his writings, particularly his three epistles. Along with Simon Peter (another temperamental fisherman!), the sons of Zebedee became Jesus' closest followers, sharing with him significant experiences not shared by the other disciples (Mark 5:37; 9:2; 14:33). John seems to have done his writing—his Gospel, his three brief epistles, and the book of Revelation—later in a long life. Most students date these writings toward the end of the first century.

John's Gospel is different from the other three in several respects. It says nothing of Jesus' birth or early life; it tells more of his ministry in Judea and less of his work in Galilee; it focuses on Jesus' discourses rather than his parables; it includes more of Jesus' one-on-one encounters; and it highlights strong contrasts—life and death, light and darkness, spirit and flesh, truth and falsehood, love and hate. John's prologue, the text for today's lesson, is also unique. Nothing in the other Gospels (or elsewhere in Scripture) compares with the description of God's revelation of himself found in these verses.

I. THE ETERNAL WORD (JOHN 1:1-5)
A. THE WORD AND GOD (vv. 1, 2)

1, 2. In the beginning was the Word, and the Word was with God, and the Word was God. He was with God in the beginning.

The beginning echoes the thought of Genesis 1:1. God has always been. He is without beginning, without end, and without change. Many in the scientific world can see nothing before time except more time. John declares plainly what they cannot even imagine: God's *Word*, who was Jesus (v. 14), is before and beyond all of it!

The term *word* was important in Hebrew thought as God's vehicle of creation. He spoke, and things came into being (Psalm 33:6). *Word* also designated his command; the "Ten Commandments" is literally, in the Hebrew text, "ten words." Prophets often introduced God's messages with "Hear the *word* of the Lord."

To first-century Greeks the term *logos*, which is the Greek term rendered *word*, signified thought and reason, as well as a unit of speech or writing. It is difficult to determine whether John had a specific idea in mind by his use of this concept. Perhaps he simply chose a term that people had been using for years and declared its true meaning and fulfillment in Jesus.

The Word was with God. The Word was God's companion before anything else existed. A distinct being is recognized, as Genesis 1:26 indicates: "Let *us* make man in *our* image." The Word was with God—not only in his presence but with him in the sense of agreeing with all his purposes and doings. Jesus speaks of "the glory I had with you before the world began" (John 17:5).

The Word was God. Scripture consistently affirms the deity of him who came to earth as Jesus of Nazareth (John 20:28; Acts 20:28; Romans 9:5; Colossians 2:9; Hebrews 1:1-4).

WHAT DO YOU THINK?

Some people will admit that Jesus was a tremendous teacher or a bold crusader for social reform or a compassionate humanitarian, but they balk at the idea of his being the Son of God. John leaves no room for such unbelief. At the outset he makes the reader aware that the human Jesus he is about to describe was present "In the beginning"—at creation and even before. How could you use this text to help someone who believes Jesus was merely a great teacher to come to faith in him as the Son of God? What would you do differently for one who is willing to accept the Bible's record as true from what you would do with one who does not necessarily accept the Bible?

WHAT DOES THIS WORD MEAN?

In the marvelous opening phrases of his record of the "good news" of Jesus, the apostle John uses the word *logos*—a word of profound significance to the Greeks. Several words reflected the Greek view of the universe. For example, *chaos* was believed to be the primary and original state of the universe. *Logos* was the divine principle that imposed order and arrangement upon this wild confusion.

The concept of the *logos* as that which organizes and systematizes reality is seen in the large number of our English words by which we characterize various disciplines of knowledge. We speak of psycho*logy*, bio*logy*, ornitho*logy*, archaeo*logy*, etc. All these words contain the element of *logos* to describe an ordered, systematized study of some area of our universe.

John defines the *logos*, not as a concept, but as a person. He declares that the *logos* "became flesh and made his dwelling among us" (John 1:14). Genesis tells us that the original creation was "formless and empty" until God spoke (Genesis 1:2). It was his *Word* that brought order out of chaos. Jesus is the divine *Word*, who brought order not only in the beginning, but brings it to all human chaos now.

—J. G. V. B.

B. THE WORD AND CREATION (v. 3)

3. Through him all things were made; without him nothing was made that has been made.

Some philosophers in John's day thought matter was evil; they did not believe a righteous God could have created anything material. John insists that *all things*, including material items, were brought into being by the Word of God and are to be used with thanksgiving to his glory. As the agent of creation, the eternal Word brought into orderly existence the world and all that is in it (Colossians 1:16, 17; Hebrews 1:2). Our universe with its design and order is no accident!

C. LIGHT IN THE DARKNESS (vv. 4, 5)

4. In him was life, and that life was the light of men.

Life and *light* are terms used often and meaningfully by the apostle John— more than by any other writer of Scripture. The living Word of God is the source of the human life that was breathed into Adam, so that he became a living being (Genesis 2:7). Eternity is part of the life that God intended for mankind, and Jesus came to make such eternal life possible.

Light was the first item spoken into existence (Genesis 1:3). This light was intended to benefit mankind by dispelling darkness. There is also a moral light of goodness and purity dispelling the kind of darkness that is loved by wicked men because their deeds are evil (John 3:19). Only in Jesus, however, is there "the light of the knowledge of the glory of God" (2 Corinthians 4:6).

5. The light shines in the darkness, but the darkness has not understood it.

The deeper the *darkness*, the brighter a *light* will shine (even the small light of a candle will seem bright in the deep darkness of a cave). The light of Christ continues to shine amidst the moral and spiritual darkness of our times, just as it did in the darkness of first-century paganism. If his light is not dispelling the darkness around it, it is because its handlers have kept it hidden!

The Greek word rendered *understood* can also mean "overcome." Either word describes something that the darkness has never been able to do with the light of Jesus. That light will lead men to salvation as long as there are men to lead, despite the failures of its followers and the attacks of its foes.

II. THE FAITHFUL WITNESS (JOHN 1:6-13)

A. GOD'S MAN FOR THE WORK (vv. 6-8)

6. There came a man who was sent from God; his name was John.

Having introduced the Word as eternal with God, and having touched on the impact of the Word's earthly ministry, John calls attention to the messenger who prepared men to receive the Word. That was another *man* named *John*, son of a priest named Zechariah and his wife Elizabeth. The angel Gabriel had appeared to Zechariah, assigning the name *John* to the child not yet conceived and describing his ministry (Luke 1:8-17). John the Baptist was thus indeed *sent from God*,

VISUALS FOR THESE LESSONS

The Adult Visuals *packet contains classroom-size visuals designed for use with the lessons in the Spring Quarter. The packet is available from your supplier. Order No. 392.*

DAILY BIBLE READINGS

Monday, Mar. 1—In the Beginning Was the Word (John 1:1-5)

Tuesday, Mar. 2—The Witness of John the Baptizer (John 1:6-9)

Wednesday, Mar. 3—John Baptizes Jesus (Mark 1:1-11)

Thursday, Mar. 4—To All Who Received Him (John 1:10-13)

Friday, Mar. 5—Believe on the Lord Jesus (Acts 16:25-34)

Saturday, Mar. 6—The Word Became Flesh and Lived Among Us (John 1:14-18)

Sunday, Mar. 7—Before the Foundation of the World (Ephesians 1:3-14)

WHAT DO YOU THINK?

When John calls Jesus the "true light," he suggests there were other so-called lights in the world, claiming to provide enlightenment but failing. The same is true today. What are some of the false lights in our world, and how can we shine the true light in such a way as to expose them as mere darkness?

What about false lights within the church? How can these be replaced by the true light?

WHAT DO YOU THINK?

Jesus' own people, particularly their leaders, refused to accept Jesus because he did not fit their idea of a Messiah, or because they feared they would lose their own power, or because they "loved praise from men more than praise from God" (John 12:43). In what ways may Christians sometimes be guilty of not accepting Jesus as Lord of our lives? Seeking acceptance from our peers, do we sometimes compromise our faith? How can we be more bold? When confronted with biblical teaching that challenges our opinions or behavior, how can we find the inner power to make the proper adjustments instead of clinging tenaciously to our comfortable patterns?

and he lived up to his appointed mission. Jesus once described him as "a prophet . . . and more than a prophet." He declared, "Among those born of women there has not risen anyone greater than John the Baptist" (Matthew 11:7-11).

7, 8. He came as a witness to testify concerning that light, so that through him all men might believe. He himself was not the light; he came only as a witness to the light.

John the Baptist's primary purpose was "to make ready a people prepared for the Lord" (Luke 1:17). In doing so he preached and practiced the baptism of repentance and remission of sins (Luke 3:3). His hearers were told to *believe* in Jesus *through* John the Baptist's testimony. When asked to identify himself and explain his mission, John answered with a firm negative: "I am not the Christ" (John 1:20).

B. GOD'S LIGHT FOR THE WORLD (v. 9)

9. The true light that gives light to every man was coming into the world.

Jesus said of John the Baptist, "John was a lamp that burned and gave light, and you chose for a time to enjoy that light" (John 5:35). Jesus, however, is the *true light*, whose influence is worldwide. *World* is another of John the apostle's powerfully inclusive words. It can designate the universe, the earth, the people on the earth, most people, or the human system opposed to God's purposes. Here it signifies the population of the earth, including all those multitudes yet to be born into the world. The Light of life had come to save all by giving his life for "the sins of the whole world" (1 John 2:2).

C. THE LIGHT REJECTED (vv. 10, 11)

10, 11. He was in the world, and though the world was made through him, the world did not recognize him. He came to that which was his own, but his own did not receive him.

In spite of the fact that the *world* had come into being through Jesus, he was not recognized when he came to it. "No room . . . in the inn" (Luke 2:7) describes how Jesus was treated not only as a baby, but throughout his life. For the most part, *his own* people (the Jews) did not acknowledge him—a fact Pilate noted when Jesus stood before him (John 18:35).

What about us? Do our words and works always recognize Jesus for who he really is? Or have we treated him as if he were a stranger?

D. THE LIGHT RECEIVED (vv. 12, 13)

12, 13. Yet to all who received him, to those who believed in his name, he gave the right to become children of God—children born not of natural descent, nor of human decision or a husband's will, but born of God.

John the Baptist was among the first and most influential of those who gladly welcomed Jesus as "the Lamb of God, who takes away the sin of the world" (John 1:29). Those who follow in doing so receive the privilege of becoming what no one can become in any other way—members of God's family. Until then, although they are creatures of God and beloved by God, they are not his children.

To *believe on* the *name* of Jesus is to recognize and confess by word and deed the sonship, saviorhood, and lordship implied in his name. "There is no other name under heaven given to men by which we must be saved" (Acts 4:12). Full commitment to him brings much to celebrate: "How great is the love the Father has lavished on us, that we should be called children of God!" (1 John 3:1).

This family relationship comes through a process parallel to, but very different from, the birth that makes us members of human families. That birth is physical and takes place in accordance with the willing participation of the parents. The new birth from above (John 3:3-6) is spiritual and is the product of the work of God through his Word (1 Peter 1:23).

III. THE WORD MADE FLESH (JOHN 1:14-18)

A. "FULL OF GRACE AND TRUTH" (vv. 14-16)

14. The Word became flesh and made his dwelling among us. We have seen his glory, the glory of the One and Only, who came from the Father, full of grace and truth.

Here is one of Scripture's most definitive statements of the incarnation: *the Word became flesh.* (See also Philippians 2:5-8.) He *made his dwelling among us* (literally, "pitched his tent among us"). Jesus' stay on earth was temporary, as though in a tent instead of a permanent dwelling.

John includes himself among those who *have seen his glory.* Along with Peter and James, John saw certain incidents that the others did not, such as Jesus' transfiguration (Matthew 17:1-8). With the other disciples, John saw the risen Lord ascend to Heaven (Luke 24:51; Acts 1:9-11).

Jesus demonstrated a perfect balance of tender mercy and moral perfection (*full of grace and truth*). Since he who dwelt for a time *among* us now dwells within us (Colossians 1:27), we must demonstrate a similar balance in our daily conduct and our dealings with others. Paul introduced his passage about the incarnation by saying, "Your attitude should be the same as that of Christ Jesus" (Philippians 2:5). It's a big order, but eternally worth working on!

15. John testifies concerning him. He cries out, saying, "This was he of whom I said, 'He who comes after me has surpassed me because he was before me.'"

Again John the apostle calls attention to the testimony of *John* the Baptist, who was assured when he baptized Jesus (by a voice from Heaven and a dove) that this was God's beloved Son (Matthew 3:16, 17; John 1:32-34). The first two verbs in this verse are properly in the present tense: *testifies* and *cries out.* John the Baptist's testimony was not meant to be a one-time event; it still speaks to all who will listen.

Jesus is the eternal Word, infinitely greater than the great man who introduced him. John the Baptist was six months older than Jesus in the flesh (Luke 1:24-31), but he knew that the Word was *before* either of them was born (see John 1:30).

16. From the fullness of his grace we have all received one blessing after another.

Here the apostle speaks for himself and countless other followers of the Lord. All have gained immeasurably from a humble acceptance of Jesus' overflowing *grace* and mercy. That has been a continual source of *one blessing after another* to every Christian.

B. SUPERIOR TO LAW (vv. 17, 18)

17. For the law was given through Moses; grace and truth came through Jesus Christ.

This continues the subject of *grace and truth* that was begun in verse 14. John is not downplaying *Moses* or *the law* that was given through him; however, Jesus is the divine means by which God conveys what was impossible through the law. The law provided God's directives and indicated the consequences of following or disobeying them. Jesus provides the example of perfect obedience, the means of cleansing and forgiveness for the transgressor, and the power to live a daily life of godliness.

The visual for this lesson illustrates verse 14. Display it as you begin to discuss section III (*The Word Made Flesh*).

WHAT DO YOU THINK?

John says we have received "one blessing after another." What are some of the blessings you have received as a follower of Jesus? How can you use these blessings to testify of Jesus?

18. No one has ever seen God, but God the One and Only, who is at the Father's side, has made him known.

Exodus 33:20 records God's statement to Moses: "You cannot see my face, for no one may see me and live." It is impossible for the mortal to comprehend that which is eternally divine. But as there is one God, there is also "one mediator between God and men, the man Christ Jesus" (1 Timothy 2:5). He is *God the One and Only*—the divine Son of God who entered the world by birth, interrupting an eternity of being in the very presence of God. Thus he could describe and demonstrate the Father, and declare, "Anyone who has seen me has seen the Father" (John 14:9; see also Colossians 1:14, 15; 1 Timothy 6:14-16; Hebrews 1:1-4).

IV. JOHN'S PURPOSE FOR WRITING (JOHN 20:30, 31)

We come now to a summary statement of the apostle's pattern and purpose for writing his Gospel. He has just told of Jesus' meeting with his disciples a week after his resurrection. Thomas, absent from an earlier and similar meeting, was firmly convinced by seeing for himself the proofs of the resurrection. In reverent faith he declared, "My Lord and my God!" (John 20:26-29).

30. Jesus did many other miraculous signs in the presence of his disciples, which are not recorded in this book.

Present with Thomas on this occasion were the other *disciples*, chosen to observe and bear witness to this and other "convincing proofs" (Acts 1:3) of Jesus' deity. John's *book* includes other *signs* observed by the disciples, with others also present on most occasions. *Many other* similar pieces of evidence could have been set forth, but what is included is sufficient for the sincere seeker after truth.

31. But these are written that you may believe that Jesus is the Christ, the Son of God, and that by believing you may have life in his name.

John's purpose in writing is clear. *You* are the readers of his Gospel. Not having seen the risen Christ, they must come to *believe* through the word of those who have seen. Their faith will be especially blessed (John 20:29).

What are they to believe? Faith must have an object, and in this case the object is *Jesus* (John 3:16). But notice also that one must believe a specific truth about Jesus: that he is *the Christ, the Son of God*, as Peter confessed earlier (Matthew 16:16). In other words, faith must have content. One who possesses such faith must then accept the truth about Jesus and make a commitment of his life to him. *Believing* in this manner brings to the believer new *life* (Romans 6:1-11)—life that continues beyond the grave.

Let us never forget that the purpose of every gospel presentation is to lead another person from death to life.

CONCLUSION

The apostle John has said that the eternal Word became flesh in the person of Jesus. The life of Jesus provided a convincing demonstration that this was so. John has also declared that he wrote his Gospel in order that you, the reader, might believe and find life in Christ. A reading of the Gospel will provide a convincing demonstration that this also is true. But how well do *you* know that demonstration? Have you read the Gospel of John lately? The next few weeks will provide an excellent opportunity to study selected passages from John. Why not go a step further and read his account completely and repeatedly for yourself during this quarter? Give John a chance to demonstrate the worth of his writing. Each journey through John will take no longer than sitting through an ordinary baseball game. Let John demonstrate his purpose for writing to *you*!

Discovery Learning

This page contains an alternate lesson plan emphasizing learning activities. Classes desiring such student involvement will find these suggestions helpful. The next page is a reproducible activity page to further enhance discovery learning.

LEARNING GOALS

After this lesson students should be able to:

1. State the identity and mission of Jesus as the incarnate Word.

2. Compare Jesus' mission with John's purpose for writing his Gospel.

3. Express a commitment to living in harmony with Jesus' identity and mission.

INTO THE LESSON

Review briefly the theme of the new quarter: that we may believe that Jesus is Lord. Mention the four units that are included, especially the second one—the death, burial, and resurrection of Jesus, which comprise the essence of the gospel (cf. 1 Corinthians 15:1-4). The other three units explore Jesus' call to faith, his declaration of God's message, and his concern for his followers as his death drew near.

Distribute index cards or small slips of paper, each with one of the following expressions written on it: "I give you my *word*." "The *word* on the street." "I need a *word* with you." "Wait until I give the *word*." "He is a man of his *word*." "That's the final *word* on the subject." "Put in a good *word* for me." "Send us *word* when you arrive." If you have a large class, ask people with the same expressions to get together and discuss the significance of the word *word* in their expressions; then discuss them together as a class. If your class is smaller, have individuals read their expressions and tell what is significant about *word* in each one. Discuss the expressions together.

Next, do a similar activity based on the word *light*. Use expressions like the following: "Significant facts were brought to *light*." "I saw the *light*!" "This will shed some *light* on the situation." "She is the *light* of his life!" "He saw things in a different *light* today." "In *light* of the circumstances." "Turn on the *light*."

Note that these terms are important to understanding Jesus' identity and mission. We'll see how in today's lesson.

INTO THE WORD

Ask, "What is needed for us to have faith in something or someone?" As the class discusses this question, the idea should emerge that faith requires knowledge; it cannot be groundless or completely emotional. Then have someone read John 20:30, 31. Observe that John recognized the need for a solid foundation of evidence for faith to develop. He attempts to provide that foundation in his Gospel. Take a minute or two to explain how the Gospel of John differs from the others. (See the introductory material on page 238.)

Ask a volunteer to read John 1:1-18. Discuss, "Why is Jesus called the 'Word'?" Prompt the discussion by having students read Psalm 33:6; Isaiah 55:11; 1 John 1:1; Revelation 19:13. Observe that John identifies Jesus as eternal, one with God and yet distinct in personality, the Creator of all things, the One who leads us to the Father, and the One who became like us in order to do that but was not recognized by the world.

Discuss also the *work* of the "Word." Compare the concept here with the different expressions using the term *word* that you discussed earlier. Note how Jesus' role as the "Word" suggests that he is God's ultimate revelation (cf. Hebrews 1). He brings a message from God, but he is more than a mere messenger. He himself is the Word.

Note that Jesus is also described as the "light" and as the "true light." Discuss the significance of Jesus as light. Again, use ideas from the introductory activity to help. Ask volunteers to read the following Bible verses and explain what they mean regarding Jesus: Psalm 119:105; Proverbs 4:18; Isaiah 9:2; 1 Corinthians 4:5.

INTO LIFE

Recall again John's purpose for writing (John 20:30, 31). Ask, "In view of John's purpose, what is significant about where John starts with his Gospel?" As you discuss, note the importance of identifying Jesus' identity and mission as the incarnate Word in order to give substance to the readers' faith. Our faith is not merely in a great teacher or good moral example, but in the eternal God who took on human flesh to save us!

Ask, "How does Jesus' identity and mission make a difference in your own life?" Encourage believers to make a statement of their own faith in Jesus and their own involvement in ministry in his behalf. If there are non-Christians in your class, challenge them to consider seriously the faith messages of John over the next twelve weeks of your study together. His purpose is as valid at the close of the twentieth century as it was in the first!

John and Jesus

Both John the Baptist and Jesus were remarkable figures. Each had quite a following among the people of Judea and Galilee. But, of course, they were quite different. Compare the two by exploring the Scriptures below.

JOHN

John 1:6-8, 15, 19, 20, 23

JESUS

John 1:1-3, 9-11, 18, 26, 27

Many Other Signs

John tells us that Jesus did many other miraculous signs besides the ones he wrote about, but his report gives us enough information to come to faith in Christ. What are some of the miracles he and the other three Gospel writers tell us about? List as many as you can from memory. Then use a concordance or topical Bible to see how many more you can find.

Which does the most to build your faith? Why?

JOHN THE BAPTIST TESTIFIES OF JESUS

LESSON 2

Mar 14

WHY TEACH THIS LESSON?

Most entertainment stars use "opening acts" to precede and to introduce their performances. These "second bananas" often become celebrities in their own right, with headliner shows similarly preceded by acts of lesser-known artists. Few are content to remain in a secondary position; they aspire to become the featured performers. John the Baptist is a notable exception. He never failed to focus the spotlight on Jesus, always "decreasing" so that the Messiah could "increase."

Since the mission of all Christians is to "prepare the way of the Lord," John's example is instructive and inspiring. Our personal testimonies must focus attention upon Jesus only, never upon ourselves, our goodness or our achievements. This lesson will remind "forerunners" to first be *followers*, humbly pointing seekers to their Leader, the Light of Life.

INTRODUCTION

A. WHO ARE YOU, ANYWAY?

An amusing television commercial showed a young man chatting with his mother in his place of work. After a brief time she mentioned some business she had come to transact. "Do you have any identification?" he demanded. The rules required documentary proof that she was who she claimed to be, and not even her son could allow her to conduct her business without it!

This raises a more complicated question that disturbs many insecure persons: Who are you, anyway? The answer may take any of several forms, depending on the viewpoint of the questioner. It was even asked of Jesus. Neighbors identified him by family as son of Joseph and Mary, or by occupation as a carpenter. Judeans identified him by residence as a Nazarene or Galilean. He became widely known as teacher, prophet, healer, and friend of tax collectors and other disreputable people. None of these labels, however, came close to his true identity as Messiah, Son of God, and Savior of mankind.

How, then, is any of us to be identified concerning his or her innermost character, purpose, and program in life? How, indeed, except in relation to him who makes life meaningful and eternal? *Christian* or *non-Christian* is the real "ID." And while *Christian* would not be used for some time yet, John the Baptist was way ahead of us in choosing that focus for his identity. He possessed an unshakable conviction that his calling in life was to glorify Jesus and point others to him.

B. LESSON BACKGROUND

Matthew 3:1—4:11; Mark 1:1-13; and Luke 3:1-22; 4:1-13 lay important foundations for today's lesson. They recount the ministry of John the Baptist as he preached to multitudes and baptized many who came to the wilderness along the Jordan River to hear him. Some even speculated that John could be

DEVOTIONAL READING:
EPHESIANS 4:25—5:2.

LESSON SCRIPTURE:
JOHN 1:19-42.

PRINTED TEXT:
JOHN 1:19-34.

LESSON AIMS

After this lesson students should be able to:

1. Identify and explain the mission of John the Baptist.

2. Compare John's mission with that of Christians today.

3. Determine one way to be a better witness of Christ and seek to implement it in the coming week.

KEY VERSE

The next day John saw Jesus coming toward him and said, "Look, the Lamb of God, who takes away the sin of the world!"
—John 1:29

LESSON 2 NOTES

The visual for lesson 2 will help you locate for your class the sites mentioned in this lesson and throughout the quarter. (It is similar to the map on page 235.)

DAILY BIBLE READINGS

Monday, Mar. 8—John's Testimony (John 1:19-23)

Tuesday, Mar. 9—I Baptize With Water (John 1:24-28)

Wednesday, Mar. 10—Here Is the Lamb of God (John 1:29-34)

Thursday, Mar. 11—What Do You Want? (John 1:35-42)

Friday, Mar. 12—Jesus Must Become Greater (John 3:22-36)

Saturday, Mar. 13—Jesus Commends John (Luke 7:18-28)

Sunday, Mar. 14—John Is Beheaded (Mark 6:14-29)

the Messiah (Luke 3:15). Matthew, Mark, and Luke detail John's demand for repentance and the practical application of godliness. They tell how Jesus came from Galilee to be baptized by John, who hesitated at first but finally yielded. They report that when Jesus was baptized, the Holy Spirit in the form of a dove came down on him, and a voice from Heaven acknowledged Jesus as God's beloved Son. Then Jesus retired into the wilderness for forty days of fasting and temptation, ending with victory over the tempter.

Today's text from John's Gospel tells of events that most likely accompanied Jesus' return to the area around the Jordan after his temptation. John 1:19-42 tells what happened there during three successive days.

I. JOHN THE ANNOUNCER (JOHN 1:19-23)

John 1:18 says that the eternal Word, which "became flesh" (v. 14) as the only begotten Son of God, proceeded to reveal the nature of God. The Son was then made known through the testimony of John the Baptist. Our printed text begins with the testimony given by John the Baptist under persistent questioning.

A. IDENTIFICATION DEMANDED (v. 19)

19. Now this was John's testimony when the Jews of Jerusalem sent priests and Levites to ask him who he was.

Here John speaks of *the Jews*, not as a body of people, but as a designation of the religious rulers in *Jerusalem*. There the Sanhedrin sat as a ruling body of seventy men, including the chief priests, elders, and scribes (the high priest served as president). Its duty was to oversee religious practices and activities among the people. The Sanhedrin became increasingly resistant to Jesus during his ministry. Its opposition is reflected in the approximately seventy times that *the Jews* are mentioned in John's Gospel.

These rulers were understandably concerned at news of the popular response to the preaching of John the Baptist. This new development in matters where they were the authorities called for investigation. The delegation included *priests*, who conducted worship and offered sacrifices, and *Levites*—members of the tribe of Levi who were usually temple helpers, but occasionally assisted in teaching (Nehemiah 8:7-9).

It is to these leaders' credit that they decided to go to John himself *to ask him who he was*. They may, however, have exhausted other sources in their previous investigations of the matter.

B. MESSIAHSHIP DENIED (vv. 20-22)

20. He did not fail to confess, but confessed freely, "I am not the Christ."

John the Baptist seems to have been aware of the rumors that he might be the *Christ* (Luke 3:15)—the "anointed One," empowered with divine authority beyond that of other anointed individuals, including kings (1 Samuel 16:13) and priests (Exodus 40:13-15). The preacher at the Jordan silenced immediately any suggestion of his being the Messiah. The structure of his statement emphasizes the I. The anticipated Christ was not he, but one immeasurably greater. Jesus was the One he wanted to talk about.

21. They asked him, "Then who are you? Are you Elijah?" He said, "I am not." "Are you the Prophet?" He answered, "No."

The Baptizer's replies became increasingly brief as the questions continued. The first answer had addressed the examiners' primary concern. What was left?

Students of the Scriptures knew that the prophet *Elijah* had been taken to Heaven without dying (2 Kings 2:1) and that Malachi (Malachi 4:5) had predicted

Elijah's return before "that great and dreadful day of the Lord comes." Zechariah was told that his son's ministry would demonstrate the "spirit and power of Elijah" (Luke 1:17). Jesus testified that John the Baptist fulfilled Malachi's prophecy (Matthew 17:10-13). However, the popular expectation was for a literal return of Elijah, and John was not that. He answered the question as it was asked.

Moses had predicted the coming of a *Prophet* like himself, who was to be given a most respectful hearing (Deuteronomy 18:15). John the Baptist was not that Prophet; Jesus was (Acts 3:19-23). Neither was John or any of the other prophets who had been expected to return in the messianic age (Matthew 16:14). The investigators were wrong on all counts.

22. Finally they said, "Who are you? Give us an answer to take back to those who sent us. What do you say about yourself?"

These committeemen were in an embarrassing situation. They had been sent to get information, and all they had thus far was disappointment in their expectations and denial of their allegations. At this point, they had to let the object of their investigation speak for himself.

C. PURPOSE DECLARED (v. 23)

23. John replied in the words of Isaiah the prophet, "I am the voice of one calling in the desert, 'Make straight the way for the Lord.'"

In answer to the investigators from Jerusalem, John needed only to declare himself a herald proclaiming the King's arrival. He was content with nothing more. Such a response from the Jordan was not likely to satisfy the Sanhedrin in Jerusalem. For us, however, it glows with the singleness of purpose that we need to establish our own self-identity and sense of worthwhile living. Thank God for John the Baptist!

HOW TO SAY IT

Bethany. BETH-uh-nee.
Elijah. Ee-LYE-juh.
Galilean. Gal-uh-LEE-un.
Isaiah. Eye-ZAY-uh.
Levites. LEE-vites.
Malachi. MAL-uh-kye.
Nathanael. Nuh-THAN-yull.
Nazarene. NAZ-uh-reen.
Pharisees. FAIR-ih-seez.
Sanhedrin. San-HEED-run or SAN-huh-drin.
Zechariah. Zek-uh-RYE-uh.

A VOICE IN THE WILDERNESS

With words taken from Isaiah 40:3, John the Baptist identified himself as "the voice of one calling in the desert" (John 1:23). He was preaching in the arid, inhospitable land along a stretch of the Jordan River. It seemed a forlorn and unlikely place to draw crowds, yet many came to hear John.

It was in the late 1890s that Dr. Susie Rijnhart (*Rine*-hart) and her husband went as missionaries of the churches of Christ to the faraway, desolate land of Tibet. After a brief time there, her husband was murdered, and her only child died and was buried in a small box at the foot of the Dang-La Mountains. Such sacrifices as these inspired others to follow in Dr. Rijnhart's steps.

In 1908 Dr. Zenas S. Loftis left the United States as another witness to "cry" in the vast wilderness of Tibet. He began working as a medical missionary with Dr. A. L. Shelton. Dr. Loftis died of typhoid fever and smallpox on August 12, 1909. Through these dedicated missionary lives, voices were calling out in a remote "desert" to point to the Redeemer.

Amidst the rising tide of secularism, negativism, and false religions around us, we too are seemingly in a "desert" that is alien to the Christian faith. However, if we, like John, lift our voices in faith and dedication on behalf of the Christ, transformed and obedient lives will be the result. —J. G. V. B.

II. JOHN THE BAPTIZER (JOHN 1:24-28)

A. PHARISEES' QUESTION (vv. 24, 25)

24, 25. Now some Pharisees who had been sent questioned him, "Why then do you baptize if you are not the Christ, nor Elijah, nor the Prophet?"

Pharisees, not mentioned previously in our text, are introduced here to provide background for their question about John's baptism. They were eager guardians

THOUGHT TO REMEMBER

Who am I? The answer to that question depends on my relationship to Jesus Christ.

of the law of Moses and the traditions of the elders. They seem to have been rather persistent in their interrogation of John.

The *Christ*, or even a returning prophet, would have recognizable authority to introduce to the people a new religious practice (such as John's baptism seemed to be) or even to require a ceremonial cleansing of those who were regarded already as good Jews. But what right had a mere proclaimer of another's arrival to practice such an invasion of lawful and traditional procedure? This was a question that resurfaced during the ministry of Jesus: did John's practice of baptism have divine authority, or was it merely a human invention (Matthew 21:23-27)? The Sanhedrin could not (or, rather, would not) answer, but Jesus accepted John's testimony. He knew that John was not the Messiah, but he did speak God's message.

B. POINTING TO JESUS (vv. 26, 27)

26, 27. *"I baptize with water,"* John replied, *"but among you stands one you do not know. He is the one who comes after me, the thongs of whose sandals I am not worthy to untie."*

What kind of answer was this to the Pharisees' question? They had asked why John baptized; he admitted that he did indeed *baptize*, but there was a larger issue. The Pharisees still needed to become acquainted with the greater One whom he had come to introduce. The baptism *with water* (literally, "in water") was a purposeful part of the introduction. It provided a link with Christian baptism, which symbolizes the death, burial, and resurrection of Jesus—the events that form the core of the gospel (1 Corinthians 15:3, 4).

Jesus had been *among* the people who came to John to be baptized, and he would be among the crowds again on the following day. Until now, however, they had no idea of his real identity. Jesus came *after* John the Baptist, being six months younger (Luke 1:24-26) and just now entering his public ministry when John was at the height of his popularity.

To loosen or tighten the *thongs* of another person's *sandals* was regarded as the most menial of services, to be done only by slaves—as when they washed the other's feet. But John considered himself *not worthy* of even that degree of contact with the magnificent One whom he proclaimed.

BEARING WITNESS

In spite of the adulation of crowds and the great success that John the Baptist enjoyed in leading many to be baptized in the river Jordan, he still kept his task in perspective. He remembered that he was testifying of another greater than he was. We need to evaluate our own Christian service and to understand that we are not seeking honor and glory for ourselves, but for our Savior.

One of the most famous biographers in English literary history was James Boswell (1740-1795). He dedicated himself to the recording and transcribing of the deeds, writings, and above all the "table talk" and conversational remarks of Samuel Johnson. Johnson was a novelist, biographer, and lexicographer. His *English Dictionary* was a landmark achievement. Boswell preserved so many of Johnson's interesting and perceptive observations that his *Life of Samuel Johnson* became a classic. His dedication to the presentation of Johnson's wisdom made Boswell famous as well.

In the same way, our testimony to Jesus also enlarges and ennobles our lives. We seek to make his words known. We remind others of his deeds of mercy and power, and we do what we can to enlist others as his followers. James Boswell simply sought to make Samuel Johnson known and loved. This is exactly what we seek to do in our presentation of Jesus—to make him known and loved.   —J. G. V. B.

WHAT DO YOU THINK?

One prominent characteristic of John the Baptist was his humility, and his humility seems to have been related to his sense of purpose. When some of John's disciples pointed out how Jesus' popularity was growing, while John's own popularity was apparently waning, he responded, "He must become greater, but I must become less" (John 3:30). How important is it for us to be humble? Why? How can maintaining a clear sense of purpose assist us in being properly humble? How can we keep our purpose clearly in focus?

C. PLACING THE EVENT (v. 28)

28. This all happened at Bethany on the other side of the Jordan, where John was baptizing.

Since this *Bethany* was located *on the other side of the Jordan*, or east of the river, it should not be confused with the Bethany near Jerusalem, where Mary, Martha, and Lazarus lived. Apparently it was one of several places along the Jordan Valley where John the Baptist was preaching and *baptizing* (John 3:23).

We can only wonder what the investigating committee reported to the Sanhedrin when they returned home.

III. JOHN THE WITNESS (JOHN 1:29-34)

A. "HERE HE IS!" (vv. 29, 30)

29. The next day John saw Jesus coming toward him and said, "Look, the Lamb of God, who takes away the sin of the world!

It was now *the next day*, but enough of the same audience remained for John to address them with a reference to previous comments. Note the timing of Jesus' coming: the committee from Jerusalem was gone. Having dealt with their questions, John could now freely and enthusiastically point to the promised One.

The Lamb of God! What a treasure of meaning that opens! In faith Abraham had assured Isaac that "God himself will provide the *lamb*" as an alternative to the sacrifice of Isaac (Genesis 22:8). A *lamb* had been a part of the annual Passover observance for each family in Israel whenever the nation celebrated its deliverance from bondage in Egypt (Exodus 12:1-11). The sacrifice of a *lamb* was part of the morning and evening ritual in the tabernacle and the temple (Exodus 29:38, 39). Isaiah spoke of the sacrificial *lamb* in his prophecy of the Suffering Servant (Isaiah 53:7). The final book of the Bible pictures the glorified *Lamb*, standing though looking as if it had been slain, and recognized in Heaven as the only one worthy to open the sealed scroll (Revelation 5). John the Baptist was indeed "a prophet . . . and more than a prophet" (Matthew 11:9).

30. "This is the one I meant when I said, 'A man who comes after me has surpassed me because he was before me.'

Jesus, the living Word, was unquestionably and immeasurably *before* John, by virtue of both his pre-incarnation existence in eternity and his standing as God's Son on earth. John could not say that often enough, or strongly enough. But how did John know all that? Keep reading.

B. "HE IS THE REASON I BAPTIZE" (v. 31)

31. "I myself did not know him, but the reason I came baptizing with water was that he might be revealed to Israel."

John had told his hearers the previous day that they did not recognize the One standing among them (v. 26). Now he admits that except for his commission to baptize *with water* (or "in water," as in verse 26), he himself would not have known Jesus as God's Son.

This son of Zechariah was "sent from God" (John 1:6) to preach and baptize. When Jesus came to be baptized, the occasion revealed his true identity to John. Then and only then did John the Baptist understand why he had been commissioned to conduct his ministry as he did.

C. "THIS IS HOW I KNOW HIM" (vv. 32, 33)

32, 33. Then John gave this testimony: "I saw the Spirit come down from heaven as a dove and remain on him. I would not have known him, except that the one

WHAT DO YOU THINK?

For John to call Jesus "the Lamb of God" would have attracted Jewish hearers in his time. We still use the expressions "innocent as a lamb" and "sacrificial lamb" today, though they fail to communicate the fullness of meaning they would have for Jewish observers of Passover.

How can we help believers, especially young believers and those new to the faith, understand the rich imagery of biblical metaphors like "Lamb of God"? What new or fresh metaphors might we use to attract unbelievers who do not understand the biblical metaphors?

WHAT DO YOU THINK?

John had his own disciples, but his mission was to point them and everyone else to Christ. To what extent is it a problem for some to follow a religious leader instead of the Christ to whom that leader intended to point? What can such a leader do about it? Think in terms of a parent as a leader as well as someone in a church position of leadership.

What should followers do if a leader seems to be inadvertently drawing some people more to his personality than to his Lord? What should they do if the leader seems to be deliberately drawing people to himself?

WHAT DO YOU THINK?

John saw the dove descend on Jesus and was assured that he is the Son of God. We don't have to see the dove; if we accept the New Testament as reliable, then there is sufficient evidence for us to be sure of Jesus' identity. But what of those not convinced of the reliability of the New Testament? How would you answer a doubter in order to give him assurance that the Jesus of the New Testament is for real and is the only source of eternal salvation?

WHAT DO YOU THINK?

The lesson writer mentions introducing Jesus to a friend. How can we share our faith in a way that is as natural as introducing someone to a friend and at the same time credible to the person with whom we are sharing?

PRAYER

Thank you, Father, for sending your faithful forerunner to prepare the way for Jesus. May we follow the example of John the Baptist, so that we too will become instruments through which others come to know Jesus. May we develop the degree of commitment that will say, "Jesus is more important to me than anything or anyone else." Grant us grace to introduce Jesus as we know him to friends who have not yet made his acquaintance. In his name. Amen.

who sent me to baptize with water told me, 'The man on whom you see the Spirit come down and remain is he who will baptize with the Holy Spirit.'

God, who had brought John into the world to be the forerunner of the Christ, revealed to him that the Christ would be identified as the one on *whom you see the Spirit come down and remain.* As the other three Gospels clearly show, this sign occurred when Jesus was baptized (Matthew 3:16, 17; Mark 1:9-11; Luke 3:21, 22). This visible sign included spoken testimony from the Father concerning his Son.

In addition, God revealed to John that as he had baptized *with water,* the Christ would baptize *with the Holy Spirit.* Jesus made such a promise specifically to his chosen apostles (Luke 24:49; Acts 1:5) and fulfilled it on the Day of Pentecost (Acts 2:3, 4). Later Peter reflected on this fulfillment when he first brought the gospel to Gentiles (Acts 10:45-47).

D. "NOW I TELL YOU" (v. 34)

34. I have seen and I testify that this is the Son of God."

Having seen and heard the evidence that God had promised to provide him, John the Baptist began immediately to testify to the fact established by that evidence. He was delighted to become known for all time as the voice announcing *the Son of God.* That sonship became the theme, not only of the preaching of John the Baptist, but also of the writing of John the apostle, as noted in the previous lesson: "These are written that you may believe that Jesus is the Christ, the Son of God, and that by believing you may have life in his name" (John 20:30).

CONCLUSION

There was still a third day for the testimony of John the Baptist to be heard. Following the day of *announcement* in response to the committee from Jerusalem, and the day of *introduction* when Jesus himself came near, there was a day of *direction* when John led some of his disciples to follow Jesus (John 1:35-42). Among these were the brothers Andrew and Simon (Peter), and one not named who almost certainly was John, the author of this Gospel. On "the next day" (v. 43) Philip and Nathanael, who also became apostles, were added to the group. Obviously John the Baptist meant it when he said of Jesus, "He must become greater, but I must become less" (John 3:30).

The steps just observed are natural, coming logically one after the other, yet seldom in so brief a span. Most of us can recall the day when we chose to be known as *Christian.* Then came the time when we had the opportunity to introduce Jesus to a friend, and a friend to Jesus, saying, "He is the really important One in my life; he is the reason I choose as I do among the daily options of saying and doing and spending."

A more difficult day may follow, when we face the full implications of the question, "How far am I willing to go in my commitment to Jesus as God's Son?" Perhaps we must say to a friend or a family member, "Follow and serve Jesus, no matter where that may take you, or how far you must travel from the close associations and frequent contacts we have so greatly enjoyed. Your love for Christ is not complete until you love him more than you love me."

We need have no fear that the choice we have recommended will lead someone to abandon the responsibilities of caring for family members or friends in need. Genuine love of the Lord will, in fact, make one increasingly attentive to those responsibilities.

For how many of these days, then, have we walked with John the Baptist? Is it our continuing desire that Jesus "become greater" while we "become less"?

Discovery Learning

This page contains an alternate lesson plan emphasizing learning activities. Classes desiring such student involvement will find these suggestions helpful. The next page is a reproducible activity page to further enhance discovery learning.

LEARNING GOALS

After this lesson a student should be able to:

1. Identify and explain the mission of John the Baptist.

2. Compare John's mission with that of Christians today.

3. Determine one way to be a better witness of Christ, and seek to implement it in the coming week.

INTO THE LESSON

In advance ask someone to give a short talk on what it means to be a witness in a court of law. Have that person point out the importance of eyewitness testimony as opposed to hearsay.

Invite two more class members to portray John the Baptist on the witness stand and a lawyer who questions him about his ministry and its purpose. Assist these two students in preparing a script. A brief sample follows.

Lawyer: What is your name?

J. B.: John the Baptist.

Lawyer: Your occupation?

J. B.: Prophet and advance preparer.

Lawyer: Who is your employer?

J. B.: God.

Lawyer: Where do you work?

J. B.: In the wilderness.

Lawyer: What is your purpose?

Add other appropriate questions. Conclude by noting that there is a "John the Baptist" in the life of every one of us who is led to the Lord. Someone acted as a witness for the Lord, and we accepted his or her testimony. Perhaps there were several witnesses. Ask for accounts of who played that role in the lives of class members. What qualities made these people point to the Lord? Was it encouraging, teaching, helping, example? (A good way to get this discussion going is to tell who led you to the Lord. What qualities made the testimony of this person—or these people—credible?)

INTO THE WORD

Begin with a brief description of John the Baptist, tying in last week's text with this, and noting information from the Introduction (page 245). Then, citing Malachi 4:5, ask for a comparison of John with Elijah, in appearance, in the nature of their ministries, in their messages, in where they preached, and in how they lived.

Have class members read through John 1:19-34 to identify the testimonies of John. (I am not the Christ; I am the voice; compared to the Christ I am the lowliest; Jesus is the Passover Lamb.)

Arrange two columns on the chalkboard with the headings "A Witness" and "John." Referring back to the material in "Into the Lesson," ask for the characteristics of each. Bring out the unique role of John in calling God's people to repent, baptizing them, and identifying Jesus as the One for whom they had been waiting.

INTO LIFE

John the Baptist had a clear sense of his identity, of his mission and purpose. Discuss, "In what ways is a clear sense of identity important to us as followers of Christ?" If your church has a published "Mission Statement," read it and discuss it together. What demands does it make on the members? What biblical support can be found for such demands? In what ways was John's mission similar to that of your church?

If your church does not have a mission statement, discuss the concept together. Say, "If we had been asked by the elders to write a mission statement, what would it include?"

Write what class members have to say on a chalkboard and then use the notes to frame a statement about your church's sense of identity. Compare your mission with that of John the Baptist. How is it alike? How is it different? (You might take a little time to contrast John's baptism with Christian baptism. See Acts 19:1-5.)

You might conclude with a challenge to each Christian to become a John the Baptist and introduce others to Jesus. To make this concept more concrete, distribute copies of the reproducible activity "Who? Me?" from the next page and ask students to do the following:

1. Think of one person to whom you could give your testimony about Jesus this week—someone who is not a Christian.

2. Write some things you might say as part of your testimony.

3. When will you make contact with this person to share your testimony of the Lord?

Close with prayer that the Spirit of the Lord will be with your "John the Baptists" as they give their testimonies this week.

My John the Baptist

John the Baptist pointed people to Jesus. Because of his testimony many people—including some of Jesus' twelve apostles—became followers of Jesus. Whose testimony led you to faith in Jesus? How did it happen?

Write the name or names of whoever significantly influenced you to become a Christian. Write a brief summary of how the person(s) influenced your faith.

Who? Me?

You, too, can be a "John the Baptist" for someone who does not know the Lord. Below list the names of several people with whom you have contact who do not, as far as you know, profess any faith in the Lord Jesus Christ. Then choose one or two of the names and write what you can do this week to begin sharing your testimony of Jesus with them to lead them to the Lord.

Cut out the face from a photograph of yourself and glue it on to this picture of "John the Baptist." Keep the picture as a reminder to point the way to Jesus.

NICODEMUS VISITS JESUS

LESSON 3

DEVOTIONAL READING:
1 CORINTHIANS 15:17-22

LESSON SCRIPTURE:
JOHN 3:1-21

PRINTED TEXT:
JOHN 3:1-17

Mar
21

WHY TEACH THIS LESSON?

John 3:16 is often called the Golden Text of the Bible. It is the first, and often the *only*, verse of Scripture many people ever learn. Even non-church people can quote it or, at least, remember its general thrust. It captures and capsulizes the good news of the gospel.

The world wants to know that we are loved unconditionally. We need to know Jesus paid our penalty for sin. The assurance of everlasting life has universal appeal. People need the Lord! Those are the best reasons this lesson must be taught.

INTRODUCTION

A. INCREDIBLE? NOT WITH GOD

Incredible bargains! Incredible values! Unbelievable quality! These and other phrases are dinned into our ears and blazoned before our eyes as advertisers try to make us believe and buy on the basis of what they have just told us is past belief! I tend to accept their acknowledgment of reckless exaggeration and keep my money in my pocket, believing the maxim: "If it seems too good to be true, it probably is."

The Bible, on the other hand, speaks with unrestrained enthusiasm about God's *amazing* grace, his *marvelous* power, and his *indescribable* gift of love in Christ Jesus. It does not call it unbelievable, though, and then ask us to believe it. In fact, the word *incredible* appears only once in the Bible: "Why should any of you consider it incredible that God raises the dead?" (Acts 26:8). What God says and does is not incredible! We can believe it!

In today's printed text is a truth that appeared unbelievable. Twice Nicodemus asked *how* what Jesus was telling him could happen. Jesus' words, however, were not too good to be true; they related a truth too important to ignore.

B. LESSON BACKGROUND

The first chapter of John's Gospel tells us of Jesus' coming to earth as God's eternal Word in human form. It also tells of the introductory ministry of John the Baptist, and of John's directing some of his own disciples to follow Jesus. The second chapter tells of Jesus' first miracle at a wedding in Cana of Galilee, then of his going to Jerusalem for the Passover. There Jesus saw the way in which some were using the temple as a marketplace, and he drove them out. Certain Jews who were present demanded a sign demonstrating Jesus' authority to do such a thing, and he told them that if they destroyed the temple (meaning his body) he would restore it (by rising again) in three days. Jesus' disciples did not understand the meaning of this statement until after his resurrection. But they did recall the Scripture that said, "Zeal for your house consumes me" (Psalm 69:9).

While in Jerusalem, Jesus worked a number of miracles and "many believed in his name." They were so shallow in their belief, however, that Jesus did not proceed any further in revealing himself to them (John 2:23-25). One observer among the Jews considered the matter seriously enough that he determined to learn more from Jesus himself about him and his teaching. He may have been

LESSON AIMS

After this lesson students should be able to:

1. Summarize what Jesus said to Nicodemus about the new birth.

2. Explain from this and related texts what it means to be "born again" or "born from above."

3. Thank God for the privilege of being born again and commit himself or herself to a pattern of consistent growth.

KEY VERSE

For God did not send his Son into the world to condemn the world, but to save the world through him.   —John 3:17

especially interested in Jesus' statement: "The kingdom of God is near" (Mark 1:15). We meet that observer, Nicodemus, in our lesson today.

I. THE NEEDY VISITOR (JOHN 3:1, 2)

1. Now there was a man of the Pharisees named Nicodemus, a member of the Jewish ruling council.

Pharisees (a term meaning "separated ones") were known for their strict interpretation of the law of Moses and their rigid adherence to the traditions surrounding it. Unfortunately, their zeal for the law resulted in an obsession with outward conformity rather than a concern "to act justly and to love mercy and to walk humbly with your God" (Micah 6:8).

As we saw in last week's lesson, certain Pharisees had already queried John the Baptist about his baptism (John 1:24, 25). They would clash frequently with Jesus about his nonconformity to their regulations and traditions, particularly regarding the Sabbath. A Pharisee tended to take great pride in what he saw as his own assured position in the kingdom of God.

That Nicodemus was *a ruler of the Jews* indicates that he was a member of the Jewish ruling council, or Sanhedrin. This was composed of seventy priests, scribes, and elders who exercised authority over the religious community. Yet, in spite of his distinguished position, recognized a deficiency in his understanding of spiritual matters. He was curious about what Jesus had to say.

2. He came to Jesus at night and said, "Rabbi, we know you are a teacher who has come from God. For no one could perform the miraculous signs you are doing if God were not with him."

Many Pharisees brought questions designed to trap Jesus into making public statements that could be used against him. Not Nicodemus. He appears to have been seeking a private and leisurely conversation with Jesus to find out more about his teaching. *Rabbi* and *teacher* are terms that were precious to the Pharisees (Matthew 23:1-10). Nicodemus's use of the terms appears to have been a sincere attempt at showing respect.

Evidently Nicodemus had discussed Jesus' miracles and teaching with some of his peers. His assertion *we know* indicates that he was not alone in his beliefs about Jesus. (Perhaps he intended to report this conversation to his peers.) The teaching aspects of Jesus' ministry would be important to a Pharisee, but he would also consider the working of genuine *miracles* as evidence that God was *with him*. Jesus acknowledged the value of miracles as credentials of his authority (John 10:37, 38).

So what did this God-sent teacher have to offer a God-fearing Pharisee? Nicodemus had not yet asked any questions of Jesus. He did not have to. Jesus knew what the man needed to know and what was on his mind. (See John 2:25.)

II. THE NEW BIRTH (JOHN 3:3-8)

A. NECESSITY OF THE NEW BIRTH (v. 3)

3. In reply Jesus declared, "I tell you the truth, no one can see the kingdom of God unless he is born again."

Jesus' emphatic *I tell you the truth* is a translation of the double use of *amen* in the Greek text. (In the *King James Version* it is rendered "verily, verily.") It appears twenty-five times among the words of Jesus recorded in John's Gospel and always introduces a statement of extraordinary importance.

The kingdom, or reign, *of God* was a theme familiar to the Pharisees. Daniel 2:44 and 7:27 spoke of an eternal kingdom that God would establish, and John the Baptist had declared that "the kingdom of heaven is near" (Matthew 3:2).

Now Jesus was claiming that God's kingdom could not be perceived without a radical change from one's natural viewpoint. This change required beginning an entirely new life, so new that Jesus described it as being *born again* or "born from above" (both meanings are possible renderings of the Greek term). Paul would later write, "If anyone is in Christ, he is a new creation" (2 Corinthians 5:17).

B. NATURE OF THE NEW BIRTH (vv. 4-6)

4. *"How can a man be born when he is old?" Nicodemus asked. "Surely he cannot enter a second time into his mother's womb to be born!"*

Nicodemus took Jesus' language literally and materially. This was the natural response to many of Jesus' statements. (See John 2:18-21; Matthew 16:5-7, 12.)

5. *Jesus answered, "I tell you the truth, no one can enter the kingdom of God unless he is born of water and the Spirit.*

Water and *Spirit* had been dramatically linked in the baptism of Jesus when the Spirit's visible presence testified to God's acceptance of his baptism in water (Matthew 3:13-17). The same linking appears in the events of Pentecost, inaugurated by the Spirit (Acts 2:1-4) and completed with the promise that the Spirit would be given in response to believers' baptism into Christ (Acts 2:37-41). Titus 3:5 makes a similar connection between the water and the Spirit: "he [God] saved us, not because of righteous things we had done, but because of his mercy. He saved us through the washing of rebirth and renewal by the Holy Spirit."

Romans 10:17 and 1 Peter 1:23 tell us that the means through which the Spirit begets new life is the Word of God. Romans 6:3-6 indicates that the moment of entering a "new life" comes when in baptism we reenact Jesus' burial and resurrection.

"BORN AGAIN"

The moment of birth ushers us into this world as separate, breathing individual beings. Of course, we are living before the time of birth, but not as persons separate from our mothers. Jesus was saying that we must come into the world of spiritual life by the process of birth, just as by physical birth we come into the world of breathing, eating, seeing, hearing, and other experiences.

Occasionally there are certain events or circumstances that lead us to think in terms of a "new birth." So it was that in his famous "Gettysburg Address," Abraham Lincoln spoke of his hope "that this nation, under God, may have a new birth of freedom." From the old system that allowed millions of Americans to be held as slaves, Lincoln challenged the nation to become a society where all were free, with none treated as the property or the chattel of another.

Sometimes we witness the rise of new modes of thought or expression in art, literature, politics, world views, or religion, which seem to be so revolutionary as to be called a new birth. Such a movement took place in western Europe between 1450 and 1550, and came to be called the *renaissance*. In essence, this means a new birth, a renewal, a completely new beginning.

Just as there is in physical birth a passage from life in the mother's womb to a new and different life in the world, so in spiritual birth we pass into a new and different life in Christ. As Paul describes it, "The old has gone, the new has come!" (2 Corinthians 5:17).

—J. G. V. B.

6. *Flesh gives birth to flesh, but the Spirit gives birth to spirit.*

Here was Jesus' answer to Nicodemus's question regarding the repetition of physical birth. Physical birth and bodily life are God-given and they are good, but they are material and temporal; they are not spiritual and eternal. The latter qualities must come from another source. "Flesh and blood cannot inherit the

WHAT DO YOU THINK?

One commentator says there was a longing in Nicodemus's question, "How can a man be born when he is old?" He wanted a new birth, a fresh start, but he did not know how to attain it. How much do you think people today long for a "new birth" or a fresh start? How can we use that longing to win them to Christ?

WHAT DO YOU THINK?

What comparisons and contrasts can we make between physical birth and spiritual rebirth? For each of the following ideas related to physical birth, suggest a similarity or a difference in connection with spiritual birth. How can these points help an unbeliever or new Christian better appreciate the concept of the new birth?

• A baby has no control over the time or circumstances of his or her birth.

• Physical birth results from an act of love between two parents.

• A newborn requires nourishment and nurture from others.

• Birth is a dramatic step in a process of growth and development into a mature being, not the climax.

kingdom of God" (1 Corinthians 15:50). John 1:12, 13 emphasizes the spiritual source of the spiritual life: "Yet to all who received him, to those who believed in his name, he gave the right to become children of God—children born not of natural descent, nor of human decision or a husband's will, but born of God."

C. MYSTERY OF THE NEW BIRTH (vv. 7, 8)

7, 8. You should not be surprised at my saying, 'You must be born again.' The wind blows wherever it pleases. You hear its sound, but you cannot tell where it comes from or where it is going. So it is with everyone born of the Spirit."

You should not be surprised—as though something wholly unreasonable is being presented. All around us are commonly accepted happenings for which we have no ready explanation.

The words are addressed to *you*—Jesus was speaking to Nicodemus alone. But the obligation to be *born again* is stated in the plural: *you*—all of you—in the Sanhedrin, in Israel, and throughout the world!

Since *wind* and *spirit* are both translations of the same Greek word, *pneuma*, this passage offers a fascinating play on words. We should not be surprised that we cannot grasp all the intricacies of spiritual truth as well as we would like. We cannot fully understand the movements of natural phenomena such as the wind. However, since we hear its *sound* and see its impact, we do not doubt that it is real. In the same way, we cannot observe the Spirit at work or actually see the processes of faith and repentance taking place, but we can see the Spirit's influence in the transformed lives of *everyone born of the Spirit*.

A person can welcome and yield to the Spirit, or he can stifle and "put out" the Spirit (1 Thessalonians 5:19), just as one can erect barriers against the wind. The new life generated by God's Spirit must not be aborted before it comes to fruition in the new birth.

III. THE VISITOR'S PROBLEM (JOHN 3:9-12)

9. "How can this be?" Nicodemus asked.

Nicodemus did not understand Jesus' words, but he was not giving up. He still asked *how*.

10. "You are Israel's teacher," said Jesus, "and do you not understand these things?

In the Greek text the definite article appears before the word *master* ("*the* master of Israel"), calling attention to Nicodemus's standing as a highly respected scholar. However, there are things that even a presumed expert does not know, especially if he has allowed form to take precedence over substance—as the Pharisees so often did. Nicodemus should not have found this information so amazing. After all, Ezekiel had announced God's promise: "I will give you a new heart and put a new spirit in you" (Ezekiel 36:26, 27). Was a new birth more amazing than that?

11. "I tell you the truth, we speak of what we know, and we testify to what we have seen, but still you people do not accept our testimony.

We most likely includes Jesus' disciples. You refers to the group of which Nicodemus is a part. Most of the Jewish leaders rejected Jesus' claims and teachings. Thus they were refusing Heaven's ambassador and his authoritative *testimony* concerning the kingdom of God.

12. "I have spoken to you of earthly things and you do not believe; how then will you believe if I speak of heavenly things?

Jesus had spoken, as he did in his parables, of common and familiar items—birth, wind, and water. These *earthly things* receive their permanent value from heavenly and spiritual concepts, such as love, mercy, faith, truth, and goodness.

WHAT DO YOU THINK?

Jesus almost chided Nicodemus—a teacher of Israel—for not understanding what he was saying. Why is it that those who ought to have spiritual insight often seem not to have any? How can such insight be gained?

WHAT DO YOU THINK?

Nicodemus was a Pharisee, a sect that collectively had become so enamored with the form of the law that they had lost sight of its substance. What happens when church leaders or church members in general lose sight of the substance of the faith and see only the form? What are we doing to prevent this condition? What more can we do?

A fuller understanding of *heavenly things* would have to await Nicodemus's further observation of Jesus' ministry.

IV. DIVINE PROVISION (JOHN 3:13-17)

A. GOD'S SON (v. 13)

13. *"No one has ever gone into heaven except the one who came from heaven—the Son of Man.*

Biblical writers did not use quotation marks to indicate words spoken by a certain person at a certain time, so we don't know whether Jesus spoke these and the following words to Nicodemus that night or whether John added them as additional explanation. In any case they provide additional insights into what is needed for entrance into God's kingdom. Man's only hope of salvation was for God to provide it. We could never have reached Heaven on our own merit or effort. As the *Son of man* who *came from heaven,* Jesus justified the claim of verse 11 that he bore witness to what he knew. Ephesians 4:9, 10 speaks both of Jesus' coming from Heaven and his returning to Heaven after his resurrection.

B. GOD'S SACRIFICE (vv 14, 15)

14. *"Just as Moses lifted up the snake in the desert, so the Son of Man must be lifted up.*

On one occasion God punished the children of Israel in the wilderness for their thankless complaints by sending serpents whose bite proved fatal. Penitent prayer followed, and God commanded *Moses* to set up a brass *snake* on a pole, directing those bitten by the serpents to look upon it and live (Numbers 21:4-9).

This incident became a symbol of Jesus' crucifixion, which brings salvation from the venom of sin to those who look in obedient faith to Christ. Jesus said, "But I, when I am lifted up from the earth, will draw all men to myself" (John 12:32). And the explanation follows: "He said this to show the kind of death he was going to die" (v. 33). That prediction of Jesus' atoning death was an immediate part of the "heavenly things" that Nicodemus was not yet able to understand.

15. *". . . that everyone who believes in him may have eternal life.*

The term *everyone* means that the benefits of Jesus' death are available to all persons everywhere. All sinners are invited to faith—belief and trust in the uplifted One—and thus to faith in the Father who provided his Son as our sacrifice. The *eternal life* to which the obedient faith leads begins with the knowledge of Jesus as Savior (John 17:3); it has no end, for death is merely the means of passage into the presence of God.

C. GOD'S SALVATION (vv. 16, 17)

16. *"For God so loved the world that he gave his one and only Son, that whoever believes in him shall not perish but have eternal life.*

Jesus' crucifixion was not the tragic murder of a good man. His death was the result of the fact that God looked in compassion on the world of mankind, created in his own image as the climax of all his creation (Genesis 1:26-28). His love was so great that *he gave his one and only Son* for man's redemption. Before Jesus came we were doomed to *perish;* now we can *have eternal life.*

Every word in this verse is stretched to the full capacity of its meaning: *God . . . loved . . . the world . . . whoever believes . . . perish . . . eternal . . . life.* You cannot grasp this on the run. You have to linger and let its truth soak in. And you must take the time to substitute your own name in place of the word *whoever!*

17. *"For God did not send his Son into the world to condemn the world, but to save the world through him."*

The visual for today's lesson portrays Jesus pleading for the defense of those who by faith have accepted him and received the new birth.

For God sent not his Son into the world to condemn the world, but that the world through him might be saved.
—John 3:17

WHAT DO YOU THINK?

God's intentions are clear. (See 1 Timothy 2:4; 2 Peter 3:9.) It is not his desire to condemn the world. Too often, however, his people act as if they would be glad to see some people condemned. When we become better known for what we are against than what we are for, we fail to convey the Lord's desire that "whoever believes in him" should have eternal life. How clearly are we communicating the truth that God wants everyone to be saved? How can we do it better?

PRAYER

Thank You, Father, for our Savior Jesus, who used this personal conversation with Nicodemus as an opportunity to teach eternal truth to all of us. Help us to be faithful in following that truth by living the new life in Christ for time and eternity. Help us in leading others to their own experience of the new birth. Amen.

THOUGHT TO REMEMBER

"No one can enter the kingdom of God unless he is born of water and the Spirit" (John 3:5).

DAILY BIBLE READINGS

Monday, Mar. 15—Nicodemus Comes to Jesus (John 3:1-10)

Tuesday, Mar. 16—God So Loved the World (John 3:11-21)

Wednesday, Mar. 17—Nicodemus Takes a Stand (John 7:45-52)

Thursday, Mar. 18—Joseph and Nicodemus Claim Jesus' Body (John 19:38-42)

Friday, Mar. 19—A Contrasting Response to Jesus (Matthew 19:16-22)

Saturday, Mar. 20—Another Contrasting Response (Acts 24:22-27)

Sunday, Mar. 21—God Cares for All (Psalm 91:1-16)

Since the law of Moses was not perfectly kept by anyone, it became a tool of condemnation, an agency of divine judgment. Jesus, on the other hand, was God's expression of love and grace, providing a way by which *the world* could be saved. He was sent on a rescue mission to live among the inhabitants of earth for the purpose of removing their condemnation.

However, condemnation has not been entirely set aside. Some persons are not interested in the salvation that God has offered, and so by their own choice they judge themselves as unsuited to receive it. Paul said to some of that kind, "We had to speak the word of God to you first. Since you reject it and do not consider yourselves worthy of eternal life, we now turn to the Gentiles" (Acts 13:46). John 3:18-21 (not included in our printed text) announces freedom from condemnation for the believer in Christ, but condemnation "already" for the unbeliever. He has rejected the "true light" (John 1:9).

CONDEMNATION OR SALVATION?

Probably John 3:16 is the most familiar verse in all the Bible. It has been quoted and lauded as "the New Testament in miniature." It may come as a surprise, then, to learn about a preacher who, given liberty to choose whatever text he pleased as the basis for what would surely be a once-in-a-lifetime sermon, chose John 3:17 instead of John 3:16. It was on June 2, 1850, that Alexander Campbell spoke from John 3:17 to both houses of the United States Congress in the chamber of the House of Representatives. Although he spoke for some ninety minutes, it was said that during this time, Campbell held his audience "in the most fixed attention."

How vital to know that God did not send Jesus to *condemn* the world, but to *save* it. It is such a temptation to attack the grossness, the insensitivity, and the moral decay of the world. It seems its many sins need to be itemized and denounced. But Jesus came to save men. To declare Jesus' love, his grace, his sacrifice, and his salvation is the true task of those who are his. As Dora Greenwell wrote:

He did not come to judge the world,
   He did not come to blame;
He did not only come to seek—
   It was to save he came;
And when we call him Savior,
   Then we call him by his name.

The message of the gospel is not bad news about human failures (we get enough of that from the world every day!). No, the gospel is good news about God's love in Jesus. It is the loving appeal of a Father, who longs for the wanderer to come home.

—J. G. V. B.

CONCLUSION

Whatever happened to Nicodemus after that memorable night visit with Jesus? John's Gospel mentions Nicodemus twice more, identifying him as the one who came to Jesus "earlier." In the first of these, Nicodemus cautioned his fellow rulers in the Sanhedrin not to condemn Jesus before they heard his teaching. That comment was not well received (John 7:45-52). On the other occasion, Nicodemus and Joseph of Arimathea claimed and cared for the body of Jesus after his crucifixion (John 19:38-42). That was expensive, and it required some courage. A tradition says that Nicodemus later became a part of the church in Jerusalem. The Holy Spirit, however, did not provide the rest of the story in the record of Scripture, so we do not really know just how far Nicodemus's admiration for Jesus led him. A more important issue for you and me is how far our admiration for Jesus will lead us.

Discovery Learning

This page contains an alternate lesson plan emphasizing learning activities. Classes desiring such student involvement will find these suggestions helpful. The next page is a reproducible activity page to further enhance discovery learning.

LEARNING GOALS

After this lesson students should be able to:

1. Summarize what Jesus said to Nicodemus about the new birth.

2. Explain from this and related texts what it means to be "born again" or "born from above."

3. Thank God for the privilege of being born again and commit himself or herself to a pattern of consistent growth.

INTO THE LESSON

Before class prepare a poster with a large question mark [?] in the middle. Across the top write, "You Have Questions." Across the bottom write, "Who Has Answers?"

Post this in a conspicuous place in the classroom. When it's time to begin, ask, "How do you go about getting answers to difficult questions?" Allow everyone who wants to suggest answers to do so. Write each one without evaluation on the chalkboard or on the poster. Responses such as seeking experts, looking in reference books, or using a computer network may be expected.

Observe that in today's lesson we shall meet a man with questions. He went to the best source of all for answers. He went to Jesus.

INTO THE WORD

Assign a class member to prepare in advance a background check on Nicodemus. A good Bible dictionary should provide sufficient information. Start the Bible study with that report. You might also have someone prepared to provide some information about the sect of the Pharisees, who they were, what they believed and practiced, and how influential they were in Jesus' time.

Next, have a volunteer read John 3:1-17. Make some brief remarks about the passage, noting three metaphors in Jesus' discourse: new birth, the wind, and the serpent in the wilderness. Divide the class into at least three small groups and ask each group to explore the meaning of each metaphor. (If you have more than eighteen members in your class, make more groups, giving duplicate assignments as needed.) Give the groups about six or eight minutes, then call for reports. Below are some suggestions for what the groups should report.

Group 1: New Birth. As birth marks a great new beginning for the child who has been living in his mother's womb, so life in Christ is radically new and different from one's life before becoming a Christian.

Group 2: The Wind. As the wind is invisible and yet obvious in its power and effect, so the Spirit works in ways unseen by the human eye yet producing visible and powerful results.

Group 3: The Serpent. This is a reference to an historical event from the wilderness wanderings. See Numbers 21:4-9. As the people of Israel could not save themselves from the serpents, so no one today can save himself from the guilt of sin. But God has raised up a Deliverer!

After the groups report, move into a study of Scriptures having to do with being born again. Begin with Romans 6:3-11. Draw out ideas of what this rebirth means, what is involved in the process, and what the distinction is between born "of water" and born "of the Spirit." (Use information from the lesson commentary to clarify this concept.)

Have a Bible drill aimed at clearing up why Jesus said Nicodemus should know about the new birth. Begin with the following: 1 Samuel 10:6; Isaiah 32:15; Jeremiah 31:33; Ezekiel 36:25-27; Joel 2:28, 29. These passages will reveal that, for many centuries, God's people were taught to expect a new heart and new spirit, that it would come from on high, that it would be for all humanity, and that it would be part of a personal covenant that stressed individual responsibility.

INTO LIFE

Nicodemus asked a good question: "How can a man be born [again] when he is old?" Studies show that, if a person does not make a decision for Christ by the time he or she turns eighteen, it is rare that the person does so at all! Discuss how your class can reach adults with the message of Jesus and the new birth. If you have some students who came to the Lord as adults, ask them what attracted them to the Lord. Suggest ways you and your class can make this a more common experience.

Discuss also what your church is doing to nurture new converts—and long-time believers as well. How well are most people taking advantage of these opportunities? Challenge your class members to commit themselves to taking advantage of every opportunity that will help them develop a pattern of consistent growth. Close with a prayer of thanks for the new birth available in Christ Jesus.

It's Like This

In John 3:1-17 Jesus used a variety of metaphors to describe the new birth and the work of the holy Spirit. It's like being born; it's like the wind; it's like the bronze snake. Explain what Jesus meant by each metaphor.

New Birth.

The Wind.

The Serpent

If an unbeliever could visit with Jesus some evening the way Nicodemus did, what metaphors might Jesus use to communicate to the following kinds of people? Explain the metaphor in each case.

A stock broker

A stay-at-home mom

A pilot

A dairy farmer

How might you use one of these metaphors to talk with someone you know about the Lord?

A WOMAN BRINGS HER VILLAGE TO JESUS

WHY TEACH THIS LESSON?

"Happy are those who are hungry and thirsty for righteousness," said Jesus. The truth of that Beatitude is illustrated by the divine-human encounter recorded in today's lesson text. The Samaritan woman was not all that happy when she walked out to the well that day. But she was elated before the day was over because she had discovered the Living Water that completely satisfied her spiritual thirst. She experienced the fulfillment of the promise: "for they shall be filled."

The world is full of people who are dying of thirst today. Some of them will attend classes where this lesson is taught and discussed. Some may be present in your class. Your teaching can supply the spiritual springs that will satisfy forever their craving for Christ. That's why you will teach this lesson.

INTRODUCTION

A. JUST BETWEEN THE TWO OF US

Trivial!

You meet by chance in the shopping mall and you "pass the time of day." What do you talk about? The weather? Last night's ball game? Probably nothing very important, thus the origin of our word *trivial*. This word is derived from a Latin word that means "three ways." It described a place where paths intersected and neighbors paused to engage in small talk. When the conversation is "just between you and me," we may not feel as responsible for what we say.

Not so with Jesus, for whom every conversation was an opportunity to bring someone closer to his Father.. The third and fourth chapters of John provide examples, one with a religious leader who came to Jesus by night, and the other with a woman he met by a well in Samaria. In each person he saw a need and addressed that need through teaching that went far beyond the hearer's immediate understanding. Now all of us can also learn from those one-on-one conversations. We met Nicodemus last week. Today we meet the woman of Samaria.

B. A HISTORY OF HOSTILITY

A business establishment in our city operates a "Samaritan van" that patrols streets and highways and offers help to travelers in need. This service is named for the unlikely hero of Jesus' parable in Luke 10:25-37.

The Jews in Jesus' day did not consider Samaritans as heroes. A succinct statement of relations between the two groups is found in John 4:9: "Jews do not associate with Samaritans." Tensions between the two can be traced to events that occurred some seven hundred years earlier. In 722 B.C., when the Assyrians conquered the northern kingdom of Israel and its capital of Samaria, they scattered its people to other parts of the empire, replacing them with foreigners. The people who resulted from this mixture of populations came to be called Samaritans.

DEVOTIONAL READING:
REVELATION 7:13-17

LESSON SCRIPTURE:
JOHN 4:1-42

PRINTED TEXT:
JOHN 4:7-15, 28-30, 39, 40

LESSON AIMS

This study should help the class member to:

1. Tell how the Samaritan woman's life and village were changed by an encounter with Jesus.

2. List several principles for evangelism demonstrated by Jesus and the woman.

3. Form a specific plan to tell others of Jesus, using one or more of the principles from this text.

KEY VERSE

"Whoever drinks the water I give him will never thirst. Indeed, the water I give him will become in him a spring of water welling up to eternal life." —John 4:14

Years later in 538 B.C., following seventy years of captivity in Babylon, the Jews from Judah were allowed to return to Jerusalem and rebuild their temple. Samaritans in the area expressed an interest in helping with the temple, but their offer was refused because they did not worship Yahweh exclusively. Eventually the Samaritans established their own religious practices, based on the five books of Law (Genesis to Deuteronomy). They built their own temple on Mount Gerizim, located within sight of "Jacob's well." That temple was destroyed during the period between the Old and New Testaments, but the site continued to be considered holy ground by the Samaritans. (A Samaritan group worships at the base of Mount Gerizim to this day!)

By the time of Christ, mutual resentment between Jews and Samaritans had intensified. Jesus, however, refused to be a part of it, taking notable occasions to show that God's love and mercy included Samaritans. One of these occasions is the subject of today's lesson.

C. LESSON BACKGROUND

Jesus' conversation with Nicodemus was a significant event in his early ministry in Judea, where he is said to have baptized some of his hearers (John 3:22). Soon the disciples of John the Baptist began to express their concern that Jesus was gaining a larger following than John (v. 26). John was pleased to see this happening, saying, "He must become greater; I must become less" (3:30). Certain Pharisees were eager to transfer their criticism and opposition of John to Jesus, but Jesus knew the time was not right for that. So Jesus and his disciples headed north to Galilee (4:1-3). Instead of following the Jews' popular detour around Samaritan territory (traveling east and crossing the Jordan River, then crossing again north of Samaria), he went directly northward through Samaria. At "about the sixth hour" (noon by Jewish reckoning) the group arrived "near the plot of ground Jacob had given to his son Joseph" (v. 5; see Genesis 33:18, 19; Joshua 24:32). Jacob's well, still usable, was a familiar landmark.

Jesus was not one to seek favors, but at this point he was "tired . . . from the journey" (John 4:6). He sat to rest by the well while his disciples went to buy food in the town of Sychar, about half a mile away.

I. TALKING ABOUT WATER (JOHN 4:7-15)

It was time for refreshment, physical and spiritual. Both were on the agenda.

A. JESUS ASKS FOR WATER (vv. 7-9)

7. *When a Samaritan woman came to draw water, Jesus said to her, "Will you give me a drink?"*

The *Samaritan woman* was a citizen of the region, not the city, of Samaria. (To come from the city would have required about a two-hour walk.) She had come *to draw water.* From verse 28 we gather that she was carrying a "water jar," either on her head or on her shoulder.

Jesus saw this woman as a person having more than one kind of thirst. He could help her with her spiritual thirst, and the best possible opportunity to do this was through asking her to help him with his physical thirst. He would put himself in debt to her for a kindness that she could easily render. What could be more natural than for a thirsty person to ask for a *drink?* But under the social circumstances, what could be more startling?

8. *(His disciples had gone into the town to buy food.)*

We can only guess how many disciples were with Jesus on this journey, and why or whether they all went *into the town.* The rift between Jews and Samaritans

WHAT DO YOU THINK?

Jesus, a Jewish man, engaged in evangelistic discussion with a Samaritan woman. Given the social norms of the day, this was startling. (Note the disciples' reaction when they saw it, v. 27.) What are some principles to keep

did not prevent their doing business on commercial levels, but it might limit what *food* a Jew would buy in a Samaritan market.

9. The Samaritan woman said to him, "You are a Jew and I am a Samaritan woman. How can you ask me for a drink?" (For Jews do not associate with Samaritans.)

The *woman* did not refuse the request, but she was in no hurry to grant it. The stranger's Jewishness would have been evident from his physical appearance, his clothing, and his speech, at least. Jews did not fraternize with Samaritans, and Jewish men did not talk in public places with women at all! What Jew would acknowledge a need that she could supply? Yet Jesus had asked her for a *drink*!

We are left to wonder when or whether the woman actually drew water from the well and supplied the drink that Jesus had requested. The conversation moved swiftly to more important matters.

B. Jesus Offers Living Water (vv. 10-14)

10. Jesus answered her, "If you knew the gift of God and who it is that asks you for a drink, you would have asked him and he would have given you living water."

The woman's need was greater than Jesus' need, and he lost no time in pointing this out. Her need was spiritual, and it would be met by God's provision rather than by her ability. The phrase *gift of God* is not used elsewhere in John's Gospel, but John 3:16 carries the same idea when it describes God's love as a love that "gave his one and only Son." He is the source of the *living water* that he was offering to the woman. But it was too early in the conversation for her to recognize this link.

Living water should be understood as a fresh, flowing stream (as from a spring or artesian well), in contrast to the standing and stagnant water in a pond or cistern. The water that Jesus offers is as necessary to spiritual life as water is to physical life. It is *living* water in a double sense, in kind and in movement: "If anyone is thirsty, let him come to me and drink. Whoever believes in me, as the Scripture has said, streams of living water will flow from within him" (John 7:37, 38).

11. "Sir," the woman said, "you have nothing to draw with and the well is deep. Where can you get this living water?

Just as Nicodemus had found difficulty with the idea of being born again (John 3:4), so this woman found it hard to think beyond the difficulties related to providing water from a deep *well* without a rope and a bucket. (The well at this site has been measured at more than a hundred feet in total depth.)

Nevertheless, she had observed qualities in Jesus that commanded her respect. She addressed him as *Sir* (the Greek form is *kurie*, frequently translated, "lord"). Perhaps his courtesy toward her had something to do with her respect of him. Still, she obviously suspected this man of promising more than he could deliver. Did she dare to think that he had another source for the *water* that he offered?

12. Are you greater than our father Jacob, who gave us the well and drank from it himself, as did also his sons and his flocks and herds?"

The patriarch *Jacob* was acknowledged as *father* by both Jews and Samaritans. He had shown remarkable resourcefulness in providing a dependable source of water for his family and his flocks. Was this Jewish stranger suggesting that he could outdo the respected ancestor of both Jew and Samaritan?

13, 14. Jesus answered, "Everyone who drinks this water will be thirsty again, but whoever drinks the water I give him will never thirst. Indeed, the water I give him will become in him a spring of water welling up to eternal life."

The woman had suggested a comparison between Jacob and Jesus. Jesus chose instead to contrast the kinds of water that each was able to provide. The

in mind when we have evangelistic contacts across racial and gender lines? What social norms ought we to ignore? Are there some we should maintain? If so, what ones, and why?

What Do You Think?

It is amazing to see how Jesus was able to use everyday sights and experiences like water as vehicles for spiritual teaching. How can we turn casual conversation into opportunities to share Christ with our companions? What helps can you suggest to aid us in this approach to sharing the gospel?

Consider 1 Peter 3:15; Colossians 4:2-6 in your discussion.

The visual for lesson 4 illustrates our Key Verse, John 4:14.

WHO
SO
EVER
drinketh of the water that I shall give him shall never thirst; but the water that I shall give him shall be in him A WELL OF WATER springing up into everlasting life.

water from Jacob's well could satisfy a physical thirst for a time, but that thirst would return to make repeated demands. And that water could never slake the spiritual thirst that was even now tormenting the woman who came to draw from the well.

There is something better about the water of life, however, than simply providing a permanent supply that keeps a person going and going indefinitely. Ordinary water satisfies the person who drinks it, and no one else. Christ's water of life is a constantly renewed and overflowing supply, affecting not only the believer in Christ, but also those with whom the believer comes into contact. That quality was to be demonstrated within the hour as the Samaritan woman's enthusiasm for Jesus spilled over to her neighbors as she brought them to meet him, too.

A SPRING WELLING UP

It was at Jacob's well that Jesus met and conversed with the woman of Samaria. Despite their many differences, both Jews and Samaritans obtained water from this well (the well can still be visited and used).

Jesus told this woman that the "living water" he could give her would be "a spring of water welling up to eternal life"—always refreshing, enlivening, and never running dry! There is something mysterious and marvelous about everflowing springs of water. They gush forth from the earth, pouring forth constantly, day and night, year after year, in every season.

In Florida there are many such springs, which *every day* pour out over four billion gallons of water. Some of these seemingly inexhaustible springs are: Silver Springs, five miles northeast of Ocala, which emits 808 cubic feet of water per second; Rainbow Springs, four miles northeast of Dunnellon (699 cubic feet per second); and Ichatuckee Springs, near Hildreth (335 cubic feet per second).

Just as this abundance of water flows in a torrent of clear and continual freshness, so Jesus' presence and power constantly revives us within. Whatever the drabness and dreariness of the outer life, inwardly all is green and fresh and beautiful for the Christian.

—J. G. V. B.

WHAT DO YOU THINK?

The more Jesus talked, the more this woman wanted whatever it was he had to offer! What can we do to stimulate a spiritual thirst in the hearts of our friends and acquaintances?

C. THE WOMAN ASKS FOR WATER (v. 15)

15. The woman said to him, "Sir, give me this water so that I won't get thirsty and have to keep coming here to draw water."

Without hearing the words spoken, it is hard to say what the woman meant here. Perhaps she was sincere, not understanding yet what Jesus was talking about but liking what she heard. The idea of not having to draw water was very appealing. Her thirst for spiritual water, if recognized, was not yet on her mind. On the other hand, she may have been sarcastic with her remark. If she was thinking about physical water, Jesus' promise surely sounded too good to be true!

Whatever her intent, when Jesus raised the issue of her chaotic marital status (vv. 16-18), his insight convinced her that he was a prophet (v. 19). Probably embarrassed, especially if she had spoken rudely, she changed the subject from husbands to religion. For Jews and Samaritans, this raised the question of Jerusalem versus "this mountain" (Mount Gerizim, which would have been visible from where Jesus and the woman were) as the place of acceptable worship. Jesus promised the time when the spirit, rather than the location, would determine acceptable worship before God. The woman was willing to leave such matters to the Messiah at his sometime-in-the-future arrival. Jesus then told her plainly that he was that Messiah! (v. 26).

At this point the Lord's disciples returned. They were amazed, but politely silent, at finding their Master in conversation with this woman.

II. TALKING ABOUT JESUS (JOHN 4:28-30)
A. "COME AND SEE" (vv. 28, 29)

28, 29. Then, leaving her water jar, the woman went back to the town and said to the people, "Come, see a man who told me everything I ever did. Could this be the Christ?"

The disciples' arrival may have startled the woman into recognizing that others also needed to hear the remarkable things that she had just heard. Her priorities suddenly changed. She set aside her *water jar* (perhaps still empty), for she had found something vastly more important than that for which she came. She did not return home, but went to where others were, to share with them her remarkable experience.

What was so exciting? She had met a *man* so wonderful that they must meet him, too. The quality that impressed her most was not that he spoke of giving the water of life, or of God caring more for the spirit of one's worship than the place where it was offered. No! This wonderful man understood *her*, and talked about *her*! He knew all about her and still respected her!

Could this be the long-anticipated *Christ*? Limiting their use of Scripture to the books of the Law, the Samaritans lacked the clear messianic prophecies found in Isaiah and other writers; but they would have known, for example, what Moses had said about a Prophet whom God would one day "raise up" (Deuteronomy 18:15). The woman's question served well to stir curiosity in her hearers, who then wanted to find out about this remarkable individual for themselves.

EVERYTHING I EVER DID

The Samaritan woman claimed that Jesus had told her everything "I ever did" (John 4:29, 39). Of course, Jesus did not literally tell her about every act she had ever done. But he did tell her about her five husbands and the man with whom she was living who was not her husband (v. 18). These unhappy situations had probably been the repeated source of frustrated hopes, days of discord, and nights of tension (perhaps even of terror).

Perhaps such a checkered past affected this woman's standing in the community and alienated her from her family. We do not know what children she may have borne to her various husbands, or what rifts might have occurred in her relationships with their families. In any case, Jesus had quietly touched on the things she had done, but he had done so in such a way as to give her a hope, not despair.

Have we not sometimes heard a teacher or preacher who seemed to "lay bare" for us our most basic fears and hopes and questions? Often we are not really aware of these until a speaker or writer seems to strike a certain key. Suddenly all the music of our life is revealed as more discordant than we realized. However, as the Samaritan woman came to discover, Jesus can bring harmony to even the most out-of-tune life. May we let similar moments of self-awareness lead us to Jesus as well.

> Let words of Jesus reach your heart,
> Let vision clear and healing start;
> All can be cleansed, but nothing hid,
> For He knows everything you did.
>
> —J. G. V. B.

B. INVITATION ACCEPTED (v. 30)

30. They came out of the town and made their way toward him.

As the multitudes had gone out of Jerusalem to hear John the Baptist in the wilderness, so the people of Sychar "were coming" (a literal translation of the Greek text) to Jesus at the well. It is an amazing result from a single invitation. As an evangelist, this woman was an *amateur* in the best sense of that term (the word comes from a root meaning "to love"); for she was acting out of love for

DAILY BIBLE READINGS

Monday, Mar. 22—Jesus Goes Through Samaria (John 4:1-6)

Tuesday, Mar. 23—Jesus' Encounter With a Samaritan Woman (John 4:7-15)

Wednesday, Mar. 24—I Am the Messiah (John 4:16-26)

Thursday, Mar. 25—Jesus' Disciples Are Astonished (John 4:27-42)

Friday, Mar. 26—Even a Cup of Cold Water (Matthew 10:37-42)

Saturday, Mar. 27—Take the Water of Life As a Gift (Revelation 22:16-21)

Sunday, Mar. 28—Jesus Rides Into Jerusalem (Mark 11:1-11)

WHAT DO YOU THINK?

The Samaritan woman's excitement about Jesus stirred her neighbors to come hear him. Jesus himself said the harvest was ready (v. 35). How can we be more eager and effective in sharing the gospel and reaping this harvest?

What are we already doing? Are there ways we can improve on those efforts? What are we doing to publicize our church and the ministries we offer, the needs we meet? What are we doing

specifically for outsiders? How
are we training people for evangelism? How can we improve?

*What new fields can we
enter? What special needs are
there in our community, or what
areas of the community have
been largely neglected? Can we
take the gospel there? How?*

WHAT DO YOU THINK?

*The Samaritans came out to
investigate Jesus for themselves
and were convinced. What do
you think is the most convincing
thing about who Jesus is today?
How can we help people see that
for themselves?*

what she was doing, and not for any hope of gain. Her effectiveness came from her obvious passion rather than from the logic of her arguments.

The sight of many people coming toward Jesus became the basis for discussion between Jesus and his disciples. The disciples wanted him to eat of the food they had brought; he said he was enjoying a different kind of nourishment (vv. 31-34). The disciples saw prospects for a future harvest in the grainfields around them; he saw a spiritual crop ready for immediate harvest (vv. 35-38).

III. TALKING WITH JESUS (JOHN 4:39, 40)

We turn now from the conversations of Jesus with the Samaritan woman and with his disciples to the reaction of the residents of Sychar after their encounter with Christ.

39. Many of the Samaritans from that town believed in him because of the woman's testimony, "He told me everything I ever did."

The woman's testimony to the townspeople had been convincing. Even allowing for some exaggeration that Jesus recounted *everything I ever did*, it is clear that they accepted her evaluation of Jesus as a prophet of God, and perhaps *the* prophet anticipated by Moses. Their faith is the more remarkable in light of the handicaps it had to overcome. It was a Jew—not a Samaritan—who just might be the Messiah, and the suggestion was coming from a person whose track record for dependability was less than perfect.

If this woman could be so effective in representing Jesus, who of us can say, "I could never bring anyone to Christ"? Perhaps we're simply not as excited about him as she was!

40. So when the Samaritans came to him, they urged him to stay with them, and he stayed two days.

It seems that the *Samaritans* who came to see Jesus for themselves reached the same conclusion about him that the woman had. They wanted to know more, and they insisted on his staying for a time among them.

The fruits of Jesus' brief two-day stay with the Samaritans were as remarkable as the events leading to it. They are reported briefly in the two verses immediately following our printed text: "And because of his words many more became believers. They said to the woman, 'We no longer believe just because of what you said; now we have heard for ourselves, and we know that this man really is the Savior of the world'" (vv. 41, 42). But first, someone had to tell them about Jesus. The Samaritan woman had done her part in pointing others to him.

CONCLUSION

Jesus talked, one-on-one, with a scholar named Nicodemus, whose acquaintance many would have been eager to make. He also talked with an unnamed Samaritan woman, whose acquaintance many would have shunned. In each conversation he planted seeds of truth that the other was not yet prepared to understand, but which finally became intensely meaningful to countless generations.

Ironically, the results from the less promising conversation with the Samaritan woman were much more fruitful (at least immediately) than those from the conversation with the religious leader. What was the difference? Nicodemus pondered the matter and kept it to himself. The woman became excited about Jesus and told everyone she met about him. They, in turn, inquired for themselves and came to believe for themselves, thus providing early evidence that the gospel was meant to break down the walls that had divided Jews and Samaritans for hundreds of years. And it all began with a conversation beside a well.

What conversations for Christ can you begin today?

PRAYER

*Father, we praise you for your
Son Jesus, who is to us the water
of life, slaking our spiritual thirst
now and forever. Thank you for
faithful witnesses who brought
the good news of the gospel to us.
Grant us boldness to share it
with others. In Jesus' name.
Amen.*

THOUGHT TO REMEMBER

Come with me and see Jesus!

Discovery Learning

This page contains an alternate lesson plan emphasizing learning activities. Classes desiring such student involvement will find these suggestions helpful. The next page is a reproducible activity page to further enhance discovery learning.

LEARNING GOALS

This lesson should equip students to:

1. Tell how the Samaritan woman's life and village were changed by an encounter with Jesus.

2. List several principles for evangelism demonstrated by Jesus and the woman.

3. Form a specific plan to tell others of Jesus, using one or more of the principles from this text.

INTO THE LESSON

Before class prepare a poster with the words, "I just have to tell you . . ." written in large letters. Add some pictures to the poster, either drawn or cut from magazines, of items that would suggest someone has great news to tell. You might include an engagement ring ("I'm getting married!"), a house ("We sold our house!" or "We've just bought/built a home"), a limousine (an important official is coming to town), money (got a scholarship, an inheritance, etc.), and several other items. Ask the students to guess what news each item might represent. Invite volunteers to tell about times they have had exciting news to tell. After some discussion, ask, "How excited are we to tell people about Jesus?" Discuss why we are sometimes not as excited about that as we are to tell other news. Make the transition to Bible study by noting that today's lesson introduces us to a woman who just had to tell the good news about Jesus.

INTO THE WORD

At the outset, it would be helpful to have someone brief the class on the Samaritans: who they were, what they believed. A Bible dictionary or a Bible encyclopedia should provide enough details for a quick survey.

It would also be informative to ask the class to read aloud the entire fourth chapter of John and then compare the Samaritan woman with Nicodemus. Two columns on the chalkboard can be used to visualize the reactions. For example, he was of high status in that society and she was of low. He was very "religious" and she was not. She was somewhat cynical and he was not. Their needs were not the same. What were they?

With the assistance of the entire class, outline the conversation between Jesus and the woman, as well as the results. Write the outline on a flip sheet or chalkboard.

- The request for a drink (v. 7)
- The cross-cultural communication (v. 9)
- The shift to "spiritual" water and to Jesus (vv. 10-15)
- A look at the woman's spiritual condition (vv. 16-18)
- Her change of subject to the appropriate place of worship (vv. 19-24)
- His revelation that he is the Messiah (vv. 25, 26)
- The woman shares the good news (vv. 27-30)
- Response of the city (vv. 39, 40)

Ask, "What made the woman want to tell others about Jesus?" After a brief discussion, ask, "How can we have the same desire and excitement to share the good news?"

INTO LIFE

In order to make some applications to our lives today, review the conversation between Jesus and the woman, noting some timeless principles for evangelism that Jesus followed. Discuss how we can observe the same principles today. Some suggested principles follow:

1. Begin a conversation in a natural manner. (Jesus' request for a drink was natural enough, given the climate and the proximity of a well.)

2. Don't be afraid to cross cultural barriers. (What was unusual about Jesus' request was that it ignored the prejudice that existed between Jews and Samaritans.) You might use the reproducible page that follows to enhance this point.

3. Appeal to felt needs. (Jesus' talk of living water appealed to the woman, as it seemed it would make her life easier.)

4. Stay focused. (When the woman tried to change the subject, Jesus kept the conversation focused on the message he had for her.)

5. Point to the Christ. (See vv. 25, 26.)

Compare how the woman followed some of the same principles in telling the people of her city about Jesus. For example, with the anticipation of the coming Messiah, her question, "Is not this the Christ?" appealed to their felt need for his arrival.

Ask the class to plan and organize some ways that Jesus can be shared today. Then distribute index cards and ask each student to get specific. Each one should write the name of someone who needs to know the Lord and write two or three steps that can be taken in the coming week to share him with that person.

Bring the Walls Down

Several barriers could have separated Jesus from the woman at the well, but Jesus refused to let them. Unscramble the words below to see what they were.

care _____

drenge _____

ilionger _____

fysletile _____

gutafie _____

What barriers prevent Christians from sharing their faith today? Why? How can we tear these walls down even as Jesus tore down the walls in his day?

It's a Start

What barriers keep you from sharing your faith?

Think of one person you know who needs to know the Lord. (Write his or her name here.)

Now write two or three ideas of what you can do to begin to share your faith with this person in spite of any potential barriers.

Answers to **Bring the Walls Down:** race, gender, religion, lifestyle, fatigue

JESUS IS CRUCIFIED AND RESURRECTED

WHY TEACH THIS LESSON?

"I come to the garden alone. . . ." So begins the familiar hymn "In the Garden," which is based on the poignant encounter between Mary Magdalene and the risen Lord. "And the voice I hear, falling on my ear, the Son of God discloses." One of the most tender scenes in all the Bible is this one where Mary recognizes the voice of the Master and turns and cries, "Rabboni!" It was his voice that disclosed his identity to Mary.

How can we hear that voice? What is it that will disclose to us the presence of the risen Lord? It is the study of passages just like this one! We, too, need to have confidence that the Lord is risen, he is risen indeed. You need that confidence, and your students need it, too. That is the reason it is so important to teach this lesson today.

INTRODUCTION

A. WHY ARE YOU CRYING?

She was in college far from home, and in rehearsal for the prime dramatic event of the season. Today, however, she had learned that her mother's mysterious health problem appeared to be a long-term incurable disease. So between "takes" the girl was seeking quiet comfort in a darkened corner with a box of facial tissues. First to see her there was a seminary student with whom she shared a speaking acquaintance.

"Problems?" he wanted to know.

"You might say so," she replied.

"Do you want to talk about it?" he persisted.

"Not really," she said between sniffles.

But the young man was persistent. "Have you prayed about it?" This "preacher's kid" then brought out a clean handkerchief to replace the soggy tissues.

"I haven't done much else all day," she sobbed. She figured that if this pushy pest wanted a problem, she would lay it on him. So she did, and he listened and shed a few tears himself. The young man could at least weep with those who weep. Finally, with her permission, he laid it on the Lord.

A year or so later the girl's parents visited the college and had dinner with her and the "pushy preacher" student. They rejoiced together as an engagement ring went on the appropriate finger. Mother commented, "I'm so glad that someone could benefit from my illness."

"Why are you crying?" That's a good question to ask anyone in tears. Both angels and Jesus himself asked the question of Mary Magdalene. The risen Christ then changed Mary's tears of sorrow to tears of joy—an experience that has been repeated numerous times in the lives of other followers of Jesus.

DEVOTIONAL READING:
ACTS 2:32-39
LESSON SCRIPTURE:
JOHN 18:1—20:18
PRINTED TEXT:
JOHN 19:16-18, 28-30;
20:11-18

Apr
4

LESSON AIMS

This lesson should equip the student to:

1. Recount the details of Jesus' death and his postresurrection appearance to Mary.

2. Explain why the death and resurrection of Jesus must continue to be the focus of the church's message to the world.

3. Suggest one or two ways the student or class can tell in a fresh way the good news of Jesus' resurrection.

KEY VERSE

"Don't be alarmed," [the angel] said. "You are looking for Jesus the Nazarene, who was crucified. He has risen! He is not here. See the place where they laid him. —Mark 16:6

LESSON 5 NOTES

B. JOHN AND HIS FRIENDS

When the apostle John wrote his inspired record of Jesus in the fourth Gospel, he was surely aware of what had been written earlier by his fellow apostle Matthew, by Peter's friend Mark, and by the careful historian Luke. Each had written in his own way for a special audience. John, the "disciple whom Jesus loved," could still supply important information as an intimate witness of Jesus' life and ministry. His focus on Mary Magdalene as the first witness of the risen Christ is a case in point.

Mary Magdalene is mentioned earlier by Luke as one of the women from Galilee who were blessed by Jesus' healing ministry and expressed their gratitude by supporting his work financially (8:1-3). The designation "Magdalene" distinguishes this Mary from other Marys mentioned in the Gospels. It probably indicates that she came from Magdala, a town located on the southwest shore of the Sea of Galilee. Luke specifically notes that Jesus cast out seven devils from Mary (Luke 8:2). It is fruitless to speculate about the nature of the devils or their influence on Mary, but her deliverance obviously identified her as one who had received much from the Lord and therefore loved much in return (Luke 7:47). That great love became increasingly evident during the events of Jesus' death and resurrection.

HOW TO SAY IT

Aramaic. Air-uh-MAY-ic.
Barabbas. Buh-RAB-us.
Cleopas. KLEE-uh-pass.
Emmaus. Em-MAY-us.
Golgotha. GAHL-guh-thuh.
Magdala. MAG-duh-luh.
Magdalene. MAG-duh-leen or
  Mag-duh-LEE-nee.
Rabbi. RAB-eye.
Rabboni. Rab-O-nye.
Sanhedrin. San-HEED-run or
  SAN-huh-drin.

C. LESSON BACKGROUND

Assigned for background reading this week are two and one-half chapters: John 18:1—20:18. These are important to the understanding of our printed text from John 19 and 20. Thus a brief survey of the events recorded within these chapters is in order. After Jesus' memorable Passover with his disciples in the upper room in Jerusalem, he led them to the Mount of Olives. There he engaged in intense prayer, after which Judas came with temple officers to arrest him (John 18:1-11).

Jesus was then subjected to a series of "trials" before the high priest and the Sanhedrin (who pronounced him guilty of blasphemy against God), before Herod, and before Pilate, the Roman governor of Judea. Pilate, questioning Jesus privately, was quickly convinced of his innocence and made a series of weak efforts to set him free. He finally tried to accomplish this by a Passover tradition of releasing one prisoner; however, Jesus' accusers "stirred up the crowd to have Pilate release Barabbas instead" (Mark 15:11). When the Jewish leaders linked the governor's desire to release Jesus with sedition against Rome (John 19:12-15), Pilate, whose position with Rome was rather shaky, gave in to their demands to put Jesus to death.

I. JESUS' CRUCIFIXION (JOHN 19:16-18)

16. Finally Pilate handed him over to them to be crucified. So the soldiers took charge of Jesus.

Pilate handed . . . over two prisoners to different fates: guilty Barabbas to freedom, and innocent Jesus *to be crucified.* The Romans executed the most despised criminals by fastening them to crosses, where they were exposed to maximum shame and pain before death. The Jewish leaders' fury against Jesus was so intense that they welcomed the opportunity to expose him to the most degrading punishment. Since Rome did not permit the Jews to execute anyone, Jesus' sentence of crucifixion was carried out by the Romans.

17, 18. Carrying his own cross, he went out to the place of the Skull (which in Aramaic is called Golgotha). Here they crucified him, and with him two others—one on each side and Jesus in the middle.

WHAT DO YOU THINK?

Suppose, while studying this passage with a friend, your friend says, "Hey! This says Jesus carried his own cross. I thought one of the other Gospels said that they made a guy named Simon

The victim of crucifixion was required to carry at least one beam of the *cross* to the place of execution. Luke 23:26 indicates that Jesus, apparently exhausted and unable to continue carrying the cross, was relieved of this duty. A bystander named Simon was seized from the crowd to finish the task.

Jewish law forbade executions within the walls of a city (Acts 7:58); thus Jesus was *crucified* outside Jerusalem at *Golgotha*, meaning *the place of the Skull*. Such a name could indicate the use of this site for executions, or it may have called attention to the appearance of the location. (A proposed site of the crucifixion, known as Gordon's Calvary, contains two hollow spaces on the side of the hill that resemble two eyes.) The Latin equivalent of the name, *Calvary*, is perhaps more pleasant to the ear than the harsher *Golgotha*, and so *Calvary* appears more frequently in song and story. But there is nothing pleasing or appealing to the physical senses in what happened to Jesus at Golgotha.

That *two others*, called "robbers" by Matthew (27:38) and Mark (15:27) and "criminals" by Luke (23:32), should be crucified *one on each side* of Jesus was an evident attempt to discredit him by association. Instead, it fulfilled a messianic prophecy (Isaiah 53:12) and provided an opportunity for Jesus, even in dying, to show the way of life to a penitent transgressor (Luke 23:39-43).

THE SCORNED BECOMES SACRED

When the idea was first suggested of building a memorial to honor the American military personnel who had been killed in the Vietnam War (more than fifty thousand of them), it was determined that a contest would be held to decide what type of memorial it should be. The winning idea was one presented by a young Chinese-American girl, Maya Lin, and selected over 1,420 other entries. Her proposal was to construct a wall on which would be engraved the name of every American serviceman or servicewoman who had lost his or her life during the Vietnam War.

At first the idea of a wall engraved with names seemed so ordinary that many thought it an insult to the soldiers rather than a tribute. Many bitterly objected to its construction. With the passing of time, however, the Vietnam Wall has become deeply revered and greatly respected. People now glory in what was once scorned.

Crucifixion was the most scorned and severe form of execution in the world of Jesus' day. However, Jesus' death on a cross for the sins of the world transformed something hideous and repulsive into an emblem of victory and freedom. Paul was unashamed to glory in the cross of Christ (Galatians 6:14), and so are Jesus' followers today. What was once despised and scorned remains a means of transformation, blessing, and renewal of life.

—J. G. V. B.

II. JESUS' DEATH (JOHN 19:28-30)

Verses 19-27, not included in our printed text, tell us that Pilate refused to change the inscription he had displayed above Jesus' head: "Jesus of Nazareth, the King of the Jews." The attending soldiers divided Jesus' garments among them and cast lots for his clothing, as Psalm 22:18 had said they would. Jesus consigned the care of his mother to "the disciple whom he loved," apparently a reference to John. Thus Jesus was serving and thinking of others, even while he was dying for the sins of the world.

28. Later, knowing that all was now completed, and so that the Scripture would be fulfilled, Jesus said, "I am thirsty."

From extreme loss of blood and sheer exhaustion, Jesus suffered a burning, ravishing thirst. Even now, *Scripture* continued to be *fulfilled*: "My strength is dried up like a potsherd, and my tongue sticks to the roof of my mouth; you lay me in the dust of death" (Psalm 22:15). No one would begrudge Jesus' giving a

carry it. That's why I just can't believe the Bible: it's full of contradictions!" How would you respond?

(The other accounts are in Matthew 27:31, 32; Mark 15:20, 21; and Luke 23:26.)

WHAT DO YOU THINK?

John notes in verse 28, as in other places, that Jesus' actions came "that the Scripture would be fulfilled." What significance do you find in this? How does it help your faith in Jesus?

Daily Bible Readings

Monday, Mar. 29—*Judas Betrays Jesus (John 18:1-14)*

Tuesday, Mar. 30—*Peter Denies He Is a Disciple (John 18:15-27)*

Wednesday, Mar. 31—*Pilate Gives the People a Choice (John 18:28-40)*

Thursday, Apr. 1—*Jesus Is Condemned to Crucifixion (John 19:1-16a)*

Friday, Apr. 2—*Jesus Is Crucified (John 19:16b-30)*

Saturday, Apr. 3—*The Day of Preparation (John 19:31-42)*

Sunday, Apr. 4—*I Have Seen the Lord (John 20:1-18)*

Thought to Remember

"Christ died for our sins according to the Scripture, . . . he was buried, . . . he was raised on the third day according to the Scriptures" (1 Corinthians 15:3, 4).

little attention to his own need at this point, but even his request for refreshment may have been not only for himself. As he prepared for his victory cry (v. 30), it may be that he wanted to be sure it was clear and understood. A little moisture in his mouth would help him to speak more loudly and clearly.

29. A jar of wine vinegar was there, so they soaked a sponge in it, put the sponge on a stalk of the hyssop plant, and lifted it to Jesus' lips.

At hand was a container of *vinegar*—a cheap, sour wine possibly present for the soldiers' refreshment. This was not the mixture containing a pain-deadening drug that Jesus had earlier rejected (Mark 15:23). The present meager relief was made available by dipping a *sponge* in the wine, placing it on the tip of a *stalk* from the *hyssop plant*, and lifting it to *Jesus' lips*. Psalm 69:21 had said with prophetic foresight, "They . . . gave me vinegar for my thirst."

30. When he had received the drink, Jesus said, "It is finished." With that, he bowed his head and gave up his spirit.

Jesus had laid down his heavenly glory to come to earth. He had laid down his rights and interests and concerns to serve and teach others. He could say to God his Father, "I have brought you glory on earth by completing the work you gave me" (John 17:4). Now that work—the work of saving lost humanity by bearing "our sins in his body on the tree" (1 Peter 2:24)—was *finished*.

Seldom did a crucified person die in so short a time. For this reason the Roman authorities verified Jesus' death by piercing his side with a spear (John 19:31-37). This also fulfilled Scripture (Psalm 34:20; Zechariah 12:10). The Lord's body was taken from the cross and entombed by loving hands. His friends then dispersed to observe the Sabbath (John 19:38-42).

III. MARY MAGDALENE SEES THE RISEN LORD (JOHN 20:11-18)

The first ten verses of John 20 tell us that Mary Magdalene came to the tomb very early on the first day of the week and found the stone at the entrance of the tomb removed. (Other women accompanied her in this journey, but John does not mention them.) Mary Magdalene hurried to report the apparent grave robbery to Peter and John, who ran to the site and found the tomb empty except for the linen grave clothes. Then the men went home. The other women had also left, and Mary was left there alone—but not alone for long.

A. Angels Inquire (vv. 11-13)

11, 12. But Mary stood outside the tomb crying. As she wept, she bent over to look into the tomb and saw two angels in white, seated where Jesus' body had been, one at the head and the other at the foot.

The *crying* represented here is loud wailing, which might be expected of Mary Magdalene in her present grief and frustration. She had lost the one who had delivered her from a hopeless, demon-possessed existence and given meaning to her life. Now she had come to anoint his body and it was not to be found. Apparently she had not yet examined the interior of the tomb, so *she bent over to look* through the low doorway. There on the shelf designed to accommodate the body were *two* individuals. John tells us they were *angels*, but he does not tell us whether Mary realized that fact or not.

13. They asked her, "Woman, why are you crying?"

"They have taken my Lord away," she said, "and I don't know where they have put him."

Why are you crying? In reply Mary repeated what she had already told Peter and John (v. 2). She had expected to shed tears as she anointed the body. Now she sobbed in total frustration at finding no body to anoint.

They have taken my Lord away. It did not occur to Mary to speak of the "body" or the "remains" of one who had died. This was still the Friend whom she had known and loved.

B. JESUS MAKES HIMSELF KNOWN (vv. 14-16)

14. At this, she turned around and saw Jesus standing there, but she did not realize that it was Jesus.

We can only guess why Mary *turned* away from the angels. Was it a gesture of hopelessness to end the conversation? Did she sense that someone was behind her? Did the angels suddenly vanish from sight?

And why did she not recognize Jesus when she saw him? Were her eyes blurred with tears? Did she see him indistinctly as she turned halfway around? We are reminded, however, that Jesus appeared "in a different form" (Mark 16:12) to Cleopas and his companion on the way to Emmaus, "but they were kept from recognizing him" (Luke 24:16).

While we may question why Mary could not recognize Jesus any sooner than she did, we should stop and ask: are any of us more prepared in times of major stress to recognize the presence of Jesus to help us overcome our difficulties?

15. "Woman," he said, "why are you crying? Who is it you are looking for?"

Thinking he was the gardener, she said, "Sir, if you have carried him away, tell me where you have put him, and I will get him."

Again Mary Magdalene was asked to explain her distress. But this time Jesus' query went a step further: "You're looking for *someone*—who is it?" That question is appropriate to address to anyone in trouble. Healing can come with the finding, not of some *thing*, but of some *one*; and that someone is always Jesus.

The questioner was obviously a friendly person, perhaps, thought Mary, the *gardener*, or caretaker, of the grounds. (This indicates that the resurrected Christ had a common human appearance.) Mary addressed him respectfully as *Sir*. She assumed that he already knew the answer to the question he had just raised: that she was looking for the occupant of the tomb. Perhaps he knew where the body was. Perhaps it was he who *carried* it somewhere else. She would gladly take care of the body if he would simply *tell* her where it was. However, the promise found in Matthew 5:4 was about to be fulfilled: "Blessed are those who mourn, for they will be comforted."

16. Jesus said to her, "Mary."

She turned toward him and cried out in Aramaic, "Rabboni!" (which means Teacher).

The sound of her name spoken in Jesus' familiar tones was all the identification Mary needed! The Good Shepherd, who had laid down his life for his sheep and then taken it again, had called one of his own by name (John 10:3, 14-17). Mary *turned* to look directly at him, instantly calling out the affectionate title: *Rabboni!* While this meant the same as the more common *Rabbi* ("my teacher"), it was a more respectful form of address (in fact, it was often used in referring to God). Thus with audio-visual proof, Mary Magdalene became the first to see Jesus alive after his resurrection.

JESUS SAID TO HER, "MARY"

This is one of the most tender and beautiful passages in the New Testament. When Mary did not recognize the risen Jesus, but mistook him for a gardener, he spoke just one word to her—her own name. It is not hard to imagine the quick gasp of breath and the wonder of recognition in her eyes as she reverently addressed him as *Rabboni!* or "Master!"

Visual for lesson 5

RABBONI!

Today's visual tries to express the love, awe, and complete amazement that were Mary's as she realized she was speaking to the risen Lord.

PRAYER

We praise you, Father, for the privilege of weeping again with those who wept at Jesus' death, and of sharing in their joy at reporting the glorious news of his resurrection. Equip us with the courage and the willingness to tell this life-giving story to others. In Jesus' name. Amen.

Most of us in the intimacy of family life give and receive "pet" names or nicknames. Examples are "Shorty," "Sunshine," "Pug," "Kiddo," and "Cutie." As the years go by, some of us may acquire titles or degrees and may be addressed by many as "Doctor," "Judge," or "Professor." Yet when we go back home and get back in touch with those who are nearest and dearest to us, we are still "Pug" or "Kiddo." And when we hear a certain person call us by one of those names, we know almost immediately who it is.

So it was with Mary. No one else had ever spoken her name in just the way Jesus did. Warm, tender, compassionate—*Mary*. So it will be when we hear our name spoken in the eternal city whose builder and maker is God. We will hear our name as our Savior knows it and, like Mary, we shall know fulfillment, reunion, and ecstasy as we reply, *Master*.

—J. G. V. B.

C. JESUS SENDS MARY (vv. 17, 18)

17. Jesus said, "Do not hold on to me, for I have not yet returned to the Father. Go instead to my brothers and tell them, 'I am returning to my Father and your Father, to my God and your God.'"

The translation of Jesus' command as *do not hold on to me* correctly renders the tense of the verb as it appears in the Greek text, where it implies continual action. (The *New American Standard Bible* reads, "Stop clinging to Me.") Rather than to linger with Jesus, Mary was to go immediately and tell others that he had risen. Much was yet to be done in the days before Jesus ascended into Heaven.

The term *brothers* most likely refers to Jesus' disciples (Matthew 28:7). They were to be the primary witnesses of the good news of his resurrection (Luke 24:47-49). The word signaled the new and special relationship that followers of the living Lord are meant to have with him (Psalm 22:22; Hebrews 2:11, 12).

Since Jesus and his followers are brothers, he can now refer to God as *my Father and your Father*. However, God's relationship to Jesus as his Father is quite different from God's relationship to us in the same capacity. He is the Son of God by nature; we are sons of God by adoption (Romans 8:14-17; Galatians 4:4-7).

18. Mary Magdalene went to the disciples with the news: "I have seen the Lord!" And she told them that he had said these things to her.

In this summary statement is a vital link in the gospel chain from fact to faith, from Jesus to each of us. The first witness to the resurrection is identified as *Mary Magdalene*. In obedience to Jesus she went to his *disciples*, bearing witness that she had *seen the Lord*. Her report was faithful in fact and in word. John, the "disciple whom Jesus loved," kept in memory what Mary told and preserved, through the guidance of God's Spirit, the vivid details. He recorded them that others may read and believe and find eternal life in Christ (John 20:30, 31).

CONCLUSION

"Blessed are your eyes," said Jesus to his disciples, "because they see, and your ears because they hear" (Matthew 13:16). Seeing eyes and hearing ears were exemplary faculties of the disciples and their companions, such as Mary Magdalene. They saw what Jesus did, they heard what he said, and they reported accurately what they observed. It was no ordinary experience that they talked about; it was the knowledge of the one and only Son of God. The object of their seeing and hearing and telling—Jesus, God's Son—is what made their report so effective in serving God and annoying his enemies. Men such as Peter and John, who saw and heard Jesus both before and after his death and resurrection, refused to yield to others' efforts to silence them: "We cannot help speaking about what we have seen and heard" (Acts 4:20). All that they and Mary Magdalene saw and heard in Jesus demands and deserves telling again and again—until he returns.

WHAT DO YOU THINK?

The lesson writer calls John's summary in John 20:18 "a vital link in the gospel chain from fact to faith, from Jesus to each of us." This metaphor illustrates the importance of evangelism. How can we add more links to this chain—as a church and as individuals?

WHAT DO YOU THINK?

We are not eyewitnesses to the resurrection. We cannot, like Mary and Peter and John, speak about "what we have seen and heard" (Acts 4:20) when we tell of Jesus' resurrection. So what can we tell?

Discovery Learning

This page contains an alternate lesson plan emphasizing learning activities. Classes desiring such student involvement will find these suggestions helpful. The next page is a reproducible activity page to further enhance discovery learning.

LEARNING GOALS

This lesson should equip the student to:

1. Recount the details of Jesus' death and his postresurrection appearance to Mary.

2. Explain why the death and resurrection of Jesus must continue to be the focus of the church's message to the world.

3. Suggest one or two ways the student or class can tell in a fresh way the good news of Jesus' resurrection.

INTO THE LESSON

Begin the lesson by asking one or more of the following questions: (1) What does it take for you to accept something as a fact? Explain how you decide that a statement is a fact. (2) What is required for you to accept a prediction as true?

The answers will vary, based as they are on personal experiences and viewpoint. Out of the responses, you should draw a distinction between fact and belief, pointing out that beliefs should be *based on* facts. (A similar activity appears in the student book.)

Observe that today's lesson involves the most "incredible" fact of history: the resurrection of Jesus Christ. Yet, in spite of the unbelievable nature of the report, the evidence is overwhelming. Jesus is alive! We'll look at some of the evidence for this fact in today's lesson.

INTO THE WORD

Begin with a description of crucifixion as a form of capital punishment (a Bible dictionary will be useful). Distinguish it from other forms used in modern times (hanging, beheading, firing squad, electrocution, lethal injection, gas). All of these methods, if done properly, result in instant death, whereas crucifixion was a deliberately slow and brutally painful death. Establish the fact that the Roman soldiers were experts in death. No one came down off a cross alive!

Have a volunteer read John 19:16-18, 28-30. Ask the others to listen while the text is read and list all the details they can about Jesus' death; list these on the chalkboard as students report them after the reading. (Pilate turned Jesus over to the soldiers ["Finally Pilate handed him over to them"], v. 16; the order was "to be crucified," v. 16; the soldiers took him as ordered, v. 16; Jesus carried his own cross—at least for a while, v. 17; he went to Golgotha, v. 17; Jesus was crucified, v. 18; two others were crucified with him, v. 18; Jesus said he was thirsty, v. 28; he was given wine vinegar, vv. 29, 30; Jesus declared his work "finished," v. 30; Jesus yielded up his spirit, v. 30.) Use the comments in the exposition section to note the significance of these details as they are reported.

Ask another volunteer to read John 20:11-18. This tells of Jesus' appearance to Mary Magdalene. Again, have the class list details as the text is read and then summarize. (Mary waited alone outside the tomb, v. 11; she was crying, v. 11; she saw two angels inside the tomb, v. 12; the angels asked her why she was crying, and she said Jesus' body had been moved to an unknown location, v. 13; when Jesus first appeared, Mary did not recognize him, v. 14; Jesus repeated the angels' question, v. 15; Mary thought Jesus was the gardener and asked him to direct her to Jesus' body, v. 15; at the sound of her name, Mary recognized Jesus, v. 16; she addressed Jesus as "Master," v. 16; Jesus would not allow Mary to hold on to him, but told her to go to the disciples, v. 17; Mary obeyed and went to report the resurrection to them, v. 18.)

INTO LIFE

Ask your students to cite some things they believe to be true that they have not verified by personal observation or experience. (They may suggest the existence of historical characters like national heroes; the presence of microscopic organisms like germs, viruses, and bacteria; historical events; etc.). Discuss why we believe in these. (Note the importance of eyewitness testimony.)

Observe that we have no living eyewitnesses today to testify of Jesus' resurrection. But we have the written record of eyewitnesses, like the ones we have noted today. (See also Acts 4:20 and 1 John 1:1-3.) Ask a volunteer to read 1 Corinthians 15:1-11. Note how Paul appealed to eyewitness testimony to plead for the truth of the resurrection. (Use the reproducible activity "Signs of Faith" on the next page to explore additional evidence of the resurrection.)

Divide the class into groups of four or five. Ask each group to develop a way to present the good news of Jesus' death and resurrection in a fresh and meaningful way. (Use the reproducible activity "Spreading the Faith" on the next page to facilitate the discussion.) Share these ideas at the conclusion of your class time.

Signs of Faith

John wrote so people would believe in Jesus Christ. Of course, the most significant set of facts one can believe is that Jesus died for our sins, was buried, and rose again. Read John 19:16—20:18 and list below the evidence John compiles to make his case.

Fulfilled prophecy:

Physical evidence:

Eyewitness testimony:

Spreading the Faith

Having been convinced by the evidence ourselves, we want others to know why they can believe in the resurrection of Jesus. Suppose you were going to start a Bible study in your home through which you hoped to introduce non-Christians to the evidence of the resurrection. How would you promote the study? What would you say to people in inviting them to come?

Now that you know how to invite people, why not start such a study?

JESUS APPEARS TO HIS DISCIPLES

LESSON 6

WHY TEACH THIS LESSON?

A Christian student at a state university was struggling to keep his faith. He was overheard praying before his open Bible: "Lord, I know this is true; help me to believe it."

Surely every Christian can relate to that struggle—the same struggle experienced by the apostle Thomas. In our heart of hearts, we want to believe that Jesus lives. In lieu of logical proof, we want at least enough evidence to produce a psychological certainty.

Sometimes our faith is fragile. These texts, however, are so valuable in confirming Christian convictions that students should be prompted to respond to this lesson with the declaration of Thomas: "My Lord and my God!" Teachers should expect such a positive response.

INTRODUCTION

A. "HE IS RISEN"

We sat enthralled for five hours in the great theater at Oberammergau in Bavaria, watching the village's dramatic presentation of the life and death of Jesus. The production was the renowned "Passion Play," emphasizing Jesus' suffering for our sins. It lingered on a scene not at all found in Scripture—Mary, Jesus' mother, holding and weeping over his body after it was removed from the cross. A hurried acknowledgment of Jesus' resurrection concluded the play, but the lasting impression was not a triumphant one. It lacked the angel's victorious announcement at the empty tomb: "You are looking for Jesus the Nazarene, who was crucified. He has risen! He is not here" (Mark 16:6).

A large segment of the "Christian" world still clings to its crucifixes—artistic representations of Jesus dying or dead on the cross—and bids us weep with them there. Today we join with the Lord's disciples in finding him alive. Let us rejoice in the angel's glorious news: "He has risen! He is not here."

B. LESSON BACKGROUND

Early in his ministry, Jesus spoke of his eventual death and resurrection. He did this using symbolic language that the disciples did not grasp. The first record of such a warning was at the Passover in Jesus' first year of ministry (John 2:19). Another came midway through the Lord's ministry (Matthew 12:40). In the last months of his ministry, and following Peter's Good Confession, Jesus began to speak "plainly" (Mark 8:32) about this. Matthew 16:21 notes that Jesus told the disciples that he "must go to Jerusalem and suffer many things . . . and that he must be killed and on the third day be raised to life." This emphasis is also found in Matthew 17:22, 23; 20:17-19; Mark 8:31; 9:31; 10:32-34; Luke 9:22, 44, 45; 18:31-33. Yet the disciples seem to have rejected so vigorously the idea of Jesus'

DEVOTIONAL READING:
MARK 9:14-24
LESSON SCRIPTURE:
JOHN 20:19-29
PRINTED TEXT:
JOHN 20:19-29

Apr
11

LESSON AIMS

As a result of this lesson, each student should be able to:

1. Summarize the events of the two postresurrection appearances included in today's printed text.

2. Cite several "convincing proofs" for believing in Jesus' resurrection.

3. Give encouragement to someone this week who, like the doubting disciples, needs reassurance regarding his or her faith.

KEY VERSE

Blessed are those who have not seen and yet have believed.
—John 20:29

LESSON 6 NOTES

death that they did not even hear him say he would rise again. In none of them do we find any trace of expectation that this would happen. Only after they saw Jesus alive after the crucifixion and were assured by "many convincing proofs" (Acts 1:3) that he was indeed alive, did they recall his earlier predictions (John 2:22).

The risen Lord appeared first to Mary Magdalene, then to the other women who came early to the tomb (Mark 16:1; Luke 24:1), then to Peter (Luke 24:34; 1 Corinthians 15:5), and then to Cleopas and his friend on the road to Emmaus (Luke 24:13-35). These last two returned to Jerusalem to tell their news to the disciples, whom they found discussing the reports from the women and from Peter.

I. JESUS AND THE DISCIPLES (JOHN 20:19-23)

A. COMING AMONG THEM (v. 19)

19. On the evening of that first day of the week, when the disciples were together, with the doors locked for fear of the Jews, Jesus came and stood among them and said, "Peace be with you!"

Resurrection day was marked by important events from early dawn until *evening*. Ever since then, the *first day of the week* has been special to believers in the risen Lord. Gathered that evening—perhaps in the upper room where they had observed the Passover with Jesus (Luke 22:12, 13)—*the disciples* were concerned for their own safety. *The Jews* who had pursued Jesus to his death could be expected to press their campaign against any of his known companions. They had already tried to turn Rome's officers against the disciples by reporting the resurrection as a case of grave robbery (Matthew 28:11-15). The two from Emmaus and any others in the present gathering (Luke 24:33) must have been carefully identified before they were admitted. Security was of the utmost concern.

However, there was no need (and no possibility!) of securing the place against the risen Lord. Suddenly he *stood among* those who were discussing the reports of his resurrection. His familiar, reassuring greeting of *peace* was most timely.

B. CONVINCING PROOF (v. 20)

20. After he said this, he showed them his hands and side. The disciples were overjoyed when they saw the Lord.

Luke 24:36-43 provides a more detailed account of this incident. At first the disciples were frightened, thinking they were seeing a ghost. To allay these fears Jesus said, "Look at my hands and my feet. It is I myself! Touch me and see; a ghost does not have flesh and bones, as you see I have" (v. 39). Instead of Jesus' feet, John mentions Jesus' *side*, which was pierced by a spear in the hands of a soldier certifying Jesus' death. This is a detail of the crucifixion mentioned only by John (John 19:31-37). Luke also notes that, to remove any lingering doubts the disciples had, Jesus asked for food and ate it in their presence (Luke 24:42).

Many years later the apostle John wrote, "That which was from the beginning, which we have heard, which we have seen with our eyes, which we have looked at and our hands have touched—this we proclaim concerning the Word of life" (1 John 1:1-3). Thus the apostles *saw the Lord*, risen from the dead. Their eyes took in the details; their hands verified that they were not dreaming or hallucinating; their minds accepted the marvelous fact. This was indeed the same Jesus with whom they had walked and worked, and whom they had come to know as Lord and Master. They had reason to be *overjoyed!*

C. COMMISSION GIVEN (vv. 21-23)

Jesus' Great Commission was given on a number of occasions following his resurrection. Here we see him giving it in Jerusalem on the same evening as the

---

WHAT DO YOU THINK?

While "Peace" (Hebrew *shalom*) *was the traditional Jewish greeting, that surely is not the only reason that Jesus' first word to the assembled apostles on resurrection evening was "Peace." The apostles were experiencing profound grief and great fear at the same time. They needed the "peace" that only Jesus could provide. This peace would also be significant to them in the future. In the midst of persecution and turmoil, they would be able to enjoy "the peace of God, which transcends all understanding"* (Philippians 4:7).

What kind of peace does the risen Jesus give you?

resurrection itself (Luke 24:46-49 notes this as well). In Mark 16:14-16 it appears immediately following the account of Jesus' appearances on that day, but without indication of time or place. In Matthew 28:18-20, it is spoken to the apostles on a mountain in Galilee. In Acts 1:7, 8 it is given immediately before Jesus' ascension from the Mount of Olives.

21. Again Jesus said, "Peace be with you! As the Father has sent me, I am sending you."

Here were echoes and reinforcements of Jesus' Passover conversation with the disciples: "Peace I leave with you; my peace I give you. I do not give to you as the world gives. Do not let your hearts be troubled and do not be afraid" (John 14:27). Later Jesus prayed for the disciples: "As you have sent me into the world, I have sent them into the world" (John 17:18).

An awesome responsibility accompanied the comparison of the disciples' commission from Jesus with the commission that *sent* Jesus from Heaven to earth! Their need for inner *peace* and practical courage would apply to matters far more important and more lasting than any immediate fear of trouble from the Jews.

SENT!

In 1803 United States President Thomas Jefferson sent out Meriwether Lewis and William Clark on an expedition to the Pacific coast. They were to cross rivers, deserts, and mountains in a journey of many thousands of miles. They explored territory that no other white men had ever seen. They returned in 1806.

These men and their companions were sent out on a definite mission. The president who dispatched them had authority to do so and exercised it. In the same way, our Lord sent out his apostles—bound for a mission more difficult, but more rewarding and more vital than that of Lewis and Clark. Lewis and Clark wanted to extend the boundaries of their country. Jesus' apostles were to extend the boundaries of the kingdom of God.

Today are we not also sent? Does not the command to go forth to save men from sin also come to us? Jesus' church today is called to send his valiant disciples to every corner of the earth, however distant, difficult, or daunting, to bring under his sway every tribe and nation. We are sent to seek the lost and proclaim good news—just as Jesus was.

—J. G. V. B.

22, 23. And with that he breathed on them and said, "Receive the Holy Spirit. If you forgive anyone his sins, they are forgiven; if you do not forgive them, they are not forgiven."

The act of breathing on the disciples seems to have been a symbolic gesture, reminiscent of God's bestowing on Adam the breath of life so that he became a living soul (Genesis 2:7). During Jesus' evening with the disciples in the upper room, he had promised that after his departure the Counselor (*the Holy Spirit*) would come to them (John 16:7). Now the promise was reaffirmed; however, its fulfillment awaited Jesus' departure into Heaven. Luke 24:49 records Jesus' command that the apostles remain in Jerusalem "until you have been clothed with power from on high," and Acts 1:5 records his promise that this power would come "in a few days." It came on the Day of Pentecost ten days after Jesus' ascension (Acts 2:1-4).

The Spirit-empowered apostles followed Jesus' instruction that "repentance and forgiveness of sins will be preached in his name to all nations, beginning at Jerusalem" (Luke 24:47). On the Day of Pentecost the apostles (Peter specifically) preached Christ in Jerusalem in a way that caused hearers to ask what they could do to gain forgiveness for their sins. Peter's Spirit-led response was, "Repent and be baptized, every one of you, in the name of Jesus Christ for the forgiveness of

HOW TO SAY IT

Aramaic. Air-uh-MAY-ick.
Cleopas. KLEE-uh-pass.
Cornelius. Kor-NEEL-yus.
Didymus. DID-uh-mus.
Emmaus. Em-MAY-us.
Magdalene. MAG-duh-leen or
    Mag-duh-LEE-nee.
shalom (Hebrew). shah-LOME.

DAILY BIBLE READINGS

Monday, Apr. 5—Peace Be With You (John 20:19-23)

Tuesday, Apr. 6—Unless I See (John 20:24-29)

Wednesday, Apr. 7—On the Road to Emmaus (Luke 24:13-27)

Thursday, Apr. 8—Then Their Eyes Were Opened (Luke 24:28-35)

Friday, Apr. 9—Touch Me and See (Luke 24:36-43)

Saturday, Apr. 10—He Opened Their Understanding (Luke 24:44-52)

Sunday, Apr. 11—Jesus Showed Himself Again (John 21:1-14)

your sins. And you will receive the gift of the Holy Spirit. The promise is for you and your children and for all who are far off—for all whom the Lord our God will call" (Acts 2:38, 39).

To *forgive* or *not forgive* an individual's *sins* was not within the judgment of any man—not even the apostles. These men were simply to announce and apply the conditions that were established by divine authority. God would not be bound by apostolic decree; apostolic decree would be bound by God's direction. The apostles were to announce what God had determined. And that is exactly what Peter did at Pentecost.

II. JESUS AND THOMAS (JOHN 20:24-29)

A. SKEPTICAL ABSENTEE (vv. 24, 25)

24. Now Thomas (called Didymus), one of the Twelve, was not with the disciples when Jesus came.

Didymus is the Greek form of the Aramaic name *Thomas*, meaning "twin." Thomas had been chosen by Jesus as *one of the Twelve* who were to share in his ministry and report it—especially his resurrection—as eyewitnesses (Mark 3:14-19; Acts 1:21, 22).

Thomas's absence on the evening of the resurrection is not rebuked, praised, or even explained in Scripture. It did give the others an opportunity to tell of Jesus' appearance to them, and it gave Thomas an opportunity to receive dramatic proof of the resurrection.

There are two other references to Thomas in the Gospels, both of which are found in John's record. One is found in John 11:16, where he believes (mistakenly) that Jesus is going to Bethany to die. Thomas suggests that the Twelve go with Jesus to face his enemies and "die with him." The other reference is in John 14:5, where we find Thomas asking Jesus, "Lord, we don't know where you are going, so how can we know the way?" He asked this in response to Jesus' statement that he was going away to prepare a place for the disciples so that they might join him there one day.

It appears from these incidents that Thomas was someone who desired facts, and, if given sufficient evidence, would give his total commitment to a cause.

25. So the other disciples told him, "We have seen the Lord!" But he said to them, "Unless I see the nail marks in his hands and put my finger where the nails were, and put my hand into his side, I will not believe it."

The Greek verb rendered *told* indicates that this was not a one-time report. Literally, *the other disciples* "kept telling" Thomas, *We have seen the Lord!* Perhaps they spoke to him each day of the next week, trying to convince him that what they were claiming was true. But he had not experienced what they had; why should he share their conviction?

Thomas's reference to *the nail marks* indicates that Jesus was nailed, rather than bound with cords, to the cross. This also tells us that Jesus' wounds left a vivid impression on Thomas. Perhaps he remained at or near the cross until after Jesus died. He may have cringed at the size of the wound that was caused when Jesus' *side* was pierced by a Roman spear. Now Thomas wanted proof that the One whom his companions claimed was alive still bore the marks of his shameful treatment.

B. SECOND APPEARANCE (v. 26)

26. A week later his disciples were in the house again, and Thomas was with them. Though the doors were locked, Jesus came and stood among them and said, "Peace be with you!"

WHAT DO YOU THINK?

Thomas is best known for his doubt, but our lesson writer says, "It appears . . . that Thomas was someone who desired facts, and, if given sufficient evidence, would give his total commitment to a cause." Thomas knew that following Jesus was a life-or-death decision. In many parts of the world believers still appreciate this fact, and every year great numbers of them are martyred for their faith. In places where Christianity is accepted as one choice among many, commitment is often only halfhearted or weak. How can we help modern believers to demonstrate the same kind of commitment as Thomas displayed?

The phrase *a week later* is literally "after eight days" in the Greek text. John seems to have employed the Jewish method of including the first and last days in reporting a given length of time (as musicians count both the first and last notes of the scale in counting an octave). Thus this second meeting with the *disciples*, like the first, was also on the first day of the week. They had time to ponder, discuss, and investigate the events of Resurrection Day before those events were reinforced by this additional appearance.

Repetition characterized most of the details in this second meeting. The place was evidently the same, with the same concern for security. Jesus appeared again without announcement, suddenly standing *among* his friends and bidding them be at *peace*. Of course, there was one important difference. This time, *Thomas was with them*.

JESUS' GREETING OF "PEACE"

John notes that after Jesus' resurrection, he greeted his disciples three times with the salutation, "Peace be with you" (John 20:19, 21, 26). This was likely a form of the Hebrew greeting *shalom*, which means "peace." Certain standard words or phrases are used in many languages as a means of friendly expression when people meet. Usually the French say, *Bonjour*; the Spanish say, *Buenos dias*; the Italians say, *Ciao*; and those in Hawaii say, *Aloha*. Americans may say, "How are you?" "Hello," or just "Hi!" The British often say, "Cheerio," and in Australia it's, "G'day."

Jesus' greeting of *peace* was particularly significant, since he came to make peace "through his blood, shed on the cross" (Colossians 1:20). The angels over Bethlehem had spoken of peace as part of the purpose of his coming to earth (Luke 2:14). Jesus enables us to know peace with God and the peace of God as well. It is significant that in telling Cornelius the meaning of Jesus' coming, Peter said, "You know the message God sent to the people of Israel, telling the good news of peace through Jesus Christ, who is Lord of all" (Acts 10:36).

Peace is part of the greeting at the beginning of every one of Paul's letters. Let us give thanks that in the midst of a warring, restless, agitated world, Jesus not only brings the greeting, but the reality of *peace*! —J. G. V. B.

C. SEEING AND ACKNOWLEDGING (vv. 27, 28)

27. Then he said to Thomas, "Put your finger here; see my hands. Reach out your hand and put it into my side. Stop doubting and believe."

Earlier in his Gospel, John had noted that Jesus "knew all men. He did not need man's testimony about man, for he knew what was in a man" (John 2:24, 25). Thus Jesus knew what Thomas had thought and said in response to the other disciples' report; and Jesus responded to all of it in precise detail.

The word *see* clearly includes more than merely the exercise of one's vision. It is an invitation to learn what one wants to know by firsthand experience. Thomas had demanded to feel and examine the wounds in Jesus' *hands* and side. Now he was free to do so.

We should therefore note that the wounds that had been inflicted on Jesus at the crucifixion remained open and unhealed in his resurrection body. Some have proposed that this may be the case even in Heaven. The renowned hymn writer, Fanny Crosby, suggested this in one of her hymns: "I shall know Him by the print of the nails in His hand" ("My Savior First of All"). John's vision of Heaven does speak of "a Lamb, looking as if it had been slain," standing in the midst of God's attendants around his throne (Revelation 5:6).

28. Thomas said to him, "My Lord and my God!"

Did Thomas actually touch and examine the Lord's hands and side as he had said he must do? If so, it is not recorded. He seems to have been convinced as

PRAYER

Father, we are thankful for the "many convincing proofs" by which the disciples were finally convinced and by which we are persuaded. We pray for courage to declare openly what they declared—that Jesus is the Christ, our Savior and Lord. Amen.

THOUGHT TO REMEMBER

The living Lord, who appeared to his disciples after his resurrection, will appear to all mankind when he comes in judgment.

WHAT DO YOU THINK?

Thomas was convinced of Jesus' resurrection and, in a dramatic moment, cried out, "My Lord and my God!" Recall that dramatic moment in your life when you first acknowledged Jesus as Savior and Lord. What led you to that moment? What can you, our class, or our church do to be more effective at leading others to that realization?

much by Jesus' perfect knowledge of his inmost thoughts as he was by the physical evidence that this was indeed the Lord whom he had followed in Galilee and Judea. Thomas left no doubt as to the deity of God's one and only Son. He was ready to concur with the introductory statement in John's Gospel: "In the beginning was the Word, and the Word was with God, and the Word was God. . . . The Word became flesh and made his dwelling among us" (John 1:1, 14). He was also ready to echo John's conclusion: "These are written that you may believe that Jesus is the Christ, the Son of God, and that by believing you may have life in his name" (John 20:31).

Thomas was not easily convinced of Jesus' resurrection, but when he became fully convinced he was fully committed, never to be shaken. His kind will always be at the core of Christ's ongoing body, his church.

D. BLESSING OF BELIEVING (v. 29)

29. Then Jesus told him, "Because you have seen me, you have believed; blessed are those who have not seen and yet have believed."

You have seen me. As noted earlier, nothing is said here about Thomas's touching and feeling Jesus' resurrected body, as the other disciples had done. That may have been included in what was *seen*, but it is not necessarily so. In any case Thomas was now in the same situation as the rest of the disciples who had seen the risen Lord and were prepared to say so, even at the risk of their lives.

Jesus next turned his attention to those who would hear and accept the apostles' testimony concerning him. These future believers would be especially *blessed!* In his Sermon on the Mount Jesus declared those *blessed* who reflect the character and actions they see in him (Matthew 5:3-12). Here he used the same word to describe those who would believe in him on the basis of the spoken and written Word, without demanding a special revelation to themselves. Don't waste time envying Thomas and the other apostles, or even those latter-day mystics who claim miraculous visions. Jesus' special blessing rests with all those common people whom he welcomes as members of his family when they hear, believe, and follow him as he is revealed in his Word.

CONCLUSION

In describing the reaction of the disciples to Jesus' first appearance to them following his resurrection, John 20:20 says, "The disciples were overjoyed." That sense of celebration swept onward, wave upon wave, over the followers of Jesus as they became convinced that "the Lord has risen indeed" (Luke 24:34). Later, when persecution came upon them, they were persistently and continuously joyous (Acts 5:41)

Followers of sporting events are familiar with "the thrill of victory and the agony of defeat," as successes and failures follow one another in the constant struggle to overcome various kinds of opposition. Something better is available in the blessings that come through steadfast faith in the risen Christ. Victory is offered, not sometimes or to some contestants, but consistently to all who look to Jesus in their wrestling not against flesh and blood, but against the forces of Satan in high places (Ephesians 6:12). They are blessed with the removal of guilt through Jesus' death for their sins at the cross. They are blessed with a clear purpose in life, focused on the goal of eternity with God. They are blessed with a warm family relationship with the children of God. Moreover, they can celebrate all these victories with a joy far greater and more lasting than the celebration of any sports championship, and without any letdown on the following day!

"Rejoice in the Lord always. I will say it again: Rejoice!" (Philippians 4:4).

Discovery Learning

This page contains an alternate lesson plan emphasizing learning activities. Classes desiring such student involvement will find these suggestions helpful. The next page is a reproducible activity page to further enhance discovery learning.

LEARNING GOALS

As a result of this lesson each student should be able to:

1. Summarize the events of the two postresurrection appearances included in today's printed text.

2. Cite several "convincing proofs" for believing in Jesus' resurrection.

3. Give encouragement to someone this week who, like the doubting disciples, needs reassurance regarding his or her faith.

INTO THE LESSON

Before class tape red, yellow, and blue index cards under the chairs where the students will sit, one card per chair. On the red cards, have this question written: "Have you ever feared for your life or for your safety? When?" On the yellow cards print the following: "We all have doubts about what to believe. What is your biggest doubt?" And on the blue cards should be written, "What was the biggest change of mind you ever experienced? What convinced you to change your mind?"

To begin the class, ask the students to retrieve the cards from under their chairs to form three groups by joining others with the same color cards as theirs. Have them discuss the questions on their cards in the groups and to choose which of the stories they will report to the class. Allow five minutes for discussion and then call for reports. (Don't spend too much time on this. You just want to introduce the concepts.)

Observe that the disciples of Jesus, just after the resurrection, experienced all of these: fear, doubt, and a great change of mind. Their experience will help us to put our faith unwaveringly in the risen Lord Jesus Christ!

INTO THE WORD

Raise this question with the class: How would you prove something in a court of law? Legal procedures will be familiar enough to the class on the basis of courtroom dramas on television, both real and fictional.

Next, have a volunteer read John 20:19-25. As the class suggests items, list on the chalkboard the "evidence" for the resurrection, from a legal point of view. The following should be noted: physical evidence: the disciples saw and heard Jesus (19); they saw his wounds, so they knew this was not an impostor (20);

eyewitness testimony: the ten disciples told Thomas about Jesus (25).

(If you have time, expand this activity by having the class examine what Luke 24:36-43 says about this same incident and adding to the evidence list what they find.)

Ask a volunteer to read the rest of today's text, John 20:26-29. Ask the following questions: 1. What evidence did Thomas receive? (The same as the other apostles, vv. 25-27.) 2. What was Thomas's response? (Confession of faith, v. 28.) 3. What blessing did Jesus pronounce? (Blessing on those who accept the testimony of those who did see Jesus, without seeing him for themselves, v. 29.)

Option. Use the reproducible activity page that follows to guide the class in an exploration of today's text.

INTO LIFE

Read Acts 1:1-3 to the class, then ask students to cite as many of the "many convincing proofs" of Jesus' resurrection as they can. (Several have already been noted in this lesson.) Ask, "What is significant about the variety of witnesses and occasions by which Jesus showed himself alive?" (The accumulated evidence becomes impossible to explain away as hallucination, wishful thinking, or any other alternative except that it is the truth.)

Note Thomas's doubt. Remind the class that Thomas's need for conclusive evidence answers our need for evidence today. Thomas was not going to be swayed by sentimentality or wishful thinking. He demanded evidence and was convinced. Jesus really must have been present for Thomas to have made his confession of faith!

Discuss the problem of doubt in the church today. How does this passage help erase our doubts? How does it help us to encourage others who may be doubting? Note how the other apostles continued to fellowship with Thomas even as he was doubting. How is that a model for us when friends or loved ones have doubts? Ask the students to think of people who need some encouragement this week to help them come to a stronger faith. Ask each student to write the name of one person whom he or she could encourage to have greater faith in the risen Lord.

Close with prayer that your students will have greater faith in the risen Jesus, and that they will translate that faith into action by encouraging others to believe.

Doubting Disciples (First Century)

   Thomas is known as the "doubting disciple" because of his refusal to believe in Jesus' resurrection when the others told him they had seen Jesus. Is this fair? After all, weren't all the disciples doubters before they personally saw Jesus? Use the chart below to compare the faith/doubt of Thomas with that of the other ten disciples.

	THE TEN	*THOMAS*
Reaction to Testimony	Luke 24:10, 11	John 20:24, 25
Reaction to Seeing Jesus	Luke 24:36-43	John 20:26-28

   Many people today doubt our testimony about the resurrection, but we are unable to arrange a personal appearance by the risen Lord to erase their doubts. What can we do to give credence to our testimony?

Doubting Disciples (Twentieth Century)

   Even believers are sometimes beset with doubt. What are the most common doubts that come to your mind on occasion?

How do you deal with these doubts?

What would you say or do to reassure another believer who was experiencing doubt?

JESUS, THE BREAD OF LIFE

LESSON 7

WHY TEACH THIS LESSON?

With the fall of the USSR, *Communism* is no longer the threat that it was for some seventy years. *Atheism* has fewer advocates today, it seems, than in some eras. Secular humanism, however, is the "philosophy of choice" for millions. And of all the "isms" embraced by society in this age, *consumerism* (with its first cousin, *materialism*) is perhaps the most perilous.

Earn/spend, buy/pay, charge/owe—these describe the goals and lifestyle of current culture. Carelessly investing life and resources in "food that spoils," the masses desperately need to hear the call of Christ to a higher road: "laying up treasures in heaven." The fruits of materialism will only depreciate, and finally disintegrate. But the "Bread of Life" will sustain and bless with compounding appreciation into eternity. This lesson needs to be taught as never before.

INTRODUCTION

A. WHAT DO WE REALLY NEED?

Along with bright skies, birds' songs, and beautiful blooms, springtime occasionally brings some very turbulent weather. Tornadoes and torrential rains often inflict severe destruction, which, if we allow it to, can teach us a lesson about what we really need in the way of material possessions. When everything is lost and one is at the mercy of others for such basics as food and shelter, he or she comes to appreciate anew what most of us take for granted. "Give us today our daily bread," Jesus taught his followers to pray (Matthew 6:11).

In every age, bread of one kind or another has been a basic food. In fact, the Hebrew word for *bread* is often used for food or sustenance of any sort. The New Testament word for *bread* indicates more definitely a loaf—usually about an inch thick and easily broken and shared—but this word is also used to describe food or nourishment in general. We still use the term in a general sense: we speak of a wage earner as a "breadwinner" or as someone who "keeps bread on the table."

How appropriate it is, then, that bread should appear in our text first as Jesus' miraculous provision for a hungry multitude and then as the symbol of Jesus himself—the necessary and all-sufficient source of life eternal for mankind!

B. LESSON BACKGROUND

Jesus' feeding of the five thousand with five loaves and two small fishes is the only one of his miracles (except his own resurrection) that is recorded by all four Gospel writers (Matthew 14:13-21; Mark 6:30-44; Luke 9:10-17; John 6:1-15). It took place at the height of his popularity in Galilee, when great crowds were following him to witness his miracles and teaching. Matthew relates the event to John the Baptist's death by order of King Herod Antipas. Matthew 14:13 tells us that when Jesus heard of John's death, "he withdrew by boat privately to a solitary place." Luke notes that this was "a town called Bethsaida" (Luke 9:10), located on the northeast shore of the Sea of Galilee.

Despite Jesus' efforts to obtain privacy, multitudes from a wide area followed him. He taught the crowds for the greater part of a day. Then the disciples

DEVOTIONAL READING:
ISAIAH 55:1-11
LESSON SCRIPTURE:
JOHN 6:1-59
PRINTED TEXT:
JOHN 6:10-14, 26, 27, 35-40

LESSON AIMS

This study should help each student to:

1. Tell the story of the feeding of the five thousand, and summarize Jesus' sermon on the bread of life, which followed.

Apr
18

2. Compare the people's desire for literal bread and an earthly kingdom with some of the wrong priorities of people today.

3. Make spiritual matters a higher priority in his or her daily choices.

KEY VERSE

I am the living bread that came down from heaven. If anyone eats of this bread, he will live forever.   —John 6:51

LESSON 7 NOTES

suggested that he send the people home since "it was late in the day" and there was nothing for them to eat (Mark 6:35, 36). Inquiry led to Andrew's discovery of a lad who had "five small barley loaves and two small fish" (John 6:8, 9). That seemed hopelessly inadequate. But Jesus knew what was available and what he would do with it.

I. JESUS FEEDS A MULTITUDE (JOHN 6:10-14)

A. DIRECTING THE CROWD (vv. 10, 11)

10. Jesus said, "Have the people sit down." There was plenty of grass in that place, and the men sat down, about five thousand of them.

The people may have been standing to be near Jesus as he sat to teach (John 6:3). Now Jesus invited them to be more comfortable. Mark 6:39, 40 says that the *grass* was green and that the people sat in "groups of hundreds and fifties." The result may have looked like a spring garden, with plots separated by paths to allow movement among the people. The mention of *men* leaves one to guess how many women and children may have been present. (See Matthew 14:21.)

11. Jesus then took the loaves, gave thanks, and distributed to those who were seated as much as they wanted. He did the same with the fish.

Mark 6:41 says Jesus, "looking up to heaven, . . . gave thanks and broke the loaves. Then he gave them to his disciples to set before the people." The giving of *thanks* was evidently similar to what was done by the head of each family at the Passover. (John 6:4 notes that the Passover "was near.") This was likely a brief prayer, but with great meaning and power. The result was enough food to satisfy those with the healthiest appetites and others who seldom had enough to eat.

B. SAVING THE SURPLUS (vv. 12, 13)

12. When they had all had enough to eat, he said to his disciples, "Gather the pieces that are left over. Let nothing be wasted."

Nothing of God's provision is to be despised, but all of it at all times is to be treated with respect. *Let nothing be wasted* is a divine purpose to be applied most seriously to God's highest creation—persons made in his own image.

13. So they gathered them and filled twelve baskets with the pieces of the five barley loaves left over by those who had eaten.

Most likely each of the *twelve* disciples was supplied with a basket, since the number of *baskets* matches the number of disciples. These *twelve baskets* were then used to collect the remaining *pieces* of the *loaves*. Nothing is said here about any leftover fish, but we know from Mark's account that there was some (Mark 6:43). Where they got the baskets and what they did with all those leftovers is not stated, but it would have been difficult and awkward for the disciples to have kept them. The Greek word used here most often refers to a large, heavy basket, not a small handbasket. Since the Lord's purpose in collecting the fragments was to "let nothing be wasted," and since the group of disciples probably could not have eaten that much food before the fish spoiled, we may surmise that the food was given to some nearby who were in need.

C. REACTING TO JESUS (v. 14)

14. After the people saw the miraculous sign that Jesus did, they began to say, "Surely this is the Prophet who is to come into the world."

The people were mostly Jews. They were familiar with Moses' promise that God would raise up a *Prophet* like himself, who would merit full attention (Deuteronomy 18:15). They saw in Jesus' *miraculous* provision of bread a similarity to Moses' bringing of manna from Heaven to feed the Israelites in the wilderness

WHAT DO YOU THINK?

What would you say to a fellow Christian who said, "It was easy for Jesus to help people; he just did a miracle. But I can't do miracles! All these hurting, hungry, homeless people—and what can I do to help? It's hopeless"?

In your discussion, remind students that we are to be faithful according to what we have, not according to what we don't have. Try to lead the discussion to a frank evaluation of whether we are using all the available technology to full advantage to help the hurting and to win the lost.

(Exodus 16). These people were on the right track in their thinking, but they were wrongly focused. The principal ministry of both Moses and Jesus was to make known God's covenant will for his people. The provision of emergency rations was a relatively small matter in both instances.

Jesus' observers were a prime example of zeal without knowledge (Romans 10:2). They planned to take Jesus by force and make him their kind of king (John 6:15), probably hoping he would lead and supply an army to overthrow the Romans. Knowing their intentions, Jesus escaped into the nearby hills alone.

II. JESUS OFFERS LASTING FOOD (JOHN 6:26, 27)

While Jesus went to the hills, the disciples set out to cross the Sea of Galilee. On the way, they encountered a severe storm, and as they struggled against it Jesus came to them walking on the water. Eventually the disciples landed and entered Capernaum. The next day they were approached by amazed crowds who had followed, looking for Jesus. "When did you get here?" they asked him. Jesus responded to their need rather than to their question.

26. Jesus answered, "I tell you the truth, you are looking for me, not because you saw miraculous signs but because you ate the loaves and had your fill.

Jesus was more interested in addressing the people's motives than their questions about his mobility. In his miracles they had seen, not the power and generous love of God, but only a free meal. They had eaten *loaves* without cost. They liked the sample, and they wanted more.

We may criticize the people's shortsightedness, but is our perception much better than theirs? When we quote Jesus' pattern prayer (Matthew 6:9-13), what gets the emphasis: God's name, kingdom, will, and glory, or our daily bread? And when we hear requests for prayer, do we give more attention to physical needs than we do to Jesus' own request that we pray for laborers to go into the harvest (Matthew 9:38)?

27. Do not work for food that spoils, but for food that endures to eternal life, which the Son of Man will give you. On him God the Father has placed his seal of approval."

The people's energy would have been better spent, Jesus said, in following his teachings than in chasing after a free lunch. Any kind of *food* eventually *spoils* if it is not eaten. And if it is eaten, it builds a physical body that is but temporary. The spiritual nourishment that Jesus came to give *endures to eternal life.*

The benefit Jesus offers must be received as a gift; it can never be earned by man's *work.* So when Jesus told the crowd to *work . . . for food that endures,* he was not suggesting a regimen of works by which they could find *eternal life.* The "works of God" that he was talking about was to put their faith in Jesus as God's Son (vv. 28, 29).

III. JESUS SERVES GOD'S PURPOSE (JOHN 6:35-40)

Jesus had told his hearers to believe in him. But why should they? What credentials did he offer? Could he provide anything similar to Moses' manna from Heaven? Jesus answered that God was providing better bread from Heaven. That caught their attention; it was just what they thought they wanted (John 6:34).

A. HE IS THE BREAD OF LIFE (v. 35)

35. Then Jesus declared, "I am the bread of life. He who comes to me will never go hungry, and he who believes in me will never be thirsty.

Here is the grand, sweeping announcement to which the entire conversation had been leading. It begins as one of Jesus' seven great declarations of his divine

WHAT DO YOU THINK?

The lesson writer suggests that the content of our prayers demonstrates whether or not we allow physical and material concerns to override spiritual ones. How can we put more emphasis on spiritual matters?

Observe the role of the "model prayer" (Matthew 6:9-13) and Paul's prayers recorded in Ephesians 1:15-23; 3:14-21 as patterns to follow in our prayers.

WHAT DO YOU THINK?

Jesus as the bread of life assures us that if we come to him, we will never hunger. What kind of hunger does Jesus satisfy? How do we develop such a hunger in ourselves and others?

Consider Matthew 5:6; Philippians 4:11-13; 1 Timothy 6:6-8 in your discussion.

HOW TO SAY IT

Antipas. AN-tih-pus.
Bethsaida. Beth-SAY-uh-duh.
Canaan. KAY-nun.
Capernaum. Kuh-PER-nay-um.
Nazareth. NAZ-uh-reth.
Zacchaeus. Zack-KEE-us.

being. Others, equally bold, are: "I am the light of the world" (John 8:12; 9:5); "I am the gate" (John 10:7, 9); "I am the good shepherd" (John 10:11, 14); "I am the resurrection and the life" (John 11:25); "I am the way and the truth and the life" (John 14:6); and "I am the true vine" (John 15:1).

Jesus was offering himself to the people: *the bread of life.* The two promises that follow emphasize one combined thought. Coming to Christ and believing in Christ belong together—in acceptance, trust, commitment, and action. One finds in him a satisfaction of spiritual needs that can come through no other source. Thus is fulfilled the promise of Matthew 5:6: "Blessed are those who hunger and thirst for righteousness, for they will be filled." Their need will not go unmet. However, as Jesus proceeded to point out, some cannot claim that promise.

B. NOT ALL ACCEPT HIM (vv. 36, 37)

36. But as I told you, you have seen me and still you do not believe.

Seeing is not always believing. In verses 26 and 27 are Jesus' earlier words of rebuke to those who had seen his miracles but had rejected his message. These people were not interested in learning and adjusting to the truth, but chose rather to twist the truth so as to support their own agenda. Let us pray that we may not yield to the same temptation.

In contrast to those unbelieving who have *seen* are those who are blessed for believing, even though they have not seen (John 20:29). That is good company in which to be included.

37. All that the Father gives me will come to me, and whoever comes to me I will never drive away.

The bad news has been heard; now for the good news. In all places and all times there are those who with honest hearts hear the message of Christ, believe it, and commit themselves to following him. *The Father* knows in advance who will accept Christ and follow him faithfully. On this basis God gives such individuals to Jesus. That this does not do away with an individual's choice is clear from Jesus' reference to *whoever comes to me.* Each person must choose whether or not to be a part of what the Father has given to his Son. Watch the rich young ruler go sadly with his wealth rather than gladly with Christ (Mark 10:17-22). Watch Zacchaeus make the opposite choice to part with his wealth and make Jesus his Master (Luke 19:8-10). Mark the destiny of those who change their minds and turn away after having followed Christ for a time (Hebrews 6:4-6).

C. HE DOES GOD'S WILL (vv. 38-40)

38. For I have come down from heaven not to do my will but to do the will of him who sent me.

The only way we can understand or explain Jesus is by accepting his bold claim: *I have come down from heaven.* Jesus pressed that claim five times in this context alone (vv. 33, 38, 50, 51, 58). The purpose of his coming provides a second emphasis in the Gospel of John: Jesus' commitment *to do the will of him who sent me.* This was more important to him than eating: "My food," said Jesus, "is to do the will of him who sent me and to finish his work" (John 4:34).

39. And this is the will of him who sent me, that I shall lose none of all that he has given me, but raise them up at the last day.

This provides another aspect of Jesus' concern to "let nothing be wasted," spoken earlier of the miraculously multiplied loaves (v. 12). Here his emphasis is on people. This theme is sounded throughout the Bible, as in Ezekiel 33:11: "As surely as I live, declares the Sovereign Lord, I take no pleasure in the death of the wicked, but rather that they turn from their ways and live." Compare

WHAT DO YOU THINK?

In verse 38 Jesus emphasized his commitment to doing his Father's will. How can we demonstrate a similar commitment? What would happen if every Christian displayed a Christlike commitment to obeying the Father?

What do the following passages suggest as helps in maintaining such commitment? (Matthew 4:1-11; Luke 4:1-12; Luke 22:40, 42).

2 Peter 3:9: "The Lord is . . . not wanting anyone to perish, but everyone to come to repentance."

However, the Father's *will* is not always fulfilled, because some are not willing to follow it. Some choose the path destined for punishment and will therefore perish. Even among Jesus' disciples was one who insisted on his own and opposite way: "While I was with them, I protected them and kept them safe by that name you gave me. None has been lost except the one doomed to destruction so that Scripture would be fulfilled" (John 17:12).

The last day evidently refers to the time of Christ's coming in glory and judgment, when the dead in Christ will rise first and living saints will be caught up to meet and be with him (1 Thessalonians 4:16, 17).

40. For my Father's will is that everyone who looks to the Son and believes in him shall have eternal life, and I will raise him up at the last day."

Here the object of the divine *will* is described as *everyone* (each individual) rather than "all" (the entire group of the saved), as in verse 37. *Eternal life* is for those who both see and believe, in contrast to those whose seeing does not produce belief (v. 36). Attentive looking at God's revelation, and believing on the basis of what is seen, is required.

No matter how long the great *last day* may be delayed according to our calendar, the time will be as nothing from God's perspective (2 Peter 3:8). Jesus' promise is totally dependable.

IV. JESUS IS THE TRUE BREAD (JOHN 6:47-51)

Verses 41-46 tell us that some who knew Jesus' family in Nazareth were inclined to doubt that he came from Heaven. Their problem could be solved only by recognizing Jesus for what the evidence showed him to be—the Son of God.

A. THE SOURCE OF LIFE (vv. 47, 48)

47, 48. I tell you the truth, he who believes has everlasting life. I am the bread of life.

I tell you the truth, as already noted (see page 254), introduces a statement of utmost importance. Again Jesus insists on the personal application of his message. Believing, or faith, is at the core of any claim to God's eternal gifts. Faith has always been the key identifying mark in all God's heroes (Hebrews 11).

B. SUPERIOR TO MANNA (vv. 49-51)

49, 50. Your forefathers ate the manna in the desert, yet they died. But here is the bread that comes down from heaven, which a man may eat and not die.

The eager eaters in Jesus' audience had earlier referred to how their *forefathers* had been fed by *manna in the desert.* They had asked Jesus, "What miraculous sign then will you give that we may see it and believe you?" (John 6:30, 31). Jesus pointed to the obvious fact that the manna eaters had died before or soon after they reached Canaan.

Moses had summarized the people's experience in these words: "He [God] humbled you, causing you to hunger and then feeding you with manna, to teach you that man does not live on bread alone but on every word that comes from the mouth of the Lord" (Deuteronomy 8:3). Jesus himself was the Word of God who came *from heaven* to be the *bread* of life. He provides life that does not end. He could truly say, "I am the resurrection and the life. He who believes in me will live, even though he dies; and whoever lives and believes in me will never die" (John 11:25, 26).

51. I am the living bread that came down from heaven. If anyone eats of this bread, he will live forever. This bread is my flesh, which I will give for the life of the world."

The visual for lesson 7 contrasts Jesus, "the bread of life," with the manna gathered by the Israelites in the wilderness.

WHAT DO YOU THINK?

The Jews were proud that their ancestors in the wilderness had eaten manna, but Jesus declared himself to be better than that manna. In what are people trusting today? How can we demonstrate that Jesus can satisfy more completely than anything else?

PRAYER

We thank you, our Father, for Jesus, the bread of life eternal. Thank you for the abundance of your grace, which is limited only by our unwillingness to receive it. Give us an ever-increasing appetite for Jesus and the life he provides. In his name. Amen.

THOUGHT TO REMEMBER

Lord, evermore give us the living Bread—Jesus himself for our nourishment and growth, for now and eternity.

DAILY BIBLE READINGS

Monday, Apr. 12—*There Is a Boy Here* (John 6:1-15)

Tuesday, Apr. 13—*"It Is I; Don't Be Afraid"* (John 6:16-21)

Wednesday, Apr. 14—*Give Us This Bread Always* (John 6:22-34)

Thursday, Apr. 15—*I Am the Bread of Life* (John 6:35-51)

Friday, Apr. 16—*This Bread Came Down From Heaven* (John 6:52-59)

Saturday, Apr. 17—*Israel Was Given Bread From Heaven* (Nehemiah 9:6-15)

Sunday, Apr. 18—*Mortals Ate the Bread of Angels* (Psalm 78:17-29)

Jesus built his whole discussion toward the climax found in this verse. The miracle of the loaves and fishes was not an end in itself; it was only a prelude to a greater spiritual reality to come. The *bread* of life, or *living bread . . . from heaven*, is Jesus himself. Just as any food must be eaten, digested, and assimilated to build one's physical body, so Jesus—his teaching, life, and personality—must be assimilated as a part of oneself to build eternal life.

One startling fact was now added: the bread Jesus offers is not only himself; it is his *flesh!* The fleshly body in which he lived (John 1:14) was to be offered as a sacrifice on the cross. His body became the gift, the basis of *life* for the believer—in time and eternity. This truth is etched in the believer's mind and memory at the Lord's table, where we recall Jesus' words at the breaking and presenting of the bread: "This is my body given for you; do this in remembrance of me" (Luke 22:19).

BREAD AND LIFE

Bread is one of the most basic necessities of life. Prepared and served in various ways, bread appears almost everywhere. One sees it in the shape of long, thin loaves in France, in a black color in Russia, and in a somewhat heavy white variety in England.

Jesus' description of himself as "the bread of life" (John 6:35) is one to which most anyone can relate. He compared the "bread" of his salvation with the manna that the Hebrews ate during their wilderness wandering. Jesus also came down from Heaven (v. 38), but with the "true bread" (v. 32). Whereas the Hebrews died, though they had eaten "bread from heaven" (v. 31), anyone who eats the bread Jesus provides "will live forever" (v. 51). Jesus also linked the provision of this bread to his death on the cross (v. 51). We recognize this link through the Lord's Supper, in which we partake of the bread that symbolizes Jesus' body given "for the life of the world" (v. 51).

We are to pray for our "daily bread" and eat it, as a way to continue our mortal life. Jesus gives us a bread with immortal life in it: "If anyone eats of this bread, he will live forever."

"We taste thee, O Thou living Bread,
    And long to feast upon Thee still;
We drink of Thee, the Fountainhead,
    And thirst our souls from Thee to fill."
                  (Anonymous)   —J. G. V. B.

CONCLUSION

Many who want to play a particular sport never get into the game. They are cut from the squad before the team takes the field. John 6 is the account of a similar "cut" that took place among prospective followers of Christ. Thousands came, enjoyed eating of the food Jesus provided, and wanted more of the same. But the number dwindled rapidly during the follow-up coaching sessions; and when Jesus pressed the matter of accepting him as the source of life, most of them left. The idea of eating his flesh and drinking his blood was too much for them, and they were not ready to consider words that were "spirit" and "life" (John 6:63).

The twelve apostles, though, stayed on. There was still much about Jesus that they did not understand, but faced with the alternatives they said, "Lord, to whom shall we go? You have the words of eternal life. We believe and know that you are the Holy One of God" (John 6:68, 69). That should be enough to reassure any of us.

Discovery Learning

This page contains an alternate lesson plan emphasizing learning activities. Classes desiring such student involvement will find these suggestions helpful. The next page is a reproducible activity page to further enhance discovery learning.

LEARNING GOALS

This study should help each student to:

1. Tell the story of the feeding of the five thousand, and summarize Jesus' sermon on the bread of life, which followed.

2. Compare the people's desire for literal bread and an earthly kingdom with some of the wrong priorities of people today.

3. Make spiritual matters a higher priority in his or her daily choices.

INTO THE LESSON

On the chalkboard or on a large poster write *Hunger.* Ask the class to suggest characteristics of hunger. Write down these suggestions under the heading. Then write the headings *Physical* and *Spiritual* next to the word *Hunger.* Ask the class how each item you noted earlier applies to physical and/or spiritual hunger. Note these under the appropriate headings and next to the items listed under *Hunger.* You can expect such responses as pain, lethargy, weakness, and hallucinations. These are obvious in the physical realm; how does spiritual hunger induce such problems in a figurative way?

Make the transition to today's Bible study by noting the devastating effects of hunger on the human body. Observe that, in today's lesson, we'll see that the risks of spiritual hunger are even more frightening.

INTO THE WORD

Ask in advance for four volunteers who will read today's text: John 6:10-14; 26, 27; 35-40; 47-51. Ask the first reader to read John 6:10-14 now. (This is the only miracle, outside of Jesus' own resurrection, that is cited in all four of the Gospels. If you have time, have the records of Matthew, Mark, and Luke read also to provide fuller details of this miracle. You may use the reproducible activity on the next page to facilitate a four-Gospel study of the feeding of the five thousand.)

Note the background events (see pages 285, 286); then ask a volunteer to provide a very brief summary of the feeding of the five thousand. Discuss the purpose of the miracle (meet the immediate need of hunger; demonstrate Jesus' power/authority—see v. 14). Note verse 15 (not in the printed text). The people saw only the physical and wanted to exploit Jesus' power by making him an earthly king; but Jesus shunned their efforts.

Ask your second reader to read verses 26 and 27. Provide background to connect this event with verses 10-15. Discuss, "Why did Jesus seem to be rebuking the crowd in this text?" (They were missing the point, focusing on physical bread.) Discuss how this still happens today. Ask, "How much of the trouble in the world is a result of people's pursuit of what satisfies their physical appetites instead of what satisfies their spiritual hunger?"

Ask your third reader to read John 6:35-40. This is the heart of Jesus' message. Divide the class into groups of five or six and ask each group to paraphrase this text. Give them five minutes, then ask each group to read its paraphrase. Compare the results and make any necessary comments based on the lesson exposition.

Note that this was not an easy sermon for the people to hear. Many were offended. But Jesus did not back down. Have your final reader now read verses 47-51. Ask your small groups to compare this section with verses 35-40. Ask half of the groups to list new information and the other half to list information that is repeated from the earlier section. Allow five minutes and then ask for reports.

INTO LIFE

Ask, "Wouldn't it have been great to hear Jesus give this sermon? How do you think you would have reacted if you had been there?" Discuss briefly, then read verses 60-70. Most of the people abandoned Jesus after this, but the Twelve knew that he had "the words of eternal life."

Challenge the class, "This sermon presents a crisis for each of us. We, too, have to choose how we will respond to Jesus. Some of us have been too focused on material things: our jobs, money, our homes and cars and boats. Maybe we've been too focused on our families, wanting them to be happy and comfortable but not giving attention to their spiritual needs." Have a time of silent prayer, asking each student to ask God's help to make spiritual matters a higher priority in his or her daily choices.

After a few moments, point out that this text presents a crisis for our church too. The world, by and large, has abandoned the church, but the church still has Jesus' "words of eternal life." Discuss ways your church can reach out with renewed vigor to help your community hear the words of life.

Four Reports

Outside of the resurrection of Jesus, the feeding of the five thousand is the only miracle recorded in all four Gospels. On the chart below, look at the list of events associated with this miracle. Cite the verse or verses of each Gospel that tells of each event in the appropriate column.

EVENT	MATTHEW 14:13-21	MARK 6:30-44	LUKE 9:10-17	JOHN 6:1-15
Jesus and the disciples cross the lake, but a crowd follows.				
Jesus teaches the crowd.				
Jesus heals the sick in the crowd.				
The disciples urge Jesus to dismiss the crowd to go buy food.				
Jesus tells the disciples to feed the crowd.				
The disciples say they don't have enough unless they buy some.				
Philip is asked about buying food.				
Philip says they don't have enough money.				
Jesus tells the disciples to see how much food they have.				
Andrew brings a boy to Jesus.				
The boy gives his small lunch to Jesus.				
The people are told to sit down.				
Jesus blesses the loaves and fish.				
Jesus gives food to the disciples to give to the crowd.				
Everyone eats as much as he or she wants.				
Jesus commands that the leftovers be gathered.				
Twelve basketfuls of leftovers are collected.				

TRUTH THAT SETS PEOPLE FREE

LESSON 8

WHY TEACH THIS LESSON?

Pontius Pilate would feel at home among the humanists and hedonists who proliferate here at the close of the twentieth century. He and they could wonder together, "What is truth?" Millions of pseudo-sophisticates declare that truth is relative and situational, not absolute and unconditional. Such phony philosophers also are confused about *freedom*, supposing that it means being free from responsibility and from accountability.

The teaching of Jesus Christ can clear up the confusion. Absolute truth is whatever God says about something, and true freedom is spiritual liberation from slavery to sin. The text under consideration in today's lesson can stimulate right thinking among students about the truth personified by Jesus, and about the freedom made possible by his supreme sacrifice.

INTRODUCTION

A. WHAT DO YOU MEAN—"FREE"?

What is freedom? Try asking the kids.

"It's when you get into the movies without having to pay any money."

"It's when there's a lot of snow and no school."

"It's like when the guy in Jesus' story got his money from his dad and went a long way from home to do whatever he wanted to."

"It's like when slaves got away from their masters, and couldn't be brought back to be slaves anymore."

"It's when some dictator is thrown out of office, and the people get to vote for the leader they want."

However, the greatest liberty is enjoyed by numerous individuals who don't have any of the "freedoms" just described. They have a living relationship with Christ Jesus, who is the truth that sets people free. Because of his love, they choose to live in a better way than any law could compel them to live.

B. LESSON BACKGROUND

The autumn Feast of Tabernacles brought Jesus to Jerusalem some six months before his crucifixion. It was a time of tension and controversy. The ruling hierarchy of the Jews had already determined that the troublesome preacher from Nazareth must be destroyed. Other Jews from many places, in Jerusalem for the feast and hearing Jesus for the first time, were astonished and impressed by him. Many were even inclined to believe in him as the Christ (John 7:31; 8:30).

John 8:12-59 tells of a discussion that took place soon after Jesus declared himself to be the water of life (John 7:37-44; compare with John 4:10-15). Such a bold assertion created sharp differences of opinion among his hearers. A similar result could be expected from the discourse that followed.

DEVOTIONAL READING:
PSALM 51:1-9

LESSON SCRIPTURE:
JOHN 8:12-59

PRINTED TEXT:
JOHN 8:12, 21-36

LESSON AIMS

After this lesson students should be able to:

1. Summarize Jesus' sermon at the Feast of Tabernacles.

2. Compare and contrast what Jesus said about truth and freedom with the way today's world views these concepts.

3. Tell how to counter the world's false views with the truth found in Jesus and the Scriptures.

Apr 25

KEY VERSE

If you hold to my teaching, you are really my disciples. Then you will know the truth, and the truth will set you free.
—John 8:31, 32

WHAT DO YOU THINK?

Some have suggested that Jesus used the lighting of the great lamps in the temple during the Feast of Tabernacles as an opportunity to declare himself to be the true light of the world. We should be able to find some apt metaphors to contrast Jesus with the things of the world and demonstrate that he is far greater. The Christian football player might suggest that Jesus is the real "goal" in life. The Christian politician might suggest that Jesus is the ultimate "ruler." The Christian teacher can show that Jesus is the "Master Teacher." What symbols can you suggest to demonstrate the superiority of Jesus today?

Perhaps each of your students can suggest a metaphor particularly appropriate to his or her profession or situation in life. Discuss strategies for sharing these metaphors effectively.

I. THE LIGHT OF THE WORLD (JOHN 8:12)

12. When Jesus spoke again to the people, he said, "I am the light of the world. Whoever follows me will never walk in darkness, but will have the light of life."

Jesus began this discourse with another of his great "I am" declarations with which he had already shaken the religious community. Some commentators suggest that the lighting of four huge golden lampstands in the temple during the Feast of Tabernacles provided an appropriate background for his reference to himself as *the light of the world*.

From the dawn of creation, light has been recognized as essential to life. The glory of God is essentially light (1 Timothy 6:16). The contrast between light and darkness is symbolic of the contrast between knowledge and ignorance, joy and sorrow, and good and evil. John 1:4 says of the eternal Word who became flesh in the person of Jesus, "In him was life, and that life was the light of men."

The Jewish establishment was not pleased with the idea of Jesus' being light for the entire *world*. They expected the Messiah to lead and serve the Jews, opposing and conquering their enemies. Yet Jesus expected his followers to reflect the light they found in him without limitations of any kind. To them also he said, "You are *the light of the world*" (Matthew 5:14).

There is a twofold significance to living by *the light of life* rather than having to *walk in darkness*. First, he who walks in the light can see where he is going and can travel safely. Jesus is the ideal guide, providing continual light to lead our way. No one can stumble or be lost while following him.

Second, he who walks in the light will be living daily according to Jesus' teaching and example. "Whoever claims to live in him must walk as Jesus did. Dear friends, I am not writing you a new command but an old one, which you have had since the beginning. This old command is the message you have heard" (1 John 2:6, 7).

Pharisees in the temple charged Jesus with offering unsupported testimony about himself. In response Jesus pointed to the testimony of his Father, as seen in his words and in the miracles that he enabled Jesus to do. However, as Jesus pointed out, the Pharisees did not know his Father (John 8:13-20).

II. FURTHER DISCUSSION (JOHN 8:21-30)

A. WORDS OF WARNING (vv. 21-24)

21. Once more Jesus said to them, "I am going away, and you will look for me, and you will die in your sin. Where I go, you cannot come."

Jesus knew that his time was short. Only the presence of a friendly crowd prevented the Jewish establishment from arresting him immediately—that and the fact that "his time had not yet come" (John 7:30; 8:20; see also 7:6, 44; 8:59). Jesus would choose the time and would arrange the circumstances for his going to the cross. He had spoken earlier of going to a place where the Jews could not find him, and they had speculated that he might be going to foreign lands to teach among the scattered Jews and their Gentile neighbors (John 7:34-36).

In bold contrast to Jesus' words *where I go, you cannot come* is his promise to his followers. He told them he was going to prepare a place for them and would come again to receive them. "You know the way to the place where I am going. … I am the way and the truth and the life. No one comes to the Father except through me" (John 14:4, 6).

22. This made the Jews ask, "Will he kill himself? Is that why he says, 'Where I go, you cannot come'?"

Just how would Jesus arrange his own departure so that he could not be found or followed? There was in his comment a note of finality that suggested death to his hearers. They were right to think of death, but it would not be at Jesus' own hand as they supposed.

23. But he continued, "You are from below; I am from above. You are of this world; I am not of this world.

Jesus said they misunderstood him because they did not have the proper frame of reference by which to know—as we say today—"where he was coming from." Their worldly interests, ambitions, and pride clearly marked the Pharisees as drawing from earthly sources and acting on an earthly level. In contrast, Jesus was *from above*, fully committed to the will and purpose of his Father.

24. "I told you that you would die in your sins; if you do not believe that I am the one I claim to be, you will indeed die in your sins."

These scoffers would *die* in their *sins* because they did not *believe* in the only one who could save them from their sins. They were in the position of being "condemned already" because of their unbelief (John 3:18).

The phrase *the one I claim to be* is not in the original Greek text but is supplied because the linking verb seems to need a complement. The statement says only, *if you do not believe that I am.* "'Believe I am' what?" In the previous verse Jesus had said, "I am from above," so "from above" might be the proper understanding. He had also said, "I am not of this world," so perhaps "not of this world" is the proper complement. In verse 12 he said, "I am the light of the world." Should we read "light of the world" here? The New International translators apparently tried to supply a complement that would be faithful to both the meaning of the passage (that Jesus had made claims that they needed to accept) and to the rather vague tone of the passage (as the verb without any complement is vague).

What is lost, however, is the clever play on words. The expression sounds much like God's answer to Moses, "I am who I am" (Exodus 3:14). It anticipates Jesus' later and more controversial claim: "Before Abraham was born, I am!" (v. 58). Salvation from sin is possible only through a complete confidence and trust in him who is the way, the truth, and the life, and whose claims are securely established by his resurrection from the dead: "If Christ has not been raised, your faith is futile; you are still in your sins" (1 Corinthians 15:17).

B. WORDS OF SELF-REVELATION (vv. 25-27)

25. "Who are you?" they asked.

"Just what I have been claiming all along," Jesus replied.

Baffled by Jesus' refusal to identify himself more clearly, the questioners demanded (literally), "You, who are you?" Again Jesus chose not to give a brief answer in plain words, lest they mistake the short phrase for the whole truth and never learn what they really needed to know. Instead, he chose to provide the means by which they could discover the truth for themselves, if they were willing. Besides, it was not yet time for Jesus to provide his enemies with a quotable declaration of his deity. That would come later when he was ready to die for what they would call "blasphemy."

All along (that is, throughout his ministry) Jesus had been providing evidence that convinced his earliest followers that he was the Christ, the Son of the living God (Matthew 16:16). This continually drew others into the circle of faith. He had claimed to be the water of life, the bread of life, and the light of the world. Let these questioners draw their own conclusions from the evidence available to everyone else.

26. "I have much to say in judgment of you. But he who sent me is reliable, and what I have heard from him I tell the world."

WHAT DO YOU THINK?

When the woman at the well mentioned the Messiah, Jesus told her plainly that he was the Messiah (John 4:26). But with the Pharisees he was much less clear, forcing the hearers to think carefully about his words. Of course, the woman at the well was ready to accept Jesus as the Christ; the Pharisees were not. How can we know when to give someone a direct answer about Christ and when we need to be more cautious or force them to think more carefully?

Accepting the Lord is a matter of both mind and heart. How do we know the right mix of emotional and intellectual appeal?

DAILY BIBLE READINGS

Monday, Apr. 19—"I Am the Light of the World" (John 8:12-20)

Tuesday, Apr. 20—Many Believed in Him (John 8:21-30)

Wednesday, Apr. 21—If You Continue in My Word (John 8:31-38)

Thursday, Apr. 22—Abraham's Children Do the Works of Abraham (John 8:39-47)

Friday, Apr. 23—Whoever Keeps My Word Will Never See Death (John 8:48-59)

Saturday, Apr. 24—Live As Children of Light (Ephesians 5:1-14)

Sunday, Apr. 25—Let Your Light and Your Truth Lead Me (Psalm 43:1-5)

WHAT DO YOU THINK?

As disciples we must "hold to" Jesus' teachings. What are you doing that you would say is holding to his teaching?

Jesus knew that what he said and did would disturb and offend many. However, he also knew that he was not acting alone; God had *sent* him to accomplish a particular task. Any unpopular deeds or words were a part of what the righteous and unchangeable Father in Heaven had commissioned him to do and to say for the salvation of mankind.

27. They did not understand that he was telling them about his Father.

The questioners had heard Jesus' insistence that his message had its source in the One who sent him; but they did not, or would not, recognize that he was talking about God, and that his message was from God. The Pharisees revealed much about themselves by their slowness to recognize who Jesus is.

C. WORDS OF PROMISE (vv. 28-30)

28. So Jesus said, "When you have lifted up the Son of Man, then you will know that I am the one I claim to be and that I do nothing on my own but speak just what the Father has taught me.

The discussion continued, with Jesus speaking in parable-like terms and his hearers still not understanding what he was talking about. If they had understood, they likely would have demanded his death—at that very moment!

The subject of *the Son of Man*'s being *lifted up* was to recur some six months later during Jesus' last week in Jerusalem. At that time he said, "I, when I am lifted up from the earth, will draw all men to myself." John adds, "He said this to show the kind of death he was going to die" (John 12:32, 33). Jesus' enemies would cause him to be "lifted up" on the cross to die, but that was part of the eternal plan of God (Acts 2:23). Through Jesus' death and resurrection salvation for lost mankind would become possible.

The statement *then you will know that I am the one I claim to be* indicates that Jesus' death and resurrection would demonstrate that the controlling hand of God was in all Jesus had said and done. (Again, as in verse 24, *the one I claim to be* is not found in the Greek text.) His critics would have all the evidence needed to conclude that Jesus was who he claimed to be, that he was, indeed, the divine Son of God. If not, they would forfeit any hope of salvation (Acts 4:10-12).

29. "The one who sent me is with me; he has not left me alone, for I always do what pleases him."

God was *the one* who had both sent his Son into the world and constantly attended and empowered Jesus in his ministry. That truth would later be stated in even bolder terms: "I and the Father are one" (John 10:30). That is a source of contention to unbelievers, then and now. It was this very claim that moved the Sanhedrin to pronounce the death sentence on Jesus (Matthew 26:63-66).

Now, as then, Jesus' claims make it impossible for anyone to be neutral or indifferent in regard to Jesus. The serious thinker must either believe and follow him, or disbelieve and reject him.

30. Even as he spoke, many put their faith in him.

Decision time had come, and a significant number decided in favor of Jesus. We are not told how many *put their faith in him*, or how the fact that they did so was expressed. At any rate, there were enough to pose a threat to the Jewish leaders in their determination to seize and do away with Jesus. They did not dare move against him when too many people were around.

III. THE WAY TO FREEDOM (JOHN 8:31-36)

A. BY KNOWING THE TRUTH (vv. 31-33)

31. To the Jews who had believed him, Jesus said, "If you hold to my teaching, you are really my disciples.

The previous discussion had been heavily influenced by the Pharisees' opposition to Jesus. Now Jesus addressed *the Jews who had believed him*. His teaching is appropriate to any stage of a believer's spiritual development. The beginning of discipleship, like the beginning of physical life, must be followed by nourishment and growth if it is to accomplish its purpose. It is one thing to follow Jesus with an initial burst of enthusiasm; it is another to *hold to* his *teaching*. Following Jesus is a never-ending learning process.

32. *"Then you will know the truth, and the truth will set you free."*

Here is an important step in the pathway of discipleship. The way of freedom, Jesus declared, is an intimate acquaintance with him who is the *truth* (John 14:6). Truth is much more than mere facts or data; it is a Person. Pilate's cynical question, "What is truth?" (John 18:38), is answered by a *who*, and the who is Jesus.

Jesus' linking of truth with being *free* is significant, especially in today's world where freedom is often equated with not adhering to any kind of absolute truth. The knowledge of Christ frees one from ignorance, superstition, and bad habits; but more to the point, it frees from the slaveries of pride, self, and sin. These latter enslavements are more binding than any chains. Consider Paul and Silas, who did not let the restrictions of a maximum security prison silence their praise (Acts 16:25). In reality, they were free before their chains were broken!

Without Christ, on the other hand, the pursuit of philosophical "truth" (even within the mysteries of Scripture) can become an enslavement to self-centered pride. Paul writes of those who are "always learning but never able to acknowledge the truth" (2 Timothy 3:7).

33. *They answered him, "We are Abraham's descendants and have never been slaves of anyone. How can you say that we shall be set free?"*

This question surprises us if it came from the believers whom Jesus urged toward a more mature discipleship (v. 31). Apparently the Pharisees were still present and were listening as Jesus addressed the new believers. We know Jesus was addressing them when he said that they were intending to kill him (vv. 37, 40) and called them children of the devil (vv. 38, 41, 44). He stated clearly that they had refused to believe him (vv. 45, 46). John's use of the term "the Jews" (vv. 48, 52, 57) is a reference to the disbelieving Jewish leaders, not to Jews in general. Probably it was these same leaders who challenged Jesus' statement, even though Jesus had been speaking to the ones who believed in him.

Never been slaves of anyone? No Jew could be so ignorant of his national history as to deny Israel's slavery in Egypt, captivity in Babylon, or current subjection to Rome. The Pharisees' claim reflected a fierce insistence that *Abraham's descendants* might be enslaved politically, but they would never become voluntary slaves. From a religious standpoint, they would remain the chosen people and the "holy nation" that God had originally called them to be (Exodus 19:5, 6). To them, this was all the freedom they needed. What more could Jesus offer?

"NEVER IN BONDAGE"

The religious leaders who were listening to Jesus as he talked about freedom were curiously unaware of the relevance of what he was saying. They felt they were far from lacking in freedom—there was no way they could be called slaves.

As we read the account of the leaders' conversation with Jesus, we are amazed at their lack of perception. Were they not at that very moment under the control of imperial Rome? Furthermore, they claimed that as "Abraham's descendants" they had "never been slaves of anyone" (John 8:33). Had they forgotten the years of slavery in Egypt? Had they forgotten the years in Babylon? How inaccurate their answer was!

The visual for lesson 8 illustrates our Key Verse. Discuss the kind of freedom that comes by the truth.

If ye continue in my word, then are ye my disciples indeed: and ye shall know the truth, and the truth shall make you free. John 8:31, 32

WHAT DO YOU THINK?

Many in our culture believe they have found freedom in the abandonment of the idea of absolute truth. Jesus, however, declared that it is the truth, not the absence of truth, that gives freedom. How can we communicate to people who do not believe in truth the concept that it is the truth which brings freedom?

Today those who would venture to make a similar claim of having "never been slaves" ought to stop and think. Have we lost sight of the great numbers who are actually enslaved to the use of tobacco? Are not millions held in bondage to alcohol? What about all who are becoming more and more addicted to the habit of gambling? What of those who are enslaved by drugs, such as cocaine, heroin, and other substances? Others are bound with chains of indebtedness due to credit card purchases or other forms of financial mismanagement.

Jesus still speaks to any who are bearing heavy chains of habits and attitudes that bind, imprison, and stifle. He alone can break such chains and set free those who are held captive.

—J. G. V. B.

What Do You Think?

The Jews told Jesus they were Abraham's descendants and, thus, slaves to no one—and nothing, we may be certain. In that they are like so many today who refuse to see their own shackles. Even people with addictions to substances such as alcohol, nicotine, or narcotics often deny that they have lost the freedom to act on their own.

How can we get people to see that they are enslaved to sin and in need of the freedom Jesus offers?

B. By Turning From Sin (v. 34)

34. Jesus replied, "I tell you the truth, everyone who sins is a slave to sin.

Jesus' answer was introduced with *I tell you the truth*, which to his hearers was a clear signal of its importance. These descendants of Abraham, like the Gentiles they despised, were in need of liberation because they really were in bondage—*to sin*. By serving sin they had made themselves its bondservants. Paul states the issue in these words: "Don't you know that when you offer yourselves to someone to obey him as slaves, you are slaves to the one whom you obey—whether you are slaves to sin, which leads to death, or to obedience, which leads to righteousness?" (Romans 6:16).

C. By Accepting the Son (vv. 35, 36)

35. "Now a slave has no permanent place in the family, but a son belongs to it forever.

He who has yielded himself in obedience to sin is not only in bondage, but until a more lasting relationship is established, he is without a home. *A slave has no permanent place in the family* whom he serves. He may be turned out at any time. The situation is quite different where a *son* is concerned; and Jesus, as God's one and only Son, possesses an eternal claim on the rights and riches of Heaven. He shares these freely with those who come to the Father in his name and thus become members of the family by adoption. "How great is the love the Father has lavished on us, that we should be called children of God!" (1 John 3:1).

36. "So if the Son sets you free, you will be free indeed."

Freedom is not living the way we want to live and doing what we want to do. Freedom is living the way we *ought* to live and doing what *God* wants us to do. By his life Jesus demonstrated this kind of freedom; by his death he made it possible for us to have it.

CONCLUSION

Our world today is filled with those who like to boast of being free because they live in a country where a particular document declares that they are free, or whose brave men and women have fought and died to keep their freedoms alive. The Western world seems sadly to have forgotten the God and the Bible that were once freely acknowledged as the basis of mankind's laws and of the liberties that we prize.

The New Testament gives its own directive for keeping alive the spiritual freedoms we treasure: "You, my brothers, were called to be free. But do not use your freedom to indulge the sinful nature; rather, serve one another in love" (Galatians 5:13). Let us never forget the one who set us free and the tremendous price he paid for our freedom!

Prayer

Thank you, Father, for the love that willingly paid the price for our freedom from guilt and self and sin. Grant us courage to follow in the way lighted and led by him who is the way of truth and life and liberty. Amen.

Thought to Remember

"So if the Son sets you free, you will be free indeed" (John 8:36).

Discovery Learning

This page contains an alternate lesson plan emphasizing learning activities. Classes desiring such student involvement will find these suggestions helpful. The next page is a reproducible activity page to further enhance discovery learning.

LEARNING GOALS

After this lesson students should be able to:

1. Summarize Jesus' sermon at the Feast of Tabernacles.

2. Compare and contrast what Jesus said about truth and freedom with the way today's world views these concepts.

3. Tell how to counter the world's false views with the truth found in Jesus and the Scriptures.

INTO THE LESSON

A few weeks before the lesson ask several children and/or teens the question, "What does it mean to be free?" Record their answers and make a poster with as many of them as you can. Display this poster in your classroom for today's lesson.

If you have several repeated answers, list the three most common answers in random order. Ask the class to guess which answer was the most common.

Option: If you aren't able to do the survey in advance, ask your class members the question and record their responses.

Review the list of answers (from your class or the earlier survey) and ask, "Why are there so many different answers for this question?" Discuss the variety of concepts of freedom: political freedom, freedom from responsibility, freedom from a habit, and others. Note that Jesus gives freedom of a sort that the world cannot match. It is that freedom which we will discuss today.

INTO THE WORD

Ask someone to read John 8:12, 21-36. Divide the class into four study groups and assign the following topics: (1) What does Jesus teach us about light? (2) What does Jesus teach us about sin? (3) What does Jesus teach us about freedom? (4) What does Jesus teach us about truth?

The groups may want to use marginal notes in their Bibles or other references available to them to find related Scriptures and ideas about their topics. After ten minutes, allow some time for sharing what each group has uncovered. Use comments from the exposition section of the lesson to fill in any gaps you feel are left after the groups report.

Write this statement on the board: "What the world calls real is many times false." Ask the class to suggest examples that support the truth of this statement. (One example is found in science. The secular world's "real answer" for the origin of the universe is false.)

Option: If you have an amateur magician in your congregation, ask that person to be present and to perform one or two illusions for your class at this time to show that what seems real may not be.

Write the headings *Jesus* and *World* on the chalkboard. Have the students return to their study groups and ask two of the groups to compare and contrast what Jesus said about truth with the way today's world views it. The other two groups should make the same comparisons/contrasts regarding freedom.

Allow the groups about five minutes, then call for reports. (The second group reporting on each topic should report only new information and not repeat what the previous group has already stated.)

Observe that there is a clear difference between the world's view of truth and freedom and Jesus' view. Ask, "Is the church influencing the world on these issues more or less than the world is influencing the church? Why?" After some discussion ask the class to help you make a list: "In what ways have the world's views of truth and freedom infiltrated the church?" List as many answers as possible on the chalkboard.

INTO LIFE

Have the class return once again to the study groups. Ask each group to come up with some ways to counter the world's intrusions on the church (the list referred to above). Assign one-fourth of the list to each group.

After a few minutes call for reports. Suggest ways to implement some of the more promising ideas that have been suggested. Are there some items common to several groups? Perhaps these should receive first priority.

Invite individuals to find and read these Scriptures: Deuteronomy 6:7; Ezra 7:10; Psalm 100:5; Galatians 3:26-29; and 4:22-31. The ensuing comments should include the following: (1) we must study, do, and teach God's Word; (2) we must teach our children God's Word; (3) God is faithful to all generations; (4) if we have put on Jesus, we are God's children and heirs of the promise of eternal life; (5) we are not the children of a bondservant, but of the free.

Close the lesson by having a volunteer read Psalm 119:159, 160 as a prayer.

Cryptic Message

Jesus' words at the Feast of Tabernacles were hard for the people to understand. They were confused and asked each other what he meant. Fill in the blanks from John 8 below. Then look in the shaded column to discover who Jesus said he was.

1. "I am going away, and . . ." (v. 21).
2. Jesus told the unbelievers, "You will . . ." (v. 21).
3. Further, he told them, "___ ___ ___, ___ ___ ___" (v. 21).
4. The Jews wondered, "___ ___ ___ ___?" (v. 22).
5. Jesus said, "You are of this world; ___ ___ ___ ___ ___" (v. 23).
6. "You will die in your sins ___ ___ ___ ___ ___ that I am the one I claim to be" (v. 24).
7. The people did not understand that Jesus was telling them about ___ ___ ___" (v. 27).
8. "When you have ___ ___ the Son of Man, then you will know" (v. 28).
9. "You will know that I am the one I clam to be, and that I do ___ ___ ___ ___" (v. 28).
10. "I ___ just what the Father has taught me" (v. 28).
11. "The one who sent me is ___ ___" (v. 29).
12. "He has not ___ ___ ___" (v. 29).
13. "If you hold to my teaching, you are . . ." (v. 31).
14. "Then ___ ___ ___ ___, and the truth will set you free" (v. 32).
15. The Jews claimed to be ___ ___, and slaves to no one (v. 33).

1. ___ ___   ___ ___ ___
2. ___ ___   ___ ___ ___
3. ___ ___   ___ ___ ___
4. ___ ___ ___   ___ ___ ___   ___ ___ ___
5. ___ ___ ___   ___ ___ ___ ___
6. ___ ___ ___   ___ ___ ___ ___
7. ___ ___ ___   ___ ___ ___
8. ___ ___ ___ ___   ___
9. ___ ___ ___   ___ ___ ___
10. ___ ___ ___   ___ ___ ___
11. ___ ___ ___
12. ___ ___ ___
13. ___ ___ ___ ___
14. ___ ___ ___   ___ ___ ___ ___
15. ___ ___ ___   ___ ___ ___ ___

Now write the words revealed in the highlighted section; Jesus is the ___ ___ ___ ___.

DEATH THAT GIVES LIFE

WHY TEACH THIS LESSON?

"The trouble with 'living sacrifices,'" someone has said, "is that they keep crawling off the altar!" Indeed they do, as each of us can probably testify. We want to do as Paul says in Romans 12:1, and we determine that we will do it. But then the flames get hot, and we notice some friend who is not on the altar, and he seems to be having a great time. Before we know it, we've sneaked off the altar.

This lesson will be a reminder for all "living sacrifices" of the need to stay on the altar. The example of Jesus will be our guide. The one who could very well have come down from the cross, but didn't—who could have called twelve legions of angels to keep him from the cross, but didn't—will help us stay on the altar. In so doing, we will find life even greater than we had imagined. Best of all, we, like Jesus, will glorify God.

If you have some students who have been thinking of crawling off the altar, this lesson is just what they need today!

INTRODUCTION

A. MORE THAN GOOD-BYE

"Of all the dispositions and habits that lead to political prosperity, religion and morality are indispensable supports. . . . Whatever may be conceded to the influence of refined education in minds of peculiar structure, reason and experience both forbid us to expect that national morality can prevail in exclusion of religious principle."

Thus spoke George Washington, first President of the United States, in his thoughtful and thorough farewell address on September 19, 1796. That, rather than political or military accomplishments, was the contribution through which Washington chose to be remembered by future generations. When one has to say good-bye, it is the kind of gift that is more important than any material legacy.

Jesus is our perfect pattern for concluding a life of service with words of admonition. John 13–17 recounts his "family" conversation with his disciples just before his crucifixion. John 12:20-50, portions of which form today's printed text, records what apparently was Jesus' last public discourse. It served as a final appeal to a nation that, for the most part, had rejected him.

B. LESSON BACKGROUND

When Jesus raised Lazarus from the dead at Bethany, excitement about him grew in nearby Jerusalem. He became immensely popular with the masses (John 11:45; 12:11) and intensely unpopular with the religious leaders of the Jews (11:53, 57). For a time Jesus stayed away from Jerusalem and "no longer moved about publicly among the Jews" (v. 54). He returned, however, to a tumultuous welcome as he rode on a borrowed donkey into Jerusalem. By then Jews from near and far had crowded into Jerusalem for the Passover, and the enthusiasm regarding Jesus was intensifying (12:12-19). During the daytime Jesus taught in the temple area, where the presence of the multitudes protected him from attack. At night he retired to Bethany.

DEVOTIONAL READING:
ROMANS 5:1-11
LESSON SCRIPTURE:
JOHN 12:20-50
PRINTED TEXT:
JOHN 12:23-37, 42, 43

LESSON AIMS

After this lesson students will be able to:

1. Explain what Jesus said in today's text about death and life.

2. Tell how Jesus' demands for his disciples imitate his own death and resurrection.

3. Conduct their lives in a way that demonstrates death to the world and life through Christ.

May
2

KEY VERSE

"But, I, when I am lifted up from the earth, will draw all men to myself." —John 12:32

Among those in the city for the Passover were some Greeks—worshipers who were denied certain temple privileges because they were not Jews. They wanted to meet Jesus and attempted to make arrangements to do so through the disciples Philip and Andrew. Scripture does not say what purpose they had in mind, nor does it indicate how or whether Jesus received them (John 12:20-22). His message may have been conveyed to the Greeks by Philip and Andrew. Jesus seems to have responded to these inquirers as was his custom—not in words directed to their questions, but in principles suited to their needs.

I. LIFE FOUND THROUGH DEATH (JOHN 12:23-26)

A. JESUS' COMING DEATH (v. 23)

23. Jesus replied, "The hour has come for the Son of Man to be glorified.

Son of man was Jesus' most frequently used title to describe himself. Here the term possessed special significance. Jesus' messiahship involved "being made in human likeness" (Philippians 2:7) with all its difficulties. Now he would be *glorified*. His disciples must have viewed recent events (particularly the triumphal entry) as long-overdue recognition of Jesus. But here he spoke of a very different kind of glory. That glory would come from God in response to Jesus' total self-sacrifice to the point of "death—even death on a cross!" (Philippians 2:8-11).

Previously John has noted that Jesus' enemies did not arrest him because his *hour*, or time, had not yet come (7:6, 8, 30; 8:20). Now we have reached a pivotal point: Jesus announces that *the hour has come*. He recognizes that his death is near and will speak in a similar manner in later settings (13:1; 16:32; 17:1).

B. AN ILLUSTRATION (v. 24)

24. "I tell you the truth, unless a kernel of wheat falls to the ground and dies, it remains only a single seed. But if it dies, it produces many seeds.

As noted in previous lessons, Jesus' *I tell you the truth* (or "verily, verily" in the *King James Version*) gives emphasis to the words that follow. Here he uses an analogy of a *kernel of wheat* that may be preserved indefinitely in a dry granary, but will produce life only when it *dies* in moist soil. There its potential is released and it grows into a stalk, with a head full of many kernels.

MANY SEEDS FROM ONE

Jesus spoke of one seed dying and, through its death, producing many seeds. He was, of course, thinking of the vast influence that his death would have through the blessing of new life that would come as a result.

This principle also applies to our service for Jesus. In the latter part of the nineteenth century, a young preacher caught a vision of the need for a college where young men without much money could study to become preachers. With very little in financial resources, the young man began such an institution in a rural area of Tennessee. In spite of the setbacks he often encountered, the determined young preacher persevered and finally won support for his venture.

This young man, Ashley Johnson, gave his life—all his efforts and hopes—to develop a school that would advance the cause of Christ. Following his death the school was named after him: "Johnson Bible College." Today there are hundreds of students at the school. The campus is a beautiful one, including several buildings worth hundreds of thousands of dollars. Across the world there have been and are hundreds of ministers and missionaries who owe their education to this institution. As a kernel of faith, hope, and love, Ashley Johnson gave his life, and much fruit has come from that gift.

Such an example challenges all of us to lose our lives for Christ's sake. The resulting blessings will be more than we could ever have imagined.   —J. G. V. B.

WHAT DO YOU THINK?

Jesus taught a spiritual lesson by referring to a seed's being planted in the soil. What are some ways in which the work of farming or gardening illustrates the kind of sacrifices we must make as Christians?

Farming metaphors are common in the Bible because the culture in which it was written was heavily dominated by agriculture. What metaphors might you suggest to reach people in a non-agrarian culture?

C. JESUS' CHALLENGE (vv. 25, 26)

25. *"The man who loves his life will lose it, while the man who hates his life in this world will keep it for eternal life.*

The principle demonstrated in Jesus and illustrated by the grainfield is now expanded and applied to persons, one and all. The hate required by Jesus is best understood by comparing Luke 14:26 (which refers to one hating his family) with Matthew 10:37 (which speaks of one wrongly loving his family more than he loves Jesus). Jesus is saying that the disciple must hold his own life in comparative disregard, in view of the priority that he is to give to spiritual matters. In other words, the disciple is to follow the example of Jesus, who hated his own life in comparison with his desire to accomplish the will of God through his atonement for our sins.

It has been said that until one has something worth dying for, he does not really have anything worth living for. Christ is the only one ultimately worthy of total commitment.

26. *"Whoever serves me must follow me; and where I am, my servant also will be. My Father will honor the one who serves me."*

A disciple is one who learns from and follows his teacher. Jesus was going in the direction of death to accomplish the purpose for which he had come into the world. Were others willing to follow him in the same path? To *follow* Jesus summarizes the *duty* of the disciple; to be with Jesus, now and forever, is the *reward* of the disciple (John 14:2, 3; 17:24; 1 Thessalonians 4:17; Philippians 1:23).

II. JESUS FACES DEATH (JOHN 12:27-31)

Jesus had made it clear that life must come through death, and he knew that his own death—by crucifixion—was fast approaching. That was disturbing to Jesus, and it could be confronted only by calling upon his Father.

A. COMMITMENT TO THE FATHER (vv. 27, 28a)

27, 28a. *"Now my heart is troubled, and what shall I say? 'Father, save me from this hour'? No, it was for this very reason I came to this hour. Father, glorify your name!"*

The word *troubled* brings to mind the inner turmoil that Jesus experienced later in Gethsemane. Here we see foreshadowed the struggle between apprehension and commitment that would become the subject of fervent prayer.

For what should he pray? That God would *save* him from suffering? He did pray, "Father, if you are willing, take this cup from me" (Luke 22:42). Yet the suffering for others' sins was the *very reason* for which he had come to earth. Thus, the Lord prayed, "Not my will, but yours be done." We should understand that as the same prayer Jesus here expressed by saying, *Father, glorify your name!*

We, too, struggle between apprehension and commitment. In difficult times it is proper to ask for relief, even as Paul prayed for removal of his "thorn" (2 Corinthians 12:7-10). May we learn to pray also, "Let this matter glorify you, Father; your will be done." Sometimes he will be glorified by our deliverance; at other times he will be glorified when we endure patiently through the grace he supplies.

B. ENCOURAGEMENT FROM THE FATHER (vv. 28b-30)

28b. *Then a voice came from heaven, "I have glorified it, and will glorify it again."*

Jesus' voice lifted in prayer to Heaven was answered by the Father's assuring *voice . . . from heaven*. Scripture records two other comparable events: at Jesus' baptism (Luke 3:21, 22) and at his transfiguration (Luke 9:28-36). Jesus was praying on both occasions.

WHAT DO YOU THINK?

Jesus commanded that we follow him. But just what does it mean to "follow" Jesus? What is different about your life because you follow Jesus than would be true if you made no claim to follow him?

WHAT DO YOU THINK?

The lesson writer notes that both Jesus and Paul faced situations when the Father was glorified, not by delivering them, but by enabling them to accomplish greater good through endurance. How have you found the same to be true in your own life?

The visual for lesson 9 illustrates the grand truth of verse 32.

WHAT DO YOU THINK?

Our lesson writer suggests that the failure of Jesus' followers to lift him up can constitute one reason why some people are not attracted to him. What can we do to lift up Jesus in a more attractive manner?

Without criticizing any of the persons involved, evaluate your church's evangelistic efforts. Are services designed to appeal to the

The Father's name had been *glorified* in all that Jesus had said and done. It would be glorified especially in Jesus' suffering and death.

29. The crowd that was there and heard it said it had thundered; others said an angel had spoken to him.

Voices from Heaven are apparently clearest to the ones addressed. Thus at Jesus' baptism it was not the words of God, but rather the lingering of the Spirit on Jesus (in the form of a dove) that revealed him to John the Baptist as the promised Messiah (John 1:32-34). And when Jesus spoke from Heaven to Saul of Tarsus on the Damascus road, Saul's companions saw the blinding light but did not hear the spoken message (Acts 22:9). So here the voice was thought by many to be a coincidental sound from nature, and by others to be a heavenly message to Jesus. All, however, knew that something had happened in response to Jesus' prayer.

30. Jesus said, "This voice was for your benefit, not mine.

In certain instances the meaning of *not* is perhaps better understood as "not only." This is the case, for example, with Jesus' statement: "When a man believes in me, he does not believe in me only, but in the one who sent me" (John 12:44). It was not only to encourage Jesus in his need that God's *voice* spoke, but especially to affirm him in the presence of witnesses.

C. JUDGMENT ON SATAN (v. 31)

31. "Now is the time for judgment on this world; now the prince of this world will be driven out.

The voice of God had expressed his approval of his Son in all his doings. That was an affirmative *judgment*. At the same time and with the same voice, it was a judgment that stood in condemnation of all that was opposed to Jesus, beginning with the source of such opposition—*the prince of this world* (John 14:30; 16:11; Ephesians 2:2).

The means by which Jesus' enemies thought they could destroy him worked instead to glorify God and to destroy Satan and his reign. The essential judgment of the archenemy has occurred already. It is now up to each person to choose how he or she will be judged, whether with the redeemed or with the condemned.

III. PURPOSE OF JESUS' DEATH (JOHN 12:32-36)

A. HIS DEATH IS FOR ALL (vv. 32-34)

32, 33. "But I, when I am lifted up from the earth, will draw all men to myself." He said this to show the kind of death he was going to die.

Jesus had centered thus far on his coming death; these words indicated the way in which it would happen. That Jesus was to be *lifted up* revealed *the kind of death he was going to die*—the Roman procedure of fastening a victim to a cross, where he was lifted up and exposed to torture and ridicule as he died a slow and agonizing death.

Jesus spoke of the power of his death to *draw all men* to himself. Through his sacrificial death Jesus is universally attractive, freeing from the guilt of the universal curse of sin. Why, then, do not all hearers of the gospel respond equally to its appeal? Consider that not all objects are equally drawn to the attraction of a magnet. The key factor is the resistance of the object drawn. The drawing power of Jesus does reach out to all, but some are held back by their wrong expectations of Jesus or their prejudices toward him. Of course, the failure of Jesus' followers to lift him up can constitute another reason why others are not attracted to him.

34. The crowd spoke up, "We have heard from the Law that the Christ will remain forever, so how can you say, 'The Son of Man must be lifted up'? Who is this 'Son of Man'?"

The crowd understood the connection between Jesus' designation as the *Son of Man* and the *Christ* (Messiah) who was prophesied in the Old Testament (here referred to as *the Law*). Yet Jesus was predicting his death. How could this be, since Isaiah 9:7 said, "Of the increase of his government and peace there will be no end," and Daniel 7:14 declared, "His dominion is an everlasting dominion that will not pass away"? There may have been nothing but honest inquiry in the minds of some who referred to the *Son of Man*—the only time in the Gospels that this term is used by anyone except Jesus. Some, however, likely attempted to draw from Jesus a controversial statement that they could take to the Sanhedrin.

B. HE IS THE LIGHT (vv. 35, 36)

35. Then Jesus told them, "You are going to have the light just a little while longer. Walk while you have the light, before darkness overtakes you. The man who walks in the dark does not know where he is going.

Now Jesus issued a final appeal to the people to ponder what he had said, find understanding, and shape their behavior according to the teaching he had given. As the *light* of the world (John 1:4; 8:12), Jesus had shown the way. Let his hearers now use that light, lest nightfall find them stumbling and becoming lost.

36. "Put your trust in the light while you have it, so that you may become sons of light." When he had finished speaking, Jesus left and hid himself from them.

Trust in the light that is available to you! Depend on the guidance given by Jesus, the light of the world! To us the light of life is available through our personal knowledge of Jesus, and also through what we can learn of him through further study of the Bible, prayer, and daily practice of his teachings.

IV. RESPONSE TO JESUS (JOHN 12:37, 42, 43)

A. UNBELIEF DESPITE EVIDENCE (v. 37)

37. Even after Jesus had done all these miraculous signs in their presence, they still would not believe in him.

Earlier the skeptics had demanded *miraculous signs*, suggesting that such signs would constitute sufficient evidence for believing in Jesus (John 6:30). But their implied promise was worthless. John's Gospel describes fewer than a dozen miracles, but makes reference to others that Jesus did (John 2:23; 3:2; 4:45; 7:31; 20:30; 21:25). Unbelievers, however, remained adamant in their rejection of Jesus. In the case of Lazarus, for example, the Jewish leaders chose to try to destroy the evidence—that is, to kill Lazarus—rather than be convinced by it (John 12:10, 11). And this in spite of the fact that they admitted, "Here is this man performing many miraculous signs" (John 11:47)!

STILL UNBELIEVING

It seems impossible that people could see many of the miraculous works that Jesus performed and still not believe in him as the promised Messiah. People will find every possible way to discount, minimize, evade, and explain away things supernatural and marvelous.

An incident that occurred some time ago illustrates this hardness of heart. Many of the students at a Christian college took courses at a state university located nearby. The philosophy department at the university had several professors who were in some cases indifferent and in other cases openly hostile to the Christian faith.

newcomer and visitor or only to the long-time members? What percentage of your programming is devoted to outreach, and how much is for the benefit of the membership? Does the community know you? Respect you? What can be done to increase your community exposure?

HOW TO SAY IT

Arimathea. AIR-uh-muh-THEE-uh (TH as in THIN).
Damascus. Duh-MASS-kus.
Gethsemane. Geth-SEM-uh-nee.
Herodians. Heh-ROE-dee-unz.
Jairus. JYE-rus or JAY-ih-rus.
Lazarus. LAZ-uh-rus.
Nicodemus. Nick-uh-DEE-mus.
Pharisees. FAIR-ih-seez.
Sadducees. SAD-you-seez.
Sanhedrin. San-HEED-run or SAN-huh-drin.
synagogue. SIN-uh-gog.
Tarsus. TAR-sus.

PRAYER

We praise and thank you, heavenly Father, for Jesus, who endured a horrible death to give us a glorious life. We love you because you first loved us. We pray for wisdom and courage to choose the way of life eternal, no matter what it may cost in terms of this present world, for Jesus' sake. Amen.

WHAT DO YOU THINK?

Still today some love "praise from men more than praise from God." Certain prominent people in our time are more concerned about being politically correct than biblically correct. What are some examples? Is this condition present in the church? If so, what can be done about it?

(Perhaps we need more emphasis on such passages as 1 John 2:15-17 to encourage timid believers. Role-playing in a friendly environment may also help them feel more comfortable in the more hostile one.)

THOUGHT TO REMEMBER

Jesus died and rose, providing the way of eternal life. In him we die to self and to sin, that we may live in him and with him forever.

A debate, or at least a discussion, was arranged between a professor from the university's philosophy department and a professor from the Christian college. The philosophy professor presented arguments to prove that all "God talk" was meaningless, and that all ideas about God were part of man's search for meaning. He scoffed at any idea of God's revealing himself to man.

When the Christian college professor gave a powerful argument for the resurrection of Jesus, affirming that this proved God's existence and Jesus' divinity, the philosophy professor remained unpersuaded. He said that even if someone were in fact to be raised from the dead, it would prove nothing!

Such was the attitude of many of those in Jesus' day who, despite the impressive array of evidence before them, "would not believe in him."   —J. G. V. B.

B. SECRET BELIEF (vv. 42, 43)

42. Yet at the same time many even among the leaders believed in him. But because of the Pharisees they would not confess their faith for fear they would be put out of the synagogue.

Opposition to Jesus was not unanimous even among members of the Sanhedrin. Friends of Jesus included Nicodemus, who pleaded with his colleagues for fairness toward Jesus (John 7:45-52), and Joseph of Arimathea, who joined with Nicodemus in caring for the dead body of Jesus and placing it in Joseph's new tomb (John 19:38-42). Named also is Jairus, a synagogue ruler in Galilee whose daughter Jesus restored to life (Luke 8:40-56).

Most adamant in their opposition to Jesus were the *Pharisees*, eager guardians of the laws and traditions of the elders. They decreed that anyone who acknowledged Jesus as Messiah would be *put out of the synagogue* (John 9:22, 34). That meant ostracism from the Jewish community, socially as well as religiously. For *many* it was an effective deterrent.

43. For they loved praise from men more than praise from God.

A friend of Jesus among the membership of the Sanhedrin was a bit like a Christian on a city council representing a predominantly non-Christian constituency, or a Christian student in a class taught by a cynical atheist. God's will is clear enough in the Bible, but God doesn't vote in a local election or record this semester's grade. Often *praise from men* carries much less personal risk than seeking *praise from God.*

Jesus warned against doing even the most praiseworthy things, such as praying, fasting, and giving, for the purpose of pleasing the neighbors. What is done for human approval, he said, will bring no added honor from God (Matthew 6:1-18). If the purpose is to please and honor God, however, that should be evident to the neighbors as well (Matthew 5:16). God's opinion must come first, because his judgment is the one that matters!

CONCLUSION

Jesus' message in the temple concluded with his departure from the crowds in Jerusalem (v. 36). John notes disappointing responses to Jesus: rejection (v. 37) and a weak and timid faith (vv. 42, 43). In an appended paragraph (vv. 44-50) John records words of Jesus addressing those instances. What he had spoken was from God. It was final, and it would be the basis on which his hearers would be judged. His words would remain forever as the unchanging message of the unchanging God—to be considered, responded to, and applied as the basis of life everlasting.

God and his Word cannot change, conforming to us. By his grace we can change, conforming to him, and live. Will we?

Discovery Learning

This page contains an alternate lesson plan emphasizing learning activities. Classes desiring such student involvement will find these suggestions helpful. The next page is a reproducible activity page to further enhance discovery learning.

LEARNING GOALS

After this lesson students will be able to:

1. Explain what Jesus said in today's text about death and life.

2. Tell how Jesus' demands for his disciples imitate his own death and resurrection.

3. Conduct their lives in a way that demonstrates death to the world and life through Christ.

INTO THE LESSON

Bring a few grains of wheat to class and give some to each student. Explain that these seeds, which seem to be dead, are actually full of life. Ask, "What is required for life to spring from these seeds?" Several answers should be given, such as being planted, light, warmth, and water. Tell the class, "Jesus used a grain of wheat as an example to teach that his own death was really the beginning of life. Included in his lesson was the concept that we, as his disciples, will also find life only when we are willing to lay down our lives—like seeds planted in a fertile field."

INTO THE WORD

Ask a volunteer to read John 12:23-43. Then divide the class into four groups. Give each group one of the following assignments:

Group 1. Study verses 23-26; explain how Jesus' parable of the kernel of wheat applied to Jesus' own experience and how it applies to his followers—including us.

Group 2. Study verses 27-31; explain how Jesus' death would bring glory to the Father. Suggest also how Jesus' prayer is a model for us as we face difficulty for the sake of Christ.

Group 3. Study verses 32-36; explain the expression "lifted up" in both a literal and figurative manner. Tell what demands this passage puts on believers today.

Group 4. Study verses 37-43. Compare and contrast the different responses to Jesus that are described here. How are the same responses seen today?

Allow about ten minutes for study, then ask the groups to report. Supply additional information from the commentary pages as needed. Use the discussion questions on the next page to further explore the issues brought up in the reports. Be sure the following summaries are expressed in connection with the group reports:

Group 1. Jesus' death was followed by burial and resurrection, just as a seemingly dead seed is buried and then new life springs forth. As his disciples, we must lay down our lives in service; he will raise us up.

Group 2. Jesus' death fulfilled God's plan of redemption. It proved God to be more powerful than death, and that brought God glory. See the commentary section to note how Jesus' prayer is a model for us (page 303).

Group 3. Literally, Jesus was talking about being "lifted up" on a cross to die. By doing so he opened the way of salvation to all. Figuratively, he is "lifted up" when we tell what he has done so people may hear the Word and come to faith.

Group 4. The response to Jesus then was mostly negative (unbelief) even as it is today. Even those who believed were afraid to confess their faith. Are we as timid as they?

INTO LIFE

Write this question on the board: "What areas of our lives should die?" As the ideas emerge, list them on the board. (Pride, selfishness, fear, fleshly lust, anger, disbelief and doubt, worldly ways of thinking, and others may be suggested.)

When the class seems to run out of ideas, ask the class to arrange the ones given in the order of importance. Then take the top three and ask for ways that dying to these can be accomplished. Call for a commitment to act, and ask for a report next Sunday of what was accomplished.

Ask the class, "Are you more or less vulnerable to peer pressure now than you were ten years ago?" We often think about the problems teens face with peer pressure, but we all wrestle with it to some extent. Ask, "What is something you have done because of peer pressure that you now wish you hadn't?" (If possible, offer a humorous example about yourself.) Sometimes we get into trouble because of peer pressure, but none is worse than the peer pressure described in our text. Note verses 42 and 43 and ask how many of the students know of examples where believers have been afraid to express their faith because of other people. Discuss practical ways of resisting such peer pressure.

Close with a prayer circle, asking God for his strength to resist peer pressure and to take a stand of faith in the coming week.

Responses to Jesus

Statisticians often use pie charts to demonstrate the relative size of different groups with differing responses to some person or issue. The pie chart in figure A below suggests what might have been the response to Jesus' ministry. The vast majority of people were curious onlookers—eager to be present to see a miracle or hear Jesus silence his critics, but not willing to make any commitment. A small but vocal group was openly hostile to Jesus. These included the Pharisees and Sadducees, the Herodians, and possibly some others. Of course, there was also the small band of disciples, openly supportive of Jesus. Our text suggests another small group, the secret disciples. These were believers in Jesus, but they were afraid to admit their faith because they feared the response of the vocal and powerful hostile group.

On the chart in figure B diagram the modern response to Jesus as you see it. Use the following labels or come up with your own: Openly committed to Jesus; Nominally committed; Apathetic (they have no opinion); Skeptical about Jesus; Openly hostile toward Jesus.

Finally, use figure C to suggest the amount of time, effort, and resources the church ought to use to reach each of the groups in figure B. Is there an exact correlation—the biggest group gets the most effort—or should a smaller, more open group be left out entirely? Why or why not? After you diagram the effort you feel should be applied to each group, suggest one or two programs that you would like to see initiated in your church to help in this effort. What are you willing to do to see these programs get started?

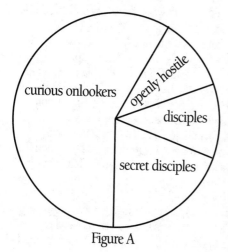

Figure A

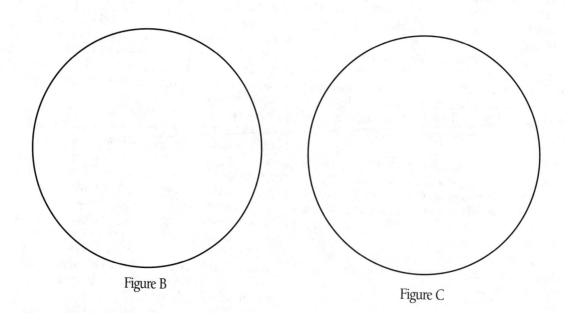

Figure B

Figure C

JESUS TEACHES SERVANTHOOD

LESSON 10

WHY TEACH THIS LESSON?

An old adage says that the man who holds the ladder at the bottom is just as important as the man at the top. Though it's the man at the top who gets noticed and who gets the credit for the work that is done, he could not do any of it without the man at the bottom.

Many Christians want to be great in God's kingdom; they aspire to be high-profile leaders in the church. Some people like to be seen and heard by the crowd. They want to work at the top of the ladder.

Jesus offers us the contrast. He does so in many ways, but the incident in today's text is the most memorable. The Son of God, who was *with* God and *was* God—this divine Creator and Redeemer—stooped to do a slave's work.

If you or any of your students aspires to be the one at the top of the ladder, this lesson will be a timely reminder that the one at the bottom is essential, too. Perhaps our Lord would have us fill a role at the bottom—right next to him!

INTRODUCTION

A. THE GLORY OF SERVING JESUS

The Slavic peoples of today make up many nations in Eastern Europe. During the early Middle Ages, these nations did not exist. There were only Slavic tribes, who were often in conflict with Germanic tribes from central Europe. When the Slavs lost, the captives were sold to other peoples as slaves. In fact, our word *slave* comes from the word *slav*. In the Slavic languages, however, the word *slav* means "glorious."

While we think of slavery and glory as two quite opposite ideas, they come together beautifully in Jesus Christ. As we will learn today, it is a glorious thing to be a servant (slave) of Jesus.

B. LESSON BACKGROUND

John is the only Gospel writer to record the unforgettable demonstration of servanthood that occurred in the upper room—Jesus' washing of his disciples' feet. This visual aid served to reinforce what Jesus had been trying to teach his disciples all along about greatness in his kingdom. It was a lesson that the Twelve had been extremely slow to learn. Even in the upper room, with the cross fast approaching, "a dispute arose among them as to which of them was considered to be greatest" (Luke 22:24). The lesson Jesus taught them was one they desperately needed. It is one we must heed as well.

I. SETTING THE SCENE (JOHN 13:1-5)

In any drama it is important to set the stage. The upper room where the events in our text took place did not look at all like the paintings of the Last Supper that

DEVOTIONAL READING:
MATTHEW 25:31-40
LESSON SCRIPTURE:
JOHN 13:1-35
PRINTED TEXT:
JOHN 13:1-17

LESSON AIMS

After this lesson students will be able to:

1. Tell the story of Jesus' washing the disciples' feet in the upper room.

2. Explain why it is difficult either to serve or to be served by another.

3. Resolve to do something each day this week in service to another, and to receive the service of others graciously.

May 9

KEY VERSE

I tell you the truth, no servant is greater than his master, nor is a messenger greater than the one who sent him. —John 13:16

we often see. Luke describes it as a large room (Luke 22:12). Access to the room was made by means of an outside stairway. (In Jesus' day one did not take up precious space inside the house with steps.) As was the custom in that time, the men sat on couches or cushions arranged around a low table.

We do not know who owned this upper room. Apparently he was a follower of Jesus not named by any of the Gospel writers. This may have been the same room where the disciples met after the resurrection and where the risen Christ appeared to them (John 20:19).

A. The Timing (vv. 1-3)

1. It was just before the Passover Feast. Jesus knew that the time had come for him to leave this world and go to the Father. Having loved his own who were in the world, he now showed them the full extent of his love.

What does John mean by *before the Passover Feast?* Most Bible students believe that this refers to the time just before the meal began. Some think that it means "before the day" of this Passover. They contend that Jesus died at the same time that Passover lambs were being killed on the temple altar (1 Corinthians 5:7). If this were the case, then Jesus and the Twelve shared an earlier meal as a substitute for the Passover. This may appeal to our poetic side; but it is not necessary to take this view, and most find the arguments for it unconvincing. Most likely the phrase simply means "before they sat down for the meal."

John refers to three other Passovers besides this one. (See John 2:13; 5:1; 6:4; the feast mentioned in John 5:1 is generally considered to have been a Passover, though that is not specified.) From these feasts, we determine that the ministry of Jesus lasted between three and three and a half years. (See the chart on page 236.) Since Luke tells us that Jesus was "about thirty years old" at the beginning of his ministry (Luke 3:23), we deduce that he died at the age of thirty-three.

The Passover commemorated the Jews' departure from Egypt and their establishment as a nation. It is important to note that at the time when the most solemn Jewish ceremony was observed, Jesus instituted the most solemn Christian ceremony. Not only are the two alike in their solemnity, but both are also highly symbolic. Everything on the Passover table was symbolic of something that the Jews experienced during their exodus from Egypt. Everything on the Communion table is symbolic, too. We must also remember that the Passover commemorated the Jews' deliverance from bondage in Egypt. Our Communion commemorates our deliverance from the bondage of sin. This is obviously more than a happy coincidence. In fact, the Passover was a "type" or a foreshadowing of the deliverance from sin Jesus would effect through his death, burial, and resurrection. Thus the Passover finds its fulfillment in the Communion service, for both ceremonies ultimately point to the same event!

We have noted in previous lessons the significance of the term *hour* in John's Gospel. On certain occasions during his ministry, Jesus stated (or John noted) that his hour had not yet come (2:4; 7:6, 8, 30; 8:20). In last week's lesson we saw how Jesus began to declare, "The hour has come" (12:23). Clearly *Jesus knew* what lay ahead. The cross was no surprise to him. He said, "I lay down my life—only to take it up again. No one takes it from me, but I lay it down of my own accord" (John 10:17, 18).

The expression *he now showed them the full extent of his love* is a very beautiful description of the depth of Jesus' love for his disciples. The Greek word for *extent* may also be translated "completion," so the expression may rightly be translated "loved them completely." A footnote in the *New American Standard Bible* has "loved them 'eternally.'"

The visual for lesson 10 cites nearly all of today's printed text in a manner that reminds us that the full extent of Jesus' love was seen, not only in the upper room, but at Calvary.

Iscariot. Iss-CARE-ee-ut.
Rabbi. RAB-eye.

Note the contrast between the words *his own* as used here and as they are used in the first chapter of John's Gospel (John 1:11). There the emphasis is on the rejection of Jesus by *his own*. Here *his own* describes the closeness that had developed between Jesus and the Twelve during the years of his ministry. They were truly his own; they belonged to Jesus in the strongest sense of the word because they had chosen to believe in him, follow him, and obey him.

2. *The evening meal was being served, and the devil had already prompted Judas Iscariot, son of Simon, to betray Jesus.*

John moves directly to the time during which *the evening meal was being served.* He notes that *the devil had already prompted Judas Iscariot . . . to betray Jesus.* By now Judas had begun the betrayal process, for he had already contacted and contracted with the enemies of Jesus (Matthew 26:14-16). He had only to decide on the proper time to carry out his plan and have Jesus arrested. It was obvious from the triumphal entry that Jesus was still immensely popular with the people. To try to arrest him during the daytime could cause a disturbance. But on this night all the people were in their homes for the Passover observance. It was the ideal moment to apprehend Jesus without incident. Later John notes that after Jesus gave to Judas the "bread" that had been dipped in a bowl of gravy or sauce, "Satan entered into him" (v. 27).

3. *Jesus knew that the Father had put all things under his power, and that he had come from God and was returning to God.*

That someone who had been instrumental in the creation of the universe (John 1:3) and was one day to sit down at the right hand of God (Hebrews 1:3) should kneel to wash men's feet is amazing. *Jesus knew* that he was on his way to the cross, but he also knew that he was on his way to the crown. At a time when we might expect the greatest pride, we see instead the greatest humility.

That should not surprise us. It was Jesus' knowledge of who he was that freed him to serve his disciples. People whose sense of identity and self-worth come from externals are continually worried about what others think of them. They will not do anything that might make another think less of them. But Jesus knew he was God's Son and that he would soon rejoin his Father in Heaven. Washing his disciples' feet did not make him any less divine.

We who follow Jesus can have the same freedom. We know that in Jesus we belong to God and will one day go to him to live with him forever. Such knowledge should fortify us against pride and temptation. It should never become a source of vanity. When we are so concerned about our own status and position that we are not willing to stoop to do common deeds for common people, we show how insecure we really are in our relationship to Christ.

STOOPING TO SERVE

At a church I once served in Pittsburgh, Pennsylvania, it was customary for baptisms to be administered during the morning worship service. This required a quick change of clothing by the minister so he could prepare for the baptisms. An elder of the church went into the minister's dressing room and helped him don the boots that he wore while in the baptistery.

The elder who did this, often kneeling on the floor to help with this task, was the chief engineer with the Bell Telephone Company in Pittsburgh. Here was an important executive performing a humble task. He was doing it because he believed that the work of God at that time and place required this particular service.

This man probably made significantly more money than most people in the church. He had status, power, prestige—but he laid all of this aside so he could serve another. We should possess a similar dedication to any task that God may need us to accomplish.

—J. G. V. B.

WHAT DO YOU THINK?

Jesus' confidence in who he was freed him to act as a servant and wash his disciples' feet. Do you think it is a lack of confidence in our standing in Christ that often prevents us from serving in menial ways? If so, how can such confidence, and thus service, be encouraged? If confidence is not the issue, then what is? How can the problem be addressed to encourage more service after the pattern of Christ?

WHAT DO YOU THINK?

Certainly the lesson Jesus was teaching here was that we ought to be servants (see verse 14), and most of us have more trouble with serving than with being served. However, sometimes, in our zeal to play the servant, we resist when someone else tries to perform some service in our behalf—just as Peter was initially resistant to the idea of Jesus' washing his feet. Have you ever tried to do something to help another, but that person resisted? Why do you think some people have so much difficulty in accepting service? How do you balance the need to be a servant and the need to allow another to serve you?

B. JESUS' PREPARATION (vv. 4, 5)

4. So he got up from the meal, took off his outer clothing, and wrapped a towel around his waist.

As noted earlier, only John tells us about Jesus' washing of the disciples' feet. He is also the only Gospel writer who says nothing about Jesus' institution of the Lord's Supper in the upper room. In this case John (whose Gospel was most likely the last of the four to be written) seems to be supplementing what Matthew, Mark, and Luke had already recorded.

That Jesus *took off his outer clothing* indicates that he took off his outer robe. Beneath this robe he would have been wearing a sleeveless tunic and a loincloth. Some believe he also removed the tunic, though that is not certain. Either way, he suddenly appeared before the disciples in the role of a servant instead of the host.

Jesus then *wrapped a towel* (a long linen cloth) *around his waist*. No doubt the towel and basin were provided by the owner of the upper room for use by his guests. That was customary. What was clearly not customary was for Jesus to do what he proceeded to do.

5. After that, he poured water into a basin and began to wash his disciples' feet, drying them with the towel that was wrapped around him.

In Jesus' day people did not wear shoes but open sandals. They walked in dust if the weather was dry and in mud if it was wet. Travelers generally arrived at a house with dirty feet. It was considered the responsibility of a household servant to wash the feet of the guests. But there was no servant in the upper room on this occasion, and none of the Twelve had been designated as such. So Jesus *began to wash his disciples' feet.*

We do not know to which of the Twelve Jesus went first, nor do we know the reaction of any except that of Peter. It is possible that one of them thought, "Why didn't someone think of that?" We hope that one of them may have said to himself, "Why didn't I think of that?" We must ask ourselves, "If I had been in that upper room, would I have volunteered for this task before Jesus did it? Would I have taken the towel from him when he began to do it? Would I have accepted his service in silence, or would I have protested as Peter did?"

II. EXCHANGE WITH PETER (JOHN 13:6-11)

A. PETER'S RELUCTANCE (vv. 6-9)

6. He came to Simon Peter, who said to him, "Lord, are you going to wash my feet?"

Peter was astonished at what Jesus was doing, and he expressed his astonishment with a question: *Lord, are you going to wash my feet?* He may have put the emphasis on the word *my*, especially if he was the last to have his feet washed. Or he may have put the emphasis on *you*. Both pronouns are emphasized in the Greek text, and it is interesting to think of Peter stressing both in his question.

7. Jesus replied, "You do not realize now what I am doing, but later you will understand."

Jesus knew what he was doing and why he was doing it, but none of the Twelve did. He reassured them that *later* they would *understand*. After the crucifixion and the resurrection, they would realize what Jesus had done and what he wanted to teach them. Looking back on that night, the disciples would remember that they had been quarreling over who would be the greatest in Jesus' kingdom (Luke 22:24). Jesus had responded to their vain ambitions with an unforgettable gesture of service.

8. "No," said Peter, "you shall never wash my feet." Jesus answered, "Unless I wash you, you have no part with me."

Perhaps others of the Twelve felt the same way as *Peter*, but he was always quick to speak up. His *you shall never* sounds as harsh as his earlier "This shall never happen to you!" following Jesus' prediction of his death (Matthew 16:22). Jesus' reply to Peter was equally strict: if he did not wash Peter, Peter would *have no part with* Jesus. Obviously far more was involved than the mere washing of feet. On the surface Peter's words appeared to express an attitude of humility. In reality he was defying Jesus' authority, seeking to tell him what to do. True fellowship with Jesus was impossible if Peter's attitude did not change.

9. **"Then, Lord," Simon Peter replied, "not just my feet but my hands and my head as well!"**

Peter still did not understand. He wanted to remain a devoted follower of Jesus. So, misunderstanding what Jesus had just said, he changed his reluctance to an eager acceptance: *not just my feet but my hands and my head as well*. Whatever blessing was involved, Peter wanted more of it. Again, his attitude may appear admirable, but Peter was still trying to tell Jesus what to do. This is a mistake we all make: trying to serve Jesus on our terms instead of accepting his.

B. JESUS' RESPONSE (vv. 10, 11)

10. **Jesus answered, "A person who has had a bath needs only to wash his feet; his whole body is clean. And you are clean, though not every one of you."**

Here Jesus shifted from physical cleansing to the more critical matter of spiritual cleansing. However, as he applied this to the disciples, he added these sad words: *though not every one of you*. Obviously Jesus was referring to Judas Iscariot. Was he still present? It is difficult to tell from the accounts in the four Gospels at what specific point Judas left the group in the upper room. It is clear from John's Gospel that Judas did not leave the room until after Jesus had given him the bread (v. 30). If John's account is chronological, this would have been after the events related here. Many believe that Judas was present when Jesus washed the disciples' feet and that it was immediately after his departure that Jesus instituted the Lord's Supper with the remaining disciples.

11. **For he knew who was going to betray him, and that was why he said not every one was clean.**

Again John notes that Jesus *knew who was going to betray him*. Yet Jesus not only sat at the same table with this man, but even offered him a special token of friendship. He took a piece of bread and gave it to Judas (v. 26). This was recognized in that time as a gesture of close, personal friendship—and Jesus extended it to his betrayer! Jesus' handing of the bread to Judas was an act that was every bit as remarkable as his washing of the disciples' feet.

III. JESUS' APPLICATION (JOHN 13:12-17)

A. THE LORD IS ALSO A SERVANT (vv. 12, 13)

12. **When he had finished washing their feet, he put on his clothes and returned to his place. "Do you understand what I have done for you?" he asked them.**

The disciples had just watched Jesus do something truly remarkable. But did they *understand* its significance?

13. **"You call me 'Teacher' and 'Lord,' and rightly so, for that is what I am.**

The Greek word translated *Teacher* is closely related to the term "Rabbi," as John 1:38 indicates. Rabbis were held in great respect among Jews of that day, even as they are today. *Lord* indicates authority or even ownership, as in a lord's relationship to a slave. Jesus did not condemn the Twelve for calling him by either of these titles. He only intended to show that they had not yet fully grasped the meaning of either title.

WHAT DO YOU THINK?

We do not know whether Judas Iscariot was present when Jesus washed the disciples' feet, but if he was, then Jesus washed his feet as well. Imagine the scene as Jesus washed Judas's feet. Imagine the penetrating look Jesus must have had as he looked Judas in the eye. What lessons does that suggest to you?

What does this scene teach us about our own level of service? What would it take for a modern believer to be able to perform loving acts toward one who has spread gossip about the person or otherwise worked to his or her harm? How can we follow Jesus' example?

WHAT DO YOU THINK?

The washing of a guest's feet was a part of the welcome extended to him (see Luke 7:44-46). So we should be able to find some counterparts in the way we welcome one another in the church. Let's not limit this concept to activities performed at the church building, however. There are many ways we can serve one another. What are some modern-day counterparts to footwashing?

WHAT DO YOU THINK?

Anyone who has from a pure heart rendered service in Jesus' name can surely tell of blessings received. What blessings have you received from serving others?

PRAYER

O Lord, forgive the pride that robs us of the joy of service. Forgive as well the pride that makes us hesitate to accept the loving service of others. Keep ever before us the example of Jesus. We pray in his name. Amen.

THOUGHT TO REMEMBER

Both in serving and in being served we follow the example of our Lord.

B. AN EXAMPLE TO FOLLOW (vv. 14, 15)

14, 15. Now that I, your Lord and Teacher, have washed your feet, you also should wash one another's feet. I have set you an example that you should do as I have done for you.

Did Jesus intend for us to take these words literally? Some believe that he did, and thus footwashing as a part of worship is practiced in some churches today. Those who do so maintain that Jesus instituted this ceremony as surely as he instituted the Lord's Supper in the upper room.

However, while there is further mention of the Lord's Supper in the letters of the New Testament, footwashing as a part of worship is never mentioned again. The only other time it is mentioned at all is in 1 Timothy 5:10, where it is one of several "good deeds" to be done for someone in need. Therefore, most believers understand Jesus' words as a challenge to follow his example of humility and service, not as the institution of an act of public worship.

C. TRUE GREATNESS (v. 16)

16. I tell you the truth, no servant is greater than his master, nor is a messenger greater than the one who sent him.

If Jesus as Lord was willing to do the work of the lowest servant, then the men in that room must be prepared to do the same. They would soon be leaders in Jesus' church, of course. But they would fulfill that duty most effectively only if they were willing to be servants. Jesus remains the supreme example of servant leadership (Matthew 20:28; Philippians 2:5-8).

D. TRUE HAPPINESS (v. 17)

17. Now that you know these things, you will be blessed if you do them."

To know what is right is commendable. However, knowledge alone, as Paul reminds us, puffs us up (1 Corinthians 8:1). To do what is right produces a sense of fulfillment and the blessing of true happiness. (The word for blessed is the same one used in the Beatitudes in Matthew 5:3-11.) When we are faithful to Jesus and to the example he has set for us to follow, we will indeed be blessed.

CONCLUSION

A. THE NEED FOR HUMILITY

Humility is surely the most elusive of virtues. Just when we think we have attained it, we've lost it! Real humility is expressed in serving, in not insisting on our own way or supposing that we have all the answers, and in not insisting that we be given praise or preference. We should not be surprised that 1 John 2:16 (King James Version) places "the pride of life" alongside "the lust of the flesh" and "the lust of the eyes" as one of the taproots of sin.

B. TWO KINDS OF HUMILITY

Whenever we read or study the incident recorded in today's text, we usually focus on Jesus, who was not too proud to wash men's feet. We also need to focus on Peter, who at first was too proud to allow Jesus to wash his feet.

In a monastery in Austria, at each end of a long colonnade is a wood carving. One shows Jesus kneeling to wash Peter's feet. The other shows a woman kneeling to wash Jesus' feet. Ordinarily we do not think of those two scenes together, but we should. It took as much humility for Jesus to permit that woman to wash his feet as it took for him to wash the disciples' feet.

Certainly we need to develop a spirit of humility that is willing to serve in any capacity. At other times, however, we need the humility to allow others to serve us.

Discovery Learning

This page contains an alternate lesson plan emphasizing learning activities. Classes desiring such student involvement will find these suggestions helpful. The next page is a reproducible activity page to further enhance discovery learning.

LEARNING GOALS

After this lesson students will be able to:

1. Tell the story of Jesus' washing the disciples' feet in the upper room.

2. Explain why it is difficult either to serve or to be served by another.

3. Resolve to do something each day this week in service to another, and to receive the service of others graciously.

INTO THE LESSON

Write on the chalkboard or a large poster the words, "Jobs I Hate to Do." Encourage students, as they arrive, to write answers under the heading. You'll probably get responses like "take out the garbage," "clean the toilet," or "scrub the floor." Parents of young children may add "changing diapers."

When it is time to begin, ask the class to vote on the worst job on the list. Ask, "Why are these jobs so distasteful?" Some of the jobs on the list will be difficult. Many will require handling or being near something dirty. But the worst thing is that they are thankless jobs. Everyone expects them to get done, but the doing of them seems to be taken for granted.

Point out that, in New Testament times, people walked on dusty or muddy roads and streets in open sandals. They removed the sandals in Oriental fashion when they entered a home, but their feet were still dirty. So it was customary to greet one's guests with a footwashing to remove the soil. This job went to the lowest of servants. If a visitor from the first century were present at the beginning of today's class, "washing feet" is probably what he or she would have written on the "Jobs I Hate to Do" list. In today's lesson we'll see how Jesus used this thankless job to teach a valuable lesson.

INTO THE WORD

Assign someone in advance to be prepared to read John 13:1-17. Distribute to the class a chart with the following headings across the top: Forget Yourself (vv. 1-5); How Can I Wash Your Foot When It's in Your Mouth? (vv. 6-11); I'd Rather See a Sermon Than Hear One (vv. 12-17). Ask the students to reflect on verses 1-5 and write how one's self-esteem is related to his or her willingness to serve. Ask them to write their thoughts in the first column.

After a few minutes, ask the class to look at verses 6-11 and write what was wrong with Peter's protest (v. 8) and his later exclamation (v. 9). Ask them to summarize what Jesus wanted the disciples to learn about serving and about being served.

Again allow a few minutes for the students to work; then ask them to consider the remaining six verses of the text. Ask them to suggest practical ways of following Jesus' example as he commanded, and to suggest at least one blessing that might result (v. 17).

Allow a few more minutes for the students to respond; then ask them to get into pairs to review their answers in column 1. Ask for volunteers to share some interesting items from their partners' answers. (No one may share his or her own answers.) Use information from the commentary section to supplement this discussion.

Repeat this same procedure to review the texts related to columns 2 and 3, asking the students to find new partners for each section.

INTO LIFE

From the responses offered under column 3, make a list on the chalkboard of tasks that Christians can do to follow Jesus' example of humble service. Ask for more ideas if the list seems short. (You need at least six.)

When your list is complete, distribute sheets of paper on which you have written the days of the week, Monday through Saturday, down the left side. (Or use the reproducible activity page that follows.) Ask each student to write one activity from your list next to each day and to plan to do at least one act of loving service each day. Remind them to be ready to accept service from others as well.

Then ask the class to choose one item from the list that might make a good class project. Plan a time when your class can accomplish it. Perhaps "washing windows for an elderly person" was cited. Organize a time your class can get together and wash windows for several older members. You could meet at the church building and send teams of three or four people to different homes. Then meet back at the church building or a member's home for some fun and fellowship.

Conclude the class session by reading verses 14-17. Close with prayer that God would give you the grace to serve, and to accept the service of others, in the true spirit of Christ.

Day by Day With Jesus

Jesus' example in the upper room is one he told us to follow. On the chart below list six tasks that you can do to follow Jesus' example of humble service each day the rest of this week. Use the space to the right of each item to write any details needed to plan to do each item.

	TASK	PLANS
Monday		
Tuesday		
Wednesday		
Thursday		
Friday		
Saturday		

Let's Get Together

Is there a job on your list above—or some other that you can think of—that would be better done by a group than by an individual? Write that one below and plan to round up a team of "servant-helpers" to get the job done!

JESUS, THE TRUE VINE

LESSON 11

WHY TEACH THIS LESSON?

The New York Philharmonic Orchestra was practicing Beethoven's Ninth Symphony. The conductor, Arturo Toscanini, led them through the entire work without interruption. When they finished, there was a long silence; everyone was too moved by the music to speak. Then Toscanini broke the silence. "Who am I?" he said. "Who is Toscanini? I am nobody. It is Beethoven. He is everything."

That attitude, with a refined focus, is what you want to cultivate in your students today. Of course, it is not Beethoven, but Jesus, who is everything. "Apart from me you can do nothing," he told us. With him, you and your students can do anything he has called you to do. Today's lesson will help you to communicate that fact.

INTRODUCTION

A. A FAMILIAR PICTURE

Perhaps nothing in the landscape of Israel was more familiar to the Jews of Jesus' day than the vine. Vineyards could be seen almost everywhere. The vine was also prominent in their history. The twelve spies sent by Moses to explore the promised land spoke of clusters of grapes so large that it would take two men to carry them (Numbers 13:23). In addition the vine was prominent in the Jews' architecture: over the front of the temple in Jerusalem was a golden vine. And it was prominent in their Scriptures, for both the vine and the vineyard were often used in the Old Testament to represent the nation of Israel. So when Jesus called himself the "vine," he was using a symbol quite familiar to his hearers.

B. LESSON BACKGROUND

Last week's lesson focused on Jesus' washing of his disciples' feet in the upper room (John 13:1-17). At some point during the evening, Jesus made it clear to Judas that he knew of his plot to betray him, and Judas left the group. Probably it was after Judas left that Jesus instituted the Lord's Supper.

Jesus then gave a lengthy discourse to his disciples, calming their fears, promising the Holy Spirit to aid them, and praying for both them and future believers (John 14–17). Some of these words were spoken in the upper room, but some may have been spoken on the way to Gethsemane, where Jesus prayed and was later arrested. (See Jesus' words, "Come now; let us leave," in John 14:31.) If so, perhaps the disciples noticed on the way the golden vine on the temple or passed some growing vines. On the other hand, some believe that all the discourse was given in the upper room and that John 18:1 refers to the group's leaving the upper room. If that is so, perhaps they were simply preparing to leave at the end of chapter 14. In that case, the cup from which Jesus and the disciples had drunk of "the fruit of the vine" could have suggested the object lesson of the vine.

I. CULTIVATING A FRUITFUL LIFE (JOHN 15:1-6)

A. THE VINE (v. 1)

1. "I am the true vine, and my Father is the gardener.

DEVOTIONAL READING:
PSALM 1
LESSON SCRIPTURE:
JOHN 15:1-17
PRINTED TEXT:
JOHN 15:1-17

LESSON AIMS

After this lesson each student should be able to:

1. Summarize Jesus' message of the vine and the branches.

2. Explain the relationship that believers, as "branches," are to maintain with Jesus, the "Vine."

3. List one or two "fruits" that he or she is seeking to cultivate, based on a relationship with the Vine.

May
16

KEY VERSE

I am the vine; you are the branches. If a man remains in me and I in him, he will bear much fruit; apart from me you can do nothing. —John 15:5

LESSON 11 NOTES

Often the Old Testament references to Israel as a vine are negative (Isaiah 5:1-7; Jeremiah 2:21; Ezekiel 15:1-6; Hosea 10:1). Jesus referred to himself as *the true vine*, in contrast with disobedient Israel, which was an imperfect foreshadowing. Recall how elsewhere John records Jesus' statement that he is the "true bread" compared with the manna that God provided for the Israelites (6:31, 32). At the beginning of his Gospel, John calls Jesus the "true light" compared with the light provided by John the Baptist (1:6-9).

Earlier in the week, Jesus had spoken a parable about a vineyard and the wicked tenants who abused their responsibility to care for it (Mark 12:1-12). He was speaking of the Jewish leaders. Here Jesus refers to his *Father* as the *gardener*. Whatever the "wicked tenants" among the Jews may seek to do to him, his Father's higher purpose will be fulfilled.

B. THE BRANCHES (vv. 2, 3)

2. "He cuts off every branch in me that bears no fruit, while every branch that does bear fruit he prunes so that it will be even more fruitful.

Some claim that the branches that were removed were never really connected. However, *in me* indicates a connection to, or relationship with, Christ. Some say the unfruitful branch refers only to Judas, but what, then, of the word *every*?

Jesus was stating a principle by which God continues to operate: as a gardener prunes away the dead branches, so God will cut off those who are unproductive. In addition, he also *prunes* (cuts back) the good branches. This suggests the removal of all that would hinder us from wholesome Christian living. Thus does God trim and shape the fruitful branches so that they *will be even more fruitful*. Note the importance of God's "discipline," as described in Hebrews 12:5-11.

Sometimes the term *fruit* refers to converts to Christ (Romans 1:13). Here, however, it more likely refers to one's character, as it does frequently in the New Testament. (See, for example, Matthew 3:8; 7:16-20; 12:33; Galatians 5:22, 23.)

3. "You are already clean because of the word I have spoken to you.

The Greek word rendered *clean* comes from the same root as the verb meaning "to prune." Jesus says that we are made *clean*, or pruned, by *the word*. Concerning the church, Paul writes that it is Jesus' desire to "sanctify and cleanse it with the washing of water by the word" (Ephesians 5:26).

C. NECESSITY OF ABIDING (vv. 4, 5)

4. "Remain in me, and I will remain in you. No branch can bear fruit by itself; it must remain in the vine. Neither can you bear fruit unless you remain in me.

Jesus commands all followers to *remain* in him. The *branch* that is cut off from the *vine* loses its source of life. In some countries where spring comes slowly, people will cut budding branches off fruit trees and bring them inside. The branches bloom in the indoor warmth, but they can never *bear fruit* as long as they are cut off from the parent stock.

5. "I am the vine; you are the branches. If a man remains in me and I in him, he will bear much fruit; apart from me you can do nothing.

There is a mutual union stated in the words of verse 4: *Remain in me, and I will remain in you. If we remain connected to Jesus, he will not sever the connection. But if we choose to disconnect ourselves from him, he will not force himself on us.* Here, of course, the illustration of the vine falls short (as all illustrations do). In the vineyard the branches have no choice. In life we "branches" do have a choice.

The result of abiding in Christ will be bountiful. It is not just that we will bring forth fruit, but that we will bring forth *much fruit*. No believer will ever be embarrassed that he connected himself to Jesus Christ.

WHAT DO YOU THINK?

Jesus said that the Father not only cuts off the dead branches but also prunes the good ones. He does this, Jesus said, through "the word" (John 15:3). How has the Word of God helped you to cut away unproductive attitudes and actions?

With what kind of attitude must we approach the hearing of a sermon or Bible lesson or our devotional reading of the Word? It's easy to listen for interesting facts or comforting promises, but how do we prepare ourselves to let the Word reveal our hidden sins and challenge us to eliminate them?

WHAT DO YOU THINK?

"Remain in me," Jesus said. That means to stay connected to him. What do you do to be sure you are staying connected to Jesus? What are some things you will not do because doing them may make remaining in him more difficult?

Encourage the students to be as specific as possible in their suggestions.

[handwritten: Are You receiving the nourishment & life offered by Christ? the vine]

As every coin has two sides, so every truth has a positive and a negative side. The negative side of this illustration is that without Christ we *can do nothing*. No real spiritual good can be accomplished without him.

D. COST OF NOT ABIDING (v. 6)

6. "*If anyone does not remain in me, he is like a branch that is thrown away and withers; such branches are picked up, thrown into the fire and burned.*

When a *branch* is cut off from a vine, it *withers* and dies. With certain plants one can cut off a branch, put it in water, and it will develop roots and become another plant. The vine is not like that. The follower of Jesus is not like that. If he cuts himself off from Christ, he withers and dies.

Branches pruned from a grapevine have no further use. One cannot build anything from them. He cannot carve anything out of them. They are simply worthless, so the best thing one can do is to see that they are *thrown into the fire and burned*. Such a fate reminds us of the Scriptures' frequent warnings about the punishment of the wicked (Matthew 13:42, 50; Mark 9:48; Luke 16:24; 2 Thessalonians 1:8; Jude 7; Revelation 20:14, 15).

THE IMPORTANCE OF REMAINING

According to John 15, one of the most important aspects of bearing fruit is the need to "remain" in Christ. It is obvious, as Jesus pointed out, that a branch separated from its vine quickly loses its life and becomes good for nothing except fuel for the fire.

While the illustration of a vine is not nearly as familiar to our society as it was to Jesus' audience, we can think of several modern examples that illustrate the importance of "remaining in," or staying connected to, a source of power. When an electric wire is disconnected from a wall plug, it becomes useless. When something hinders the circulation of blood to a hand or finger, it becomes stiff, numb, and useless. If a telephone wire is cut, the phone will not work. Its connection has been severed. Sometimes a gas or an oil pipeline will be cut or broken; the result is that fuel cannot be carried to homes, schools, or factories.

Sometimes a Christian, through disobedience or apathy, loses his connection with Jesus. The consequences are far more tragic than those in the above illustrations of being "disconnected." Someone once observed, "If you are not feeling as close to God as you once did, who do you think moved?" In light of Jesus' words in John 15, we could alter the question to ask, "If you haven't remained in Christ, the true Vine, who do you think broke the connection?" —J. G. V. B.

II. BLESSINGS OF A FRUITFUL LIFE (JOHN 15:7-17)

A. A PRAYER-FILLED LIFE (v. 7)

7. "*If you remain in me and my words remain in you, ask whatever you wish, and it will be given you.*

The little word *if* is a significant one: it tells us that it is possible for a believer to turn away from Christ so that he does not *remain in him*. We avoid this tragic condition by allowing his *words* to *remain in us*. Long ago David said, "I have hidden your word in my heart that I might not sin against you" (Psalm 119:11). Later, the apostle Paul wrote to the Colossians, "Let the word of Christ dwell in you richly" (Colossians 3:16).

Jesus gives an additional promise to those who remain in him: *ask whatever you wish, and it will be given you*. Whenever we read such promises as this (similar ones are found in Matthew 21:22; Luke 11:9; and John 16:23), we may immediately think of instances where our personal experience with prayer did not seem to confirm Jesus' promise. However, let us keep in mind the condition stated by

I am the vine, ye are the branches. He that abideth in me, and I in him, the same bringeth forth much fruit for without me ye can do nothing. John 15:5

[handwritten: key Christ? the vine]

The visual for lesson 11 illustrates verse 5 of the text. Discuss the kind of fruit Jesus expects of his followers today.

[handwritten: How do remain in Him. One of most important aspects of bearing fruit is to remain in Christ. If we remain in Jesus He will not sever the connection. If we choose he will not force himself on us.]

WHAT DO YOU THINK?

Suppose a Christian brother came to you and said, "What about this promise in John 15:7? I prayed that my wife and I would work out our problems, but we got divorced anyway. Why didn't God answer my prayers?" How would you answer?

Would you suggest the brother might be at fault (Psalm 66:18; James 4:3)? Why or why not—or under what circumstances? Would you blame the wife? Why or why not—or under what circumstances? What encouragement could you give this brother now?

HOW TO SAY IT

agape (Greek). uh-GAH-pay.
Gethsemane. Geth-SEM-uh-nee.

Jesus: *if you remain in me and my words remain in you.* The petitions of those who abide in Christ will reflect his will and his purpose (note the promise in 1 John 5:14). Jesus was certainly not promising to satisfy each and every one of our whims. No wise and loving parent gives a child everything the child asks for—and God is our Father. Those occasions when we do not receive what we prayed for should strengthen our faith, not weaken it.

B. A PURPOSEFUL LIFE (v. 8)

8. "This is to my Father's glory, that you bear much fruit, showing yourselves to be my disciples.

Remaining in Christ enriches our own lives and brings *glory* to God. It should amaze us that our lives can be used to bring glory to God. We can understand how "the heavens declare the glory of God" (Psalm 19:1). We can understand how sacred music glorifies God. We can understand how certain forms of art, literature, and architecture glorify God. But God is glorified most of all through the holy lives of the *disciples* of Jesus.

KINDS OF FRUIT

In the first few verses of John 15, Jesus stresses how important it is for his disciples to be fruitful. He speaks of bearing "fruit" and being "fruitful." Most likely the "fruit" of which he speaks includes the deeds of kindness, acts of love, and evidences of caring that his love inspires in us.

What kinds of fruit do we see in the world because Jesus' disciples are doing his will? Consider the hospitals, the orphanages, and the special schools for the blind, the deaf, and those who have mental retardation. Consider the people and organizations ministering faithfully to those in prison. Consider the soup kitchens and food pantries operated by churches in areas where few people care enough to get involved. Consider the nursing homes and retirement facilities that churches have started and staffed in order to provide adequate care and housing for the elderly.

If we desire a summary of the "fruit" that Jesus desires to see in his followers, we should examine Matthew 25:31-46. There we find a description of the conduct that Jesus will reward on Judgment Day. It includes feeding the hungry, giving hospitality to strangers, clothing the naked, looking after the sick, and ministering to prisoners. This is the kind of fruit that those who remain in Christ are to bear before a watching world.

—J. G. V. B.

C. A JOYFUL LIFE (vv. 9-11)

9. "As the Father has loved me, so have I loved you. Now remain in my love.

The coming crucifixion did not cause Jesus to think that God no longer *loved* him. Nor should our suffering cause us to think that God does not love us. The love that God had for Jesus was the same *love* Jesus had for his disciples. They were to *remain in* that love. Of course, Jesus would continue to love them if they turned away from him; but if they did, they would forfeit the blessings that walking in his love can bring. (By this time, Judas had already turned away from Jesus and resolved to carry out his plans of betrayal.)

The word translated *love* is a Greek word with which many are familiar—*agape*. It emphasizes the will more than the emotions and implies that love is shown by one's actions. That idea is developed in the next verse.

10. "If you obey my commands, you will remain in my love, just as I have obeyed my Father's commands and remain in his love.

For all who follow Jesus Christ, the evidence of love is obedience. Jesus' question, "Why do you call me, 'Lord, Lord,' and do not do what I say?" (Luke 6:46), will not go away.

John records other instances where Jesus declared his obedience to the *Father's commands*. "I seek not to please myself but him who sent me" (John 5:30). "The one who sent me is with me; he has not left me alone, for I always do what pleases him" (John 8:29). In John 14:31 is recorded Jesus' words: "I do exactly what my Father has commanded me."

11. "I have told you this so that my joy may be in you and that your joy may be complete.

Surely we have lived long enough and learned enough from the experiences of others to know that the world's *joy* can never *be complete*. It is always shallow and superficial. It is always followed by regret and guilt. As Jesus wants us to have a more abundant life (John 10:10), so he wants us to have a fuller joy.

D. A LIFE OF FRIENDSHIP (vv. 12-15)

12. "My command is this: Love each other as I have loved you.

If love were simply an emotional feeling, we could hardly be commanded to *love each other*. But when we understand love as a commitment, we can see how it can be commanded. Perhaps we can never love one another as much as Jesus loves us, but we can strive to demonstrate the same kind of love.

In John 13:34 Jesus called the *command* to love a "new command." It must have seemed to the disciples that there were already enough commands. Why did they need another one? However, as Jesus had explained earlier (Matthew 22:34–40), two basic commandments embrace all the rest. When one loves God, and his neighbor as himself, keeping the other commandments naturally follows.

13. "Greater love has no one than this, that he lay down his life for his friends.

In only a few hours Jesus will in fact *lay down his life*. The crucifixion was much more than the evil scheme of Jesus' enemies. He voluntarily allowed himself to be put to death (John 10:18), and that remains the ultimate evidence of his love for mankind. John, who was present on this occasion, wrote in his first letter, "This is how we know what love is: Jesus Christ laid down his life for us. And we ought to lay down our lives for our brothers" (1 John 3:16). (We ought to memorize 1 John 3:16 as well as John 3:16.)

14. "You are my friends if you do what I command.

In any friendship there are always mutual obligations. Jesus will fulfill his part by dying on the cross. His followers are to fulfill their part by doing what he commands them to do.

15. "I no longer call you servants, because a servant does not know his master's business. Instead, I have called you friends, for everything that I learned from my Father I have made known to you.

Jesus had indeed *called* his disciples *friends*. One of these occasions is recorded in Luke 12:4 (there may have been other times). Now he will explain the word and the relationship. The Greek word translated *servant* means "slave." A servant is not expected to maintain an intimate friendship with his *lord*. The relationship is strictly business; the servant's task is to carry out the master's orders.

Friends, however, make plans together and discuss matters that they would never talk about with someone else. Jesus' disciples would continue to serve him, but they would share his mission of taking good news to a lost world. Thus the relationship would be far more intimate than that of servant to lord.

We should not suppose that the word *everything* means that the disciples knew all that Jesus knew. Most likely it indicates that they understood all things necessary to carry out their work. Later, during this same discourse, Jesus promised to send the Holy Spirit, who would guide the disciples "into all truth" (John 16:13).

WHAT DO YOU THINK?

The world's joy is shallow; it will eventually fail. The joy of the Lord sustains us even when we have trouble, just as it did Jesus at the cross (Hebrews 12:2). How can we attract people of the world, who believe they have joy without Jesus, to the fullness of joy that Jesus offers?

E. A LIFE OF SECURITY (vv. 16, 17)

16. "You did not choose me, but I chose you and appointed you to go and bear fruit—fruit that will last. Then the Father will give you whatever you ask in my name.

From among his many followers, Jesus specifically *chose* twelve. This choosing, or being *appointed*, refers to the specific calling to be an apostle. It does not refer to these men's original decision to follow Jesus. That is always a personal choice, made freely, both in Jesus' time and in our time.

The purpose to which these men were called was not an idle one. They were to *bear fruit*. They were also given the assurance that their fruit would *last*. How that must have been a comfort to them! They may not succeed in every city or in every effort, but their cause would succeed. These words are also a great comfort to us. God's Word will not return to him void; it will accomplish the purpose he has assigned to it (Isaiah 55:11). The apostle Paul had great confidence in the gospel as "the power of God for the salvation of everyone who believes" (Romans 1:16).

Once again we have Jesus' promise that *whatever you ask* shall be given. Here he adds the phrase *in my name*. It is common to close our prayers by saying "in Jesus' name" or similar words. This is a good way to pray and a proper thing to say. However, when we read the prayers of the New Testament, we find such language missing. Therefore, *in my name* must refer to something else besides the actual contents of a prayer. At the same time, it should warn us against praying for something that we cannot properly ask for in Jesus' name. The phrase thus limits our prayer requests to items that are consistent with a life of obedient faith.

Also, the word *name* usually suggests authority. Christ authorizes us to pray. He is our mediator, "bridging the gap" between us and God (1 Timothy 2:5; Hebrews 9:15; 12:24). It is good that we acknowledge this fact in the closing words of our prayers by praying "in Jesus' name." Were it not for his work on our behalf, we would not be able to approach God as our Father.

17. "This is my command: Love each other."

In light of the jealous bickering that had gone on earlier in the upper room (Luke 22:24), this *command* was most appropriate. This was the third time during the evening that Jesus had given it (13:34, 35; 15:12).

CONCLUSION

We have heard or sung the hymn "Amazing Grace" so often that we can easily forget how "amazing" God's love and grace really are. We do not deserve the love of God. In fact, if we received from God what we truly deserved, condemnation for eternity would be the result. God loves us, not because of all the good we have done, but in spite of all the bad we have done. This is grace—unmerited favor—at work.

It is also important to read the four verses (18-21) that follow today's printed text. The love of Jesus for his followers and of his followers for one another is placed alongside the hate that both they and Jesus will experience in the world. Why did some people hate Jesus? The answer is that his perfect life served as a condemnation of their own. Similarly, the lives of genuine Christians stand in such contrast to the ways of the world that they too are sometimes hated by the world that both they and Jesus love.

While we should never lose our amazement at Jesus' love for us, neither should we ever be amazed when the world responds to it with hostility. As Jesus said, "No servant is greater than his master" (John 15:20).

Discovery Learning

This page contains an alternate lesson plan emphasizing learning activities. Classes desiring such student involvement will find these suggestions helpful. The next page is a reproducible activity page to further enhance discovery learning.

LEARNING GOALS

As a result of participating in this lesson, each student will be able to:

1. Summarize Jesus' message of the vine and the branches.

2. Explain the relationship that believers, as "branches," are to maintain with Jesus, the "Vine."

3. List one or two "fruits" that he or she is seeking to cultivate, based on a relationship with the Vine.

INTO THE LESSON

Ask your students how many of them are making use of the Internet—that vast network of computers and file servers by which a person with a personal computer can access information, send electronic messages to other computer owners, and even make long-distance phone calls with the proper software. Ask those using the Internet, "How many of you have had problems getting connected or staying connected?"

Many Internet service providers have found demand for their services to be greater than they are able to deliver. Thus, several of your Internet users will probably say they have had some trouble. Busy signals, slow response, and loss of connection are frequent complaints. Ask, "What good is the Internet to you if you cannot connect or stay connected?" Obviously, it is of no value; it's as if the Internet were not there.

Tell the class, "Staying connected is the theme of our lesson today. But we're not talking about staying connected to the Internet. We're not even talking about staying connected to a vine—though that is the metaphor Jesus used to communicate the truth we want to explore today. We're talking about staying connected to Jesus himself. It's frustrating when a computer user loses his or her connection with the Internet. But it's absolutely tragic when a believer loses the connection with Christ!"

INTO THE WORD

Ask a volunteer to read John 15:1-17. Then divide the class into groups of three to five each. Give one-third of your groups one of the following assignments. (If you cannot form at least three groups, have the entire class work on all the activities together.)

Assignment 1: Read verses 1-6. Jesus used a metaphor familiar to people who knew about grapevines. What metaphor might he have used if he had been speaking to people of our time and place? Write a paraphrase of verses 1-6 with a different metaphor.

Assignment 2: Read verses 7-11. List all the promises Jesus gives in this section. If a promise is conditional, note the condition. Suggest at least one specific way a believer can comply with each condition you find. (The promises are as follows: "ask whatever you wish, and it will be given you" [conditioned on "if you remain in me and my words remain in you"]; "showing yourselves to be my disciples" [conditioned on "that you bear much fruit"]; "you will remain in my love" [conditioned on "if you obey my commands"].)

Assignment 3: Read verses 12-17. This section begins and ends with a command to "love each other." In between, Jesus emphasizes the themes of self-sacrifice, obedience, prayer, and bearing fruit. Explain how these themes are related to loving one another.

Allow about eight minutes for the groups to choose a reporter and to write their responses. Then ask each group to have its reporter summarize the group's findings. Supplement the reports with additional information from the commentary section as needed.

INTO LIFE

Challenge the class to think of ways in which they can love and serve one another in the week ahead. Make a list of these suggestions on the chalkboard. Suggest that these activities comprise some of the "fruit" Jesus calls us to bear.

Ask, "Why do we not always demonstrate this kind of fruit in our lives?" Make a list on the board of the class's answers. Call for suggestions on how to reduce or remove each of these hindrances.

Make copies of the reproducible page that follows, one for each member of the class. Distribute the copies and ask each class member to write on the back one or two "fruits" that he or she is seeking to cultivate, based on a relationship with the Vine, Jesus. Encourage the students to post their grape clusters where they will see them and be reminded of the need to bear fruit for the Lord Jesus Christ.

End the lesson with a circle prayer of thanksgiving and rejoicing that we can abide in the Vine and bear fruit for his glory.

I Will Bear Fruit

Write on the back of this sheet one or two "fruits" that you are seeking to cultivate, based on a relationship with the Vine, Jesus. Then post this cluster of grapes in a place where you will see it and be reminded of the need to bear fruit for the Lord Jesus Christ.

THE SPIRIT EMPOWERS LOVING OBEDIENCE

LESSON 12

WHY TEACH THIS LESSON?

A businessman was preparing to go to Thailand to expand his company's business overseas. First, he had to learn the Thai language, a slow and tedious process. He enrolled in a class taught by a former missionary to Thailand. The missionary was amused when the businessman, after only a few sessions, pleaded, "What are the shortcuts so I can get a handle on this faster?"

It seems we are always looking for shortcuts, something to make a difficult task easier. We are like the art student who, discouraged by his failure to develop his talent more quickly, picked up the master's brush and began to use it. The results were no better than with his own brush. A fellow student remarked, "It's not the master's brush you need, but the master's spirit."

This lesson will remind your students that Jesus did not give us any shortcuts on the road of faithful service. He provides no gimmicks or gadgets. What he has given us is his Spirit.

INTRODUCTION

A. THE CHRISTIAN'S "COACH"

The next time you attend an athletic competition, keep your eyes on the coach. Whether the sport is being played on a high school, college, or professional level, good coaches pursue the same goals. They want their players to do their best and to perform at maximum efficiency. Whenever a player does something well or puts forth a particularly strong effort, the coach is enthusiastic in his praise. At other times, the coach may appear stern and demanding, wanting to know why a player failed to carry out an assignment correctly. He may even "bench" the player and let him think about the error of his ways! But whatever the coach does, he does it with the player's best interests in mind.

Recognizing that all illustrations have limitations, we may compare the work of the Holy Spirit in the Christian's life with that of a coach. As we will see in today's text, the Spirit serves as the Christian's constant guide and companion, "coaching" him in the process of becoming more like Jesus. He provides encouragement in doing right, and conviction when the Christian is on the verge of embarking on the wrong path.

Whatever he does, the Holy Spirit wants only what is best for us. We need to learn the discipline of following our "Coach."

B. LESSON BACKGROUND

Today's lesson is taken from another portion of Jesus' discourse with his disciples on the night before his arrest and crucifixion. Last week's text was taken from the part of the discourse concerning the vine and the branches (John 15:1-17). Today's text focuses on Jesus' promise of the Holy Spirit. Jesus made it clear

DEVOTIONAL READING:
HEBREWS 2:10-18
LESSON SCRIPTURE:
JOHN 14:15-31; 16:4B-15
PRINTED TEXT:
JOHN 14:15-18, 24-26; 16:7-15

LESSON AIMS

After this lesson the students should be able to:

1. Summarize the Holy Spirit's role as companion, teacher, and evangelist.

2. Compare the apostles' need for "another Counselor" with our need for the Spirit.

3. Pinpoint aspects of their lives where they need to depend more completely on the Holy Spirit.

KEY VERSE

The Counselor, the Holy Spirit, whom the Father will send in my name, will teach you all things and will remind you of everything I have said to you. —John 14:26

May 23

LESSON 12 NOTES

The visual for lesson 12 shows the breadth of meaning in the word Jesus used to describe the promised Holy Spirit. Discuss the significance of the different terms noted here.

WHAT DO YOU THINK?

The literal meaning of the word "Counselor" in John 14:16 is "one called alongside." It can refer to one called to help, to defend (as in a court of law), to rebuke, to encourage, or to comfort. All of these concepts fit the work of the Holy Spirit. Each one makes it clear to us that the Spirit is on our side—a companion who is with us constantly to help us in many ways. Which one do you find especially significant? Why?

to his disciples that he was going to leave them (John 14:1-4). However, he assured them that they would not be left alone, for he would send to them "another Counselor . . . the Spirit of truth" (vv. 16, 17). The Spirit would empower the disciples for the monumental task that they were to accomplish in Jesus' name. Such power would become especially important to them in light of the hostility that the world would demonstrate toward both them and their message (15:18-25; 16:1-4). The promise still has application to Jesus' disciples today.

I. CONSTANT COMPANION (JOHN 14:15-18)

A. A TEST OF LOVE (v. 15)

15. "If you love me, you will obey what I command.

Someone once summarized the Bible's teachings as facts to be believed, commands to be obeyed, promises to be enjoyed, and warnings to be heeded. Here we see a command to be obeyed placed in the midst of promises to be enjoyed. The preceding verses include the promise of answered prayer (vv. 13, 14). In the succeeding verses we read Jesus' promise of the Holy Spirit.

In another portion of our printed text (v. 24), we will note words very similar to these about the importance of obedience to God. John stresses this theme in his first epistle: "We know that we have come to know him if we obey his commands. The man who says, 'I know him,' but does not do what he commands is a liar, and the truth is not in him" (1 John 2:3, 4).

B. A WONDERFUL PROMISE (v. 16)

16. "And I will ask the Father, and he will give you another Counselor to be with you forever.

Jesus introduces the Holy Spirit by describing him as a *Counselor*. The Greek word, *paraklete*, is difficult to translate. Besides *Counselor*, it is rendered in other translations as "Helper" and "Comforter." The word is used of Jesus in 1 John 2:1, where it is translated "one who speaks . . . in our defense." The term actually means "one who is called alongside another." Imagine, by way of illustration, a person standing before a judge in the courtroom with his attorney standing alongside him. But the Spirit's presence is not limited to any one particular situation. He will be alongside the followers of Jesus *forever*—in whatever situation they are facing. Such a promise would have been especially meaningful to the disciples, for Jesus had just told them he would be leaving them (v. 3).

Notice that Jesus described the Holy Spirit as *another Counselor*. The word for *another* does not mean a different kind of companion, but another of the same kind. While the disciples will miss the companionship of Jesus, the Spirit will be their unseen companion. He will be to them what Jesus was while he was present with them.

C. LIMITATIONS OF THE PROMISE (v. 17)

17. ". . . the Spirit of truth. The world cannot accept him, because it neither sees him nor knows him. But you know him, for he lives with you and will be in you.

Earlier Jesus had declared himself to be "the truth" (v. 6). Now he describes the Holy Spirit as the *Spirit of truth*. *The world*, referring to those who are under the sway of the "prince of this world" (John 16:11), or Satan, *cannot accept* the Spirit. As long as the "god of this age" blinds them to spiritual truth (2 Corinthians 4:4), the message of the Spirit will mean little or nothing to them.

The words *you know him* call attention to the fact that the Holy Spirit is never referred to by the pronoun "it." Always he is described with the personal pronouns "he" and "him." The Holy Spirit is a person, just as God is a person and

Jesus is a person. He has the characteristics of a person; for example, he can be grieved (Isaiah 63:10; Ephesians 4:30) and tested (Acts 5:9).

Jesus' words also pointed to the intimate relationship between his followers and the Spirit: the Spirit would live *with* them and *in* them. The fact that the Holy Spirit dwells in believers receives constant emphasis in the New Testament (Acts 2:38; 5:32; Romans 8:9-17; 1 Corinthians 3:16; 6:19; 2 Corinthians 5:5; Ephesians 5:18; 1 Thessalonians 4:8; 2 Timothy 1:14; 1 Peter 4:14).

D. ASSURANCE OF THE PROMISE (v. 18)

18. *"I will not leave you as orphans; I will come to you."*

The idea of being left *as orphans* is a vivid one. Perhaps that is just how the disciples felt, knowing that Jesus would be leaving them.

Certainly Jesus did *come* to the disciples following his resurrection. This promise, however, is linked to his promise of the Holy Spirit. Through the presence of the Spirit, Jesus would be with his followers—"to the very end of the age," as he said (Matthew 28:20).

NEVER ALONE

Jesus promised that he would provide a *paraklete* for his followers. This Greek word means "someone who is called to stand beside another." It pictures someone who assists or encourages another. The term is translated "Comforter" in the *King James Version* and "Counselor" in the *New International Version*. One may think of the task of an attorney, an intercessor, a mediator, or anyone whose role involves being a helper to another. This is the work that the Holy Spirit has been sent to accomplish.

In promising the Spirit Jesus said, "I will not leave you as orphans" (John 14:18). Just as an orphan is bereft of father and mother, and thus without an adult to offer comfort, consolation, and spiritual companionship, so we would be in this world without God's Spirit to indwell, bless, admonish, and encourage us.

The assurance of never being left "as orphans" is captured in this hymn, cherished by many:

> I've seen the lightning flashing,
>   I've heard the thunder roll,
> I've felt sin's breakers dashing,
>   Which almost conquered my soul;
> I've heard the voice of my Savior
>   Bidding me still to fight on;
> He promised never to leave me,
>   Never to leave me alone!
>   (Author unknown)

—J. G. V. B.

II. INSPIRING TEACHER (JOHN 14:24-26)

A. AUTHORITY OF JESUS' WORDS (v. 24)

24. *"He who does not love me will not obey my teaching. These words you hear are not my own; they belong to the Father who sent me.*

Here we have the negative side of that which was presented positively in verse 15. As far as Jesus is concerned, the test of whether someone truly loves him is always obedience. This is especially clear in Jesus' parable of the two sons (Matthew 21:28-32). Even in the Old Testament, God put a high premium on obedience (1 Samuel 15:22; Jeremiah 7:23). His concern in the New Testament era is no less.

HOW TO SAY IT

Gideon. GID-ee-un.

paraklete (Greek). PAIR-uh-kleet.

WHAT DO YOU THINK?

Some say that obedience is not important as long as one loves Jesus. "Obedience," they claim, "goes with the Old Covenant of law-keeping, but we live in the age of grace." How would you respond, based on today's text?

THE PRIORITY OF OBEDIENCE

In the first portion of today's printed text, Jesus speaks about the importance of doing what he commands (John 14:15). He repeats this theme in the second segment (v. 24). The primary test of our loyalty to Christ is our obedience to him. Merely addressing Jesus as "Lord, Lord" is a waste of words if we do not treat him as Lord in the way we live (Matthew 7:21; Luke 6:46).

The word *obey* may seem harsh or unfeeling to many. However, it is an essential element in many areas of our lives. What does a coach expect when he tells his team to execute a certain play in a specific situation? He wants them to *obey* his instructions. A parent tells a child that he wants him home for lunch at a certain time. The child's duty is to *obey*. When a teacher asks for a report to be prepared and turned in on a specific date, the student's duty is to *obey*. When a government says that a certain type of stamp is required for a first-class letter, the citizen's responsibility is to *obey*. Is the standard any lower concerning our relationship with God?

—J. G. V. B.

B. AUTHORITY OF THE SPIRIT (vv. 25, 26)

25, 26. "All this I have spoken while still with you. But the Counselor, the Holy Spirit, whom the Father will send in my name, will teach you all things and will remind you of everything I have said to you."

The Spirit would *remind* the disciples of what Jesus *said*. Not one of us can remember completely the sermon he heard last Sunday. But the apostles were able to recall the teachings of Jesus several years after his earthly life and then write them down accurately. They could do this by the inspiration of the Holy Spirit.

That the Spirit would teach the apostles *all things* is not to suggest that the apostles were omniscient. Only God knows everything. But they would be taught all that they needed to know, and they would thus convey to future generations all that they would need to know of Jesus and the way of salvation. We should keep in mind that this promise was given only to the apostles, in keeping with their role as part of the foundation of the church (Ephesians 2:20). Some have claimed to receive new revelations of truth through the Holy Spirit; but when these revelations contradict what the inspired writers of Scripture have taught, we must conclude that the alleged revelations are false. Truth cannot contradict truth, nor can God contradict himself.

This is not to diminish the importance of the measure of the Spirit that Christians receive, for we are to be "filled" with him (Ephesians 5:18). However, we need the Holy Spirit, not to receive knowledge (which is found in the Scriptures), but to empower us to live lives of holiness (1 Thessalonians 4:7, 8).

III. CONVINCING EVANGELIST (JOHN 16:7-15)

A. FOLLOWING JESUS' DEPARTURE (v. 7)

7. "But I tell you the truth: It is for your good that I am going away. Unless I go away, the Counselor will not come to you; but if I go, I will send him to you.

Jesus' departure must not have seemed to the disciples to be for their *good*; in fact, it appeared to put them at a serious disadvantage. What would they do without their Master? But Jesus' leaving would be a blessing in disguise, for it would be followed by the coming of the *Counselor*.

This is not to say that the Holy Spirit was not active prior to Jesus' departure into Heaven. The Spirit was present at creation (Genesis 1:2). The Spirit empowered men such as Moses (Numbers 11:17), Joshua (Deuteronomy 34:9), Gideon (Judges 6:34), Samson (Judges 14:6, 19; 15:14), David (1 Samuel 16:13; 2 Samuel 23:1, 2), and the Old Testament prophets (Nehemiah 9:30). John wrote that to Jesus, "God gives the Spirit without limit" (John 3:34).

DAILY BIBLE READINGS

Monday, May 17—*If You Love Me, Keep My Commandments* (John 14:15-24)

Tuesday, May 18—*The Holy Spirit Will Teach You* (John 14:25-31)

Wednesday, May 19—*When the Spirit of Truth Comes* (John 16:4b-15)

Thursday, May 20—*The Spirit of the Lord Brings Freedom* (2 Corinthians 3:12-18)

Friday, May 21—*No Longer a Slave But a Child* (Galatians 4:1-7)

Saturday, May 22—*Strengthened With Power Through His Spirit* (Ephesians 3:14-19)

Sunday, May 23—*We Are Children of God* (Romans 8:12-17)

However, Jesus' departure marked a new stage in the ministry of the Spirit. This is clear from John 7:39: "By this he meant the Spirit, whom those who believed in him were later to receive. Up to that time the Spirit had not been given, since Jesus had not yet been glorified." Only after Jesus was "glorified" in his ascension was the Spirit given (Acts 2:1-4, 33, 38).

B. REPROVING THE WORLD (vv. 8-11)

8. "When he comes, he will convict the world of guilt in regard to sin and righteousness and judgment.

It is because of this verse that we can say that the Holy Spirit works in the role of an evangelist, for he is involved in the process of bringing people to Christ. It used to be said that people whose conscience was bothering them and who were considering accepting Christ were "under conviction." Several translations use the word "convince" instead of *convict*.

While human voices and personalities must do their very best to lead people to Christ, ultimately it is the Holy Spirit who convicts and brings a response to the gospel. This does not mean that we should remain passive in the area of evangelism. We must be untiring in our efforts to lead people to Christ, but we must also humbly recognize that the Spirit takes our efforts and uses them.

9-11. ". . . in regard to sin, because men do not believe in me; in regard to righteousness, because I am going to the Father, where you can see me no longer; and in regard to judgment, because the prince of this world now stands condemned.

Here Jesus elaborated on the threefold conviction that is brought by the Spirit. The first step is to convince people that they are guilty of *sin*. No one can be saved until he knows that he is lost. This may be the hardest task we have in evangelism, particularly in today's world where "tolerance" of one another often appears to be the noblest virtue. People will admit to making mistakes, but they find it hard to confess that they are sinners in need of a Savior.

The second step is to be convinced of the need for *righteousness*. People need to know that there is a better way to live than what the world offers. They need to see that life exemplified in Jesus. They must also realize that they "fall short" of God's standard of righteousness (Romans 3:23) and that they can never, by their own efforts, reach that standard. Their only hope of attaining it is through Jesus' efforts—his death for their sins (2 Corinthians 5:21).

Finally, people must be convinced of the reality of a coming *judgment*. Judgment is sometimes a neglected theme today (again, because of our excessively tolerant society), but it is a prominent theme in the New Testament (Matthew 25:31-46; Romans 14:12; 2 Corinthians 5:10; Hebrews 9:27; Revelation 20:12).

All of Jesus' references to *the prince of this world* (Satan) occurred during his final week, as the time of his crucifixion grew closer (John 12:31; 14:30). While we can indeed sing the great hymn, "This Is My Father's World," it is also true that Satan has usurped God's position as rightful ruler of this world. Jesus came in order to reclaim what was lost because of man's sin. This is the significance of his description of someone who enters a house and "ties up the strong man" (Matthew 12:29). First John 3:8 tells us, "The reason the Son of God appeared was to destroy the devil's work." Those who accept Christ as Savior choose to leave Satan's domain in order to follow Jesus as Lord.

C. REVEALING THE TRUTH (vv. 12, 13)

12. "I have much more to say to you, more than you can now bear.

The word *bear* means "grasp" or "understand." Just as one goes through different levels in obtaining an education, so the Master Teacher gradually revealed

WHAT DO YOU THINK?

Since it is the Holy Spirit who reproves or convicts of sin, righteousness, and judgment, some people might assume that we humans need to do nothing to win the lost, that the Holy Spirit will do that. What would you say about this idea?

WHAT DO YOU THINK?

Jesus knew that the apostles needed much more information than they had, but they were not ready for it. They did not yet comprehend that Jesus was going to die and be raised again. There was no way, then, that they could understand the purpose for those events. The Spirit would have to guide them into these and other truths at a later time. Even so, many people today do not have a proper frame of reference to understand the gospel. For example, people who have been abandoned by their fathers have a difficult time appreciating God as a heavenly Father.

What happens when we try to give people more spiritual information than they are ready for? How can we tell how much a person is ready and able to understand?

WHAT DO YOU THINK?

The Holy Spirit's ministry is to glorify Jesus. That should be our aim as well, but it will not happen by accident. We must be deliberate about our ministries and plan for Jesus to be exalted. How can we be sure that Jesus has the preeminence in all of our programs and personal efforts?

PRAYER

O Lord, thank you for the blessed assurance that we are not spiritual orphans in a lonely and sometimes friendless world. Thank you for keeping your promise to be with us. May we welcome your Holy Spirit as a Holy Guest and make room for him in our lives. Amen.

THOUGHT TO REMEMBER

"The one who is in you is greater than the one who is in the world" (1 John 4:4).

his truth to his followers. The same principle is noted elsewhere regarding Jesus' teaching method: "With many similar parables Jesus spoke the word to them, as much as they could understand" (Mark 4:33).

13. "But when he, the Spirit of truth, comes, he will guide you into all truth. He will not speak on his own; he will speak only what he hears, and he will tell you what is yet to come.

The Holy Spirit would not *speak* a different message from that which the disciples had received from Jesus. As the *Spirit of truth*, his message would be entirely consistent with what Jesus had taught. The word *guide* is most interesting here, for it is the first indication of the divine inspiration that the apostles would be granted in the writing of the New Testament Scriptures. Second Peter 1:21 says that biblical writers were "carried along by the Holy Spirit." Paul claims that what he taught was what the Holy Spirit taught (1 Corinthians 2:13). He also declares in 2 Timothy 3:16 that "all Scripture is God-breathed."

The phrase *what is yet to come* could refer to the insights given to the apostles regarding events surrounding the second coming of Christ. (Consider, for examples, 2 Peter 3:1-13 and the book of Revelation.) It may also be describing the body of Christian truth and doctrine that the apostles, as part of the church's foundation, would be instrumental in communicating.

D. EXALTING JESUS (vv. 14, 15)

14. "He will bring glory to me by taking from what is mine and making it known to you.

Here Jesus says that the Spirit *will bring glory to me*. The Spirit will not come to promote himself. Often we hear some claim that there is not enough teaching on the Holy Spirit. The opposite may be the case. The Holy Spirit inspired Paul to write that in all things Jesus should have the preeminence (Colossians 1:18).

15. "All that belongs to the Father is mine. That is why I said the Spirit will take from what is mine and make it known to you."

There is complete unity between the *Father*, the Son, and the *Spirit*. The three are one; there is no rivalry. The best minds down through the ages have wrestled with the doctrine of the Trinity. Various illustrations have been used to explain it, though such illustrations must fall short of adequately explaining something so profound. However, we can believe in what Paul describes as "the mystery of godliness" (1 Timothy 3:16) without fully comprehending it.

CONCLUSION

The promise of today's lesson was repeated by Jesus after his resurrection. As the time neared for him to leave his disciples, he promised never to leave them. "And surely I am with you always, to the very end of the age," he said (Matthew 28:20). Believers down through the years are quick to confess that Jesus' promise has been kept in every era and in all places. This is one of the reasons Jesus had to leave this world and allow the Spirit to fulfill his appointed task. Jesus, because of his physical body, was limited in time and space. On the other hand, the Holy Spirit is not subject to such limitations and can dwell in believers throughout the world in every subsequent period of time.

Many Christians have avoided the topic of the Holy Spirit because it tends to be so controversial. This is a tragic mistake, because the Spirit is meant to be the Christian's ever-faithful Friend and Companion—his "Coach." While we should never presume to claim for ourselves promises meant only for the apostles, we should be quick to claim for ourselves and all believers the promise that the Spirit will supply us with the power we need and the comforting presence we cherish.

Discovery Learning

This page contains an alternate lesson plan emphasizing learning activities. Classes desiring such student involvement will find these suggestions helpful. The next page is a reproducible activity page to further enhance discovery learning.

LEARNING GOALS

After this lesson the students should be able to:

1. Summarize the Holy Spirit's role as companion, teacher, and evangelist.

2. Compare the apostles' need for "another Counselor" with our need for the Spirit.

3. Pinpoint aspects of their lives where they need to depend more completely on the Holy Spirit.

INTO THE LESSON

Write the word *Good-bye* on the chalkboard or on a large poster. As students arrive, ask them to describe how they feel when they have to tell a loved one good-bye. The occasion may have been a death or alienation or a geographic separation. How do they deal with such a situation? Is there one good way to handle the situation or are there many good ways?

Have each student write on a card the hardest parting he or she ever faced. (These descriptions should remain anonymous.) Collect the cards and read three or four, asking for short reactions from the class.

Tell the class, "In our lesson today we'll look at a time when Jesus' disciples were facing the hardest separation of their lives: Jesus would soon be leaving them. While our circumstances are not the same, it is helpful to note how the hope that Jesus offered his disciples applies to us in our difficulties—not only in times of separation from loved ones, but in many similar situations. Jesus promised the Counselor—a Helper, the Holy Spirit—and he will help us to cope with whatever difficult times come our way."

INTO THE WORD

Ask three volunteers to read these three passages without interruption: John 14:15-18; 24-26; 16:7-15.

Distribute sheets of paper to the class. Ask each student to write the headings *Role, Apostles,* and *Believers* at the top of his or her paper and to draw vertical lines separating the page into three columns. In the "Role" column, ask the students to write the word *Companion* near the top, *Teacher* about a third of the way down, and *Evangelist* about two-thirds down the page.

Option: Use the reproducible activity page that follows to facilitate a Scripture study of the Holy Spirit.

Have the students work individually or in small groups to note the promises connected with the Spirit's

role as companion (John 14:15-18), teacher (John 14:24-26), and evangelist (John 16:7-15), noting specific applications to the apostles and to believers generally by writing ideas in the two remaining columns. For example, in the "teacher" section, students should note verse 26. Under the "apostles" column they should note that this is a promise of inspiration so that the apostles could teach, preach, and write accurately and without error. Under the "believers" column they should note that we still have the benefit of this promise from what has been written in the New Testament. (See 2 Timothy 3:16, 17; 2 Peter 1:21.)

Allow time for the students to work—about five to seven minutes for each section. (If time is short, assign different sections to different groups.) Then discuss each section. Use information from the commentary section to help you sort out the differences between what Jesus promised the apostles and what applies to us.

Note that Jesus' farewell is much like many we face; separation from a loved one is always difficult. But his was unique in that he was able to promise "another Counselor." As your study has shown, we continue to benefit from that promise, but we need to depend on the Spirit for the promise to be of any help to us.

INTO LIFE

Ask the students how the promise of a "Counselor" makes them feel. What about this promise is most significant to them? After a brief discussion, note the wider meaning of the word translated "Counselor" (see the commentary section, page 326, or today's visual). How does this expanded meaning help them as they consider the Spirit's role in helping them to live for the Lord?

Distribute index cards to the class. Ask the students to use these cards to write down some of the things they are trying to do for the Lord. These might include breaking a bad habit, cultivating a closer relationship with a spouse, developing a better devotional time, serving in a ministry position in the church, or something else. Then ask each student to look at his card and to ask himself: "Am I depending on the power of the Spirit to help me with each of these items?" Encourage each student to choose one or two items where he or she needs to depend more completely on the Holy Spirit and to seek to do that this week.

Getting to Know the Spirit

Look up each of the following Scripture passages and make a brief notation of what it teaches you about the Holy Spirit.

Genesis 1:2

Numbers 11:17

Deuteronomy 34:9

Judges 6:34

Judges 14:6, 19

1 Samuel 16:13

2 Samuel 23:1, 2

Nehemiah 9:30

John 14:16, 17

John 14:18-25

Acts 2:1-4, 33

Ephesians 5:18

1 Thessalonians 4:7, 8

2 Timothy 3:16, 17

2 Peter 1:21

JESUS PRAYS FOR HIS DISCIPLES

LESSON 13

WHY TEACH THIS LESSON?

Have you ever had someone pray for you? Perhaps you were sick, maybe even in the hospital, and someone from the church stopped by and, after a brief visit, prayed for your recovery. Or perhaps there was a significant decision to be made, and someone from your family prayed with you and for you. How do you feel when someone prays for you? Isn't it one of the most moving experiences in your Christian life? If the person praying is known for mature spirituality, the experience is even more powerful.

Your students need to know someone has prayed for them, someone whose spiritual depth is unmatched. The Son of God himself prayed—not just for the little band of Galileans who followed him across the Palestinian landscape for three years—but for them. This lesson will allow them to reflect on that. It should encourage their faith and bind them together in the love of the Lord.

INTRODUCTION

A. THE TRUE "LORD'S PRAYER"

It is often moving to listen to the public prayers of certain individuals. It can be especially moving to listen in on someone's private prayers, for they usually are offered with greater intensity and emotion. The prayer of Jesus found in today's lesson text was not a public prayer, but he meant for his disciples (both then and now) to overhear it. It is one of the most moving passages, not only in the Gospels but in the New Testament.

It is not wrong to call the prayer that Jesus taught us in Matthew 6 the Lord's Prayer. However, when we call it that, we must also realize that strictly speaking it is the disciples' prayer: "This, then, is how *you* should pray," Jesus said (Matthew 6:9). John 17 records the true Lord's Prayer; for it is Jesus' own personal prayer, deliberately prayed in the hearing of his closest followers. In it we learn much about Jesus and about ourselves. When we examine its contents, we are truly walking on holy ground, like Moses before the burning bush. We should approach this lesson with a special measure of reverence.

B. LESSON BACKGROUND

The lessons in this final unit of our studies from John's Gospel have all been drawn from the events that took place on the evening before Jesus' crucifixion. We have noted that of all the Gospel writers, only John records Jesus' words of warning and encouragement to his disciples and the prayer from which today's text is taken (chapters 14–17).

At what point Jesus and the disciples left the upper room and began to make their way to the Garden of Gethsemane is not clear. Jesus told the disciples to get up so they could leave just after he promised the coming of another Counselor,

DEVOTIONAL READING:
EPHESIANS 6:10-20

LESSON SCRIPTURE:
JOHN 17

PRINTED TEXT:
JOHN 17:1-5, 9-11, 15-24

LESSON AIMS

After this lesson students should be able to:

1. Tell what Jesus prayed for in John 17.

2. Explain why the unity of believers, for which Jesus prayed, must continue to be a priority for the church today.

3. Suggest steps that individuals and congregations can take to work for that unity.

KEY VERSE

Holy Father, protect them by the power of your name—the name you gave me—so that they may be one as we are one.
—John 17:11

May
30

the Holy Spirit, and before his discourse on the vine (John 14:31). John notes, however, that it was "when he had finished praying" that "Jesus left with his disciples" (John 18:1). Either their departure was delayed after Jesus said "let us leave" in 14:31 or John's mention of leaving in 18:1 refers to leaving the city and not the upper room. He notes at that point that they crossed the Kidron Valley, which separates the city of Jerusalem from the Mount of Olives. Many believe, then, that Jesus and the disciples left the upper room (14:31) and continued the discourse as they walked. Somewhere along the way, before they crossed the brook Kidron (18:1), Jesus offered the prayer recorded in John 17.

I. JESUS FACES DEATH (JOHN 17:1-5)

A. THE TIME IS NEAR (v. 1)

1. *After Jesus said this, he looked toward heaven and prayed: "Father, the time has come. Glorify your Son, that your Son may glorify you.*

Many of us are familiar with the hymn "In the Cross of Christ I Glory." We should never forget what a strange thing that would have been to believe and profess in the first century. No cross was ever said to *glorify* someone until Jesus died on one. Crosses were instruments of abject humiliation and shame. But Jesus, who reversed the world's thinking in so many areas, reversed it here as well. Paul was not ashamed to glory in the cross (Galatians 6:14).

We have cited several occasions, earlier in Jesus' ministry, where John noted that Jesus' enemies did not make a move against him because his hour, or *time*, had not yet *come* (7:30; 8:20). Then, as the cross drew near, Jesus began to change his language to say that his hour had come (12:23; 13:1; 16:32). This is how he speaks as he begins his prayer. The cross did not come as a surprise to Jesus. He knew that it was near. But he also knew that what men were plotting to do to shame him would in fact bring glory both to him and to his *Father*.

B. HE SPEAKS OF LIFE (vv. 2, 3)

2, 3. *"For you granted him authority over all people that he might give eternal life to all those you have given him. Now this is eternal life: that they may know you, the only true God, and Jesus Christ, whom you have sent.*

Here Jesus speaks of himself in the third person (*he* and *him*). (In the fourth verse he will switch back to the first person.) It is remarkable that Jesus, though facing certain death, speaks not of death at all, but of life—of *eternal life*. As Jesus shared in God's giving of physical life at creation (John 1:1-4), so here he is involved in the provision of eternal life.

Life is one of the prominent themes in John's Gospel. Jesus declares himself to be the source of "a spring of water welling up to eternal life" (4:14); the "bread of life" (6:35); the source of the "light of life" (8:12); "the resurrection and the life" (11:25); and "the way and the truth and the life" (14:6).

To experience this life, one must *know . . . the only true God*. It is not enough to know about God. One must have a personal acquaintance with him. Notice that Jesus does not define eternal life in terms of endless years in Heaven. It is not a relationship with time, but with God.

C. HIS WORK IS FINISHED (vv. 4, 5)

4, 5. *"I have brought you glory on earth by completing the work you gave me to do. And now, Father, glorify me in your presence with the glory I had with you before the world began."*

In one sense, of course, Jesus' *work* was not yet completed. The cross was still before him. On the cross he would cry, "It is finished." However, at this point

Jesus saw the cross not as a future event but as something already accomplished. His words indicate his readiness to proceed with this ultimate step in fulfilling the will of his *Father*. He was moving toward the last hours of his earthly work—the work God had given him to do. That work *brought . . . glory* to God, and it would soon bring glory to the Son, as the *glory* that Jesus *had with God before the world began* would be given back to him. When Jesus had completed everything necessary, he would sit once again at God's right hand (Hebrews 1:3; 12:2).

GLIMPSES OF GLORY

The glory of God is a prominent theme in both Old and New Testaments. The seraphim whom Isaiah saw in his vision of God in the temple cried out, "The whole earth is full of his glory" (Isaiah 6:3). When the temple of Solomon was dedicated, "the glory of the Lord filled the temple. The priests could not enter the temple of the Lord because the glory of the Lord filled it" (2 Chronicles 7:1, 2). When the angel of the Lord appeared to the shepherds on the night of Jesus' birth, "the glory of the Lord shone around them" (Luke 2:9); and the host of angels who soon appeared cried, "Glory to God in the highest" (v. 14). Paul tells us we have "the light of the knowledge of the glory of God in the face of Christ" (2 Corinthians 4:6).

Glory is a prominent theme in Jesus' high priestly prayer in John 17, too. The words *glory* and *glorify* appear nine times in this prayer. Jesus prayed in John 17:24, "Father, I want those you have given me to be with me where I am, and to see my glory, the glory you have given me because you loved me before the creation of the world." May we so give our lives to the Son of God, and to others in his name, that his petition may be answered. The fulfillment of this is found in the Holy City, which "shone with the glory of God" (Revelation 21:11).   —J. G. V. B.

II. JESUS PRAYS FOR THE TWELVE (JOHN 17:9-11, 15-19)

A. A FOCUSED PRAYER (vv. 9, 10)

9. "*I pray for them. I am not praying for the world, but for those you have given me, for they are yours.*

Imagine how these disciples felt when they heard Jesus say, *I pray for them*. They did not know what dangers they would face in serving him, but he did. Already one of them (Judas) had fallen prey to temptation and was at that very moment carrying out his betrayal of Jesus.

Why did Jesus say, *I am not praying for the world*? It was not that Jesus was unconcerned about the world (John 3:16). But here he was concentrating more on those whom he would leave in the world to carry on his work. Only through their efforts would the world begin to hear the message of salvation.

10. "*All I have is yours, and all you have is mine. And glory has come to me through them.*

When Jesus said *all I have is yours, and all you have is mine*, he was describing the complete unity that exists between the Father, the Son, and the disciples of the Son. There is no rivalry or division between Father, Son, and followers.

Jesus' statement *glory has come to me through them* should be studied alongside earlier references to Jesus' prayer that God glorify him (vv. 1, 5). God "glorified his servant Jesus" (Acts 3:13), ushering him back to the glory of Heaven following his resurrection. Christians are called to live "that the name of our Lord Jesus may be glorified" in us (2 Thessalonians 1:12).

B. A PRAYER FOR PROTECTION AND UNITY (vv. 11, 15-17)

11. "*I will remain in the world no longer, but they are still in the world, and I am coming to you. Holy Father, protect them by the power of your name—the name you gave me—so that they may be one as we are one.*"

HOW TO SAY IT

Calvary. KAL-vuh-ree.
Galileans. Gal-ih-LEE-unz.
Gethsemane. Geth-SEM-uh-nee.
Kidron. KID-ron.
Pilate. PIE-lut.
Wycliffe. WIK-lif.

WHAT DO YOU THINK?

In John 17:9 Jesus contrasted prayer for his disciples with prayer for the world. How are your prayers for non-Christians different from those you offer for Christian brothers and sisters?

Once again Jesus was looking ahead. The next day he would be crucified. After three days he would rise from the dead. He would appear to his followers for a period of forty days; then he would ascend to the Father and would *remain in the world no longer.* Of course, Jesus meant that physically—in a visible, tangible form—he would no longer be in the world. In the person of the Holy Spirit Jesus keeps his promise, "Surely I am with you always" (Matthew 28:20).

Jesus continued his prayer for his disciples, knowing how vulnerable they would be by remaining *in the world.* He knew the hazards they would face because the world would be, for the most part, as hostile to them as it had been to him (John 15:18-21). The concern of Jesus for his own did not end with his departure from this earth. It continued—and it continues still.

This concern was also demonstrated by Jesus' prayer to *protect them by the power of your name.* Among Jews, the ideas of "name" and "power" were closely linked, as they are by us when we say, "in the name of the law." As we will see shortly (v. 15), Jesus did not intend for his followers to be secluded from the world, but to remain untarnished by the world's evil influences.

Jesus also prayed for his disciples *that they may be one as we are one.* At this point the unity of the group was fragile. Even in the upper room, they had been arguing about which of them was greatest (Luke 22:24). This temptation to place selfish interests above kingdom interests still surfaces. It is sobering to consider that when we drive wedges of division between God's people, we are frustrating the prayer of Jesus!

15, 16. "My prayer is not that you take them out of the world but that you protect them from the evil one. They are not of the world, even as I am not of it.

The disciples would not be taken *out of the world.* To do so would be like taking the salt out of the food and the light out of the darkness. Jesus never meant for his followers to separate themselves physically from the world. He did want them to be spiritually separated from the world, or, more specifically, *from the evil one* (Satan). Thus are Christians to be in the world, but *not of the world.*

17. "Sanctify them by the truth; your word is truth.

The word *sanctify* means "to make holy" or "to set apart for a holy purpose." In the Old Testament, both objects and people were thus sanctified. Whenever we think of sanctification, two prepositions must follow. We are set apart *from* something—the world—and we are set apart *for* something—the service of God.

In only a few hours Pilate would cynically ask Jesus, "What is truth?" (John 18:38). Here is the answer: *your word is truth.* Earlier Jesus had told the disciples, "I am . . . the truth" (John 14:6). In a world that has rejected the very idea of absolute truth, the church is called to proclaim without fear or hesitation where truth can be found: the written Word of God and the living Word of God.

C. A PRAYER FOR THEIR WORK (vv. 18, 19)

18. "As you sent me into the world, I have sent them into the world.

The word *apostle* means "one who is sent." While we do not have exactly the same purpose or power that the apostles possessed, we too are *sent . . . into the world* by Jesus. Certainly we must gather faithfully in worship with other Christians (Hebrews 10:25), but we are not to remain isolated from those who need the salt and light that we can provide. Our lives have purpose and meaning only when we dedicate them to involvement in Christ's ministry. We are *sent* to continue the ministry that God began when he *sent* Jesus.

19. "For them I sanctify myself, that they too may be truly sanctified.

Jesus was already sanctified in the sense of being set apart from the world. He was without sin and could not become holier in that sense. He could, however, *sanctify* himself by committing himself to the task that lay ahead—laying down his life in accordance with his Father's will (John 10:18).

III. JESUS PRAYS FOR US (JOHN 17:20-24)

A. FOR OUR UNITY (vv. 20-22)

20. *"My prayer is not for them alone. I pray also for those who will believe in me through their message.*

Having prayed for those men who were to become his apostles, Jesus now focused his prayer on future followers. Certainly we who are Christians today are included among those who *believe* on Jesus *through their message.* "Faith comes from hearing the message, and the message is heard through the word of Christ" (Romans 10:17). It is the testimony of the apostles, written for us in the New Testament, that brings us to faith in Christ as Savior and that forms the only foundation upon which genuine Christian unity can rest. We should possess the confidence that Jesus had in the power and the priority of the apostolic message.

It is always touching and encouraging to know that someone is praying for us. How much more so to know that Jesus prayed for us! How much more so to know that he prays for us still! He is at the right hand of God interceding for us even now (Romans 8:34; Hebrews 7:25).

21. *". . . that all of them may be one, Father, just as you are in me and I am in you. May they also be in us so that the world may believe that you have sent me.*

There is a purpose in Jesus' desire for the unity of believers: *that the world may believe that you have sent me.* Jesus saw the lack of unity as a hindrance to evangelism. We know from our own experiences that non-Christians often cite the division in the church as a reason for their lack of interest in the Christian message.

That all of them may be one is not an organizational unity accomplished by man-made resolutions or the decisions of ecclesiastical bodies. Jesus described our unity in this manner: *as you [Father] are in me and I am in you.* This unity is spiritual in nature—a oneness in mind, will, and purpose that is expressed in our love for God and for all who have accepted Christ and are therefore God's children. We need to recognize this oneness and seek to "keep the unity of the Spirit through the bond of peace" (Ephesians 4:3).

"THAT ALL OF THEM MAY BE ONE"

One of Jesus' most earnest petitions in his beautiful prayer was that those who would believe in him in the future would be united—"that all of them may be one" (v. 21). One of the major tragedies in the history of the church is the division among Jesus' followers and the sheer hatred that they at times have shown to one another.

An example of this may be seen in the reactions many church authorities had to the first complete translation of the Bible into English in the late 1300s under the influence of John Wycliffe. Wycliffe was viciously castigated by these leaders, being called (in the spelling of that era) "the Devells Instrument . . . Peoples Confusion, Hereticks Idoll."

How terrible that someone who was trying to put the Word of God into peoples' hands and in a language they could understand was considered an enemy of the God he loved and served. Several years after his death, Wycliffe was publicly condemned as a heretic, and his bones were dug up and burned. The ashes were then scattered in a nearby river.

Today the animosity between Christians is usually not as intense as that between Wycliffe and his critics. However, it does not have to be to have the effect of alienating a lost world that desperately needs Jesus.

—J. G. V. B.

WHAT DO YOU THINK?

The current state of denominationalism must certainly be confusing to unbelievers! Perhaps some of you have been challenged with, "How can people who claim to follow the same Lord hold such differing views on things? And if you cannot get along with each other, what is so special about your faith anyway?" What did you say? What could you say?

What difference do you think a greater measure of unity among Christians would make in an unbeliever's attitude about accepting Christ? Why?

WHAT DO YOU THINK?

What can we do to promote unity within our own congregation?

Encourage your students to suggest specific actions that will bring healing to whatever situation most threatens the unity of your congregation. Many divisions result from a lack of communication. What can be done to improve the lines of communication? What other issues can you address?

Use the visual from lesson 9 to illustrate today's lesson. It demonstrates Jesus' concern for the whole world, as expressed in John 17:23.

PRAYER

Dear God, we thank you for letting us listen to Jesus' prayer. Forgive us when anything we do or say frustrates the desires of Jesus or hinders the cause of world evangelism. In Jesus' name, amen.

22. *"I have given them the glory that you gave me, that they may be one as we are one:*

Jesus lived in heavenly *glory* before he came to earth (v. 5). Eventually he would return to that glory at the Father's right hand. This is the glory that Jesus wants to share with his followers, as verse 24 indicates. However, they must be willing to travel the path of humble service as Jesus did, realizing the glory of living in this manner. If all Christians would seek such glory, rather than glory for themselves, how much greater the possibility that we would *be one!*

B. FOR OUR WITNESS (v. 23)

23. *"I in them and you in me. May they be brought to complete unity to let the world know that you sent me and have loved them even as you have loved me.*

Such *complete unity* as that for which Jesus prayed will be a powerful witness to *the world*—one that it cannot ignore. The world will then *know* that Jesus came from God. The world will also know that God loves those who commit their lives to Jesus. Many in our society today are starving for such love.

C. FOR OUR FUTURE (v. 24)

24. *"Father, I want those you have given me to be with me where I am, and to see my glory, the glory you have given me because you loved me before the creation of the world."*

Jesus now looked beyond his departure from his disciples, beyond the days of their service, and into eternity. He has been with these men for three and a half years. But he wants to be with them forever! The rewards of Heaven are not grudgingly given. Jesus wants all his followers to spend eternity in *glory* with him.

Then Jesus moved from thinking of the future to considering the distant past. He spoke of the Father's love for him *before the creation of the world*. These words about an eternal love deepen the mystery of creation in our minds. Why did God bother to create the world, knowing that the Son, whom he loved, would need to enter the world, live in it, and die for it? How could God love his Son and yet love the world so much that he gave his Son to die for it? This is a great mystery. It should give us reason to ponder the greatness of God's grace and the greatness of his desire to be loved by us.

CONCLUSION

A. FACING DEATH WITH COURAGE

The first part of today's lesson shows us how Jesus faced death with courage. The last part directs our minds to the glory of Heaven so that we too may face death with courage. Yet we are not to be so set on Heaven that we are discontent with earth. God wants us to live full, rich, and purposeful lives here. First Timothy 6:17 tells us, "God . . . richly provides us with everything for our enjoyment."

Sooner or later, however, all of us must face death. We need to face it with courage as Jesus did—looking forward with anticipation, not backward with regrets.

B. WORKING FOR CHRISTIAN UNITY

After reading of Jesus' burden for the unity of his followers, we need to ask, "What attitudes of mine hinder Christian unity? Do I have a divisive spirit that works contrary to the fervent prayer of our Lord?" We may not be able to work for unity in large ways, but we all can promote it in small ways. We can make sure that our spirit is gracious because we have been saved by grace, and that our attitude is loving because Christ first loved us—in our sins!

Discovery Learning

This page contains an alternate lesson plan emphasizing learning activities. Classes desiring such student involvement will find these suggestions helpful. The next page is a reproducible activity page to further enhance discovery learning.

LEARNING GOALS

After this lesson students should be able to:

1. Tell what Jesus prayed for in John 17.

2. Explain why the unity of believers, for which Jesus prayed, must continue to be a priority for the church today.

3. Suggest steps that individuals and congregations can take to work for that unity.

INTO THE LESSON

Write the word UNITY vertically on the chalkboard. As students arrive, ask them to suggest a word or phrase that starts with each letter of *unity* and denotes a similar concept or a means of either achieving or maintaining unity. Here are some suggestions in case you get stuck:

> Understanding
> Not being selfish
> In the world, but not of it
> Truth
> Yearning for harmony

Make a transition to the Bible study by noting that unity should not simply be a lofty ideal that we talk about but never achieve. At least in our own congregation we should be committed to achieving it. Whether that unity will spread beyond us is more than we can control, but we can do our part. Unity was the focus of Jesus' prayer in John 17, from which today's lesson is drawn. If unity was important to Jesus the last night that he was with his disciples before his crucifixion, then it must become important to us.

INTO THE WORD

Review briefly the preceding events recorded in John 16 (Jesus warns the disciples of persecution, and he promises the Holy Spirit). Note that all the events in John 13–18 happened the same night and into the next morning. The events of John 13 and 14 occurred in the upper room where Jesus and the disciples observed the Passover. The events of chapters 15–17 may have occurred on the way to Gethsemane (see 14:31), though John 18:1 suggests that the group may not have left the room until after Jesus' prayer. (See the commentary background on pages 333 and 334 for more details on this issue.)

Have a volunteer read John 17:1-5, 9-11, 15-24. Ask the rest of the class to listen to the reading and to write down everything Jesus prayed for. (For the glorification of the Son and the Father [vv. 1, 5]; for the disciples [v. 9]; that the disciples be kept through God's name and that they be one [v. 11]; that they be protected from the evil one [v. 15]; that they be sanctified by the truth [vv. 17, 19]; for those who would believe in Jesus from the apostles' testimony [v. 20]; for the unity of believers with other believers and with God, in order that the world may believe in Jesus [vv. 21-23]; that believers may be with Jesus [v. 24].)

Review the lists the students develop, commenting on the significance of the items and discussing their importance. Use information from the commentary section as well as the "What Do You Think?" questions in the margins to assist in this.

Divide the class into groups of four or five, and ask each group to write a statement of the importance of unity in the church.

INTO LIFE

Distribute copies of the reproducible activity "Let's Get Together" from the next page. Ask the class to name some characteristics of a united church. (This can be done as a class activity or in the small groups formed earlier.) What does a united church do that a church with division does not? What attitudes are apparent in a united church? Compile a list based on the students' responses and write it on the chalkboard.

Assign each of the small groups one or two of the items on the list. Ask them to decide whether each characteristic is a *result* of unity or a *cause*. That is, will unity result if the church works to develop this characteristic, or must the church have real unity before the characteristic can be present?

Ask the class to use the results of this activity, as well as any other insights they may have, to suggest specific ways a church or an individual Christian can work for unity in the church. Ask the students to make a commitment to implement at least one of the ideas suggested. Look also for an idea that might make a good class project so your class can take the lead in working for unity in the church.

Since this lesson is about Jesus' prayer for unity, it is especially appropriate that you close this session with a similar prayer. Have the students stand and join hands around the perimeter of the room for this closing prayer.

Let's Get Together

What are some of the necessary components or characteristics of a united church? Label each of the jigsaw pieces below with a word or description that represents an essential element of church unity.

Cause and Effect

Some of the characteristics of a united church happen because the church has unity; these are results or "effects" of unity. Others are fundamental to unity—unless they are present, the church will not have unity. These are "causes" of unity.

Choose one or more items from above that you believe are *causes* of unity. What can you do to bring it to be (or to improve on it if it is already present) in your church?

Summer Quarter, 1999

Genesis: Beginnings

Jun 6

Jun 13

Jun 20

Jun 27

Jul 4

Jul 11

Jul 18

Jul 25

Aug 1

Aug 8

Aug 15

Aug 22

Aug 29

Special Features

Lessons

Unit 1: In the Beginning

Unit 2: The Beginnings of a People

Unit 3: A People Tested

About These Lessons

This quarter launches our chronological study of the Old Testament. Of course, we begin with that book of beginnings, Genesis. We'll see that, right from the start, God's people had their ups and downs, yet God was faithful through it all. May it encourage us to know that God is with us, too, through all of our own ups and downs.

Roots

by John W. Wade

A little over twenty years ago, *Roots* became a popular television miniseries. Alex Haley, the author of the book on which the series was based, went back to Africa in an attempt to find the beginnings and history of his family. As a result of watching this program, many people became interested in their own roots and began to investigate their family ancestry. The lessons in this quarter take us back to the "roots" of humanity. They are drawn from Genesis—the book of beginnings.

IN THE BEGINNING

JUNE

Unit 1 of this quarter consists of four lessons taken from the early chapters of Genesis. **Lesson 1** deals with the story of God's creation of the heaven and the earth, climaxing in the creation of human beings in the image of God. **Lesson 2** tells how all the animals had companions, but Adam was alone. Then God created Eve to be Adam's helper and companion. In **lesson 3** tragedy strikes. Adam and Eve have already been forced to leave their beautiful home because of sin, but evil reaches a new low when Cain kills his brother Abel. Evil continues to escalate until God has to act in judgment on the world with the great flood. **Lesson 4** has that story.

THE BEGINNINGS OF A PEOPLE

JULY

Lessons five through thirteen of this quarter focus on one family—the family of Abraham and his descendants—that exhibited many of the problems that are quite common in modern families. This family began approximately four thousand years ago in the city of Ur of the Chaldees, in the southeastern part of modern Iraq. In **lesson 5** we learn of God's call to Abraham (then known as Abram) to launch out on a venture of faith that led him to Canaan. **Lesson 6** tells how God gave Abraham and Sarah a child, Isaac, even though they were both advanced in years. **Lesson 7** tells how Abraham's faith was severely tested when God told him to offer his son Isaac as a sacrifice. **Lesson 8**, "Deceit and Blessing," deals with strife in the family of Isaac involving his two sons, Jacob and Esau. Use this as an opportunity to allow your students to share some ideas about how they have dealt with conflicts in their own families.

A PEOPLE TESTED

AUGUST

In **lesson 9**, as Jacob fled the wrath of his brother, God confronted him in a dream and renewed the covenant he had made with Abraham and Isaac. Twenty years later Jacob was confronted by God again, this time in the person of an angel who wrestled with him through the night. **Lesson 10** tells the story. There is more discord in this family, which comes to a head in **lesson 11**, as Jacob's ten oldest sons take vengeance on the favored Joseph by selling him into slavery. The events in **lesson 12** show God's hand at work in the life of faithful Joseph, who is able to rise to prominence in Egypt just in time to save his own family. **Lesson 13** brings this series of lessons to a heartwarming conclusion with the reunion of Joseph to his family and the forgiveness of his brothers.

Our Sunday schools often suffer a "slump" during the summer months. Attendance may be down, but don't let those who attend get "turned off" by lessons from the Old Testament. These narratives can make for exciting teaching, and the applications can be just as contemporary as this morning's newspaper.

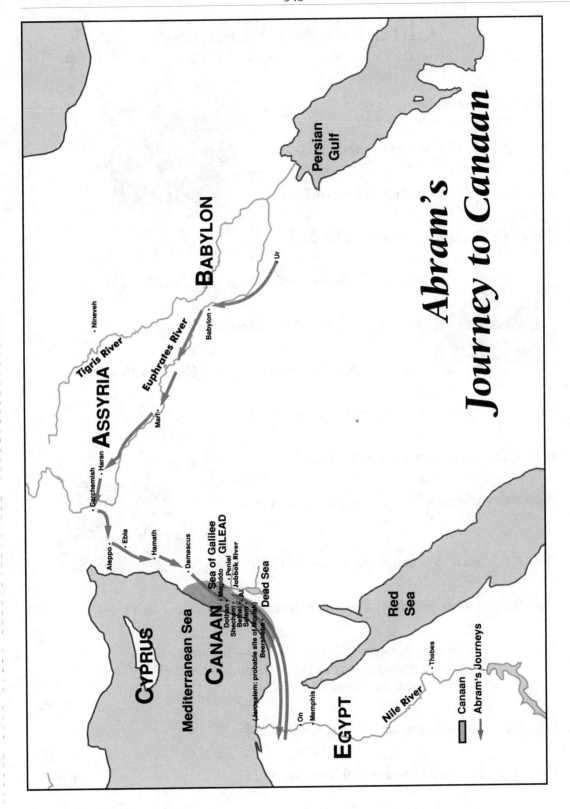

Abram's Journey to Canaan

Chronology of Genesis
From the Call of Abraham to the Death of Joseph

2167 B.C.   **Abram born**

2092 B.C.   **Call of Abram (Genesis 12:1-5)**

2081 B.C.   **Ishmael born (Genesis 16:15, 16)**

2067 B.C.   **Isaac born (Genesis 21:1-3)**

2050 B.C.   **Abraham offers Isaac (Genesis 22:1-19)**

2007 B.C.   **Jacob and Esau born (Genesis 25:24-26)**

1992 B.C.   **Abraham dies at age 175 (Genesis 25:7)**

1930 B.C.   **Jacob flees to Haran (Genesis 28:10)**

1916 B.C.   **Joseph born (Genesis 30:22-24)**

1899 B.C.   **Joseph sold into Egypt at age 17 (Genesis 37:2, 28)**

1887 B.C.   **Isaac dies at age 180 (Genesis 35:28)**

1886 B.C.   **Joseph interprets Pharaoh's dream at age 30 (Genesis 41:46)**

1877 B.C.   **Jacob goes to Egypt (Genesis 46:5, 6)—Beginning of the Israelites' 430-year stay in Egypt (Exodus 12:40, 41), leading to the exodus in 1447 B.C.**

1860 B.C.   **Jacob dies at age 147 (Genesis 47:28)**

1806 B.C.   **Joseph dies at age 110 (Genesis 50:26)**

GOD'S GOOD CREATION

LESSON 1

WHY TEACH THIS LESSON?

Ken Hamm of "Answers in Genesis" makes a good point in his presentations of evidence for creation. He notes that Christians spend a lot of time hammering away at such issues as abortion, euthanasia, homosexuality, and other important matters while humanists attack the Judeo-Christian ethic at its foundation: "In the beginning God." This foundational issue determines in advance where a person will come out on other issues. If God is the Creator, then his word on a subject is binding. If he says the taking of innocent lives is wrong, then it is. If God made a man and then provided a woman as the helper suitable for him, then homosexuality is wrong.

This lesson, and the series that follows, provides a good chance for your class to return to the basics. Providing your students a solid foundation on which to position other matters of faith is your goal in teaching today's lesson.

INTRODUCTION

A. CREATION COMMOTION

"In the beginning God created the heavens and the earth" (Genesis 1:1). The first verse of the Bible is strikingly simple. Yet things can get awfully confusing when one ventures to investigate various aspects of the creation-evolution controversy, theories about the duration of the days of creation, and other related issues that surface in the early chapters of Genesis. Brilliant students and scholars, coming from opposing viewpoints, make impressive, persuasive, and often highly technical arguments to try to support their ideas. At times the scientific, philosophical, and linguistic arguments can be bewildering, to say the least. What is the student of God's Word to do?

Not everyone feels comfortable with the often complicated discussions surrounding God's creative activity. Certainly these should not be allowed to overshadow the basic simplicity of the biblical record, nor should they minimize the necessity of faith. "By faith," the writer of Hebrews reminds us, "we understand that the universe was formed at God's command, so that what is seen was not made out of what was visible" (Hebrews 11:3).

At the same time, we must seek to develop the discernment necessary to be able to distinguish truth from error. Creation and related issues constitute an area where we should "always be prepared to give an answer to everyone who asks [us] to give the reason for the hope that [we] have" (1 Peter 3:15). Our defense should include a concern for Christlike character and communication, avoiding the harsh words that can accompany such a controversial subject. It should also include a sensitivity for how best to reach the world with the message of the Creator's reality and redemption.

B. LESSON BACKGROUND

In the beginning God. . . . Today's lesson on creation deals with one of the grandest, most significant themes in all of Scripture. Without the biblical doctrine of creation, man is left to see himself as the product of blind force and

DEVOTIONAL READING:
PSALM 104:24-35

LESSON SCRIPTURE:
GENESIS 1:1-24

PRINTED TEXT:
GENESIS 1:1, 2, 20-31

LESSON AIMS

After this lesson the students will be able to:

1. Summarize the account of God's creative activity in the first chapter of Genesis.

2. Explain why the biblical record of creation is superior to other explanations of man's origin.

3. Give thanks that he or she is not an "accident," but an individual created in the image of God.

KEY VERSE

God saw all that he had made, and it was very good.
—Genesis 1:31

The visual for lesson 1 should be on display as you begin the class session. It is a beautiful reminder that God created our universe.

WHAT DO YOU THINK?

Suppose a member of your church said, "You don't believe all that stuff about God creating the world, do you? Science has proved the universe is the result of millions of years of chance process. Genesis is a record of ancient man's view of the origin of things. We can't take it literally today." How would you answer?

WHAT DO YOU THINK?

Many theories are proposed that seek to reconcile contemporary scientific opinion and the Scriptures. The lesson writer has noted the "gap theory" and pointed out some shortcomings in that view. Besides, scientific opinion is constantly shifting, so that the "science" one harmonizes the Bible with today may be rejected by scientists tomorrow. How then

chance. He is virtually alone in a universe without meaning and without purpose.

We learn from Genesis 1 that a loving God created man as part of a wonderful plan, and as the "crowning glory" to everything he had made. He declared each phase of his creative process as "good" and concluded his activity by declaring all that he had made "very good" (Genesis 1:31).

The truths found in the early chapters of Genesis are foundational to Christian faith. Jesus referred to events found in the early chapters of Genesis (1-11) and treated them as historical events, not as fables or myths (Matthew 19:4, 5; 23:35; 24:37-39). Every New Testament writer refers to at least one event found in the early chapters of Genesis. Recall how Paul, in presenting the gospel to the philosophers on the Areopagus in Athens, began by proclaiming "God who made the world and everything in it" (Acts 17:24).

While we often speak of the "Genesis account" of creation, the theme of creation is prominent throughout the Old Testament. The command to the Israelites to observe the Sabbath on the seventh day was grounded in the creation week (Exodus 20:8-11). Significant portions of the book of Job (38–41), the Psalms (8; 19:1-6; 33:6; 139:14-16; 148; and especially 104), and the prophets (Isaiah 40:26, 28; 42:5; 45:12, 18; Jeremiah 10:10-12; Amos 4:13; 5:8; 9:6; Malachi 2:10) call attention to the glory and majesty of all that God has created.

In today's lesson we examine the fundamental teachings of Genesis 1, with a view toward understanding some of the key issues that surround this portion of Scripture.

I. IN THE BEGINNING (GENESIS 1:1, 2)
A. CREATION INTRODUCED (v. 1)
1. In the beginning God created the heavens and the earth.

The fact of divine creation is affirmed in the opening statement of Scripture. Debate over the *how* or *when* should not overshadow the primary emphasis of this verse: the entire universe owes its existence to the will and power of Almighty God. The existence of God is not explained or analyzed; it is simply set forth as a foundational truth of Scripture. Ultimately it is a matter of faith (Hebrews 11:3); however, the evidence for believing in God as Creator is far more substantial than the evidence for not believing.

B. INITIAL CHAOS (v. 2)
2. Now the earth was formless and empty, darkness was over the surface of the deep, and the Spirit of God was hovering over the waters.

This verse describes the state of the *earth* before order was established. Later distinctions and specializations would be made: light and darkness; air and water; dry land and seas; plants and animals, and others. The work of *the Spirit of God* in creation is emphasized here. In the New Testament we find that Jesus was also involved in the creation (John 1:3; Colossians 1:16, 17; Hebrews 1:2).

Some have suggested that there is an enormous time span between Genesis 1:1 and 1:2. This "gap theory" of creation holds that Satan and his followers were defeated during this time, and in the process the original created order was ruined. Dinosaurs, animals evidenced by the fossil records, and "cave men" are all relegated to the time of the "first creation." The events described after Genesis 1:2 refer to an alleged *second* creation. This approach, also called the re-creation view or the ruin-reconstruction view, seeks to harmonize modern scientific belief in an old earth with a literal approach to the events recorded in Genesis.

However, nowhere in Scripture is there any firm indication that Genesis speaks of two creations. In fact, certain Scriptures cause serious problems for the gap theory. For example, Exodus 20:11 says, "For in six days the Lord made the heavens and earth, the sea, and all that is in them." In other words, *everything* was created within the six days described in Genesis; there appears to be no room for any previous creative activity in the biblical account.

Perhaps more damaging to the theory is Romans 5:12, which says, "Sin entered the world through one man, and death through sin, and in this way death came to all men, because all sinned." Under the gap theory, death would have occurred *before* Adam's sin. But Paul's statement is clear that there was no death prior to Adam's sin. Thus the gap theory, while it may appear to provide another way of understanding the creation account, challenges other important biblical teaching. It is far more preferable to view Genesis 1 as describing a single period of creation.

II. DAY FIVE (GENESIS 1:20-23)

Our printed text now brings us to the events of the fifth day of creation. The six days of creation can be divided into two groups of three. During the first three days, God created what we might call the territories where created objects or creatures should go; then during the last three days he created the objects and creatures to fill the space he had made. Note, according to the chart below, the correspondence between the first three days and the last three. One writer has called the first three days "days of forming," and the last three, "days of filling."

Day		Day	
1	light	4	sun, moon, stars
2	heavens	5	fish, birds
3	earth, vegetation	6	land animals, man

A. GOD CREATES (vv. 20, 21)

20, 21. And God said, "Let the water teem with living creatures, and let birds fly above the earth across the expanse of the sky." So God created the great creatures of the sea and every living and moving thing with which the water teems, according to their kinds, and every winged bird according to its kind. And God saw that it was good.

The phrase *let the water teem* captures well the incredible quantity and variety of aquatic life. The same Hebrew term that is here translated *living creatures* is also used to describe man in Genesis 2:7, where it is rendered "living being." As we shall see, it is the fact that man is created in the image of God that distinguishes him from all other living creatures in God's creation.

Note also the important phrase *according to their kinds*, which appears elsewhere in Genesis 1 (vv. 11, 12, 24, 25). Whatever biological class is designated by a "kind" (whether a species or a broader group), the various *kinds* of creatures did not evolve from a common ancestor, as evolutionists claim. Each kind was made unique and distinct from every other. There was no need to evolve to some higher form of life, for *God saw* that what he had made *was good.*

B. GOD BLESSES (vv. 22, 23)

22, 23. God blessed them and said, "Be fruitful and increase in number and fill the water in the seas, and let the birds increase on the earth." And there was evening, and there was morning—the fifth day.

With this form of life, mating is in order, so God bids these creatures to *be fruitful and increase in number.* This same imperative is given to mankind in verse

should we view alleged discrepancies between science and the Bible? Can a person accept both "scientific truth" and "biblical truth"? If so, how?

WHAT DO YOU THINK?

One of the key questions in this debate is how life started. Even the simplest life form is unimaginably complex. No accident could have produced such a result. The evidence of careful design is everywhere. In spite of the evidence, many people refuse to accept the existence of God because they do not want to accept accountability to him. How, then, would you attempt to share your faith with someone who refused to accept the existence of God, but chose to believe some other explanation for the existence of life?

HOW TO SAY IT
adam (Hebrew). *uh-DAHM.*

28. Of course, with regard to the *birds* and sea creatures, it was not a "command" to be obeyed; it simply indicates God's purpose and design for the propagation of these living beings.

III. DAY SIX (GENESIS 1:24-31)

A. LAND ANIMALS CREATED (vv. 24, 25)

24, 25. And God said, "Let the land produce living creatures according to their kinds: livestock, creatures that move along the ground, and wild animals, each according to its kind." And it was so. God made the wild animals according to their kinds, the livestock according to their kinds, and all the creatures that move along the ground according to their kinds. And God saw that it was good.

The three terms used to describe the land animals are of a general nature. The first group named is that of the larger herd animals (*livestock*), some of which would become domesticated. The second group is composed of *creatures that move along the ground*, a term that would include such reptiles as lizards and snakes. Finally there are the *wild animals*, an expression that is simply "living things" in Hebrew, but likely designates any undomesticated animals.

B. MAN CREATED (vv. 26, 27)

26. Then God said, "Let us make man in our image, in our likeness, and let them rule over the fish of the sea and the birds of the air, over the livestock, over all the earth, and over all the creatures that move along the ground."

The Hebrew word translated *man* (*adam*, which is also the name given to the first man) can also be translated "mankind." Being made in the *image* of God does not include physical characteristics. Involved instead are attributes such as intellect, self-consciousness, emotion, self-determination, and the capacity to love, communicate, and have fellowship with God. We might include the capacity to "create," or think independently and originally, as something we share with God.

Being made in God's image also involves a shared authority, by which man is granted *rule* over the rest of the created order. Man was created to be a ruler; as David wrote, "You made him a little lower than the heavenly beings and crowned him with glory and honor" (Psalm 8:5). But he is to rule out of compassion, not greed. Thus was Adam placed in the garden of Eden "to work it and take care of it" (Genesis 2:15).

What does *let us make man* indicate? Most likely this is an early indication of the doctrine of the Trinity, a plurality of persons within the divine being. (As we have already noted, both Jesus and the Spirit of God were present at creation.) Others believe that the plural pronoun reflects what is called a "plural of majesty"—the use of the plural to express the grandeur of something or someone. Similar language appears in Genesis 11:7 ("Let *us* go down") and Isaiah 6:8 ("Who will go for *us*?").

Another question involves the significance of the terms *image* and *likeness*. Most likely these are simply interchangeable terms, as seen by a comparison of Genesis 1:27 with Genesis 5:1. They indicate that man is set apart from the rest of creation and is given a position of honor above everything else God has made.

WHAT DO YOU THINK?

Our text declares that God made mankind, both male and female, in his image. What significance does that fact have to you? Why? How does it affect your self-esteem and sense of purpose?

27. So God created man in his own image, in the image of God he created him; male and female he created them.

Here *man* is defined as comprising both *male and female*. Both share the blessings and responsibilities of being made in *the image of God*. Next week's lesson will focus on the more detailed description of man and woman's creation in Genesis 2.

C. A MANDATE GIVEN (28)

28. God blessed them and said to them, "Be fruitful and increase in number; fill the earth and subdue it. Rule over the fish of the sea and the birds of the air and over every living creature that moves on the ground."

The words *subdue* and *rule* describe the responsibility given man as a result of his being made in God's image. They encompass the realms of science and technology. Man is to seek to understand the created order and then utilize that knowledge, not selfishly or thoughtlessly, but to the glory of his Creator.

Psalm 8 refers to this "creation mandate," as David marvels at the glorious position bestowed on man at creation. However, man's fall has diminished his ability to fulfill such a mandate. Hebrews 2:5-9 teaches that only through Jesus Christ, whom the Father has "crowned with glory and honor," can man's dominion over creation be realized.

TOP OF THE LINE

Serious car enthusiasts know the names of the finest automobiles manufactured by the major manufacturers: Eldorado, Continental, Aurora, Imperial, Roadmaster, and others. These are called "top of the line," and they are roomier, safer, more luxurious, more powerful, and more comfortable than the other models. Only a certain affluent segment of society can afford these cars; the rest of us merely fantasize about driving one.

When God created the world, he saved his best till last. He created humans in his image and gave them dominion over the rest of creation. Humans possess features surpassing the characteristics of all other species in the animal kingdom. Self-consciousness and superior intelligence endow us with capabilities that are unique and unsurpassed. We are God's "top of the line." As such we exercise dominion over the earth and its inhabitants, subduing even creatures much larger, stronger, and faster than we.

We are "fearfully and wonderfully made" (Psalm 139:14). God made us just "a little lower than the heavenly beings" and has "crowned [us] with glory and honor" (Psalm 8:5). How else can we respond except to say, "O Lord, our Lord, how majestic is your name in all the earth!" (Psalm 8:1, 9).   —R. W. B.

D. GOD'S PROVISION (vv. 29-31)

29, 30. Then God said, "I give you every seed-bearing plant on the face of the whole earth and every tree that has fruit with seed in it. They will be yours for food. And to all the beasts of the earth and all the birds of the air and all the creatures that move on the ground—everything that has the breath of life in it—I give every green plant for food." And it was so.

These verses suggest that initially both man and animals fed only on *plant* life. Only after the flood is animal flesh specified for human consumption (Genesis 9: 2, 3). The significance of these instructions lies in God's gracious provision for what he has created.

31. God saw all that he had made, and it was very good. And there was evening, and there was morning—the sixth day.

At the culmination of his creative work—after man, the crown of his creation was fashioned—God pronounced it all as *very good*. A perfect world, unmarred by sin and its consequences, was in place. A being created in God's image was given dominion over this world.

An important element of man's being created in the image of God was his freedom of choice. Tragically, we know how man abused his freedom to disobey God—an abuse that continues to the present day. Apart from his Creator, man cannot become better; he can only grow worse.

VISUALS FOR THESE LESSONS

The Adult Visuals *packet contains classroom-size visuals designed for use with the lessons in the Summer Quarter. The packet is available from your supplier. Order No. 492.*

WHAT DO YOU THINK?

Several events are listed for the sixth day. Some skeptics claim there would not have been enough time in a day, especially considering the twelve-hour daylight portion of the day as the time span of activity. How would you respond to a skeptic with such a view?

PRAYER

God of Heaven and earth, we marvel as we consider the power and wisdom that you have displayed in the handiwork of your creation. We are privileged to be created in your image. May we use our lives to glorify you—our great Creator. Amen.

THOUGHT TO REMEMBER

"You are worthy, our Lord and God, to receive glory and honor and power, for you created all things, and by your will they were created and have their being" (Revelation 4:11).

DAILY BIBLE READINGS

Monday, May 31—Day One of Creation (Genesis 1:1-5)

Tuesday, June 1—Days Two and Three of Creation (Genesis 1:6-13)

Wednesday, June 2—Day Four of Creation (Genesis 1:14-19)

Thursday, June 3—Day Five of Creation (Genesis 1:20-23)

Friday, June 4—Day Six of Creation (Genesis 1:24-31)

Saturday, June 5—Day Seven; God Finishes Creation (Genesis 2:1-4a)

Sunday, June 6—How Many Are Your Works, O Lord! (Psalm 104:24-35)

GOD THROUGH GLASS

I looked at the moon through a telescope recently, and I didn't see the "man in the moon." But I did see God—that is, I saw convincing evidence of God's design and creative excellence.

There were no shadows across the moon that night; the moon was "full." I could see one whole face of the entire sphere, brilliantly white. Craters were visible, too; the telescope's powerful magnification brought it all up close and beautiful.

To believe that our solar system, let alone the infinite universe beyond, came into existence as the result of some cosmic accident stretches my imagination too far. What I saw through the telescope confirmed my faith in a world created by an omniscient, benevolent, Supreme Being.

I've seen God through a microscope, too. Viewing the world that is invisible to the naked eye is another revelation of remarkable design and precision. Microscopic organisms deliver "sermons from science." The intricacies of form and function that one can see with the aid of powerful lenses speak of purposeful, intelligent creation.

Perhaps the most convincing argument for the truth of the biblical account of creation is what one sees in the glass of a mirror. The only power that could possibly create such a remarkable specimen as man is Almighty God. He alone is responsible for the beauty of the earth.

—R. W. B.

CONCLUSION

Today there is much controversy over whether both creation and evolution should be taught in public schools. Those who hold the evolutionary viewpoint often depict their view as scientific while portraying the biblical account of creation as nothing more than religious folklore.

The simple fact is that both those who support the theory of evolution and those who believe in creation must come to their respective positions by faith. The Christian believes in divine creation because he considers the Bible to be the Word of God, and this is clearly an act of faith. However, one who believes in evolution must also come to his position by faith, since obviously there were no eyewitnesses to the beginning of living things.

Which, then, of these two faiths has more to commend it? One way to address this question is to ask which of them produces the most desirable results. If the physical universe and man came into existence by blind chance, then clearly there is no purpose in the universe. Without purpose, there can be no logical basis for morality. Man may propose rules for his own protection, but if there is no God behind the rules to give them authority, then man may break them whenever he "feels like it" or whenever he thinks he can get away with it.

On the other hand, if we believe that God created the universe with moral as well as physical laws to govern it, then our approach to life will be drastically different. When we have a sense of identity (Who am I?), origin (Where did I come from?), and destiny (Where am I going?), we will live lives that are filled with meaning and purpose, not despair and disillusionment.

How should we respond to the attacks that are often mustered against the creation viewpoint? First, we should seek to acquaint ourselves with the key issues and facts, recognizing (as noted earlier) that not everyone will be comfortable with the more technical aspects of the discussion. Second, we should seek God's wisdom as we try to discern that which is important for our faith and that which is not. Third, we should exhibit a gracious spirit in our discussions on the subject, whether verbal or written. We must contend for the revealed truth, not for man-made theories and opinions. God will bless our efforts as we commit our study of this subject to him.

Discovery Learning

This page contains an alternate lesson plan emphasizing learning activities. Classes desiring such student involvement will find these suggestions helpful. The next page is a reproducible activity page to further enhance discovery learning.

LEARNING GOALS

As a result of participating in this session, the student will be able to:

1. Summarize the account of God's creative activity in the first chapter of Genesis.

2. Explain why the biblical record of creation is superior to other explanations of man's origin.

3. Give thanks that he or she is not an "accident," but an individual created in the image of God.

INTO THE LESSON

As students arrive, give each one a copy of the following scrambled sentence.

"was visible made by the universe so that God's command, we understand that was formed at what faith is seen was not out of what."

Ask the students to try to unscramble the sentence, which is a verse of Scripture. After a few minutes, ask someone to read Hebrews 11:3, which is the solution. Ask how many had correctly unscrambled the verse. Award these a small prize, like a stick of gum or a bookmark.

Ask all the students, "What is the most confusing thing to you about the current evolution-creation debate?" Some may suggest the conflicting reports about what the fossil record indicates. Others may be confused about the "old earth" or "young earth" debate.

Point out that you will not resolve all the differences between the various views of creation in this class session. What we must all agree on is that the Bible certainly conflicts with any worldview that starts without a Creator. The most important thing to know about creation is not its exact process but its origin. The world is not a product of blind chance and probability; God created it!

INTO THE WORD

Begin the exploration of Genesis 1 by asking your students to form small groups and complete the right-hand column of the chart shown below. (Note: the chart below has been filled in for you. A copy of the incomplete chart can be found in the student book, *NIV Bible Student*, or you can make your own worksheet leaving the "Creative Act" column blank.) This will help the students to work through the basic outline of the biblical account of creation.

Text	Day	Creative Act
Genesis 1:1-5	Day 1	Light & darkness/day & night
Genesis 1:6-8	Day 2	Earth's atmosphere (the firmament)
Genesis 1:9, 10	Day 3	Dry land and seas separated
Genesis 1:11-13	Day 3	Plants & trees
Genesis 1:14-19	Day 4	Sun, moon, & stars; seasons, days, years
Genesis 1:20-23	Day 5	Sea creatures & birds
Genesis 1:24, 25	Day 6	Land animals
Genesis 1:26-31	Day 6	Man

After a few minutes briefly summarize the creative acts so that you can be sure each group was able to complete the activity successfully.

Ask your students to return to their small groups and answer the following question: "What do we learn about God from the account of creation?" They will probably notice at least three things: (1) God is the Creator of all things, including man; (2) God is distinct from his creation; (3) God is eternal and is in control.

INTO LIFE

Make the transition to application of the text by encouraging your students to answer the "so what?" questions about creation. What does it mean to them that God created the world? How do they live differently? How do they worship God differently? How do they view nature differently? How does it change the way they look to the future? (Distribute copies of the reproducible page that follows to facilitate this discussion.)

If you have time, a similar exercise can be done in the small groups with the question: "What do we learn about ourselves from the biblical account of creation?" At least two responses may be (1) we are valuable to God since he chose to make us; and (2) we are more precious to him than all of the rest of his creation.

Observe that after all their research is in, many scientists have found themselves in an undesirable position of staring in the face of the God whom they have desperately tried to avoid. Then lead your students in a prayer of praise that God has revealed himself as the Creator and sustainer of our world. If time allows, ask each small group to spend some time offering sentence prayers of praise for the way in which God has created and cared for them.

So What?

What does the doctrine of creation mean to you personally? What difference does it make in your perspective, in your behavior, or in your relationships?

Use the following chart to contrast the logical result of accepting either the creation explanation for the origin of things or the accidental-chance explanation.

	CREATION	CHANCE
What is the basis for "moral" behavior?		
What is the basis for self-esteem?		
What is the logical view of one's purpose on the earth?		
What demands are placed on you about how you treat other people?		
What basis is there for medical ethics?		
What reason do you have for optimism regarding the future?		
What is the basis for conservation of the earth and its resources?		
What purpose does religion or worship have in one's life?		
To whom is one ultimately accountable?		

Genesis: Beginnings
Unit 1. In the Beginning
(Lessons 1-4)

GOD'S PURPOSE FOR PEOPLE

LESSON 2

Jun 13

WHY TEACH THIS LESSON?

"Why?" The question seems to be a natural part of the human personality. From the two-year-old's "Why? . . . Why? . . . Why?" to the grieving widow's "Why was my husband taken?" the same question rolls off our lips again and again.

The question of why has no answer, of course, unless there is a purpose to the present order of things. Purpose comes from an intelligent Designer, not from blind chance. So it is only the one who believes in a Creator who can hope to find an answer to the persistent question, "Why?"

Perhaps some of your students are asking, "Why?" Any number of reasons or circumstances may have prompted the question, and you probably will not be able to give specific answers tailored to their individual needs. But this lesson will point them in the right direction. God does have a purpose for people, and it is only as we seek to fulfill that purpose that all the other "whys" will ever make sense.

INTRODUCTION
A. WHAT IS MAN?

The year 1997 marked the spectacular appearance of an infrequent visitor in the skies above North America. The Hale-Bopp Comet, which is visible approximately every 2400 years, produced a dazzling display as the glow of its tail shone brightly in the heavens. For some, its appearance was a bit overwhelming. Our eleven-year-old daughter became rather unsettled by the sight and didn't even like to look at it. The comet's mystique was heightened by the bizarre mass suicide of thirty-nine members of a cult known as Heaven's Gate near San Diego, California. They believed that their deaths would somehow allow them to travel to Heaven by means of a spaceship in the tail of the comet.

In ancient times, the psalmist David understood the meaning of the heavens far better than many moderns do. In Psalm 8 he extols the majesty and splendor of God as revealed in the heavens. In verse 4 he asks an appropriate question, in view of the vast, impressive heavenly array above: "What is man that you are mindful of him, the son of man that you care for him?" To view man as the centerpiece of God's magnificent work of creation is truly mind-boggling. And yet that is what Genesis 1 states. Man alone was made "in the image of God" as the crown of his creation (Genesis 1:26, 27). In today's lesson from Genesis 2, we find further evidence of that wonderful truth.

B. LESSON BACKGROUND

With grand and forceful style, the opening verses of the Bible provide the reader with a panoramic overview of God's act of creation. In six successive days,

DEVOTIONAL READING:
EPHESIANS 5:22
LESSON SCRIPTURE:
GENESIS 2:4-25
PRINTED TEXT:
GENESIS 2:7-9, 15-25

LESSON AIMS

After completing this lesson, each student will:
1. Describe the creation of, and the relationship between, the first man and woman.
2. Explain how the belief that we are created in God's image gives purpose to living.
3. Choose an area of life in which he or she needs to reflect God's purpose better, and take steps to do so.

KEY VERSE

The LORD God formed the man from the dust of the ground and breathed into his nostrils the breath of life, and the man became a living being.
—Genesis 2:7

LESSON 2 NOTES

The visual for lesson 2 illustrates verse 7 of the text. Display it at the beginning of the class session.

Introduce the text with the crossword puzzle on page 360. The solution is shown above.

OPTION

all that comprises our precious planet and the indescribable universe that surrounds it was created by "the word of the Lord" (Psalm 33:6). God spoke, and it was so.

The sixth day begins with the creation of the land animals and culminates in the creation of man and woman. It is clear on several counts that woman's creation is a part of day six: (1) We are told that God created "male and female" on the sixth day (Genesis 1:27), then blessed "them" and commanded "them" to be fruitful and increase in number (v. 28). (2) God pronounced the result of his work at the end of day six as "very good" (v. 31), implying that his creation of everything, including mankind, was finalized. (3) God's seventh-day rest from his creative activity indicates that his work is done, so the female counterpart of Adam must already have been on the scene. Thus it is clear that the events of Genesis 2:7-25 were all a part of day six and followed the creation of land animals earlier that day.

Not all Christians agree on the nature and length of the days in Genesis 1. It is best to view them as twenty-four-hour days in light of Exodus 20:8-11. There God tells Israel to observe the seventh day as a sabbath, "for in six days the Lord made the heavens and the earth." This command makes sense only if we are thinking in terms of literal twenty-four-hour days.

It has been pointed out that the events recorded in Genesis 2 make for a rather full day, since it includes the following events: land animals are brought forth; Adam is created and placed in the garden; he is prohibited from eating of the tree of the knowledge of good and evil; he is commissioned with the task of naming all the creatures brought before him; he is put into a deep sleep, awakens to find the woman God has fashioned from his rib, and names her. Still, it would not have been impossible for all of this to occur. The largest objection is that of naming all the varieties of animals. However, we do not need to think of every subcategory of animal species as being involved in Adam's naming of the creatures; he could have named broad categories.

The sixth day thus included not only man's special creation, but also a series of events that reinforced his special place in God's creative purpose.

I. MAN'S SPECIAL CREATION (GENESIS 2:7)

A. THE PROCESS (v. 7a)

7a. The LORD God formed the man from the dust of the ground and breathed into his nostrils the breath of life.

The shift in focus from the first chapter to the second chapter of Genesis is much like switching from a wide-angle panoramic lens to a close-up "zoom" lens. Several features in chapter 2 accentuate this transition. The phrase "the heavens and the earth," found in Genesis 1:1; 2:1, 4 is replaced by "the earth and the heavens" (end of verse 4), as the emphasis now shifts to man's dwelling place. The name shift from *God* (the Hebrew word *Elohim*, used throughout chapter 1) to *Lord God* (*Yahweh Elohim*) throughout chapters 2 and 3 is also significant. While the name *God* designates God in his power (as reflected in his creative activity in chapter 1), the name *Lord* (*Yahweh*) is often used to emphasize God's covenant relationship with his people. From Genesis 4 to the end of the book *Lord* (*Yahweh*) is frequently used, but the term *Lord God* (*Yahweh Elohim*) does not appear at all. This suggests a special "linking" function of this compound name in chapters 2 and 3.

God *formed the man from the dust of the ground.* The Hebrew word rendered *formed* signifies that God fashioned or shaped man, much as the potter works a lump of clay. *Dust* is both the original source and ultimate state of man's physical existence (Genesis 3:19; Job 34:15). Man is made of the stuff of this world. Even today, the human body's survival depends on some sixty minerals derived from the ground. We are still closely tied to the earth from which we came. The similarity in the Hebrew words *adam* ("man") and *adamah* ("ground") serves to emphasize this association.

B. THE RESULT (v. 7b)

7b. And the man became a living being.

As noted in last week's lesson, the Hebrew phrase translated *living being* ("living soul" in the *King James Version*) is the same one rendered "living creatures" in Genesis 1:20 (also in 1:24; 2:19; 9:10, 12, 16). Thus we should not use this phrase to defend man's superiority to the rest of creation or his immortality. Man's uniqueness is indicated by the special process through which God formed him (for example, God did not breathe life into the nostrils of any other creature) and, especially, by the fact that man alone is created in the image of God (Genesis 1:26, 27).

II. MAN'S SPECIAL ENVIRONMENT (GENESIS 2:8, 9, 15-17)

A. A SPECIAL TERRITORY (vv. 8, 9)

8. Now the LORD God had planted a garden in the east, in Eden; and there he put the man he had formed.

The *garden* into which Adam was *put* was located in *Eden*. The paradise conditions described there apparently did not exist elsewhere outside the garden area. One suggestion for the location of *Eden* is the region at the northern tip of the Persian Gulf, in what is now the country of Iraq. The 1991 Gulf War was fought in this same area (although many speculate that modern-day Kuwait would have been under water in earliest times, with the shoreline being to the north of it).

From what we know concerning the terrain of that part of the world at present, it is hard to imagine a luxuriant, natural garden flourishing there. However, some climatologists now argue that this part of the world was much wetter in earlier times, with a major shift to a much drier climate occurring after 3000 B.C. or so.

9. And the LORD God made all kinds of trees grow out of the ground—trees that were pleasing to the eye and good for food. In the middle of the garden were the tree of life and the tree of the knowledge of good and evil.

The *garden* is described as a beautiful and beneficial place. Two special trees are noted as being provided by God. It is unclear whether these were specially created or were simply ordinary trees endowed with extraordinary meaning. Not everything in the garden is simply laid out for man to enjoy, however. Many of the benefits will come only from the work of his hands, as the next verse of our printed text indicates.

B. A SPECIAL TASK (. 15)

15. The LORD God took the man and put him in the Garden of Eden to work it and take care of it.

Even in paradise, *work* was involved! Work was not part of the curse placed on man following the fall; it was part of the Creator's intention for him from the beginning. Adam was assigned the task of cultivating and caring for the *Garden of Eden* in which God placed him. See verse 5, where it is noted that, prior to God's creation of Adam, "there was no man to work the ground." Adam's task filled this void. His responsibility in the garden was the beginning of the process of subduing the earth, in accordance with God's design (Genesis 1:28).

WHAT DO YOU THINK?

Self-esteem is talked about and promoted in virtually every aspect of our society today, but low self-esteem remains a problem. Perhaps the reason for that is the acceptance of evolutionary theories about the origin of man. If we are but accidents of nature, we are no better than the beasts of the field.

In the Bible, however, we see God's creation of man to be a special event, with God taking a more intimate role than in his creation of the animals. First he formed man out of dust, suggesting a more "hands-on" approach than merely speaking the words to create. Then he breathed the breath of life into man's nostrils.

How might you use this description of man's creation to encourage a friend who suffers from low self-esteem?

HOW TO SAY IT

adam (Hebrew). uh-DAHM.
adamah (Hebrew). ad-uh-MAH.
Elohim (Hebrew). El-owe-HEEM.
ishah (Hebrew). ish-AH.
Yahweh (Hebrew). YAH-weh.

WHAT DO YOU THINK?

Man's free will required at least one ethical choice in order to function. This was the way man's obedience was to be tested. That was the purpose of the tree of the knowledge of good and evil. What ethical choices do you find hardest to make today? Why? How can you consistently make right choices?

C. A SPECIAL TEST (vv. 16, 17)

16, 17. And the LORD God commanded the man, "You are free to eat from any tree in the garden; but you must not eat from the tree of the knowledge of good and evil, for when you eat of it you will surely die."

The *garden* was not only a place of pleasure, but also a place of probation. Man's continued enjoyment of the blessings there was conditioned on his adherence to God's rules. His love for his Creator was to be demonstrated by obedience to his will. Woman was not yet created at this point, so she would not have heard this initial prohibition. Either God repeated it for her, or it was communicated to her by her husband.

The tree of life is not mentioned in the prohibition given to man. Later we learn that once man disobeyed God and ate of the *tree of the knowledge of good and evil*, he no longer was permitted access to the tree of life. That access will be restored in the renewed paradise described in Revelation 22:1, 2.

Spiritual death, that is, separation from God, occurred immediately upon Adam and Eve's transgression. This separation was symbolized by their expulsion from the garden. They did not *die* physically at the very instant of their rebellion, but the principle of death began to operate within their mortal bodies. This physical "death penalty" was then passed on to all future generations of Adam and Eve's descendants (for "all sinned," according to Romans 5:12), but the curse is ultimately removed in Christ (Romans 5:12-21; 1 Corinthians 15:21, 22).

TALE OF TWO TREES

A Tale of Two Cities may not be the best known or most read work of Charles Dickens (*A Christmas Carol* probably is), but many can at least recognize that title as the name of a literary classic. In the same way, the names of two specific trees in the garden of Eden are recognized by many who are otherwise unfamiliar with much of what the Bible says. We could call those trees "The Tree of Life" and "The Tree of Temptation."

These two trees represent man's free moral agency—our choice and our dilemma. The conflict between good and evil began as soon as God planted that second tree, the one with a "No Trespassing" sign on it. He planted the tree to encourage man to exercise his freedom of choice wisely by obeying his Creator. Satan used the tree to plant the idea of disobeying the Creator.

Life-or-death choices are still a part of our daily experience. Without them we would be reduced to mere puppet-like clones with no personality and no opportunity for independent decisions and individual action.

When God planted his garden, he provided for all of our needs, including the freedom of choice. That is part of being made in his image. We exercise that freedom best when we choose to obey our Creator. —R. W. B.

III. MAN'S SPECIAL ROLE (GENESIS 2:18-20a)

A. A HELPER NEEDED (v. 18)

18. The LORD God said, "It is not good for the man to be alone. I will make a helper suitable for him."

Dominion over the rest of creation was given by God to both male and female (Genesis 1:27, 28). God knew that this task would require a team effort and purposed to provide the newly created *man* with a companion and helper. While everything else in God's creation had been declared "good" thus far, here was a situation that was *not good*.

The phrase *helper suitable for him* suggests the supportive role of woman and calls attention to her role as one who complements man and supplies what he

WHAT DO YOU THINK?

Suppose a Christian brother is thinking of asking an unbeliever to marry him. "I know the Bible says we are not to be 'yoked together with unbelievers,' he says, but the Bible also says, 'It is not good for the man to be alone.' What choice do I have?" What advice would you give?

lacks. Interestingly, the person in the Old Testament most frequently referred to as a helper is God (particularly in the Psalms).

B. AN AUTHORITY EXERCISED (vv. 19, 20a)

19, 20a. *Now the LORD God had formed out of the ground all the beasts of the field and all the birds of the air. He brought them to the man to see what he would name them; and whatever the man called each living creature, that was its name. So the man gave names to all the livestock, the birds of the air and all the beasts of the field.*

God had formed out of the ground the land animals and *birds*, just as he made man "from the dust of the ground" (v. 7). He now *brought them to the man to see what he would name them.* As noted earlier, it is not necessary to think of every subcategory of animal species as being involved here. The term *livestock* likely designates larger domesticated animals, while the phrase *all the beasts of the field* describes wild animals.

The fact that the man was given the task of naming the animals emphasized his authority over the animal kingdom. Apparently Adam was created as an intelligent adult who looked like he had reached that stage through the normal process of being conceived, born, and nurtured to adulthood. We do not need to envision a lengthy learning process prior to Adam's being able to assign a multitude of names to the animals. He came into this world with a mind that possessed the capacity to think and reason on a high level.

It should be noted that this concept of "apparent age" has interesting ramifications if applied to other created objects besides man. For example, the stars could have been given an age of several thousand years at the time God created them. Thus the fact that they reflect that age does not indicate that they are actually that old.

IV. MAN'S SPECIAL COMPANION (GENESIS 2:20b-25)

A. SUITED FOR MAN (v. 20b)

20b. *But for Adam no suitable helper was found.*

One may wonder why there was a delay in the creation of woman, since God knew that she was a necessary part of the picture. Several suggestions come to mind. One is that her separate creation emphasized her importance. Another is that she was created only after the man recognized his need for her. Nothing in the animal parade over which Adam officiated came close to filling the bill! The fact that God had said that it was not good for the man to be alone (v. 18) signified how vital this final creative act really was. The woman was just the *helper* and companion the man needed—and still needs.

B. FASHIONED FROM MAN (vv. 21, 22)

21, 22. *So the LORD God caused the man to fall into a deep sleep; and while he was sleeping, he took one of the man's ribs and closed up the place with flesh. Then the LORD God made a woman from the rib he had taken out of the man, and he brought her to the man.*

God caused the man to fall into a deep sleep. The word for *deep sleep* indicates a state in which one is oblivious to any nearby sounds (a "dead to the world" kind of sleep). The Hebrew term is used in two other places where specific individuals are said to fall into a deep sleep (Abram in Genesis 15:12; Saul and his army in 1 Samuel 26:12).

The use of a *rib* suggests someone who is close to man's heart and who stands by his side to fulfill the role of helper. The Hebrew verb used in the phrase *made*

DAILY BIBLE READINGS

Monday, June 7—The Lord God Planted a Garden (Genesis 2:4b-14)

Tuesday, June 8—Therefore a Man Clings to His Wife (Genesis 2:15-25)

Wednesday, June 9—Husbands, Love Your Wives (Ephesians 5:18-33)

Thursday, June 10—Honor Your Father and Your Mother (Matthew 15:1-9)

Friday, June 11—Claiming to Keep the Commandments (Matthew 19:16-22)

Saturday, June 12—God Made Them Male and Female (Mark 10:1-9)

Sunday, June 13—Perishable to Imperishable (1 Corinthians 15:42-49)

PRAYER

Our Lord and Father, we marvel at how much we mean to you as the crown of your creation. We thank you for your provisions and blessings—for human love and companionship; for noble purposes and important tasks; for the freedom to serve you out of choice, not compulsion. Help us in our marriages and other relationships as we strive to fulfill your plan for our lives. In the name of Jesus we pray. Amen.

a woman means "to build." It carries the idea of a planned, precise construction of man's special companion.

C. UNITED WITH MAN (vv. 23-25)

23. The man said, "This is now bone of my bones and flesh of my flesh; she shall be called 'woman,' for she was taken out of man."

Bone of my bones and flesh of my flesh. This expression has a ring of exclamation to it. The close physical similarity between man and woman as a result of God's creation is reinforced by the language in verse 24 describing the marriage bond. Another sound correspondence in Hebrew (similar to *adam* and *adamah* noted under the study of Genesis 2:7a) is found here in the words translated *woman* (Hebrew, *ishah*) and *man* (Hebrew, *ish*). (The similarity in the English words "woman" and "man" occurs because the term "woman" is derived from the phrase "wife [of] man.")

24. For this reason a man will leave his father and mother and be united to his wife, and they will become one flesh.

Jesus indicates that the words of this verse are directly from God, and not a continuation of Adam's speech (Matthew 19:5). In the context Jesus employs the designation *one flesh* as a prohibition against divorce. Indeed, in marriage it is God who joins man and woman together in a bond that is not to be broken. The words *be united* further depict the closeness that marriage is to entail. For *a man* to *leave his father and mother* marks the establishment of a new relationship of love and devotion that is to supersede all previous relationships.

25. The man and his wife were both naked, and they felt no shame.

Adam and Eve initially enjoyed a wonderful innocence and intimacy with one another as well as with God. The phrase *the man and his wife* signifies the special relationship of marriage that God designed to be a part of his creation order. At the beginning man and woman were truly "good," not only in design and origin, but in actual thought and deed.

CONCLUSION

We learn much concerning God's plan and purpose for man in the opening chapters of Genesis. Made in the "image of God," men and women are to reflect the glory of God in their lives. Our lesson text for today singles out man as the capstone of God's creation. As the psalmist David proclaimed, we have been "crowned . . . with glory and honor" by our Creator (Psalm 8:5).

Although marriage is set forth as the divine model in our text, Christians who are unmarried, including those who do not plan to be married, should not see themselves as excluded from God's divine program for man as described in Genesis. The apostle Paul even notes that undistracted devotion to God may be best achieved in the unmarried state, since marriage carries with it other obligations and priorities (1 Corinthians 7:32-35).

Adam and Eve were created pure and sinless, yet there was no guarantee that they would remain so. Free will and self-determination were part of being made in God's image. Conditions were attached to Adam and Eve's continued enjoyment of God's blessings. Their control over the rest of creation would depend on their measure of self-control—their conscious decision to love and obey their Creator.

To look at today's text is to look into our own hearts. It seems that daily, as we recall God's provision and blessings toward us, we find ourselves standing beneath forbidden fruit in one form or another. We must ask ourselves whom we will serve. We can experience the glory and honor that we were created to possess only when we live to bring glory and honor to our Creator.

WHAT DO YOU THINK?

Our text records that God instituted marriage when he presented Eve to Adam to be his mate. What do these verses teach us about the nature and intent of marriage?

WHAT DO YOU THINK?

According to the Bible, all mankind has descended from Adam and Eve. Incredible as it may seem, God made the human genetic code so complex and yet so flexible that billions of humans could come from just two individuals; yet each of these people is unique. Apparently geographical isolation caused certain traits, such as color and other body features, to concentrate in different peoples, giving rise to the races. Yet all human beings are descended from these two original people. What lesson does this teach us in regard to race relationships? How ought we to treat others who are different from ourselves?

THOUGHT TO REMEMBER

We receive our greatest sense of fulfillment when we do what God wants, not what we want.

Discovery Learning

This page contains an alternate lesson plan emphasizing learning activities. Classes desiring such student involvement will find these suggestions helpful. The next page is a reproducible activity page to further enhance discovery learning.

LEARNING GOALS

As a result of participating in this session, the student will be able to:

1. Describe the creation of, and the relationship between, the first man and woman.

2. Explain how the belief that we are created in God's image gives purpose to living.

3. Choose an area of life in which he or she needs to reflect God's purpose better, and take steps to do so.

INTO THE LESSON

Ask the married couples in your class to form at least two small groups of no more than six—with husbands and wives in *separate* groups. Ask the members of each group to tell what they first found attractive about their mates and what they now appreciate most. If the two are not the same, explain why.

Have the singles form small groups, too. These should tell what they are looking for in a prospective mate. What physical, spiritual, intellectual, and emotional qualities do they hope to find? Which is most important? Why?

After a few minutes, tell the class that today's lesson looks at the origin of marriage. "Dating" in today's world can be confusing. The many people trying to give advice on marriage can make that relationship rather confusing as well. Things were much simpler in the garden of Eden. The one man met the one woman in the world, and God made them "one flesh." Let's see how that relationship can help us understand our own situations more clearly.

INTO THE WORD

Lead into the Bible study portion of the lesson by asking a volunteer to read Genesis 2:7-9, 15-25 aloud. Distribute copies of the reproducible page that follows and give the students time to work the puzzle. Then use the following questions to lead a discussion of the text.

1. What do you think Moses (the author of Genesis) is trying to convey to us about the creation of mankind when he uses the imagery "breathed into his nostrils the breath of life"? (God creates mankind in a very special, intimate way when compared with the way in which he created all that was created previously.)

2. The word "garden" literally means "a protected area" and "Eden" means "delight." In what way did the garden of Eden live up to its name? (Encourage your students to visualize the garden as it was before man sinned. Be sure to emphasize the fact that it was a place specially prepared by God for man, that it provided every physical thing necessary for life, and that man had the opportunity for intimate fellowship with God there.)

3. Why did God plant the tree of life in the garden? (He intended that man would not die but live forever.)

4. Why did God plant the tree of the knowledge of good and evil in the garden of Eden? (God desired man's obedience. In order to obey, Adam needed to have real choice. Without choice, Adam was a prisoner in the garden. True love and worship are not possible without choice.)

5. What was man's "job" in the garden? ("To work it and take care of it." This was part of the mandate to subdue and have dominion over the earth. Work is not part of the curse; it was part of man's God-ordained role even before there was sin.)

6. What was the one thing that was "not good" in God's creation? (Man was alone. He needed companionship. He needed a mate with whom to reproduce and fill the earth with people.)

7. What is significant about the manner in which woman was created? (She was taken from man's side; so she was like him—made of the same stuff. She was to be at his side as a companion. The word for "made" in verse 22 suggests the idea of a planned, precise construction, much as the word "formed" suggests God made man in a special way. The man and the woman were both very special in design and in relationship to God.)

INTO LIFE

Point out to your students that Adam and Eve lived in the garden of Eden as they were created to live—in a delightfully intimate relationship with each other and with their Creator. Ask, "How can we restore something of that purpose and relationship?" In your discussion, note that Adam and Eve had to choose to obey God. (Next week we'll see what happened when they did not.) We too can choose to obey God and act in a way that reflects the image of God.

Then lead in a time of prayer thanking God for creating us in his image. Seek his help in reflecting that image more clearly.

Creation Crossword

Use the following clues and Genesis 2:7-9, 15-25 to complete the crossword puzzle below.

The LORD God formed the man from the [16 Down] of the ground and breathed into his [9 Down] the breath of life, and the man became a [11 Down] being.

Now the LORD God had planted a [2 Across] in the east, in Eden; and there he put the man he had formed. And the LORD God made all kinds of trees grow out of the ground—trees that were pleasing to the eye and [15 Across] for food. In the middle of the [2 Across] were the tree of life and the tree of the knowledge of [15 Across] and [3 Down].

The LORD God took the man and put him in the [2 Across] of Eden to [10 Down] it and take [8 Down] of it. And the LORD God commanded the man, "You are free to eat from any tree in the [2 Across]; but you must not eat from the tree of the knowledge of [15 Across] and [3 Down], for when you eat of it you will [12 Across] [13 Across]."

The LORD God said, "It is not [15 Across] for the man to be [5 Down]. I will make a [21 Across] [12 Down] for him."

Now the LORD God had formed out of the ground all the [20 Across] of the field and all the [19 Across] of the air. He brought them to the man to see what he would [1 Down] them; and whatever the man called each [11 Down] [8 Across], that was its [1 Down]. So the man gave names to all the [11 Across], the [19 Across] of the air and all the [20 Across] of the field.

But for Adam no [12 Down] [21 Across] was found. So the LORD God caused the man to fall into a deep sleep; and while he was sleeping, he took one of the man's ribs and closed up the place with [14 Down]. Then the LORD God made a [6 Across] from the [17 Down] he had taken out of the man, and he brought her to the man.

The man said,

> "This is now bone of my bones
>   and [14 Down] of my [14 Down];
> she shall be called '[6 Across],'
>   for she was taken out of man."

For this reason a man will [7 Down] his father and mother and be [18 Across] to his wife, and they will become one [14 Down].

The man and his wife were both [4 Across], and they felt no shame.

CONSEQUENCES OF SIN

LESSON 3

DEVOTIONAL READING:
1 JOHN 3:11-18

LESSON SCRIPTURE:
GENESIS 4

PRINTED TEXT:
GENESIS 4:1-16

Jun
20

WHY TEACH THIS LESSON?

Every spring motorists in the midwest find a new "sport" on the highways: pothole dodging! Every winter, moisture finds its way down into small cracks in the pavement and then freezes. This freezing moisture expands and breaks up the pavement. Soon the small crack is a large crack, and then a hole.

Homeowners can face the same problems with their driveways, so smart homeowners will regularly apply a sealer to their driveways. This closes the cracks and prevents the moisture from getting into the pavement. It thus prevents the potholes that are the natural consequence.

Sin is like that moisture seeping into the pavement. If it is allowed to be present, as it was in Cain's life, the destructive consequences will follow. Cain could have mastered the situation, but he failed to do so. You can use this lesson to help your students apply a coat of "sealer" so they do not have to deal later with harmful consequences.

INTRODUCTION

A. PARADISE LOST

A tiny island dots the western Pacific Ocean just south of the equator between Australia and Hawaii. At one time abundant wildlife, lush foliage, and food-laden trees made the eight-square-mile island of Nauru (Nah-*oo*-roo) a delight for its seven thousand native inhabitants. But then "progress" replaced paradise. Nauru was discovered to be situated on one of the richest stores of phosphate rock on the globe. Millions of tons have been mined during this century, creating vast wealth—and untold misery. Greed and government intervention have combined to turn what was once a dreamland into a nightmare.

Although the island gained its independence in 1968, its new and improved status was quickly followed by the nationalization of the phosphate mines. Wasteful affluence soon manifested itself in many ways, and continues to do so today: thousands of cars, loads of high-tech gadgetry, multiple televisions per family, and the list goes on. The government subsidizes everything—health care, education, housing, and utilities, to name but a few items.

Major problems now exist on Nauru. Changes in diet have destroyed the health of the people. Nine out of ten are obese, and heart disease and diabetes are on the rampage. The average life expectancy is only fifty-five. Government handouts have created a lazy welfare state, and its misuse of earnings from the now nearly depleted mines has left a mortgage on the future that may bankrupt the island in a few years. Much of the once lush terrain now resembles a lunar landscape, and the excess heat from all the exposed rock has even severely lessened the rainfall on the island. For Nauru, paradise has indeed been lost—a victim of greed and folly.

B. LESSON BACKGROUND

Last week's lesson focused on God's creation of Adam and Eve. Placed in a beautiful garden in Eden, they enjoyed the blessings of their Creator. However,

LESSON AIMS

After completing this lesson each student should:

1. Summarize the details surrounding Cain's murder of Abel.

2. Cite examples from modern society or personal experience that demonstrate the destructive consequences of sin.

3. Identify someone to whom he or she is (or will be) accountable in order to minimize the danger of falling prey to sin.

KEY VERSE

"If you do what is right, will you not be accepted? But if you do not do what is right, sin is crouching at your door; it desires to have you, but you must master it."
—Genesis 4:7

HOW TO SAY IT

Bathsheba. Bath-SHE-buh.
Enosh. EE-nosh.
Lamech. LAY-mek.
Septuagint. Sep-TOO-ih-jent.

Satan, in serpent form, succeeded in enticing them to eat from the tree of the knowledge of good and evil. He promised them that they would become like God with the knowledge gained from the tree's forbidden fruit. But loss, not gain, was the result of Adam and Eve's transgression. A spiritual separation from God occurred alongside the introduction of the process of physical death into their bodies. They were driven out of the garden (Genesis 3:23, 24). Their wonderful paradise was lost.

Amidst the punishment that God pronounced on the man and woman was a glimmer of hope. Through the promised seed of the woman, Satan would one day taste ultimate defeat. The curse upon man would be removed by a triumphant Redeemer, who would crush Satan's head (Genesis 3:15).

For the present, however, Adam and Eve would continue to experience the devastation caused by sin. Today's lesson shows how much heartache sin brought to the first family. It will remind us that sin always yields bitter fruit, particularly when it affects a home.

I. CAIN AND ABEL (GENESIS 4:1-5a)
A. TWO SONS (vv. 1, 2a)
1, 2a. Adam lay with his wife Eve, and she became pregnant and gave birth to Cain. She said, "With the help of the LORD I have brought forth a man." Later she gave birth to his brother Abel.

The intimate relations between a husband and *wife* were ordained prior to the Fall, for on the sixth day God had commanded, "Be fruitful and increase in number; fill the earth" (Genesis 1:28). The name *Eve* means "living" or "life," for she was to be "the mother of all the living" (Genesis 3:20). She recognized that being able to conceive and give birth to *Cain* was a result of God's blessing. In contrast, very little information is given regarding the birth of *Abel*.

B. TWO OCCUPATIONS (v. 2b)
2b. Now Abel kept flocks, and Cain worked the soil.

Whether by necessity or by personal preference, *Abel* and *Cain* found themselves in different occupations. Both labors were valuable in providing for their family. Contrary to the picture painted by evolutionists (of man as a primitive being whose intelligence slowly "evolved"), the Bible portrays mankind as being involved from the beginning with advanced tasks such as soil cultivation and animal domestication.

C. TWO OFFERINGS (vv. 3, 4a)
3, 4a. In the course of time Cain brought some of the fruits of the soil as an offering to the LORD. But Abel brought fat portions from some of the firstborn of his flock.

When and why did the first act of worship occur? Did God command the offerings mentioned here, or were they spontaneous? Had Adam made similar offerings? Were these the first offerings that *Cain* and *Abel* offered? And what was the exact purpose of such offerings: to atone for sins or to accomplish some other purpose? No definite answer can be given to any of these questions, so we must be cautious about whatever conclusions we draw based on our understanding of the offerings.

We should make two observations from our text. First, each man gave from the produce of his individual labors. Cain brought a grain or vegetable *offering*, while Abel brought an animal offering. Second, the phrase *firstborn of his flock* may have some significance. Such an offering by Abel would have been consistent with laws later given to Israel (Exodus 13:12; 34:19). Cain, however, *brought some of the fruits of the soil.* The text does not say that he brought of the "first-fruits"—another practice later commanded of Israel (Exodus 23:16, 19; Nehemiah 10:35). Of course, only at certain times of the year could a farmer bring of the firstfruits, or first results, of his harvest.

D. TWO RESPONSES (vv. 4b, 5a)

4b. The LORD looked with favor on Abel and his offering.

What caused the Lord to have *looked with favor on* Abel's *offering* but not on Cain's? Usually two answers are suggested. One is that Abel provided a blood sacrifice, presumably according to God's specific command. Cain's was only a grain offering. We later learn that apart from the shedding of blood, there is no forgiveness of sins (Hebrews 9:22). However, we cannot be certain that a sin offering was involved here. The Hebrew word rendered *offering* here is the same one used in verse 5, and is also used to describe the grain offering in Leviticus 2.

More likely the heart of the offerer was the key factor distinguishing the two offerings. An offering can be made according to exact specifications and yet be accompanied by an evil heart. The New Testament contrasts Cain and Abel with regard to their righteousness. We learn that it was "by faith" that Abel offered a "a better sacrifice than Cain did" and was thus commended as righteous (Hebrews 11:4). First John 3:12 states that Cain's actions were evil, while his brother's were righteous. Most likely Abel's act of worship arose from a right relationship with God, thus *the Lord looked with favor on Abel and his offering.*

5a. But on Cain and his offering he did not look with favor.

Cain's angry reaction to God's rejection of his *offering* (verse 5b) provides a clue to the real problem here. Rather than view Cain's offering as a well-intentioned but misguided attempt to approach God, we should see it as symptomatic of a deeper crisis in his spiritual life.

The problem of empty ritual in Israel was frequently addressed by the prophets. They endeavored to drive home the point that merely going through the motions of worship, unaccompanied by genuine devotion to God, is an abomination to the Lord. "To obey is better than sacrifice," Samuel scolded a disobedient Saul (1 Samuel 15:22). "For I desired mercy, not sacrifice," God chastened Israel through the prophet Hosea (Hosea 6:6). Following his sin with Bathsheba, David realized that multitudes of animal sacrifices would not restore his relationship with God: "The sacrifices of God are a broken spirit; a broken and contrite heart, O God, you will not despise" (Psalm 51:17). See also Isaiah 1:11-20; Jeremiah 7:21-23; Amos 5:21-24; Micah 6:6-8; and Malachi 1:10-14.

Cain's corrupted offering casts a long, dark shadow. His failure is a foretaste of similar experiences in the history of Israel, and is even cited in the New Testament (Jude 11). It is sobering to think that the first acts of worship described in Scripture produced such tragic results.

II. CAIN AND GOD (GENESIS 4:5b-16)

A. CAIN'S ANGER (v. 5b)

5b. So Cain was very angry, and his face was downcast.

Rebellion was followed by resentment. How God communicated his displeasure with Cain is not clear, but in the next verse he spoke directly with Cain.

B. GOD'S RESPONSE (vv. 6, 7)

6, 7. Then the LORD said to Cain, "Why are you angry? Why is your face downcast? If you do what is right, will you not be accepted? But if you do not do what is right, sin is crouching at your door; it desires to have you, but you must master it."

WHAT DO YOU THINK?

Some have alleged that God was unfair to Cain. Both he and Abel brought offerings from their own field of endeavor—Abel from his flock and Cain from his harvest—yet God accepted only the blood offering, which Cain was unable to give. How would you respond to such criticism?

WHAT DO YOU THINK?

Cain's reaction shows us much about his heart. Rather than accept responsibility and repent, he became angry. Some people still respond that way when their sins are exposed. How do you deal with such people? How can we lovingly lead them to repentance?

WHAT DO YOU THINK?

Cain's offering was rejected, but God's loving counsel with Cain shows that God still loved him. Christians are sometimes accused of hating those they believe guilty of sin (e.g., homosexuals, abortionists, etc.). How can we demonstrate that we truly do hate the sin but love the sinner?

The visual for lesson 3 dramatizes the danger Cain was in, and the danger each of us faces when temptation urges us to sin. Display it as you discuss verse 7.

God reasoned with Cain in an apparent attempt to restore him. Could Cain justify his anger? Had God been unclear or unfair in his dealings with him? We might categorize this confrontation as the Bible's first recorded counseling session. It is clear that the changes in attitude were Cain's to make. He had a problem; would he face it and deal with it? Sin is depicted as a savage beast, *crouching at Cain's door* to devour him. However, Cain could still resist if he would make the effort. God's final words to him indicated that he had a choice concerning this "beast": *you must master it.*

C. Cain's Violence (v. 8)

8. Now Cain said to his brother Abel, "Let's go out to the field." And while they were in the field, Cain attacked his brother Abel and killed him.

The Hebrew text literally reads, "And Cain said to Abel his brother." Curiously, the Hebrew words, "said to," are normally followed by what was said, but not here. Thus the *King James Version* translates the verb *talked*: "Cain talked with Abel his brother." However, several ancient versions, including the Septuagint (the Greek text of the Old Testament), include the expected quotation of Cain's words: *"Let's go out to the field."* The *New International Version* has followed these ancient versions in producing the reading we find here.

Although a Jewish tradition states that Abel's death was the result of an argument that broke out between the brothers in the field, another view is that an angry, jealous Cain invited Abel to go with him to the field with the intent to kill him once they were there.

D. God's Curse (vv. 9-12)

9. Then the Lord said to Cain, "Where is your brother Abel?"

"I don't know," he replied. "Am I my brother's keeper?"

Perhaps Cain had buried his brother's body to hide his evil deed, but he could not hide it from God, who then confronted him. Cain's question, *Am I my brother's keeper?* is one of the most familiar (and quoted) questions from Scripture. It is also one of the most tragic. It conveys an attitude of contempt and neglect that sadly characterizes many in society today.

What Do You Think?

Cain asked, "Am I my brother's keeper?" Such a flippant question revealed that his heart contained no love for his brother. He does not appear to have been remorseful in the least for his terrible deed. What do you think it means to be your brother's—or sister's—keeper? How do you perform such a role?

(Perhaps some in your class can share specific acts done to help a brother or sister in need.)

Like Father, Like Son

Fathers hope their sons will imitate only their good and honorable characteristics and habits. Unfortunately, most sons don't exercise such discretion. They become just like Dad, "warts and all." A father's influence on his offspring exerts itself negatively as well as positively. From his father a son may learn dishonesty as well as integrity, profanity as well as purity, laziness as well as ambition.

Cain apparently developed shortcomings similar to Adam's. When confronted with his own transgression, Adam tried to shift the blame, refusing to accept responsibility for his own actions: "The woman you put here with me—she gave me some fruit from the tree, and I ate it" (Genesis 3:12).

When Cain killed Abel and was subsequently confronted with his sin, he tried the same gambit: "Am I my brother's keeper?" He had learned the "art" of dodging responsibility for his personal behavior and choices.

As members of the human race, we are all, in a sense, sons and daughters of Adam. We too have learned to shirk responsibility, to play the "blame game," and to resist repentance and confession of our sins. Christians, however, are "children of God" (1 John 3:1). When we acknowledge our sin and seek forgiveness, we are promised that Christ will "purify us from all unrighteousness" (1 John 1:9).

Let us pursue the holiness of our heavenly Father so that others can readily identify us as his children.

　　　　　　　　　　　　　　　　　　　　　　　　　—R. W. B.

10. *The LORD said, "What have you done? Listen! Your brother's blood cries out to me from the ground.*

God heard a voice that no human ear could detect. As David describes so vividly in Psalm 139 (especially vv. 1-12), no one can hide an act or even a thought of the heart from God. The testimony of Abel's *blood* before an all-knowing Judge called for justice and retribution.

11. *"Now you are under a curse and driven from the ground, which opened its mouth to receive your brother's blood from your hand.*

The *ground*, which had become contaminated with Abel's *blood*, would now be a source of cursing rather than blessing by not producing a harvest for Cain. This was a particularly painful punishment for Cain, since he "worked the soil" (v. 2). Cain would not be able to survive by doing what he had become most adept at doing.

12. *"When you work the ground, it will no longer yield its crops for you. You will be a restless wanderer on the earth."*

The word *earth* at the end of this verse is different from that rendered *ground*, and indicates a much larger region or area (or the entire planet). There was no place to which Cain could travel to escape the impact of this curse. He would be forced to live as a *restless wanderer* and fend for himself as best he could.

E. CAIN'S PROTEST (vv. 13, 14)

13, 14. *Cain said to the LORD, "My punishment is more than I can bear. Today you are driving me from the land, and I will be hidden from your presence; I will be a restless wanderer on the earth, and whoever finds me will kill me."*

God's *punishment* did not set well with the volatile and violent disposition of Cain. (Adam, in contrast, offered no protest when God pronounced his punishment.) Cain complained about the severity of his sentence. He seemed to believe that he would be cut off (*hidden*) from God's presence and care, but that was not true, as Cain would soon learn. Later God declared that death was the appropriate penalty for murder (Genesis 9:5, 6; Exodus 21:12); thus Cain's punishment was actually less severe than it could have been.

Another concern expressed by Cain was the fear that he himself would be slain by an act of vengeance. We should keep in mind that all persons on the earth at this time were members of the same family, although the numbers of cousins, nephews, etc. already could have numbered into the hundreds or even thousands. We do not know how she learned of it, but Eve knew of Cain's deed (v. 25) and we assume that everyone else did as well. Cain's fears may have been well grounded (we know that feuds within families have often escalated, leaving numerous undeserving victims in their wake), but one wonders how much he read into other people's thinking the evils of his own heart. If others were like Cain, he was indeed in grave danger.

F. GOD'S PROTECTION (vv. 15, 16)

15. *But the LORD said to him, "Not so; if anyone kills Cain, he will suffer vengeance seven times over." Then the LORD put a mark on Cain so that no one who found him would kill him.*

The term *seven times over* is probably the use of the number *seven* to express completeness. Full *vengeance* will be taken on whoever *kills Cain*.

Commentators speculate about the meaning of the *mark on Cain*. The Hebrew preposition translated as *on* is best rendered as "for" or "for the sake of." The idea is probably not that a mark (literally, "sign") was placed on the body of Cain, but that a sign was given for Cain's sake either to indicate God's displeasure on

WHAT DO YOU THINK?

God's punishment was severe, but he stopped short of requiring Cain's life as he could justly have done. Nonetheless, Cain complained. His complaint clearly shows his unrepentant heart. His only concern was for the suffering he was going to experience, not for the suffering and death he had inflicted. Why is it that some people complain even when they are treated with grace? How do you deal with such people?

PRAYER

Father in Heaven, as your children may we reflect the glory of your image to a world blinded by sin's dark shadow. Help us to take sin seriously in our own lives, and to demonstrate your love and your grace to those around us who are trapped by sin. In Jesus' precious name we pray. Amen.

THOUGHT TO REMEMBER

"The sacrifices of God are a broken spirit; a broken and contrite heart, O God, you will not despise" (Psalm 51:17).

DAILY BIBLE READINGS

Monday, June 14—Sin Is Lurking at the Door (Genesis 4:1-7)

Tuesday, June 15—Cain Murders His Brother Abel (Genesis 4:8-16)

Wednesday, June 16—The Birth of Enoch and Seth (Genesis 4:17-26)

Thursday, June 17—Iniquities Are Barriers Between You and God (Isaiah 59:1-15)

Friday, June 18—Those Who Forsake Transgressions Will Obtain Mercy (Proverbs 28:9-14)

Saturday, June 19—"But I Tell You" (Matthew 5:21-26)

Sunday, June 20—Happy Are Those Whose Transgression Is Forgiven (Psalm 32:1-11)

anyone who would kill him or to warn Cain if someone seeking to take his life was approaching.

16. So Cain went out from the LORD's presence and lived in the land of Nod, east of Eden.

The name Nod means "wandering." It was a fitting location since Cain had been sentenced to live as a "wanderer." There Cain established a family line. Six generations, including the godless Lamech, are mentioned (vv. 17-24). However, it was not until Adam and Eve had Seth, and he in turn had a son named Enosh, that "men began to call on the name of the Lord" (v. 26).

MURDER MYSTERIES

Homicide cases unraveled by Sherlock Holmes, Colombo, Matlock, and others like them provide captivating drama by focusing on the psychological tension created by the presence of unknown details. Missing pieces of information make mysteries mysterious. The more question marks that punctuate the crime, the more convoluted the story line can be. Until the victim, the weapon, and the motive (as well as witnesses) are discovered, readers or viewers can only guess what the outcome will be. Usually, last-minute revelations provide surprise endings where the crime is solved and the perpetrators are brought to justice.

Genesis 4 tells of a murder mystery of sorts. Though we know who the victim and the murderer are, questions remain. Why was Cain's offering to God unacceptable? What weapon was used? What was the "mark on Cain"? Exactly where was the "land of Nod"?

We can be certain of this: God tells us all we need to know about this tragic incident. He wants us to understand something about the origins and consequences of sin, his justice and punishment for disobedience, his grace and compassion for sinners, and our accountability to him. We don't have to know any more details to be able to grasp these important concepts. About such truths as these there is no mystery.

—R. W. B.

CONCLUSION

A. LEARNING FROM CAIN

Some important truths are evident from our lesson text today. First, God desires a personal relationship with us, not merely outward compliance to his laws. God accepted the sacrifice of Abel because it was offered by a man of faith (Hebrews 11:4). Second, we are reminded of the chaos that sin can produce in our lives. For Cain, God's rejection of his sacrifice drove him to anger, bitterness, and eventually even murder. God challenged Cain to master sin (Genesis 4:7). We also must heed that charge.

Cain's question, "Am I my brother's keeper?" speaks to the issue of accountability. The message of Genesis 4 is clear: we are accountable, both to our fellowmen and to the One who created them and us in his image.

B. BLOOD THAT SPEAKS

The blood of Abel cried out from the ground calling for judgment on his murderer Cain. The one who had shed man's blood deserved for his own to be shed, since he had slain that which was made in the very image of God (Genesis 9:6). Abel's blood, therefore, cried out on behalf of justice and legal rights.

The book of Hebrews teaches that the blood of Jesus "speaks a better word than the blood of Abel" (Hebrews 12:24). The theme "better" is prominent in Hebrews, as the New Covenant through Jesus is shown to be superior to the Old in a variety of ways. Jesus' blood "speaks better" because it calls, not for vindication and justice, but for mercy and grace.

Discovery Learning

This page contains an alternate lesson plan emphasizing learning activities. Classes desiring such student involvement will find these suggestions helpful. The next page is a reproducible activity page to further enhance discovery learning.

LEARNING GOALS

As a result of participating in this session, the student will be able to:

1. Summarize the details surrounding Cain's murder of Abel.

2. Cite examples from modern society or personal experience that demonstrate the destructive consequences of sin.

3. Identify someone to whom he or she is (or will be) accountable in order to minimize the danger of falling prey to sin.

INTO THE LESSON

Ask your students to form small groups of no more than three or four to a group. Then ask each person to think of a time in his life when he had a clear choice between right and wrong and chose to do what he knew was wrong. Ask each person to describe that event to his group, tell why he chose to do wrong, and describe the result. Make this exercise less intimidating by telling the students that the choices they describe need not be examples from their adult lives but may be things they did as children. Break the ice by telling the results of some wrong choice of your own.

When every member of the class has had time to tell his or her story, ask, "Do you think you would have made a different choice if you had felt accountable to someone? Why or why not?" Allow some time for the groups to discuss this among themselves; then note that today's lesson introduces us to, perhaps, the most famous act of disobedience in the Scriptures: Cain's murder of Abel. His oft-quoted "Am I my brother's keeper?" shows he shirked accountability, and suggests the danger of our not being accountable today.

INTO THE WORD

Ask a volunteer to read Genesis 4:1-16. Then distribute a worksheet with the names Cain and Abel at the top, heading two separate columns. Ask the class to use the worksheet to note points of comparison and contrast between Cain and Abel from the first five verses of the text. (Three specific contrasts should be noted in the two occupations, two offerings, and two results.)

Discuss why Abel's offering was accepted and Cain's was not. Use Hebrews 11:4 and the Scripture exposition on page 363 to help you.

Write the word *temptation* on your chalkboard. Ask, "What is temptation? Is temptation the same as sin? Why or why not?" (Temptation is an enticement to sin. It is not, generally, sin itself—except that sometimes our sin becomes temptation to further sin.)

Read verses 5b-7. Ask, "Is Cain guilty of wrong here, or is he merely being tempted? Explain." (Cain is clearly being tempted, as God's warning that "sin is crouching at your door" reveals. His anger, and the reason his offering was rejected are also wrong, however. So he is guilty of sin, but he is being tempted to greater sin.)

Read verses 8-16 and discuss the following questions:

1. What were the results of Cain's sin? (Abel was dead, and Cain became an exile.)

2. What other examples can you cite, either from modern society or personal experience, that illustrate the destructive consequences of sin? (Increasing violence in our society, declining moral standards, broken homes, and many other general consequences might be cited. Each class member may have a story of deception or jealousy or some other sin that caused painful personal consequences. Don't pressure anyone to share, but try to get everyone to reflect on what sin has done in his or her own life in order to see the repugnance of sin.)

INTO LIFE

Point out that most of us find ourselves in the position of Cain in verse 7. Sin is "crouching at the door." Sometimes we are in that position because of our own mistakes or past unfaithfulness; at other times it is in spite of our innocence. But either way, sin is there, we are being tempted, and we must master it. Discuss some ways we can do that.

One way is by being accountable to another believer. Cain may not have believed himself to be his brother's keeper, but God did not accept that. Mutual accountability between two believers, or in a small close group, is a great help in avoiding sin.

Distribute index cards (or use the lower portion of the reproducible activity page) and ask each student to write the name of someone to whom he or she would be willing to be accountable in order to minimize the danger of falling prey to sin. Challenge the students to seek to initiate accountability relationships with the people whose names they have written. Then close your class session with prayer.

Sin Is Murder!

Cain found that his sin had bitter consequences. First his unrighteousness spoiled his sacrifice, so he and the sacrifice were rejected. Then he murdered his brother, and he became an exile.

Listed below are some common temptations that people, even Christians, sometimes give in to. What consequences have you seen follow when they do?

Gossip

Lying

Angry outbursts

Deception

Jealousy

You Need Help

Many believers have found it helpful to have an accountability partner to help them master the temptations that threaten to trip them up. Weekly, or at some other regular interval, these accountability partners get together for prayer, Bible study, confession, and encouragement.

Write below the name of someone with whom you believe you could establish such a relationship. Then write some ways you might go about it—where would you meet, at what intervals, etc.

> *"If you do what is right, will you not be accepted? But if you do not do what is right, sin is crouching at your door; it desires to have you, but you must master it."*
>
> Someone Who Could Help Me Master It Is _____
>
> Ideas for an Accountability Relationship:
>
> _____
>
> _____
>
> _____
>
> _____

JUDGMENT AND NEW BEGINNING

LESSON 4

DEVOTIONAL READING:
ISAIAH 54:8-14

LESSON SCRIPTURE:
GENESIS 6:5–9:17

PRINTED TEXT:
GENESIS 6:5-8; 7:1-4; 9:12-17

Jun
27

WHY TEACH THIS LESSON?

"Oh, we've got trouble! Right here in River City!" So sang the con man Professor Harold Hill in *The Music Man*. To Hill, that trouble was billiards, and, indeed, in an earlier day the pool hall represented all that was evil in middle America and probably many other parts of the world as well. But pool is not the trouble—not in River City, Iowa; not in America; not in the world. The problem is sin, and many Christians are growing increasingly frustrated with its growing presence.

That is the reason this lesson is important. It provides hope on two fronts for those who are concerned about the moral condition of their society. First, it reminds us that God can deal with sin—even global sin. He has judged it before, and someday he will judge it again. Second, it reassures us he can deliver the righteous from the harmful effects of sin. It is a reminder that you and your students need simply to put your faith in God and obey his Word. Like Noah and his family, that will keep you afloat above all the evil and wickedness that God will ultimately judge.

INTRODUCTION

A. SONS OF GOD?

The introductory verses of Genesis 6 demonstrate that bearing the "image of God" as a result of creation and bearing a resemblance to God in character and deed are two very different matters. In these verses we are introduced to three groups, the identity of whom remains a matter of considerable discussion: the sons of God, the daughters of men, and the Nephilim. Some Bible students believe that the Nephilim, who are described as "heroes of old, men of renown" (v. 4) may have been men who were giants (the *New American Standard Bible* suggests this meaning in a footnote). They may be linked to the sons of Anak, whom the spies who explored the land of Canaan saw (Numbers 13:33). There is also a possible connection to the family of Goliath of Gath (Joshua 11:22; 1 Samuel 17:4). The Hebrew name seems to mean "fallen ones" or "falling ones."

Three main proposals have been given for understanding the "sons of God" and the "daughters of men": (1) fallen angels who married human women; (2) human rulers who began to multiply harems of wives for themselves; and (3) the godly line of Seth that began to commingle with the more wicked descendants of Cain. The first view mentioned seems least likely since Jesus taught that angels "neither marry nor [are] given in marriage" (Matthew 22:30).

The third view, while it may possess its own difficulties, appears the most acceptable interpretation. That the line of Seth was a godly line seems to be indicated by the last verse in Luke's genealogy of Jesus, which traces Jesus' line back to the beginning: "the son of Enosh, the son of Seth, the son of Adam, the son of God" (Luke 3:38).

LESSON AIMS

As a result of completing this lesson, the student will:

1. Explain the reason for the great flood, and how God dealt with faithful Noah.

2. Compare the need for a cleansing of the earth in Noah's day with the growing need for cleansing of the earth today.

3. Make a commitment to be ready for the Lord's return and to share in his deliverance from the final cleansing.

KEY VERSE

I will remember my covenant between me and you and all living creatures of every kind. Never again will the waters become a flood to destroy all life.

—Genesis 9:15

LESSON 4 NOTES

What we must keep in mind is that bearing the image of God requires more than membership in the human race. In our lesson today, a righteous God faces the tragic task of having to pronounce judgment on a people made in his image, but who no longer reflected that image.

B. LESSON BACKGROUND

How much time elapsed from the time of creation to the flood of Noah's day? The answer cannot be known for certain. If we assume that there are no gaps in the lengthy genealogy found in Genesis 5, then 1565 years passed.

Many Bible students, however, believe that such gaps probably do exist. Other genealogies in the Bible exhibit gaps, some of them rather significant. Perhaps the most obvious instance is the genealogy of Jesus in Matthew 1. That listing moves from King Jehoram to King Uzziah (v. 8), omitting Uzziah's father, grandfather, and great-grandfather. This does not mean that the Bible is in error or that the biblical writers were careless in recording such matters. It was not always their purpose to give complete lists of names, but to call attention to prominent individuals within a genealogy.

If the genealogies of Genesis 5 and 11 are complete, several interesting situations emerge. For example, when Abraham turned fifty, Noah was still alive, while Noah's son Shem actually outlived Abraham! (To some, this appears unlikely.) In addition Methuselah, the man with the longest life recorded in Scripture (969 years), died in Noah's six hundredth year, the year of the flood (Genesis 7:11). This could be mere coincidence, but it does raise the question of whether or not Methuselah was one of those swept away by the flood. The spiritual status of Methuselah is not discussed in the Bible.

On the other hand, the spiritual status of Methuselah's grandson Noah is one of the key themes in the early chapters of Genesis. His righteous life shone brightly against the dark background of his wicked generation. Our lesson today examines the monumental events that transpired during his lifetime.

I. NEED FOR JUDGMENT (GENESIS 6:5-8)

A. MAN'S WICKEDNESS (v. 5)

5. The LORD saw how great man's wickedness on the earth had become, and that every inclination of the thoughts of his heart was only evil all the time.

As the *wickedness* of Adam and Eve's descendants grew greater and greater, the patience of God reached its limits. *The Lord saw. . . .* The same God who had observed the first sin in the garden and then the murderous deed of Cain was also now keenly aware of the woeful conditions on the *earth* in Noah's day. Not only were the actions of wicked man known to him, but also *every inclination of the thoughts of his heart.*

WHAT DO YOU THINK?

Except for Noah and his family, the people of Noah's day were in open rebellion against God. They were so alienated from God that they thought only about doing evil. It reminds us in large part of our world. Homosexuality, violence, drunkenness and drug use, immorality, corruption, and abortion are just a few of the evils rampant in our society. Many Christians believe the judgment of God cannot tarry long under these conditions.

What do you think God will do about the condition of the world of our day? What do you think the church should do about it?

(Discuss specific actions the church or individual Christians might take to address the issues that are of greatest concern to your class.)

WHAT'S ON YOUR MIND?

I recently revisited the Christian camp where I began my church camping experience at age nine. It was nostalgic to see the old buildings, the lake, the vespers site, and other familiar facilities. When I saw the boys' dorm, I remembered how much fun we had lying on our cots at night, thinking up pranks to torment the guys on the other side of the lockers. They, of course, were brainstorming how they would retaliate. Everything from pop-bottle caps to dirty socks to bars of soap were thrown over those lockers before the week was out.

Our imaginations were clearly active in those days, but generally not mean-spirited. In the days of Noah, however, most people were lying awake nights thinking of the evil that they had done, that they were doing, or that they planned to do.

It certainly was no church camp! Those people were vile and wicked; they were unrepentant sinners, giving themselves totally to devising ever-new ways to transgress God's will. God was sorry he had created mankind—so sorry, in fact, that he decided to destroy his handiwork, including both man and beast.

What's been on your mind lately? Do your imaginations satisfy or sadden your Maker? "Whatever is true, . . . noble, . . . right, . . . pure, . . . lovely, . . . admirable—if anything is excellent or praiseworthy—think about such things" (Philippians 4:8).

—R. W. B.

B. GOD'S GRIEF (v. 6)

6. The LORD was grieved that he had made man on the earth, and his heart was filled with pain.

The Lord was grieved over the way *man* had responded to his gracious actions with rebellion and wickedness. *His heart was filled with pain*, because the creature made in his image was acting so contrary to his purposes.

C. GOD'S SOLUTION (v. 7)

7. So the LORD said, "I will wipe mankind, whom I have created, from the face of the earth—men and animals, and creatures that move along the ground, and birds of the air—for I am grieved that I have made them."

The Hebrew word translated *wipe* is used in 2 Kings 21:13 to describe God's judgment against rebellious Jerusalem. Here in Genesis 6, the scope of God's judgment is stressed by listing all air-breathing forms of life created on days five and six (Genesis 1:20-31). Note that they are listed in the opposite order of that in which they were created—*men*, the land *animals*, the *creatures that move along the ground*, and the *birds of the air*. Most likely man is mentioned first because he is the creature primarily responsible for the earth's sorry condition.

Elsewhere in Scripture animals are described as suffering the consequences of man's sins (Joshua 7:24, 25). Apparently the animal world is considered to be creatures living under man's corrupted dominion; thus they share in his judgment. Note that in the book of Jonah, even the livestock of Nineveh participated in the fast of repentance and were donned with sackcloth (Jonah 3:5-8)!

D. AN EXCEPTION (v. 8)

8. But Noah found favor in the eyes of the LORD.

The name *Noah* means "rest, relief, comfort." His name was appropriate, given the relief he provided from a strife-torn world filled with men consumed by evil. Note how he fulfilled the words spoken at his birth, when his father declared, "He will comfort us in the labor and painful toil of our hands caused by the ground the Lord has cursed" (Genesis 5:29). Noah is described as "a righteous man, blameless among the people of his time," and is said to have "walked with God" as did Enoch earlier (Genesis 6:9; 5:24). The word *favor* is used frequently in the Old Testament to describe God's compassion and mercy toward man.

II. DELIVERANCE FROM JUDGMENT (GENESIS 7:1-4)

A. PROVISION OF AN ARK (v. 1)

1. The LORD then said to Noah, "Go into the ark, you and your whole family, because I have found you righteous in this generation.

Interestingly, the only other portion of the Bible where the Hebrew word translated *ark* is found is in Exodus 2:3, 5, in reference to the "basket" that held the baby Moses as it floated among the reeds of the Nile River. The dimensions of Noah's boat made it an enormous vessel: 450 feet long, 75 feet wide, and 45 feet high (Genesis 6:15).

WHAT DO YOU THINK?

From the great flood we learn that God has great, but not unlimited, mercy. We learn he is the righteous Judge of all. And we see beyond the shadow of a doubt that God has incredible power both to execute his judgment on sinners and to save the righteous. The flood is a warning to all mankind that God holds us accountable for our actions and that he can and will bring judgment on us. It warns us that none can withstand him or escape from his judgment.

How might we communicate those warnings? Do you see any other warnings in the flood that apply to people today? If so, what?

HOW TO SAY IT

Anak. AY-nak.

Canaan. KAY-nun.

Elijah. Ee-LYE-juh.

Enoch. EE-nock.

Enosh. EE-nush.

Ezekiel. Ee-ZEEK-yul or
Ee-ZEEK-ee-ul.

Isaiah. Eye-ZAY-uh.

Japheth. JAY-feth.

Jehoram. Jeh-HO-rum.

Jeremiah. Jair-uh-MY-uh.

Methuselah. Muh-THOO-
suh-luh.

Nephilim. Neff-ih-LEEM.

Nineveh. NIN-uh-vuh.

Uzziah. Uh-ZYE-uh.

WHAT DO YOU THINK?

Noah and his family entered the ark seven days before the rain started. Waiting is always hard. We like to see instant results, and not getting them can be disappointing. With or without hecklers outside, the wait must have been a strong test of their faith. But Noah had the word of God that the flood would begin in seven days after he entered the ark. Thus, even after six days of waiting, Noah could not say God had not done what he had promised—his word was still true.

What tests your faith today? What helps you to persevere, even as Noah and his family held fast to their faith even when no rain fell for seven days?

The phrase *you and your whole family* included Noah, his three sons (Shem, Ham, and Japheth), and their wives. These eight individuals entered the ark and therein found deliverance. Although only Noah's righteousness is mentioned, we may infer that this quality was present in the lives of his family as well. Perhaps they aided him in the massive undertaking of the construction of the ark. Others may have assisted as well, although apparently none heeded Noah's warnings (1 Peter 3:20; 2 Peter 2:5).

B. PROVISION FOR A FUTURE (vv. 2, 3)

2. Take with you seven of every kind of clean animal, a male and its mate, and two of every kind of unclean animal, a male and its mate.

A distinction was made regarding the animals that Noah was to gather into the ark. Although some commentators have interpreted the terminology *seven of every kind* to mean "seven each" (three pairs and an extra to be later sacrificed), it would seem best to understand that Noah was to set apart fourteen of *every kind of clean animal*—seven male-female pairs.

Leviticus 11 provides a lengthy explanation of clean and unclean animals as part of the regulations found in the law of Moses. No such analysis is given here, but a revelation of God's guidelines must have been made known to Noah. It is presumed that only the clean animals would be desirable for sacrifices (Genesis 8:20) and for food (9:3). This would explain why more of them were taken aboard the ark.

3. And also seven of every kind of bird, male and female, to keep their various kinds alive throughout the earth.

Noah was also to gather seven pairs of *every kind of bird*, in order *to keep their various kinds alive throughout the earth.*

C. PROVISION FOR CLEANSING (v. 4)

4. Seven days from now I will send rain on the earth for forty days and forty nights, and I will wipe from the face of the earth every living creature I have made."

Noah and his family boarded the ark *seven days* before the *rain* came. We can imagine that such a circumstance itself would have been a test of faith. How many mockers came by and laughed? What were the feelings of the tiny crew as they fed huge numbers of livestock sitting in dry dock, waiting for the promised deluge? Some people believe the condition described in Genesis 2:5, in which the earth was watered by "streams" coming up from the earth, continued until the time of the flood. If so, then it had never rained at all on the earth when Noah's family entered the ark. That really would have stretched their faith!

The time span of *forty days and forty nights* occurs elsewhere in Scripture in connection with certain occasions, which, like the flood, carried great spiritual significance. Examples are found in Exodus 24:18; 1 Kings 19:8; Jonah 3:4; Matthew 4:2; and Acts 1:3.

The word translated *earth* here is the word for "ground" or "soil." Those who argue against a worldwide flood and in favor of a localized one believe that this term is worth noting. However, the idea of a universal flood is suggested from other passages, such as Genesis 6:17: "I am going to bring floodwaters on the earth to destroy all life under the heavens, every creature that has the breath of life in it. Everything on earth will perish." The word *earth* in this verse does indicate the entire planet. In addition, if the flood were localized, God's promise never to destroy the earth again by a flood (Genesis 9:11) would have been broken many times since Noah's day; for many destructive localized floods have occurred since then.

III. AFTERMATH OF JUDGMENT (GENESIS 9:12-17)

At this point the flood has already taken place. God's righteous judgment has been administered. Following the departure of Noah and his family from the ark, God establishes his covenant with them.

A. A Sign Given (vv. 12-14)

12. And God said, "This is the sign of the covenant I am making between me and you and every living creature with you, a covenant for all generations to come.

God's *covenant* or promise included his assurance that he would never again destroy the earth as he had in Noah's day (8:21, 22; 9:11, 15; Isaiah 54:9). This promise was directed toward Noah and his sons (v. 8); the *you* in the verse before us is plural. The covenant was unlimited regarding subjects (*every living creature*) and duration (*for all generations to come*).

13, 14. "I have set my rainbow in the clouds, and it will be the sign of the covenant between me and the earth. Whenever I bring clouds over the earth and the rainbow appears in the clouds. . . .

A *rainbow* was to serve as the pledge or symbol of God's covenant with Noah and his descendants. The Hebrew term translated *rainbow* literally means "bow," and generally refers to a weapon for hunting or warfare. Genesis 9 (vv. 13, 14, 16) and Ezekiel 1:28 are the only places in the Old Testament where the word describes a rainbow. The symbolism of God's act may lie in the fact that he was laying aside his weapon of destruction in keeping with the promise of the next verse.

Was this the first occurrence of a rainbow in the clouds? The importance attached to its appearance indicates that this was the case. If Noah's flood represented the first rain ever experienced, then this was indeed the first time such a visual effect in the sky was present.

GOD'S PROMISE IN THE CLOUD

Is there any phenomenon in nature more beautiful than a rainbow? Especially fascinating are the so-called "double" rainbows. I've seen only two of those in my life. The first one was so breathtaking, I pulled my car off an interstate highway to the shoulder so we could safely look at the wonder with full attention.

The second double rainbow I saw appeared not long ago. There was no rain or mist in the air where I was, but apparently, moisture higher in the atmosphere diffracted light rays into two splendid spectra of color, ringing the sun. It was a truly spectacular sight.

That rainbows are singularly wonderful is no surprise. The Maker and his promises are wonderful, too. God's covenant with Noah and with all mankind was that the earth would never be destroyed by a flood again. There are many other promises in the Bible given to those who, like Noah, find "favor in the eyes of the Lord."

Imagine how thrilling it must have been for Noah and his family to have witnessed the splendor of the first rainbow. Rainbows are still the eye-pleasing reminder of God's "very great and precious promises" (2 Peter 1:4).   —R. W. B.

B. A Sign Explained (vv. 15-17)

15. "I will remember my covenant between me and you and all living creatures of every kind. Never again will the waters become a flood to destroy all life.

I will remember my covenant. The promises of God are sure. As Moses reminded Israel, "Know therefore that the Lord your God is God, he is the faithful God, keeping his covenant of love to a thousand generations of those who love him and keep his commands" (Deuteronomy 7:9).

I will remember my covenant between me and you and living creatures of every kind. Never again will the waters become a flood to destroy all life. Genesis 9:15, NIV

The visual for lesson 4 is a cheery-looking reminder of God's promise, which he sealed with the rainbow.

WHAT DO YOU THINK?

God said that the rainbow was the token of his covenant with the earth. How can we maintain this purpose of the rainbow today? Does knowing the scientific explanation for how the rainbow appears lessen this value in any way? Why or why not?

WHAT DO YOU THINK?

In the midst of such great destruction, God preserved the righteous Noah and his family. What encouragement does that give to you? Why?

Consider 2 Peter 2:4-10 in your discussion.

Father in Heaven, Judge of the living and the dead, we pray that we may lead lives that honor you in righteousness and obedience to your will. Help us to be beacons of your light in our own age of spiritual darkness. Amen.

THOUGHT TO REMEMBER

"As it was in the days of Noah, so it will be at the coming of the Son of Man. For . . . people were eating and drinking, marrying and giving in marriage, up to the day Noah entered the ark; and they knew nothing about what would happen until the flood came and took them all away. That is how it will be at the coming of the Son of Man" (Matthew 24:37-39).

DAILY BIBLE READINGS

Monday, June 21—The Earth Was Corrupt in God's Sight (Genesis 6:5-22)

Tuesday, June 22—You Alone Are Righteous Before Me (Genesis 7:1-16)

Wednesday, June 23—God Remembers Noah (Genesis 7:17—8:5)

Thursday, June 24—The Waters Are Dried Up From the Earth (Genesis 8:6-22)

Friday, June 25—God Blesses Noah and His Sons (Genesis 9:1-7)

Saturday, June 26—God Makes a Covenant With Noah (Genesis 9:8-17)

Sunday, June 27—Noah Pronounces a Curse (Genesis 9:18-28)

As noted earlier, the wording of God's promise in this verse would be weakened by any view that the flood affected only a limited region. The expressions *all living creatures* and *a flood to destroy all life* point to a catastrophe of worldwide scope.

16, 17. *"Whenever the rainbow appears in the clouds, I will see it and remember the everlasting covenant between God and all living creatures of every kind on the earth."*

So God said to Noah, "This is the sign of the covenant I have established between me and all life on the earth."

A new phase in God's dealings with mankind had begun, yet God knew that man's heart had not really changed. Hear his words from Genesis 8:21: "Never again will I curse the ground because of man, even though every inclination of his heart is evil from childhood." Accompanying God's command for man to be fruitful and multiply (9:7) was the stern warning that "whoever sheds the blood of man, by man shall his blood be shed" (9:6). God was still concerned with justice, but he would never again use a flood to administer justice.

CONCLUSION

A. PREACHER OF RIGHTEOUSNESS

Not only was Noah a portrayer of righteousness through his obedient conduct, but he was also, according to 2 Peter 2:5, a "preacher of righteousness." Thus Noah's testimony was communicated by both example and exhortation. No doubt the curiosity aroused by Noah's shipbuilding activities gave him numerous opportunities to proclaim God's message of coming judgment.

Not only was Noah the first "preacher" according to the Bible, but he was also the first to experience rejection by his audience. Of course, in this he is not alone. He is joined by a host of "failures" in the Old Testament alone: Moses, Elijah, Isaiah, Jeremiah, Ezekiel, Amos—the list could go on of men who faithfully proclaimed the truth of God regardless of popular sentiment and opinion. Today's generation also has its host of faithful heralds of God's divine revelation. For them we should be thankful, because the needs of our time are as great as they were in Noah's. His generation was "corrupt in the sight of God" and "filled with violence" (Genesis 6:11, *New American Standard Bible*). So is ours. Noah had a message of deliverance to proclaim to the people of his day. So do we.

B. SCOFFERS BE WARNED

As a precursor of the second coming of Christ, the flood offers a grim warning for those willing to heed it. Peter describes men in his day who sound a lot like a host of individuals in our present day. They are called "scoffers" (2 Peter 3:3), or mockers, who denied the supernatural, especially the fulfillment of the promise that God would bring this world to an end. "Where is this 'coming' he promised?" they jeered.

But Peter reminded the scoffers that there was once a great interruption to the regular course of things—a catastrophic event that destroyed the world of Noah's day (v. 6). Fire, not water, will be God's future instrument of devastation (v. 10). In the same way that God's patience delayed the sending of the flood waters in Noah's day, so today God's patience allows others the opportunity to "come to repentance" (v. 9). His schedule is controlled by an eternal perspective—"With the Lord a day is like a thousand years, and a thousand years are like a day" (v. 8). And yet that day will at last arrive and judgment will be rendered. In light of this fact, Peter asks us, "What sort of people ought you to be in holy conduct and godliness?" (v. 11, *New American Standard Bible*).

Discovery Learning

*This page contains an alternate lesson plan emphasizing learning activities. Classes
desiring such student involvement will find these suggestions helpful. The next page
is a reproducible activity page to further enhance discovery learning.*

LEARNING GOALS

After this session, the student will be able to:

1. Explain the reason for the great flood, and how God dealt with faithful Noah.

2. Compare the need for a cleansing of the earth in Noah's day with the growing need for cleansing of the earth today.

3. Make a commitment to be ready for the Lord's return and to share in his deliverance from the final cleansing.

INTO THE LESSON

As you prepare for today's lesson, watch for news items (from a magazine or newspaper) that would illustrate both the good and the bad in mankind. If your students generally sit at tables in small groups, place one news item in each group before class begins. As you begin the lesson, ask each group to summarize its article and give an opinion as to whether the activity reported in the story is more or less typical of human behavior.

Another possibility for getting into this lesson is to set up a debate among several class members as to whether our society demonstrates more good deeds than bad behavior. This activity should be arranged far enough in advance that those taking each side in the debate will have enough time to prepare.

Make the transition into the Bible study time by pointing out that regardless of how bad we think things may be now, there was a time in history when mankind was characterized by so much evil that God decided that he should wipe out creation and begin again with a small faithful remnant.

INTO THE WORD

Divide the class into three groups. Ask one group to read Genesis 6:1-8, a second group to read Genesis 7:1-10, and the third to read Genesis 9:8-17. Ask each group to write ten questions that can be answered by its assigned text. Have each group select one member to be its "quizmaster." This person will ask the other groups the questions the group has written.

After about eight or ten minutes, ask the quizmaster for group 1 to stand and ask group 2 the first question from his or her list. If group 2 answers correctly, score one point for them and direct the quizmaster to ask group 3 the next question. If group 2 misses the ques-

tion, group 3 gets a chance. The next question goes first to group 3 either way. Have quizmaster 1 continue alternating between groups 2 and 3 until all group 1's questions have been asked and answered. Have a volunteer read Genesis 6:1-8 aloud; then review the material to make sure everyone understands this section of Scripture before proceeding.

Next have quizmaster 2 stand and ask questions alternately of groups 1 and 3, scoring as before. Read and review the section as before, and then have quizmaster 3 stand and ask questions of groups 1 and 2. Read and review the section; then tally the scores and announce the winning group. If there is a tie, ask questions to the tying groups until you can crown a winner—or just declare a tie. If you want to award small prizes to the members of the winning group, be sure you have enough for everyone in case all the groups tie.

INTO LIFE

Ask the class, "Which generation do you think was or is worse, Noah's or our own?" Discuss the similarities between the two. Does the fact that God sent the flood indicate that Noah's generation must have been worse, or does the fact that the next judgment is final suggest God is even more patient with our generation than with Noah's?

Point out that Noah and the flood are mentioned several times in the New Testament. Have a volunteer look up and read each of these Scriptures: Matthew 24:36-39; Hebrews 11:7; 1 Peter 3:17-22; 2 Peter 2:4, 5, 9. After each text is read, ask, "What do we learn from Noah's example in this text that helps us follow the Lord today?" (Option: Distribute copies of the reproducible activity "Noah in the New Testament" to facilitate an investigation of these texts.)

One of the most important lessons we can learn is that judgment is coming when the Lord returns, and we need to be ready for that great event. Close with a prayer circle, asking any who wish to participate to pray for your church, your community, your nation, and the world at large about the need to repent and to be right with God when the Lord returns. Also ask each one to pray, whether aloud or silently as others pray, and make a commitment to be personally ready for the Lord's return and to share in his deliverance from condemnation at the final judgment.

Noah in the New Testament

Look up each of the following New Testament Scriptures and record what it says about Noah and God's judgment of sin in his day. Note also what help it gives us for following the Lord today.

Matthew 24:36-39

Hebrews 11:7

1 Peter 3:17-22

2 Peter 2:4, 5, 9

What a Year!

Genesis 7:11 tells us the flood began in Noah's six hundredth year, the second month, and the seventeenth day. Noah and his family left the ark on the twenty-seventh day of the second month of Noah's six hundred and first year (Genesis 8:13, 14). Thus the eight people and their menagerie spent just over one full year on the ark!

What do you think would have been the hardest thing about spending a year on the ark? Why?

What would you have done to pass the time?

How would you have handled personality conflicts in such a confined space?

What lesson or lessons do you think you would have learned through the ordeal?

How might you learn such a lesson without having to spend a year riding out a flood?

GOD'S CALL TO ABRAM

LESSON 5

WHY TEACH THIS LESSON?

The first people to inhabit New Zealand were Polynesians who arrived in outrigger canoes from other Pacific islands a thousand miles away. The Polynesians had known for many years that the land was there because their voyagers had seen a long white cloud on the horizon. They knew that when a cloud stayed over a place for a very long time that there was land beneath it. They didn't know exactly what they would find when they arrived at New Zealand, but they knew there was land. They knew they would find what they called "the land of the long white cloud."

Some of your students may at times feel their Christian life is a long voyage with a distant destination they cannot even see. They are looking for the long white cloud, or something to reenergize their faith. This lesson may provide what they need. Abraham (called Abram at the time) also set out on a journey with an unseen destination. He did not even know where he was going; there was no long white cloud to mark the spot. He simply trusted God. This lesson will help your students to trust God to guide them to their own promised land.

INTRODUCTION

A. BLIND FAITH

An artist and a poet once examined a painting representing Jesus' healing of the two blind men of Jericho. The poet asked, "What seems to you the most remarkable thing in this painting?"

"Everything in the painting is excellently done," replied the artist. "The form of Christ, the grouping of the individuals, the expressions in the faces of the characters—all these are marvelously executed."

But the poet found the most significant touch elsewhere in the picture. Pointing to the steps of a house in the corner of the picture, he said to his friend, "Do you see that discarded cane lying there?"

"Yes, but what does that signify?"

"Why, my friend, on those steps one of the blind men sat with the cane in his hand, but when he heard that Jesus was coming, he was so sure that he would be healed that he left his cane there. He knew he would no longer need it, and hastened to the Lord as if he could already see."

Such was the faith of Abram. His faith in God was much more than just an acknowledgment that God exists. It was so powerful that he left comfort and safety behind as he journeyed from Ur to Haran to Canaan to answer God's call.

B. LESSON BACKGROUND

The first four lessons in our study of Genesis this quarter were taken from the first eleven chapters of the book. These chapters, as we have seen, deal first with events surrounding the creation of the heavens and the earth and the creation and fall of man. They lay the groundwork for God's later dealings with mankind as he worked to offset the effects of the fall and the curse that resulted from man's disobedience in the garden.

DEVOTIONAL READING:
HEBREWS 11:8-12
LESSON SCRIPTURE:
GENESIS 11:27–12:9
PRINTED TEXT:
GENESIS 11:31–12:9

Jul
4

LESSON AIMS

After this lesson students will be able to:

1. Recount the details of God's call to Abram and the promises God made to him.

2. Compare Abram's decision to leave his homeland in answer to God's call with the decisions that followers of Jesus are challenged to make today.

3. Embark on an adventure of faith by "breaking new ground" in one area of their Christian living.

KEY VERSE

The LORD had said to Abram, "Leave your country, your people and your father's household and go to the land I will show you. I will make you into a great nation and I will bless you; I will make your name great, and you will be a blessing." —Genesis 12:1, 2

The close of chapter 11 marks the introduction of the family of Abram, through whom God planned to send the Messiah as the one who would crush the serpent's head (Genesis 3:15). It is difficult to date Abram (or Abraham, as he later came to be called) precisely. The most likely time of his birth was somewhere in the middle of the twenty-second century before Christ. (See the "Chronology of Genesis," page 344.) The details of his life and times, according to the book of Genesis, reflect practices found among ancient Near Eastern peoples of that period.

The name Abram means "exalted father." Later God changed his name to Abraham, which means "father of many nations," in reference to the great number of descendants that he promised to Abram (Genesis 17:5). Abram is introduced to us as the son of Terah, who lived in "Ur of the Chaldeans" (Genesis 11:31). Scholars disagree about the location of Ur. Some place it in northern Mesopotamia near the city of Haran. However, the work of the British archaeologist Sir Leonard Woolley, between 1922 and 1934, provided strong evidence that ancient Ur was located in southern Mesopotamia.

In its prime, Ur was a large, thriving city that provided a comfortable lifestyle for its inhabitants. It was also a city in which many gods were worshiped, with the worship of the moon god most prominent.

Today's visual is a map that traces Abram's trek from Ur to Haran to Canaan. Use the map throughout the quarter to locate important sites.

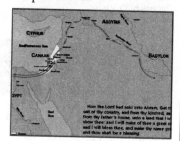

I. FROM UR TO HARAN (GENESIS 11:31, 32)

A. TERAH'S JOURNEY (v. 31)

31. Terah took his son Abram, his grandson Lot son of Haran, and his daughter-in-law Sarai, the wife of his son Abram, and together they set out from Ur of the Chaldeans to go to Canaan. But when they came to Haran, they settled there.

Terah had three sons: Abram, Nahor, and Haran (Genesis 11:27). Haran died while the family was still in Ur (v. 28). Apparently Nahor chose to remain in Ur when Terah and other members of the family moved to Haran. (The Hebrew words for Haran the person and Haran the place have a slightly different spelling that does not come through in English.) Haran was located in northwestern Mesopotamia on a tributary of the Euphrates River and on a major trade route that led from Assyria to Syria and Palestine.

Since Haran is more than six hundred miles from Ur, moving family and possessions as well as large flocks and herds from Ur to Haran must have been a slow and demanding trip. Later, members of Nahor's family also moved to that area. We know they did so because they were living there when Abraham sent his servant to find a wife for Isaac (Genesis 24:10, 15) and when Jacob fled there for refuge (28:2).

We are not told why Terah decided to move to Haran. However, we do know that God appeared to Abram while he was still in Ur, telling him to leave Ur and begin a quest for a land that God would eventually show him (Acts 7:2, 3). Perhaps Abram convinced his father to come with him on this move. Accompanying Abram and Terah were not only Sarai, Abram's wife, but also Lot, Terah's grandson and a nephew to Abram.

B. TERAH'S DEATH (v. 32)

32. Terah lived 205 years, and he died in Haran.

This verse raises a chronological question. Genesis 11:26 seems to say that Terah was seventy years old when Abram was born, which would have made Abram one hundred thirty-five years old when his father died. Yet Genesis 12:4 states that Abram was seventy-five when he left Haran (that he left Haran after his father's death is clear from Acts 7:4). The best solution to the problem is to say that Abram was not the son who was born when Terah was seventy. Apparently the order of "Abram, Nahor and Haran" that appears in Genesis 11:26 does not reflect the birth order of the three sons of Terah, but Abram's prominence in the account that follows.

II. FROM HARAN TO CANAAN (GENESIS 12:1-5)

A. GOD'S CALL (v. 1)

1. The LORD had said to Abram, "Leave your country, your people and your father's household and go to the land I will show you.

We do not know what method God used to reveal himself to Abram. It may have been through an audible voice, in a dream, or in a vision. But regardless of the method, Abram had no doubt that it was God who spoke to him, nor did he have any problem understanding what God wanted him to do. The message was simple: Go!

Answering God's call demanded great faith on Abram's part. First, he had to leave his father's household. In addition he had no road map to guide him to his destination. All God told him was that he was to go to the land I will show you. Yet Abram was equal to the challenge. The New Testament tells us, "By faith Abraham, when called to go to a place he would later receive as his inheritance, obeyed and went, even though he did not know where he was going" (Hebrews 11:8).

Some students wonder whether this call came to Abram in Ur (his original home) or in Haran (where Terah's caravan had stopped). The context of this verse seems to indicate that it took place in Haran, since this is where the group had stopped (v. 31) and from which they continued their journey according to 12:4, 5. That a previous call in Ur had occurred is clear from Genesis 15:7 and from Stephen's statement in Acts 7:2-4. Most likely the call issued to Abram in Ur was repeated in Haran, which is why our text reads, The Lord had said to Abram.

DESTINATION UNKNOWN

My youngest daughter's husband planned a surprise holiday for their first wedding anniversary. Charlotte knew that the two of them were going somewhere special, but Paul didn't reveal their destination until they boarded a plane (in Chicago) for Phoenix, Arizona! He had made all the arrangements for a fun weekend in the Southwest, including mountain hiking, sightseeing, elegant dinners, and room service breakfasts. The surprise aspect of the trip made the celebration especially exciting and memorable.

Most people are intrigued by mystery and enjoy being treated to surprises. Church youth groups like "Destination Unknown" parties, when they can only guess where sponsors are taking them.

Not knowing where we are going can be fun for a party or a holiday. Abram's experience, however, required more faith and courage. He was risking his future, and perhaps jeopardizing his family's welfare, when he heeded God's call to leave his homeland and travel to Canaan. "By faith Abraham . . . obeyed and went, even though he did not know where he was going" (Hebrews 11:8).

As Christians we know our final destiny: everlasting life in Heaven. Some of the details have not been revealed, but we can rest assured that there will be a great celebration. Not knowing when should enhance the journey!   —R. W. B.

B. GOD'S PROMISES (vv. 2, 3)

2. "I will make you into a great nation and I will bless you; I will make your name great, and you will be a blessing.

WHAT DO YOU THINK?

God's call to Abram required him to leave home and family, comfort, security, and the like in order to walk with God. When we become Christians, we pledge to follow the Lord however and wherever he leads. What has that call meant for you? Where has God led you since you answered his call? What have you left behind? What have you received?

WHAT DO YOU THINK?

God made several promises to Abram if he would follow him. Similarly, the Lord makes many promises to those who follow him today. He promises to provide food and clothing for those who seek first his kingdom and his righteousness (Matthew 6:25-33). Jesus promises he will return for his followers (John 14:3). He promises eternal life to those who believe in him (John 3:16; 6:40, 47). He promises no more death, mourning, crying, or pain (Revelation 21:4). Which of these, or others of his promises, is most significant to you? Why?

God made four distinct promises to Abram in this verse. First of all, he would make of him a *great nation*. From the world's point of view, this promise may have seemed impossible to fulfill, for at the time Abram was not only childless but was also well advanced in years. But God specializes in doing the impossible, as both Abram and Sarai were to learn. From this one man came the nation of Israel.

The second promise, *I will bless you*, was fulfilled as Abram acquired great flocks, material wealth, and servants—even in a land where he "made his home . . . like a stranger in a foreign country" (Hebrews 11:9). There was also a spiritual dimension to Abram's blessings, for he was privileged to know God as his "shield" and his "very great reward" (Genesis 15:1).

The third promise, that God would *make* Abram's *name great*, has been fulfilled beyond anything that he could ever have imagined. Today three great religions—Judaism, Christianity, and Islam, comprising a significant portion of the world's population—honor him in one way or another.

The final promise, *you will be a blessing*, had even more far-reaching implications. From among Abram's descendants God would eventually call a special people, the Jews, and through them he would send his Son, Jesus Christ, as the Savior of the world.

3. I will bless those who bless you, and whoever curses you I will curse; and all peoples on earth will be blessed through you."

Although God extended a tremendous challenge to Abram, he also gave him the assurance that he would watch over him during his travels. Those who treated Abram fairly could expect God's blessings. On the other hand, those who mistreated Abram would experience God's wrath. A good example of this is seen in Egypt when Pharaoh unwittingly prepared to make Sarai one of his wives. As a result, God brought great plagues on Pharaoh and his house. Realizing what he had done, Pharaoh quickly returned Sarai to Abram (Genesis 12:10-20). In this case God watched over Abram, even though he had tried to hide the real truth by claiming Sarai was his sister.

Here too it is important to note the broader implications of God's promise, according to the New Testament. God was calling just one man, yet with a view toward bringing *all peoples on earth* back to him. Paul goes so far as to say that God "announced the gospel in advance to Abraham" when he promised him, "All nations will be blessed through you" (Galatians 3:8). Paul then adds, "So those who have faith are blessed along with Abraham, the man of faith" (v. 9), and, "If you belong to Christ, then you are Abraham's seed, and heirs according to the promise" (v. 29).

LEAVING A LEGACY

You probably have seen the bumper sticker that reads: "I'm spending my kids' inheritance." Such a humorous thought is really true to life, because not many parents leave large legacies for their children these days. Most of us simply try to keep from becoming a burden in our final years; we try to provide for adequate retirement income, and for the possibilities of major illnesses and/or nursing home care. Leaving an inheritance of any size for the family is a luxury that average persons usually cannot afford.

Abram was by no means average. He was a wealthy patriarch with large herds and considerable possessions. However, when God promised that all his descendants (in fact, all people of the earth) would be blessed in him, he had in mind a spiritual rather than a material heritage. Among the descendants of Abram would finally come the Messiah—Jesus Christ, the Savior. No other inheritance can equal

WHAT DO YOU THINK?

The most remarkable thing about Abram, the thing that made him beloved of God, was his faith. Abram was convinced in his heart that God could and would keep his promises. Thus he was able to obey God with no more assurances of a positive outcome than God's word. How can we exhibit this faith in our Christian lives? How does this faith grow?

the faith, hope, and love bequeathed to those who are children of Abraham by faith in Christ (Galatians 3:29) and who belong to the church, the "Israel of God" (Galatians 6:16).

The legacy of faith, trust, and obedience must be passed on to each succeeding generation. Do you want to bless your children with an invaluable inheritance when you die? Leave an estate that includes Christian values and commitment. "May all who come behind us find us faithful!"   —R. W. B.

C. ABRAM'S OBEDIENCE (vv. 4, 5)

4, 5. So Abram left, as the LORD had told him; and Lot went with him. Abram was seventy-five years old when he set out from Haran. He took his wife Sarai, his nephew Lot, all the possessions they had accumulated and the people they had acquired in Haran, and they set out for the land of Canaan, and they arrived there.

Abram traveled the full length of the so-called Fertile Crescent that extended from lower Mesopotamia to upper Mesopotamia through Syria and into southern Palestine. The trade routes that connected ancient Egypt to the great kingdoms of Mesopotamia passed through this area. The shorter route connecting Egypt and Mesopotamia ran across a desert that was impassable for persons such as Abram, who was traveling with donkeys and large numbers of flocks.

Abram started this trip to *Canaan* when he was *seventy-five years old.* Accompanying him were *his wife Sarai, his nephew Lot,* and *the people they had acquired in Haran.* Since Abram and Sarai were childless at this time, these additional *people* must refer to servants and their families. We do not know how many people were with Abram at this time, but later, when he came to Lot's rescue, he was able to lead a force of over three hundred armed servants against Lot's captors (Genesis 14:14).

III. INTO THE PROMISED LAND (GENESIS 12:6-9)

A. ABRAM'S TRAVELS (v. 6)

6. Abram traveled through the land as far as the site of the great tree of Moreh at Shechem. At that time the Canaanites were in the land.

Abram and those with him journeyed from northern Canaan to the central highlands, where he stopped at the town of *Shechem.* Shechem was located about thirty miles north of Jerusalem in a valley between Mount Gerizim and Mount Ebal.

The verse concludes by noting that Abram was not the only resident in the land of promise: *the Canaanites were in the land.* If these Canaanites engaged in some of the wicked and idolatrous practices that later Canaanites did (Deuteronomy 7:1-4), then their presence may have constituted a serious test of Abram's faith in and commitment to the true God.

B. GOD'S PROMISE (v. 7)

7. The LORD appeared to Abram and said, "To your offspring I will give this land." So he built an altar there to the LORD, who had appeared to him.

This was it! After weeks, perhaps even months of travel, Abram had finally arrived at his destination. Once more God *appeared* to Abram and announced that this was the *land* that he had promised to Abram. Yet Abram would never really possess it himself; the promise was to his *offspring.* Joshua 21:43-45 records the fulfillment of this promise to Abram's descendants—the people of Israel.

Following God's revelation to him, Abram *built an altar there* and worshiped *the Lord.* On this altar he may well have offered a sacrifice, perhaps an animal, as an expression of his gratitude toward God for bringing him to this land and of his faith in God's promise that his descendants would one day possess it.

WHAT DO YOU THINK?

Abram built altars at Shechem and near Bethel. What connection do you see between worship and obedience? How important do you think regular worship is in our walk with the Lord?

C. ABRAM'S WORSHIP (vv. 8, 9)

8, 9. From there he went on toward the hills east of Bethel and pitched his tent, with Bethel on the west and Ai on the east. There he built an altar to the LORD and called on the name of the LORD. Then Abram set out and continued toward the Negev.

Abram continued to travel southward, stopping this time near *Bethel*, about a dozen miles north of Jerusalem. The name Bethel means "house of God," a name given to the place by Jacob many years later after his dream of a stairway stretching to Heaven with angels ascending and descending on it (Genesis 28:12). (In Abram's day the town was called Luz, according to Genesis 28:19.) There he once more *pitched his tent* and again *built an altar*. The town of *Ai* (Joshua 7:2) was located about two miles to the *east* of Bethel.

The altars that Abram built were probably nothing more than a few stones stacked on top of one another. Since he was constantly on the move, he had little time to build anything more elaborate. His practice should be an example for those of us who move or travel frequently. Have a place of worship wherever you are, even if your stay there is brief.

Then Abram set out and continued toward the Negev. Literally, this reads something like, "he kept pulling up stakes," indicating frequent moves. These moves brought Abram into the Negev, the arid region in southern Palestine, southwest of the Dead Sea, that provided very little pasture. Perhaps Abram was pressured by hostile Canaanites to move into this more desolate area, or God may have providentially moved him there so that he would be in a better position to move on into Egypt when a famine befell the land (Genesis 12:10).

CONCLUSION

Several years ago *Mission Impossible* was a popular television program. At the beginning of the program, the main characters were given information about an extremely difficult task. Then they were given the opportunity either to accept the mission or to reject it. Of course, experts that they were, they always accepted. What followed was a series of ingenious and daring schemes that enabled them to accomplish their assigned mission.

In a way, the venture God challenged Abram to undertake was a "mission impossible." How could a man living in Ur of the Chaldeans embark on a journey to an unknown destination hundreds of miles away? Yet Abram, like the characters in the television program, accepted the challenge.

Every one of us, like Abram, is challenged to embark upon a "mission impossible." We are called to journey through a society that subtly or often quite openly rejects the truths that Christianity embraces. More and more we feel like strangers having to make our way through spiritual and moral minefields that have been laid by Satan.

WHAT DO YOU THINK?

The lesson writer notes that "we have some advantages that Abram did not." As examples, he cites the fellowship of the church, the Scriptures, the presence of the Holy Spirit, and our knowledge of Heaven. How are these helpful to you? How can we take full advantage of them to help us on our spiritual journey?

But we have some advantages that Abram did not. We have the fellowship of the church to give us support and companionship in our journey. In addition, God has given us the Scriptures as a road map for the journey, and he has promised the Holy Spirit as a Comforter.

We have one additional advantage. While Abram "was looking forward to the city with foundations, whose architect and builder is God" (Hebrews 11:10), he did not know as much about that place as we do. We know that our ultimate destination is Heaven—an eternal "promised land" planned and built by God for us. Let's go!

Discovery Learning

This page contains an alternate lesson plan emphasizing learning activities. Classes desiring such student involvement will find these suggestions helpful. The next page is a reproducible activity page to further enhance discovery learning.

LEARNING GOALS

Having participated in this session, students will be able to:

1. Recount the details of God's call to Abram and the promises God made to him.

2. Compare Abram's decision to leave his homeland in answer to God's call with the decisions that followers of Jesus are challenged to make today.

3. Embark on an adventure of faith by "breaking new ground" in one area of their Christian living.

INTO THE LESSON

As you begin the lesson, help your students focus their thoughts on one of the themes of today's text by asking, "What is the greatest promise anyone has ever made to you?"

If your students sit in small groups, encourage them to go around the group and take time for each one to share one promise that was made to him. This will allow everyone to get involved in the lesson right away. After everyone has had time to share, ask for a show of hands to indicate whether the promise was kept.

If time allows, you might also ask them to tell some of the promises that they have received from God. Make the transition into the lesson by pointing them to the promises of God to Abram in Genesis 12. Use the reproducible page that follows to trace Abram's journey in response to God's promise.

INTO THE WORD

As a way of getting all of your students into the biblical text, ask them to work in small groups on the chart shown below. You may want to make a chart like this (except for the answers, of course) for each group (or if you have student books available, they can use the chart provided there). If you have a small class, this exercise can be done with the whole class while you write their ideas on a chalkboard.

Ask your students to read Genesis 11:31—12:9 and Hebrews 11:8-10 and list the qualities they see in Abram and the ways in which he shows them.

Abram's Qualities	How He Shows Them
1. Courageous	He was willing to set out for an unknown land.
2. Obedient	Hebrews tells us that God called Abram; apparently that was the reason for his move from Ur; he obeyed again when God repeated the call in Haran.
3. Persuasive	Abram convinced his father and nephew to make the trip from Ur with him.
4. Faithful	Abram trusted God, and that was the source of his obedience.
5. Reverent	He built altars to worship God; he "called on the name of the Lord."

Now ask your students to read the passage again and list the promises made to Abram. Write these clearly on a large piece of poster board. (1. God would make of him a great nation; 2. God would bless him and make his name great; 3. He would be a blessing—those who blessed Abram would be blessed and those who cursed Abram would be cursed; 4. In him all peoples of the earth would be blessed; 5. The land would be given to Abram's seed.) Then ask the students to read Genesis 17:1-8 and indicate how many of these promises are repeated (confirmed).

Ask, "How are the promises related to the call?" To some, the promises may seem a reward for Abram's obedience to the call. But the Bible makes clear that "Abraham [i.e. Abram] believed God, and it was credited to him as righteousness" (Romans 4:3). Abram obeyed the call because of his faith in God. Perhaps God had already made some of these promises in the original call to Abram in Ur. Abram believed them—he believed God—and so he obeyed.

INTO LIFE

Ask your students to compare Abram's call with the call that comes to each of us to follow Christ. (Both require faith; both have promises attached; both are fulfilled ultimately in Christ.)

Ask the class, "How would relying more on God and his promises affect your current decisions and priorities?" After a brief discussion, say, "I'd like each of you to focus on one area of your Christian living in which greater faith would help you to 'break new ground' in your walk with the Lord. What specifically will you do about it?" Close with prayer that your students can exhibit greater faith in these areas.

Charting the Course

On the map below, trace Abram's journey from Ur to Haran to Canaan. Then note the locations where Abram built altars to the Lord, Bethel and Shechem.

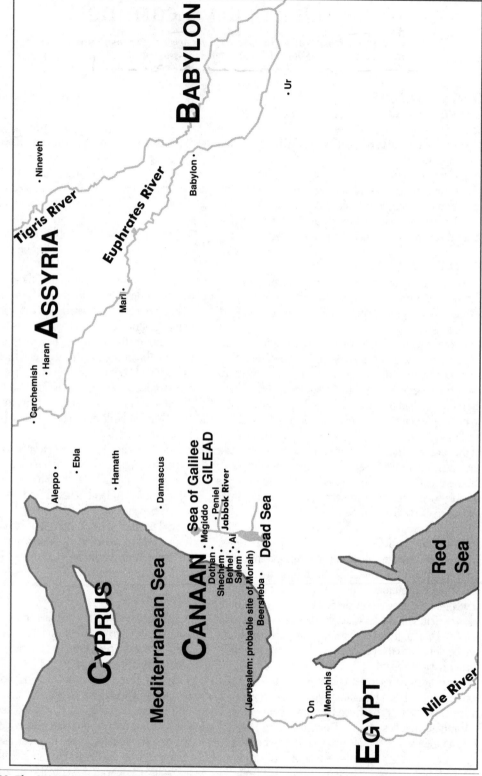

A PROMISE FULFILLED

LESSON 6

WHY TEACH THIS LESSON?

What's the biggest thing happening at your church right now? Perhaps you are in a building program, and everyone has been challenged to increase his or her financial support to expedite the construction. Or maybe you are launching a new evangelistic program to reach a neglected part of your town or city. It might be that the membership has been challenged to a closer walk with the Lord, stressing spiritual disciplines and family devotions and the like. Are you starting a new ministry to the homeless or an abortion-alternative ministry? Or maybe your church is significantly increasing your commitment to world-wide evangelism, i.e., missions.

Whatever it is, if your church is challenging its members to change the status quo, there are probably some who doubt it can be done. Or they may just doubt their own ability to be a part of it. They want to claim God's promises, but they lack confidence. Lessons like this one are designed to bolster the faith of such believers and to help them move out of doubt and into claiming the promises of our God!

INTRODUCTION

A. STOP THE BUS

A small boy riding a bus home from Sunday school was very proud of the card he had received, which had a picture and a caption that read: "Have Faith in God." Then to his dismay the card slipped from his hand and fluttered out the window. "Stop the bus!" he cried. "I've lost my 'faith in God!'"

The driver pulled the bus to a stop, and as the lad climbed out and went to retrieve his card, one of the adult riders smiled and made a comment about the innocence of youth. A more perceptive adult observed, "All of us would be better off if we were that concerned about our faith. All too often we plunge ahead on our own when we have lost our faith in God."

Abraham provides an excellent example of this truth. God promised him that he would give him a son who would be the heir of all of his promises to Abraham. However, after many years passed and the promise had not been fulfilled, Abraham attempted to take care of the matter on his own. He plunged ahead, leaving his faith behind.

B. LESSON BACKGROUND

Some years passed between the events covered in last week's lesson and the events narrated in today's lesson. During this time Abram had been forced by a famine to move into Egypt. There Sarai, who was quite attractive, caught the attention of Pharaoh, who desired to make her his wife. Fearing that Pharaoh would kill him in order to acquire her, Abram had told Pharaoh that Sarai was his sister, which was a half-truth (Genesis 20:12); and Pharaoh took Sarai into his house. But God plagued Pharaoh's house because of it, and Pharaoh sent Abram and Sarai away (Genesis 12:11-20). We are not told how Pharaoh knew the plagues were associated with Sarai. In a similar incident later God spoke in a

DEVOTIONAL READING:
DEUTERONOMY 7:7-11

LESSON SCRIPTURE:
GENESIS 15:1–18:15; 21:1-7

PRINTED TEXT:
GENESIS 15:1-6; 17:17-21; 21:1-3

LESSON AIMS

Jul
11

After completing this lesson students should be able to:

1. Summarize God's promise to Abraham and how he continually reaffirmed it even when Abraham doubted or misunderstood.

2. Tell why God's promises are no laughing matter—even when they seem incredible.

3. State a confident faith in one or more of the wonderful promises of God.

KEY VERSE

God said, ". . . Your wife Sarah will bear you a son, and you will call him Isaac. I will establish my covenant with him."
—Genesis 17:19

LESSON 6 NOTES

dream to Abimelech, king of the Philistines (Genesis 20). We assume God made some specific revelation to Pharaoh in this case as well.

Abram and his company then left Egypt and returned to Canaan (Genesis 13:1). By this time, Abram and Lot both had become rather wealthy and their flocks quite large—so large that there was not adequate pasture for the flocks of both of them. To avoid strife between the herdsmen of the two men, they agreed to go their separate ways. While Abram remained in the highlands, Lot chose to move to the Jordan Valley, which was well watered and green.

Before long this area was attacked by a group of marauders, who defeated the rulers of Sodom and Gomorrah and their allies, carrying off Lot and his family as a part of their booty. When Abram learned what had happened, he led a rescue party that defeated the raiders and rescued the captives. As he returned from his victory, Abram was greeted by Melchizedek, "king of Salem and priest of God Most High" (Hebrews 7:1), who pronounced a blessing on him. Abram then gave Melchizedek tithes of all he had obtained (Genesis 14:19, 20). It was "after this" that the events found in the first part of today's printed text took place.

I. GOD REAFFIRMS HIS COVENANT (GENESIS 15:1-6)

A. GOD'S REASSURANCE (v. 1)

1. After this, the word of the LORD came to Abram in a vision:
> **"Do not be afraid, Abram.**
>   **I am your shield,**
>   **your very great reward."**

WHAT DO YOU THINK?

The Lord appeared to Abram and described himself as Abram's "shield" and his "very great reward." Since Abram had just returned from battle, these terms were especially significant. If God appeared to you in such a way, what terms might he use to describe himself? Why?

Most likely the reassuring words *Do not be afraid* were needed because the immediate response anyone has when brought into the presence of Almighty God is one of overwhelming fear. In the presence of his holiness, man feels himself "ruined" (Isaiah 6:5). It is also possible that these words were meant to help prepare Abram for the developments that were to follow.

The Lord's description of himself to Abram was appropriate in light of recent events. He was Abram's *shield*, promising to protect him if the marauders gathered reinforcements and tried to stir up trouble again. Although Abram had refused to take any kind of reward or booty following his victory (Genesis 14:22-24), he was promised a greater spiritual treasure: God himself would be Abram's *very great reward*.

B. ABRAM'S CONCERN (vv. 2, 3)

2, 3. But Abram said, "O Sovereign LORD, what can you give me since I remain childless and the one who will inherit my estate is Eliezer of Damascus?" And Abram said, "You have given me no children; so a servant in my household will be my heir."

WHAT DO YOU THINK?

Abram questioned God about his promise. It had been a long time since God first appeared to Abram, and still he was childless. Why is waiting on God such a test of faith? What do you do to keep your faith strong even when it seems nothing is happening to bring you closer to what you want or expect from God?

(Note: Abram took his concern to the Lord. We, too, can pray and study God's Word to be sure what we want or expect is in harmony with his revealed will.)

When the Lord had spoken to Abram on previous occasions, he did the talking and Abram listened and then acted. On this occasion Abram spoke up to voice his concern. What troubled him most was not that he was *childless*, having no *heir*. His question was how God could *give* him all he had promised without an heir to help fulfill those promises. How could God make of him a "great nation" (Genesis 12:2) when he didn't even have a son? We cannot tell for certain whether Abram's faith was wavering at this point or whether he was simply asking how God planned to keep his promise. Note in the following verses that God responded to Abram, not by rebuking him for lack of faith, but by reassuring him of his promise.

Archaeological discoveries of clay tablets dated only shortly after the time of Abram show that his description of *Eliezer* referred to a common practice of the day. A childless couple would adopt a servant, who would become their heir unless a child should be born later to them, at which time that child would become the heir. Here *Eliezer of Damascus* is described as the *servant in Abram's household* (perhaps his birthplace was *Damascus*, or he had been purchased from someone who lived there). Apparently he had been adopted by Abram at some point. The phrase *servant in my household* literally reads, "the son of my house." It indicates, not that Eliezer was born into Abram's household, but that he had attained a favorable status within it.

The Scriptures do not provide us any further information about Eliezer. He may be the servant in Genesis 24 whom Abraham sent to find a wife for Isaac.

C. GOD'S ANSWER (vv. 4-6)

4, 5. *Then the word of the LORD came to him: "This man will not be your heir, but a son coming from your own body will be your heir." He took him outside and said, "Look up at the heavens and count the stars—if indeed you can count them." Then he said to him, "So shall your offspring be."*

Once more *the word of the Lord came to him*. Abram's concern necessitated a further response from the Lord. First of all, God informed him that Eliezer would *not be* his *heir*. The heir would come from his *own body*. The heir would be his own offspring.

Apparently it was night when this revelation occurred, and Abram was most likely inside a tent. So, to further assure him, God took Abram *outside* and told him to *look up* into the sky and *count the stars*. The number of his descendants, God told him, would be equally vast. Such an impressive visual aid and the accompanying explanation would give Abram the assurance he needed and calm his anxieties.

Today astronomers tell us that there are millions upon millions of stars dotting the heavens. Such information would have really impressed Abram! God used this same illustration with him later (Genesis 22:17) and with Isaac (Genesis 26:4). Moses referred to this promise when interceding for the children of Israel (Exodus 32:13) and when addressing them as they prepared to enter the promised land (Deuteronomy 1:10; 10:22).

6. *Abram believed the LORD, and he credited it to him as righteousness.*

This is the first specific reference to Abram's faith in God, although he had already exercised faith when he left his homeland in answer to God's call (as Hebrews 11:8 notes). The use of this verse in the New Testament is significant in the writings of Paul (Romans 4:3; Galatians 3:6) and James (James 2:23). Both point out that Christians are children of Abraham, for they must come to God by faith as he did. There is no other way to please God (Hebrews 11:6) or to be considered righteous before him.

THAT'S INCREDIBLE!

Can you believe what some people believe these days? Thousands of "hot-line" subscribers swallow the prognostications of so-called "psychics" every day. And what about the untold numbers who fall prey to the con man? Promising something "too good to be true," he swindles otherwise sensible people out of millions every year. It's incredible that intelligent human beings could be so naive and gullible.

Abram seems to have wondered whether he had chosen to believe something that was "too good to be true." He was an elderly man and concerned that God's promise of an heir was quickly leaving the realm of possibility. Yet God insisted that Abram would have an heir "from your own body" (Genesis 15:4). And despite all

HOW TO SAY IT

Abimelech. Uh-BIM-eh-lek.
Abram. AY-brum.
Damascus. Duh-MASS-kus.
Eliezer. El-ih-EE-zer.
Gerar. GEAR-ar.
Gomorrah. Guh-MORE-uh.
Hagar. HAY-gar.
Ishmael. ISH-may-el.
Melchizedek. Mel-KIZZ-ih-dek.
Mesopotamia. MESS-uh-puh-
   TAY-me-uh.
Sarai. SEH-rye.
Sodom. SOD-um.

DAILY BIBLE READINGS

Monday, July 5—*Your Very Own Offspring Shall Be Your Heir (Genesis 15:1-6)*

Tuesday, July 6—*The Lord Makes a Covenant With Abram (Genesis 15:12-20)*

Wednesday, July 7—*Hagar Bears Abram a Son (Genesis 16:1-16)*

Thursday, July 8—*Your Name Shall Be Abraham (Genesis 17:1-14)*

Friday, July 9—*Sarah Shall Be Her Name (Genesis 17:15-27)*

Saturday, July 10—*Sarah Laughs to Herself (Genesis 18:1-15)*

Sunday, July 11—*Sarah Bears Abraham a Son (Genesis 21:1-7)*

the probabilities to the contrary, Abram "believed the Lord" (v. 6). Now that is truly incredible—or is it?

We can believe that Abram believed because he trusted the same God whom we trust. We believe the record of Genesis because we regard the Bible as the inspired Word of God—totally true. And we believe in miracles because we know that our God can do exceedingly more than we could ever ask or think (Ephesians 3:20).

—R. W. B.

II. GOD PROMISES A SON (GENESIS 17:17-21)

A. ABRAHAM'S DOUBTS (vv. 17, 18)

17, 18. Abraham fell facedown; he laughed and said to himself, "Will a son be born to a man a hundred years old? Will Sarah bear a child at the age of ninety?" And Abraham said to God, "If only Ishmael might live under your blessing!"

In the years that passed between the events studied in the previous verses and those recorded in these, several significant things had occurred. Even though God had promised that Abram would have a son, that seemed increasingly unlikely as the years passed. Finally, Sarai suggested that Abram take her handmaid, Hagar, as a surrogate wife so that she could bear children to him. (This too was an accepted custom of that time, although it was not what God intended Abram to do.) From this union a son, Ishmael, was born.

Thirteen years later God once more appeared to Abram to reaffirm the covenant that he had previously established. In the process Abram's name was changed to Abraham, which means "father of many nations" (Genesis 17:5). At this point the circumcision of all males was introduced as a mark of the covenant. Sarai's name was changed to Sarah with the promise that she would bear a son and become the mother of nations (vv. 15, 16).

Such extraordinary promises as these seemed to raise doubts in the mind of Abraham. In the very presence of Almighty God, he *laughed* at such a thought. Of course, he was ninety-nine years old now (vv. 1, 24), so he would have to be *a hundred years old* by the time a child was born to him. Abraham's long experience told him that a hundred-year-old man did not father children with a wife who was *ninety* years old.

Some suggest that Abraham's laughter may have been the expression of joy or wonder at the thought that he and Sarah could be parents at their ages. That God repeated his promise in the next verse would indicate that Abraham entertained some doubts and needed reassuring. We ourselves who often struggle with taking God at his word can identify with Abraham at this point.

Abraham then asked God that *Ishmael might live under your blessing*. Earlier Abraham had proposed that Eliezer be his heir. Perhaps he was now proposing that Ishmael be that heir. Or Abraham's words may simply reflect his desire that God not ignore Ishmael while blessing the promised child.

B. GOD'S PLANS (vv. 19-21)

19. Then God said, "Yes, but your wife Sarah will bear you a son, and you will call him Isaac. I will establish my covenant with him as an everlasting covenant for his descendants after him.

God was tolerant of Abraham's weakness and did not rebuke him. Instead, he reaffirmed his previous promise. In spite of Abraham's doubts, God would give him *a son*. In addition, God even gave Abraham's son a name—*Isaac*, which means "he laughs" or "laughter." Was God displaying a subtle sense of humor by assigning this name just after Abraham had laughed at the idea that he would have a son?

20. *"And as for Ishmael, I have heard you: I will surely bless him; I will make him fruitful and will greatly increase his numbers. He will be the father of twelve rulers, and I will make him into a great nation.*

I have heard you. God had heard Abraham's petition on behalf of *Ishmael* and was granting it, but apparently not as Abraham had expected. God promised to do four things for Ishmael: *bless him*, *make him fruitful*, make him *the father of twelve rulers* (see Genesis 25:12-16), and *make him into a great nation*. However, God did not establish a covenant with Ishmael as he had with Abraham and would later do with Isaac. Regardless of the blessings that Ishmael would receive, he was not to be a part of God's plan to bless all the families of the earth through Abraham.

21. *"But my covenant I will establish with Isaac, whom Sarah will bear to you by this time next year."*

The *covenant* God established with Abraham did not include all of his physical descendants. It included only those who were descendants of *Isaac*. Of course, we today who are Christians are the spiritual children of Abraham, for we have come to God in faith as he did (Galatians 3:7-9, 29). Isaac is used to symbolize all Christians who live under the New Covenant (Galatians 4:21-31).

God added that the promised son of the covenant would be born *by this time next year*. In his earlier promises of a son, God had not given a specific time for their fulfillment. Now he had set a date.

LAUGHING AT GOD

Most everyone loves a good laugh. "Situation comedies" are featured on prime-time television every night. Sometimes our whole world seems locked into its own twenty-four-hour comedy channel.

No topic is sacred anymore; any subject is fair game for a laugh. Some people laugh at disabilities, misfortune, pain, religion, and sin (they may be laughing themselves right into Hell).

What was going through Abraham's mind when he laughed at God's promise of a son? Did he actually fall down laughing? Was it a laugh of amazement and wonder? Abraham had already expressed his faith in significant ways; God wanted to address the degree of unbelief that apparently he still possessed regarding this latest promise. He knew Abraham's heart was right; he knew this righteous servant *wanted* to believe. So, lovingly and patiently, God simply repeated his promise.

Do you suppose it seems to God that we laugh at him and his promises sometimes? Some say that God has a sense of humor, but God never kids around with his promises. We may misunderstand God, and we may raise our eyebrows at some of his ways and methods; but we must always take him seriously. He says what he means, and he means what he says.   —R. W. B.

WHAT DO YOU THINK?

Abraham did have a very hard test of trust, but God appeared to him repeatedly through the years and reaffirmed his promises. We do not have the same benefit. How does God reaffirm his promises to us and encourage us to keep our faith strong?

III. GOD KEEPS HIS WORD (GENESIS 21:1-3)

Genesis 18 tells of the visit of three men to Abraham. While they ate the food that he had provided for them, one of them mentioned that Sarah would have a son. Sarah overheard the remark and, not believing it, laughed within herself. When confronted, she denied that she had laughed. The chapter also tells how God revealed to Abraham that the cities of Sodom and Gomorrah would be destroyed because of their wickedness. Upon learning this, Abraham made an impassioned plea on their behalf. While God was not willing to spare Sodom and Gomorrah (not even ten righteous people could be found there), he did spare Lot and his family when he destroyed these cities (Genesis 19).

Genesis 20 reveals yet another failure by Abraham to walk in faith. During his travels Abraham came into contact with Abimelech, king of Gerar. Fearing for his

WHAT DO YOU THINK?

Though God delayed in fulfilling his promises to Abraham, his delay gave him opportunity to display his greatness, power, and glory. For Isaac to be born when Abraham and Sarah were so advanced in age was truly miraculous. The result was that Abraham's faith, though sorely tried, was greatly strengthened. What positive results have come to you when you have had to wait to see God working in your life?

PRAYER

We thank you, Father, that you called Abraham and challenged him to live a life of faith. May we have the wisdom and the courage to follow you wherever you may lead us. May the world see in our lives the same kind of faith that Abraham demonstrated. In Jesus' name we pray. Amen.

THOUGHT TO REMEMBER

The righteous shall live by faith.

life, Abraham again claimed Sarah was his sister, just as he had in Egypt. In spite of Abraham's duplicity, Abimelech sent him away with additional livestock, servants, and silver.

A. A SON IS BORN (vv. 1, 2)

1, 2. Now the LORD was gracious to Sarah as he had said, and the LORD did for Sarah what he had promised. Sarah became pregnant and bore a son to Abraham in his old age, at the very time God had promised him.

The Lord was gracious to Sarah in fulfilling the promise that he had made to Abraham earlier—the same promise that Sarah had ridiculed when she overheard it. Sarah's lack of faith did not prevent God from fulfilling his promise of *a son* in her old age.

The actual birth would not have come as a complete surprise to Sarah. *At the very time* would seem to indicate that the pregnancy covered a normal nine-month span. As the months passed, Sarah would have become increasingly aware of the new life developing within her womb. As the baby grew, so did her faith that God was able to do *what he had promised.*

B. A SON IS NAMED (v. 3)

3. Abraham gave the name Isaac to the son Sarah bore him.

It was the normal practice for the father to name a child. In this case Abraham was carrying out the order that God had given him earlier (Genesis 17:19). As has already been noted, *the name Isaac* means "he laughs" or "laughter." What an appropriate name for a son born under such impossible conditions!

CONCLUSION

In the scriptural "Hall of Faith" Abraham ranks high. His faith withstood numerous challenges during his long life. When his faith caused him to leave Ur, he had to give up a life of comfort. Archaeological findings from Ur indicate that citizens of that city, especially people of means as Abraham appears to have been, lived in comfortable, roomy houses and had numerous slaves to take the drudgery out of life. In addition, Abraham had to give up the security that people in Ur enjoyed. Evidence indicates that Ur in Abraham's day was not threatened by any outside forces and was able to provide adequate food supplies for its citizens. People of every age, ours included, desire these securities and are usually very reluctant to give them up once they have them.

Once Abraham decided to leave Mesopotamia, he had to leave behind much of his family and all of his friends. Unless one has had the experience of "pulling up stakes" and leaving behind his loved ones, he has no way to understand the pain that such separation can bring. By faith Abraham made this move, taking along only Lot and his family (and they turned out to be more of a problem than a blessing).

Most important, Abraham believed God's promises even when there was no evidence of any kind that they would be fulfilled. As the years passed, Abraham was continually challenged to trust God to do what appeared impossible, and yet he kept his faith. Through it all "Abram believed the Lord, and he credited it to him as righteousness" (Genesis 15:6).

Abraham's faith serves as a model for all of us today. Most of us have never had our faith tested as he did. Occasionally we may hit a little bump along life's highway, but these are usually not devastating. And often these challenges to our faith come because of our own carelessness or foolishness. When we do have severe tests, let us look to Abraham and take heart.

Discovery Learning

This page contains an alternate lesson plan emphasizing learning activities. Classes desiring such student involvement will find these suggestions helpful. The next page is a reproducible activity page to further enhance discovery learning.

LEARNING GOALS

As a result of participating in this session, the student will be able to:

1. Summarize God's promise to Abraham and how he continually reaffirmed it even when Abraham doubted or misunderstood.

2. Tell why God's promises are no laughing matter—even when they seem incredible.

3. State a confident faith in one or more of the wonderful promises of God.

INTO THE LESSON

Before the class arrives, write the words, *ABRAHAM BELIEVED THE LORD AND HE CREDITED IT TO HIM AS RIGHTEOUSNESS*, on fifty-seven sheets of paper (half-sheets are adequate)—one letter per sheet. Post these on a wall where everyone will be able to see them, but hang them so the letters face the wall. (Be sure to leave spaces between the words.)

As you begin the class session, divide the class into two or three teams. Each team takes a turn suggesting a letter of the alphabet. If that letter appears in the sentence, turn the appropriate sheet(s) around to display the letter(s). That team gets a chance to guess what the complete sentence is. If the letter is not present, the next team gets a chance.

When the sentence has been solved, say, "We are going to see the origin of that statement in our lesson today. What some of us may be surprised to learn is that Abraham's faith was not without a few doubts and blunders along the way. Still, God's grace was with Abraham, and we can be certain it is with us today even if our faith seems a little shaky from time to time."

INTO THE WORD

Recall last week's lesson on the promises made to Abraham (Abram) at his call. Ask a volunteer to read Genesis 12:1-3, 7. If you made the poster suggested last week (see "Into the Word" on page 383), display it and review the promises together.

Then assign each of three groups one of the following Scripture passages: Genesis 15:1-6; Genesis 17:17-21; Genesis 21:1-3. Ask each group to cite the promises from Genesis 12 that are mentioned, confirmed, or fulfilled in its assigned text. Note also signs of doubt on the part of Abraham and how God dealt with his doubt.

Allow about five minutes for the groups to work, and then ask for reports. Between reports, fill in details of what happened between the events recorded in the texts. (Use the exposition section of this book to help you.) Note how Abraham not only doubted, but at times took matters into his own hands to work things out (as with having a son by his wife's servant Hagar, Genesis 16:1-4, 15).

After the reports, ask, "When have you found yourself, like Abraham, taking matters into your own hands instead of waiting on the Lord? Have you ever acted in a way that cast doubt on your true belief in the promises of God?"

Point out that God changed Abram's name to Abraham (from "exalted father" to "father of a multitude") to constantly remind him of his promise.

Lead in to the next exercise by saying, "God's promises are no laughing matter. There were others in the Bible (in addition to Sarah) who, by the direct intervention of God, conceived when it seemed impossible." Then have the class read the following passages and see who they were: Judges 13:2-24 (*Wife of Manoah*); 1 Samuel 1:2-20 (*Hannah*); Luke 1:7-25 (*Elizabeth*); Luke 1:32-35 (*Mary*).

INTO LIFE

In Genesis 15:7 God spoke to Abram, calling himself "the Lord, who brought you out of Ur . . . to give you this land." List the promises God makes to you in each of the following passages:

- Mark 9:23 (unlimited blessing)
- Mark 11:24 (answered prayer)
- Luke 17:6 (removal of obstacles)
- John 3:16 (eternal life)
- John 12:46 (spiritual light)
- John 14:12 (power for service)
- Romans 1:16 (salvation)

Give each student a three-by-five card and these instructions: "Write on this card one of these promises that you feel you especially need to be reminded of in the coming week. Follow this format:

"Write, 'I am the Lord who . . .' and finish the statement with one of the promises. Then write an encouragement based on the promise." For example, one who is timid in his witness might write, "I am the Lord who empowers you for service. Tell your neighbor of my love."

Covenants

A covenant is a legally binding obligation (promise). Throughout history God has made covenants with his people. (That is, he would do certain things if the people would meet certain conditions.) Look up the following Scripture references and fill in the chart describing God's promise (covenant) in each one.

TEXT	PROMISE
Genesis 3:15	
Genesis 9:8-17	
Genesis 15:12-21	
Genesis 17:1-14	
Genesis 28:10-15	
Exodus 19:5, 6	
Numbers 25:10-13	
2 Samuel 7:13	

My Promise

In Genesis 28:20-22, Jacob responded to God's promise with a promise of his own. What will you promise to God in response to the wonderful promises God has made to you?

A TEST OF FAITH

LESSON 7

WHY TEACH THIS LESSON?

"Give of thy sons to bear the message glorious; Give of thy wealth to speed them on their way." These lines from "O Zion, Haste" remind us that the application of today's text is not merely figurative. Normally when we study this account of Abraham's near-sacrifice of Isaac, someone is quick to point out, "Of course, God would never ask us to sacrifice one of our own children!"

Don't be too sure about that! Especially if you have students with children about to graduate and choose a career, note how we sometimes "sacrifice" our children by giving them up to the Lord's service. If your church is encouraging the young people to go on a summer missions trip, you might use this lesson to help some parents see how important it is to let them go.

INTRODUCTION

A. COMPARING PRICE TAGS

A well-to-do merchant stood on the dock watching as final preparations were made for a ship to sail. As he stood there, he was joined by a stranger whose clothing revealed his poverty. Finally the stranger spoke up. "You seem mighty pleased about watching this ship sail," he said.

"Yes," replied the merchant. "I have seen many ships leave this harbor, but this one gives me more satisfaction than any other I can remember. You see, on this ship I am sending ten thousand dollars worth of equipment for a mission hospital in China. I just had to come down and see that it got off safely."

"Then we have something in common," said the stranger, "for I, too, have a gift on that ship."

"And what is that gift?" asked the merchant somewhat incredulously.

"My only daughter is on that ship. She's going to China as a missionary."

"Then my gift is nothing compared with yours," came the merchant's quiet reply.

Like this merchant, Abraham was a man of great wealth. His faith was so strong that he would readily have given any or all of his wealth to God. However, Abraham's material wealth was nothing compared with the gift God asked of him—his son Isaac. Yet Abraham passed even this test of faith in noble fashion.

B. LESSON BACKGROUND

After the birth of Isaac (with which last week's printed text ended), the tensions between Sarah and Hagar continued to increase. They reached the breaking point when Isaac was weaned. Sarah demanded that Hagar and Ishmael be sent away, but Abraham was reluctant to give in to his wife's demands until God told him to do what Sarah asked. Isaac was to be the child of promise, God said, but Ishmael, too, would be made a great nation (Genesis 21:9-14). We find Sarah's behavior shocking, yet she was acting within her legal rights when she made her demand. (Some of the laws of ancient Mesopotamia allowed the primary wife almost complete control over a secondary wife.) Even though Hagar and Ishmael were sent out into the desert with only a little food and water to sustain them,

DEVOTIONAL READING:
DANIEL 3:13-26
LESSON SCRIPTURE:
GENESIS 22:1-19
PRINTED TEXT:
GENESIS 22:1-14

LESSON AIMS

After this lesson students should be able to:

1. Summarize the account of how God tested Abraham's faith by commanding him to sacrifice Isaac.

2. Consider what their response would be if God commanded them to give up someone or something precious to them.

3. Explain how they have been, or are being, tested, and the lessons they have learned from the test.

Jul
18

KEY VERSE

"Do not lay a hand on the boy. . . . Do not do anything to him. Now I know that you fear God, because you have not withheld from me your son, your only son." —Genesis 22:12

God watched over them and cared for them. The young Ishmael grew to maturity in the wilderness of Paran, located in the Sinai Peninsula.

During this time, Abraham continued to travel about in southern Palestine, seeking pasture and water for his flocks. After a misunderstanding with Abimelech over a well that Abraham had dug, the two entered into an agreement that allowed them to live in peace with one another.

I. ABRAHAM IS TESTED (GENESIS 22:1, 2)

A. GOD APPEARS TO ABRAHAM (v. 1)

1. Some time later God tested Abraham. He said to him, "Abraham!"
"Here I am," he replied.

God tested Abraham. James notes how "trials of many kinds," which he describes as the "testing of [our] faith" are to be considered a source of joy because they contribute to our Christian maturity (James 1:2-4). This testing of Abraham's faith was for Abraham's benefit, not God's. God already knew Abraham's heart and knew that he was a man of faith. While Abraham had passed most of his earlier tests, his grade was not one hundred percent. Although his faith had grown through the years, the fact that his faith had wavered at times indicated that he still had room for growth. If he met the upcoming test successfully, it would mean that his faith had reached a new level of maturity and dedication.

All of us are like Abraham: we never fully understand our strengths and weaknesses until we have been tested in the fires of pain, suffering, and defeat.

B. GOD COMMANDS ABRAHAM (v. 2)

2. Then God said, "Take your son, your only son, Isaac, whom you love, and go to the region of Moriah. Sacrifice him there as a burnt offering on one of the mountains I will tell you about."

Of course, *Isaac* was not Abraham's *only* son. He had another son, Ishmael, but he had been sent away. So Isaac, the beloved son of Abraham's old age, was the *only son* with Abraham and the *only son* through whom God's covenant with Abraham would be fulfilled.

The very thought of sacrificing this son *as a burnt offering* must have struck Abraham's heart like a sledgehammer. To further complicate the matter, the idea of human sacrifice would have been abhorrent to Abraham. Some of the peoples around him practiced human sacrifice, but the God he worshiped was a life-giving God, not a life-taking God. To offer a human sacrifice would seem to contradict everything he had learned about God.

We know that God would never require us to kill one of our children to prove our faith in him. Yet through the Great Commission of Jesus, he may call one of our children to serve in some distant and dangerous mission field. Should that occasion ever arrive, would we be as steadfast and unwavering in our faith as Abraham was?

The region of Moriah was located in central Canaan. Centuries later Solomon built the temple of Jerusalem on Mount Moriah (2 Chronicles 3:1). Many believe that Abraham journeyed to that mountain or, if not there, to *one of the mountains* in the vicinity of Jerusalem.

DO YOU HAVE WHAT IT TAKES?

Reports of widespread persecution of Christians around the world are deeply troubling. Believers in Communist China must worship "underground," fearing imprisonment or worse if they are discovered. Entire villages in the Sudan have been destroyed by militant Muslims, making corpses, slaves, or refugees of the

---

WHAT DO YOU THINK?

Isaac was the most precious thing in Abraham's life. No test could have been more severe! God does not ask for burnt offerings today, but for a living sacrifice (Romans 12:1). What are some of the things that are most precious to you? How might God demand you to give them up to serve him?

HOW TO SAY IT

Abimelech. Uh-BIM-eh-lek.

Beersheba. Beer-SHE-buh.

Hagar. HAY-gar.

Ishmael. ISH-may-el.

Jehovah-jireh. Jeh-HO-vuh-JYE-ruh.

Mesopotamia. MESS-uh-puh-TAY-me-uh.

Moriah. Mo-RYE-uh.

Paran. PAIR-un.

Sinai. SYE-nye or SYE-nay-eye.

Christians who live there. In Pakistan, the "Blasphemy Law" threatens anyone who is perceived as speaking or acting in disrespect of Mohammed. Christians are being tortured and sometimes killed in these and several other countries.

One has to wonder, "Could my faith withstand such pressure and abuse? Is my Christian commitment deep enough to risk or surrender my freedom and/or life if I were forced to make such a choice?" An even bigger question comes to mind when we consider Abraham's experience: "Would I be willing to sacrifice one of my children if God commanded me to do so?"

Spiritual giants are made, not born. Abraham probably never imagined he had such faith until he was actually confronted with the challenge. That day on the mountain in Moriah he grew a spiritual mile. We must remember that though few Christians have *what* it takes to be victorious in such situations, we all have *whom* it takes; and he has overcome the world (John 16:33).   —R. W. B.

II. ABRAHAM OBEYS (GENESIS 22:3-10)

A. ABRAHAM'S JOURNEY (vv. 3-5)

3. Early the next morning Abraham got up and saddled his donkey. He took with him two of his servants and his son Isaac. When he had cut enough wood for the burnt offering, he set out for the place God had told him about.

Early the next morning seems to indicate that God had spoken to Abraham during the night. Abraham's heart must have been heavy as he made the preparations that he believed would cost him his beloved son. The struggle he must have gone through was both emotional and intellectual. It was emotional because his own son was involved; it was intellectual because he could not see any way that God could fulfill the covenant promises if Isaac were sacrificed. Hebrews 11:19 suggests a solution to Abraham's intellectual problem. He reasoned "that God could raise the dead." Thus, even if Isaac were sacrificed, Abraham believed that God would restore him to life and allow him to fulfill the covenant.

So Abraham left for Moriah, taking Isaac with him. He was also accompanied by *two of his servants.* Perhaps with their help Abraham *cut* the firewood that was to be used in the *burnt offering.* We wonder what the foursome talked about as they traveled.

4, 5. On the third day Abraham looked up and saw the place in the distance. He said to his servants, "Stay here with the donkey while I and the boy go over there. We will worship and then we will come back to you."

If Abraham started his trip at Beersheba (where he was when chapter 21 ended), then he had to journey about fifty miles to reach Moriah. Since Abraham had probably traveled over this area many times, he knew where he was going and would recognize *the place in the distance.* Taking his leave of the two *servants,* he and Isaac started toward the mountain. The duty he was about to perform was too intensely personal to have anyone else present. Furthermore, had the servants been present and realized what was about to happen, they might have interfered.

Notice how strong Abraham's faith remained, even though the moment that he dreaded was drawing ever nearer. He told the servants that both he and Isaac (*I and the boy*) would return.

B. ISAAC'S QUESTION (vv. 6-8)

6, 7. Abraham took the wood for the burnt offering and placed it on his son Isaac, and he himself carried the fire and the knife. As the two of them went on together, Isaac spoke up and said to his father Abraham, "Father?"

"Yes, my son?" Abraham replied.

WHAT DO YOU THINK?

Sometimes when we face a tough challenge, we don't refuse; we just procrastinate. Abraham, however, got up "early the next morning" to initiate his obedience. What benefits do you see in taking immediate action in order to obey? What dangers do you see in putting it off?

DAILY BIBLE READINGS

Monday, July 12—*Take Your Son, Your Only Son Isaac (Genesis 22:1-8)*

Tuesday, July 13—*"Abraham . . . Took the Knife to Slay His Son" (Genesis 22:9-14)*

Wednesday, July 14—*I Will Indeed Bless You (Genesis 22:15-19)*

Thursday, July 15—*We Will Not Serve Your Gods (Daniel 3:16-26)*

Friday, July 16—*Remove This Cup From Me (Mark 14:32-42)*

Saturday, July 17—*One Who in Every Respect Has Been Tested (Hebrews 4:14—5:4)*

Sunday, July 18—*The Greatest of These Is Love (1 Corinthians 13:1-13)*

"The fire and wood are here," Isaac said, *"but where is the lamb for the burnt offering?*

As they trudged upward, Abraham carried the *knife* that he would need to slay the sacrificial victim. He also *carried the fire*, probably a censer or pot containing live coals needed to start a fire and make the sacrifice a burnt offering. Isaac carried the *wood* for the fire.

Artists have often portrayed Isaac as a small boy at this time. Actually he was more likely an older teenager. A small child would not have been able to carry the wood, especially for as long as Isaac apparently had to. In addition, his question involved more rational thinking than one might expect from a child. At this point Isaac did not have an inkling about what Abraham was planning to do. *Where is the lamb for the burnt offering?* he asked. No doubt Isaac had witnessed other acts of worship involving a burnt offering, and so his question was reasonable enough. He may have wondered earlier about the absence of a lamb, but waited until he was alone with his father before he asked.

8. Abraham answered, "God himself will provide the lamb for the burnt offering, my son." And the two of them went on together.

Abraham may have answered calmly enough, but his heart must have experienced a turmoil of emotion. His response must have been confident enough to satisfy Isaac. (It may imply that he did not believe that God would allow him to sacrifice Isaac.) Christians recognize the prophetic significance in Abraham's statement, for God did *provide* his own Son as *the lamb* that would take away the sins of the world (John 1:29).

C. ABRAHAM'S PREPARATION (vv. 9, 10)

9. When they reached the place God had told him about, Abraham built an altar there and arranged the wood on it. He bound his son Isaac and laid him on the altar, on top of the wood.

The Scriptures do not indicate that there was any further conversation between the distraught father and the unsuspecting son. Under the circumstances it is not likely that Abraham felt much like talking. Finally they arrived at the designated *place* of sacrifice. Abraham then gathered up some large stones and *built an altar*—something he had done many times in the past. Next he laid out the *wood* upon the altar. Finally he *bound his son Isaac and laid him . . . on top of the wood*. During the process of being tied up, Isaac certainly must have realized what was about to happen. He was a young man in his physical prime and certainly could have resisted his father had he so desired, yet he humbly submitted to what was happening. This says a great deal about young Isaac's faith—both in his father and in God.

10. Then he reached out his hand and took the knife to slay his son.

The moment of truth had arrived. At every step along the way Abraham could have stopped and turned back, refusing to carry out God's order. But now "by faith . . . he who had received the promises was about to sacrifice his one and only son" (Hebrews 11:17).

III. GOD INTERVENES (GENESIS 22:11-14)

A. AN ANGEL SPEAKS (v. 11)

11. But the angel of the LORD called out to him from heaven, "Abraham! Abraham!"

"Here I am," he replied.

Just as Abraham raised his knife to plunge it into the heart of his son, *the angel of the Lord* interrupted him. In that brief moment, the call of his name must have

WHAT DO YOU THINK?

Through all of this, Abraham taught Isaac a powerful lesson in trusting God. Isaac's behavior shows that he already had a high degree of trust in God and in Abraham; otherwise he could and would have resisted. The lesson was not a new one, then, but a vivid demonstration of an old one, and proof that what Abraham had taught Isaac about his faith was completely genuine. How may we use crises to teach our children or others who look to us for guidance to trust in God?

Of course, we cannot lead where we have not gone. How can we be sure our faith is sound in order to teach valid faith lessons to others?

sent a storm of emotions surging through his heart. Were his orders being changed? Was he to receive new orders? What did it mean? God's revelations to him in the past had been frequent enough that he must have recognized the voice that was speaking, and so he quickly responded, *Here I am.*

B. GOD COMMENDS ABRAHAM (v. 12)

12. *"Do not lay a hand on the boy," he said. "Do not do anything to him. Now I know that you fear God, because you have not withheld from me your son, your only son."*

Abraham could not have heard words more wonderful than *Do not lay a hand on the boy.* When Abraham began this solemn venture, he had no idea how it would turn out. As he journeyed along, he must have hoped that somehow his son would be spared, but he had no idea how this would happen. Now all his fondest hopes were realized. God assured him that he had passed the test. Although God knew from the beginning how the test would turn out, it was necessary that Abraham go through the entire process right up to the killing of Isaac. As noted earlier, the test was for the benefit of Abraham, not God. If he had *withheld* his *only son,* then his faith in God would have remained incomplete. Referring to this incident, James writes of Abraham, "His faith and his actions were working together, and his faith was made complete by what he did" (James 2:22).

TEMPTED OR TRIED?

My wife recently took a Medical Assistant Certification test—four hours, three hundred questions. She had studied for some twenty weeks (about two hundred hours) in preparation. She won't know her score for three months, but she doesn't think she did very well. The questions did not reflect the study material or the sample quizzes that the candidates were given. One of my wife's friends said that she was confident of less than one-tenth of her answers!

This test apparently was designed to fail the testees. It was clearly unfair. By contrast, God's intent with Abraham's test was to prove his faith, not cause his failure. Certain events in life are allowed to try the quality of our trust and the courage of our convictions. We say such trials are tests of our faith. That's different from temptation.

James teaches us that God tempts no one (James 1:13). Temptation is designed by the devil to cause our failure. God allows us to be tested to strengthen our Christian character (James 1:2-4). Satan wants to destroy us; God wants to reward us with the "crown of life" (James 1:12). His purpose in our trials is positive—to temper our commitment and to harden our resolve. God wanted Abraham to be a spiritual giant, and he wants that for you and me, too. —R. W. B.

C. THE SUBSTITUTE (vv. 13, 14)

13, 14. *Abraham looked up and there in a thicket he saw a ram caught by its horns. He went over and took the ram and sacrificed it as a burnt offering instead of his son. So Abraham called that place The LORD Will Provide. And to this day it is said, "On the mountain of the LORD it will be provided."*

Earlier Abraham had told Isaac that God would provide an offering, but of course, he had no idea how this would be accomplished. Now, in God's perfect timing, a *ram* was made available as a substitute for *his son.* Again note the prophetic element in this act: God's provision suggests a sacrifice that was to occur centuries later when he substituted his Son for us at the cross.

Abraham, who only a few moments before had been filled with anguish, now experienced a joy that knew no bounds. This is the normal response when faith

Today's visual pictures that dramatic moment when the angel of the Lord called to Abraham to prevent him from slaying his son Isaac.

"Lay not thine hand upon the lad, neither do thou any thing unto him: for now I know that thou fearest God." *Genesis 22:12*

WHAT DO YOU THINK?

Though Abraham had no way of knowing it, his actions were a dramatic and powerful portrayal of God's actions some two thousand years later. Abraham was called to give his only son of promise, his beloved son; God gave his only begotten and beloved Son. Abraham took Isaac to a mountaintop in the land of Moriah, a mountain close to, or maybe even the same as, the temple mount, or perhaps Calvary. Isaac was innocent of anything that called for his death; Jesus was absolutely pure and innocent. Isaac willingly obeyed his father by accepting that he would be sacrificed; Jesus made his sacrifice of his own will, in obedience to the will of his heavenly Father.

How do these things strengthen your faith?

What Do You Think?

The lesson writer says we need to prepare for tests of our faith. How do you think one does that? What do you do to prepare for such tests?

Prayer

We thank you, dear Lord, for Abraham, whose life of faith serves as a model for us. Give us the wisdom to learn from his life and the strength to follow his example. In our Master's name we pray. Amen.

triumphs over doubt. We can know that same joy when we overcome a particularly severe temptation or a personal disaster, such as a serious illness, that tries our faith.

The Lord Will Provide was an appropriate name for a *place* where God had graciously *provided* a substitute for Isaac. Abraham was able to keep his earlier promise (v. 5): "I and the boy . . . will worship and then we will come back to you."

CONCLUSION

We live in an age of testing. Millions upon millions of dollars are spent every year on testing. Such items as the food we eat, the water we drink, and the clothes we wear are all subjected to countless tests before they are sold to us. Although these tests are expensive and often time-consuming, we accept them as a part of our complicated lifestyle. When we visit a physician's office, we are likely to be tested so that he can make a better diagnosis of our ailments. Our automobiles are safer than ever because they have been tested both in the designing and the manufacturing process. We must pass a test to receive a driver's license, and if we should be caught driving erratically, we may be tested by an officer for our sobriety. And the word *school* is one that for many students becomes synonymous with tests.

Our faith in God involves testing. Just as our everyday life involves testing, so does our relationship to God. On rare occasions that test may come in one defining moment, as did Abraham's when he was told to sacrifice Isaac. But most of us will never have an experience like that with all of its intensity and drama. Our tests usually come frequently, even daily. They arise in the seemingly small, insignificant events of life. They come when we are exasperated by another person and cut him down with a sarcastic remark. They arise when we "forget" about the posted speed limits on the highway. They occur when, in a group that may be critical of Christ or the church, we remain silent rather than speak up for our Lord. When we fail to live up to our faith in these and a thousand similar situations, we will rarely be criticized. Often our consciences won't even bother us. And in addition, when we pass these tests of faith, we will not receive an instant commendation from the Lord as did Abraham. Yet these tests are still important.

We need to prepare for tests of our faith. As a teacher I spend a great deal of time preparing, giving, and grading tests. Normally I give students advance notice of tests and tell them how to prepare for them. Some students listen, prepare, and usually make good grades. Others don't listen, or they prepare inadequately, and they suffer the consequences. Occasionally I give a "pop quiz" just to make sure that the students stay alert.

Life is much like this. We often know when and where major tests of faith will come in our lives, and we can prepare for those times. When we move or take a new job or make new friends, we should be aware that such situations often put our faith to the test. At other times, tests come like the dreaded pop quizzes—unannounced and unexpected. These are usually the most difficult tests because our guard is not up.

Tests can make our faith stronger. Most of us don't enjoy tests when we have to take them. But James reminds us to "consider it pure joy, my brothers, whenever you face trials of many kinds" (James 1:2). Abraham was able to rejoice when he successfully passed his test, and so can we. God gives us this assurance: "Blessed is the man who perseveres under trial, because when he has stood the test, he will receive the crown of life that God has promised to those who love him" (James 1:12).

Discovery Learning

This page contains an alternate lesson plan emphasizing learning activities. Classes desiring such student involvement will find these suggestions helpful. The next page is a reproducible activity page to further enhance discovery learning.

LEARNING GOALS

After this lesson students should be able to:

1. Summarize the account of how God tested Abraham's faith by commanding him to sacrifice Isaac.

2. Consider what their response would be if God commanded them to give up someone or something precious to them.

3. Explain how they have been, or are being, tested, and the lessons they have learned from the test.

INTO THE LESSON

As you begin the lesson, ask your students, "What is the most difficult test you have faced in your life?" Ask several students to share their stories if they are willing.

It might be best to do this exercise in small groups. In this way each student will have the opportunity to get involved in a less threatening environment. After allowing enough time for several to share, ask anyone in the class who is willing to tell what they learned from being tested. In what ways are they different?

Lead into the Bible study by pointing out that one of the great patriarchs of the Old Testament was greatly tested—and passed with flying colors! It is his story that we will consider today.

INTO THE WORD

Ask a volunteer to read Genesis 22:1-14 aloud. Then divide the class into groups of three to five students each and give each group one of the following three assignments:

1. Imagine that Abraham kept a journal or diary. What might he have written in it upon returning home with Isaac after this event?

2. Imagine that Isaac kept a journal or diary. What might he have written in it upon returning home with Abraham after this event?

3. Write what Abraham and Isaac might have said to each other as they walked home. What fatherly advice might Abraham have given his son based on this experience?

Encourage each group to include a review of the details of the event, something of the emotional drama that must have been present as Abraham and Isaac looked back at the experience, and any lessons they might have learned. Allow ten minutes; then have several groups share their results. You need not have every group read its work unless each one is eager to do so. A sampling will provide a good review.

Discuss the areas in the writings where the groups were speculating. Do their conclusions seem reasonable? What lessons are there for us in these events? Use information from the Scripture exposition section to explain any details that are unclear to the students or to answer their questions.

INTO LIFE

After the students have completed this exercise, read Hebrews 11:17-19. Ask the students what they think God was asking Abraham to give up by sacrificing Isaac. (He may have been asking Abraham to give up control and let God lead. At least three times before, Abraham had taken matters into his own hands—twice calling Sarah his sister to protect himself, and once by fathering a child with Hagar.) Why was this test necessary? (It demonstrated that God had Abraham's full trust and confidence–not just when Abraham could see a good purpose.) What was God really after? (Abraham's heart.) How might God make a similar demand on us? (How about when he calls our children to serve him as missionaries in far-off lands, or in ministerial professions that won't earn the kind of money they have the potential to make in secular employment?)

Say, "God has not asked any of us to sacrifice our children on an altar, but probably there are some of us who are being tested. What tests are you facing right now or have you faced? What lessons have these trials taught you?"

It appears from verse 19 that Abraham believed that even if he obeyed the Lord and killed his son, God could bring Isaac back again. Ask your students how this reflects on Abraham's faith in God to keep his promises. Then ask your students to think about what God has asked them to sacrifice (to give up). Do they believe that God can provide what was given up?

Close by reminding your class that Abraham called the place of the sacrifice "The Lord Will Provide." In Hebrew, that is "Jehovah-jireh." Tradition says that this is the same mount where the temple was later built and near the place called Golgotha, where a sacrifice was made that "provides" for us in a very special way.

Lead your class in singing the chorus "Jehovah-jireh, My Provider" before you pray.

Testing, Testing

In our text today Abraham faced a most difficult test. What is the most difficult test you have faced in your own life?

What have you learned from being tested?

In what ways are you different?

The Gospel in Genesis

Read all of the following Scripture passages and look for the parallels between any two of the words below. When you see a parallel, draw a line between the two words and write both Scripture references on the line that connects the words. For instance, comparing Genesis 22:13 with John 11:49-52 indicates that there is a parallel between Jesus and the ram. Thus there is a line between *Ram* and *Jesus* with those Scripture references written on that line.

Genesis 22:1-14
John 3:16
Luke 23:46

John 1:29
Mark 14:36
John 19:17

Mark 1:11
John 11:49-52

God

Abraham   Ram

                    Genesis 22:13
                    John 11:49-52

Jesus   Isaac

DECEIT AND BLESSING

LESSON 8

WHY TEACH THIS LESSON?

Pick up the evening's TV listings, and what will you find? On one network is a situation comedy—"good family viewing," they say. In tonight's episode Dad has gone to the ball game when he promised to go to the opera with Mom. Now he has to come up with a story to cover up his deed. The son has got a bad grade on his report card and is desperately seeking a way to keep his parents from finding out, and little sister is going out with a boy even though her parents have told her she can't date for another year. Obviously, she doesn't want them to know.

On another station is an adult drama. It's full of lies and deception, unfaithfulness, and other assorted sins. Let's skip over that one to the next! Here's an action-adventure drama. The good guys are beating the bad guys at their own game. An undercover officer has infiltrated the criminal ring and is wearing a "wire" to gather evidence.

Doesn't anybody tell the truth anymore? Your students are so bombarded by lies and deception, even in what we call entertainment, that this lesson will come as a timely warning. Deception is wrong, and the deceiver is often the one who faces the worst consequences.

INTRODUCTION

A. SISTERS WHO DIDN'T SPEAK

In many churches people have a favorite pew. Week after week they will sit in the same pew for the worship services. That was true in the small-town church in which I grew up. I remember two couples who were always in the same separate pews, one couple on the left side of the sanctuary and the other on the right.

I was grown and had left home before I learned that the two women in these couples were sisters. Years before, the two had become involved in a bitter dispute about an inheritance from their parents. One felt that the other had received an unfair share. In the years that followed they never spoke to one another though they continued to attend the same church. They always sat on opposite sides of the sanctuary and always entered and left by different doors, insuring that they would never have to speak to one another. As far as I know, they died without ever being reconciled to each other.

As we study the household of Isaac, we may be tempted to dismiss the conflict within it as just another ancient story that has little relevance in our day. However, on every hand we can see the same kind of family scheming and plotting. And in many of today's conflicts, the results are far more deadly.

B. LESSON BACKGROUND

The previous lesson (which was taken from Genesis 22) ended with Abraham passing the test of faith when he was commanded to offer up Isaac as a sacrifice. Chapter 23 records the death and burial of Sarah. Chapter 24 then tells how Abraham sent his servant back to northern Mesopotamia (to the area near Haran, where Abraham had formerly lived) to secure a wife for Isaac from among his own kinsmen. Rebekah returned with the servant and became Isaac's wife.

DEVOTIONAL READING:
LUKE 16:1-14

LESSON SCRIPTURE:
GENESIS 25:19-34; 27:1-40

PRINTED TEXT:
GENESIS 25:29-34; 27:30-37

LESSON AIMS

After this lesson the student will be able to:

1. Tell how Jacob tricked his brother and father to secure rights and blessings for himself.

2. Cite instances (from Scripture or from personal experience) of the alienation caused by deceitful words and actions.

3. Determine to live by the truth in every relationship, especially those within his or her own family.

Jul
25

KEY VERSE

[Isaac] said, "Your brother came deceitfully and took your blessing." Esau said, "Isn't he rightly named Jacob? He has deceived me these two times: He took my birthright, and now he's taken my blessing!"
—*Genesis 27:35, 36*

Some time after Isaac and Rebekah were married, Abraham died and was buried in the cave of Machpelah, where Sarah had been buried. Eventually Rebekah gave birth to twin sons—Jacob and Esau. Even before they were born, they struggled within her womb—a precursor to the events described in today's text. It should be pointed out that Isaac and Rebekah contributed to much of the tension that developed between their sons by "playing favorites." Genesis 25:28 tells us, "Isaac . . . loved Esau, but Rebekah loved Jacob."

I. JACOB SECURES A BIRTHRIGHT (GENESIS 25:29-34)

A. A Hungry Brother (vv. 29, 30)

29, 30. *Once when Jacob was cooking some stew, Esau came in from the open country, famished. He said to Jacob, "Quick, let me have some of that red stew! I'm famished!" (That is why he was also called Edom.)*

Although *Jacob* and *Esau* were twins, their personalities and interests were quite different, as verse 27 indicates. Esau was "a skillful hunter, a man of the open country." We might label him an "outdoorsman." For this reason he was his father's favorite. Contributing to Isaac's preference for Esau was his fondness of the food that Esau supplied him, described in verse 28 as "wild game."

Jacob, in contrast, was a "quiet man, staying among the tents." Apparently he was rather meek and not as aggressive as his brother. It seems he had developed some cooking skills and was quite handy around the tent. We should not be surprised, then, that he was Rebekah's favorite son.

In the rearing of children there is always a temptation for those of us who are parents to play favorites. And even when we diligently try to avoid this, our actions may be perceived as favoring one child over another. Even when we try our best to treat our children alike, we end up treating them differently simply because each child is different. However, though we cannot treat our children alike, we must try to treat them fairly. From the account of Jacob and Esau, it seems obvious that Isaac and Rebekah had failed in this critical area.

On the occasion described in our text, *Jacob was cooking some stew*. When Esau *came in from the open country* where he had been hunting or perhaps caring for the flocks, he was *famished*. The aroma from the stew no doubt whetted his appetite even more, and he had to have some of it now—right now!

These two verses tell us a great deal about the two brothers. Esau was clearly a captive of his own appetites. No doubt he was hungry after being out in the field for a time, but he was in no danger of starving to death as he would later claim (v. 32). He just thought he was! Like many today, he lived for the moment. Jacob, on the other hand, looked to the future and cleverly took advantage of his brother's weakness to provide for his own future. Had Jacob been a true brother, he would have generously offered Esau some of the stew he was preparing, not expecting any kind of personal gain from the favor.

Verse 25 of this chapter tells us that Esau received the name that he did because he was "hairy" at his birth. Now he was given another name (perhaps a nickname) based on his desire for the *stew* that Jacob was preparing (probably *red* because of the meat in the stew). The name *Edom*, meaning *red*, became the name by which Esau's descendants were known—Edomites (Genesis 36:9).

B. A Scheming Brother (vv. 31, 32)

31, 32. *Jacob replied, "First sell me your birthright."*

"Look, I am about to die," Esau said. "What good is the birthright to me?"

It was a common practice in the ancient Near East that when a man died, his oldest son received a double portion of the inheritance along with his father's

What Do You Think?

Esau and Jacob were not the first siblings to squabble over family matters, and they certainly haven't been the last. Like Isaac's twins, siblings today fight over inheritances, be it riches or sentimental mementos. In fact, some fight over what they can get from their parents while the parents are still living. They become jealous of each other and fight for their parents' affections and praise. Why do some brothers and sisters fight over such things? How can they call a halt to such bickering?

Is there anything that is worth fighting to keep? If so, what?

family responsibilities. This was the *birthright* Jacob wanted. He wanted Esau to give it to him at that very moment, while Esau was tired and hungry. Once Esau had eaten and rested, Jacob knew that he wouldn't be such an easy mark.

Esau's response must have seemed quite logical to him. After all, if he was going to *die* very shortly, why worry about a birthright that might be years in coming? Esau was not about to starve, but he was such a slave to his physical appetites that he exaggerated his need and convinced himself that he was. We wonder why he didn't appeal to Jacob's mercy, but he had probably had enough experience with Jacob to know that this would never work.

C. A CLEVER DEAL (vv. 33, 34)

33, 34. But Jacob said, "Swear to me first." So he swore an oath to him, selling his birthright to Jacob.

Then Jacob gave Esau some bread and some lentil stew. He ate and drank, and then got up and left.

So Esau despised his birthright.

According to verse 23 of this chapter, Rebekah was told that Esau, her older son, would serve Jacob, her younger son. Since Rebekah was closer to Jacob, she may have shared this revelation with him. Jacob, schemer that he was, may have seen in Esau's hunger the opportunity to fulfill what God had prophesied. In his own mind he may have justified his actions on this basis. "After all," he may have said to himself, "I'm going to come out ahead in the future. Why not cooperate with God and hurry the process along?"

This verse provides some information as to the ingredients of Jacob's stew: it was a *lentil stew*. The lentil is a member of the legume family and was widely grown in the ancient Near East. The lens-shaped seed is less than a quarter of an inch in diameter. It is nutritious, and when mixed in a stew containing meat and other vegetables it is quite delicious.

Had someone challenged Jacob's actions in this matter, he might have responded that it was a good deal for everyone involved. Esau got what he wanted—a meal—and went away satisfied; Jacob got what he wanted—the *birthright*. The concluding statement of verse 34 provides us with the correct understanding: *Esau despised his birthright.* There was no way that a bowl of stew was worth the birthright. But guided by his carnal mind, Esau was unable to keep the two items in proper perspective. The conniving Jacob understood quite well how Esau thought and cleverly took advantage of his brother's weakness.

LIVING BENEATH ONE'S PRIVILEGE

What's the value of a name? Ask "John-John" Kennedy, or Lucy Arnaz, or Franklin Graham, or any of the Rockefeller clan.

What is a family legacy worth? Ask the Walt Disney heirs, or the Hearst family, or the children of people like Jimmy Stewart, Henry Fonda, and Judy Garland.

Most people value their "birthright." Most consider it a privilege to inherit a family legacy of wealth or of character, reputation, and values. Not Esau. He "despised his birthright"—his family name and his promised inheritance. He surrendered it all for nothing more than the instant gratification of his carnal appetites.

Esau's descendants are legion. Think of the millions who sacrifice or risk integrity, purity, virginity, trust, and reputation for just a few moments of pleasure, indulgence, or adulation. Even members of the family of God are often guilty of trading Christian privileges for temporal and sensual rewards.

We are privileged to be called the children of God, and that is what we are (1 John 3:1). But so often we live beneath our privilege, selling our heavenly birthright for little more than a mess of earth's stew.

—R. W. B.

II. JACOB STEALS A BLESSING (GENESIS 27:30-37)

A. JACOB'S DEPARTURE (v. 30)

The preceding verses of chapter 27 tell how Rebekah plotted with Jacob to gain a blessing from Isaac that properly belonged to Esau. It is hard to imagine a mother and son who would plot to deceive an aged and blind husband and father as Rebekah and Jacob did. Or is it? Not really, for again, we see similar acts happening about us all the time. The plot was cleverly planned—the goatskins on Jacob's hands and neck to make him feel like his hairy brother, and Esau's clothes to make Jacob smell like a man of the field. But even with these preparations, the scheme almost failed. "The voice is the voice of Jacob," old Isaac said, "but the hands are the hands of Esau" (v. 22). Nevertheless, Isaac proceeded to bless Jacob.

30. After Isaac finished blessing him and Jacob had scarcely left his father's presence, his brother Esau came in from hunting.

Apparently Esau returned sooner than Jacob had expected, but Jacob was able to get away just in time. Otherwise, a bloody confrontation might have occurred right in the presence of Isaac. The *blessing* that Isaac pronounced on Jacob included an abundance of physical blessings. Isaac asked God to give Jacob "of heaven's dew and of earth's richness—an abundance of grain and new wine" (v. 28). But there were other blessings beyond the physical. Jacob was also given mastery over other nations and over his brothers (v. 29).

B. ISAAC'S DISCOVERY (vv. 31-33)

31, 32. He too prepared some tasty food and brought it to his father. Then he said to him, "My father, sit up and eat some of my game, so that you may give me your blessing."

His father Isaac asked him, "Who are you?"

"I am your son," he answered, "your firstborn, Esau."

Although Esau was a hunter and a man of the field, apparently he had also gained some cooking skills; for after returning from a successful hunt, he *prepared* the *tasty food* that his father loved. He may have come into his father's presence with an air of triumph. He had fulfilled Isaac's request and now he expected to receive his due reward—the coveted *blessing*.

What a shock Isaac must have received when he heard Esau's voice! He thought he had already blessed Esau, but now came the devastating realization: he had been deceived. To confirm his suspicions, he asked, *Who are you?* Perhaps he thought that it might be Jacob who had just arrived. But Esau's answer was emphatic: *I am your son . . . your firstborn, Esau.* The emphasis on being *your firstborn* suggests that he had already begun to suspect that something was amiss.

33. Isaac trembled violently and said, "Who was it, then, that hunted game and brought it to me? I ate it just before you came and I blessed him—and indeed he will be blessed!"

When Esau responded to Isaac's question, *Isaac trembled violently*, realizing that he had been deceived. The statement indicates his intense emotions. Not only was he distraught because he had been deceived by his own son, but his distress was intensified because he could not undo what had been done. He had pronounced the blessing upon Jacob: *and indeed he will be blessed!* In our culture a contract that has been agreed to under duress or fraud can be challenged in the courts. But in that day there was no legal remedy for what happened in this case. Furthermore, when Isaac blessed Jacob, he had called upon God to honor Jacob's blessing. Isaac knew there was no way that God would rescind the blessing even if he tried to.

How to Say It

Abimelech. Uh-BIM-eh-lek.

Edom. EE-dum.

Edomites. EE-dum-ites.

Gideon. GID-ee-un.

Haran. HAIR-un.

Machpelah. Mack-PEA-luh.

Mesopotamia. MESS-uh-puh-TAY-me-uh.

C. ESAU'S DISAPPOINTMENT (v. 34)

34. When Esau heard his father's words, he burst out with a loud and bitter cry and said to his father, "Bless me—me too, my father!"

Now it was Esau's turn to express his anguish. His *cry* is described as *loud and bitter*. It was a soul-wrenching cry of bitter disappointment—a spontaneous outburst at the realization of what had been taken from him. The bitterness that Esau felt would soon turn to anger, which would smolder unchecked until it burst forth in rage against his brother, calling for revenge. This family would never be the same again!

Hoping that there was still some blessing left for him, Esau pleaded, *Bless me—me too, my father!* Even though Jacob had cheated him out of his birthright and now had stolen the blessing that rightfully belonged to him, surely, thought Esau, there ought to be something left for him.

D. ISAAC'S DECLARATION (vv. 35-37)

35, 36. But he said, "Your brother came deceitfully and took your blessing."

Esau said, "Isn't he rightly named Jacob? He has deceived me these two times: He took my birthright, and now he's taken my blessing!" Then he asked, "Haven't you reserved any blessing for me?"

Isaac now realized the full impact of what had happened. He may have begun to realize something else. Even while Rebekah carried the twin brothers, God told her that "the older will serve the younger" (Genesis 25:23). She certainly must have shared this information with Isaac. Yet knowing this, Isaac had worked to secure God's blessing for Esau, who was his favorite son. His efforts to thwart the will of God had failed, even though Jacob had accomplished it by devious and unacceptable means.

There is a note of bitter sarcasm in Esau's reply: *Isn't he rightly named Jacob?* The name *Jacob* means "heel grabber" (Genesis 25:26), or one who tries to trip up, or deceive, another. Esau realized that he had been cheated *two times* by his brother. As a result, he had lost his standing as the favored son. In desperation Esau asked, *Haven't you reserved any blessing for me?*

FAVORITE SONS

I was visiting an elderly widow recently. As she spoke of her several children, she told me without apology that one of her sons was her "favorite." Such admissions make me very nervous, for I know that favoritism like that can lead—indeed, it has led—to serious problems within the family. When parents choose favorites among their children, they almost certainly will indulge their favoritism in some way or another. Equal treatment and fairness are hardly possible in such circumstances, and the result is resentment on the part of the slighted child(ren).

Rebekah preferred Jacob, and she led him to become manipulating and dishonest. Isaac loved Esau better and influenced him (perhaps inadvertently) to develop self-centered instincts and a carnal outlook on life. Values became unbalanced, relationships became jealous and competitive, and the family became, in today's jargon, "dysfunctional."

Not every case of parental favoritism results in such obvious failure. That such situations are potentially harmful, however, is clear. Every child is a gift from God (Psalm 127:3) and needs to be instructed carefully in his ways (Proverbs 22:6). Though we may feel more comfortable with the temperament and personality of some children than with others, our preferences should never be detected by any of our offspring. Nonpartisan parenting should be the aim of every mom and dad. We have the perfect model, for our heavenly Father is "no respecter of persons" in his grand family.

—R. W. B.

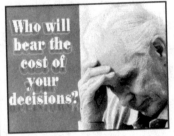

modern parents—or anyone who works with youth—learn from their poor example?

Some have said this situation proves we must treat our children alike. Others argue that individual differences in children call for individual treatment. Who is right? Why?

PRAYER

PRAYER

O God of Abraham, Isaac, and Jacob, thank you that in your infinite wisdom and bountiful grace you were able to use these men in such a way that we today enjoy your blessings of salvation. In the name of your Son and our Savior. Amen.

THOUGHT TO REMEMBER

Let spiritual priorities guide your daily living.

DAILY BIBLE READINGS

Monday, July 19—Jacob and Esau Are Born (Genesis 25:19-26)

Tuesday, July 20—Esau Sells His Birthright (Genesis 25:27-34)

Wednesday, July 21—Rebekah Schemes to Deceive Isaac (Genesis 27:1-17)

Thursday, July 22—Jacob Deceives Isaac (Genesis 27:18-29)

Friday, July 23—Esau Pleads for a Blessing (Genesis 27:30-40)

Saturday, July 24—Because He Had Acted Shrewdly (Luke 16:1-9)

Sunday, July 25—Clean Hands and Pure Hearts (Psalm 24:1-6)

37. Isaac answered Esau, "I have made him lord over you and have made all his relatives his servants, and I have sustained him with grain and new wine. So what can I possibly do for you, my son?"

Isaac's answer was not very reassuring, for it seemed to suggest that there was nothing left for Esau. In the verses that follow, Esau continued to plead for a blessing. Finally Isaac agreed to bless him, but it was not nearly what Esau had hoped.

The New Testament summarizes the tragedy of Esau in this way: "Afterward, as you know, when he wanted to inherit this blessing, he was rejected. He could bring about no change of mind, though he sought the blessing with tears" (Hebrews 12:17).

CONCLUSION
A. THE PEOPLE GOD USES

God in his infinite wisdom chose Abraham to begin the family line through which he would send his Son to bless the earth. Abraham was not perfect by any means. On two occasions he lied about Sarah's being his sister in order to save his life. Yet God was able to use him.

Isaac, Abraham's son, was a good man but did not seem to have the same high level of faith that his father did. However, he did imitate his father in one respect: he used the same ruse that Abraham had used and lied to Abimelech about Rebekah (Genesis 26:6-11). Yet God was able to use him.

The situation got worse with the third generation. As we have seen, neither Esau nor Jacob demonstrated exemplary character. Esau was a slave of his physical passions. He was impatient and lived for the moment. Because the satisfaction of his hunger meant more to him than the birthright to which he as the eldest son had claim, the Scriptures say he "despised his birthright." Jacob, on the other hand, wanted the birthright and was willing to plan ahead to secure it. To acquire it he took advantage of his brother's weaknesses. Today's texts from Genesis show Jacob to be a conniving schemer. Yet God was able to use him.

We could add others to our list of unlikely instruments of God, including Moses, Gideon, David, Peter, and Paul. Regardless of whom we choose, the lesson is the same: God uses imperfect people. There is no other kind for him to use! He still meets us where we are and challenges us to let him use us for his glory. As someone has pointed out, it isn't *ability* that God wants as much as *availability*.

B. SIBLING RIVALRIES

Esau and Jacob give us a vivid example of a sibling rivalry that was made worse because the parents, Isaac and Rebekah, took opposite sides in the conflict. Although the Bible relates only two incidents that highlight this tension, we can be certain that the conflict was an ongoing one over many years.

Such rivalries are common in families where there is more than one child. How can we deal with these in our own families? First of all, we need to treat all of our children equally and try not to play favorites. Our children will not always understand that we are being fair, but we should not allow them to manipulate us. (Also, we ought not to let them manipulate their grandparents.)

We have to do the best we can, bathe our efforts in prayer, and, above all, never give up. We can find consolation in the fact that in many cases children who were bitter rivals while they were growing up become the closest of friends when they become adults. Keep in mind that Esau and Jacob, though separated for many years, later reunited and were reconciled (Genesis 33:1-16).

Discovery Learning

This page contains an alternate lesson plan emphasizing learning activities. Classes desiring such student involvement will find these suggestions helpful. The next page is a reproducible activity page to further enhance discovery learning.

LEARNING GOALS

As a result of participating in this session, the student will be able to:

1. Tell how Jacob tricked his brother and father to secure rights and blessings for himself.

2. Cite instances (from Scripture or from personal experience) of the alienation caused by deceitful words and actions.

3. Determine to live by the truth in every relationship, especially those within his or her own family.

INTO THE LESSON

Write the words *sibling rivalry* on the chalkboard. Ask your students to list as many examples of sibling rivalry as they can. (This activity may be more effective if students work together in small groups. If at all possible, divide your students into four equal-size groups.)

Students will, no doubt, suggest many examples either from their own families or from the families of friends and neighbors they have known. After the students have shared a few stories, encourage them to suggest examples from the Bible. They may list Cain and Abel, Jacob and Esau, Joseph and his brothers, and perhaps others.

Lead into the Bible study by saying that today's story of Jacob and Esau will show that God is able to use even sibling rivalry to accomplish his purpose.

INTO THE WORD

Ask your students to read Genesis 25:27-34 aloud in their small groups and then make a list of the personality characteristics that distinguish Esau and Jacob. In what ways do these traits come from their parents? *Students should be able to identify Esau's character as a manly outdoorsman (like his country-boy father), outgoing, living for the moment, a captive of his own appetites. They should also be able to identify Jacob as quiet (like his city-girl mother), logical, patient, cunning, taking tactical advantage of others' weaknesses, and one who takes the longer view of events.*

After each group has had the opportunity to share their ideas with the rest of the class, ask your students to think of modern examples of these two personality types. They should be able to think of any number of modern personalities like Esau who live for the moment and are captives of their own appetites. They should also

easily be able to identify modern examples of Jacob's cunning—those who are more than happy to take advantage of the weaknesses of others to gain what they want in life.

Next, assign each of four small groups one of the main characters in the story (Isaac, Rebekah, Esau, and Jacob). Ask them to use the following passages to determine what each of them did wrong.

- Isaac (Genesis 25:23, 28; 27:1-4)
- Rebekah (Genesis 25:28; 27:5-17, 42-46)
- Esau (Genesis 25:29-34; 27:34, 38, 41)
- Jacob (Genesis 25:29-34; 27:11-27)

As they share their answers with the rest of the class, help them to see that even though Rebekah had been told God's plan for her sons (and she had probably shared this information with the family), none of them gracefully accepted God's desires without trying to work things out themselves.

INTO LIFE

Ask each of the four groups to write a summary of the events of chapter 27 told from the viewpoint of the character they were assigned earlier. Encourage each group to tell the story in such a way as to try to justify their character's actions. After they have each had an opportunity to tell their version, ask them, "Did God need all of this help to accomplish his purpose?"

The Bible says that Esau "despised his birthright." We could list examples of the same attitude from modern life—exchanging integrity for a pittance, trading honor for a good test grade, or a good reputation for popularity. Ask the class to take time in their small groups to share some ways in which they or people they have known have "despised their birthright"—times in which they found themselves so enslaved to their immediate desires that they were able to convince themselves to do something as illogical as trading a birthright for stew. Allow several in each group to share their thoughts.

Distribute copies of the reproducible activity page that follows. Give the students about five minutes to work; then ask volunteers to share some of their results.

Close your session by reminding your students that in spite of the dishonorable way in which any of us has acted, God still blesses and honors his covenant. Even though Jacob did not deserve God's favor, he received it—and so do we.

A Deceitful Heart

Genesis 25:26 tells us that Jacob was born holding on to Esau's heel. The name Jacob in Hebrew means something like "to follow at the heel," which means "to supplant," "to trick," or "to deceive"—a rather accurate description of a character trait Jacob received from his father and grandfather.

Later in describing the character of the descendants of Jacob, the prophet Jeremiah said, "The heart is deceitful above all things and beyond cure. Who can understand it?" (Jeremiah 17:9). The word he uses for "deceitful" is related to the word *heel*. So Jeremiah is basically saying, "The heart of everyone is Jacob-like and in desperate need of God."

In the heart-shaped space provided below, list as many Jacob-like traits as you can that are typical of modern men (and women) and that show their desperate need of God.

A Pure Heart

David prayed, "Create in me a pure heart, O God" (Psalm 51:10). Over every Jacob-like trait you listed above, write an opposite pure character trait that comes from drawing close to God. Pray that God will help you demonstrate the latter more often than the former.

JACOB'S FLIGHT AND VISION

LESSON 9

WHY TEACH THIS LESSON?

Where Is God? That is the title, or part of the title, of twelve books listed in the current issue of *Books in Print.* Some of the titles ask about specific situations: *Where Is God When It Hurts?* or . . . *When a Child Suffers?* or just . . . *When You Need Him?* Others are more general: simply *Where Is God?* Without reading them all, or at least reviews of them, it is impossible to say whether they are written by people of faith or not.

Some of them are, like *Where Is God When It Hurts?* by Philip Yancey. It is clear that even people of faith sometimes ask, "Where is God?" Especially when circumstances bring pain, sorrow, and suffering, believers wonder why God doesn't intervene and deliver them. Where is he, anyway? What's he doing? We feel like the frightened disciples in the boat, "Master, don't you care that we're going to die?"

Perhaps some of your students are hurting today. Some of them may be asking, "Where is God in all this?" Use today's lesson to encourage your students to keep their eyes open. They, like Jacob, may discover that God shows up even in places where he is not expected!

INTRODUCTION

A. THE LORD IS IN THIS PLACE

When the first Russian cosmonaut returned to earth, he triumphantly announced to the world that now he had proof that there was no God. He had circled the earth in his spacecraft, and in all of outer space he had seen nothing of God or nothing to indicate God's presence. We stand amazed at the naivete of this man, who in many other respects must have been quite intelligent.

Yet consider Jacob. He was fleeing for his life from the wrath of his brother. But it also seems obvious that he was fleeing from the presence of God. Perhaps he was deliberately fleeing God and the responsibility that the presence of God involved, like Jonah many centuries after him. Or perhaps he simply believed the God of his fathers was limited to the place where his father was—that fleeing his father's house necessitated fleeing his God. For whatever reason, it is clear from his cry of amazement when he awoke from his dream that he believed he had left God behind: "Surely the Lord is in this place, and I was not aware of it."

Now let us consider ourselves, for we are all like Jacob. Our actions occasionally betray the fact that we think we have wandered too far from God for him to reach us, or that we can deliberately run far enough to get beyond the presence of God. We ought to pray that when this happens, God will jar us back to our senses and cause us to cry out, "Surely the Lord is in this place, and I was not aware of it."

DEVOTIONAL READING:
PSALM 121

LESSON SCRIPTURE:
GENESIS 27:41–28:22

PRINTED TEXT:
GENESIS 27:41; 28:10-16, 18-22

LESSON AIMS

After participating in this lesson, each student should:

1. Summarize the details surrounding God's appearance to Jacob at Bethel.

2. Relate a personal experience in which God was at work even though he or she was initially unaware of God's presence.

3. Praise God for granting his presence and blessings even though we are undeserving.

Aug
1

KEY VERSE

"I am with you and will watch over you wherever you go, and I will bring you back to this land. I will not leave you until I have done what I have promised you."
—Genesis 28:15

B. LESSON BACKGROUND

The events described in today's lesson follow immediately after those covered in last week's lesson. That lesson ended with Esau pleading with his father for some kind of a blessing to replace the one out of which Jacob had cunningly cheated him. But the blessing that Isaac gave was more like a curse than a blessing. It included the promise that Esau would live by the sword and serve his brother (Genesis 27:40). While Esau himself did not experience the fulfillment of these words, his descendants (the Edomites) would later be in frequent submission to the descendants of Jacob (the Israelites). It is not surprising, in view of the blessing that Esau missed and the blessing that he received, that he reacted with hatred toward his brother and began to plot against him.

I. ESAU'S HATRED (GENESIS 27:41)

41. Esau held a grudge against Jacob because of the blessing his father had given him. He said to himself, "The days of mourning for my father are near; then I will kill my brother Jacob."

When Esau first learned that his brother had cheated him out of his father's *blessing,* he "burst out with a loud and bitter cry" (v. 34). With the passing of time, his disappointment grew into a seething hatred.

Driven by this hatred, Esau began to plot how he would even the score against his brother. One who acts out of passion on the spur of the moment can be a dangerous and violent person. But once the moment of rage has passed, such a person usually regains control of his emotions and begins to behave more rationally. Far more dangerous is the man who is able to control his emotions for the moment, but allows them to simmer slowly until they become intensely bitter. This type of person is able to plot his revenge calmly, often carrying it out in violence.

At this point Isaac was advanced in years, and it seemed evident that his death was not far away. Esau, who loved and respected his *father,* did not want to cause him grief by an act of violence within the family. Instead he determined to restrain his revenge until Isaac had died and *the days of mourning* for him had passed.

We do not know how long these days of mourning typically lasted. According to Genesis 50:3, Jacob was mourned seventy days by the Egyptians. Then, when his body was taken back to Canaan for burial, the caravan mourned him an additional seven days just before entering Canaan (Genesis 50:10). The seven days likely reflects the more common mourning period in the family of Abraham.

Esau's plan was to wait until his father had died and been "properly mourned," *then* he would *kill* his *brother Jacob.* However, Isaac lived for many years after this, and at his death was buried by both Jacob and Esau (Genesis 35:29). By then, Esau had put aside his anger and no longer wished to kill Jacob.

II. JACOB'S FLIGHT (GENESIS 28:10-16)

Esau felt so strongly about getting revenge that he was not able to keep his intentions to himself. He may have confided his desire to kill his brother to some of his friends, or he may inadvertently have let slip what he had in mind. In any event Rebekah learned about it and told Jacob about Esau's plan. Her advice, which made good sense under the circumstances, was for Jacob to flee to her brother Laban in Haran. Perhaps she had maintained some degree of contact with Laban and knew that Jacob could find a refuge there. Or perhaps she simply believed the family ties would be strong enough for Jacob to be welcome even though he was a stranger to Laban. After all, Abraham's servant had showed up

WHAT DO YOU THINK?

Esau had a legitimate complaint—he had been cheated! The more he thought about it, the madder he became until he hated his brother. The only thing that kept him from killing Jacob was respect for their father. That still happens today. People are wronged, hurt, or offended in some way, and they nurse their anger until it grows into hatred. It is easy to say one ought to forgive but much harder to practice it. So we begin to look for ways to exact revenge. What advice would you give someone who had been wronged by another? What would you do to help the two restore their broken relationship?

there several years earlier and had been welcomed. That was how Rebekah had come to be Isaac's wife (Genesis 24).

However, Rebekah did not want to reveal to Isaac the real purpose for Jacob's departure. Instead, she told him that she wanted Jacob to find a wife among her own people rather than from among the pagan peoples around them in Canaan. Esau had married two Canaanite wives, and Rebekah complained that they were a source of frustration to her (Genesis 27:42-46).

This seemed plausible enough to Isaac, so he called Jacob in, blessed him, and sent him on his way. When Esau learned the stated reason for Jacob's departure, he realized that his father did not approve of his taking Canaanite wives. It appears that Esau tried to get back in his father's good graces by marrying a daughter of Ishmael. He apparently believed that since Ishmael was related to Abraham, this would be acceptable to Isaac. However, God had already made very clear his intention to establish his covenant with Isaac, not Ishmael (Genesis 17:19-21). Thus Esau's marriage may only have added to the tension between him and his father.

A. JACOB'S REST (vv. 10, 11)
10. Jacob left Beersheba and set out for Haran.

Jacob's journey from *Beersheba*, located in the southern part of Canaan, to *Haran*, located in northern Mesopotamia east of the Euphrates River, would cover several hundred miles through rugged, semi-desert terrain. Furthermore, there was a good chance that Jacob would encounter some hostile tribes or individuals along the way. We are not told what provisions Jacob took along with him for the trip, which may have taken several weeks. Since he left in haste (Genesis 27:43), he probably did not have much.

11. When he reached a certain place, he stopped for the night because the sun had set. Taking one of the stones there, he put it under his head and lay down to sleep.

Beersheba, where Jacob started, was about forty-five miles southwest of Jerusalem. Luz (later named Bethel), where Jacob stopped, was about a dozen miles north of Jerusalem; thus Jacob had traveled close to sixty miles since he left home. He had been on the road probably three or four days, then, at this point. Exhausted as he must have been by a long day's journey, all he wanted was a place where he could stop and rest. At sunset, *he reached a certain place.* The Hebrew has the definite article ("*the* place"), suggesting that Jacob's arrival at this particular location was no accident. It was not by Jacob's plan that he arrived at this place, however. Jacob was soon to discover that Another was guiding his steps on this journey.

As Jacob prepared for a night's rest, he took *one of the stones there* and *put it under his head.* The Hebrew text reads, "He took from the stones of the place and set up his pillow." That one stone was used by Jacob for a pillow is clear from verse 18. His heavy outer garment likely served as bedding.

B. JACOB'S DREAM (v. 12)
12. He had a dream in which he saw a stairway resting on the earth, with its top reaching to heaven, and the angels of God were ascending and descending on it.

At some point during the night Jacob *had a dream*, but this was no ordinary dream! This is one of several accounts recorded in the Old Testament of divine revelation coming to someone through a dream. Later, Jacob's son Joseph had a number of dreams and was also given the ability to interpret dreams.

In his dream Jacob saw *a stairway resting on the earth.* The *top* of this stairway reached *to heaven.* Years before men had attempted to build their own stairway to

Heaven (the tower of Babel), and God had thwarted their efforts (Genesis 11:4-9). Now God himself opened the way. Communication between Heaven and earth must take place on God's terms, never on man's.

Apparently the vision conveyed to Jacob that no matter how far he had run, he had not moved beyond God's care and control. We are not told the significance of the angels both *ascending and descending*, but it may have symbolized the communication that was to take place between God and Jacob, as well as that which he desires with all mankind. Was Jesus thinking of this incident when he was speaking to Nathanael and referred to himself as the one upon whom the angels of God would be "ascending and descending" (John 1:51)? Jesus is the "stairway" by which God has reached down to communicate with mankind (John 1:1, 14).

C. GOD'S REVELATION (vv. 13-15)

13. There above it stood the LORD, and he said: "I am the LORD, the God of your father Abraham and the God of Isaac. I will give you and your descendants the land on which you are lying.

Above this stairway *stood the Lord*. We are not given a description of what the Lord looked like, and appropriately so, for "no one has ever seen God" (John 1:18). Jacob knew from the words spoken to him that this was no ordinary dream; it was clearly of the Lord. Probably the last thing in the world that he expected at this time was a revelation from God. And although he did not deserve such a revelation, Jacob—a cheat and a swindler—certainly needed one. In spite of his sins and failures, God intended to use him in his plan for the salvation of the human race.

When the Lord began to speak to Jacob, he identified himself as *the God of your father Abraham and the God of Isaac*. God had made a covenant with both Abraham and Isaac, promising them a large posterity and the land of Canaan as their own. How much information about this covenant Isaac had shared with Jacob we do not know, but certainly Jacob knew something about it. Now God indicated that he was renewing this covenant with Jacob. The very *land* on which Jacob was sleeping was a part of the land that God had promised to his father and grandfather. The idea that this promise could ever be fulfilled in him must have struck Jacob as highly improbable. How could Jacob—a fugitive from his brother and a stranger in the land where he traveled—ever hope to inherit anything but more trouble?

Note, too, the irony. Jacob had schemed and deceived to achieve for himself greater rights and blessings, and he had only made himself a fugitive. Now, helpless and virtually hopeless, he achieves a greater blessing than he could have imagined—simply by God's grace!

14. Your descendants will be like the dust of the earth, and you will spread to the west and to the east, to the north and to the south. All peoples on earth will be blessed through you and your offspring.

Now the dream became even more amazing. *Your descendants will be like the dust of the earth.* How could this promise ever be fulfilled in a man who not only had no children, but was not even married? Yet the situation was not entirely hopeless. After all, Jacob's own grandfather and grandmother had been blessed with a son after all hope of having a child had passed.

You will spread to the west and to the east, to the north and to the south. In every direction from where he lay, Jacob's descendants would scatter. Furthermore, *through* his *offspring, all peoples on earth* would be *blessed*. How ironic that one who was then a curse to his own family should someday be a source of blessing

HOW TO SAY IT

Beersheba. Beer-SHE-buh.

Bethel. BETH-ul.

Canaanite. KAY-nuh-nite.

Edomites. EE-dum-ites.

Esau. EE-saw.

Euphrates. You-FRAY-teez.

Haran. HAIR-un.

Ishmael. ISH-may-el.

Jeroboam. Jair-uh-BOE-um.

Laban. LAY-bun.

Luz. Luzz.

Melchizedek. Mel-KIZZ-eh-dek.

Mesopotamia. MESS-uh-puh-TAY-me-uh .

Nathanael. Nuh-THAN-yull.

to the nations! We know that blessing to be Jesus Christ, who many generations later would be born to descendants of Jacob and would draw in many "from east and west and north and south" to be part of his kingdom (Luke 13:29).

15. *I am with you and will watch over you wherever you go, and I will bring you back to this land. I will not leave you until I have done what I have promised you.*"

Jacob was just beginning a journey that would take him far from home for a long time (twenty years, according to Genesis 31:38). He certainly must have been apprehensive about what the future held for him. Now came God's reassuring words. God promised to be *with* Jacob—to *watch over* him, protect him every step of the way, and eventually return him to *this land*. He would never *leave* Jacob until he had accomplished what he had *promised*.

BETTER THAN A DREAM

Not long ago a popular retort to someone's plans or ideas was, "In your dreams!" It meant that someone's ambitions or fantasies were far less than likely to be fulfilled. Dreams that actually do come true seem to be disproportionately outnumbered by those that don't. Occasionally, however, one's dreams are realized: a girl actually marries a "knight in shining armor," a college graduate lands the perfect job, and nice guys finish first rather than last.

In some cases dreams challenge individuals to do some serious self-examination and make some long overdue changes. Consider the account of Jacob's dream in today's lesson text. We, like him, would react with awe and reverence if God spoke to us in a dream. Indeed, perhaps we wish that he *would* communicate his purposes and promises in such a direct manner or tell us personally, "I will not leave you. . . ." Jacob was truly blessed to be reassured of God's covenant through the miracle of a dream.

But think about this: we have our own miracle of God's revelation. The Bible is God's book; it is "God-breathed" (2 Timothy 3:16). In it God *has* communicated his purposes and promises to us. He *has* said that he will never leave us (Hebrews 13:5). We should treat this sacred record with awe and reverence—for through it God speaks. —R. W. B.

D. JACOB'S RESPONSE (v. 16)

16. *When Jacob awoke from his sleep, he thought, "Surely the LORD is in this place, and I was not aware of it."*

When Jacob awoke, he was a different man. Perhaps he had believed that God could operate only in a small area, specifically the area where his family lived. Now he realized that God knows no geographical limitations. Not only was God back home with his family, but God was also in the very spot where he lay!

Many today share Jacob's limited faith. Because God permits evil in the world, they believe that he has limited power. Or because he fails to extricate them from the mess they have made of their lives, they reject him as powerless. Or because they deem their sins so terrible, they refuse to believe that he can forgive them.

III. JACOB'S MEMORIAL (GENESIS 28:18-22)

A. THE ANOINTED PILLAR (v. 18)

18. *Early the next morning Jacob took the stone he had placed under his head and set it up as a pillar and poured oil on top of it.*

Verse 17 tells us that Jacob was filled with fear as a result of his experience during the night. *Early the next morning Jacob took the stone* that had been his pillow during the night and used it to construct a *pillar*. Then he *poured oil on top of it* as an act of consecration. Actually, Jacob was not consecrating the stone; he was consecrating the spot where God had revealed himself to him.

The visual for lesson 9 illustrates Jacob's dream at Bethel and highlights God's promise to protect him and bring him back to the land of promise (v. 15).

WHAT DO YOU THINK?

Jacob probably worshiped God before he had his dream, and genuinely so. But when God appeared to him, Jacob's worship took on a whole new dimension. He submitted to God, trusted in him, and attempted to walk with him. It went from ritual to real. It became important to Jacob that he know God and please him. We cannot duplicate Jacob's experience to deepen our worship, so how can we move our own worship from the ritual to the real? What impact does real worship have on your life?

PRAYER

Dear God, help us learn from the experiences of Jacob. Keep us from seeking to take advantage of our family and our friends through questionable practices or misleading words. Help us to grow in faith as Jacob finally did. In Christ's name we pray. Amen.

THOUGHT TO REMEMBER

"Where can I flee from your presence?" (Psalm 139:7).

B. A NEW NAME (v. 19)

19. He called that place Bethel, though the city used to be called Luz.

Bethel means "house of God." (The earlier name, *Luz,* means "nut tree" or "almond tree.") Jacob's encounter had so overwhelmed him that he had no doubt that God was present. Jacob was not proclaiming this spot to be the only place where God lived; like the erection of the pillar, the new name marked this location as one of great meaning for Jacob. Bethel played a significant part in later Hebrew history. It was one of the places where Samuel held court and judged Israel (1 Samuel 7:16); and it was there that Jeroboam, who ruled the northern kingdom following the division of Israel, erected a golden calf to keep the people in the north from going to Jerusalem to worship (1 Kings 12:28-33).

C. JACOB'S VOW (vv. 20-22)

20, 21. Then Jacob made a vow, saying, "If God will be with me and will watch over me on this journey I am taking and will give me food to eat and clothes to wear so that I return safely to my father's house, then the LORD will be my God.

If God will be with me . . . then the Lord will be my God. Some believe that these words show that Jacob was driving a bargain with God. His reputation would certainly leave him open to such a charge. However, at this point in Jacob's spiritual pilgrimage, we might better see this as claiming God's promise and responding to it: "If God will be with me [and I believe he will], then. . . ." Jacob obviously had some growing to do, but the next verse indicates that he was not thinking simply of getting things from God; he also wanted to give a portion of God's provisions back to him.

22. And this stone that I have set up as a pillar will be God's house, and of all that you give me I will give you a tenth."

This stone . . . will be God's house. Jacob was not affirming that he believed that God actually lived in the stone that he had set up. Such a crude form of paganism may have been accepted by some of the Canaanites in the land around Jacob, but this was not his religion. This statement may be taken as Jacob's pledge that someday he would build here a more fitting altar, monument, or structure to the glory of God. And indeed, Jacob did eventually return to Bethel, and built there an altar to mark the time when God appeared to him (Genesis 35:6, 7).

I will give you a tenth. Jacob made a second commitment. Recognizing that all of his material blessings would come from God, he pledged to return to him a tenth, or a tithe, of all those blessings. Abraham earlier had given tithes to Melchizedek (Genesis 14:18-20). These two examples indicate that tithing was an accepted practice many years before the instructions in the law of Moses were given.

CONCLUSION

An atheist wanted to proclaim his denial of the existence of God. So he hired a skywriter to write the following message across the sky: GOD IS NOWHERE. But just as the pilot finished writing the words, a shift in the wind changed the message to read: GOD IS NOW HERE.

Jacob was not an atheist, but his idea of God was a rather limited one. The way he lived his life indicated that God did not have an important place in his decision-making. When he left his home and fled for his life, he apparently left his convictions about God at home. Then God confronted Jacob in the way that God often confronts us—when we are tired, lonely, and hurting. Jacob's dream convinced him that God was not confined to one small locality but was everywhere! We too need to come to that same conclusion—and do so before we are confronted with dire circumstances.

Discovery Learning

This page contains an alternate lesson plan emphasizing learning activities. Classes desiring such student involvement will find these suggestions helpful. The next page is a reproducible activity page to further enhance discovery learning.

LEARNING GOALS

As a result of this lesson, your students should be able to:

1. Summarize the details surrounding God's appearance to Jacob at Bethel.

2. Relate a personal experience in which God was at work even though he or she was initially unaware of God's presence.

3. Praise God for granting his presence and blessings even though we are undeserving.

INTO THE LESSON

Introduce this lesson by asking your students to suggest various ways that God makes himself known. Write their answers on a sheet of newsprint. Some answers are through the Bible, through a personal tragedy (death, disease, financial reverse), through answered prayer, through another person's witness, through a sermon, through music, or through a special blessing (such as the birth of a child).

In today's lesson we will learn how God encountered Jacob and made himself known in a dream. The promises God made to Jacob in that dream still have relevance for us today, as we shall see in our lesson.

INTO THE WORD

Review the events that happened in last week's lesson. Jacob's flight to Haran in this lesson was necessitated by his acts of deception in last week's lesson, which angered Esau to the point of murderous hatred (Genesis 27:41).

In this lesson we see that God is faithful to reveal himself even when we are not looking for him. God's self-disclosure to Jacob was actually a reaffirmation of the covenant he had made with Abraham and renewed with Isaac. As such, it contained multiple promises. Ask your students to read Genesis 28:12-16 and identify and explain each promise:

• Land (v. 13). Jacob was heir to the same land God had promised to Abraham—Canaan, the land of promise.

• Descendants (v. 14a). As Israel, Jacob would give his name to the descendants of Abraham—the Israelites (Jews).

• A Descendant (v. 14b). This promise was fulfilled in Jesus Christ.

• Presence (v. 15). God promised to go with Jacob even to faraway Haran. This contradicted the popular belief that gods worked only in specific areas and functions.

Ask the class, "If God appeared to you in a spectacular vision and spoke in an audible voice, what would your response be?" Obviously, life for a person who had such an experience would be changed forever. Such was the case with Jacob. Have a volunteer read Genesis 28:18-22. Then distribute a sheet of paper with the title "Jacob's Response" at the top and verse numbers 18-22 down the left side. Working individually or in small groups, students should fill in the chart by noting what is said of Jacob's response in each verse.

18: He worshiped God by building an altar.

19: He named the place "Bethel," i.e.,"house of God."

20, 21: He acknowledged God's promises and vowed to serve God.

22: He promised to build a proper altar or sanctuary for the worship of God at Bethel and to give God a tithe of everything he received.

INTO LIFE

In Genesis 28:20-22 Jacob made what appears to be a bargain with God. Have any of your students ever tried to negotiate a deal with God? How do your students feel about making deals with God? What are the hazards?

There is a better way to look at Jacob's "bargain" with God. He may have been making a promise to God as a result of this life-changing encounter. In that case it was not so much a bargain as an expression of praise to God and an affirmation of faith in God.

Tell the class, "Jacob apparently thought he was leaving everything—including God. But in his vision he learned that God was still with him." Then ask, "What experiences have you had when you were not specifically aware of God's presence for a time but then came to realize he was with you?" Be prepared to relate a personal example to initiate the discussion. Perhaps it was when a loved one died and you found a strength not your own to hold up under your grief. Or perhaps you took on a job you feared you could not handle but found God gave you the strength to do it.

In closing, challenge your students to praise God during the coming week for all the blessings and promises that flow from his hand.

A Sibling Rivalry Without Rival!

The relationship between Jacob and Esau went way beyond sibling rivalry! This was hatred, and each brother was partly to blame. Look up the following Scriptures and note how each brother fanned the flames of hatred.

JACOB

Genesis 25:30, 31

Told Esau to sell him his birthright

Genesis 27:6-17

tricked his father

Genesis 27:18-29

tricked his father

ESAU

Genesis 25:32, 34

Esau dispised his BIRTH RIGHT

Hebrews 12:16

for single meal sold his inheritance

Genesis 27:41

Planned to Kill Jacob

My Bethel

For Jacob, a place that had formerly been called Luz became "Bethel," the house of God. It was a special place for Jacob, symbolizing a significant milestone in his spiritual life.

Perhaps there is a "Bethel" in your life. It might be a place, an object, even a memory. It symbolizes for you a time when God seemed especially close, and it has perhaps shaped your spiritual life since that time.

What is your Bethel? How does it draw you closer to God? What can you do to help others draw closer to him as well?

JACOB'S STRUGGLE AT PENIEL

LESSON 10

WHY TEACH THIS LESSON?

He was a hard man. Feeling no need for God in his own life, he ridiculed those who professed faith in Christ. His wit was sharp, and he used it mercilessly.

Then he got cancer. After surgery, he hovered between life and death. A preacher began to visit him daily and to read Scripture and to pray with him. One day the preacher told him the story of Jacob, and the sick man was intrigued.

When he was well enough, he began to attend church services. When a friend asked him what had happened, he said, "I wrestled with an angel." Comparing his earlier life with the deceptive Jacob, the man told how Jacob had wrestled with an angel and was never the same again. After looking the angel of death in the face, the man said, he could never again be what he had been.

Probably none of your students is as callous as this man was, but perhaps there are some who have been a little like Jacob in trying to get by on their own cunning. Use this lesson to challenge your students to submit to God's plan and to find God's blessing in whatever struggles they may be experiencing.

INTRODUCTION

A. FIXING THE WORKS

An old mountaineer came one day into a watchmaker's shop, bringing with him the hands from a large old-fashioned clock. "I want you to fix these," he said to the watchmaker. "They jist don't keep the right time anymore."

"But there's nothing wrong with these hands," replied the watchmaker. "The trouble is in the works. Bring the clock in; that's the only way I can fix it."

"But it's the hands that don't work," argued the old man. Nothing that the watchmaker said could convince him that the real trouble was in the works and not in the hands. Finally in anger the mountaineer cried, "I knowed it! I knowed it all along. You jist want to git that clock in here so's you kin work on it and charge me a fancy price. Well, I'm not dumb enough to let you git away with it!"

Foolish as this man was, his caution was very much like that of Jacob, who tried to control and manage his life without addressing the real problems on the inside. His promise at Bethel was a good start (recall last week's lesson), but for the next twenty years Jacob still had difficulty putting himself under God's authority. Perhaps he feared that the price would be too high. But at Peniel he finally realized that true victory would never be his unless he was willing to surrender the "works" of his life to God.

B. LESSON BACKGROUND

Rebekah had sent Jacob to her brother Laban to escape the revenge of Esau and to find a wife from among her own people. Jacob's mission was successful on both counts. He spent seven years working for Laban, after which he married his two daughters, Leah and Rachel. To complete the agreement for Rachel, Jacob had to work seven more years, and then six more years in order to have his own livestock. Rebekah had urged Jacob to stay with Laban "for a while" (Genesis 27:43, 44); that short while had turned into twenty years!

DEVOTIONAL READING:
PSALM 25:1-7

LESSON SCRIPTURE:
GENESIS 32:3–33:17

PRINTED TEXT:
GENESIS 32:9-11, 24-30; 33:1-4

LESSON AIMS

After this lesson each student will be able to:

1. Tell how Jacob was reconciled with Esau and of the prayer and divine struggle that preceded the event.

2. Explain the significance of Jacob's actions as he prepared to meet Esau, and describe the change in his character these actions represent.

3. Examine his or her own life for an occasion of struggling with God, and seek God's blessing in it.

Aug
8

KEY VERSE

I am unworthy of all the kindness and faithfulness you have shown your servant.

—Genesis 32:10

LESSON 10 NOTES

During this twenty-year period, Jacob prospered. His wives and their hand-maidens bore him eleven sons and a daughter. In addition God blessed him materially and, especially in the last six years, his flocks increased. Laban's flocks, which Jacob tended, had grown large during the first fourteen years Jacob worked for Laban. But in the last six, while Jacob's flocks were growing stronger, Laban's grew weaker. This led to growing tensions between Laban and Jacob.

Eventually God told Jacob to leave Haran and return to Canaan—"the land of your fathers" (Genesis 31:3). Jacob realized that Laban would not be happy with his leaving, and so he slipped away secretly.

Learning of Jacob's departure, Laban pursued him; but before he caught up with him, God spoke to Laban in a dream, telling him to deal cautiously with Jacob (Genesis 31:24). The meeting of the two men was not exactly congenial, but they agreed to go their separate ways. They raised a heap of stones, which they agreed would mark the boundary beyond which neither would pass. Laban's words to Jacob formed a benediction that many Christians still use: "May the Lord keep watch between you and me when we are away from each other" (Genesis 31:49). After this meeting, Jacob and his family and flocks continued to move southward toward the territory where Esau lived.

I. JACOB PRAYS (GENESIS 32:9-11)

A. A PRAYER OF HUMILITY (vv. 9, 10)

As Jacob and his company drew closer, he sent messengers to Esau, who was living in "the land of Seir, the country of Edom" (Genesis 32:3), located south and east of the Dead Sea. The messengers were instructed to convey to Esau the word that Jacob came in peace, seeking reconciliation with him. But when the messengers returned, they brought word that Esau was coming to meet Jacob with four hundred men. Jacob assumed the worst and reacted with "great fear and distress" (v. 7). He figured that Esau had organized a group of men in order to gain the revenge against Jacob that he had never been able to obtain.

9. Then Jacob prayed, "O God of my father Abraham, God of my father Isaac, O LORD, who said to me, 'Go back to your country and your relatives, and I will make you prosper,'

Jacob had good reason to go to God in prayer. He knew that the sizable group approaching him, led by Esau, could easily overpower him. And with the numbers of family and flocks accompanying him, there was really no way he could escape if Esau chose to pursue him.

Jacob began his prayer by addressing Yahweh as the *God of* his *father Isaac* and his grandfather *Abraham*. Then he mentioned the promise that God had made to him earlier during his flight from Laban. Jacob was in this precarious situation because God had told him to return to the *country* of his fathers. He claimed that God had promised to *make* him *prosper*. But that is not exactly what God had said. God had promised Jacob, "I will be with you" (Genesis 31:3). God's abiding presence with us is no guarantee that everything will "go well" or that our circumstances will always come out the way we want them to.

10. I am unworthy of all the kindness and faithfulness you have shown your servant. I had only my staff when I crossed this Jordan, but now I have become two groups.

During his twenty-year "exile," Jacob had grown in his faith. He approached God with a humility that was not evident earlier in his life. Formerly he had depended on his cleverness and cunning to get what he wanted. Now he acknowledged that God had showered his *kindness and faithfulness* on him and had opened his heart to new truth, in spite of the fact that he was so *unworthy* of such treatment. Jacob was showing signs of real spiritual growth.

WHAT DO YOU THINK?

Jacob assumed that the Lord had promised more than he actually had. Jacob claimed the Lord had promised to make him "prosper." What the Lord had actually promised was to be with Jacob. Humans have an amazing capability of believing what they want to believe. Thus people quote Scriptures that don't exist or otherwise misrepresent God's promises. "The Lord helps those who help themselves" is widely believed, but it's not in the Bible. "A God of love couldn't send anyone to Hell" is another popular but wrong belief.

Why is it so easy to assume that the Lord has promised us more than he has? What alleged promises do people put stock in that are without foundation? How can we help them see what God has actually promised?

The visual for lesson 10 (see page 419) cites Genesis 32:10 and reminds us that none of us is worthy of the grace of God. Praise God that he gives it to us anyway!

Jacob noted that when he had crossed the Jordan River during his flight from Esau, he had nothing but his *staff*. God had blessed him so that his possessions were now so many that he could divide them into *two groups*. Jacob's sentiments can be echoed by every Christian: we have been brought out of spiritual poverty into immeasurable wealth, and we are *unworthy* of such treatment.

B. A PRAYER FOR DELIVERANCE (v. 11)

11. Save me, I pray, from the hand of my brother Esau, for I am afraid he will come and attack me, and also the mothers with their children.

Jacob thought of *Esau* as he had been twenty years earlier. As far as we know, there had been no communication between the two during that time. Jacob remembered Esau as impulsive and ill-tempered, and that caused him to fear for his own safety and for the safety of his wives and *children*. Apparently it never occurred to Jacob that Esau might have changed, even as he himself had changed during that time. Still, we can understand why he felt as he did. After all, why else but for battle did Esau need a four-hundred-man escort?

II. JACOB WRESTLES WITH AN ANGEL (GENESIS 32:24-30)

A. THE STRUGGLE (vv. 24, 25)

As the moment drew near for the two brothers to meet, Jacob selected a sizable number of sheep, goats, camels, cattle, and donkeys to be sent by his servants as a gift to Esau. He also sent his family across the Jabbok River, a tributary of the Jordan that flows east, about halfway between the Dead Sea and the Sea of Galilee. Only Jacob remained behind.

24, 25. So Jacob was left alone, and a man wrestled with him till daybreak. When the man saw that he could not overpower him, he touched the socket of Jacob's hip so that his hip was wrenched as he wrestled with the man.

Jacob was left alone with his thoughts and his fears. Suddenly, or so it appears, he was attacked without warning. Here we have no description of the assailant except that he was a *man*. Hosea 12:4 tells us that he was an angel.

Jacob, in spite of the fact that he was advanced in years (according to the information provided in Genesis, he would have been close to one hundred years old), struggled valiantly and held his own until the dawning of the new day. The angel then demonstrated his supernatural ability when he *touched the socket of Jacob's hip* and *wrenched* it.

B. JACOB'S DEMAND (v. 26)

26. Then the man said, "Let me go, for it is daybreak."

But Jacob replied, "I will not let you go unless you bless me."

When the stranger touched his thigh joint and left him crippled, Jacob must have realized that he was not just an ordinary desert marauder, but was in some sense divine, or a divine messenger. (He had already encountered angels of God, according to Genesis 32:1, 2.) Thus, when the stranger asked to be released, Jacob refused to let him go unless he received a blessing.

Hosea 12:4 provides an interesting commentary on this contest. Speaking of Jacob, the prophet said, "He struggled with the angel and overcame him; he wept and begged for his favor." From wrestling, Jacob turned to supplication—a most significant change in attitude. Thus the most important wrestling that took place during this incident was spiritual, not physical. God's angel could have overpowered Jacob at any point. But when a man is struggling for God's blessing, God does not want to prevail against him and make him abandon the struggle. God may delay the giving of his blessing because the man needs the

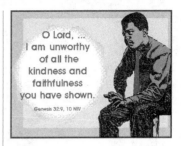

O Lord, ... I am unworthy of all the kindness and faithfulness you have shown.

Genesis 32:9, 10 NIV

WHAT DO YOU THINK?

After reading Genesis 32:10—"I am unworthy of all the kindness and faithfulness you have shown your servant"—a friend says, "I thought we were supposed to feel good about ourselves—you know, have 'good self-esteem.' This sounds like we should feel worthless!" How would you answer?

WHAT DO YOU THINK?

Though Jacob and the angel had wrestled through the night, it is obvious that the angel could have disabled Jacob at any time. It was not the physical struggle that was important here, except that it illustrated the spiritual struggle that Jacob had experienced. Jacob's struggle was not one of resisting or opposing God. Jacob had done that all his life! Here he was struggling to find God's favor, God's blessing. Jacob "overcame" in that his prayer for deliverance from Esau was answered. How have you struggled with God? What was the result?

HOW TO SAY IT

Bethel. BETH-ul.
Edom. EE-dum.
Esau. EE-saw.
Haran. HAIR-un.
Jabbok. JAB-ock.
Laban. LAY-bun.
Peniel. Peh-NYE-el.
Seir. SEE-ir.

time of waiting and struggling to help him realize his need for God and appreciate his blessing when it comes. Apparently Jacob continued to suffer the effects of his injury (v. 31), but the greater spiritual battle had been won.

C. THE ANGEL'S RESPONSE (vv. 27, 28)

27, 28. The man asked him, "What is your name?"

"Jacob," he answered.

Then the man said, "Your name will no longer be Jacob, but Israel, because you have struggled with God and with men and have overcome."

Of course, the angel knew Jacob's *name*; he asked for it only to emphasize the change that he was about to make. Jacob confessed that his name was *Jacob*, the "heel grabber," the "supplanter." The name described his earlier life quite accurately—a cheat, a clever trickster, one who had taken advantage of his blind father and his hungry brother.

Then came the dramatic announcement: *Your name will no longer be Jacob, but Israel.* This name is interpreted by some as meaning "prince of God"; however, the Hebrew term can be translated as "one who strives, or struggles, with God" and seems to be the preferred meaning among Bible students. The word is thus rendered here and in the *New American Standard Bible* ("you have striven with God and with men"). This is not to be understood in the bad sense (as though Jacob opposed God), but in the good sense (that he worked vigorously to obtain God's blessing). Jacob had learned to *overcome* through God's power, not through his own craftiness.

A NEW NAME

Names make a big difference to some people. Think of the Hollywood celebrities whose whole public persona has been shaped around their screen names. Some brides choose not to take the family name of their husbands; keeping their own name is an issue of personal independence for them. Others prefer to be called by a nickname rather than by their given name—in fact, sometimes their legal name becomes a closely guarded secret.

Names had great significance in early Hebrew culture. Names often called attention to appearance and achievements, as well as character and personality. *Jacob* meant "supplanter." The name was actually a kind of prophecy, which came to pass when the younger twin born to Rebekah and Isaac stole the birthright and blessing of his older brother. Jacob's new name, *Israel*, identified him as one who had "struggled" with God and secured divine favor.

Most Westerners don't pay that much attention to names and their meanings. Christians, however, wear the name and title of Jesus, and "there's just something about that name!" Blessed be the name of the Lord!   —R. W. B.

D. JACOB'S REALIZATION (vv. 29, 30)

29, 30. Jacob said, "Please tell me your name."

But he replied, "Why do you ask my name?" Then he blessed him there.

So Jacob called the place Peniel, saying, "It is because I saw God face to face, and yet my life was spared."

Please tell me your name. Jacob was interested in much more than his opponent's name; he wanted to know his identity, who he really was. Jacob must have already strongly suspected that his opponent was more than human. Through his question, he wanted to confirm his suspicions. The angel did not answer Jacob's question directly, but by blessing him, he confirmed that he was indeed supernatural. The blessing apparently included God's assurance that his presence would sustain Jacob through the upcoming meeting with Esau.

Peniel means "the face of God." By now Jacob had begun to understand the implications of his experience, and he was filled with awe. *I saw God face to face.* Of course, no man has actually seen God with his physical eyes (John 1:18). But Jacob's experience was as vivid as if God had been visible, and he was overwhelmed by the fact that he had survived such an intimate encounter with God.

III. JACOB MEETS ESAU (GENESIS 33:1-4)

A. JACOB'S PREPARATION (vv. 1, 2)

1, 2. Jacob looked up and there was Esau, coming with his four hundred men; so he divided the children among Leah, Rachel and the two maidservants. He put the maidservants and their children in front, Leah and her children next, and Rachel and Joseph in the rear.

As the new day dawned, the moment of truth for Jacob and his family arrived. Since Esau was accompanied by *four hundred men*, Jacob believed he had good reason to expect the worst. And yet he did not turn back because he had faith that God would protect him. Having prevailed with God the night before, he had every reason to believe that God would help him prevail against his brother.

Apparently, however, Jacob had no guarantee that he would prevail without a struggle or that the struggle would be without casualties. He began to take precautions to save some of his party from the anticipated conflict. He placed the *maidservants and their children* first, followed by *Leah and her children*, and finally *Rachel and Joseph in the rear*. This showed the order of Jacob's preference for the family members involved. Perhaps he thought that if Esau was bent on revenge, then at least his favorite wife (Rachel) and son (Joseph) could escape. We wonder what those placed in the front of the group may have thought about this strategy!

B. JACOB'S GREETING (v. 3)

3. He himself went on ahead and bowed down to the ground seven times as he approached his brother.

Whatever the different groups of his family thought about his precautions, they could not accuse Jacob of being a coward. *He himself* boldly stepped forward and placed himself at the front of his family. If violence ensued, he would be the first to suffer. Note the contrast: twenty years earlier he had fled in fear to escape his brother. Now, as he approached Esau, Jacob *bowed . . . seven times* as a gesture of respect and submission. Probably he bowed once, took a few steps toward Esau, then bowed again, repeating this action until he stood before *his brother.*

C. ESAU'S RESPONSE (v. 4)

4. But Esau ran to meet Jacob and embraced him; he threw his arms around his neck and kissed him. And they wept.

Like the father who ran to meet his prodigal son, Esau laid aside any proper protocol and *ran to meet* his long-lost brother, embracing him and kissing him in a display of his affection. In spite of his earlier treatment by Jacob, Esau obviously accepted his brother's gesture as sincere. Gone was the bitterness and hostility of the past. At first Jacob was likely taken aback by Esau's response, but he soon shared with his brother in tears of joy. In words that reflected his experience of the previous night, Jacob told Esau, "For to see your face is like seeing the face of God, now that you have received me favorably" (v. 10).

A PARABLE OF GRACE

Parables—"earthly stories with heavenly meaning"—are a frequent teaching device in the Bible. Jesus often used them (Matthew 13:34), employing both fictional

WHAT DO YOU THINK?

Jacob had finally put wholehearted faith in God. He had struggled with God and had overcome. Still, as Esau approached, he took some practical precautions. Some people say Jacob's precautions show he still didn't quite trust God one hundred percent. Others find no fault in Jacob's "plan B." What do you think? How do you mix faith and practicality? At what point is planning for a contingency simply a lack of faith, and when is it just good sense?

THOUGHT TO REMEMBER

Jacob's struggles with God taught him that the path to victory lies in surrender.

WHAT DO YOU THINK?

The lesson writer uses Jacob's experiences at Bethel and Peniel to illustrate our need for corporate worship (Bethel, "house of God") and private worship (Peniel, "face of God"). Suggest some ways to enhance either our public worship times or our private worship.

Guide the discussion to focus more on the condition of our hearts in public worship than on the style, format, and other externals. As for our private worship times, ask volunteers to share how they do this at home, either in individual or family worship. Some class members may be wanting to initiate family worship but don't know how. This could be a good time to learn!

PRAYER

O God of Abraham, Isaac, and Jacob, help us learn the lessons you have for us in the lives of these patriarchs. Let us never forget that we, like they, are pilgrims in this world, seeking our promised land. In Jesus' name we pray. Amen.

and historical parables. Old Testament parables are fewer and farther between, but they do exist.

Jacob's reconciliation with Esau may be considered an historical parable of the doctrine of grace. Jacob sins against Esau; Esau sentences the sinner to death; Jacob, acknowledging his sin, first runs in fear of retribution but then returns to Esau in humble repentance; Esau forgives Jacob, receiving him with open arms of reconciliation. The story is somewhat reminiscent of Jesus' well-known parable of the prodigal son. The rebellious and wasteful son finally comes to his senses; and when he returns home in penitent humility, the forgiving father welcomes him with love and acceptance.

In the Old and New Testaments, we find the drama of redemption prophesied, illustrated, and fulfilled according to God's will. Today we are the leading characters in the drama—as sinners saved by grace.

—R. W. B.

CONCLUSION

A. WRESTLING THROUGH THE NIGHT

Engaging in a wrestling match with an angel was a unique experience that none of us is likely to have. But most of us have at one time or another wrestled with God emotionally and spiritually. When we were younger, those prolonged wrestling matches may have come as we struggled to make a choice about our life vocations. Perhaps we struggled in choosing between an honorable profession and one that was not so honorable. Or we had to choose between two vocations, both of which were honorable. Such a match is not usually settled in one night but may go on for weeks or even months.

What about the wrestling that one addicted to alcohol must endure to free himself from its shackles? Many caught in this kind of struggle are never able to succeed on their own. They need the help of God and the faithful encouragement of others to make it.

Or perhaps a Christian is married to one who is not a Christian. This struggle may go on for months and years. Sometimes it is resolved when the Christian compromises his or her faith. But it can also come to a happy conclusion with the conversion of the non-Christian mate.

From these and similar wrestling matches we can learn at least two lessons. One of them comes from Jacob's experience. Even though he prevailed against his opponent, he was wounded in the conflict. Sometimes this happens to us. In the process of prevailing in our efforts to serve God, we may lose a friend, a job, or even a mate. But if our wounds serve the cause of Christ, then we should rejoice.

The second lesson we need to learn is that as we struggle to resist temptation or to serve the Lord more faithfully, we gain strength in victory. Each triumph makes us better equipped to win the next contest.

B. BETHEL AND PENIEL

During his first great encounter with God, Jacob was so impressed with the experience that he called the place *Bethel*, meaning "house of God." His second great encounter with God, related in today's lesson, led him to name the place *Peniel* or "face of God," because the confrontation had been so direct and so personal. It is doubtful that Jacob could have ever become a faithful, effective servant of God without this second experience.

Christians regularly visit Bethel—the house of God—where they worship and fellowship with other Christians. But Christians must also go to Peniel; they must have a personal relationship with God that goes beyond assembling each Lord's Day. This relationship must be a growing one that develops within them a mature Christian faith.

Discovery Learning

This page contains an alternate lesson plan emphasizing learning activities. Classes desiring such student involvement will find these suggestions helpful. The next page is a reproducible activity page to further enhance discovery learning.

LEARNING GOALS

As a result of this lesson, each student should be able to:

1. Tell how Jacob was reconciled with Esau and of the prayer and divine struggle that preceded the event.

2. Explain the significance of Jacob's actions as he prepared to meet Esau, and describe the change in his character these actions represent.

3. Examine his or her own life for an occasion of struggling with God, and seek God's blessing in it.

INTO THE LESSON

To introduce the lesson, distribute copies of a worksheet as follows: On the left side of the page is a vertical column of words (see below). To the right of that column and at the top of the page are the words *Positive* and *Negative*. Students are to look at each word on the left and determine whether it has a positive or negative connotation and then make a mark (✔) under the appropriate heading. (Words considered "neutral" can be marked "positive.") The words for the column on the left are as follows: *cross, desire, forward, liberal, radical, sophisticated.*

Allow a couple of minutes for the students to mark their sheets; then poll the class on each word. Probably there will not be unanimity on any of these, for each word can be taken in different ways. For example, the *cross* is a reminder of our salvation, but someone who is *cross* is hard to get along with. A conservative theologian opposes *liberal* theology, but *liberal* giving is praiseworthy. *Sophisticated* suggests education and refinement, but it also has to do with not being naive or innocent. Sometimes *sophisticated* suggests the loss of innocence that pornography represents.

Suggest the word *struggle*—is it positive or negative? In past lessons we have seen Jacob struggle in the sense of resisting God and trying to get by on cunning. Today we'll see him struggle for God's favor.

INTO THE WORD

Set the scene for this lesson by listing in scrambled order several events from Jacob's life (from Genesis 29:1 through 32:8). List these on newsprint or on a handout (or refer the students to the student book, *NIV Bible Student*) and ask the students to put them in the correct chronological order. (Begin with Jacob's journey to Haran and end with Jacob's learning that Esau is coming with four hundred men.)

Ask a volunteer to read Genesis 32:9-11. Observe that we see Jacob here dealing with a potentially threatening situation with prayer instead of cunning. Ask, "Is that how the 'old Jacob' would have handled things? What made the difference?"

Tell the students that the answer is in the text just read. Ask them to identify Jacob's character qualities that can be seen in that passage. For example: devout (v. 9), aware of his religious heritage (v. 9), humble (v. 10), thankful to God for his blessings (v. 10), dependent on God (v. 11), concerned for others (v. 11).

Ask another volunteer to read Genesis 32:24-30. Discuss what Jacob's struggle with the angel represented. Use the Scripture exposition section, as well as the second "What Do You Think?" question on page 419, to help you.

Now have another volunteer read Genesis 33:1-4. Discuss the relationship between trusting God in a difficult or dangerous situation and taking sensible precautions. At what point do our precautions suggest we are lacking in faith? Discuss also how this picture of reconciliation is similar to God's grace. (See "A Parable of Grace" on pages 421, 422.)

INTO LIFE

Observe that God wants to give us grace. Ask, "Why, then, do we sometimes have to struggle for it? Why did Jacob have to struggle with the angel in order to find God's blessing?"

Be sure to point out that we cannot struggle for grace in the sense that if we work hard enough we can earn God's favor. But God allows tests in our lives to refine and purify us (James 1:2-4; 1 Peter 1:6, 7). Jacob could have bolted and looked to some other source for security against his brother. But he realized he needed God's blessing, and he stayed with the fight to get it. When difficulties come to us, we can bolt and look for the best the world has to offer, or we can stay in the fight and seek God's blessing. It's a matter of submission to his will.

Challenge the students to think about their relationship with God. What obstacles are making it a struggle? Pray for endurance to continue to seek God's blessing through their struggles.

Jacob's Ups and Downs

Jacob did not come easily to the point where we find him in today's lesson. Look up the Scriptures that follow. For each event plot Jacob's life on the graph below. After all the points have been plotted, connect the points to form a graph of Jacob's life.

1. Genesis 25:20-34
2. Genesis 27:1-45
3. Genesis 28:1-22
4. Genesis 29:1-30
5. Genesis 30:25-43
6. Genesis 31:1-21
7. Genesis 32:1-21
8. Genesis 32:22-30

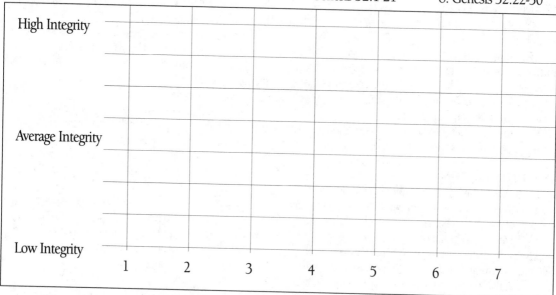

My Ups and Downs

Review your own spiritual life over the past five to ten years. Choose seven events that had significant impact on who you are today, and chart your own life. Do you like the way the graph is heading? What do you need to do?

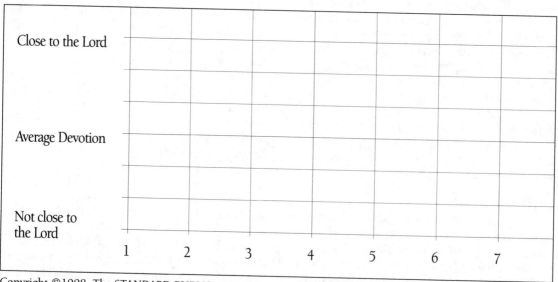

FAVORED SON TO SLAVE

LESSON 11

WHY TEACH THIS LESSON?

This is not the most encouraging lesson you will ever teach! It really needs to be kept in context with next week's lesson. If you have students who are new to the faith or for some other reason are not familiar with the story of Joseph, assure them that next week's lesson will provide "the rest of the story."

Many people in our world, however, feel their situation is grim—perhaps even hopeless. Murphy's Law seems to follow them wherever they go. It's enough to shake one's faith.

These people will identify with Joseph in today's lesson. In an exalted position because of his father's love, he typifies the new Christian. But then adversity strikes. The believer, like Joseph, wonders, "Why is this happening to me?" The situation looks hopeless.

Teach this lesson to set the stage for the demonstration of what God can do with "bad circumstances" in next week's lesson.

INTRODUCTION

A. A DEADLY ACID

A military leader in an ancient Grecian city had rendered an outstanding service to his fellow citizens, and they in turn had honored him by erecting a statue of him in the public plaza. A brother of this hero became terribly jealous and looked for a way to destroy him. Since a personal attack on the hero was out of the question, the brother decided to deface the statue honoring him. Late at night, when everyone was asleep, he secretly went to the plaza and tried to push the statue over. But try as he might, he couldn't budge it. In desperation he started digging away at the foundation supporting the statue. His efforts proved all too successful, for the next morning he was found crushed to death beneath the statue that had toppled over when its foundation was removed.

In similar fashion Joseph's brothers learned that jealousy is a destructive passion. While their jealousy did not result in their deaths, their jealous actions against Joseph wreaked havoc and heartache within their family. Like a powerful acid, jealousy, once spilled out, burns and corrodes all that it touches.

B. LESSON BACKGROUND

After the peaceful reunion between Esau and Jacob (which we studied in last week's lesson), the two brothers went their separate ways. Esau returned to Seir and Jacob moved on to Succoth, where he built a house and a shelter for his livestock (Genesis 33:16, 17). Succoth, located east of the Jordan River in the Jordan Valley, was not far from Peniel, where Jacob wrestled with an angel. Jacob then moved across the Jordan River and settled in Shechem. There occurred the shameful incident, recorded in Genesis 34, involving Dinah, the daughter of Leah. After this happened, God told Jacob to move to Bethel (35:1). Then he moved on to Ephrath (later called Bethlehem), where Rachel died while giving birth to Benjamin (35:16-19). Also during this period, Isaac died at the age of one hundred eighty and was buried by Esau and Jacob (35:28, 29).

DEVOTIONAL READING:
1 SAMUEL 18:1-9

LESSON SCRIPTURE:
GENESIS 37

PRINTED TEXT:
GENESIS 37:3, 4, 17b-28

LESSON AIMS

After this lesson students should be able to:

1. Tell why Joseph's brothers were jealous of him and what they did to him because of their jealousy.

2. Suggest some ways the sibling rivalry in Joseph's family could have been prevented by Jacob.

3. State some principles that fathers and grandfathers today can follow to promote greater peace in their families.

Aug
15

KEY VERSE

Now Israel loved Joseph more than any of his other sons, because he had been born to him in his old age; and he made a richly ornamented robe for him.
—Genesis 37:3

I. JOSEPH, A FAVORED SON (GENESIS 37:3, 4)

A. JACOB'S GIFT (v. 3)

3. Now Israel loved Joseph more than any of his other sons, because he had been born to him in his old age; and he made a richly ornamented robe for him.

As we learned last week, *Israel* was the new name given to Jacob at Peniel. In the narratives that follow, the two names are used interchangeably (Genesis 42:4, 5; 45:21, 25-28; 46:1-8).

That Jacob *loved Joseph* was admirable; the problem was that he loved him *more than any of his other sons, because he had been born to him in his old age*. Within many families the youngest child often receives special privileges. However, Benjamin was younger than Joseph, and yet at this point was apparently not as favored as Joseph. This leads us to believe that Joseph may have had other qualities that endeared him to his father. Probably the favoritism began as soon as Joseph was born, while Rachel was still alive and before Benjamin was born. Benjamin's birth, then, did not change Jacob's feelings for Joseph.

Jacob showed his preference for Joseph by giving him *a richly ornamented robe*, perhaps more commonly known as a "coat of many colors" (*King James Version*). Some commentators suggest that this was a tunic with long sleeves, designed more for leisure than for work. Others have suggested that such a robe designated its owner as the son whom the father desired to become the future leader of the family—a privilege normally given to the firstborn. From his own experience (Genesis 25:28), Jacob should have known that this obvious partiality to Joseph would kindle resentment among the other sons.

B. REACTION OF JOSEPH'S BROTHERS (v. 4)

4. When his brothers saw that their father loved him more than any of them, they hated him and could not speak a kind word to him.

Strong feelings and impulsive actions came easily to Joseph's brothers. Their behavior in the case involving their sister Dinah (Genesis 34) showed how violent they could become. Concerning Joseph, they *could not speak a kind word to him*. How, then, did they speak to him? Did they tease and taunt him? Were they openly hostile? Did they just not speak to him at all? The second option seems least likely since Jacob and Joseph both seemed unaware of the danger Joseph would be in by being in their presence far from home (v. 18). That the Scripture says they "could not *speak a kind word to him*" suggests they did speak to Joseph, but it was not nice. Probably their speech was filled with innuendo and sarcasm, and they must have delighted to point out any mistake he might have made, no matter how trivial.

Joseph did not help matters by some of his own actions. Genesis 37:2 tells us he brought a "bad report" to his father about four of his brothers. We do not know whether this was a case of "tattling" some misdemeanor or whether it was a serious case of wrongdoing that needed to be reported. Either way, his brothers would not have appreciated it. What really angered his brothers, however, was his relating of his dreams (v. 5). In them his brothers and even his parents were subservient to Joseph (vv. 6-11). Did Joseph realize even at the young age of seventeen that these were messages from God? If so, perhaps he felt an obligation to report them. Or was he trying to get even with his brothers for their hatred toward him? Or was Joseph simply naive about the way his brothers would take these reports? These are questions we cannot answer with certainty, but it appears that Joseph might have used better judgment even if he was not particularly vindictive. His father rebuked him, but even so he seems to have felt there might be something worth noting in the dreams (vv. 10, 11).

WHAT DO YOU THINK?

We might have expected that Jacob, knowing firsthand what it felt like to have his father favor his brother, would have been careful not to repeat this mistake. But he did just as his father did. Adults often repeat the mistakes of their parents. Why is this? How can adults break with the patterns of the past?

WHAT DO YOU THINK?

Jealousy is a form of coveting: we want what the other person has. It might be a talent, our father's favor, a more winsome personality, or any number of things. What kinds of things make people jealous of others today? How can parents and grandparents help prevent this within the family?

JOSEPH'S SIN

I once heard a powerful sermon about Joseph in which the preacher proclaimed, "If Joseph ever sinned, the Bible doesn't tell us about it!" That statement and that sermon made an impact on me and on hundreds of youth at a huge rally. Joseph remained faithful to the Lord despite many trials and temptations. That makes him a fitting role model for modern teens who struggle with all sorts of seductions in today's world.

Upon reflection and further study, however, I see at least one potential flaw in Joseph's character. This seventeen-year-old told his older brothers about dreams that unmistakably predicted that Joseph would one day rule over his own family. Such news would hardly be welcomed, especially since the brothers already were jealous and resentful. We don't know whether Joseph was vindictive or simply naive, but it seems he could have used better judgment.

Whatever the case, Joseph was not perfect. In that, he is like all of us, for "all have sinned" (Romans 3:23). This truth is not meant to serve as an excuse for the sins we commit. What it should do is drive us to the recognition of how much we need God's mercy and forgiveness.   —R. W. B.

This visual, for use with this week's lesson and next week's, depicts Joseph's fall from "favored son" to "slave," and then his elevation to second to Pharaoh over all of Egypt.

II. THE PLOT AGAINST JOSEPH (GENESIS 37:17b-22)

A. THE BROTHERS' PLAN (vv. 17b-20)

17b. So Joseph went after his brothers and found them near Dothan.

Jacob's family was dwelling at Hebron at this time (Genesis 35:27; 37:14), but apparently the pastures there became barren. So the older brothers took their father's flock to Shechem, more than fifty miles north of Hebron. After some time had elapsed, Jacob decided to check up on the brothers, and he sent Joseph to find them and then report back to him. It seems strange that Jacob would send his teenage son (Joseph was seventeen, according to Genesis 37:2) all alone on such a mission. Apparently Jacob was unaware of how the older brothers felt about Joseph—or, at least, he underestimated how bitterly they hated him.

When Joseph reached Shechem, however, his brothers were not there. A stranger told him that they had moved on to *Dothan*, about a dozen miles to the north and located on a major caravan route connecting northern Palestine and Egypt. Later it was the scene of a great miracle by Elisha (2 Kings 6:11-18). Near Dothan Joseph *found them.*

18, 19. But they saw him in the distance, and before he reached them, they plotted to kill him.

"Here comes that dreamer!" they said to each other.

Although the brothers were not expecting Joseph, they were able to recognize him at a distance, probably because of his robe. Even before he arrived *they plotted to kill him.* Their jealousy and bitterness had been growing and festering and now had an opportunity to come to the surface.

Contemptuously the brothers referred to Joseph as *that dreamer.* They resented the special treatment that Joseph had received from their father, but it was Joseph's dreams that really "stuck in their craw." Had their attitudes been different, they might have been able to laugh off their teenage brother's dreams. Or if they had been more sensitive to spiritual matters, they might have seen that God had special plans for their brother, and was revealing that through the dreams. But now those dreams had become the basis of all their hatred. Most of us have been guilty of similar attitudes when we have allowed one incident or one act by another person to become the catalyst of a continuing resentment.

Even though the brothers seem to have made their feelings about Joseph obvious to him, he appears to have felt no apprehension as he approached them.

HOW TO SAY IT

Bethel. BETH-ul.
Bilhah. BILL-ha.
Dothan. DOE-thun.
Elisha. Ee-LYE-shuh.
Ephrath. EF-rath.
Esau. EE-saw.
Gilead. GIL-ee-ud.
Hagar. HAY-gar.
Hebron. HEE-brun or HEB-run.
Ishmaelites. ISH-may-el-ites.
Keturah. Keh-TOO-ruh.
Midianites. MID-ee-un-ites.
Peniel. Peh-NYE-el.
Reuben. ROO-ben.
Seir. SEE-ir.
Shechem. SHEK-em or SHEE-kem.
Succoth. SOO-kawth.

Joseph was basically a decent person and, harboring no ill will toward his brothers, was not suspicious of their motives.

20. "Come now, let's kill him and throw him into one of these cisterns and say that a ferocious animal devoured him. Then we'll see what comes of his dreams."

The temptation to *kill* Joseph, which may have begun as a momentary impulse, quickly grew into a full-blown scheme. We are shocked to hear such threats coming from the mouths of one's brothers! Probably none of the brothers acting alone would have carried out such a violent act; but in a group of men with similar feelings, the wicked thoughts of each one stimulated the wicked thoughts of the others. "Evil companionships corrupt good morals" (1 Corinthians 15:33, *American Standard Version*). For this reason, all of us ought to be concerned about the company we keep. We need to be especially concerned about the company our children or our grandchildren keep.

As their plot began to develop, the brothers even came up with a plausible cover-up: *a ferocious animal devoured him*. At that time lions and bears still roamed the land, and either one could pose a deadly threat to a person traveling alone or sleeping outdoors.

B. REUBEN'S SUGGESTION (vv. 21, 22)

21. When Reuben heard this, he tried to rescue him from their hands. "Let's not take his life," he said.

Reuben was certainly not a model of high moral character. On one occasion he had slept with Bilhah, his father's concubine—an act that Jacob never forgot (Genesis 35:22; 49:3, 4). But now, in the face of his brothers' sinister plot, Reuben demonstrated a commendable degree of responsibility. As the oldest son he would normally be looked to for leadership, and his opinion would be given some respect by his brothers. He certainly realized the grief that Joseph's death would cause Jacob. Perhaps his conscience grieved him because of his own sin against his father, and thus he was more sensitive to his father's feelings than were the others.

22. "Don't shed any blood. Throw him into this cistern here in the desert, but don't lay a hand on him." Reuben said this to rescue him from them and take him back to his father.

Perhaps the mention of shedding *blood* would focus the brothers' attention on the heinous nature of the crime they were about to commit. How horrible it would be to have the blood of their own brother on their heads! Instead, Reuben suggested that they *throw him into this cistern*. Cisterns were hewn out of the ground to collect water during the rainy season. They were usually shaped like a bottle with a wide basin at the bottom and a narrow opening at the top that could be covered by a stone. It would have been very difficult for a person to escape from one without help from someone else.

Had Joseph been left in the cistern, he almost certainly would have died; but at least the brothers would not have felt the guilt of actually shedding his blood. They agreed with Reuben's suggestion, and so Joseph was thrown in the cistern. Reuben planned to return secretly later and *rescue* Joseph and *take him back to his father.*

III. JOSEPH TAKEN TO EGYPT (GENESIS 37:23-28)

A. JOSEPH SEIZED (vv. 23, 24)

23, 24. So when Joseph came to his brothers, they stripped him of his robe—the richly ornamented robe he was wearing—and they took him and threw him into the cistern. Now the cistern was empty; there was no water in it.

WHAT DO YOU THINK?

Reuben's intention to rescue his brother is commendable even if his method is not. After all, he failed! What do you think would have happened if Reuben had simply said, "No! We must not do anything to harm Joseph, for to do so would be sin"? Have you ever had to stand up to a crowd and say no—to act as the conscience of the group? What does it take to do so? What risks are involved? What potential benefits?

Even before Joseph reached *his brothers*, they had discussed their two plans and had decided to follow Reuben's suggestion. Joseph had no forewarning of their intentions; as soon as he arrived, they seized him. The first thing they did was to strip him of his beautiful *robe*, which perhaps symbolized all their jealousy toward him. Joseph must have pleaded with his brothers not to do this to him, but his protests fell on deaf ears. Even Reuben, who seemed not to favor their actions, did not speak up in his defense at this point. Perhaps he felt that his brothers' willingness to go along with his plan was about the only concession he could hope to get from them.

Without hesitation, the brothers carried out their plan and *threw* Joseph *into the cistern*. Fortunately for him *there was no water in it*; otherwise he probably would have drowned within just a few minutes.

B. ISHMAELITES PASS BY (vv. 25-27)

25. As they sat down to eat their meal, they looked up and saw a caravan of Ishmaelites coming from Gilead. Their camels were loaded with spices, balm and myrrh, and they were on their way to take them down to Egypt.

The reader is shocked by the callousness of Joseph's brothers. In a matter of minutes they plotted to kill their brother, took action that seemed certain to ensure his death, and then calmly *sat down to eat*. As they ate, they saw *a caravan of Ishmaelites* approaching. The Ishmaelites were descendants of Abraham through Hagar (Genesis 16:15). However, the term was sometimes applied more broadly to all the nomads who roamed the desert areas east of the Jordan River and south of the Dead Sea. Some were engaged in the lucrative business of carrying various *spices* to Egypt. *Gilead*, a fertile territory southeast of the Sea of Galilee, was famous for its *balm* that reputedly possessed outstanding medicinal properties (Jeremiah 8:22; 46:11). *Myrrh* was used not only as a spice, but also in pain-relieving medicines (Mark 15:23). It was brought to Jesus as a gift following his birth (Matthew 2:11), and was applied to his body after his death (John 19:39, 40).

Since Dothan was on a major trade route that went to Egypt, it was not surprising that a caravan should be passing by. The timing of its arrival, however, was surely by divine providence, to send Joseph to Egypt (Genesis 45:5).

26, 27. Judah said to his brothers, "What will we gain if we kill our brother and cover up his blood? Come, let's sell him to the Ishmaelites and not lay our hands on him; after all, he is our brother, our own flesh and blood." His brothers agreed.

Once these men had a little time to think about how cruelly they were treating their *brother*, they may have had some second thoughts. But they had a problem. If they took Joseph out of the pit and allowed him to return to their father, he would certainly report to him what they had done. That could only make the family situation worse.

The sight of the passing caravan of *Ishmaelites* gave the brothers a way out of their dilemma. *Judah* suggested that they *sell* Joseph to the Ishmaelites. That way they could get rid of "the dreamer" and *gain* some profit for themselves as well. Note the brothers' twisted reasoning: they did not want to kill Joseph, for *after all, he is our brother, our own flesh and blood*; but that fact did not prevent them from selling him into slavery!

C. JOSEPH SOLD INTO SLAVERY (v. 28)

28. So when the Midianite merchants came by, his brothers pulled Joseph up out of the cistern and sold him for twenty shekels of silver to the Ishmaelites, who took him to Egypt.

WHAT DO YOU THINK?

It is one thing to be jealous and have hard feelings toward someone, but Joseph's brothers acted violently and, when they were done, he was as good as dead. And they didn't even lose their appetites! How could they be so cold? What precautions do we need to take to be sure we don't get to that point?

WHAT DO YOU THINK?

Joseph was sold into slavery by his brothers. Many people are unfairly put in difficult situations by the evil deeds of others. Thieves and swindlers can rob people of most everything that they have, placing them in very hard economic situations. Spouses walk out and cause great emotional and economic hardship for the one who is left behind. When the sin of another leaves us in difficulty, what is a proper response?

PRAYER

Gracious God, we are appalled at the tragedy we have seen unfolding in the family of Jacob. Help us to learn ways to avoid such situations in our own families. Give us the knowledge and the wisdom that it takes to rear godly families, united in their desire to please you. May we seek, in every circumstance of life, to live so that you are honored by our words and actions. In Jesus' name we pray. Amen.

THOUGHT TO REMEMBER

Anger long smoldered can burst into a consuming flame at the slightest provocation and scorch everyone in its path.

DAILY BIBLE READINGS

Monday, Aug. 9—Joseph, the Tattletale and Dreamer (Genesis 37:1-11)

Tuesday, Aug. 10—Joseph's Brothers Become Jealous of Him (Genesis 37:12-24)

Wednesday, Aug. 11—Joseph Is Sold to Ishmaelites (Genesis 37:25-28)

Thursday, Aug. 12—Jacob Mourns Joseph's Imagined Death (Genesis 37:29-36)

Friday, Aug. 13—Saul Is Jealous of David (1 Samuel 18:1-9)

Saturday, Aug. 14—The First Workers Are Jealous of the Last (Matthew 20:1-16)

Sunday, Aug. 15—The Disciples Wonder Who Is the Greatest (Luke 14:7-11)

The Midianites were descendants of Abraham by Keturah (Genesis 25:1, 2). They lived in the same general area as the Ishmaelites and apparently were considered as part of the larger Ishmaelite group. (That *Midianites* and *Ishmaelites* could be used interchangeably is clear from a comparison of Genesis 37:36 and 39:1.) When the brothers began to negotiate with the Midianites, Joseph realized what the future held in store for him. He pleaded with his brothers not to carry out their plan. Years later in Egypt the brothers admitted this: "We saw how distressed he was when he pleaded with us for his life, but we would not listen" (Genesis 42:21).

The brothers received *twenty shekels of silver* for Joseph, which was later recognized in the law of Moses as the price of a male slave five to twenty years old (Leviticus 27:5). We wonder how long the brothers kept these grim reminders of their terrible crime!

THREE WRONGS MAKE ONE RIGHT?

When youngsters justify some act of meanness with "He hit me first!" conscientious parents are likely to respond with a maxim so familiar it has become a cliché: "Two wrongs don't make a right." Children later see the wisdom of such instruction when they acknowledge the sinfulness of vengeance and retaliation.

The scenario in today's text presents at least three wrongs. Jacob was wrong when he showed favoritism to one son over the others. Joseph was wrong when he provoked greater animosity among his already jealous brothers by relating his dreams of his superiority and their submission to him. The angry brothers were wrong when they retaliated hatefully and violently against Joseph.

None of these wrongs can be excused, regardless of the circumstances. But God ultimately brought right out of all these wrongs. In Egypt, Joseph providentially was promoted to a position that allowed him to save Israel (Jacob and his growing family) from the effects of famine, thereby furthering God's plan for his chosen people.

None of our wrongs ever makes a right, but our Father's will prevails even when his children sin.

—R. W. B.

CONCLUSION

Today's lesson ends on a tragic note. Even those of us who have become hardened by the frequency of violent crime all about us cannot avoid being shocked by what Joseph's brothers did to him. However, before we spend too much time bemoaning this act of violence, we need to step back and take a look at the big picture.

God did not force the brothers to mistreat Joseph, and he did not condone their actions. Yet in spite of their crimes, God was able to use their actions to achieve a greater purpose. Years later in Egypt, the brother who had been sold into slavery became the instrument whom God used to save the family of Jacob from a severe famine. Joseph recognized that God, not his brothers, was responsible for his coming to Egypt when he did: "You intended to harm me," Joseph later told his brothers, "but God intended it for good to accomplish what is now being done, the saving of many lives" (Genesis 50:20). Furthermore, God used Joseph as a model for us of remaining morally upright and determining to trust in him through all kinds of adversity.

Central to the Christian faith is the truth that our God allows us individual freedom of choice, yet, at the same time, he is also able to control the flow of history. When bad things happen to us, we need to step back a bit and try to see the big picture. Situations may seem out of control, but God is always in control.

Discovery Learning

*This page contains an alternate lesson plan emphasizing learning activities. Classes
desiring such student involvement will find these suggestions helpful. The next page
is a reproducible activity page to further enhance discovery learning.*

LEARNING GOALS

After this lesson, your students should be able to:

1. Tell why Joseph's brothers were jealous of him and what they did to him because of their jealousy.

2. Suggest some ways the sibling rivalry in Joseph's family could have been prevented by Jacob.

3. State some principles that fathers and grandfathers today can follow to promote greater peace in their families.

INTO THE LESSON

Some of your students may be old enough to remember Tom Smothers' lament to his brother that "Mom always liked you best." In reality, however, parental favoritism is no laughing matter. Ask your students to suggest some of the harmful results and consequences of parental favoritism. For example: jealousy, resentment, pride, arrogance, negative self-image, broken relationships, shattered family, even violence.

In today's lesson we see what happened when Jacob lavished special attention on his favorite son, Joseph, the first child born to Rachel, his beloved wife.

INTO THE WORD

Fill in the biblical background for this lesson by asking one of your students (in advance, early in the week) to summarize the events that happened in Jacob's life since last week's lesson. See Genesis 33:5—37:2 and the "Lesson Background" on page 425.

Dysfunctional is a word that psychologists and family counselors use when describing a family in which the relationships are not healthy and do not work. Jacob had been raised in a dysfunctional family, and now largely as a result of his own errors in judgment his own family was dysfunctional.

Ask your students to read Genesis 37:3-28 in search of indicators that this family was dysfunctional. Write their responses on the chalkboard or newsprint. (You may choose to distribute copies of the reproducible activity page that follows to assist in this exercise.)

Here are some suggested responses:

• parental favoritism—by Jacob (v. 3).

• sibling jealousy and hatred—by Joseph's brothers (v. 4).

• pride or insensitivity—by Joseph (vv. 5-10).

• envy—by Joseph's brothers (v. 11).

• hatred to the point of deciding to murder their brother—by Joseph's brothers (vv. 18-20).

• violence—by Joseph's brothers (vv. 23, 24).

• callous insensitivity—by Joseph's brothers (v. 25).

• willingness to sell a brother into slavery—by Joseph's brothers (v. 28).

Provide a copy of the lower portion of the reproducible activity page to each student. Then divide your class into three groups. Ask one group to think about what Jacob could have done differently to have prevented the horrible tragedy that struck his family when Joseph was sold into slavery.

Assign the second group to think about what Joseph could have done differently. Was he so naive that he didn't realize that relating the content of his dreams would incense his brothers? Or didn't he care?

The third group can think about what Joseph's ten older brothers could have done differently. Were they so out of touch with godly values that they didn't realize that their jealousy and murderous hatred would inevitably lead to violence? Or didn't they care?

After about five minutes, call for reports from each group. If there were things that Jacob, Joseph, and the brothers could have done to avert disaster, why didn't they? What do your students think?

INTO LIFE

Use the following "case study" to help your students talk about what parents (and/or grandparents) can do to promote peace and positive, healthy relationships in their families.

Alan has two sons. Steve is a natural athlete, and is on the high school football team. Jeff is more interested in computers and music than in sports. Since Alan was a high school football star himself, he naturally has more in common with Steve.

• How can Alan prevent his natural preference from becoming a problem?

• What can he do to demonstrate that he is not showing favoritism?

• What might happen if Alan shows more interest in Steve than in Jeff?

In closing, challenge the parents in your class to be aware of the temptation to play favorites. What will they do during this coming week to assure all their children that they are loved and valued?

Dysfunctional Families

Read Genesis 37:3-28 in search of evidences or indicators that this family was dysfunctional. List your findings below:

• v. 3

• v. 4

• vv. 5-10

• v. 11

• vv. 18-20

• vv. 23, 24

• v. 25

• v. 28

If I Had It to Do Over . . .

• What might Jacob have done differently to have prevented the horrible tragedy that struck his family when Joseph was sold into slavery?

• What might Joseph have done differently? Was he so naive that he didn't realize that his dream stories would incense his brothers? Or didn't he care?

• What might Joseph's ten older brothers have done differently? Were they so out of touch with godly values that they didn't realize that their jealousy and murderous hatred would inevitably lead to violence? Or didn't they care?

Genesis: Beginnings
Unit 3. A People Tested
(Lessons 9-13)

OPPORTUNITY TO SERVE

LESSON 12

WHY TEACH THIS LESSON?

This one will be a little tricky. You want to be careful you don't make any guarantees that God is not planning to honor! It is easy, and very tempting, to treat Joseph's situation as the norm. "Just be faithful to God," we deduce, "and everything will work out fine." That's true if we allow God to define what it means to "work out fine." The promise of Romans 8:28 is true, but sometimes the "good" for which God works is not realized this side of glory! Just ask the martyrs.

This is an important lesson, and it must be taught. Some of your students are under a lot of pressure to give up, or at least to compromise, their faith. Sometimes they feel like their faith isn't doing them any good, so why not? At other times they think, "Who would know?" Joseph resisted both of those temptations, and he becomes a good role model for us. Just don't promise your students they will find themselves on top of the heap in this life if they persevere a little longer.

Some of them will. Some of them won't.

But God *will* work for the good of them all if they, like Joseph, remain faithful.

INTRODUCTION

A. I'LL BE HONEST

Years ago in a slave market in the American South, a young man was to be sold at an auction. Before the bidding began, he was examined by several prospective buyers. Most of them were concerned about his health and his strength. One man, after examining him, told him, "I will be a kinder master to you than some of the other slave owners. But I want to know one thing. If I buy you and you become my slave, will you be honest?"

The young man drew himself up to his full height, looked the man in the eye, and said, "Sir, I'll be honest whether you buy me or not!"

Joseph would have echoed this young man's sentiment. Sold into slavery by his brothers, Joseph experienced difficult, faith-trying times. He suffered imprisonment because he refused to compromise his integrity. Eventually, however, his honesty was rewarded.

B. LESSON BACKGROUND

The Ishmaelites who purchased Joseph from his brothers took him to Egypt where he was sold to Potiphar, an official in Pharaoh's government. Joseph prospered for a time; but when he resisted the seductive advances of Potiphar's wife, he was falsely accused and thrown into prison. There Joseph was able to gain the respect of the jail keeper. Later Pharaoh's baker and cupbearer were imprisoned, and during their imprisonment each had a dream. Joseph was able to interpret their dreams, each of which came true in the way Joseph had said it would.

Some time after this, Pharaoh had a dream that none of his wise men could interpret. The cupbearer, by now restored to Pharaoh's favor, remembered Joseph and mentioned to Pharaoh his ability to interpret dreams. Upon learning this, Pharaoh sent for Joseph to have him interpret his dream.

DEVOTIONAL READING:
ACTS 21:7-14

LESSON SCRIPTURE:
GENESIS 39–41

PRINTED TEXT:
GENESIS 41:14-16, 25-40

LESSON AIMS

After completing this lesson each student should:

1. Recount Joseph's interpretation of Pharaoh's dreams and the favorable treatment he then received.

2. Compare Joseph's situation and his faith in God's providence with the situation many Christians face at the workplace.

3. Make a commitment to live with integrity and to serve with honor wherever God places him or her.

KEY VERSE

Pharaoh said to Joseph, "Since God has made all this known to you, there is no one so discerning and wise as you. You shall be in charge of my palace, and all my people are to submit to your orders. Only with respect to the throne will I be greater than you." —Genesis 41:39, 40

Aug
22

LESSON 12 NOTES

Display again the visual used with last week's lesson, which depicts Joseph's fall from "favored son" to "slave," and then his elevation to second to Pharaoh over all of Egypt.

WHAT DO YOU THINK?

Joseph said, "God will give Pharaoh the answer." Pharaoh did not accept the God of the Hebrews. He could have refused to hear Joseph. Joseph did not know how Pharaoh would receive his remark about God's having the answer, but he gave credit to God nonetheless. People who reject God today often refuse to hear Christians when they appeal to God or the Bible. How can we take a stand for God and his Word in such a way as to be heard and to have influence for him?

I. PHARAOH SUMMONS JOSEPH (GENESIS 41:14-16)

A. JOSEPH'S PREPARATION (v. 14)

14. So Pharaoh sent for Joseph, and he was quickly brought from the dungeon. When he had shaved and changed his clothes, he came before Pharaoh.

When *Pharaoh sent for Joseph*, the servants acted *quickly* to bring him *from the dungeon*. However, there were special preparations that Joseph had to make before he could present himself to Pharaoh. First of all he *shaved* himself. Hebrew men ordinarily wore beards. The Egyptian men, on the other hand, shaved their beards (they are thus depicted in ancient statues, monuments, and paintings). It is likely that Joseph followed the Egyptian custom in deference to Pharaoh. Joseph also changed from his prison *clothes* to more appropriate garments.

B. PHARAOH'S PROBLEM (v. 15)

15. Pharaoh said to Joseph, "I had a dream, and no one can interpret it. But I have heard it said of you that when you hear a dream you can interpret it."

Pharaoh immediately told *Joseph* of his predicament. He was disturbed by the fact that none of the Egyptian wise men could *interpret* his *dream*. Then he had learned from the cupbearer who had been in prison with Joseph that Joseph could interpret dreams.

When Joseph had interpreted the cupbearer's dream, he had asked that the cupbearer remember him when he was restored to Pharaoh's favor. The cupbearer, however, promptly forgot about Joseph when he returned to his post. Two years passed before the cupbearer mentioned Joseph (Genesis 40:23—41:1), and that was only after none of the Egyptians could interpret Pharaoh's dream—an incident that apparently jogged the cupbearer's memory.

C. JOSEPH'S REPLY (v. 16)

16. "I cannot do it," Joseph replied to Pharaoh, "but God will give Pharaoh the answer he desires."

Joseph's immediate response was to deny that he himself possessed any special powers that allowed him to interpret Pharaoh's dream. He then acknowledged that the *answer* would come from *God*. His affirmation that there was but one God was a significant statement of faith in Egypt, where the people worshiped many gods. In fact, even Pharaoh himself was considered to be a god. Joseph also assured Pharaoh that the answer he would receive would be *the answer he desires*. Even though Pharaoh had not yet revealed the contents of his dream to Joseph, God had given Joseph enough knowledge about it for him to know that it conveyed information of value to Pharaoh.

II. JOSEPH INTERPRETS THE DREAM (GENESIS 41:25-36)

A. FEAST, THEN FAMINE (vv. 25-32)

Verses 17-24 give the details of Pharaoh's dream, which was in two parts. In the first part, Pharaoh was standing on the bank of a river (most likely the Nile) when he saw seven cows, or cattle, "fat and sleek" come up out of the river. They were followed by seven other cows—"scrawny and very ugly and lean." Then an amazing thing happened—the lean cows devoured the fat cows, yet even after such a bountiful feast they still looked lean and ugly. Obviously in the real world cows are not cannibalistic, eating other cattle. But dreams know no such limitations.

In the second dream, Pharaoh saw seven heads of grain (probably wheat), "full and good." Then seven more heads of grain sprang up, but they were "withered and thin and scorched by the east wind." This most likely described the east wind that came in from the Arabian Desert and was hot and dry, withering much of the vegetation in its path. The withered heads of grain then attacked and swallowed up the good heads of grain. Cannibalistic grain is even stranger than cannibalistic cattle. But then again, even stranger things than these sometimes happen in dreams.

25. Then Joseph said to Pharaoh, "The dreams of Pharaoh are one and the same. God has revealed to Pharaoh what he is about to do.

Although Pharaoh had two *dreams*, the message they brought was *one and the same*. He would soon see a demonstration of the power of the *God* whom Joseph served. God in his providential mercy was using Joseph to inform Pharaoh of what he was *about to do*.

26, 27. The seven good cows are seven years, and the seven good heads of grain are seven years; it is one and the same dream. The seven lean, ugly cows that came up afterward are seven years, and so are the seven worthless heads of grain scorched by the east wind: They are seven years of famine.

Again Joseph emphasized that Pharaoh's *dream* conveyed one message. Both the *good cows* and *grain* and the inferior cows and grain represented *seven years*. Pharaoh was about to learn how these years would affect his country and the people whom he governed.

28. "It is just as I said to Pharaoh: God has shown Pharaoh what he is about to do.

Joseph also stressed once more that even though he was speaking to Pharaoh in answer to his inquiry, his words described what *God* was *about to do*. Joseph was only God's spokesman.

29-31. Seven years of great abundance are coming throughout the land of Egypt, but seven years of famine will follow them. Then all the abundance in Egypt will be forgotten, and the famine will ravage the land. The abundance in the land will not be remembered, because the famine that follows it will be so severe.

The seven fat cattle and the seven good heads of grain represented *seven years of great abundance* in Egypt. Egypt was richly blessed by the Nile River, which stretched the full length of the country. At almost exactly the same time each year, the Nile rose and flooded the land, not only providing water for the crops but also renewing the fertility of the soil by the silt it carried from upstream. Egyptians could normally count on a good crop, and rarely did they experience a famine. As a result, for centuries their country served as the breadbasket of the ancient world. Earlier Abram had traveled to Egypt because of a famine in Canaan (Genesis 12:10); eventually the brothers of Joseph would be forced to do the same.

However, in this case the coming famine would hold Egypt in its grip as well. The seven years of abundance would be followed by *seven years of famine* so *severe* that *all the abundance in Egypt will be forgotten*. The famine would not be just a local or regional one; it would *ravage the land*. Likely no one in Egypt would be able to recall a famine of this magnitude.

Quite often in the Old Testament, when disasters were predicted or came to pass, they were acts of God against sinful people. There is nothing in the Scriptures to indicate that any kind of divine judgment was being administered through this famine. However, as later chapters in Genesis reveal, this famine was providentially used of God to bring Joseph's family to Egypt.

32. The reason the dream was given to Pharaoh in two forms is that the matter has been firmly decided by God, and God will do it soon.

For a *dream* to be *given to Pharaoh in two forms* emphasized its importance. Joseph's dream concerning his brothers was thus repeated (Genesis 37:5-11).

HOW TO SAY IT
Abram. AY-brum.
Darius. Duh-RYE-us.
Egyptians. Ee-JIP-shuns.
Elohim (Hebrew). El-o-HEEM.
Ishmaelites. ISH-may-el-ites.
Nebuchadnezzar. NEB-uh-kad-NEZZ-er .
Pharaoh. FAIR-o or FAY-ro.
Potiphar. POT-ih-far.

(See another example of this in Amos 7:1—8:3.) Here the repetition of Pharaoh's dream signaled its certainty (*the matter has been firmly decided by God*) and its imminence (*God will do it soon*). Clearly there was nothing *Pharaoh* could do that would change God's decree. The best he could do was to prepare for the coming famine.

It may seem surprising that the Egyptian magicians and wise men, who had earlier failed to interpret Pharaoh's dream, raised no objections to Joseph's interpretation. They had every reason to be suspicious and jealous of him; not only was he a foreigner, but he also did not belong to their group of "experts." Apparently the logic and clarity of Joseph's interpretation (and of his subsequent suggestion for dealing with the famine) were such that they had no basis for objection.

B. JOSEPH'S ADVICE (vv. 33-36)

33. And now let Pharaoh look for a discerning and wise man and put him in charge of the land of Egypt.

In this situation Joseph functioned both as a *foreteller*, predicting future events, and as a *forthteller*, giving advice about how to deal with the situation. Many of the prophets in Israel's later history functioned in this same double capacity. Joseph advised Pharaoh to select a *discerning and wise man* who would have the responsibility of directing Egypt's efforts to meet the coming crisis. There is nothing to indicate that Joseph was seeking the job for himself.

34. Let Pharaoh appoint commissioners over the land to take a fifth of the harvest of Egypt during the seven years of abundance.

Joseph's suggestion included not only a leader, but also a plan that this leader could begin to implement. *Commissioners* would be in charge of collecting and storing the grain produced *during the seven years of abundance. A fifth of the harvest* may be considered as a kind of tax, or "double tithe," levied against the people. Or perhaps the government could *take* that portion of the grain by offering to pay for it. In a plentiful year the price of grain would be low, allowing the government to buy it up cheaply. In either case, the grain would be collected and stored for future use rather than allowed to go to waste as it might have otherwise.

35, 36. They should collect all the food of these good years that are coming and store up the grain under the authority of Pharaoh, to be kept in the cities for food. This food should be held in reserve for the country, to be used during the seven years of famine that will come upon Egypt, so that the country may not be ruined by the famine."

The *grain* was to be stored *in the cities* where it would be most needed and where it could be better protected. While Joseph did not mention the subject at this point, his plan probably necessitated building many new storage facilities. However, these tasks could be undertaken and completed within the seven prosperous years that would come first.

SAVING UP FOR A DRY DAY

Thoughtful people have always considered it prudent and thrifty to "save up for a rainy day." Laying back money and other resources to provide for leaner times is sensible. Insurance policies, annuities, IRAs, savings accounts, mutual funds, and investments of every kind are generated by a cautious, plan-ahead spirit.

Joseph's resourceful strategy to supply Egypt with food during the coming famine years could be called, "Saving Up for a Dry Day." The seven-year drought was inevitable. The Egyptians, however, had a seven-year period of plenty to prepare for the "dry day" that was sure to come.

WHAT DO YOU THINK?

Pharaoh did not ask for advice but for information; Joseph gave him advice anyway. When someone asks for information about the Bible or about our faith, is it okay to give advice as well, or should we wait until the person asks for it? Explain why you think it is proper or improper to give unsolicited spiritual advice.

DAILY BIBLE READINGS

Monday, Aug. 16—Joseph Resists Potiphar's Wife (Genesis 39:1-18)

Tuesday, Aug. 17—Joseph Is Imprisoned (Genesis 39:19—40:8)

Wednesday, Aug. 18—Joseph Interprets Dreams of Fellow Prisoners (Genesis 40:9-23)

Thursday, Aug. 19—The King's Cupbearer Remembers Joseph (Genesis 41:1-13)

Friday, Aug. 20—Pharaoh Relates His Dream (Genesis 41:14-24)

Saturday, Aug. 21—Joseph Interprets Pharaoh's Dream (Genesis 41:25-45)

Sunday, Aug. 22—Joseph Stores Grain for Egypt (Genesis 41:46-57)

We do not possess the supernatural foresight to know when our rainy or dry days will come, but we do know that they will come at some point. Jesus predicted, "In this world you will have trouble" (John 16:33). Since we know that tests, trials, and hardships are certain, "saving up" spiritually in preparation for them makes good sense. During all of our good days, when "heaven comes down and glory fills our souls," we should store up as many spiritual resources as possible to sustain us in bad times.

Then, like Joseph, we can remain faithful—rain or shine.   —R. W. B.

III. PHARAOH'S RESPONSE (GENESIS 41:37-40)

A. JOSEPH COMMENDED (vv. 37, 38)

37, 38. The plan seemed good to Pharaoh and to all his officials. So Pharaoh asked them, "Can we find anyone like this man, one in whom is the spirit of God?"

Apparently Pharaoh had made no comment about Joseph's interpretation of his dream. Perhaps he was so overwhelmed by the interpretation that he was left speechless. But when Joseph began to suggest some practical ways to address the famine that Egypt would one day face, Pharaoh immediately began to show an interest. Both he and his *officials* were impressed with the suggestions that Joseph made.

Joseph had gained administrative experience in the household of Potiphar when he was made the overseer in charge of all Potiphar's affairs (Genesis 39:1-6). He gained similar experience in prison where he was put in charge of all the other prisoners (vv. 21-23). This was all part of how "the Lord was with Joseph" (vv. 2, 21), preparing him for a task that would require such leadership. Pharaoh realized that Egypt needed someone uniquely qualified to head up the program that Joseph had just suggested.

Among all the other qualifications, such a person had to be *one in whom is the spirit of God*. The Hebrew word for *God* is *Elohim*, which can be translated "gods" as well as "God." It is difficult to know exactly what the pagan Pharaoh meant by this statement. He may have meant nothing more than a man "in whom is a divine spirit," (the translation found in the *New American Standard Bible)*. Perhaps, however, Pharaoh had heard and seen enough of Joseph to realize that he worshiped a God who was different from the Egyptian gods. Like King Nebuchadnezzar in Daniel 3:28-30 and King Darius in Daniel 6:25-27, he may have been admitting the superiority of the God of the Hebrews, the true and living God.

B. JOSEPH GIVEN AUTHORITY (vv. 39, 40)

39. Then Pharaoh said to Joseph, "Since God has made all this known to you, there is no one so discerning and wise as you.

After conferring with his advisors, *Pharaoh* immediately selected *Joseph* as the man for this new and important position. From the advisors, he may have learned that Joseph was a man of integrity—a man who could command the respect of those who served under him, and (probably most important) a man who had no personal ambitions. Autocratic rulers are usually fearful of having ambitious people around them who might try to take their jobs.

40. "You shall be in charge of my palace, and all my people are to submit to your orders. Only with respect to the throne will I be greater than you."

What a dramatic change had occurred in Joseph's status in only a few hours! When the day began, he was a despised prisoner. Now he was second only to the Pharaoh of Egypt. If there were any objections to his rapid elevation to such a high position, no one voiced them in the presence of Pharaoh. Apparently Joseph was one of those persons who impressed everyone he met as a man of

WHAT DO YOU THINK?

Probably the last thing that Joseph expected that fateful day was to be elevated from the dungeon to the palace. Unexpected challenges may happen in our lives, too. Unexpected challenges and unsought responsibilities may come upon us at work when we are tapped for an important assignment. They may come upon us in the family, perhaps through a birth or someone's death or illness. They may come upon us in the church when something important needs to be done, and no one else is able to do it. In one way or another, most of us shoulder more responsibility as we get older. How should we react to unexpected challenges? How can we prepare for them?

WHAT DO YOU THINK?

Who would have expected Joseph, a teenager sold into slavery, to end up as the second in command of all Egypt? God did! God did not force Joseph's brothers to sell him. He could have accomplished his purposes in other ways. But once it was done, God preserved Joseph until it was time to face Pharaoh. No matter what man does, God is able to work his plans and accomplish his goals. What assurance does that give you today? How does that assurance apply to some situation about which you have been especially concerned?

PRAYER

Father God, you know the struggles that we sometimes face. When trials come, may we not despair. Instead, like Joseph, may we have the strength to trust you even in our defeats. Keep us strong in the faith and prepared to accept any task you have for us. Through Christ, amen.

WHAT DO YOU THINK?

The Bible points out two critical things that Joseph did. First, he maintained his faith in God even when it appeared that God had forsaken him. Second, he maintained his integrity. What situations challenge your faith and integrity? How can you imitate Joseph's example in these situations?

(Each person will have different areas that are most challenging, but there will be much in common as well. One may have a co-worker making sexual advances. Resisting may be especially difficult if the forward one is in a supervisory position. A student may have a professor who takes delight in ridiculing his or her faith. Let the ones in your class who have weathered some of these storms encourage the others.)

THOUGHT TO REMEMBER

May each of us strive to be God's man or woman in whatever circumstances we face.

integrity and ability. Of course, behind all of this was the hand of God, who had blessed Joseph in the house of Potiphar and in prison.

ALL THINGS FOR GOOD

Was the apostle Paul simply stating a theory when he wrote Romans 8:28? Does God really work in all things for the good of those who love him? Paul had earned the right to write such a powerful truth. He could testify from experience to its authority. Despite almost constant trials and persecutions, God worked through all Paul's circumstances to bless his life and ministry in ways the apostle had never asked nor imagined.

Joseph suffered much, too. Hated and ridiculed by his own brothers, he was threatened, abused, and finally sold into slavery. Though faithful to God and to Potiphar in Egypt, he was wrongfully accused by Potiphar's wife and imprisoned for something he didn't do. He could have complained bitterly and wondered, "Why me, Lord?" But there is no record of self-pity or doubt on Joseph's part.

In the end, Joseph's integrity was vindicated, and all things did work out for his good. His example should encourage all of us. If we continue to trust God's promises and determine to fulfill his purposes, we can depend upon his faithfulness in making all things work out for our good and his glory.   —R. W. B.

CONCLUSION

Some persons come to power by virtue of birth into a ruling family. Some do so by violence and intrigue, others just by accident, and some because of their ability, along with a helping hand from some other person or persons. Joseph belonged to the latter class. He was a person of great leadership ability; and he had the best kind of helping hand, for it was the hand of God.

As a young man, Joseph's prospects of reaching the top certainly seemed dim or even nonexistent. Sold into slavery as a teenager and then unjustly thrown into prison and forgotten, what chance did he have? Yet through all of his experiences Joseph never forgot that he belonged to God. At times he certainly must have wondered why his faithfulness always seemed to be rewarded by suffering, but he never wavered in his commitment to God. Deep in his heart he must have nurtured the belief that somewhere, sometime, God would use him for a significant purpose. He had to have great patience to survive many years of disappointment. Great leaders must learn such patience, for God never seems to be in a big hurry to accomplish his purposes in history. But the years that Joseph spent as a slave and as a prisoner were not wasted years. God was training him and disciplining him for a crucial task. When the time came, Joseph was ready and willing.

God has a plan for every one of us. That fact presents us with some sobering responsibilities. First of all, we must be willing to surrender our lives to God and seek and accept his plan for us. If we are not willing to make that effort, then we can never be effectively used by him. Second, we must have the patience to prepare for carrying out that plan, whatever it may be. Moses spent forty years in Egypt and another forty years in the wilderness of Sinai before God could use him.

Perhaps the most difficult part of all of this is discovering the exact place where God wants us to serve. Sometimes we have to choose among several places or avenues of service, all of which seem equally good. At other times we are forced to choose from a set of options, none of which seems to be good. Joseph's options seemed quite limited until the very moment he was thrust into the place where God wanted him. When that time came, Joseph was ready because he never lost faith that God was still there, caring for him and planning his destiny.

Discovery Learning

*This page contains an alternate lesson plan emphasizing learning activities. Classes
desiring such student involvement will find these suggestions helpful. The next page
is a reproducible activity page to further enhance discovery learning.*

LEARNING GOALS

As a result of this lesson, each of your students
should be able to:

1. Recount Joseph's interpretation of Pharaoh's
dreams and the favorable treatment he then received.

2. Compare Joseph's situation and his faith in God's
providence with the situation many Christians face at
the workplace.

3. Make a commitment to live with integrity and to
serve with honor wherever God places him or her.

INTO THE LESSON

Much of the success—or failure—of one's life has to
do with time and place. The person who is in the right
place at the right time gets the opportunity. The person
who appears on the scene too soon or too late misses
the opportunity.

Your students no doubt can give examples of this
from their own lives. For example, some people have
been annoyed when they missed a plane—later they
learned that the plane crashed. Or two people bump
into each other in the grocery store, and before long a
romance develops. Ask your students to tell their stories.

Ask, "Do you see God's hand in such things? Do you
think God controls events to put the right person in the
right place at just the right time? Why or why not?"

In today's lesson we see that Joseph was always in
the right place at the right time. At the beginning of the
lesson he was in an Egyptian prison, but that was just
where God wanted him.

INTO THE WORD

To begin the Bible-study portion of the lesson, draw
the following "wave" on newsprint:

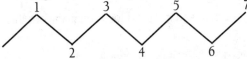

Point out that Joseph's life was a series of ups and
downs. When things were going well for him, something bad happened to reverse his situation. When
things looked hopeless, something good happened to
turn things around again.

With the students' help, chart Joseph's ups and
downs on the "wave" you have drawn. Have them read
each of the following Bible passages to discover the up
or down event in Joseph's life. (A similar exercise appears in the student book, *NIV Bible Student*.)

1. UP: Genesis 37:3 *(receives robe)*; 2. DOWN: Genesis 37:23-28 *(sold to Ishmaelites)*; 3. UP: Genesis 39:1-6
(became Potiphar's steward); 4. DOWN: Genesis 39:7-20
(falsely accused and imprisoned); 5. UP: Genesis 39:21-23
(put in charge of prisoners); 6. DOWN: Genesis 40:12-
15, 20-23 *(forgotten)*; 7. UP: Genesis 41:39-44 *(made
second to Pharaoh)*.

Ask: "What do these ups and downs tell you about
God's involvement in Joseph's life?" (God was continually with Joseph. Even the "down" events were necessary to put Joseph in position for the "ups.")

Next, ask the students to read Genesis 41:14-16, 25-
40 and call out Joseph's positive character traits that
they see demonstrated. Write these traits on the chalkboard as they are called out. Here are some ideas: humility (vv. 16, 25, 28), Joseph knew God was the one
who interpreted the dreams; courage (vv. 25, 28),
Joseph was a Hebrew and a prisoner, but he had the
courage to stand before Pharaoh and declare God's message; insightful (vv. 33-36), Joseph had a plan, which he
was bold enough to share with Pharaoh; discrete (v. 33),
Joseph could have pushed himself forward and said,
"I'm your man," but he didn't.

INTO LIFE

Begin the life-application section of the lesson by writing this open-ended sentence on newsprint: "I could be a
dynamic, powerful, and successful Christian if only . . ."

Ask the students to write a completion of that sentence on a card or piece of paper. No doubt every person in your class will have a different idea. Without
asking anyone to reveal what he or she wrote, complete
the sentence this way: "I trusted God the way Joseph
did."

Observe that many of us sit around waiting for our
situation to be ideal. When everything is just right and
working perfectly, then we will be able to serve Christ effectively. But if Joseph had waited for everything to be
perfect, he never would have served the Lord. Instead,
he had the courage and the determination to serve the
Lord wherever he was and no matter how dark his situation. Challenge your students to serve Christ in this less-
than-ideal world. Distribute copies of the reproducible
activity page that follows to explore this issue further.

Serving God—In the Prison or in the Palace

Joseph did not let his circumstances affect his devotion to God. He served the Lord as faithfully in the prison as he did in the palace.

You may know some people whose circumstances have them "imprisoned." They are thinking of giving up. Consider the following situations. How would a renewed commitment to Christ help in each one?

• Tom hates his job. It's not so much the work as it is the people. They have such a secular or pagan outlook on life that it is hard for Tom to get along with them. What can he do during the coming week to serve Christ on the job? How might that new commitment change his attitude toward his job?

• Betty's marriage seems to be coming apart at the seams. She and her husband haven't spoken in days. "It's better that way," she says. "When we do speak, we just argue."

What can Betty do during the coming week to serve Christ in her marriage? How might her new commitment change her attitude toward her mate and her marriage?

• Ed is floundering in financial distress. What can he do during the coming week to serve Christ in spite of his debt? How might a new commitment to Christ change his attitude toward his financial situation?

• Mary has a severe case of rheumatoid arthritis. She is a virtual prisoner of pain. What can she do during the coming week to serve Christ in spite of her illness? How might that new commitment change her attitude toward her illness?

In closing, challenge your students to look beyond their current situation and focus on living out their relationship with Christ during the coming week.

FORGIVENESS AND REUNION

LESSON 13

DEVOTIONAL READING:
PSALM 105:7-22

LESSON SCRIPTURE:
GENESIS 42–45

PRINTED TEXT:
GENESIS 44:16-20, 33, 34;
45:1-7

WHY TEACH THIS LESSON?

The story is told about a preacher who one Sunday morning repeated his sermon from the week before. A few church members noticed, but they didn't say anything. The next week the preacher repeated the sermon again. This time more people noticed, and there was some discussion among them, but still no one said anything to the preacher.

After the preacher repeated the sermon again the next week, however, the elders called a special meeting. The minister was brought in, and they demanded to know why he had preached the same sermon four Sundays in a row. "When you start to do what I said in this sermon," the preacher replied, "then I'll preach another!"

Some may find it a little bit strange to have a lesson on forgiveness so soon after the lesson on Jacob and Esau's reconciliation (lesson 10). After all, wasn't forgiveness a main theme in that lesson? Are there no other themes worthy of our pursuit?

Of course, there are, but we have so much trouble with this one that it's worth a second look. Perhaps no one in the Old Testament more beautifully illustrates the concept of forgiveness than Joseph. In fact, we see in him a type of Christ. If there is anyone in your class who needs to forgive another—and you know there is!—then this lesson is needed today.

INTRODUCTION

A. FROM MANLINESS TO GODLINESS

A man once approached his minister, terribly upset over something that a fellow church member had done to him. After the man had explained the nature of the incident, the minister readily agreed that he had good reason to be upset. Then the man began to tell the minister his plans for gaining revenge. When it became obvious from the minister's expression that he did not approve of the plans for revenge, the man blurted out, "Well, don't you consider it manly to seek revenge for such an insult?"

"Certainly," replied the minister, "it is quite manly to seek revenge. But it is *godly* to forgive such an offense."

Joseph surely had good reason to seek revenge for the insults and injuries he had suffered at the hands of his jealous brothers. In his day it would have been perfectly acceptable for him to have exacted vengeance on his brothers once he had them under his authority. Yet Joseph was able to rise above the "manliness" of revenge to the "godliness" of forgiveness.

B. LESSON BACKGROUND

Famine had struck Egypt and many of the surrounding lands, including Canaan. Because of Joseph's wise stewardship of Egypt's crops during its seven good years of harvests, Egypt had food enough not only for its own people but even for some of its neighbors. In Canaan Jacob learned that grain was available in Egypt, so he sent his ten oldest sons to Egypt to purchase some.

LESSON AIMS

After this lesson each student should:

1. Summarize the process by which Joseph made himself known to his brothers and the words of reconciliation that he spoke to them.

2. Explain how God's providence was accomplished through Joseph's forgiving spirit.

3. Make a commitment to forgive someone who has wronged him or her, being confident that God's providence is at work in this effort.

KEY VERSE

Do not be distressed and do not be angry with yourselves for selling me here, because it was to save lives that God sent me ahead of you. —Genesis 45:5

Aug
29

When Joseph saw them, he recognized them, but they did not recognize him. Joseph accused them of being spies and said they would have to bring their youngest brother, Benjamin, to prove that they were not. Simeon was held as a hostage until they returned. Joseph then provided them the grain that they needed but secretly returned their money in their grain sacks.

The nine brothers returned home and told their father what had happened, but he refused to allow Benjamin to accompany them back to Egypt. But the supply of grain ran out, and the famine remained severe. Faced with starvation, Jacob finally gave permission for the brothers, including Benjamin, to go to Egypt.

In Egypt the brothers were reunited with Simeon and were able once again to purchase grain. Again Joseph secretly had their money returned to them; but this time he also had his silver cup placed in Benjamin's sack. After the men had left, Joseph sent his steward to overtake them and search for the cup. When it was found in Benjamin's sack, the brothers were forced to return to Joseph and try to explain what had happened.

I. JUDAH'S DEFENSE (GENESIS 44:16-20)

A. JUDAH'S ADMISSION (v. 16)

16. "What can we say to my lord?" Judah replied. "What can we say? How can we prove our innocence? God has uncovered your servants' guilt. We are now my lord's slaves—we ourselves and the one who was found to have the cup."

At this point, the brothers must have been beside themselves, fearing not so much what might happen to them, but what would happen to Benjamin. All of them fell on the ground before Joseph (v. 14), dreading the judgment that seemed certain to fall on them.

The evidence against Benjamin seemed so obvious that there was no way that they could *prove* their *innocence*. Judah, who became their spokesman, did not even try to deny the evidence. He volunteered the whole family to become Joseph's *slaves*. They were not willing to leave Benjamin to suffer the consequences alone.

Note Judah's confession of *your servants' guilt,* apparently referring to the brothers' cruel treatment of Joseph. Judah's admission marked a significant change from the man who had so callously suggested that they ought to make a profit from Joseph's misery (Genesis 37:26, 27).

B. JOSEPH'S RESPONSE (v. 17)

17. But Joseph said, "Far be it from me to do such a thing! Only the man who was found to have the cup will become my slave. The rest of you, go back to your father in peace."

Joseph further tested his brothers by asserting that only the one in whose sack the *cup* had been *found*—Benjamin—would be punished. Apparently Joseph was trying to find out if they were the same selfish, jealous men that they had been years before when they mistreated him. They could return to their *father in peace* if they left Benjamin behind to suffer for the alleged theft. If they were willing to go along with Joseph's offer, that would indicate that they had not changed.

What would Joseph have done if the brothers had accepted his offer? Perhaps he had already heard enough to convince him that they had changed. If so, he knew that they would refuse. Or perhaps he felt, if they had not changed, that Benjamin was in the same kind of peril he had been in. In that case, this plan would have rescued Benjamin from them.

WHAT DO YOU THINK?

Even though he and his brothers were innocent of stealing from Joseph, Judah did not pursue that. Instead he said that God had found out their iniquity, referring to their treatment of Joseph so many years earlier. His guilty conscience had condemned him. He knew they were reaping exactly what they had sown. Judah and the others were facing up to their terrible sin, perhaps for the first time. No forgiveness and no healing can occur, whether from man or from God, until a person faces and admits his sin. How does that happen today? Can we help people face their sin, or must people come to that point on their own? If so, how?

WHAT DO YOU THINK?

Joseph offered his ten brothers an easy way out in verse 17. They could return to Jacob, tell him Benjamin had stolen the cup— they themselves had seen it in his sack—and put the whole mess behind them. What situations tempt us to take the easy way out today? How can we have the character to stand up under pressure, even at risk of personal loss?

C. JUDAH'S URGENT PLEA (vv. 18-20)

18. Then Judah went up to him and said: "Please, my lord, let your servant speak a word to my lord. Do not be angry with your servant, though you are equal to Pharaoh himself.

The brothers must have been shaken by Joseph's rejection of their offer to remain as his slaves. Judah was not willing to accept Joseph's decision; he *went up to him* so that he could make his appeal even more personal. He recognized that Joseph was *equal to Pharaoh himself*, with the power of life and death over them. To approach such a powerful official could mean signing his own death warrant, but Judah was willing to take the chance.

19, 20. "My lord asked his servants, 'Do you have a father or a brother?' And we answered, 'We have an aged father, and there is a young son born to him in his old age. His brother is dead, and he is the only one of his mother's sons left, and his father loves him.'

When it became apparent that Joseph was going to allow Judah to speak, he recounted the events of their first visit to Egypt. On that occasion Joseph had asked them about their *father*. Naturally he had an interest in learning about Jacob, for since the day that he had been sold into slavery he had not seen his father nor heard any word about him. For all Joseph knew at that time, his father was dead; and so he must have rejoiced when he first learned that Jacob was still alive.

Judah went on to remind Joseph how he and his brothers had told him about their youngest *brother*, Benjamin, whom they described as *a young son born to Jacob in his old age*. Judah also mentioned Benjamin's *brother*, who was *dead*. At this point in the conversation, Joseph must have had to restrain himself to avoid giving away his secret.

In the verses that follow this portion of the printed text, Judah went on to recount how Joseph had demanded that the brothers bring Benjamin with them if they returned for more grain. When the famine forced them to do so, their father permitted Benjamin to accompany them with great reluctance and only after much persuasion. Judah pointed out Jacob's great love for Benjamin and that Jacob was certain to die if Benjamin were not returned safely. Judah was appealing to Joseph's sense of compassion for an old man who would be devastated at the loss of the son with whom his life was "closely bound up" (v. 30). This argument was much more forceful than Judah realized at the time, because he did not know that he was talking to Joseph. Joseph was the last person in the world who would have wanted anything bad to happen to his father.

II. JUDAH'S PROPOSAL (GENESIS 44:33, 34)

A. JUDAH'S OFFER (v. 33)

33. "Now then, please let your servant remain here as my lord's slave in place of the boy, and let the boy return with his brothers.

Judah had a stronger reason for returning Benjamin to his father than his brothers did. Verse 32 tells us that he had made a personal pledge to his father that he would be responsible for Benjamin's safe return. Perhaps Judah originally made this promise because of the pressure of having to buy grain a second time in Egypt. However, his willingness to keep his word shows that he had not taken his pledge lightly.

The irony of this situation surely would not have escaped Joseph. Judah was the one who had suggested that the brothers sell Joseph into slavery (Genesis 37:26, 27). Now this same man was willing to become a slave that his younger brother might go free.

The visual for today's lesson portrays Joseph's brothers kneeling before him, just as his dreams had predicted they would do.

Now therefore
be not grieved, nor angry with yourselves,
that ye sold me hither:
for God did send me before you
to preserve life.

WHAT DO YOU THINK?

Judah's plea to be taken as Joseph's slave in the place of his brother Benjamin is a very powerful example of self-sacrifice. His love for his brother and his father made it intolerable to him that Benjamin be lost. Judah's noble and selfless deed looks forward to the self-sacrifice of his greatest descendant, Jesus Christ. Under what conditions would you sacrifice your own life or freedom in behalf of another? To what extent have you sacrificed self in behalf of Christ?

HOW TO SAY IT

Canaan. KAY-nun.
Egyptians. Ee-JIP-Shuns.
Goshen. GO-shun.
Pharaoh. FAIR-o or FAY-ro.
Simeon. SIM-ee-un.

B. JUDAH'S CONCERN FOR JACOB (v. 34)

34. "How can I go back to my father if the boy is not with me? No! Do not let me see the misery that would come upon my father."

When Judah had been a party to selling Joseph into slavery, he had shown no concern for how his action would affect his *father*. He and his brothers possessed such an intense hatred for Joseph that they completely disregarded any consideration for Jacob. Now that had changed. Judah was unwilling to do anything that would bring Jacob's "gray head down to the grave in misery" (Genesis 44:29).

III. JOSEPH'S DISCLOSURE (GENESIS 45:1-7)

A. WEEPING (vv. 1, 2)

1, 2. Then Joseph could no longer control himself before all his attendants, and he cried out, "Have everyone leave my presence!" So there was no one with Joseph when he made himself known to his brothers. And he wept so loudly that the Egyptians heard him, and Pharaoh's household heard about it.

This is certainly one of the most moving scenes in the entire Bible. Joseph's test of his brothers had been completed. Judah's speech clearly demonstrated that they were no longer the heartless villains who sold him into slavery. When it became obvious to Joseph that his brothers had truly changed, he could no longer hold back his emotions. Earlier during his brothers' first visit and later when he had first seen Benjamin, he had been able to recover his composure (Genesis 42:24; 43:29-31), but not this time. His test of his brothers had turned out the way that he had hoped, and when it did, he *could no longer control himself.*

As Joseph prepared to reveal his identity to his brothers, he sent all the *attendants* from the room. This was to be a private family moment that he was not ready to share with anyone else. That would come later at a more appropriate time.

When Joseph was alone with his brothers, *he wept . . . loudly.* His pent-up emotions burst forth with such force that those who had just left the room could hear him, along with *Pharaoh's household.* From the nature of his crying, those outside the room knew that he was in no physical danger from the "strangers" who were with him. Otherwise they might have burst into the room to rescue him.

WHAT DO YOU THINK?

Joseph had been separated from his father for over twenty years, but his affection was still strong. Joseph's separation from his family was very unusual, but today families frequently become separated for a variety of reasons. Children leave out of anger or a desire to be free of the restraints of home. Others may go to college and then settle far from home. Some move seeking a better job. In modern society frequent moves are a fact of life. The result is that many of our families are separated by hundreds of miles. How can we keep this separation from causing our families to disintegrate or become alienated?

B. REVEALING HIS IDENTITY (vv. 3, 4)

3. Joseph said to his brothers, "I am Joseph! Is my father still living?" But his brothers were not able to answer him, because they were terrified at his presence.

Now came the climactic moment—the moment that Joseph had postponed until the time was just right. A bolt of lightning striking in the brothers' midst could not have produced a greater shock than the words they heard: *I am Joseph!* Joseph followed this introduction with a question about Jacob. Judah's previous speech had already indicated that their *father* was still living. Thus Joseph's question was not so much for information as it was to confirm what he had hoped all along was true.

The brothers were still so shocked at what they had just heard that they could not talk. They may also have been *terrified* about what would follow, and for good reason. They realized that Joseph had the authority to do anything he wanted to with them. Had they been in his situation, they might very well have thought about exacting revenge.

4. Then Joseph said to his brothers, "Come close to me." When they had done so, he said, "I am your brother Joseph, the one you sold into Egypt!

More than twenty years had passed since the brothers had last seen Joseph, so no doubt they had difficulty believing what they were hearing. To reassure them that they had heard him correctly, Joseph asked them to *come* closer, and then told them again who he was . Then he added *the one you sold into Egypt*, indicating the knowledge of a detail that validated his claim. These words may have frightened the brothers, but no doubt Joseph's tone was gentle, even forgiving, rather than harsh.

C. Explaining God's Purpose (vv. 5-7)

5. *"And now, do not be distressed and do not be angry with yourselves for selling me here, because it was to save lives that God sent me ahead of you.*

Joseph did not mention anything about forgiving his brothers for the way they had treated him. But he did not have to. From the tone of his voice and his explanation of what had happened, it was obvious that he had already forgiven them. There was no need for them to feel burdened by a sense of guilt.

Here we see a marvelous statement of the faith that sustained Joseph during his ordeal. Joseph's faith in God permitted him to see beyond his brothers' wicked deeds to God's larger purposes. *It was to save lives that God sent me ahead of you.* What a profound theological statement! How did Joseph come to this conclusion? It is not likely that he had held such a view as a seventeen-year-old who had just been sold into slavery. There is nothing to indicate that Joseph had received a special revelation from God about this matter. The fundamentals of the faith that he had learned in his father's household followed by many years of experience, some of them very painful, had brought Joseph to this conclusion.

Joseph likely knew of the covenant that God had made with Abraham, Isaac, and Jacob. Through the eyes of faith he understood that what had happened to him had not occurred by chance. Only by God's providence had he been brought to Egypt so that when the time of famine came he was able *to save lives* and thus keep alive God's covenant family.

6. *For two years now there has been famine in the land, and for the next five years there will not be plowing and reaping.*

Joseph then informed his brothers that the present period of *famine* had only begun. It had lasted *two years* thus far, but there were still *five years* (a total of seven, in accordance with Pharaoh's dream) during which there would be neither *plowing* nor *reaping*.

7. *But God sent me ahead of you to preserve for you a remnant on earth and to save your lives by a great deliverance.*

God sent me. Joseph's brothers sent him to Egypt as a slave, but in time he was able to see the bigger picture. It was God who actually sent him to Egypt by using their evil intentions to accomplish his purposes. The idea that God works through a *remnant* persists throughout the entire Bible (Isaiah 1:9; Jeremiah 23:3; Joel 2:32; Romans 9:27; 11:5; Revelation 12:17).

The verses that immediately follow our printed text tell how Joseph sent his brothers back to Canaan in order to bring their father Jacob to Egypt. There they, along with their children and their flocks, would live in the land of Goshen during the five years of famine that remained. However, that five years stretched into four hundred years before the children of Israel were again able to leave Egypt under the leadership of Moses.

Forgiveness Begins With Grace

A lady counselee says that she feels no obligation to notify two of her siblings when her mother dies. She reasons that since this brother and sister have shown

What Do You Think?

Joseph told his brothers not to be grieved with themselves for selling him, but the brothers had difficulty finding peace because of their heinous deed. Guilt has a way of eating at our hearts and destroying our peace. Our sins don't seem so terrible when we commit them, but later their true ugliness becomes undeniable. Our consciences condemn us even when no man knows or accuses us. Guilt becomes a beast that stalks at every turn. How do you deal with guilt and overcome it?

PRAYER

Loving and forgiving Father, we thank you for revealing to us the life of Joseph, a man who knew how to forgive and forget. Show us how to follow his example and the even greater, nobler example of your Son. In his name, amen.

THOUGHT TO REMEMBER

"Forgive as the Lord forgave you" (Colossians 3:13).

DAILY BIBLE READINGS

Monday, Aug. 23—*Jacob Sends His Sons to Buy Grain (Genesis 42:1-17)*

Tuesday, Aug. 24—*Joseph Arranges to See Benjamin (Genesis 42:18-38)*

Wednesday, Aug. 25—*Jacob Agrees for Benjamin to Go to Egypt (Genesis 43:1-15)*

Thursday, Aug. 26—*Joseph Arranges a Meal for His Brothers (Genesis 43:16-34)*

Friday, Aug. 27—*Benjamin Is Threatened With Slavery in Egypt (Genesis 44:1-17)*

Saturday, Aug. 28—*Judah Offers to Take Benjamin's Place (Genesis 44:18-34)*

Sunday, Aug. 29—*Joseph Reveals His Identity (Genesis 45:1-28)*

absolutely no interest in their aging and ill mother for several years, they have forfeited their right to know. "Besides," she adds, "they probably won't care anyway."

This counselee's attitude is understandable, but not justifiable. All children have a right to know of a parent's death. No good can come from adding another wrong to the wrongful neglect and indifference of these guilty children.

Everyone would have understood if Joseph had sentenced his brothers to imprisonment or even execution. They did not deserve anything better. But Joseph graciously forgave them of their hateful deeds and sinful offenses. Nothing would have been gained by seeking vengeance.

The bitter sister in the situation described earlier finally agreed to telegram *all* the children when her mother dies. It's the right thing to do; it's the forgiving thing to do. The unloving brother and sister don't deserve to be forgiven, but grace is *always* undeserved. None of us merits God's love and redemption, yet "he looks beyond our fault and sees our need." That truly is amazing grace.   —R. W. B.

CONCLUSION

A. BUT GOD

Genesis 47:28 tells us that Jacob "lived in Egypt seventeen years." After his death, Joseph's brothers became fearful that Joseph would seek revenge for the evil they had done against him. But when they came before Joseph, he quickly dismissed their fears with words similar to those found in today's text: "You intended to harm me, *but God* intended it for good" (Genesis 50:20). What a very important lesson this is for all of us today! The world often views events through the narrow lens of time. Christians have a different viewpoint because they look at life through the lens of eternity. What a difference it makes to see events the way God sees them!

Paul tells us that "in all things God works for the good of those who love him" (Romans 8:28). Such a view should not lead us to a Pollyannaish attitude that never sees any evil anywhere. The truth is that we are surrounded by an evil world, full of pain and suffering. As Christians we must confront evil wherever we see it and try to alleviate as much of the suffering as we can.

Many of us have suffered because of the wicked deeds of others. During the time that we are going through such a trial, we may not see or understand how any good could come out of the situation. However, the passing of time can give us a broader view, as it did Joseph. Let us never forget that the world may declare a certain situation hopeless or useless, *but God* always has the last word.

B. TO FORGIVE IS DIVINE

Joseph stands out as one of the noblest characters in the Bible. Mistreated by his brothers, he refused to allow his life to be consumed by a burning hatred or a desire for revenge. He had every opportunity to get even with his brothers for what they had done to him. Instead, he returned good for evil.

How often we bear grudges about petty issues that don't really matter a whit! We may try to get even for these perceived offenses, and in the process cause the other person to retaliate. Over the years this little game can escalate until it becomes a festering sore that poisons the souls of those involved.

Joseph refused to allow his life to become scarred by what others had done to him. As a result he looked on his reunion with his brothers as an opportunity for restoration, not revenge. Revenge may seem sweet for a time, but that sweetness soon turns bitter. Long before Jesus stated it in the Sermon on the Mount, Joseph had learned to love his enemies, bless them that cursed him, and do good to them that hated him.